The Sport and Society Reader

Edited by
David Karen and
Robert E. Washington

Routledge
Taylor & Francis Group

LONDON AND NEW YORK

First published 2010
by Routledge
2 Park Square, Milton Park, Abingdon, Oxon, OX14 4RN

Simultaneously published in the USA and Canada
by Routledge
270 Madison Avenue, New York, NY 10016

Routledge is an imprint of the Taylor & Francis Group, an informa business

Typeset in Galliard and Frutiger by Keyword Group Ltd
Printed and bound in Great Britain by TJ International Ltd, Padstow, Cornwall

British Library Cataloguing in Publication Data
A catalogue record for this book is available from the British Library

Library of Congress Cataloging in Publication Data
The sport and society reader / edited by David Karen and Robert E. Washington.
   p. cm.
1. Sports—Social aspects. I. Karen, David. II. Washington, Robert E., 1941-
   GV706.5.S6963 2010
   306.4'83—dc22   2009012198

ISBN10: 0-415-77248-6 (hbk)
ISBN10: 0-415-77249-4 (pbk)

ISBN13: 978-0-415-77248-8 (hbk)
ISBN13: 978-0-415-77249-5 (pbk)

Contents

Acknowledgments

This undertaking reflects a labor of love: we love sports and we love sociology. Though Washington is less attached to given teams, we are both big sports fans. We hope that this volume will not only help students think differently about sport and society, we hope that it will also give them a leg up in the proverbial sports-bar discussions.

We have accumulated a number of debts in our work on this book. First and foremost, we would like to thank the many students in our Sport and Society class, who, over the years, helped us figure out which readings were most interesting and most pedagogically useful. Second, we would like to thank a long list of students who helped us organize, categorize, search, edit, and otherwise aid in the selection of articles for this book. Steve Feder, Emily Schneider-Krzys, Sasha Toten, and Amy Scott (who deserves special kudos for helping with the final push!) provided excellent support as we moved forward toward completing the manuscript. Third, we would like to thank a number of colleagues and friends who have been particularly helpful in the preparation of this book. Andy Markovits, Loïc Wacquant, Michael Messner, and Malcolm Gladwell helped us arrange either free or reduced costs for the publication of their contributions. Very early on, Doug Hartmann was very helpful in guiding us toward some interesting selections for possible inclusion; Nate Wright was helpful at a later stage. Jerry Karabel and Andy Markovits probably heard more about this book than anyone else and helped in myriad ways. Fourth, we would especially like to thank Karen Sulpizio, who provided excellent bibliographic and administrative support ... always with a smile. Fifth, Fred Courtright, contact with whom we have Steve Rutter to thank for, was a stalwart permissions editor, who guided us through a very circuitous process. Sixth, we would like to thank the Bryn Mawr College Provost's office for a grant to help defray various costs associated with this publication. Finally, we would each like to acknowledge some personal debts. Karen would like to thank his family for tolerating his endless stints in front of the computer (not that this will stop!): Rachel, Josh, and especially Katherine contributed in many ways to compensate for my various errors of omission and commission with respect to the household division of labor. Washington would like to thank Rose for her forbearance and cheerful disposition as this project took much longer to complete than anticipated.

Permissions

General introduction

Sport—the game and the field

David Karen and Robert E. Washington

This volume represents our attempt to present the best scholarly and journalistic work in the field of sport and society. We have compiled a rich array of materials across a broad range of subjects to provide the reader with a comprehensive introduction to the field. In assembling the collection, we strove to select scholarly articles with interesting content, analytical depth, and theoretical perspective. In contrast, we selected the journalistic articles with an eye toward engaging the reader's attention by highlighting the topical implications of the major issues addressed in the different sections throughout the book.

In this introduction, we highlight some key themes in the volume, beginning with a discussion of the uniqueness of sports. We suggest that sports represent a *unique* slice of social life, which provides a distinctive lens through which we can observe various aspects of the larger society. We begin with a discussion of sport as a contest and proceed to a more complex account of that contest by situating it within the surrounding social environment. In doing so, we anticipate many of the issues that are raised in the volume as a whole. At the end of the introduction, we present the Plan of the Book.

Sport as a meritocratic contest

Sports have assumed enormous importance in the modern world. The global attention paid to

sport can be assessed not only in economic terms (total revenue generated from media, attendance, apparel and equipment sales, etc.) and in time (total time spent watching, playing, reading about, etc.) but also in its impact on popular culture (advertising, journalism, movies, etc.). By any measure, sport has become a major force in modern life. From kids playing on the street to professionals playing in major stadiums and arenas, from the street vendor selling rubber balls to the global corporations selling athletic shoes, from neighborhood parents organizing pee-wee leagues to General Managers organizing professional team rosters, sports' presence extends throughout modern society. We see it among the young and old, the educated and uneducated, the rich and poor.

Its compelling nature, however, derives from our interest in the sports *contest*. We follow these contests because they are ostensibly fair competitions among relatively equal contestants, with concrete, objective outcomes; outcomes that are determined by public performances that we feel competent to evaluate. Even when one team appears to be decidedly more skilled "on paper," one can never be certain in trying to pick the winner. Phrases such as "on any given Sunday …" or "that's why they throw the ball up" (… "or drop the puck") are invoked to express that uncertainty.

But why should sports be of interest to *students of society*? Apart from its competitiveness and its suspenseful outcomes, sports should

1

interest the student of society because the most important principle determining the success or failure of sports organizations is also a central normative ideal characterizing democratic capitalist societies: the meritocratic principle. This principle states that superior performance under fair competition wins. In formal organizations, generally, it is assumed that meritocratic practices are adopted because they ostensibly embody instrumental rationality (using the best available means to attain a given goal), which produces maximum efficiency. These practices are believed to correspond to democratic values of fairness and equal opportunity. Translated into sport, this means that, in general, the best players play and the best teams win. More concretely, this means that selecting players based on objective assessments[1] of their abilities is not simply the most effective way to win; it is also the fairest way to assess and manage personnel. And teams advance toward championships based on their wins and losses (their objective record) across a season or tournament. Under these conditions, we would also expect that, literally, anyone can win, which means that long-distance social mobility should be observable. Taken together, these aspects of sport represent an ideal version of the ideological rationale that legitimates capitalist democracies; indeed, the meritocratic ideal is hegemonic.[2]

Though the meritocratic normative ideal operates as the legitimating rationale for social institutions in democratic capitalist societies, those social institutions vary widely in the extent to which they actually adhere to meritocratic practices. Sports provide a unique opportunity to study the social and cultural constraints that undermine meritocratic norms in institutions whose success depends upon adherence to meritocratic practices. Compared to consequences in other institutions, where outcomes are murkier (or assessments of efficiency and productivity are vague) and departures from meritocratic practices are less obvious, in sport the consequences of departure from meritocratic practices are evident as they directly affect the sports team's success or failure. It seems reasonable to assume, therefore, that if non-meritocratic practices exist in sport, they are also likely to exist in other institutions. What distinguishes sport is that everyone can observe and assess the role performances for her/himself, whereas, in other institutions, the results and their evaluations are

much more opaque.[3] Though sport is widely believed to exemplify the meritocratic ideal in ways that other institutions do not, close examination of sport reveals that it often diverges from this ideal. Which obliges us to ask: what alternative interests are being served when sport diverges from meritocratic practice? Under what conditions are such divergences likely to occur?

The sports contest within the field

These questions push us to look beyond the "pure" athletic contest. The contest is structured by the *institution* of sport, which is constituted within a social *field* in a given society in a global world.[4] So, while our interest in sport is compelled by the fairness of the dramatic competition in a given *contest*—which represents a unique model of hegemonic meritocratic norms, we must understand the highly structured nature of the *field* (see Bourdieu and Wacquant, 1992) within which sport exists. Here, we enter the province of the sociologist, who explores both how the contest is affected by the sports field in given societies and how the sports field in given societies affects the contest. We refer here to two levels of effects: the contest is located within a sports field and the sports field is one of many fields in a given society, which is constituted by its own, relatively autonomous, field of power.[5] Thus, we need to understand how the contest is affected by the sports field and how the sports field is affected by the larger field of power. We also expect that, under certain conditions, the contest can affect the field of sport, which can affect the larger field of power (see Figure 0.1).

The field of sport is comprised of individuals, organizations, and markets which are engaged in a competition for power and resources. The individuals and organizations in this field have unequal power and resources and different perceptions of opportunity and goals. While money is certainly at stake for both team owners and athletes, there is also a less tangible "sports capital" that they struggle over. This sports capital is convertible to the more fungible social and economic capital within the sports field and beyond. Thus, someone like David Beckham has acquired sports capital and converted it into many other types of capital (did he convert his sports capital into marital capital? And/or

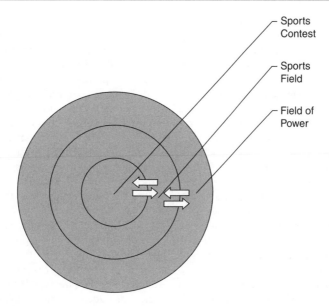

- Sports
  Contest

- Sports
  Field

- Field of
  Power

Figure 0.1. Diagram of relations among sport contests, the sports field, and the larger society's field of power.

did Victoria convert her music industry capital into marital capital?), while someone like Mark Teixeira, who signed a $180 million contract to play baseball with the New York Yankees, seems (so far) to have been content to stick with his economic conversion. There is evidence as well that institutions of higher education benefit directly from success on the athletic fields. College and university Admissions Offices in the US hope that their institutions will experience a "Flutie effect" from some sporting success that increases the visibility of their institution. Thus, sports capital can convert to increased applications, increased enrollment, and/or greater selectivity for institutions that have successful college athletic programs (Pope and Pope, 2008).[6]

The sports field is richly textured, as we can conceive of different dynamics within the field for different sports and different levels of sport. Thus, if we restricted ourselves to looking at the sport of basketball in the US, for example, we would look at high school, college, and professional basketball as somewhat separate entities, with each characterized by struggles over different resources (different championship banners; different media attention; different advertising revenue; etc.). At the same time, we can hardly ignore the reality that high school basketball feeds into college ball, which, in turn, feeds into the pros. Similarly, we must acknowledge the various

ways that even the state, through its regulation of the economy and media corporations, affects all levels of sport. Each level of the game has its own organizational logic, as different leagues represent different levels of competition and confront different structures of opportunity. Thus, in the US, Division III college programs do not orient themselves toward television exposure, while such opportunities are part of the incentives Division I coaches use to recruit top high school prospects. Moreover, the recruitment of top high school athletes by colleges is governed by rules set up by the National Collegiate Athletics Association, the organization created not only to maintain the integrity of intercollegiate athletics but also, we are led to believe, to promote the education of the student-athlete (see the NCAA's webpage: http://www.ncaa.org/wps/ncaa?ContentID=1352). And, needless to say, there are radical inequalities among the institutions that recruit these athletes.

Even while acknowledging the complexity of the field of sport, we must recognize that it is one of many fields in a given society. While each field may have its own internal dynamics and may be relatively autonomous from the dynamics of the larger society, it is, at the same time, subjected to (and often suffused with) the power relations and inequalities of the larger society. What is the effect of power relations

3

and racial/ethnic and/or class inequalities of the larger society in the sport field? As noted above, however, we would still expect the contest, somehow, to be free of these "unpure," unmeritocratic elements.

This can, perhaps, be more clearly illuminated by a contrast between sports and education. In education, we also have an ostensibly meritocratic institution that is run according to objective criteria, with the victors being designated based on how well they scored/performed on objective tests/competitions. Everyone walks into a testing room, having been provided the "same" preparation, armed with the same #2 pencils, to confront the same questions, the answers to which are objectively scored. The outcome of this competition leads the victors to certain social advantages (for example, access to selective high schools or to elite institutions of higher education) that often lead to a particular position on the society's social transmission belt. But when we examine the outcomes of this ostensibly fair competition, we discover that there is strong evidence of social reproduction, with test-takers from the most advantaged groups being much more likely than those from less advantaged groups to be among the top scorers. As Bourdieu and Passeron explain in *Reproduction* (1977), the secret, of course, is that the tests favor those with high cultural capital (those who grow up with the kind of linguistic and cultural orientations favored by dominant groups) but don't *entirely* exclude those without that kind of cultural capital. In other words, it is not a level playing field. Indeed, it is critical for the smooth operation of the system that at least a few folks from marginalized groups be successful (Bourdieu calls this "controlled mobility") so that the apparently meritocratic nature of the competition is reinforced. Parents of *both* upper and lower class kids can marvel at how hard their kids work and how they succeed, even in arenas in which they're not well-culturally-(or genetically-) endowed. Thus, we are all to understand that the tests are fair and objective, even as people witness a preponderance of social class reproduction. When these objective tests were introduced in the early part of the twentieth century, they did, indeed, change the nature of the competition: children from subordinate groups could now compete. It was no longer simply a matter of whether one knew Greek or Latin, one could actually participate in a national

competition against students from around the country. Students who previously would have been excluded based simply on where they went to school and what their school offered, now had an opportunity to compete nationally for admission to the most elite institutions of higher education. So, the move to the more objective tests was a move toward more meritocratic selection and toward a fairer, more open society.[7]

Yet this movement toward fairness, toward equality of opportunity, was only partial. While the appearance of objective, meritocratic selection has been maintained, the contest is not public and the average person is incapable of evaluating the competition. So, even if we end up with unequal, largely reproductive, outcomes, the process *seems* fair; ultimately, though, we simply assume this. It is possible that the tests (and/or grades) are rigged but since some working class students are successful, it may be that the unsuccessful ones simply didn't try hard enough. In sport, on the other hand, in an arena that is about *play* and in which everyone feels they have been involved their whole lives, we observe and understand the competition; competitions through which athletes or teams can rise to the pinnacle of their professions. Success and failure are endlessly scrutinized and debated. If an individual or team is successful, it reflects their ability to squeeze the greatest output from their talents (and, in the case of a team, that management has shrewdly evaluated, chosen, and meshed talent). If there is repeated failure, it means that they are deficient in talent or effort and that they must do something different to change the future outcome.

The focus in sports on the visible, meritocratic contest privileges all viewers to weigh in on what is wrong/right with a given team. If a Japanese hitter or pitcher is dominating his league in Japan, US teams should vie for his services. If a US soccer player is dominant, he should be recruited by the best European or South American teams. The labor market should be unfettered by immigration law and the competition for the best players should be based solely on market principles, not issues of race or ethnicity or nation. In the world of sport-as-meritocracy, if there were a working class polo player, the aristocratic team manager should recruit him, despite his lowly social origins. And the team will pay in match losses if another aristocrat is willing simply to recruit the best players. Of course, this means that those with the most resources will prevail, which is why there is such an outcry that the New York Yankees are simply buying championships. At the same time, let us remember that the Yankees have not won the World Series since 2000 and one of the lowest spending baseball teams, the Tampa Bay Rays, won the Yankees' division and made it to the World Series in 2008. Well, that's why they throw out the first pitch ...[8]

This social institution is one in which it is virtually impossible for the son or daughter of an owner to ascend though nepotism to a position on the playing field. Positions in management, instructively, reveal no such barrier. What we see, instead, among those who make it to the top of their sports, is *stunning social mobility*, which we perceive to be the accession to positions which were fairly earned in a public, visible competition with clear evaluation criteria. While our technological sophistication has progressed to the point that we can subject a given shortstop to deep statistical analyses of his fielding prowess, we have no such criteria by which we can evaluate, say, a middle manager in a business corporation. Sports games remind us that such meritocratic contests exist and reinforce our assumption that these selection norms operate in other institutions as well (Bill Clinton from a poor, single mother household becoming president, or Barack Obama, an African-American, becoming president). We certainly assume that this same situation exists in the education arena. In any case, sport tells us on an everyday basis that a high school kid from Akron can become King (Lebron) James or, reaching a few years back, that a "hick from French Lick" (Larry Bird) can rule the basketball court.

And yet, the *institution* of sport located within a social field, belies these ostensibly just, fair, consensual outcomes. The sports field is not only riven by struggles over unequal resources and power but also reflects and reinforces the dominant patterns of exclusion extant in the larger society. Yet it can maintain its claim for meritocratic purity by presenting itself as a *contest* even as it exists simultaneously as an *institution*. Needless to say, the former is what we pay for and what we pay attention to. But, as one of the players said to a coach in exasperation in "North Dallas Forty," one of the best sports movies of all time, "Every time I call it a game, you say it's a business. Every time I say it's a

business, you call it a game!" (Source: http://espn.go.com/page2/s/closer/021101.html)

Just as the structure of the contest ensures that there will be winners and losers, so, also, the structure of the field—given its inequalities—guarantees that there will be winners and losers. And the resources that accrue to winners almost guarantee their continued success. At the same time, we marvel at the success of traditional bottom-dwelling teams like the Tampa Bay Rays, or the annual surprise teams in the NCAA March Madness such as George Mason or Gonzaga. There *can* be some mobility up the hierarchy and this keeps everyone in the game.[9] And, secondarily, it is important to note that one gets some sports capital even for simply being in the game. Thus, colleges at the bottom of Division I, presumably, reap some benefits from being able to claim Division I status. Or, in the years before the Tampa Bay Rays succeeded, they could still claim "major league city" status compared to hundreds of other cities.

How is the ostensibly meritocratic institution of sport affected by class, racial/ethnic, and gender inequalities? And, how, in turn, does sport affect the inequalities in the larger society? How has this changed over time?

One of the major ways to further these inequalities in any given society is to segregate these groups in sport. What is the effect of this segregation for *institutionalizing* these inequalities? While racial/ethnic barriers have largely fallen at the elite level of sport, class and gender segregation largely remain in place. While no explicit policies exist against class-mixing, there are certainly legal and institutional barriers to gender-mixing. The general effect of gender segregation has been the denial of equal resources and opportunities to women to develop their athletic skills. This lack of access leads, of course, to the "natural" differences between men and women in orientation to sports participation. In terms of men and women playing on the same court, there have been occasional tryouts for women in the NBA and there is the famous Billie Jean King vs. Bobby Riggs tennis match. Just recently, though, a twelve-year old girl was barred from playing on her school's boys' basketball team because she was just too good (Weil, 2008). In general, though there have been calls for organizing sports by skill levels (McDonagh and Pappano, 2008), the wall between men's and women's sports is very high.

5

Despite the relative success of mixed doubles tennis, there appear to be no high-profile mixed-gender sporting competitions or interest in developing them.

The structure of opportunity in the larger society keeps class segregation in sport intact. While there are a few upper class athletes in elite level athletic competition (e.g. Bill Laimbeer, son of a corporate CEO, who played in the NBA), the road to upper class reproduction generally leads through higher education to non-athletic professional occupations (upper class sports are generally avocational).

In thinking about how the contours of class, racial/ethnic, and gender stratification appear in sport, we generally notice these more in the *field* of sport, i.e. *outside the contest* itself. Thus, when we look at management and ownership in sports, we see very clearly the inequalities extant in the larger society. We see evidence of sponsored mobility that lifts the sons (and daughters) of owners to responsible (or, at least, well-paying) positions in management (until they inherit ownership). On the field/court, however, we assume that the absolute best players are out there, unfettered by inequalities of opportunity based on social origins. Needless to say, it wasn't always this way.

We can see this illustrated in two examples of how the contest and the field of sport have affected each other. In 1947, Jackie Robinson began playing for the Brooklyn Dodgers, breaking the color line that had excluded African-Americans from Major League Baseball since the nineteenth century. As teams recognized this previously-excluded talent pool, more and more players from the Negro Leagues came to excel in Major League Baseball. Over time, the meritocratic nature of the game/contest won out over the interests of racist exclusion and cartel-oriented owners. Indeed, one could argue that the public, meritocratic nature of this baseball episode influenced both the civil rights movement and the race relations reforms in the United States.

The second example comes from a decade later and involves a trade between two National Basketball Association teams. The St. Louis Hawks made what is arguably the worst trade in the history of professional sports. In 1956, they drafted Bill Russell, a black two-time All American who had led his college team, the San Francisco Dons, to two consecutive national championships. To the Hawks, though, which had a very large southern white fan base, the prospect of having a star black player was not very appealing. So, they decided to trade Russell to the Boston Celtics for Ed Macauley, a St. Louis native toward the end of his career, who would be popular with their fans. The result? Russell went to the Celtics and led them to 11 NBA championships in 13 seasons and, by the time he retired, many sports writers ranked him as the greatest defensive basketball player of all time. Meanwhile, the Hawks declined into oblivion and eventually moved the franchise to Atlanta. Here, we have an example of a team following unmeritocratic practices (derived from the field, not the contest) and paying the price.

Let us conclude with an example of how the effects of the field of sport are manifested at the individual level. There is an interesting link between the individual and sport in thinking about the social construction of the body. Here, we see many fields converging to produce a "better" athlete. Though these sectors aren't intertwined enough to refer to a medical-athletic-industrial-entertainment complex, these powerful institutions operate within the field of sport to help produce the best bodies for given tasks on the court/field. At the same time, the individual athlete wishes to produce a body that will yield the highest possible sports capital (as well as any subsequent profits through conversion into other forms of capital). Indeed, as we suggest in the section on deviance below, the individual athlete and the doctors, trainers, coaches, and owners who are working on the athlete *all* have an objectified notion of the athlete's body, as something to be worked on and used. If a given game were a purely meritocratic contest, we could assume that all bodies have (been) prepared the same way. Yet, we know that "the game" (within the sports field) pushes some athletes to augment their strength with drugs and pushes some doctors to suggest that a player may be able to play with given injuries. Though the individual athlete may also care about her/his life and health outside of the contest and beyond the field of sport, such considerations are alien to the game.

Plan of the book

This anthology focuses on the field of sport and society. There are seven sections, each with an editorial introduction and a set of both scholarly and journalistic articles. The introductions raise theoretical and analytical issues that are relevant to the specific substantive topics in that section and highlight the ways that the selected articles address those issues. These introductory sections will help to orient the reader not only to the selected articles but also to broader research questions in that topical area.

We begin the book with a set of readings on "The Big Picture" that addresses some of the issues raised in this introduction. The selections focus on the unique nature of sport, the meaning of sport, and the compelling qualities of sport. The selections in the next three sections—on class, race/ethnicity, and gender, which focus on areas of institutionalized inequality prevalent in virtually all societies—examine the articulation between the patterns of inclusion and exclusion within sport and in the larger society, as well as the ways they are manifested at the level of individual experience. The next two sections—on deviance and sexualities—focus primarily on how pressures within sport may push individuals and organizations to affirm or resist conventional individual identities or norms of the mainstream society. The articles in these sections explore the tensions—experienced by individuals and organizations—between the demands of sport ("just win, baby!") and the constraints, demands, and values of the larger society. Finally, the section on global sport examines how sport can affect individual emotions and identities as well as mobilize nationalist sentiments. These selections allow us to examine the communal functions of sports, how these functions vary among different societies, and how processes of globalization have been changing various aspects of sport.

Although the selections are organized topically, there is much overlap across sections. For example, in Section 2 on social class, we include an excerpt from Loïc Wacquant's *Body and Soul*, an ethnographic account of a boxing gym. While Wacquant's argument about the social origins of boxers is the main focus, the piece also addresses the boxing gym as a masculine place and is therefore relevant to Section 4 on gender. Similarly, the article by Grindstaff and West in the gender section (Section 4) addresses one of the key questions that we raise in Section 1 about "what is a sport." Other examples include Lopes' (Section 2) analysis of

Brazilian football, which focuses on ethnicity and color as well as class, Thomas' (Section 2) discussion of Althea Gibson (race as well as class), Bederman (Section 3) on race as well as gender, etc. We hope that readers will use these "overlaps" to highlight the different analytical frames that exist within any given selection and to demonstrate the empirical relationships among different aspects of society.

Notes

1. *Moneyball*, by Michael Lewis (2003), discusses the tensions involved in assessing baseball players, given the increasing rationalization of sport. While old-timers marvel at the "look" of the player, the quantitatively-oriented "sabermetricians" focus on key statistical summaries of performance.

2. We suggest that the meritocratic ideal is *hegemonic* because, though it helps to cement current power relations, it is an accepted mode of recruitment, selection, and reward in capitalist democracies. Meritocracy is often the ideological basis of a society's system of social mobility.

3. Think of the difference between evaluating a basketball player's ability to shoot free throws and a middle manager's ability to maximize productivity from those s/he supervises.

4. By "institution," we mean the regular, normative patterns of interaction that occur among the individuals and organizations within sport. By using the term "field," we wish to emphasize that the institution of sport is characterized by struggles over power and resources among these actors but these struggles often include other institutions. Thus, for example, as we suggest immediately below, education and the state are involved in struggles over resources that may be waged within the sports field. For further elaboration of Bourdieu's concept of field, see Swartz (1997: 119–122).

5. According to Swartz (1997:136), the *field of power* "functions as [a] sort of 'meta-field' that operates as an organizing principle of differentiation and struggle throughout *all* fields."

6. This refers to the fact that applications to Boston College surged in the two years following Doug Flutie's "Hail Mary" pass to defeat Miami in a football game in 1984. Though there is quite a bit of anecdotal evidence for such effects across other institutions, application drops and surges are affected by so many other factors that it is difficult to firmly establish a "Flutie effect."

7. It is very easy to overstate the meritocratic effects of national testing. We are suggesting merely that this movement toward more objective testing made it *possible* for students from modest backgrounds to

gain access to elite education, *not* that selection became entirely meritocratic or fair.

8. The key here is that the Yankees and the Rays are governed by the same rules. Indeed, when the competition seems unfair, there are calls for a change in the rules, as has occurred recently in a call by the Milwaukee Brewers' management for a salary cap. Right now, Major League Baseball has a revenue sharing arrangement, whereby the teams with the highest payroll have to pay a luxury tax, which is distributed to small-market/low-payroll teams. Unfortunately, there's no proviso that the teams that receive these monies actually must spend them on the team; owners may simply pocket the extra cash.

9. So, mobility may occur at the individual level *and* at the team level. And, just as working class mobility into educational and professional success legitimates the openness of the social structure, so do big upsets legitimate our experience of sport as meritocratic.

References

Bourdieu, P. and J. Passeron. 1977. *Reproduction in Education, Society, and Culture*. London; Beverly Hills: Sage.

Bourdieu, P. and L. Wacquant. 1992. *An Invitation to Reflexive Sociology*. Chicago: University of Chicago Press.

Lewis, M. 2003. *Moneyball: The Art of Winning an Unfair Game*. New York: W. W. Norton.

McDonagh, E. and L. Pappano. 2008. *Playing with the Boys: Why Separate is not Equal in Sports*. New York: Oxford University Press.

Pope, D.G. and J. Pope. 2008. The Impact of College Sports Success on the Quantity and Quality of Student Applications. Virginia Tech Department of Agricultural and Applied Economics. Working Paper No. 2008-05. January.

Swartz, D. 1997. *Culture and Power: The Sociology of Pierre Bourdieu*. Chicago: University of Chicago Press.

Weil, E. 2008. Scary, Isn't She? *Play Magazine*. *The New York Times*. September 14. (http://www.nytimes.com/2008/09/14/sports/playmagazine/0914play-NARED.html)

Section 1

The big picture

Theorizing sports from sociological perspectives

Introduction

What makes a sport a sport? In the US, if we take ESPN's (the Entertainment and Sports Programming Network) coverage of various events as an indicator, the scope of sport has expanded over the last few decades. Not only have cheerleading competitions—which require gymnastics-type athleticism—been included in its offerings but so have spelling bees and poker tournaments. Are all of these "sports"? How does one define sport? Is it simply about competition? How physical does the activity have to be in order to be considered a sport? Can the same activity be a sport in one context and not in another? Do we consider both the Olympics softball competition (2008 may be its last year) and the beerfest in which a softball game breaks out as sports?

We also must think about the role of sport in the society. Does sport simply reflect the values—for instance, individualism or teamwork—of the larger society? What is its social significance? How many neighborhood connections are deepened (what sociologists refer to as "social capital") as parents watch their children play sports? Why and how does sport seem to unite (and divide) disparate peoples within and across nations, races and ethnicities, social classes, and genders? How has this form of *play* developed into a multi-billion dollar world-encompassing *business* that occupies the hearts, minds, and bodies of so many? According to Street and Smith's *Sports Business Journal*, "(t)he sports business industry is one of the largest and fastest growing industries in the United States. Our annual survey of the size of the industry estimated the sports business industry last year at $213 billion. It is far more than twice the size of the US auto industry and seven times the size of the movie industry" (http://www.sportsbusinessjournal.com/index. cfm?fuseaction=page.feature&featureId=43). Sport has produced a world-wide "language" that allows Chileans, Russians, Australians, Vietnamese, and Finns to compete against each other in a given event, as well as a means for white female corporate Vice Presidents to banter with Asian lunch delivery guys about the previous night's game (not that this happens *much*).

In examining the question "what is sport," we enter the realm of socially constructed and powerfully contested notions. Andy Baggott's funny, shoot-from-the-hip article raises many serious questions. Many activities have, at various times in various contexts, been categorized as sports. From games that can be played in drinking establishments (darts and pool) to competitions involving horses and cars (polo and demolition derbies), the range of activities that may be considered sports is wide indeed. Think also about how competitors interact in given sports: at one end of the spectrum and, in some ways, the essence of the sport, we see wrestlers and (American) football players grapple physically with one another to gain physical advantage and, at the other end of the spectrum, golfers bodies do not interact at all (not even via the

11

balls they hit, as in tennis) (see Bourdieu, 1988). While there are various characteristics that conventionally define a sport (e.g. some degree of physicality, competition, agreed-upon "official" rules, and an industry that supplies "official" equipment), there is, if you will, major competition among activities to *become* a SPORT.

The articles in this section suggest that it is useful to think about competition at three levels: the individual, the sport, and the national context. In each case, one sees evidence of what Eric Dunning calls "achievement-striving." At the individual level, we learn about the ways that champions arrange their lives, bodies, and minds to produce success. At the level of sport, we see the social and historical conditions that lead to the decline of amateur sports and spur attempts at professionalization. And, in a national (and even international) context, there is a highly structured "sports space"—structured especially by power relations in the given society—that develops historically and that conditions the nature of the competition among sports for greater centrality in a nation's sports space. In the piece by Tomlinson, Markovits, and Young, the concept of "sports space" is developed and its dynamics and implications are examined. In particular, we learn how soccer in the US, as opposed to virtually all other countries, is a marginal sport, played primarily by women, upper middle class white suburbanites, and immigrants. Lipsyte, in the piece included below, also pushes us to think about the implications of sport: he suggests that, by focusing on elite performance, sports tend to limit participation and to "import" the inequalities that are extant in the larger society.

What factors lead some sports to become more popular than others? Why is cricket of great interest in England but of no interest in Mexico? Why is hockey so central to daily life in Canada? What are the processes that lead some sports to develop professional leagues that produce major championship televised spectacles and other sports to flounder in regional obscurity? What is it about sport that, simply, is so compelling? Why is sport something that produces the kind of manic commitment in top athletes and in the most devoted fans? How does that commitment and devotion develop? The athletes give up friends and family in devoting themselves to their sport. The fans celebrate wildly or get depressed, depending on how their team fared.

These questions focus centrally on the relationship between sport and society. They go to the heart of the complex relations between sport and society. They deal with issues of power (compare the National Football League with the US Curling Association), culture (common idioms in the US—"Monday morning quarterback" [meaning 20-20 hindsight] or "pinch-hit" [meaning substitute]—are not common elsewhere) and inequality (think about differential participation by race, class, and gender in sports and in specific sports). We explore these issues in more detail throughout this volume.

In "The Mundanity of Excellence," Chambliss argues that, in order to produce excellence in the human practice called sport, one needs to practice (Allen Iverson's famous remarks, notwithstanding): in particular ways, with attention to detail, and in a way that makes every aspect of the activity routine. Rather than focusing on "talent," he argues that excellence in sport, as in other human practices, is rooted in the degree to which the actor is habituated to the demands of the practice. Essentially, he argues, the practice of the sport must be embedded in one's bodily habitus,[1] such that performance at any given time becomes second nature: the more routine one's engagement in the given practice in specific ways, the greater the likelihood of success. Indeed, one can argue that we learn from Chambliss' article that those who are interested in excellence in human endeavors ignore sport at their peril. If this is the case, then not only should the study of sport not be marginalized, it must be made more central to our sociological concerns.

Note

1. See the short discussion in Tomlinson *et al.* (selection in this chapter). See also Pierre Bourdieu (various works).

References

Bourdieu, P. (1988) 'Program for a Sociology of Sport', *Sociology of Sport Journal* 5(2): 153–61.

Tomlinson, A., A. Markovits, and C. Young. (2003) 'Introduction: Mapping Sports Space', *American Behavioral Scientist* 46, 11 (July): 1463–75.

The dynamics of modern sport

Notes on achievement-striving and the social significance of sport

Eric Dunning

In this piece, Eric Dunning attempts to explain the shift from sport as amateur play to sport as serious, achievement-striving. How did we move from a focus on neighbors playing a game to a focus on which country's team will win the World Cup? Dunning and his mentor, Norbert Elias, term their approach "figurational sociology"; most important for readers is to focus on Dunning's key variables. His argument is that the move toward achievement-striving is a long-term change that involved the rise of the modern state, an increase in equality among contending groups (functional democratization), and greater interdependence among people and nations. While the process of industrialization is certainly an important part of this change, Dunning claims that it is the change in relationships among people (density and scope) and the pressures that lead people to think of sport in terms of identity and prestige that truly underlie our current mania about professional sports.

Introduction

The subject of this essay is what I take to be, world-wide, the dominant trend in modern sport, namely a trend, at all levels of participation but most conspicuously in top-level sport, towards growing competitiveness, seriousness of involvement and achievement-orientation. Expressed differently, the trend I am referring to involves the gradual but seemingly inexorable erosion of 'amateur' attitudes, values and structures, and their correlative replacement by attitudes, values and structures that are 'professional' in one sense or another of that term. Viewed from yet another angle, it is a trend in which, in countries all over the world, sport is being transformed from a marginal, lowly valued institution into one that is central and much more highly valued, an institution which, for many people, seems to have religious or quasi-religious significance in the sense that it has become one of the central, if not *the* central, sources of identification, meaning and gratification in their lives.

Resistance to this trend has been offered on several occasions, in Britain perhaps most notably in the attempt since the end of the nineteenth century to maintain Rugby Union as a player-centred amateur sport based on voluntary organization and an informal framework of 'friendly' matches, that is as a sport in which the rules are designed to secure enjoyment for players rather than spectators, organization at the club, regional and national levels is undertaken as an unpaid avocation, and there is no structure of formal competition, of 'cups' and 'leagues'. However, the attempt to maintain such a structure has been conspicuously unsuccessful.

Eric Dunning, "The Dynamics of Modern Sport: Achievement Striving and the Social Significance of Sport" from *Quest for Excitement: Sport and Leisure in the Civilizing Process*. Copyright © 1986 by Norbert Elias and Eric Dunning. Reprinted with the permission of Blackwell Publishers, Ltd.

Despite strenuous efforts by the game's ruling groups, top-level matches are now played in front of large crowds and several spectator-oriented rules have been introduced. Clubs also compete annually for the John Player Cup and a number of local ones besides, and there is a system of 'merit tables' which are leagues in all but name. Moreover, the national controlling body, the Rugby Football Union, and many top clubs are financially dependent on revenue from match attendances and commercial sponsorship. The RFU also employs a number of permanent officials, and there have been repeated rumours of players who are paid. In short, in this as in other cases, the resistance has been overcome, a fact which suggests that the trend towards growing seriousness and competitiveness or, alternatively, towards the 'de-amateurization' of sport, is a compelling social process.

To say this is not to claim that resistance has died out altogether. Conflict over the issue of play-oriented, amateur versus achievement-oriented, professional forms and conceptions of sport continues in Rugby and elsewhere, hence attesting to the fact that this process is not simply a thing of the past. Moreover, besides being compelling and ongoing, this process was, and is, conflictual, a fact which shows that it is an example of what [Norbert] Elias would call a 'blind' or 'unplanned' long-term social process. That is, it is not the result of the intended acts of any single individual or group but, rather, the unintended outcome of the interweaving of the purposive actions of the members of several interdependent groups over several generations. [...]

In what follows, I want to suggest that the growing seriousness of modern sport can be in large part attributed to three interrelated processes, namely, state-formation, functional democratization and the spread of sport through the widening network of international interdependencies. The first two are, of course, the deep-structural processes, both interwoven with the lengthening of interdependency chains, by means of which Elias principally explains the sociogenesis of the civilizing process.

This suggests that there may be a connection between the civilizing process and the trend towards growing seriousness of involvement in sport; for example the latter may consist partly in the fact that, by virtue of his or her socialization into the more restraining standards of the more complex and constraining modern system of social interdependencies, the more restrained and civilized modern individual is less able to participate spontaneously and uninhibitedly in sport than his or her less civilized and more emotionally unrestrained forebear who lived in a less complex and less constraining system of social interdependencies. It seems plausible to maintain that this is so. Yet it remains necessary to spell out precisely what the connections were between, on the one hand, the growing seriousness of sports participation and, on the other, state-formation, functional democratization and the civilizing process. [...]

A figurational analysis of the trend towards growing seriousness in sport

In order to accomplish such a demonstration, I shall first discuss the amateur ethos and attempt to explain sociogenetically both it and its dissolution, that is the trend towards growing seriousness in sport. I shall then, briefly and in general terms, discuss sport in pre-industrial Britain in order to show why, in such a social figuration, it was possible for groups at all levels of the social hierarchy, to have what were, on balance, 'self-directed' or 'egocentric' forms of sports participation, that is, why it was possible for them to participate in sport for fun. Next, I shall attempt to show why, with the emergence of urban-industrial-national-states, more 'other-directed' sport-forms connected more with achievement-orientation, identity-striving and the struggle for pecuniary rewards came to develop. Finally, I shall discuss what I take to be the growing social significance of sport and the part played by its spread internationally in this overall social process.

The amateur ethos is the dominant sports ideology in modern Britain and, I think I am right in saying, of ruling groups in sport across the world, for example of the International Olympic Committee and its various national affiliates. The central component of this ethos is the ideal of playing sports 'for fun'. Other aspects, such as the stress on 'fair play', voluntary adherence to rules and non-pecuniary involvement, are essentially subordinate, designed to facilitate the achievement of that end—to make sporting contests 'play-fights' in which pleasurable excitement can be generated. The earliest example I have found of the explicit use of this ethos to criticize the trend towards growing seriousness in sport appears in a book by Trollope, published in 1868:

> [Sports] are being made too much of, and men who follow them have allowed themselves to be taught that ordinary success in them is not worth having ... All this comes from excess of enthusiasm on the matter;—from a desire to follow too well a pursuit which, to be pleasurable, should be a pleasure and not a business ... [This] is the rock against which our sports may possibly be made shipwreck. Should it ever become unreasonable in its expenditure, arrogant in its demands, immoral and selfish in its tendencies, or, worse of all, unclean and dishonest in its traffic, there will arise against it a public opinion against which it will be unable to hold its own.

It is, of course, likely that earlier examples could be found, but this mobilization of amateur values, with their stress on pleasure as the essential ingredient of sport, came at an early stage in the development of the modern forms of sport, above all at a time when professional sport as we know it today hardly existed. It was then possible for some men to earn a precarious living as prize-fighters, jockeys and cricketers, but the fact that they were only a handful suggests that Trollope's critique was directed mainly at a trend towards growing seriousness within *amateur* sport. And it is possible that one of his principal targets was what historians have called the 'public school games cult', a movement in the public schools that involved five main components: (1) a tendency to appoint and promote staff in terms of sporting rather than academic criteria; (2) the selection of prefects, that is the leading boys in a school, principally on the basis of ability at sport; (3) the elevation of sport to a prominent and, in some cases, pre-eminent position in the curriculum; (4) the educational rationalization of sport, especially team-games, as an instrument of 'character-training'; and (5) participation by members of staff in the organization and playing of their pupils' games. It is, of course, likely that such a movement could only have arisen in elite schools, the majority of whose pupils were not dependent on an academic education for their future careers. But that is less relevant for present purposes than the fact that the public school games cult shows clearly that the trend towards growing seriousness in sport in Britain

was, in its earliest stages, a phenomenon connected with amateur and not professional sport and that it did not derive its initial momentum from the conflict between amateurs and professionals adduced by Huizinga. In fact, I should like to hypothesize that the amateur ethos was articulated as an ideology in opposition to the trend towards growing seriousness and that it received its most explicit and detailed formulation when, as part of that trend, the modern forms of professional sport began to emerge.

In Britain prior to the 1880s, the amateur ethos existed in a relatively inchoate form. That is, it was an amorphous, loosely articulated set of values regarding the functions of sport and the standards believed necessary for their realization. However, with the threat posed by the incipient professionalization of new sports such as soccer and rugby, a process that began in the North and Midlands and drew low-status, regionally based, middle- and working-class groups as organizers, players and spectators into the ambit of sports that had hitherto been the exclusive preserve of the 'public school elite', the national ruling class, the amateur ethos began to crystallize as an elaborate and articulate ideology. That is, it was a collective representation developed by the members of one collectivity in opposition to the members of another which they perceived as a threat both to their organizational and playing pre-eminence and the forms of sport as they wished to see it played. In short, I am suggesting that, even though the public school elite tended to couch their pronouncements in sport-specific terms, claiming to be solely interested in preserving what they regarded as the essential, 'fun-oriented' character of sport, class and regional hostility and resentment over the loss of their erstwhile dominance played an important part in their articulation of the amateur ethos as an explicit ideology. However, if I am right, the social situation in which they found themselves was increasingly inconducive to the full-scale, unbridled realization of self-directed, pleasure-oriented forms of sport and that, in articulating and mobilizing the amateur ethos in response to the growing threat from below, they were trying to maintain forms of sports participation which they regarded as their right as members of a ruling class and which had, in fact, been possible for ruling and even subordinate groups in the pre-industrial era but which were increasingly impossible for them.

15

Support for this view comes from the fact that many of the 'abuses' that the public school elite claimed to detect in professional sport were at least equally evident in the games cult in the schools they had attended. Further support— although there were symptomatic exceptions such as 'the Corinthians' soccer team—comes from the fact that, in an increasing number of sports, the public school elite withdrew into their own exclusive circles, revealing by their fear of being beaten by professionals that they played in order to obtain the kudos of being recognized as successful sportsmen as much as they did for fun. Of course, this separatist trend was probably, in part, occasioned by the fact that contests between professional and amateur teams would frequently have been unbalanced and lacking in tone owing to the skill discrepancy that usually exists between full-time players who are following their occupation and part-time players who are merely participating in a leisure activity. But that this is not the whole story is suggested by the fact that a further separatist trend by members of the public school elite occurred within the ranks of *amateur* sport. That is, they were unwilling to submit themselves regularly to the possibility of defeat at the hands of working-class amateur teams and, by hiving off into their own exclusive circles, they showed, not only class prejudice, but that they took part in sport seriously and in order to win—the success goal had come to take precedence in their hierarchy of sporting values over the goal of participating primarily for fun. Further support for such a view comes from a figurational analysis of sport in eighteenth-century Britain.

The overall social figuration of Britain in the eighteenth century, indeed, the overall pattern of social interdependencies in pre-industrial Britain generally, was one in which there was relatively little structural pressure on groups, whether high or low in the status order, towards success-striving and achievement-orientation, that is towards 'other-directed' forms of participation, in the sporting or in other fields. The relatively low degree of state-centralization and national unification, for example, meant that 'folk games', the games of the ordinary people, were played in regional isolation, competition traditionally occurring between contiguous villages and towns or between the sections of towns. But there was no national competitive framework. The aristocracy and gentry formed

a partial exception in this regard. They were, and perceived themselves as, national classes and did compete nationally among themselves. As a result, a certain degree of other-directed competitive pressure in sporting activities was generated within their ranks. But they were subject, in a general and sporting sense, to effective pressure neither from above nor from below. The level of state-formation at that stage in the development of British society was relatively low and, in a very real sense, the aristocracy and gentry 'were the state', that is able effectively to use the state apparatus in their own interests. They had established the precedence of parliament over the monarchy and ruled over a society in which the balance of power between classes involved gross inequalities. As a result, there was no effective challenge to their position as the dominant class. The secure character of their dominance was conducive to a high degree of status security on their part and this meant, in turn, that individual aristocrats and gentlemen were, as a rule, in no way seriously threatened by contact with social subordinates. Whatever the context, they knew who was master and so did everybody else—the gross power imbalance between classes led to patterns of deference from subordinates.

Such status-security was extended to the leisure-sphere, including sport. The aristocracy and gentry took part in folk games both in an organizational and playing capacity, and used their patronage to develop forms of professional cricket, prize-fighting and horse-racing. The type of sports career that grew up under such conditions was based on unequivocal subordination of the professional to his patron and total dependency as far as life-chances were concerned of the former on the latter. No threat was posed by professionalism of that type to the interests and values of the ruling class. Professional sport was neither morally nor socially suspect and there was no need to fight against or hide the fact that pecuniary advantage could be obtained from games, whether as an occupational wage or from gambling on the outcome of contests. Above all, whether playing among themselves or with their hirelings, the aristocracy and gentry could participate in sport for fun; that is, their social situation—the power and relative autonomy they enjoyed—meant that they could develop self-directed or egocentric forms of sports participation and that, although they were not constrained to develop the amateur ethos as an explicit ideology, they came close to being amateurs in the 'ideal typical' sense of that term.

If this diagnosis is correct, it follows that the overall social figuration of pre-industrial Britain and, I think one can safely say, of other pre-industrial societies, too, was not conducive to the generation of intense competitive pressure in sporting relations, whether within or between ruling and subordinate groups. It also follows that the sociogenesis of the pressure towards other-directed, achievement-oriented forms of sports-participation has to be sought in the social figuration brought into being in conjunction with industrialization. I shall now endeavour to point out what the connections between these two social processes were, that is between industrialization and the long-term trend towards increasing seriousness of involvement and achievement-striving in sport. Briefly, and in anticipation of the analysis that follows, it can be said that the key to this relationship lies in the process that Elias calls 'functional democratization'—in the equalizing change in the balance of power within and between groups that occurs contingently upon the interrelated processes of state-formation and lengthening of interdependency chains.

Industrialization and the development of achievement-oriented forms of sport

[...]

According to Elias, the long-term social transformation usually referred to by terms denoting specific aspects such as 'industrialization', 'economic growth', the 'demographic transition', 'urbanization' and 'political modernization', is in fact, a long-term transformation of the total social structure. And, he contends, one of the sociologically most significant aspects of this total social transformation consists in the emergence of longer and more differentiated 'chains of interdependence'. That is, it involves the emergence of greater functional specialization and the integration of functionally differentiated groups into wider networks. Moreover, concomitantly with this, there occurs, according to Elias, a change in the direction of decreasing power-differentials within and among groups, more specifically, a

change in the balance of power between rulers and ruled, the social classes, men and women, the generations, parents and children. Such a process occurs because the performers of specialized roles are dependent on others and can, therefore, exert reciprocal control. The power-chances of specialized groups are further enhanced if they manage to organize since, then, they are able to disrupt the wider system of interdependencies by collective action. It is in ways such as these, according to Elias, that increasing division of labour and the emergence of longer chains of interdependence leads to greater reciprocal dependency, and, hence, to patterns of 'multipolar control' within and among groups, that is to an overall social figuration in which specific individuals and groups are subject to increasingly effective pressure from others. Such pressure is effective because of the reciprocal dependencies involved.

The relevance of this deceptively simple theory for the present analysis is manifold. Inherent in the modern structure of social interdependencies is the demand for inter-regional and representative sport. No such demand arose in pre-industrial societies because the lack of effective national unification and poor means of transport and communication meant that there were no common rules and no means by which sportsmen from different areas could be brought regularly together. At the same time, the 'localism' inherent in such societies meant that play-groups perceived as potential rivals only groups with which they were contiguous in a geographical sense. However, modern industrial societies are different on all these counts. They are relatively unified nationally, have superior means of transport and communication, sports with common rules, and a degree of cosmopolitanism' which means that local groups perceive as potential rivals, and are anxious to compare themselves with others which are not geographically adjacent. Hence, such societies are characterized by high rates of inter-area sporting interaction, a process that leads to stratification internally in specific sports—to a hierarchical grading of sportsmen, sportswomen and sports teams with those that represent the largest units standing at the top.

In its turn, this means that the reciprocal pressures and controls that operate in urban-industrial societies generally are replicated in the sphere of sport.

As a result, top-level sportsmen and women cannot be independent and play for fun but are forced to be other-directed and serious in their sports participation. That is, they are unable to play for themselves but constrained to represent wider social units such as cities, counties, and countries. As such, they are provided with material and/or prestige rewards and facilities and time for training. In return, they are expected to produce a 'sports performance', that is the sort of satisfactions which the controllers and 'consumers' of the sport demand, namely the spectacle of an exciting contest that people are willing to pay to watch or the validation through victory of the 'image' and 'reputation' of the social unit with which the controllers and/or consumers identify. The sheer numbers of people involved and the local, regional, national and international competitive framework of modern sport work in the same direction. They mean that high and sustained achievement-motivation, long-term planning, strict self-control and renunciation of immediate gratification, in other words constant practice and training, are necessary in order to get to, and stay at, the top. They also necessitate a degree of bureaucratic control and hence lead to the subordination of sportsmen in yet another respect.

In each of these ways, the social figuration, the pattern of inter-group dependencies, characteristic of an urban-industrial-nation-state generates constraints which militate against the practical realization of the amateur ethos with its stress on enjoyment as the central aim of sport. Or more properly, it generates constraints which militate against the realization of immediate, short-term enjoyment, against each sporting contest as an 'end in itself', and leads to its replacement, both for players and spectators, by longer-term goals such as victory in a league or cup, by satisfactions more centrally concerned with identity and prestige. Moreover, such constraints are not confined to top-level sport but reverberate down to the lowest levels of sporting achievement. That is partly because top-level sportsmen and women form a media-promoted reference group who set standards which others try to follow. It is also partly a consequence of the pressures generated by competition for the material and prestige rewards which can be obtained by getting to the top. However, it is by no means only due to pressures that are generated solely within sport

but also, and perhaps, more centrally, a consequence of the deep-rooted and pervasive anxieties and insecurities generated more generally in a society characterized by multipolar pressures and controls, and in which props of identity and status connected with traditional forms of class, authority, sex and age relations have all been eroded by functional democratization, that is by the equalizing process which, according to Elias, is inherent in the division of labour.

Suggestions regarding the growing social significance of sport

So far, I have provided the outlines of a figurational explanation of the trend towards increasingly serious involvement in sport. The related development in the course of which its social significance has grown remains to be discussed. This is a complex issue and can only be touched on briefly in the present context. Apart from the changing balance, ideological as well as factual, between work and leisure, a process which has increased the social significance of leisure activities generally, a constellation of at least three interrelated aspects of the emergent modern social figuration can be singled out as having contributed to the growing social significance of sport, namely: (1) the fact that sport has developed as one of the principal media for the generation of pleasurable excitement; (2) the fact that sport has come to function as one of the principal media of collective identification; and (3) the fact that sport has come to form a key source of meaning in the lives of many people.

Elias and I have suggested elsewhere that sport is a 'mimetic' leisure event in which pleasurable excitement can be generated and that, in this respect, it performs a 'de-routinizing' function. There is, however, no society without controls and routines or, as Elias has put it, no 'zero-point' of civilization. In that sense, the need for de-routinization is probably socially universal. But urban-industrial societies are highly routinized and civilized, characterized by multipolar pressures and controls. Accordingly, their members are constrained continuously to exercise a high degree of emotional restraint in their ordinary, everyday lives, with the consequence that the need for de-routinizing leisure activities such as sports in such societies is particularly intense. However, this de-routinizing process, this socially permitted arousal of emotion in public, is itself subject to civilizing controls. That is, sport is a social enclave, both for players and spectators, where pleasurable excitement can be generated in a form that is socially limited and controlled.

Nevertheless, the excitement generated can be intense, especially at top-level sports events which attract large crowds and, *pace* Huizinga who argued that sport has become 'profane', it is probably this that forms the experiential basis for the widespread perception of sport as a 'sacred' phenomenon. Durkheim argued that the collective excitement or 'effervescence' generated in the religious ceremonies of the Australian aborigines formed the principal experiential source of their idea of a 'sacred' realm, and it seems not unreasonable to suppose that the generation of 'collective effervescence' in sports events lies at the root of the fact that it is common, at least in Britain, to refer to football and cricket pitches, especially those used for representative matches, as the 'sacred' or 'hallowed' turf. Indeed, it would probably not be going too far to suggest that, at least for some groups in present-day society, sport has become a quasi-religious activity and that, viewed from a societal perspective, it has come, to some extent, to fill the gap in social life left by the decline of religion. An extreme but none the less indicative example of this quasi-religious character of modern sport is provided by the fact that it has apparently become a tradition in Liverpool for deceased supporters of Liverpool FC to have their ashes strewn on the Anfield pitch; they seem to wish to remain identified even after death with the 'shrine' or 'temple' at which they 'worshipped' during life. But even short of this extreme, it is clear that playing and/ or watching one sport or another has come to form one of the principal media of collective identification in modern society and one of the principal sources of meaning in life for many people. In short, it is by no means unrealistic to suggest that sport is coming increasingly to form the secular religion of our increasingly secular age.

It is probably the inherently oppositional character of sport, that is the fact that it is a struggle for victory between two or more teams or two or more individuals, that accounts for its prominence as a focus for collective identification. This means that it lends itself to group identification, more precisely to 'in-group' and 'out-group', or 'we-group' and 'they-group' formation on a variety of levels, such as the levels of city, county or country. The oppositional element is crucial since opposition serves to reinforce in-group identification, that is, a group's sense of 'we-ness' or unity is strengthened by the presence of a group who are perceived as 'them', the opposing team, whether local or national, and its supporters. Indeed, within the context of domestically pacified nation-states that is in societies where the state has established an effective monopoly on the right to use physical force, sport provides the only occasion on which large, complex and impersonal social units such as cities can unite. Similarly, at the international level, sporting events such as the Olympic Games and the World Cup provide the only peace-time occasions where whole nation-states are able regularly and visibly to unite. The international expansion of sport has been predicated on the growth of international interdependence and the existence, with several notable exceptions, of a fragile and unstable world peace. Contests such as the Olympics allow the representatives of different nations to compete without killing one another, though the degree to which such contests are transformed from mock-fights into 'real' ones is a function, inter alia, of the pre-existing level of tension between the particular nation-states involved. And, of course, it is in order to participate effectively at this highest level of sporting competition that the highest levels of sustained achievement-motivation, self-control and self-denial on the part of sportsmen are required.

This brings me to my final point: namely that the social pressure on sportsmen and women in countries all over the world to strive for success in international competition is a further source of the destruction of the play-element in sport. Moreover, it is that, and the increment to national prestige that success in international sport can yield, which has contributed principally to the tendency towards the involvement of the state in sport ... It has been argued that sport is a viable substitute for war but such an idea involves viewing it as an abstraction, as something independent and apart from the figurations of interdependent human beings who take part in it. That is the crucial issue: namely, whether the figurations formed by interdependent human beings, in sport and elsewhere, are conducive to co-operation or friendly rivalry, or whether they persistently generate serious fighting. [...]

19

1.3

The mundanity of excellence

An ethnographic report on stratification and Olympic swimmers

Daniel F. Chambliss

In this rewarding article, Daniel Chambliss shares with us the inner world of Olympics-level swimming. He asks the general question: where does excellence come from? He argues convincingly that one should not attribute excellence in a variety of endeavors to "talent" because "talent" is really a general description of the many little things that comprise excellence. He makes the very good point that if "talent" is the explanation, then the rest of us have an excuse for lack of excellence. Ultimately, we learn that athletic excellence is most reliably expressed when it is mundanely built into everyday bodily practice.

Olympic sports, and competitive swimming in particular, provide an unusually clear opportunity for studying the nature of excellence. In other fields, it may be less clear who are the outstanding performers: the best painter or pianist, the best business-person, the finest waitress or the best father. But in sport (and this is one of its attractions) success is defined more exactly, by success in competition. There are medals and ribbons and plaques for first place, second, and third; competitions are arranged for the head-to-head meeting of the best competitors in the world; in swimming and track, times are electronically recorded to the hundredth of a second; there are statistics published and rankings announced, every month or every week. By the end of the Olympic Games every four years, it is completely clear who won and who lost, who made the finals, who participated in the Games, and who never participated in the sport at all.

Within competitive swimming in particular, clear stratification exists not only between individuals but also between defined levels of the sport as well. At the lowest level, we see the country club teams, operating in the summertime as a loosely-run, mildly competitive league, with volunteer part-time coaches. Above that there are teams which represent entire cities and compete with other teams from other cities around the state or region; then a "Junior Nationals" level of competition, featuring the best younger (under 18 years old) athletes; then the Senior Nationals level (any age, the best in the nation); and finally, we could speak of world or Olympic class competitors. At each such level, we find, predictably, certain people competing: one athlete swims in a summer league, never seeing swimmers from another town; one swimmer may consistently qualify for the Junior Nationals, but not for Seniors; a third may swim at the Olympics, and never return to Junior

Nationals. The levels of the sport are remarkably distinct from one another.

This is convenient for the student of stratification. Because success in swimming is so definable, and the stratification system so (relatively) unambiguous (so that the athlete's progress can be easily charted), we can clearly see, by comparing levels and studying individuals as they move between and within levels, what exactly produces excellence. In addition, careers in swimming are relatively short; one can achieve tremendous success in a brief period of time. Rowdy Gaines, beginning in the sport when 17 years old, jumped from a country club league to a world record in the 100 meter freestyle event in only three years. This allows the researcher to conduct true longitudinal research in a few short years.

In short, in competitive swimming one can rather quickly learn something about stratification; here is a prime location for studying the nature of excellence.[1]

The research

From January 1983 through August 1984 I attended a series of national and international-class swimming meets conducted by United States Swimming, Inc., the national governing body for the sport. United States Swimming sanctions the selection process for American teams for international events (the Olympic Games, for example), and charters several thousand amateur swimming clubs around the country with membership of several hundred thousand athletes, by far the majority of whom are children and teenagers. These clubs provide the organizational base for amateur swimming in America. The meets attended included both the Indoor (March) and the Outdoor (August) National Championships, the USS International Meet, the Seventeen Magazine Meet of Champions, the Speedo/Dupont Meet of Champions, the 1984 Olympic Trials, and the 1984 Summer Olympic Games. I carried standard press credentials, and was free to go anywhere and talk to anyone. At most meets I traveled with the Mission Viejo (CA) Nadadores, National Team Champions at the time, sharing plane flights, hotel accommodations, meals, and in-town transportation with them. I lived with the coaches and athletes of this team in a traditional participant observer role.

It was clear to all involved that I was there as a researcher; no deception was involved at any stage of the research. During this period and several occasions since, I interviewed a total of some 120 national and world-class swimmers and coaches.[2]

Over these years I frequently spent from 3 days to a month and a half in Mission Viejo (about an hour's drive south of Los Angeles) living with coaches, visiting practices, and interviewing swimmers, coaches and officials. The Nadadores gave me complete access to their practices, weight lifting sessions, team meetings, parties, and other events. In addition, I was present in Mission Viejo during the U.S. Olympic Team Training Camp, which was held there in July of 1984, and was the only non-staff member on the pool deck during the (closed) afternoon practices of the Olympic Team. In addition, I have recently completed five years of coaching a regional-level age group swimming team (children 7–16 years old) in New York State. In that capacity I traveled to many meets, from the smallest "country club" events to the Eastern Zone Championships, as well as other large meets east of the Mississippi River. I have also coached in the southern U.S. and worked with beginners as well as National Age Group record holders.

In short, this report draws on extended experience with swimmers at every level of ability, over some half a dozen years. Observation has covered the span of careers, and I have had the chance to compare not just athletes within a certain level (the view that most coaches have), but between the most discrepant levels as well. Thus these findings avoid the usual "sociology of knowledge" problem of an observer's being familiar mainly with athletes at one level. When top-rank coaches, for instance, talk of what makes success, they are often thinking of the differences between athletes whom they see within the top level of the sport. Their ignorance of the day-to-day realities of lower levels (learn-to-swim programs, country club teams) prevents them from having a truly comparative view. Or when sports journalists write about Olympic athletes, they typically begin the research *after* the great deed is done, and so lack a legitimate longitudinal view; the athlete's memory of his or her own distant history will be distorted.

This study of Olympic swimmers, by contrast, (1) looks at different levels of the sport,

21

and (2) was begun well in advance of the Games, when no one (obviously) knew who would win and who not; it was designed with the explicit idea of seeing how the plant grew before the flower bloomed. The research was both cross-sectional (looking at all levels of the sport) and longitudinal (over the span of careers).

The nature of excellence

By "excellence" I mean "consistent superiority of performance." The excellent athlete regularly, even routinely, performs better than his or her competitors. Consistency of superior performances tells us that one athlete is indeed better than another, and that the difference between them is not merely the product of chance. This definition can apply at any level of the sport, differentiating athletes. The superiority discussed here may be that of one swimmer over another, or of all athletes at one level (say, the Olympic class) over another. By this definition, we need not judge performance against an absolute criterion, but only against other performances. There are acknowledged leaders on every team, as well as teams widely recognized as dominant.

[…]

So where does excellence—consistent superiority of performance—come from?

Excellence requires qualitative differentiation

Excellence in competitive swimming is achieved through qualitative differentiation from other swimmers, not through quantitative increases in activity. This means, in brief, that levels of the sport are qualitatively distinct; that stratification is discrete, not continuous; and that because of these factors, the swimming world is best conceived of not as a single entity but as multiple worlds, each with its own patterns of conduct.

Before elaborating on these points, I should clarify what is meant here by "quantitative" and "qualitative." By quantity, we mean the number or amount of something. Quantitative improvement entails an increase in the number of some one thing one does. An athlete who practices 2 hours a day and increases that activity to

4 hours a day has made a quantitative change in behavior. Or, one who swims 5 miles and changes to 7 miles has made a quantitative change. She does more of the same thing; there is an increase in quantity. Or again, a freestyle swimmer who, while maintaining the same stroke technique, moves his arms at an increased number of strokes per minute has made a quantitative change in behavior. Quantitative improvements, then, involve doing *more of the same thing*.

By quality, though, we mean the character or nature of the thing itself. A qualitative change involves modifying what is actually being done, not simply doing more of it. For a swimmer doing the breaststroke, a qualitative change might be a change from pulling straight back with the arms to sculling them outwards, to the sides; or from lifting oneself up out of the water at the turn to staying low near the water. Other qualitative changes might include competing in a regional meet, instead of local meets; eating vegetables and complex carbohydrates rather than fats and sugars; entering one's weaker events instead of only one's stronger events; learning to do a flip turn with freestyle, instead of merely turning around and pushing off; or training at near-competition levels of intensity, rather than casually. Each of these involves doing things differently than before, not necessarily doing more. Qualitative improvements involve doing *different kinds of things*.

Now we can consider how qualitative differentiation is manifested:

Different levels of the sport are qualitatively distinct. Olympic champions don't just do much more of the same things that summer-league country-club swimmers do. They don't just swim more hours, or move their arms faster, or attend more workouts. What makes them faster cannot be quantitatively compared with lower level swimmers, because while there may be quantitative differences—and certainly there are, for instance in the number of hours spent in workouts—these are not, I think, the decisive factors at all.[3]

Instead, they do things differently. Their strokes are different, their attitudes are different, their group of friends are different; their parents treat the sport differently, the swimmers prepare differently for their races, and they enter different kinds of meets and events. There are numerous discontinuities of this sort between, say, the swimmer who competes in a local City League meet and one who enters the Olympic Trials. Consider three dimensions of difference:

1 Technique: The styles of strokes, dives and turns are dramatically different at different levels. A "C" (the lowest rank in United States Swimming's ranking system) breaststroke swimmer tends to pull her arms far back beneath her, kick the legs out very wide without bringing them together at the finish, lift herself high out of the water on the turn, fail to take a long pull underwater after the turn, and touch at the finish with one hand, on her side. By comparison, a "AAAA" (the highest rank) swimmer, sculls the arms out to the side and sweeps back in (never actually pulling backwards), kicks narrowly with the feet finishing together, stays low on the turns, takes a long underwater pull after the turn, and touches at the finish with both hands. Not only are the strokes different, they are so different that the "C" swimmer may be amazed to see how the "AAAA" swimmer looks when swimming. The appearance alone is dramatically different, as is the speed with which they swim.

   The same is true for all the other strokes (to a greater or lesser degree), and certainly for starts (dives) and turns. Olympic-class swimmers, to make one other observation, are surprisingly quiet when they dive into the water—there is little splash. Needless to say, this is not true for a novice 10-year old.

2 Discipline: The best swimmers are more likely to be strict with their training, coming to workouts on time, carefully doing the competitive strokes legally (i.e., without violating the technical rules of the sport)[4], watch what they eat, sleep regular hours, do proper warmups before a meet, and the like. Their energy is carefully channeled. Diver Greg Louganis, who won two Olympic gold medals in 1984, practices only three hours each day—not a long time—divided up into two or three sessions. But during each session, he tries to do every dive perfectly. Louganis is never sloppy in practice, and so is never sloppy in meets.[5]

3 Attitude: At the higher levels of competitive swimming, something like an inversion of attitude takes place. The very features of the sport which the "C" swimmer finds unpleasant, the top-level swimmer enjoys. What others see as boring—swimming back and forth over a black line for two hours, say—they find peaceful, even meditative[6], often challenging, or therapeutic. They enjoy hard practices, look forward to difficult competitions, try to set difficult goals. Coming into the 5.30 AM practices at Mission Viejo, many of the swimmers were lively, laughing, talking, enjoying themselves, perhaps appreciating the fact that most people would positively hate doing it. It is incorrect to believe that top athletes suffer great sacrifices to achieve their goals. Often, they don't see what they do as sacrificial at all. They like it. (See also, Hemery 1986).

These qualitative differences are what distinguish levels of the sport. They are very noticeable, while the quantitative differences between levels, both in training and in competition, may be surprisingly small indeed. David Hemery, who won a Gold Medal in the 400-meter intermediate hurdles at the 1968 Olympics, reports the results of interviewing world-class athletes in 22 different sports. "In many cases, the time spent training [a quantitative factor, in our terms] did not alter significantly from the start of specialization right up to the top level." Yet very small quantitative differences in performance may be coupled with huge qualitative differences: In the finals of the men's 100-meter freestyle swimming event at the 1984 Olympics, Rowdy Gaines, the gold medalist, finished ahead of second-place Mark Stockwell by .44 seconds, a gap of only 8/10 of 1%. Between Gaines and the 8th place finisher (a virtual unknown named Dirk Korthals, from West Germany), there was only a 2.2% difference in time. Indeed, between Rowdy Gaines, the fastest swimmer in the world that year, and a respectable 10-year old, the quantitative difference in speed would only be about 30%.

Yet here, as in many cases, a rather small *quantitative* difference produces an enormous *qualitative* difference: Gaines was consistently a winner in major international meets, holder of

23

the world record, and the Olympic Gold Medalist in three events.

Stratification in the sport is discrete, not continuous. There are significant, qualitative breaks—discontinuities—between levels of the sport. These include differences in attitude, discipline, and technique which in turn lead to small but consistent quantitative differences in speed. Entire teams show such differences in attitude, discipline, and technique, and consequently certain teams are easily seen to be "stuck" at certain levels.[7] Some teams always do well at the National Championships, others do well at the Regionals, others at the County Meet. And certainly swimmers typically remain within a certain level for most of their careers, maintaining throughout their careers the habits with which they began. Within levels, competitive improvements for such swimmers are typically marginal, reflecting only differential growth rates (early onset of puberty, for instance) or the jockeying for position within the relatively limited sphere of their own level.

I am suggesting here that athletes do not reach the top level by a simple process of "working their way up," by accumulating sheer time in the sport; improvements across levels of the sport are not generated through quantitative changes. No amount of extra work *per se* will transform a "C" swimmer into a "AAAA" swimmer without a concurrent qualitative change in how that work is done. It is not by doing increasing amounts of work that one becomes excellent, but rather by changing the kinds of work. Beyond an initial improvement of strength, flexibility and feel, there is little increasing accumulation of speed through sheer volume of swimming. Instead, athletes move up to the top ranks through *qualitative jumps*: noticeable changes in their techniques, discipline, and attitude, accomplished usually through a change in settings, e.g. joining a new team with a new coach, new friends, etc, who work at a higher level. Without such qualitative jumps, no major improvements (movements through levels) will take place.

[...]

It may be hard to believe this completely. It seems to contradict our "common sense," what we know from daily experience. The fact is, when people around us do more, they do tend to do better. When we play in a weekend softball game, sheer increased effort (at running the bases, say) brings increased success ("Would

a bunch of guys really go at it this hard just for a beer?"). Children in Little League are told—and their coaches believe—that hard work is the major cause of success (Fine 1987), and swimming coaches widely believe that those who stay in the sport the longest and swim year-round will be more successful. The top swimming coaches in America fall into the same prejudice, attributing success often to "hard work" or "talent." Since they habitually, unreflectively, live at the top level (having spent almost their entire coaching career there), they never see what creates the differences between levels. The fact is, quantitative changes do bring success— but only *within* levels of the sport.[8] Doing more of the same pays off, but only in very limited, locally visible ways. One can achieve a slight advantage over peers by doing more without changing the quality of what is done.

Having seen that "more is better" within local situations, we tend to extrapolate: If I work this hard to get to my level, how hard must Olympic swimmers work? If I sacrifice this much to qualify for the State Championships, how much must they sacrifice? We believe, extrapolating from what we learn about success at our own level, that they must work unbelievably hard, must feel incredible pressure, must sacrifice more and more to become successful. Assuming implicitly that stratification in sports is continuous rather than discrete (that the differences are quantitative) we believe that top athletes do unbelievable things. In short, we believe that they must be superhuman.

This is really several worlds, each with its own patterns of conduct. The analysis pursued above can be taken one step further. If, as I have suggested, there really are *qualitative* breaks between levels of the sport, and if people really don't "work their way up" in any simple additive sense, perhaps our very conception of a single swimming world is inaccurate. I have spoken of the "top" of the sport, and of "levels" within the sport. But these words suggest that all swimmers are, so to speak, climbing a single ladder, aiming towards the same goals, sharing the same values, swimming the same strokes, all looking upwards towards an Olympic gold medal. But they aren't.[9] Some want gold medals, some want to make the Team, some want to exercise, or have fun with friends, or be out in the sunshine and water. Some are trying to escape their parents. The images of the "top" and the "levels" of swimming which I have used until now may simply reflect the dominance of a certain faction of swimmers and coaches in the sport: top is what *they* regard as the top, and their definitions of success have the broadest political currency in United States Swimming. Fast swimmers take as given that faster is better—instead of, say, that more beautiful is better; or that parental involvement is better; or that "well-rounded" children (whatever that may mean) are better. The very terminology of "top" and "level" then, reifies the current ranking system.

Such reification is not only analytically suspect, it is also empirically incorrect. Most swimmers don't want to win an Olympic gold medal. Some may have, at most, a vague, un-acted upon desire to go someday to the National Championships. Of course, if an adult asks what a child wants to accomplish in swimming, the child may say "I want to win the Olympics," but this is more to impress or please the adults than really to announce the child's own intentions. When younger athletes talk about such goals, they are sharing fantasies, not announcing plans; and fantasies are more often enjoyed in their unreality than in their fulfillment.

So we should envision not a swimming world, but multiple worlds[10] (and changing worlds is a major step toward excellence), a horizontal rather than vertical differentiation of the sport. What I have called "levels" are better described as "worlds" or "spheres." In one such world, parents are loosely in charge, coaches are teenagers employed as life guards, practices are held a few times a week, competitions are scheduled perhaps a week in advance, the season lasts for a few weeks in the summertime, and athletes who are much faster than the others may be discouraged by social pressure even from competing, for they take the fun out of it.[11] The big event of the season is the City Championship, when children from the metropolitan area will spend two days racing each other in many events, and the rest of the time sitting under huge tents playing cards, reading, listening to music, and gossiping. In another world, coaches are very powerful, parents seen only occasionally (and never on the pool deck), swimmers travel thousands of miles to attend meets, they swim 6 days a week for years at a time, and the fastest among them are objects of respect and praise. The big event of the season may be the National Championships,

where the athletes may spend much time—sitting under huge tents, playing cards, reading, listening to music and gossiping.[12]

Each such world has its own distinctive types of powerful people and dominant athletes, and being prominent in one world is no guarantee of being prominent in another.[13] At lower levels, the parents of swimmers are in charge; at the higher levels, the coaches; perhaps in the Masters teams which are made up only of swimmers over 25 years old, the swimmers themselves. Each world, too, has its distinctive goals: going to the Olympics, doing well at the National Junior Olympics, winning the City Meet, having a good time for a few weeks. In each world the techniques are at least somewhat distinct (as with the breast-stroke, discussed above) and certain demands are made on family and friends. In all of these ways, and many more, each so-called "level" of competitive swimming is qualitatively different than others. The differences are not simply quantifiable steps along a one-dimensional path leading to the Olympic Games. Goals are varied, participants have competing commitments, and techniques are jumbled (again, see March and Olsen, 1976).

This notion of the horizontal differentiation of the sport—of separate worlds within competitive swimming, rather than a hierarchy—may appear to be refuted by the obvious fact that moving "up" to the Olympic level is very difficult, while moving "down" is apparently easy, as if a sort of gravity obtained. We all know that people don't become Olympic champions in a day. It takes time to learn all those skills, pick up the techniques, develop the stamina, change the attitudes, practice the discipline. The physical work as well as the social and psychological readjustments are significant. This difficulty seems to suggest an asymmetry to these worlds.

Less obvious, though, is that "sliding back down" is empirically difficult indeed. For one thing, techniques once learned and habitualized don't deteriorate overnight. Quite a few swimmers, years past retirement from the sport, can come out and with a few months' practice do quite well. In 1972 a 16-year old named Sandra Nielson won three gold medals in the Munich Olympics in swimming. In 1984, just after turning 29, she entered the National Long Course Championships, placed in the finals, and swam faster than she had 12 years earlier—and with far less training.[14] At that point she had been away from competition for 10 years, returning only months before the Nationals. Nielson had lost very little of her ability.

Then too, there seem to be permanent or at least persistent effects of hard training; attitudes of competitiveness and strategies for racing once learned are rarely forgotten.[15] And finally—perhaps as significantly—the social pressures are strongly against "going back" to a lower level of competition. Hotshots simply are not welcome in the country club leagues while they are hotshots, and if their skills do begin to deteriorate, embarrassment will more likely lead one simply to quit the sport rather than continue. This may be roughly akin to the older professor who, rather than attempt to compete with younger colleagues in a fast-moving field, begins to fill his or her time with more committee duties and foundation consultantships. Graceful senior retirement is preferable to humiliating decline.

All of this (admittedly provocative) argument is to suggest that the swimming world is really several different worlds, and the "top" performers are better seen as different than as better. Even that formulation suggests that at one point the excellent performer could have been dominant at a lesser level in that other world. But as Clausewitz pointed out, in comparing the highest commanders in Napoleon's army with a colonel,

> There are Field Marshals who would not have shone at the head of a cavalry regiment, and vice versa.
> (Clausewitz 1984, p. 198).

Some people don't even begin to shine, that is, until they reach the higher levels. For our purposes here, Clausewitz's "vice versa" in the quotation above reminds us of the separation of subworlds, and of the major points made: "levels" of swimming are qualitatively distinct; stratification in the sport is discrete, not continuous; and the sport is most accurately seen as a collection of (relatively) independent worlds.

Why "talent" does not lead to excellence

Up to now, I have suggested that there are discrete social worlds of competitive swimming, and that an athlete joins those different worlds by adopting the behavior patterns of members.

This argument implies, first, that most people actually don't want to belong to the highest rank, and second, that the role of effort is exaggerated. I am suggesting that athletic excellence is widely attainable, if usually unsought. Many people—let us say, hundreds of thousands in this country—have the physical wherewithal to belong to the Olympic class. While there may be an "entry level" of physical characteristics necessary for Olympic performances, that level may be quite low, and in any case is not measurable.

At this point most readers will ask, *But what about talent?* "Talent" is perhaps the most pervasive lay explanation we have for athletic success. Great athletes, we seem to believe, are born with a special gift, almost a "thing" inside of them, denied to the rest of us—perhaps physical, genetic, psychological, or physiological. Some have "it," and some don't. Some are "natural athletes," and some aren't. While an athlete, we acknowledge, may require many years of training and dedication to develop and use that talent, it is always "in there," only waiting for an opportunity to come out. When children perform well, they are said to "have" talent; if performance declines, they may be said to have "wasted their talent". We believe it is that talent, conceived as a substance behind the surface reality of performance, which finally distinguishes the best among our athletes.

But talent fails as an explanation for athletic success, on conceptual grounds. It mystifies excellence, subsuming a complex set of discrete actions behind a single undifferentiated concept. To understand these actions and the excellence which they constitute, then, we should first debunk this concept of talent, and see where it fails. On at least three points, I believe, "talent" is inadequate.

Factors other than talent explain athletic success more precisely. We can, with a little effort, see what these factors are in swimming: geographical location, particularly living in southern California where the sun shines year round and everybody swims; fairly high family income, which allows for the travel to meets and payments of the fees entailed in the sport, not to mention sheer access to swimming pools when one is young; one's height, weight, and proportions; the luck or choice of having a good coach, who can teach the skills required; inherited muscle structure—it certainly helps to be both strong and flexible; parents who are interested in sports. Some swimmers, too, enjoy more the physical pleasures of swimming; some have better coordination; some even have a higher percentage of fast-twitch muscle fiber. Such factors are clearly definable, and their effects can be clearly demonstrated. To subsume all of them, willy-nilly, under the rubric of "talent" obscures rather than illuminates the sources of athletic excellence.

It's easy to do this, especially if one's only exposure to top athletes comes once every four years while watching the Olympics on television, or if one only sees them in performances rather than in day-to-day training. Say, for instance, that one day I turn on the television set and there witness a magnificent figure skating performance by Scott Hamilton. What I see is grace and power and skill all flowing together, seemingly without effort: a single moving picture, rapid and sure, far beyond what I could myself do. In phenomenological terms, I see Hamilton's performance "monothetically," at a single glance, all-at-once. (Schutz and Luckmann, 1973, p. 75) "His skating," I may say, referring to his actions as a single thing, "is spectacular." With that quick shorthand, I have captured (I believe) at a stroke the wealth of tiny details that Hamilton, over years and years, has fitted together into a performance so smoothly that they become invisible to the untrained eye.[16] Perhaps, with concentration, Hamilton himself can feel the details in his movements; certainly a great coach can see them, and pick out the single fault or mistake in an otherwise flawless routine. But to me, the performance is a thing entire.

Afterwards, my friends and I sit and talk about Hamilton's life as a "career of excellence," or as showing "incredible dedication," "tremendous motivation"—again, as if his excellence, his dedication, his motivation somehow exist all-at-once. His excellence becomes a thing inside of him which he periodically reveals to us, which comes out now and then; his life and habits become reified. "Talent" is merely the word we use to label this reification.

But that is no explantion of success.

Talent is indistinguishable from its effects. One cannot see that talent exists until after its effects become obvious. Kalinowski's research on Olympic swimmers demonstrates this clearly:

> One of the more startling discoveries of our study has been that it takes a while to recognize swimming talent. Indeed, it usually takes being

successful at a regional level, and more often, at a national level (in AAU swimming) before the child is identified as talented.
> (p. 173)

> "They didn't say I had talent until I started to get really good [and made Senior Nationals at sixteen]; then they started to say I had talent ..."
> (p. 174)

> ... despite the physical capabilities he was born with, it took Peter several years (six by our estimate) to appear gifted. This is the predominant, though not exclusive, pattern found in our data on swimmers. Most of them are said to be "natural" or "gifted" after they had already devoted a great deal of time and hard work to the field.
> (p. 194)

> ... whatever superior qualities were attributed to him as he grew older and more successful, they were not apparent then [before he was thirteen].
> (p. 200)

The above quotations suggest that talent is *discovered* later in one's career, the implication being that while the athlete's ability *existed* all along, we were unaware of it until late. Kalinowski, like many of us, holds to the belief that there must be this thing inside the athlete which precedes and determines success, only later to be discovered. But the recurring evidence he finds suggests a different interpretation: perhaps there is no such thing as "talent," there is only the outstanding performance itself. He sees success and immediately infers behind it a cause, a cause *for which he has no evidence other than the success itself.* Here, as elsewhere, talent (our name for this cause) cannot be measured, or seen, or felt, in any form other than the success to which it supposedly gives rise.

In Kalinowski's analysis, then—and the lay view is much the same as his—there lies an analytic error of the first degree: the independent and the dependent variables cannot be measured separately.[17]

The "amount" of talent needed for athletic success seems to be strikingly low. It seems initially plausible that one must have a certain level of natural ability in order to succeed in sports (or music, or academics). But upon empirical examination, it becomes very difficult to say exactly what that physical minimum is. Indeed, much of the mythology of sport is built around people who lack natural ability who went on to succeed fabulously. An entire genre of inspirational literature is built on the theme of the person whose even normal natural abilities have been destroyed: Wilma Rudolph had polio as a child, then came back to win the Olympic 100 Meter Dash. Glenn Cunningham had his legs badly burned in a fire, then broke the world record in the mile. Such stories are grist for the sportwriter's mill.

More than merely common, these stories are almost routine. Most Olympic champions, when their history is studied, seem to have overcome sharp adversity in their pursuit of success. Automobile accidents, shin splints, twisted ankles, shoulder surgery are common in such tales. In fact, they are common in life generally. While some necessary minimum of physical strength, heart/lung capacity, or nerve density may well be required for athletic achievement (again, I am *not* denying differential advantages), that minimum seems both difficult to define and markedly low, at least in many cases. Perhaps the crucial factor is not natural ability at all, but the willingness to overcome natural or unnatural disabilities of the sort that most of us face, ranging from minor inconveniences in getting up and going to work, to accidents and injuries, to gross physical impairments.

And if the basic level of talent needed, then, seems so low as to be nearly universally available, perhaps the very concept of talent itself— no longer differentiating among performers—is better discarded altogether. It simply doesn't explain the differences in outcomes. Rather than talk about talent and ability, we do better to look at what people actually do that creates outstanding performance.

The concept of talent hinders a clear understanding of excellence. By providing a quick yet spurious "explanation" of athletic success, it satisfies our casual curiosity while requiring neither an empirical analysis nor a critical questioning of our tacit assumptions about top athletes. At best, it is an easy way of admitting that we don't know the answer, a kind of layman's slang for "unexplained variance." But the attempt at explanation fails. What we call talent is no more than a projected reification of particular things done: hands placed correctly in the water, turns crisply executed, a head held high rather than low in the water. Through the notion of talent, we transform particular actions that a human being does into an object possessed, held in trust for the day when it will be revealed for all to see.

This line of thought leads to one more step. Since talent can be viewed only indirectly in the effects that it supposedly produces, its very existence is a matter of faith. The basic dogma of "talent" says that what people do in this world has a cause lying behind them, that there is a kind of backstage reality where the real things happen, and what we, you and I, see here in our lives (say, the winning of a gold medal) is really a reflection of that true reality back there. Those of us who are not admitted to the company of the elect—the talented—can never see what that other world of fabulous success is really like, and can never share those experiences. And accepting this faith in talent, I suggest, we relinquish our chance of accurately understanding excellence.

Still, we want to believe in talent. As Jean-Paul Sartre put it, "What people would like is that a coward or a hero be born that way",[18] knowing that it protects us by degrading the very achievements that it pretends to elevate (Staples 1987); magically separating us from those people who are great athletes, ensuring that we are incomparable to them; and relieving those of us who are not excellent of responsibility for our own condition. "To call someone 'divine'," Friedrich Nietzsche once wrote, "means 'Here we do not have to compete.'" (Nietzsche, 1984, p. 111) In the mystified notion of talent, the unanalyzed pseudo-explanation of outstanding performance, we codify our own deep psychological resistance to the simple reality of the world, to the overwhelming mundanity of excellence.[19]

The mundanity of excellence

"People don't know how ordinary success is," said Mary T. Meagher, winner of 3 gold medals in the Los Angeles Olympics, when asked what the public least understands about her sport. She then spoke of starting her career in a summer league country club team, of working her way to AAU meets, to faster and faster competitions; of learning new techniques, practicing new habits, meeting new challenges.[20] What Meagher said—that success is ordinary, in some sense—applies, I believe, to other fields of endeavor as well: to business, to politics, to professions of all kinds, including academics. In what follows I will try to elaborate on this point, drawing some examples from the swimming research, and some from other fields, to indicate the scope of this conception.

Excellence is mundane. Superlative performance is really a confluence of dozens of small skills or activities, each one learned or stumbled upon, which have been carefully drilled into habit and then are fitted together in a synthesized whole. There is nothing extraordinary or superhuman in any one of those actions; only the fact that they are done consistently and correctly, and all together, produce excellence. When a swimmer learns a proper flip turn in the freestyle races, she will swim the race a bit faster; then a streamlined push off from the wall, with the arms squeezed together over the head, and a little faster; then how to place the hands in the water so no air is cupped in them; then how to lift them over the water; then how to lift weights to properly build strength, and how to eat the right foods, and to wear the best suits for racing, and on and on.[21] Each of those tasks seems small in itself, but each allows the athlete to swim a bit faster. And having learned and consistently practiced all of them together, and many more besides, the swimmer may compete in the Olympic Games. The winning of a gold medal is nothing more than the synthesis of a countless number of such little things—even if some of them are done unwittingly or by others, and thus called "luck."

So the "little things" really do count. We have already seen how a very small (in quantitative terms) difference can produce a noticeable success. Even apparent flukes can lead to gold medal performances:

> In the 100 Meter Freestyle event in Los Angeles, Rowdy Gaines, knowing that the starter for the race tended to fire the gun fast, anticipated the start; while not actually jumping the gun, it seems from video replays of the race that Gaines knew exactly when to go, and others were left on the blocks as he took off. But the starter turned his back, and the protests filed afterwards by competitors were ignored. Gaines had spent years watching starters, and had talked with his coach (Richard Quick) before the race about this starter in particular.
>
> (Field notes; see Chambliss, 1988 for full description)

Gaines was not noticeably faster than several of the other swimmers in the race, but with this one

extra tactic, he gained enough of an advantage to win the race. And he seemed in almost all of his races to find such an advantage: hence the gold medal. Looking at such subtleties, we can say that not only are the little things important; in some ways, the little things are the only things.

[…]

In swimming, or elsewhere, these practices might at first glance seem very minimal indeed:

> When Mary T. Meagher was 13 years old and had qualified for the National Championships, she decided to try to break the world record in the 200 Meter Butterfly race. She made two immediate qualitative changes in her routine: first, she began coming on time to all practices. She recalls now, years later, being picked up at school by her mother and driving (rather quickly) through the streets of Louisville, Kentucky trying desperately to make it to the pool on time. That habit, that discipline, she now says, gave her the sense that every minute of practice time counted. And second, she began doing all of her turns, during those practices, correctly, in strict accordance with the competitive rules. Most swimmers don't do this; they turn rather casually, and tend to touch with one hand instead of two (in the butterfly, Meagher's stroke). This, she says, accustomed her to doing things one step better than those around her—always. Those are the two major changes she made in her training, as she remembers it.[22]

Meagher made two quite mundane changes in her habits, either one of which anyone could do, if he or she wanted. Within a year Meagher had broken the world record in the butterfly.

Here, then, is an area ripe for research in organizational studies: to what extent do mundane considerations lead to the success or failure of organizations, let alone individuals? A willingness to spend ten minutes a year writing a Christmas card can maintain an old friendship for decades; a faulty telephone system, which cuts off one-quarter (or even one-tenth) of all incoming calls can ruin a travel agency or mail-order house; a president who simply walks around the plant once in a while, talking with the workers, can dramatically improve an organization's morale—and its product (Peters and Waterman, 1982); a secretary, that archetypal manager of mundane work, can make or destroy an executive, or even an entire division. At the lowest levels of competitive swimming, simply showing up for regular practices produces the greatest single speed improvement the athlete will ever experience[23]; and at the lower levels of academia, the sheer willingness to put arguments down on paper and send it away to a journal distinguishes one from the mass of one's colleagues in the discipline.[24] Again, the conclusion: the simple doing of certain small tasks can generate huge results. Excellence is mundane.

Motivation is mundane, too. Swimmers go to practice to see their friends, to exercise, to feel strong afterwards, to impress the coach, to work towards bettering a time they swam in the last meet. Sometimes, the older ones, with a longer view of the future, will aim towards a meet that is still several months away. But even given the longer-term goals, the daily satisfactions need to be there. The mundane social rewards really are crucial (see Chambliss, 1988, Chapter 6). By comparison, the big, dramatic motivations—winning an Olympic gold medal, setting a world record—seem to be ineffective unless translated into shorter-term tasks. Viewing "Rocky" or "Chariots of Fire" may inspire one for several days, but the excitement stirred by a film wears off rather quickly when confronted with the day-to-day reality of climbing out of bed to go and jump in cold water. If, on the other hand, that day-to-day reality is itself fun, rewarding, challenging, if the water is nice and friends are supportive, the longer-term goals may well be achieved almost in spite of themselves. Again, Mary T. Meagher:

> I never looked beyond the next year, and I never looked beyond the next level. I never thought about the Olympics when I was ten; at that time I was thinking about the State Championships. When I made cuts for Regionals [the next higher level of competition], I started thinking about Regionals; when I made cuts for National Junior Olympics, I started thinking about National Junior Olympics ... I can't even think about the [1988] Olympics right now ... Things can overwhelm you if you think too far ahead.
> (Interview notes)

This statement was echoed by many of the swimmers I interviewed. While many of them were working towards the Olympic Games, they divided the work along the way into achievable steps, no one of which was too big. They found their challenges in small things: working on a better start this week, polishing up their backstroke technique next week, focusing on better sleep habits, planning how to pace their swim. They concentrate on what Karl Weick has called "small wins": the very definable, minor achievements which can be rather easily done but which produce significant effects,[25] not the least of which is the confidence to attempt another such "small win." Weick's article on the subject is, typically, insightful and suggestive. He says:

> A small win is a concrete, complete, implemented outcome of moderate importance. By itself, one small win may seem unimportant. A series of wins at small but significant tasks, however, reveals a pattern that may attract allies, deter opponents, and lower resistance to subsequent proposals. Small wins are controllable opportunities that produce visible results.
> (Weick 1984, p. 43).

For instance, many top swimmers are accustomed to winning races in practice, day after day. Steve Lundquist, who won two gold medals in Los Angeles, sees his success as resulting from an early decision that he wanted to win every swim, every day, in every practice. That was the immediate goal he faced at workouts: just try to win every swim, every lap, in every stroke, no matter what. Lundquist gained a reputation in swimming for being a ferocious workout swimmer, one who competed all the time, even in the warmup. He became so accustomed to winning that he entered meets knowing that he could beat these people—he had developed the habit, every day, of never losing. The short-term goal of winning this swim, in this workout, translated into his ability to win bigger and bigger races. Competition, when the day arrived for a meet, was not a shock to him, nothing at all out of the ordinary.[26]

This leads to a third and final point.

In the pursuit of excellence, maintaining mundanity is the key psychological challenge. In common parlance, winners don't choke. Faced with what seems to be a tremendous challenge or a strikingly unusual event such as the Olympic Games, the better athletes take it as a normal, manageable situation[27] ("It's just another swim meet," is a phrase sometimes used by top swimmers at a major event such as the Games) and do what is necessary to deal with it. Standard rituals (such as the warmup, the psych, the visualization of the race, the taking off of sweats, and the like) are ways of importing one's daily habits into the novel situation, to make it as normal an event as possible. Swimmers like Lundquist who train at competition-level intensity therefore have an advantage: arriving at a meet, they are already accustomed to doing turns correctly, taking legal starts, doing a proper warmup, and being aggressive from the outset of the competition. If each day of the season is approached with a seriousness of purpose, then the big meet will not come as a shock. The athlete will believe "I belong here, this is my world"—and not be paralyzed by fear or self-consciousness. The task then is to have training closely approximate competition conditions.

[...]

The mundanity of excellence is typically unrecognized. I think the reason is fairly simple. Usually we see great athletes only after they have become great—after the years of learning the new methods, gaining the habits of competitiveness and consistency, after becoming comfortable in their world. They have long since perfected the myriad of techniques that together constitute excellence. Ignorant of all of the specific steps that have led to the performance and to the confidence, we think that somehow excellence sprang fullgrown from this person, and we say he or she "has talent" or "is gifted." Even when seen close up, the mundanity of excellence is often not believed:

> Every week at the Mission Viejo training pool, where the National Champion Nadadores team practiced, coaches from around the world would be on the deck visiting, watching as the team did their workouts, swimming back and forth for hours. The visiting coaches would be excited at first, just to be here; then, soon—within an hour or so, usually—they grew bored, walking back and forth looking at the deck, glancing around at the hills around the town, reading the bulletin boards, glancing down at their watches, wondering, after the long flight out to California, when something dramatic was going to happen. "They all have to come to Mecca, and see what we do," coach Mark Schubert said. "They think we have some big secret."
>
> (Field notes)

But of course there is no secret; there is only the doing of all those little things, each one done correctly, time and again, until excellence in every detail becomes a firmly ingrained habit, an ordinary part of one's everyday life.

Conclusions

The foregoing analysis suggests that we have overlooked a fundamental fact about Olympic-class athletes; and the argument may apply far more widely than swimming, or sports. I suggest that it applies to success in business, politics, and academics, in dentistry, bookkeeping, food service, speechmaking, electrical engineering, selling insurance (when the clients are upset, you climb in the car and go out there to talk with them) and perhaps even in the arts.[28] Consider again the major points:

1 *Excellence is a qualitative phenomenon.* Doing more does not equal doing better. High performers focus on qualitative, not quantitative, improvements; it is qualitative improvements which produce significant changes in level of achievement; different levels of achievement really are distinct, and in fact reflect vastly different habits, values, and goals.

2 *Talent is a useless concept.* Varying conceptions of natural ability ("talent," e.g.) tend to mystify excellence, treating it as the inherent possession of a few; they mask the concrete actions that create outstanding performance; they avoid the work of empirical analysis and logical explanations (clear definitions, separable independent and dependent variables, and at least an attempt at establishing the temporal priority of the cause); and finally, such conceptions perpetuate the sense of innate psychological differences between high performers and other people.

3 *Excellence is mundane.* Excellence is accomplished through the doing of actions, ordinary in themselves, performed consistently and carefully, habitualized, compounded together, added up over time. While these actions are "qualitatively different" from those of performers at other levels, these differences are neither unmanageable nor, taken one step at a time, terribly difficult. Mary T. Meagher came to practice on time; some writers always work for three hours each morning, before beginning anything else; a business-person may go ahead and make that tough phone call; a job applicant writes one more letter; a runner decides,

31

against the odds, to enter the race; a county commissioner submits a petition to run for Congress; a teenager asks for a date; an actor attends one more audition. Every time a decision comes up, the qualitatively "correct" choice will be made. The action, in itself, is nothing special; the care and consistency with which it is made is.

Howard Becker has presented a similar argument about the ordinariness of apparently unusual people in his book *Outsiders* (1961). But where he speaks of deviance, I would speak of excellence. Becker says, and I concur:

> We ought not to view it as something special, as depraved or in some magical way better than other kinds of behavior. We ought to see it simply as a kind of behavior some disapprove of and others value, studying the processes by which either or both perspectives are built up and maintained. Perhaps the best surety against either extreme is close contact with the people we study.
>
> (Becker, p. 176).

After three years of field work with world-class swimmers, having the kind of close contact that Becker recommends, I wrote a draft of some book chapters, full of stories about swimmers, and I showed it to a friend, "You need to jazz it up," he said. "You need to make these people more interesting. The analysis is nice, but except for the fact that these are good swimmers, there isn't much else exciting to say about them as individuals." He was right, of course. What these athletes do was rather interesting, but the people themselves were only fast swimmers, who did the particular things one does to swim fast. It is all very mundane. When my friend said that they weren't exciting, my best answer could only be, simply put: *That's the point.*

Notes

1. The general approach taken here derives from symbolic interactionism and phenomenology, as practiced by Berger and Luckmann (1966), Blumer (1986), Schutz (1971), and Schutz and Luckmann (1973).

    The sociology of sport literature is thin on swimming: however, the following are either classics or recent work which was helpful: Elias and Dunning (1986), Fine (1979, 1987), Goffman (1961), Guttmann (1978), Lever (1983), and Rigauer (1981). Perhaps one of the finest pieces of social critique of sport appears woven throughout David Halberstam's *The Breaks of the Game* (1981).

2. Interviews were either recorded on tape (in the early stages of the research) or in written notes. Tape recording had a somewhat inhibiting effect on when and where interviews could be conducted, and so was abandoned. Interviews proceeded from a base of a few standard questions—e.g. "How did you begin in swimming?". "When did you first achieve national standing?" to a more open-ended conversation around issues of becoming a champion, finding the right coach, etc. For further details, see "Sources and Acknowledgements" in Chambliss, 1988.

3. True, the top teams work long hours, and swim very long distances, but (1) such workouts often begin after a swimmer achieves national status, not before, and (2) the positive impact of increased yardage seems to come with huge increases, e.g. the doubling of workout distances—in which case one could argue that a *qualitative* jump has been made. The whole question of "how much yardage to swim" is widely discussed within the sport itself.

    Compare the (specious, I think) notion that a longer school day/term/year will produce educational improvements.

4. One day at Mission Viejo, with some sixty swimmers going back and forth the length of a 50-meter pool, coach Mark Schubert took one boy out of the water and had him do twenty pushups before continuing the workout. The boy had touched the wall with one hand at the end of a breast stroke swim. The rules require a two-handed touch.

    One hundred and twenty hands *should have* touched, one hundred and nineteen *did* touch, and this made Schubert angry. He pays attention to details.

5. From an interview with his coach, Ron O'Brien.

6. Distance swimmers frequently compare swimming to meditation.

7. For example: several well-known teams consistently do well at the National Junior Olympics ("Junior Nationals," as it is called informally), and yet never place high in the team standings at the National Championships ("Senior Nationals"), the next higher meet.

    These teams actually prevent their swimmers from going to the better meet, holding them in store for the easier meet so that the team will do better at that lesser event. In this way, and in many others, teams choose their own level of success.

8. Increased effort, for instance, does bring increased success. But at the higher levels of the sport, virtually everyone works hard, and effort *per se* is not the

determining factor that it is among lower level athletes, many of whom do not try very hard.

9. March and Olsen make a similar point with regard to educational institutions and organizations in general: organizations include a variety of constituents with differing goals, plans, motivations, and values. Unity of purpose, even with organizations, cannot simply be assumed. Coherence, not diversity, is what needs explaining. March and Olsen, 1976.

10. See Shibutani in Rose, 1962, on "social worlds"; Blumer, 1969.

11. These fast swimmers who come to slow meets are called hot dogs, showoffs, or even jerks. (Personal observations.)

12. Again, personal observations from a large number of cases. While there are significant differences between swimmers of the Olympic class and a country club league, the basic sociability of their worlds is not one of them.

13. "Indeed, prestige ladders in the various worlds are so different that a man who reaches the pinnacle of success in one may be completely unknown elsewhere." Shibutani in Rose, 1962.

    Similarly in academia: one may be a successful professor at the national level and yet find it difficult to gain employment at a minor regional university. Professors at the regional school may suspect his/her motives, be jealous, feel that he/she "wouldn't fit in," "won't stay anyway," etc. Many top-school graduate students discover upon entering the markets that no-name colleges have no interest in them; indeed, by attending a Chicago or Harvard Ph.D. program one may limit oneself to the top ranks of employment opportunities.

14. The training information comes from her coach and, later, husband, Dr. Keith Bell.

15. Some anecdotal evidence from swimmers (e.g. Steve Lundquist) and coaches (e.g. Terry Stoddard) suggests that the physical effects of hard training can last for years, so that a swimmer in effect "rachets up" to higher levels with better training, and will not slow down appreciably once the training load is reduced.

16. "Now, no one can see in an artist's work how it evolved: that is its advantage, for wherever we can see the evolution, we grow somewhat cooler. The complete art of representation wards off all thought of its solution; it tyrannizes as present perfection." (Nietzsche 1984, p. 111)

17. I am *not* saying "natural ability doesn't matter." I am saying that to use "talent" as a way of explaining performance is to resort to tautology. The action of performing is reified—turned into a thing—and we call it "talent."

18. Sartre 1957, p. 34.

19. To coin an ungainly but accurate phrase. I borrow the term. "mundanity" from phenomenological philosopher Maurice Natanson, in *The Journeying Self.*

20. Meagher's entire career is described in detail in Chambliss, 1988.

21. Such techniques are thoroughly explained in Maglischo (1982) and Troup and Reese (1983).

22. Interview notes.

23. In teaching swim lessons, I have seen children make improvements of 20 and more seconds for a 50-yard swim (which takes about a minute) during the course of a single lesson. At the top level, swimmers spend years to improve one second in the same event.

24. The fact that the reader might not believe this reveals more about the reader's own social world—namely of professionally active scholars—than the realities of life for the bulk of college professors. For many, simply participating in scholarship is a huge step.

25. For an application of this notion to college education, see Chambliss and Ryan, 1988.

26. Interview notes.

27. An interesting parallel: some of the most successful generals have no trouble sleeping before and after major battles. For details on Ulysses Grant and the Duke of Wellington, see Keegan, p. 207.

28. Professor Margaret Bates, an opera enthusiast, tells me that this "mundanity of excellence" argument applies nicely to Enrico Caruso, the great singer, who carefully perfected each ordinary detail of his performance in an effort to overcome a recognized lack of "natural ability."

References

Becker, Howard S. 1973. *Outsiders: Studies in the Sociology of Deviance*. New York: Free Press.

Berger, Peter, and Luckmann, Thomas. 1966. *The Social Construction of Reality*. Garden City: Doubleday.

Bloom, Benjamin S. ed., 1985. *Developing Talent in Young People*. New York: Ballantine.

Blumer, Herbert. 1969. *Symbolic Interactionism*. Englewood Cliffs: Prentice Hall.

Chambliss, Daniel F. 1988. *Champions: The Making of Olympic Swimmers*. New York: Morrow.

——. and Ryan, Daniel J., Jr. "Big Problems Demand Small Solutions: Toward a General Strategy for Excellence in Education," presented at the annual meetings of the New England Educational Research Organization, April, 1988.

Clausewitz, Carl von. 1968. *On War*. Edited with an Introduction by Anatol Rapoport. New York: Penguin.

Drucker, Peter F. 1985. *The Effective Executive*. New York: Harper and Row.

———. 1986. *Managing for Results*. New York: Harper and Row.

———. 1954. *The Practice of Management*. New York: Harper and Row.

Durkheim, Emile. 1965. *The Elementary Forms of the Religious Life*. New York: Free Press.

Elias, Norbert, and Dunning, Eric. 1986. *Quest for Excitement*. Oxford: Basil Blackwell.

Fine, Gary Alan. 1979. "Small Groups and Culture Creation: The Idioculture of Little League Baseball Teams." *American Sociological Review* 44: 733–745.

———. 1987. *With the Boys: Little League Baseball and Preadolescent Culture*. Chicago: University of Chicago Press.

Goffman, Erving. 1961. "Fun in Games." Pp. 13–81 in *Encounters*. Indianapolis: Bobbs-Merrill.

Guttmann, Allen. 1978. *From Ritual to Record: The Nature of Modern Sports*. New York: Columbia University Press.

Halberstam, David. 1981. *The Breaks of the Game*. New York: Knopf.

Hemery, David. 1986. *The Pursuit of Sporting Excellence: A Study of Sport's Highest Achievers*. London: Willow.

Kalinowski, Anthony G. "The Development of Olympic Swimmers," and "One Olympic Swimmer," in Bloom (1985), Pp. 139–210.

Keegan, John. 1987. *The Mask of Command*. New York: Viking.

Lever, Janet. 1983. *Soccer Madness*. Chicago: University of Chicago Press.

Maglischo, Ernest W. 1982. *Swimming Faster*. Palo Alto: Mayfield.

March, James G. and Johan P. Olsen. 1976. *Ambiguity and Choice in Organizations*. Bergen, Norway: Universitetsforlaget.

Natanson, Maurice. 1970. *The Journeying Self: A Study in Philosophy and Social Role*. Reading, Massachusetts: Addison-Wesley.

Nietzsche, Friedrich. 1984. *Human, All Too Human*. Lincoln, Neb.: University of Nebraska Press.

Peters, Tom and Waterman, Robert. 1982. *In Search of Excellence*. New York: Warner.

Rigauer, Bero. 1981. *Sport and Work*. New York: Columbia University Press.

Rose, Arnold M. 1962. *Human Behavior and Social Process*. Boston: Houghton Mifflin Company.

Sartre, Jean-Paul. 1957. *Existentialism and Human Emotions*. New York: Philosophical Library.

Schutz, Alfred. 1971. *Collected Papers I: The Problem of Social Reality*. Edited and Introduced by Maurice Natanson. The Hague: Martinus Nijhoff.

———. and Luckmann, Thomas. 1973. *Structures of the Life-World*. Evanston: Northwestern University Press.

Shibutani, T. "Reference Groups and Social Control," in Rose, Arnold M. 1962. *Human Behavior and Social Process*. Boston: Houghton Mifflin Company, Pp. 128–147.

Staples, Brent. 1987. "Where Are the Black Fans?" *New York Times Magazine*, vol. 136, May 17, pp. 26–36.

Troup, John and Reese, Randy. 1983. *A Scientific Approach to the Sport of Swimming*. Gainesville, Florida: Scientific Sports, Inc.

Weick, Karl. 1984. "Small Wins: Redefining the Scale of Social Problems." *American Psychologist* 39: 40–49.

Varsity syndrome

The unkindest cut

Robert Lipsyte

Though originally published in 1979, this article by Robert Lipsyte is as insightful as ever. Lipsyte's evocation of SportsWorld and the "varsity syndrome" that it spawns provides us with a lens that highlights the ways that the institution of sports in the United States reinforces various patterns of exclusion and commercialism. In contrast to the argument in the article by Tomlinson, Markovits, and Young (also in this chapter), Lipsyte *does* believe that sports reflect the society of which it is a part. It is useful to push these contrasting theoretical ideas to see what each yields.

Americans must win back the natural birthright of their bodies, a birthright which has been distorted and manipulated by political and commercial forces that have used sports and physical education for purposes that often negate the incredible potential for individual and community progress that is inherent in sports—the one human activity that offers health, fun, and cooperation with the chance to combine physical, mental, and emotional energy.

Sports is the single most influential currency of mass communication in the world. Unlike so many other activities—music, art, literature—sports easily hurdles the barriers of age, education, language, gender, social and economic status that tend to divide a population.

Sports has the potential to bring us together but the evidence suggests it rarely does. In fact, it often further divides communities by promoting overzealous competition, violence, specialization, professionalization and an attitude of "win at all costs" that spills over into other aspects of daily life.

Over the years there have been changes, hopeful changes, in sport. The emergence of the black athlete, the emergence of the woman athlete, the proliferation of serious academic studies of athletes and of their impact on our culture are examples. Yet, there has been no real breakthrough in the attempt to reduce the effects of a pervasive pattern of emphasis and expectations which keeps us from realizing the intensive pleasures of sport. I call that pattern the "varsity syndrome."

We experience the effects of the varsity syndrome in childhood and its influence is lifelong. It begins in kindergarten with "organized games" and culminates each year when more than eighty million Americans watch perhaps eighty men act out our fantasies—The Super Bowl, a celebration, we are conditioned to believe, of manliness, courage, fruitful labor,

Robert Lipsyte, "Varsity Syndrome: The Unkindest Cut" from *Annals of the American Academy of Political and Social Science* 445.1 (1979): 15-23. Reprinted with the permission of the author.

pain, endurance, strength and achievement, all characteristics to which every man would aspire to hold to some degree.

Varsity syndrome—sexism

Confrontation with the varsity syndrome starts early for boys in any neighborhood, the killer word is "fag." Call a boy a fag and he will have to fight or slink away. The homosexual connotation of the word is implicit, though not primary. Since we were taught that homosexuals were unmanly, somehow "feminine," the word really meant to us that a boy was "girlish," unfit for the company of men. We all "knew" that girls were smaller, weaker, less physically skilled. They had no place or future in the big leagues of life. Sports taught us that.

A boy tried very hard to avoid being labeled a fag. He might play games in which he found no pleasure; he might root for teams that bored him; he paid constant lip service to sports. In my day it was, "Who you like better, fella, Mantle or Mays?" You could answer anyway you wanted to, you could even say "Duke Snider," just so long as you didn't say, "who cares?" The schoolyard—that no-womans land—was a male sanctuary, and the first of many arenas in which a man would be tested for his ability to perform under stress, with skill and with the ruthlessness that passes for pragmatism.

Sports was the first great separator of the sexes. Sometime after kindergarten, a girl was handed (symbolically or literally) the majorette's baton and told to go in the corner and twirl. Her athletic moment was over. She now existed only as an encourager of males. There were, of course, girls who dropped the baton and picked up the bat and beat males at their own games. However, the culture had prepared a way to combat this seeming inconsistency. Athletically superior boys might be considered supermen, but athletically superior women were something less than real women. They were locker-room jokes. Boys would tell each other, she's playing because she can't get a date; she's a tomboy; or, most devastatingly, she's a dyke. And if she turned out to be world-class, the world was quick to suspect her chromosomes.

Reading about Babe Didrikson in Paul Gallico's popular 1938 book, "Farewell to Sport," I had no reason to disbelieve his statement that she became one of the greatest of all American athletes merely as an "escape, a compensation."[1] Gallico wrote that Didrikson "Would not or could not compete with women at their own best game ... man-snatching."[2] Most sportswriters, observers, and participants accepted Gallico's statement as fact, or at the least as a manifestation of routine sexism. After all, women were barred from press boxes, locker rooms, and anything other than cheerleader positions in sport. Only recently, while researching a book, I came across an even simpler explanation for Gallico's slur. A fine and vain athlete himself, Gallico once raced Didrikson across a golf course. She ran him into the ground. And he never again wrote about her without mentioning her prominent adam's apple, or the down on her upper lip. I assume his rationalization was traditional: A woman can't beat a man unless he's a fag or she's not really a woman.

The usual justification for restricting women from sports competition—the very first manifestation of the varsity syndrome—was that their delicate bodies needed protection from physical harm. More realistically, I believe, women were rejected to protect the delicate egos of men who have been taught that their manhood depends on the presence of an underclass. James Michener, a respected writer and an avid sports fan and participant, recently published a book called *Sports in America,* which contained a concept that I feel is very dangerous because it is so widely held.[3] Michener wrote that between the ages of about eleven and twenty-two men and women should not compete against each other in sports because of the possible damage to the male's ego should he lose.[4] No consideration is given to the ego of the young female who is striving to exhibit and stretch to the outer limits her own talents and skills.

The sexism of the varsity syndrome transcends sports. Athletics give youngsters an opportunity to learn the positive values of leadership, of cooperation and dedication and sacrifice for a goal. Games are a source of skill development, whether it be physical, mental, or social. Many women have been stunted in their growth toward full citizenship because they were denied an opportunity routinely afforded to every male. The woman who does succeed in American sports does so at a certain cost. I recall one afternoon in the middle sixties, coming off a tennis court after a victory, sweaty, rackets under her arm, Billie Jean King was intercepted by a male spectator from the stands who asked, "Hey, Billie Jean, when are you going to have children?" Billie Jean answered, "I'm not ready yet." The man continued, "Why aren't you at home?" Billie Jean snapped right back "Why don't you go ask Rod Laver why *he* isn't at home?"

Varsity syndrome—elite deference

Another component of the varsity syndrome, learned on the streets and reinforced throughout school, is elitism. Special privileges are afforded athletes, including a special psychological aura or deference that ultimately proves to harm the athlete as well as the non-athlete. This aspect of the varsity syndrome is so pernicious it finds its supporters at both poles of the playing field, from neanderthal coaches on the right, whose authoritarian methods squeeze out joy of sports, to so-called sports revolutionaries on the left who see athletes as a higher order of human beings.

Traditionally, soon after fifty-one percent of the potential athletes—the women—were cut from the team, the process of winnowing the boys begins. This process, which George Sauer, the former New York Jets wide receiver, has called a form of social darwinism, has many ramifications.[5] First of all, it separates boys into worthy and unworthy classes just at a time in their lives when they are most confused about their bodies and their relationships with their peers. Those anointed as athletes often drop away from other social and intellectual pursuits, and it becomes harder and harder for them to catch up when they, too, are eventually cut from the team. It happens to everyone eventually, and no matter the age or level of competition, the cut is hard to take. Those who are marked as failures at critical times in their lives often seem to spend the rest of their lives measuring up. Those who measure up early and last for awhile become jocks. In our society the jock is often the male equivalent of the stereotyped female, the broad.

The jock and the broad are selected and rewarded for beauty and performing skills. They are used to satisfy others and to define themselves by the quantity and quality of that satisfaction whether it be as a Heisman Trophy winner or Miss America, rookie of the year or starlet, all-America or prom queen. When they grow too old to please they are discarded.

One of the cruelest ramifications of the elitist component of the varsity syndrome is the way it has been used to turn black athletes into a gladiator legion in American sports. Contrary to prevailing opinion, sports success has probably been detrimental to black progress. By publicizing the material success of a few hundred athletes, thousands, perhaps millions of bright young blacks have been swept toward sports when they should have been guided toward careers in medicine or engineering or business. For every black who escaped the ghetto behind his jump shot, a thousand of his little brothers were neutralized, kept busy shooting baskets, until it was too late for them to qualify beyond marginal work.[6]

Those who do make it big, white or black, male or female, are generally lionized out of all proportion to their intrinsic worth, or to their importance to society. The athlete is damaged by the exaggerated adulation and the rest of us are given a pantheon of heroes on a nest of false laurels. An example from my own experience illustrates this point. When I was about twenty-one, a brand-new reporter at *The New York Times,* I was sent to Yankee Stadium to interview Mickey Mantle. Several nights earlier, a fan jumped out of the stands and traded some punches with Mantle. This was years before the advent of what psychiatrists' now call "recreational violence," and it was quite unusual. Apparently Mantle had gotten the worst of the scuffle; he couldn't chew very well for a day or two. No one had dared interview him about the incident. I was sent because I was expendable as a cub reporter and I asked him about it because I didn't know any better. So, in my most polite reportorial tones I asked Mickey if his jaw still hurt. Mickey looked at me contemptuously and made an obscene and physically impossible suggestion. Somehow, after years of reading about Mantle in newspapers and magazines and books, I was not exactly prepared for his answer. So I rephrased it and tried again. He then signalled to Yogi Berra, another all-star charmer, and they began throwing a baseball back and forth an inch over my head. I sensed that the interview was over.

I don't want to make too much of this because I think a celebrity has the right (within limits that apply to us all) to act any way he or she wants. But, I also think the rest of us have a right not to be deceived. That little incident at Yankee

Stadium was a real consciousness-raiser for me. If this was the real Mickey Mantle, I thought, then we haven't been getting the right information. Like so many athletes in our culture, Mantle had been isolated early by virtue of the varsity syndrome, given privileges denied the rest of us. Those privileges begin with favors and gifts in grade school, little presents in high school such as an unearned diploma, perhaps a college scholarship. Athletes are waved, as it were, through the toll booths of life. And then, as celebrities, they are given a whole new identity as heroes.

Of course, to publicize any frailties in athletic character structure is to bring down a wave of criticism and often categorical rejection. When Jim Bouton's book, *Ball Four,* came out a few years ago, the big rap against the book wasn't its stories or that major league shenanigans were untrue, but that kids shouldn't hear them—that the false image of athletes as somehow a super race apart, must be retained, even at the price of truth.[7] Why is it so important that kids look up to false heroes as models of behavior? Why not know the truth and learn to separate what people do from what they are; to appreciate athletes as dedicated specialists, as entertainers, but not as gods.

Varsity syndrome—athletes as salesmen

There are, of course, so many components of the varsity syndrome we could never even touch them all in this limited space. But there is one other significant dimension that deserves mention—the use of athletics and athletes to sell a product. At its lowest form, athletes sell shoes or panty hose, breakfast cereals or underarm deodorant. They sell colleges that have four books in the library but a multi-million dollar fieldhouse. Athletes sell cities which mortgage their futures to build ball-parks in order to be plunged into a national entertainment network which is valuable for tourism and investment. And, on the highest and perhaps most grotesque level, athletes are used to sell ways of life, ideologies.

This is the most distorted level, not only because worldclass athletic competitions, like the Olympic Games, are such major events, but because they would not be possible without the varsity syndrome, that careful and calculated selection process that starts in kindergarten. This narrow elitism makes most of us failed athletes long before we've had the chance to really feel the sensous delights of the wind in our hair while running, or the water lapping at our bodies while swimming, or the almost orgasmic pleasures of that one perfect shot or catch or leap that comes to everyone involved in sport. Sport is the best thing you can do with your body in public.

The Olympic Games are grotesque within themselves. As is probably known, the modern Olympics were the brainstorm of a French baron from a military family who never got over France's defeat in the Franco-Prussian War. Baron DeCoubertin wanted a rematch and he thought French youth could get in shape for the rematch through sports. That kind of nationalistic taint has never been removed from the games. In 1968 we saw the spectacle of black athletes, who raised their fists in protest against racism in America, thrown off the team even though theirs was an individual gesture in a context that is supposed to exist for individualistic expression. In 1972 the hideous extension of DeCoubertin's nationalism—the use of the Olympics as a showcase for the strength of democracy or the goodness of socialism or the love of the Junta—resulted in the murder of a team of competitors from Israel. In 1976, the various machinations over China and South Africa reenforced the Olympics as *Politics in a Sweatshirt.*

The Olympics not only represents a major political event, it also is a significant entertainment and commercial event. The most poignant lesson, to me, came at a press conference prior to the 1976 games. The president of ABC sports at the time, Roone Arledge, a very powerful man in international sports, was asked by an idealistic journalist why the opening event of the Games, the ceremonial parade of athletes, couldn't be run for its full hour or more without commercial interuptions. Arledge replied quite amiably that it wouldn't be commercially feasible ... "after all, sponsors pay for telecasts."

But the questioner continued. ... "Many countries which use the Olympics as a showcase or as a statement of identity, might never be seen except in that opening parade. After all, many countries win no medals at all. And some sports, like field hockey, water polo, and volleyball, are not well covered. So some countries, lost in a commercial, might never get on the world television feed at all."

"That's true," said Arledge.

"How do your pick candidates for obscurity?" asked the journalist.

"Well," said Arledge, "we have to make judgements. Suppose we've just had two little South American countries, and its time for a commercial, and here comes a third South American country ... sooooooo, sorry about that Chile."

That third little South American country, or that little midwestern college, betting its identity on the ephemeral possibility of national or international exposure, is putting a kind of graffiti on the windows of the world, shouting, "I'm here, we're alive."

They are in the trap of the varsity syndrome. The payoff can be great, but the price to pay is also great and, for most, rarely worth the gain. The struggle to success may be stalemated prematurely by the whim of a television producer or the vagaries of the system itself. Win or lose, the country and the college invariably sell their souls cheap to a system that uses them up and moves on.

This is a system in which, for the past one hundred years or so, most Americans have been taught to believe that playing and watching competitive games are not only healthful activities, but exert a positive force on our national psyche. Through sports, they have been led to believe, children will learn courage and self-control; old people will find blissful nostalgia; families will discover non-threatening ways to communicate among themselves, immigrants will find shortcuts to recognition as Americans, and, rich and poor, black and white, educated and unskilled, we will all find a unifying language with democratization the result: The melting pot may be a myth in real life, but in the ballpark or on the playing field we are one community, unified in common purpose. Even for ballgames, these values, with their implicit definitions of courage and success and manhood, are not necessarily in the individual's best interests. But for daily life they tend to support a web of ethics and attitudes, part of that amorphous infrastructure called *SportsWorld* ... that acts to contain our energies, divert our passions, and socialize us for work or war or depression.

In 1928, a Columbia University historian named John Krout wrote: "During depressions, with thousands out of work, sports helps refocus our attention on the great American values and ideals and also helps us to remember that life does not begin and end with the dollar."[8]

This infrastructure, SportsWorld, is neither an American nor a modern phenomenon. The Olympics of ancient Greece were manipulated for political and commercial purposes. SportsWorld is no classic conspiracy, but rather an expression of a community of interest. In the Soviet Union and East Germany, for example, where world-class athletes are the diplomat-soldiers of ideology, and where factory workers exercise to reduce fatigue and increase production, it is simple to see that the entire athletic apparatus is part of government.

In this country, SportsWorld's power is less visible, but no less real. In America, banks decide which arenas and recreational facilities will be built; television networks decide which sports shall be sponsored and viewed; the press decides which individuals and teams will be celebrated; municipal governments decide which clubs will be subsidized through the building of stadiums; state legislatures decide which universities and which aspects of their athletic programs, will prosper; and the federal government, through favorable tax rulings and exemptions from law, helps develop and maintain sports entertainment as a currency of communication that surpasses patriotism and piety while exploiting them both.

Conclusion

Educators and journalists are at fault for their support of this system. And we are often in the position of being the fall guys. It sometimes seems as though we are in what the play-by-play announcers call a no-win situation. By working within the rules of the system, preparing athletes and teachers to function smoothly in SportsWorld, and to prosper with the varsity syndrome, we are perpetuating a pattern that is basically anti-sports, that deprives the joy of healthy play and competition to the society as a whole. By trying to beat the system by de-emphasizing big-time sports and cutting back on the massive construction of arenas that are wasteful in terms of human use, in favor of some broad-based physical education programs, we are often in danger of jeopardizing the financial health of our institutions and discriminating against the really talented athletes who deserve the chance to develop to their limits just as surely as do the young poets in the English Department or the student engineers. Educators and journalists are the fall guys because when things go wrong they are often blamed, and sometimes fired—even though the ultimate decisionmaking power in SportsWorld is never theirs.

Sports is, has always been, and will always be, a reflection of the mainstream culture or the society. Those who claim that we could or should keep sports free of politics, or free of commercialism, or free of ideology are fools. If sports were not such a reflection, it would be nothing more than an isolated sanctuary, an irrelevant little circus, and hardly worth considering. But sports is, as I firmly believe it should be, a critical part of the lives of every man, woman, and child in the country and in the world. Furthermore, it should be accessible, inexpensive, and fun.

Activists have always seen sports as a tool to change or direct society, and they have been criticized for it. Yet when establishment politicians and coaches talk about sports as preparation for life or about football as a way of training young men for war or for corporate positions, they are using sports as a tool just as surely as is anyone who calls for a boycott of an all-white South African rugby team. The answer, of course, is that society must be changed before sports can be changed. But that, too, can sometimes be a self-defeating answer. It allows too many of us to sit back and throw up our hands. Changing society seems like an incomprehensible, much less possible, task.

However, things are happening in sports, exciting things, some progressive, some reactionary, some scary. First, there's a growing awareness of the importance of sports in our lives. Second, the increasing academic interest in sports is a hopeful sign. Institutes, both independent and on campuses, are being created with the explicit goal of investigating, analyzing, and understanding the role of sport and society. Third, there are new laws to help end the systematic exclusion of women. (But care must be taken that the varsity syndrome does not permeate the organization of women's sport.) Fourth, there's a growing body of work exposing the so-called Lombardi ethic of "Winning isn't the Most Important Thing, it's

the Only Thing" (A phrase, by the way, which Lombardi didn't invent) as appropriate for the professional Green Bay Packers, but a crippler, physically and psychologically, when applied to youngsters just starting in sports.

Despite the enormous amount to be accomplished, there are little contests each of us can engage in that will win for us all: one little community recreation program for older people; one totally non-sexist grade school sports program; one high-school program which involves every student regardless of skill level; a girls team that doesn't use the JV's left-over shoes and the gym at dinner time; a college pool that doesn't discriminate against non-varsity swimmers; a little league that defuses the pressures of joyless competition; and a university classroom that openly approaches the possibility of new games, new methods, and fresh concepts in sport studies. Each victory will shed some light on sports and will help shape our lives through its cultural impact. Each victory will help dispel the darkness of SportsWorld, the varsity syndrome, and a system that separates people by calling some athletes and some non-athletes. When this beautiful and good thing we call sports allows each person to be an athlete forever, then it will have been true to its original purposes.

Notes

1. Paul Gallico, *Farewell to Sports* (New York: Alfred A. Knopf, 1945), p. 229.
2. *Farewell to Sports*, p. 229.
3. James Michener, *Sports in America* (Chicago: Random House, 1976).
4. *Sports in America*, p. 129.
5. Robert Lipsyte, *SportsWorld* (New York: Quadrangle, 1975), p. 51.
6. Rick Telander, *Heaven is a Playground* (New York: Grosset and Dunlap, 1976).
7. Jim Bouton, *Ball Four* (New York: World, 1970).
8. John Krout, "Some Reflections on the Rise of American Sport," Proceedings of the Association of History, #26 1929. Reprinted in *The Sporting Set*, ed. Leon Stern, (New York: Arno Press, 1975), Pp. 84–93.

Mapping sports space

Alan Tomlinson, Andrei S. Markovits, and
Christopher Young

In this article, originally published as an introduction to a special issue of the *American Behavioral Scientist,* Tomlinson, Markovits, and Young aim to discredit approaches to the study of sport—which are rooted in a variety of theoretical perspectives—that view sport as, essentially, a simple (or, even, not so simple) reflection of society. They summarize, very briefly and usefully, a number of authors who have introduced new ideas to the understanding of the relationship between sport and society. Their focus, though, is on the concept of "sport space," a concept that they develop most directly from the work of Pierre Bourdieu. Elucidating how this concept helps us understand the relationship between particular sports and particular societies (by focusing primarily on soccer's presence in the US), the article emphasizes the importance of focusing on culture and power relations and their interrelations over time.

Sports forms (the shape that sports has taken) and practices (the activities that constitute the sport itself) have been seen as interesting but not of great importance: In such a view, sport has some interest as a reflection of the society itself, but by definition, from such a perspective, sport is not of real social significance. It is a kind of reminder of the broader social analysis: The values found in sport or a particular sports culture are those that characterize the wider society. One would typically expect an advanced industrial democracy to support those sports that embody the core values of the society. In classic structural-functionalist fashion, this framework locates sport as mere reflection—a cultural reflex, no more, of the wider social body.

Purportedly, more critical approaches claim to have broken with this tradition. Three classic critiques of contemporary sport adopted radical, almost insurrectionist, postures toward contemporary sport. Paul Hoch, working within the revolutionary left networks of the 1960s and 1970s, published *Rip Off the Big Game: The Exploitation of Sports by the Power Élite* in 1972. In France, linked to the radical movement of 1968 and its associated cultural politics, Jean-Marie Brohm collected together some of his provocative essays in the arrestingly titled volume *Sport: A Prison of Measured Time* (1978). East of Brohm, in the Federal Republic of Germany, Bero Rigauer was the first to take its logical conclusions toward the analytical emphases of the Frankfurt School: As the first graduate student of Theodor W. Adorno to work on the topic of sport, Rigauer produced *Sport and Work* (first published in German in 1969, English edition 1981), in which he argued that sport was simply analogous to work/labor and the values and ideologies represented by the latter in an advanced capitalist society/economy. The problem with such approaches—however sophisticated the intellectual framework, however trenchantly argued the case—is that the theory overdetermines the cultural analysis. It is no longer worth asking what sport means, represents, or symbolizes. The answer comes ready-made, generated by the theory itself. This kind of radical work—broadly culturally Marxist—expresses the worst extremes of meta-theory: Sport is just the superstructure, a predictable reflection of the determining infrastructure of the economic, and the more significant elements of the superstructure such as the sphere of the political. In the end, such eloquent—and, it has to be said, in part convincing—radical analyses said little more about the nuances and complexities of sport cultures than the redundant functionalist approaches that they so assertively sought to displace.

Other approaches to the analysis of sport gave more credibility to the cultural distinctiveness of sports themselves. Allen Guttmann (1978, 1988) placed the comparative sociology of Max Weber at the center of his studies of sport. In comparing the key features of sport across "primitive," classical (Greek and Roman), mediaeval, and modern societies, Guttmann articulated the socially discrete nature of sports in different times and places. It is tempting to see such a listing of the characteristics of sports in various ages as yet another oversimplistic account, but in line with a Weberian recognition on the generative nature of culture and beliefs, Guttmann's powerful comparative analysis lent to the sport cultures themselves a sense of real significance in the respective society. Norbert Elias and Eric Dunning, in their work on the *Quest for Excitement: Sport and Leisure in the Civilizing Process* (1986),[1] proposed a developmental, process-sociological approach to locating sport: Sport is always to be understood in terms of the changing cultural patterns of affect control, the control of the emotions and associated behaviors, and the interdependent configurations that make up a society at a particular time and place. Seeking to avoid the excesses of vulgar Marxism, work in British-based cultural studies blended the more culturally nuanced potential of cultural Marxism, and some aspects of the structuration theory of Anthony Giddens (1984), in interdisciplinary mixes of the social historical, the cultural, and the literary. Seminal works by John Hargreaves (1986, 1987) and Richard Gruneau (1983) were highly influential here, locating culture, and sport as an example of culture, as a

contested sphere, vital to the production of ideology and the core power relations of a society. Tomlinson's (1999) work consistently championed such an eclectic critical mix. Combining a geographer's interest in space with a sensitivity to the insights of Michel Foucault on the patterns of power and surveillance mobilized within the structures of modern societies, John Bale (1989, 1993, 1994) pioneered, within sports scholarship, a spatially aware study of sport. And in all of these approaches, the increasingly central importance of the study of the body, and the ways in which bodily practices take place and are performed, was impossible to ignore.

Van Ingen (2003) has noted the coming together of some of these developments in *Sport and Space*, a 1993 double issue of the *International Review for the Sociology of Sport* (IRSS). [...] In her introduction, Van Ingen (2003) notes the potential importance of the thinking of Henri Lefebvre, particularly his *The Production of Space*. [...] For Van Ingen (2003), Lefebvre's approach to the production of space calls for an examination of "the relation between identity and the spaces through which identity is produced and expressed" (p. 208) [...] Van Ingen singles out John Bale's article (1993) for special praise, demonstrating as it does "the ways in which stadiums are highly territorialized spaces" and "the way it explores how bodies are regulated and constrained in space and for asserting that space increasingly matters as a vantage point of critical insight (p. 209)." Van Ingen insists, quite rightly, that those researching sport

> cannot ignore the ways in which spaces are inexorably linked to the social construction of dominant ideologies and to the politics of identity. Today a key challenge facing those who study sport and space is to develop more nuanced inquires into the intersections of gender, sexuality, and race *in place*.
>
> (p. 210)

One of the most prominent of contemporary social theorists/sociologists to have prioritized the study of sport is the late Pierre Bourdieu. In several short pieces (Bourdieu, 1978, 1988, 1999), he has reiterated his view that sport has been a seriously neglected area of study for sociologists, and in his major work *Distinction: A Social Critique of the Judgement of Taste* (1986), based on empirical data in France in

1963 and 1967–1968, he gave sport, and the corporeal or bodily practices that sport comprises, great prominence in his analysis of the class and gendered basis of sports practices and forms.[2] He talks of the different physical manifestations exhibited in different sports: body-building for the working class, leisure water sports for the *haut bourgeois*. But he also talks of the way in which one sport can express a different culture. To understand the meaning of a sporting practice, it is necessary to look at when and how a sport was learned, how it is played, what context it is played in, and how often it is played—considerations that lead Bourdieu to note that much available statistical data are therefore very difficult to interpret (p. 211). So in the case of tennis, new players will flaunt dress codes of traditional tennis players, and this reveals the complexity of the question of the meaning and social significance of the sport: "Tennis played in Bermuda shorts and a tee shirt, in a track suit or even swimming trunks, and Adidas running shoes, is indeed another tennis, both in the way it is played and the satisfactions it gives," and of course where it is played and how it is viewed (Bourdieu, 1986, p. 212). For this is, if anything, about how sport space is conceded and valued in the wider culture, as well as about the literal physical spaces in which sporting activities take place. For Bourdieu, the central analytical concept for cultural analysis is "habitus." Bourdieu states that the habitus is a system of dispositions:

> It expresses first the *result of an organizing action*, with a meaning close to that of words such as structure; it also designates a way of being, a habitual state (especially of the body) and, in particular, a *predisposition, tendency, propensity* or *inclination*.
> (Bourdieu, 1986, p. 562, Note 2)

The critical emphasis here is that within the one concept, structure and action are embraced as interrelated elements, without any one-sided determinism: "The habitus is not only a structuring structure, which organizes practices and the perception of practices, but also a structured structure" (Bourdieu, 1986, p. 170). This is a theoretical principle underlying the whole of Bourdieu's framework, and empirical studies alone have the capacity to identify the balance between the structuring and the structured in any given case. "Life-styles are thus the systematic products of habitus, which … become sign systems that are socially qualified" (p. 173). And habitus must, for Bourdieu, be analyzed in terms of a heuristic model of "social space," which is "to the practical space of everyday life … what geometrical space is to the 'travelling space' (*espace hodologique*) of ordinary experience" (p. 168). Sports embody lifestyles and speak not just of the social. Lifestyles are expressions of social space. Bourdieu's sociology of taste and consumption is thus an implicit sociology of (status-ridden) space and place. His overall project in *Distinction* is to promote, in his own words, a "model of the relationship between the universe of economic and social conditions and the universe of lifestyles" (p. xi). This could easily be seen as overdeterminist, reducing the significance of the cultural. But Bourdieu always recognizes the shifting parameters of the habitus: New sporting activities can emerge, with "the dynamics of the dream of social weightlessness" (p. 220): "foot-trekking, pony-trekking, cycle-trekking, motor-bike trekking, boat-trekking, canoeing, archery, windsurfing, cross-country-skiing, sailing, hang-gliding, micro-lights etc." (p. 220), all dependent on serious investment of time and money and the verbalization of the experience, and, Bourdieu might have added, a confidence in claiming the cultural space for the new sport and the actual physical space(s) in which to do it.

We need not mention and trace all such approaches. This is not an attempt at a comprehensive essay in the history of an idea or a definitive genealogy of critical work in the field. Important feminist work (Hall, 1996; Hargreaves, 1994) was of course also critical to rethinking the parameters of a persistingly patriarchal sport culture. Postmodern analyses have, as have globalization approaches, raised many questions concerning time-space relations and compression. Queer theory has politicized all of cultural space in terms of sexual power relations. Suffice it to say that in the social sciences' analysis of sport, scholars recognized more and more widely the centrality of understanding sport as culture and locating the sport culture in terms of particular aspects of time and space. Sport *as* culture was an early version of what some sociologists (Chaney, 1994) came to call the "cultural turn"—a recognition of the inherently cultural nature of sport invited scholars to analyze things way beyond the field of play; to understand the discourse and related practices around sport, physical culture, and the body; and to understand sport's relation to the wider culture and the space for sports that might be established within that culture.

It is on the basis of this very theme that Andrei Markovits's analysis of soccer (association football) in U.S. sports space assumed a significance far beyond the study of one sport in one society. When the soccer World Cup was staged in the United States, Joseph "Sepp" Blatter, then the Fédération Internationale de Football Association (FIFA) general secretary, commented, "The 1994 World Cup produced a turnover of $4 billion with 32 billion television viewers. I mean no disrespect to other sports by saying that even the Olympic Games cannot compare. The World Cup was a fabulous success" (cited in *World Soccer*, Vol. 35, Issue 3, p. 10); this may be hyperbole but it is still a gauntlet to analysts of sport culture and the globalization process. Markovits had already been thinking through the critical questions concerning the strange relationship between dominant U.S. sports—the Big Three of gridiron American football, baseball, basketball, and parvenu ice hockey—and their poor cousin, soccer, the most popular sport on the globe. Alongside this canon of U.S. sport culture, soccer had long looked unquestionably minor league. And yet, at the World Cup Finals of 1994, ticket sales exceeded those of any previous World Cup, the games were widely recognized as splendidly entertaining, and television recording and reproduction techniques guaranteed high-quality coverage of and feedback on almost any aspect of the game, its players, and the tournament. How was this possible? Understanding the nature of sport space and cultural space more generally was a key to providing viable answers.

Globally framed historical scholarship also has noted the importance and distinctiveness of sport in its complex relationship to political domination and cultural standardization. In his survey of "The Arts 1914–1945," Hobsbawm (1995) asserts that in "the field of popular culture the world was American or it was provincial," but with one exception: "The unique exception was sport" (p. 198). He recognizes soccer as a "genuinely international" sport:

> The sport the world made its own was association football, the child of Britain's global economic presence. ... This simple and elegant

game, unhampered by complex rules and equipment, and which could be practised on any more or less flat open space of the required size, made its way through the world entirely on its merits.

(Hobsbawm, 1995, p. 198)

But not in the United States. In this context, the Markovits (1990), Sugden (1994), Sugden and Tomlinson (1994), and Tomlinson (1994) theses on the marginality of soccer in the sports space of the United States were revealing, in general conceptual and not merely empirical terms.

Classic sources on the history and sociology of American sports have, until Markovits's work and his book-length study (Markovits and Hellman, 2001), paid little heed to the story of soccer in the United States, although enthusiasts for the game have sought to remedy this. Foulds and Harris (1979) retrieve some of this ignored if not hidden history and report that the American League of Professional Football Clubs opened its season on October 6, 1894. An early blend of professional and amateur players in Boston drew on the textile communities of the region, players emerging from "large, immigrant soccer-educated populations" (Foulds and Harris, 1979, p. 13). Only 6 years after the formation of the professional Football League in England, teams such as the Boston Beaneaters, the Brooklyn Superbas, the Washington Senators, and the New York Giants were competing (under the name *football)* in soccer matches. Despite optimistic reception in some quarters of the press, matches staged on weekday afternoons failed to capture a large following. As Foulds and Harris (1979) put it, "The failure of the promoters to realize that the basic support in the initial stages of the league rested with the large soccer addicted foreign-born blue collar working population of the Eastern industrial states was unfortunate" (p. 13). Despite evidence of subcultural popularity—among Jewish communities and teams in the New York area, for instance, in the 1920s (Murray, 1994, p. 262)—attempts to introduce high-profile professional soccer remained short-lived if successful, or merely marginal (Murray, 1994, pp. 265–272). As Markovits and Sugden have demonstrated, the historical, social, and cultural odds were stacked against football/soccer becoming a mainstream professional sport in the United States. The explanation for this, as Markovits (1988, 1990) so presciently noted, was the nature of U.S. sport space.

For Markovits, the lack of American response to soccer World Cups (particularly when the finals took place in a contiguous neighboring country) has been intriguing. He noted that when the 1986 World Cup Finals were hosted by Mexico, "This event failed to capture the imagination of the American public," and described the American interest in "the world's most important media event" as "strikingly minute in comparison to that exhibited in virtually every country in the world" (Markovits, 1988, p. 125). His explanation for the failure of soccer to gain a hold in U.S. sports culture revolves around a notion of sports space and the argument that in the formative period of U.S. nation-building, three vigorously characteristic American sports took shape—baseball, American football, and basketball. This had the consequence that "America's bourgeois hegemony and legacy of the 'first new nation' ... contributed substantially to the continued absence of the world's most popular team sport as a major presence in American popular culture" (Markovits, 1988, p. 125). The sports space, Markovits argues, was occupied early in the United States, so that a fully matured form of association football or soccer (as developed formatively in Britain and its imperial and trading networks) had little chance of gaining any serious foothold in U.S. sports territory. Soccer was crowded out, from below by baseball, with its mythlike resonance of rural community, and from above by American football, with its initially college-based rationalistic personification of the new industrial order. Indoors, basketball also took a hold on the sports consciousness of the expanding nation—very much, although Markovits did not expand on this, in waiting for its development in its professional form by Black Americans (George, 1992; Novak, 1976).

Where soccer took hold, Markovits reminds us, pre-World War I, it "remained closely associated with immigrants, a stigma which proved fatal to soccer's potential of becoming a popular team sport in the 'new world'" (Markovits, 1988, p. 135). Even on its reintroduction as a university/college sport in the latter half of the 20th century, "soccer has remained largely the domain of foreigners and recent immigrants, both as players and spectators" (Markovits, 1988, p. 136).

Sugden and Tomlinson (1994), referring to other spheres beyond just sport, have commented that "as a nation," the United States "has often appeared reluctant to import cultural forms which might highlight its own cultural and ethnic diffuseness" (p. 9); this theme dominated Sugden's discussion of the United States and soccer. Taking Markovits's insights further, and citing Oriard's work on images of sports in American culture, Sugden (1994) developed more fully the notion that the quest for distinctive forms of homegrown sport represented a thrusting new nation's yearning for self-identity, not least by evolving nativist cultural forms. Indeed, one might go further still from this perspective and note that the United States's Big Three are evidence of a unique society's quest for an appropriately unique sports and popular culture. With "the working class and middle class 'sport space' of the American public already crowded ... there was little or no room for another outdoor team ball game, particularly one, like soccer, which could be readily associated with anti-American traditions" (Sugden, 1994, p. 235). Sugden emphasizes the notion of American nativism, which is manifest in the celebration of one's own identity and, simultaneously, the denigration of the Cultural Other, shown in "an intense distaste for and suspicion of foreign subcultures and alien traditions" (Sugden, 1994, p. 235). He also argues that when soccer did take hold in American high schools in the 1970s and the 1980s, alongside its "elevated status as an intercollegiate sport," it did so on a middle-class base and on the basis of "a youth caucus which was not so obviously dependent on immigrant and ethnic involvement" (Sugden, 1994, p. 243). Soccer, ironically (given its status across the world as a proletarian and working-class rooted sport in its professional spectator form), now offered the indigenous American middle-class a positive, and essentially reconstituted amateurist, alternative to the excesses of violent professional sports and, especially, American football.

Compounding this antimasculinist, non-American status of soccer in the perception of the American public, the U.S. women's team became world champions in 1991, beating Norway 5-2 in China. Norway avenged this defeat with a 1-0 semifinal victory in the 1995 Women's World Cup in Sweden and went on to become champions, defeating Germany in the final. The U.S. team secured third place with a 2-0 win over China and went on to win

45

the inaugural women's soccer event in the 1996 Atlanta Olympics, defeating China 2-1 in the final. In 1999, the United States again defeated China, this time in a penalty shoot-out after a 0-0 reciprocal shutout, to win the Women's World Cup in the United States. Norway kept this three-way battle for world supremacy going, winning gold in the Sydney 2000 Olympics. Nothing in the later 1990s occurred to challenge Sugden's conclusion that

> no matter ... how well the World Cup is organized, and regardless of how many tickets are sold, so long as soccer in America continues to be viewed as a game for foreigners, rich white kids and women, its chances of becoming established as a mainstream professional sport there are minimal.
>
> (Sugden, 1994, p. 250)

These analyses do not suggest that space is simply full, like some popular restaurant with a waiting list for reservations. The concept of sports space should be understood as referring to that which is culturally constructed, not merely physically determined. And the sport space refers to the resonances of the sport form throughout the culture: the folklore of the game, the debates on outcomes in the bars and workplaces of the nation, and the way in which the sport is featured in the press and broadcast media. There is no reason why any particular society should have two rather than three, or three rather than four or five, dominant sports, and of course, this is particularly true of advanced societies with large populations, such as the United States. But sports space refers to the cultural meanings of a sport and to the capacity of a society to value a particular kind of sport and render it meaningful and of real social and cultural significance. There are socially determined and culturally specific conditions in which cultural forms such as sport are established and developed in particular societies and times. In Cuba, for instance, the postrevolutionary sports culture could harness well-established sports such as boxing and baseball to the explicit values of the revolutionary society (Sugden, Tomlinson, and McCartan, 1990). Other societies keen to excel at Olympic level also have demonstrated how the available sports space can be reallocated. These include not just the communist societies of Cuba, the former Soviet Union, the former East Germany, and China, for instance, but also Spain, when hosting the Barcelona 1992 Olympics, and the hugely successful Australian host nation in Sydney 2000, among liberal democratic capitalist societies. Sports space should therefore be seen not in any oversimplified spatio-physical terms but in the context of culture and power relations in particular societies.

Criticisms have been made of the concept of sports space and of its explanatory limitations. Waddington and Broderick criticize both Markovits and the football historian Tony Mason for what they call "an implicit—and therefore unexamined—assumption that in each society there is a limited amount of 'space' for sports, and that once this 'space' has been 'filled' by one sport, there is no room for other sports" (Waddington and Broderick, 1996, p. 45). But space is not filled simply on a first-come, first-served basis. It is disputed and contested by social groups and actors with particular sets of interests. Positions within any society's sports space can thus be denied by dominant groups and alliances of interests. This sense of sports space as contested cultural territory as well as a sphere of established institutional interests is fundamental not just to the conceptualization of soccer in the United States but also to an understanding of how particular sports become part of an established culture and are reproduced—or not—within that culture. [...]

Notes

1. See the article by Dunning from this book elsewhere in this chapter. [Eds.]
2. See the selection from Bourdieu's *Distinction* in Part 2 of this volume. [Eds.]

References

Bale, J. (1989). *Sports geography.* London: E & FN Spon.

Bale, J. (1993). The spatial development of sport. *International Review for the Sociology of Sport, 28*(2/3), 122–133.

Bale, J. (1994). *Landscapes of modern sport.* Leicester, UK: Leicester University Press.

Bourdieu, P. (1978). Sport and social class. *Social Science Information, 17*(6), 819–840.

Bourdieu, P. (1986). *Distinction: A social critique of the judgement of taste*. London: Routledge & Kegan Paul.

Bourdieu, P. (1988). Program for a sociology of sport. *Sociology of Sport Journal, 5*(2), 153–161.

Bourdieu, P. (1999). The state, economics and sport. In H. Dauncey & G. Hare (Eds.), *France and the 1998 World Cup: The national impact of a world sporting event* (Pp. 15–21). London: Frank Cass.

Brohm, J. M. (1978). *Sport: A prison of measured time*. London: Ink Links.

Chaney, D. (1994). *The cultural turn*. London: Routledge.

Elias, N., & Dunning, E. (1986). *Quest for excitement: Sport and leisure in the civilizing process*. Oxford, UK: Basil Blackwell.

Foulds, S., & Harris, P. (1979). *America's soccer heritage: A history of the game*. Manhattan Beach, CA: Soccer for Americans.

George, N. (1992). *Elevating the game: Black men and basketball*. New York: HarperCollins.

Giddens, A. (1984). *The constitution of society: Outline of the theory of structuration*. Cambridge, UK: Polity.

Gruneau, R. (1983). *Class, sports and social development*. Amherst: University of Massachusetts Press.

Guttmann, A. (1978). *From ritual to record: The nature of modern sports*. New York: Columbia University Press.

Guttmann, A. (1988). *A whole new ballgame*. Chapel Hill: University of North Carolina Press.

Hall, M. A. (1996). *Feminism and sporting bodies: Essays on theory and practice*. Champaign, IL: Human Kinetics.

Hargreaves, J. (1986). *Sport, power and culture: A social and historical analysis of popular sports in Britain*. Cambridge, UK: Polity.

Hargreaves, J. (1987). The body: Sport and power relations. In J. Horne, D. Jary, & A. Tomlinson (Eds.), *Sport, leisure and social relations* (Pp. 139–159). London: Routledge & Kegan Paul.

Hargreaves, J. (1994). *Sporting females: Critical issues in the history and sociology of women's sports*. London: Routledge.

Hobsbawm, E. (1995). *Age of extremes: The short twentieth century 1914–1991*. London: Abacus.

Hoch, P. (1972). *Rip off the big game: The exploitation of sports by the power élite*. New York: Doubleday Anchor.

Markovits, A. S. (1988). The other "American Exceptionalism": Why is there no soccer in the United States? *Praxis International, 8*(2), 125–150.

Markovits, A. S. (1990). The other "American Exceptionalism": Why is there no soccer in the United States? *International Journal of the History of Sport, 7*(2), 230–264.

Markovits, A. S., & Hellerman, S. L. (2001). *Offside: Soccer and American exceptionalism*. Princeton, NJ: Princeton University Press.

Murray, B. (1994). *Football: A history of the world game*. Aldershot, UK: Scholar.

Novak, M. (1976). *The joy of sports: End zones, bases, baskets, balls, and the consecration of the American spirit*. New York: Basic Books.

Rigauer, B. (1981). *Sport and work*. New York: Columbia University Press. (Original work published 1969).

Sugden, J. (1994). USA and the World Cup: American nativism and the rejection of the people's game. In J. Sugden & A. Tomlinson (Eds.), *Hosts and champions: Soccer cultures, national identities and the USA World Cup* (Pp. 219–252). Aldershot, UK: Ashgate.

Sugden, J., & Tomlinson, A. (Eds.). (1994). *Hosts and champions: Soccer cultures, national identities and the USA World Cup*. Aldershot, UK: Ashgate.

Sugden, J., Tomlinson, A., & McCartan, E. (1990). The making and remaking of white lightning in Cuba: Politics, sport and physical education 30 years after the revolution. *Arena Review, 14*(1), 101–109.

Tomlinson, A. (1994). FIFA and the World Cup: The expanding football family. In J. Sugden & A. Tomlinson (Eds.), *Hosts and champions: Soccer cultures, national identities and the USA World Cup* (Pp. 13–33). Aldershot, UK: Ashgate.

Tomlinson, A. (1999). *The game's up: Essays in the cultural analysis of sport, leisure and popular culture*. Aldershot, UK: Ashgate.

Van Ingen, C. (2003). Geographies of gender, sexuality & race: Refocusing the focus on space in sport sociology. *International Review for the Sociology of Sport, 38*(2).

Waddington, I., & Broderick, M. (1996). American exceptionalism: Soccer and American football. *Sports Historian, 16*, 42–63.

1.6 Journalistic view

Ten reasons why sports aren't sports

Andy Baggot

We need to get something straight here before things get out of hand.

Not everything you see on a certain all-sports cable TV network is necessarily a sport.

For some reason, people are actually debating whether the World Series of Poker and the National Spelling Bee, recent fixtures on ESPN, are sports.

Yeah, and Al Franken is going to replace Dick Cheney as President Bush's running mate.

I can understand the confusion. There seem to be a lot more "activities" trying to pass themselves off as actual sports these days, stuff like disc golf, ice dancing and cheerleading.

It doesn't help that the dictionary definition of "sport" leaves a lot open to interpretation.

"An activity involving physical exertion and skill, governed by rules or customs and often undertaken competitively" could mean basketball to you and me, but it could just as easily mean a belching contest to someone else.

To try to make the line less blurry, I have come up with 10 guidelines for identifying a real sport.

1 If you can drink alcohol and smoke a cigar while competing, then it's not a sport. Examples: Horseshoes, golf, bass fishing.

2 If the winner is determined solely by the work of judges, then it's not a sport. Examples: Gymnastics, figure skating, cheerleading, ballroom dancing.

3 If an animal dies or does the heavy lifting, then it's not a sport. Examples: Iditarod, horse racing, hunting.

4 If you sit on your butt for hours at a time, then it's not a sport. Examples: Chess, poker.

5 If an engine does the work, then it's not a sport. Examples: Auto, truck, boat and motorcycle racing.

6 If you wear a watch, long pants and a collared shirt while competing, then it's not a sport. Examples: Pool, bowling.

7 If there's a script, then it's not a sport. Examples: WWE, RAW.

8 It's possible to be an athlete, but yours may not be a sport. Gymnasts, golfers, cheerleaders and rodeo clowns are good examples of this.

9 The need for great eye-hand coordination doesn't automatically mean it's a sport. That's why marbles, juggling and croquet are out.

10 Competing against someone doesn't automatically mean it's a sport. If it did, getting the number of the woman at the end of the bar before your buddy would have leagues.

Off the top of my head, I would say the biggest opposition to this list will come from those who follow the Matt Kenseths of the world.

Andy Baggot, "Ten Reasons Why Sports Aren't Sports" from *Wisconsin State Journal* (August 7, 2004). Reprinted with the permission of the Wisconsin State Journal.

The cheerleaders will be a close second, followed by the golfers.

Auto racing is extremely dangerous. It requires tremendous eye-hand coordination. It demands quick reflexes and a sense of stamina. But a parent faces all that and more driving the Beltline at rush hour with three toddlers yelping from the backseat.

If cheerleading is a sport, then so is ballet.

Golf? Grab a beer, fire up a cigar and we'll discuss it over 18.

Section 2

High brow and low brow contests

Sports with—more or less—class

Introduction

The research has not yet been done but the likelihood that there have been great polo stars who hailed from the early twentieth century ghettoes of the lower East Side of New York City, from Brazilian *favelas*, or from Kibera in Kenya, is extremely low. Even if sport facilitates cross-class competition (think of the Williams sisters in the country club sport of tennis) and communication (think of the range of social classes that shows up at stadia and arenas), it does not necessarily produce total democratization. Certain sports are associated with athletes, and sometimes fans, from specific social class backgrounds. Polo, obviously, is an extreme example but we still see a disproportionate share of wealthy people oriented to tennis and golf and a disproportionate share of the less wealthy oriented toward NASCAR (although this is changing a bit) and basketball. In the US, basketball has drawn most heavily from poor, urban working class communities, whether Eastern-European Jews in the first half of the twentieth century or African-Americans since that time. Professional sport, as a relatively meritocratic and public social space, has famously been a source of upward social mobility for the fortunate few, even if, overall, the chances that any given high school or collegiate athlete will make it into the professional ranks are extremely slim.

Depending on their theoretical perspective, sociologists tend to emphasize different aspects of the relationship between social class and sport. For those who see society as constituted by a consensus of shared values, sport is seen as integrating people across classes in common activities and providing additional grease for the wheels of social mobility. Sociologists who see group conflict as fundamental to the structure of society are more likely to see sport as a site of struggle for advantage among classes and status groups. In looking at the vast class differences among those who attend a baseball game, the consensus sociologists would emphasize the fact that, no matter the social background, all classes are going to enjoy the game and, most likely, root together for the home team. The conflict-oriented sociologists, on the other hand, will focus on the different experiences of the "bleacher bums" compared to the patrons of the "diamond club suites." At the same time, because the fans who are in "opposite" parts of the ballpark are rooting for the same team, they "forget" their sometimes structurally-opposed (e.g., worker vs. employer) existences.

Social class manifests itself in the sports knowledge and participation of most people. Upper class people are much more likely than working class folks to understand the intricacies of yachting. At the same time, working class children are much more likely to have played stickball and stoopball than those from upper class backgrounds. Before it became professionalized, US football was a relatively upper class sport because the key locus of football socialization was college, a place that was largely reserved for upper class players. By the time football became a national obsession, however, colleges were already admitting less academically qualified, but highly athletic, working class students so as to better compete with other higher education institutions. This pattern of democratization is seen with other sports as well. The two journalistic articles, by Syed and Thomas, address issues of sport, social class, and social mobility.

Pierre Bourdieu has, perhaps, gone farthest in arguing that, in a continual quest for distinction in the larger status culture, one's social origins largely determine one's dispositions, orientations, and cultural tastes and, accordingly, one's preferences in the realm of sports. In the excerpt below from *Distinction*, among other emphases, Bourdieu suggests a relationship between one's social class and the degree to which one's sport involves bodily contact. Essentially, he proposes a direct negative relationship between the amount of bodily contact and one's social class: in upper class sports, bodies do not come into contact with one another at all (e.g., tennis and golf). At the same time, he recognizes the different forms that any given sport may take: for example, golf on a public course vs. golf at a restricted-membership club. Subtle differences in the way that one practices sport both reflect one's social position and signal one's strategy for social distinction.

Wacquant's description and analysis of the social origins of the boxers in a Chicago gym reveals in empirical terms some of the theoretical points made by Bourdieu in the previous selection. A key point—at odds with commonsensical notions—is that boxers do not (Wacquant implies that they *can* not) come from the underclasses. Almost parallel to Marx's argument that the lumpenproletariat is unreliable politically, Wacquant suggests that, in order to become a serious boxer, one must have the resources and discipline that are most often absent among those from unstable backgrounds. Even the meager funds necessary to take up the sport and the demands of regular training are often beyond those who live from meal to meal or from odd-job to odd-job.

Individual-level strategies are, of course, embedded in larger social processes. The article by Leite Lopes on the historical development of Brazilian football (soccer) reveals a number of important issues in how sport and class (and, as the title suggests, ethnicity and color) develop together in given historical and institutional contexts. The specific patterns that he describes about Brazil and football/soccer are common in other countries and for other sports, as well. The study demonstrates the ways that dominant groups (e.g., employers, those with aristocratic origins) and subordinate groups (e.g., workers, nonwhites, etc.) struggle with one another to attempt to realize their (opposed) interests. In the course of this struggle, new avenues of social mobility are created, new forms of social exclusion and social control are attempted, and a new relationship between a sport and a national identity is developed.

Distinction

A social critique of the judgement of taste

Pierre Bourdieu

This excerpt from *Distinction* by Pierre Bourdieu is a demanding but rewarding contribution. It lays out how sport articulates with social class in the struggle for status distinction in the larger society. Though most of his references are to France, readers should try to apply his ideas to their own society. Are the same relationships among sport participation, bodily practices, and social class prevalent?

Bourdieu uses three concepts in this piece that need explication: field, habitus, and capital. Field, for Bourdieu, is a highly complex, structured space in which conflicts among persons (and organizations) take place through practices within a given set of power relations. In the field of sport (within which exists everything from the somewhat obscure curling to the everyday basketball), for example, people play different sports in different ways, thereby insinuating (or attempting to insinuate) themselves into particular parts of the status structure that are connected to those sporting practices. To clarify this, it might help to think about the music field: who plays classical music vs. who plays country-western and what do they gain/lose by those practices. Individuals' orientations to the sports field are determined by their habitus, a set of conscious and unconscious predispositions toward the world that is rooted in their social origins. So, people from different social classes (races/ethnicities/genders) see different sports opportunities in the world and have different senses of what's in the realm of the possible. Finally, social classes (and class fractions) are determined for Bourdieu by individuals' locations in the distribution of social, economic, and cultural capital. Briefly, and somewhat cryptically, economic capital is wealth, cultural capital is education and familiarity with dominant cultural forms, and social capital is defined by the capital embedded in your social networks. One's leisure/sport choices, therefore, are determined by the resources you have at hand and your aspirations for future status—in the context of your perception of the opportunity structure, which is determined both by the constraints of your social class and by the larger field of power relations (for sport and for the larger society).

The universes of stylistic possibles

[...]

The spaces defined by preferences in food, clothing or cosmetics are organized according to the same fundamental structure, that of the social space determined by volume and composition of capital. Fully to construct the space of life-styles within which cultural practices are defined, one would first have to establish, for each class and class fraction, that is, for each of the configurations of capital, the generative formula of the habitus which retranslates the necessities and facilities characteristic of that class of (relatively) homogeneous conditions of existence into a particular life-style. One would then have to determine how the dispositions of the habitus are specified, for each of the major areas of practice, by implementing one of the stylistic possibles offered by each field (the field of sport, or music, or food, decoration, politics, language etc.). By superimposing these homologous spaces one would obtain a rigorous representation of the space of life-styles, making it possible to characterize each of the distinctive features (e.g., wearing a cap or playing the piano) in the two respects in which it is objectively defined, that is, on the one hand by reference to the set of features constituting the area in question (e.g., the system of hairstyles), and on the other hand by reference to the set of features constituting a particular life-style (e.g., the working-class life-style), within which its social significance is determined.

For example, the universe of sporting activities and entertainments presents itself to each new entrant as a set of ready-made choices, objectively instituted possibles, traditions, rules, values, equipment, symbols, which receive their social significance from the system they constitute and which derive a proportion of their properties, at each moment, from history.

A sport such as rugby presents an initial ambiguity. In England, at least, it is still played in the elite 'public schools', whereas in France it has become the characteristic sport of the working and middle classes of the regions south of the Loire (while preserving some 'academic' bastions such as the Racing Club or the Paris Universite Club). This ambiguity can only be understood if one bears in mind the history of the process which, as in the 'elite schools' of nineteenth-century England, leads to the transmutation of popular games into elite sports, associated with an aristocratic ethic and world view ('fair play', 'will to win' etc.), entailing a radical change in meaning and function entirely analogous to what happens to popular dances when they enter the complex forms of 'serious' music; and the less well-known history of the process of popularization, akin to the diffusion of classical or 'folk' music on LPs, which, in a second phase, transforms elite sport into mass sport, a spectacle as much as a practice.

[...] The 'aristocratic' image of sports like tennis, riding or golf can persist beyond a—relative—transformation of the material conditions of access, whereas *pétanque* [a game similar to bocce—Eds.] doubly stigmatized by its popular and southern origins and connections, has

a distributional significance very similar to that of Ricard or other strong drinks and all the cheap, strong foods which are supposed to give strength.

But distributional properties are not the only ones conferred on goods by the agents' perception of them. Because agents apprehend objects through the schemes of perception and appreciation of their habitus, it would be naive to suppose that all practitioners of the same sport (or any other practice) confer the same meaning on their practice or even, strictly speaking, that they are practising the same practice. It can easily be shown that the different classes do not agree on the profits expected from sport, be they specific physical profits, such as effects on the external body, like slimness, elegance or visible muscles, and on the internal body, like health or relaxation; or extrinsic profits, such as the social relationships a sport may facilitate, or possible economic and social advantages. And, though there are cases in which the dominant function of the practice is reasonably clearly designated, one is practically never entitled to assume that the different classes expect the same thing from the same practice. For example, gymnastics may be asked—this is the popular demand, satisfied by body-building—to produce a strong body, bearing the external signs of its strength, or a healthy body—this is the bourgeois demand, satisfied by 'keep-fit' exercises or 'slimnastics'—or, with the 'new gymnastics', a 'liberated' body—this is the demand characteristic of women in the new fractions of the bourgeoisie and petite bourgeoisie. Only a methodical analysis of the variations in the function and meaning conferred on the different sporting activities will enable one to escape from abstract, formal 'typologies' based [...] on universalizing the researcher's personal experience; and to construct the table of the sociologically pertinent features in terms of which the agents (consciously or unconsciously) choose their sports.

The meaning of a sporting practice is linked to so many variables—how long ago, and how, the sport was learnt, how often it is played, the socially qualified conditions (place, time, facilities, equipment), how it is played (position in a team, style etc.)—that most of the available statistical data are very difficult to interpret. This is especially true of highly dispersed practices, such as pétanque, which may be played every weekend, on a prepared pitch, with regular partners, or improvised on holiday to amuse the children; or gymnastics, which may be simple daily or weekly keep-fit exercises, at home, without special equipment, or performed in a special gymnasium whose 'quality' (and price) vary with its equipment and services (not to mention athletic gymnastics and all the forms of 'new gymnastics'). But can one place in the same class, given identical frequency, those who have skied or played tennis from early childhood and those who learnt as adults, or again those who ski in the school holidays and those who have the means to ski at other times and off the beaten track? In fact, it is rare for the social homogeneity of the practitioners to be so great that the populations defined by the same activity do not function as fields in which the very definition of the legitimate practice is at stake. Conflicts over the legitimate way of doing it, or over the resources for doing it (budget allocations, equipment, grounds etc.) almost always retranslate social differences into the specific logic of the field. Thus sports which are undergoing 'democratization' may cause to coexist (generally in separate spaces or times) socially different sub-populations which correspond to different ages of the sport. In the case of tennis, the members of private clubs, long-standing practitioners who are more than ever attached to strict standards of dress (a Lacoste shirt, white shorts or skirt, special shoes) and all that this implies, are opposed in every respect to the new practitioners in municipal clubs and holiday clubs who demonstrate that the ritual of clothing is no superficial aspect of the legitimate practice. Tennis played in Bermuda shorts and a tee shirt, in a track suit or even swimming trunks, and, Adidas running-shoes, is indeed another tennis, both in the way it is played and in the satisfactions it gives. And so the necessary circle whereby the meaning of a practice casts light on the class distribution of practices and this distribution casts light on the differential meaning of the practice cannot be broken by an appeal to the 'technical' definition. This, far from escaping the logic of the field and its struggles, is most often the work of those who, like physical-education teachers, are required to ensure the imposition and methodical inculcation of the schemes of perception and action which, in practice, organize the practices, and who are inclined to present the explanations they produce as grounded in reason or nature.

In any case, one only needs to be aware that the class variations in sporting activities are due as much to variations in perception and appreciation of the immediate or deferred profits they are supposed to bring, as to variations in the costs, both economic and cultural and, indeed, bodily (degree of risk and physical effort), in order to understand in its broad outlines the distribution of these activities among the classes and class fractions. Everything takes place as if the probability of taking up the different sports depended, within the limits defined by economic (and cultural) capital and spare time, on perception and assessment of the intrinsic and extrinsic profits of each sport in terms of the dispositions of the habitus, and more precisely, in terms of the relation to the body, which is one aspect of this.

The relationship between the different sports and age is more complex since it is only defined—through the intensity of the physical effort called for and the disposition towards this demand, which is a dimension of class ethos—in the relationship between a sport and a class. The most important property of the 'popular' sports is that they are tacitly associated with youth—which is spontaneously and implicitly credited with a sort of temporary licence, expressed, inter alia, in the expending of excess physical (and sexual) energy—and are abandoned very early (generally on entry into adult life, symbolized by marriage). By contrast, the common feature of the 'bourgeois' sports, mainly pursued for their health-maintaining functions and their social profits, is that their 'retirement age' is much later, perhaps the more so the more prestigious they are (e.g., golf.).

The instrumental relation to their own bodies which the working classes express in all practices directed towards the body—diet or beauty care, relation to illness or medical care—is also manifested in choosing sports which demand a high investment of energy, effort or even pain (e.g., boxing) and which sometimes endanger the body itself (e.g., motor cycling, parachute jumping, acrobatics, and, to some extent, all the 'contact sports').

Rugby, which combines the popular features of the ball-game and a battle involving the body itself and allowing a—partially regulated—expression of physical violence and an immediate use of 'natural' physical qualities (strength, speed etc.), has affinities with the most typically popular dispositions, the cult of manliness and the taste for a fight, toughness in 'contact' and resistance to tiredness and pain, and sense of solidarity ('the mates') and revelry ('the third half') and so forth. This does not prevent members of the dominant fractions of the dominant class (or some intellectuals, who consciously or unconsciously express their values) from making an aesthetico-ethical investment in the game and even sometimes playing it. The pursuit of toughness and the cult of male values, sometimes mingled with an aestheticism of violence and man-to-man combat, bring the deep dispositions of first-degree practitioners to the level of discourse. The latter, being little inclined to verbalize and theorize, find themselves relegated by the managerial discourse (that of trainers, team managers and some journalists) to the role of docile, submissive, brute force ('gentle giant', etc), working-class strength in its approved form (self-sacrifice, 'team spirit' and so forth). But the aristocratic reinterpretation which traditionally hinged on the 'heroic' virtues associated with the three-quarter game encounters its limits in the reality of modern rugby, which, under the combined effects of modernized tactics and training, a change in the social recruitment of the players and a wider audience, gives priority to the 'forward game', which is increasingly discussed in metaphors of the meanest industrial labour ('attacking the coal-face') or trench warfare (the infantry man who 'dutifully' runs headlong into enemy fire).

Everything seems to indicate that the concern to cultivate the body appears, in its elementary form—that is, as the cult of health—often associated with an ascetic exaltation of sobriety and controlled diet, in the middle classes (junior executives, the medical services and especially schoolteachers, and particularly among women in these strongly feminized categories). These classes, who are especially anxious about appearance and therefore about their body-for-others, go in very intensively for gymnastics, the ascetic sport par excellence, since it amounts to a sort of training (*askesis*) for training's sake. We know from social psychology that self-acceptance (the very definition of ease) rises with unselfconsciousness, the capacity to escape fascination with a self possessed by the gaze of others (one thinks of the look of questioning anxiety, turning the looks of others on itself, so frequent nowadays among bourgeois women who *must not* grow old); and so it is understandable that middle-class women are disposed to sacrifice much time and effort to achieve the sense of meeting the social norms of self-presentation which is the precondition of forgetting oneself and one's body-for-others.

But physical culture and all the strictly health-oriented practices such as walking and jogging

are also linked in other ways to the dispositions of the culturally richest fractions of the middle classes and the dominant class. Generally speaking, they are only meaningful in relation to a quite theoretical, abstract knowledge of the effects of an exercise which, in gymnastics, is itself reduced to a series of abstract movements, decomposed and organized by reference to a specific, erudite goal (e.g., 'the abdominals'), entirely opposed to the total, practically oriented movements of everyday life; and they presuppose a rational faith in the deferred, often intangible profits they offer (such as protection against ageing or the accidents linked to age, an abstract, negative gain). It is therefore understandable that they should find the conditions for their performance in the ascetic dispositions of upwardly mobile individuals who are prepared to find satisfaction in effort itself and to take the deferred gratifications of their present sacrifice at face value. But also, because they can be performed in solitude, at times and in places beyond the reach of the many, off the beaten track, and so exclude all competition (this is one of the differences between running and jogging), they have a natural place among the ethical and aesthetic choices which define the aristocratic asceticism of the dominated fractions of the dominant class.

Team sports, which only require competences ('physical' or acquired) that are fairly equally distributed among the classes and are therefore equally accessible within the limits of the time and energy available, might be expected to rise in frequency, like individual sports, as one moves through the social hierarchy. However, in accordance with a logic observed in other areas—photography, for example—their very accessibility and all that this entails, such as undesirable contacts, tend to discredit them in the eyes of the dominant class. And indeed, the most typically popular sports, football and rugby, or wrestling and boxing, which, in France, in their early days were the delight of aristocrats, but which, in becoming popular, have ceased to be what they were, combine all the features which repel the dominant class: not only the social composition of their public, which redoubles their commonness, but also the values and virtues demanded, strength, endurance, violence, 'sacrifice', docility and submission to collective discipline—so contrary to bourgeois 'role distance'—and the exaltation of competition.

[The data in this paragraph come from a table that is not included—Eds.] Regular sporting activity varies strongly by social class, ranging from 1.7 per cent for farm workers, 10.1 per cent for manual workers and 10.6 per cent for clerical workers to 24 per cent for junior executives and 32.3 per cent for members of the professions. Similar variations are found in relation to educational level, whereas the difference between the sexes increases, as elsewhere, as one moves down the social hierarchy. The variations are even more marked in the case of an individual sport like tennis, whereas in the case of soccer the hierarchy is inverted: it is most played among manual workers, followed by the craftsmen and shopkeepers. These differences are partly explained by the encouragement of sport in schools, but they also result from the fact that the decline in sporting activity with age, which occurs very abruptly and relatively early in the working classes, where it coincides with school-leaving or marriage (three-quarters of the peasants and manual workers have abandoned sport by age 25), is much slower in the dominant class, whose sport is explicitly invested with health-giving functions (as is shown, for example, by the interest in children's physical development). (This explains why, in the synoptic table—table 2.2.1— the proportion who regularly perform any sporting activity at a given moment rises strongly with position in the social hierarchy, whereas the proportion who no longer do so but used to at one time is fairly constant and is even highest among craftsmen and shopkeepers.)

Attendance at sporting events (especially the most popular of them) is most common among craftsmen and shopkeepers, manual workers, junior executives and clerical workers (who often also read the sports paper *L'Equipe*); the same is true of interest in televised sport (soccer, rugby, cycling, horse-racing). By contrast, the dominant class watches much less sport, either live or on TV, except for tennis, rugby and skiing.

Just as, in an age when sporting activities were reserved for a few, the cult of 'fair play', the code of play of those who have the self-control not to get so carried away by the game that they forget that it is 'only a game', was a logical development of the distinctive function of sport, so too, in an age when participation is not always a sufficient guarantee of the rarity of the participants, those who seek to prove their

excellence must affirm their disinterestedness by remaining aloof from practices devalued by the appearances of sheep-like conformism which they acquired by becoming more common. To distance themselves from common amusements, the privileged once again need only let themselves be guided by the horror of vulgar crowds which always leads them elsewhere, higher, further, to new experiences and virgin spaces, exclusively or firstly theirs, and also by the sense of the legitimacy of practices, which is a function of their distributional value, of course, but also of the degree to which they lend themselves to aestheticization in practice or discourse.

All the features which appeal to the dominant taste are combined in sports such as golf, tennis, sailing, riding (or show-jumping), skiing (especially its most distinctive forms, such as cross-country) or fencing. Practised in exclusive places (private clubs), at the time one chooses, alone or with chosen partners (features which contrast with the collective discipline, obligatory rhythms and imposed efforts of team sports), demanding a relatively low physical exertion that is in any case freely determined, but a relatively high investment—and the earlier it is put in, the more profitable it is—of time and learning (so that they are relatively independent of variations in bodily capital and its decline through age), they only give rise to highly ritualized competitions, governed, beyond the rules, by the unwritten laws of fair play. The sporting exchange takes on the air of a highly controlled social exchange, excluding all physical or verbal violence, all anomic use of the body (shouting, wild gestures etc.) and all forms of direct contact between the opponents (who are often separated by the spatial organization and various opening and closing rites). Or, like sailing, skiing and all the Californian sports [e.g. Surfing, hang-gliding, etc.—Eds.], they substitute man's solitary struggle with nature for the man-to-man battles of popular sports (not to mention competitions, which are incompatible with a lofty idea of the person).

Thus it can be seen that economic barriers—however great they may be in the case of golf, skiing, sailing or even riding and tennis—are not sufficient to explain the class distribution of these activities. There are more hidden entry requirements, such as family tradition and early training, or the obligatory manner (of dress and behaviour), and socializing techniques, which keep these sports closed to the working class

Table 2.2.1. Class variations in sports activities and opinions on sport, 1975

Sports characteristics of respondents	Positive responses (%) by class fraction					Positive responses (%) by sex	
	Farm workers	Manual workers	Craftsmen, small shopkeepers	Clerical, junior execs.	Senior execs., professions	Men	Women
Attend sports events fairly or very often	20	22	*24*	18	16	26	10
Watch or listen to sports events (on TV or radio) often or fairly often	50	*62*	60	60	50	71	47
Would like their child to become sports champion	50	*61*	55	44	33	52	47
Think that physical education ought to have a bigger place in the school curriculum	23	48	41	60	*71*	47	39
Regularly practise one or more sports (other than swimming if only on holiday)	17	18	24	29	*45*	25	15
Practise no sport now but used to	26	34	*41*	34	33	42	21
Have never regularly practised any sport	*57*	48	35	37	22	33	64
Regularly practise:							
tennis	0	1.5	2.5	2.5	*15.5*	2	2.5
riding	1.5	0.5	1	1.5	*3.5*	1	1
skiing	3.5	1.5	6.5	4.5	*8*	3	3
swimming	2.0	2.5	3.5	6.5	*10*	4	3
gymnastics	0.5	3	0.5	5	*7*	1.5	4
athletics	0	1.5	0.5	2.5	*4*	2	0.5
football	2.5	6	4.5	4	4	7	0.5

a. The statistics available only indicate the most general tendencies, which are confirmed in all cases, despite variations due to vague definition of the practice, frequency, occasions etc. (It may also be assumed that the rates are over-estimated, to an unequal extent in the different classes, since all the surveys are based on the respondents' statements and are no substitute for surveys of the actual practitioners or spectators.) For this reason a synoptic table is used to show the proportion of each class or sex of agents who present a given characteristic according to the most recent survey on sporting activities and opinions on sport. Italic figures indicate the strongest tendency in each row.

and to upwardly mobile individuals from the middle or upper classes and which maintain them (along with smart parlour games like chess and especially bridge) among the surest indicators of bourgeois pedigree.

In contrast to belote (and, even more so, manille), bridge is a game played more at higher levels of the social hierarchy, most frequently among members of the professions. Similarly, among students of the grandes écoles, bridge, and especially intensive playing, with tournaments, varies very strongly by social origin. Chess (or the claim to play it) seems less linked than bridge to social traditions and to the pursuit of the accumulation of social capital. This would explain why it increases as one moves up the social hierarchy, but chiefly towards the area of social space defined by strong cultural capital.

The simple fact that, at different times, albeit with a change in meaning and function, the same practices have been able to attract aristocratic or popular devotees, or, at the same time, to assume different meanings and forms for the different groups, should warn us against the temptation of trying to explain the class distribution of sports purely in terms of the 'nature' of the various activities. Even if the logic of distinction is sufficient to account for the basic opposition between popular and bourgeois sports, the fact remains that the relationships between the different groups and the different practices cannot be fully understood unless one takes account of the objective potentialities of the different institutionalized practices, that is, the social uses which these practices encourage, discourage or exclude both by their intrinsic logic and by their positional and distributional value. We can hypothesize as a general law that a sport is more likely to be adopted by a social class if it does not contradict that class's relation to the body at its deepest and most unconscious level, i.e., the body schema, which is the depository of a whole world view and a whole philosophy of the person and the body.

Thus a sport is in a sense predisposed for bourgeois use when the use of the body it requires in no way offends the sense of the high dignity of the person, which rules out, for example, flinging the body into the rough and tumble of 'forward-game' rugby or the demeaning competitions of athletics. Ever concerned to impose the indisputable image of his own authority, his dignity or his distinction, the bourgeois treats his body as an end, makes his body a sign of its own ease. Style is thus foregrounded, and the most typically bourgeois deportment can be recognized by a certain breadth of gesture, posture and gait, which manifests by the amount of physical space that is occupied [...] in social space; and above all by a restrained, measured, self-assured tempo. This slow pace, contrasting with working-class haste or petit-bourgeois eagerness, also characterizes bourgeois speech, where it similarly asserts awareness of the right to take one's time—and other people's.

[...]

And just as a history of the sporting practices of the dominant class would no doubt shed light on the evolution of its ethical dispositions, the bourgeois conception of the human ideal and in particular the form of reconciliation between the bodily virtues and the supposedly more feminine intellectual virtues, so too an analysis of the distribution at a given moment of sporting activities among the fractions of the dominant class would bring to light some of the most hidden principles of the opposition between these fractions, such as the deep-rooted, unconscious conception of the relationship between the sexual division of labour and the division of the work of domination. This is perhaps truer than ever now that the gentle, invisible education by exercise and diet which is appropriate to the new morality of health is tending to take the place of the explicitly ethical pedagogy of the past in shaping bodies and minds. Because the different principles of division which structure the dominant class are never entirely independent—such as the oppositions between the economically richest and the culturally richest, between inheritors and parvenus, old and young (or seniors and juniors)—the practices of the different fractions tend to be distributed, from the dominant fractions to the dominated fractions, in accordance with a series of oppositions which are themselves partially reducible to each other: the opposition between the most expensive and smartest sports (golf, sailing, riding, tennis) or the most expensive and smartest ways of doing them (private clubs) and the cheapest sports (rambling, hiking, jogging, cycling, mountaineering) or the cheapest ways of doing the smart sports (e.g., tennis on municipal courts or in holiday camps); the opposition between the 'manly' sports, which may demand a high energy input (hunting, fishing, the 'contact' sports, clay-pigeon shooting), and the 'introverted' sports, emphasizing self-exploration and self-expression (yoga, dancing, 'physical expression') or the 'cybernetic' sports (flying, sailing), requiring a high cultural input and a relatively low energy input.

Thus, the differences which separate the teachers, the professionals and the employers are, as it were, summed up in the three activities which, though relatively rare—even in the fractions they distinguish, appear as the distinctive feature of each of them, because they are much more frequent there, at equivalent ages, than in the others. The aristocratic asceticism of the teachers finds an exemplary expression in mountaineering, which, even more than rambling, with its reserved paths (one thinks of Heidegger) or cycle-touring, with its Romanesque churches, offers for minimum economic costs the maximum distinction, distance, height, spiritual elevation, through the sense of simultaneously mastering one's own body and a nature inaccessible to the many. The health-oriented hedonism of doctors and modern executives who have the material and cultural means of access to the most prestigious activities, far from vulgar crowds, is expressed in yachting, open-sea swimming, cross-country skiing or underwater fishing; whereas the employers expect the same gains in distinction from golf, with it aristocratic etiquette, its English vocabulary and its great exclusive spaces, together with extrinsic profits, such as the accumulation of social capital.

Since age is obviously a very important variable here, it is not surprising that differences in social age, not only between the biologically younger and older in identical social positions, but also, at identical biological ages, between the dominant and the dominated fractions, or the new and the established fractions, are retranslated into the opposition between the traditional sports and all the new forms of the classic sports (pony trekking, cross-country skiing, and so on), or all the new sports, often imported from America by members of the new bourgeoisie and petite bourgeoisie, in particular by all the people working in fashion—designers, photographers, models, advertising agents, journalists—who invent and market a new form of poor-man's elitism, close to the teachers' version but more ostentatiously unconventional.

The true nature of this counter-culture, which in fact reactivates all the traditions of the typically cultivated cults of the natural, the pure and the authentic, is more clearly revealed in the equipment which one of the new property-rooms of the advanced life-style—the FNAC ('executive retail' shops), Beaubourg, *Le Nouvel Observateur,* holiday clubs etc.—offers the serious trekker: parkas, plus-fours, *authentic* Jacquard sweaters in *real* Shetland wool, *genuine* pullovers in *pure natural* wool, Canadian trappers' jackets, English fishermen's pullovers, U.S. Army raincoats, Swedish lumberjack shirts, fatigue pants, U.S. work shoes, rangers, Indian moccasins in supple leather, Irish work caps, Norwegian woollen caps, bush hats—not forgetting the whistles, altimeters, pedometers, trail guides, Nikons and other essential gadgets without which there can be no natural return to nature. And how could one fail to recognize the dynamics of the dream of social weightlessness

as the basis of all the new sporting activities— foot-trekking, pony-trekking, cycle-trekking, motorbike trekking, boat-trekking, canoeing, archery, windsurfing, cross-country skiing, sailing, hang-gliding, microlights etc.—whose common feature is that they all demand a high investment of cultural capital in the activity itself, in preparing, maintaining and using the equipment, and especially, perhaps, in verbalizing the experiences, and which bear something of the same relation to the luxury sports of the professionals and executives as symbolic possession to material possession of the work of art?

In the opposition between the classical sports and the Californian sports, two contrasting relations to the social world are expressed, as clearly as they are in literary or theatrical tastes. On the one hand, there is respect for forms and for forms of respect, manifested in concern for propriety and ritual and in unashamed flaunting of wealth and luxury, and on the other, symbolic subversion of the rituals of bourgeois order by ostentatious poverty, which makes a virtue of necessity, casualness towards forms and impatience with constraints, which is first marked in clothing or cosmetics since casual clothes and long hair—like the minibus or camping-car, or folk and rock, in other fields— are challenges to the standard attributes of bourgeois rituals, classically styled clothes, luxury cars, boulevard theatre and opera. And this opposition between two relations to the social world is perfectly reflected in the two relations to the natural world, on the one hand the taste for natural, wild nature, on the other, organized, signposted, cultivated nature.

[...]

Thus, the system of the sporting activities and entertainments that offer themselves at a given moment for the potential 'consumers' to choose from is predisposed to express all the differences sociologically pertinent at that moment: oppositions between the sexes, between the classes and between class fractions. The agents only have to follow the leanings of their habitus in order to take over, unwittingly, the intention immanent in the corresponding practices, to find an activity which is entirely 'them' and, with it, kindred spirits. The same is true in all areas of practice: each consumer is confronted by a particular state of the supply side, that is, with objectified possibilities (goods, services, patterns of action etc.) the appropriation of which is one of the stakes in the struggles between the classes, and which, because of their probable association with certain classes or class fractions, are automatically classified and classifying, rank-ordered and rank-ordering. The observed state of the distribution of goods and practices is thus defined in the meeting between the possibilities offered at a given moment by the different fields of production (past and present) and the socially differentiated dispositions which—associated with the capital (of determinate volume and composition) of which, depending on the trajectory, they are more or less completely the product and in which they find their means of realization—define the interest in these possibilities, that is, the propensity to acquire them and (through acquisition) to convert them into distinctive signs.

2.3

Body and soul

The boys who beat the street

Loïc Wacquant

> In this excerpt from *Body and Soul*, an ethnography of a boxing gym in Chicago, Loïc Wacquant argues—against the popular notion that boxers come from the "hungriest" sectors of the underclass—that boxing requires a discipline and stability of life that is more common in the lower levels of the working class. Wacquant suggests that the gym transforms men from the ghetto into boxers in the same way that a gang turns them into streetfighters. He also discusses the way that this working class space is highly masculinized and demonstrably marginalizes women.

It is well known that the overwhelming majority of boxers come from popular milieus, and especially from those sectors of the working class recently fed by immigration. Thus, in Chicago, the predominance first of the Irish, then of central European Jews, Italians, and African Americans, and lately of Latinos closely mirrors the succession of these groups at the bottom of the class ladder.[1] The upsurge of Chicano fighters (and the strong presence of Puerto Ricans) over the past decade, which even a casual survey of the program of the great annual tournament of the Chicago Golden Gloves immediately reveals, is the direct translation of the massive influx of Mexican immigrants into the lowest regions of the social space of the Midwest. Thus, during the finals of the 1989 edition of that joust, clearly dominated by boxers of Mexican and Puerto Rican extraction, DeeDee [DeeDee is the manager of the gym, Eds.] points out to me that "if you want to know who's at d'bottom of society, all you gotta to do is look at who's boxin'. Yep, Mexicans,

these days, they have it rougher than blacks." A similar process of "ethnic succession" can be observed in the other major boxing markets of the country, the New York-New Jersey area, Michigan, Florida, and southern California. By way of local confirmation, when they first sign up at the gym, each member of the Woodlawn Boys Club must fill out an information sheet that includes his marital status, his level of education, his occupation and those of his parents, and mention whether he was raised in a family without a mother or father as well as the economic standing of his family: of the five precoded income categories on the questionnaire, the highest begins at $12,500 a year, which is *half* the average household income for the city of Chicago.

It is necessary to stress, however, that, contrary to a widespread image, backed by the native myth of the "hungry fighter" and periodically validated anew by selective media attention to the more exotic figures of the occupation, such as former heavyweight champion Mike

Tyson,[2] boxers are generally not recruited from among the most disenfranchised fractions of the ghetto subproletariat but rather issue from those *segments of its working class that are struggling at the threshold of stable socioeconomic integration*. This (self-)selection, which tends de facto to exclude the most excluded, operates not via the constraint of a penury of monetary means but through the *mediation of the moral and corporeal dispositions* that are within reach of these two fractions of the African-American population. In point of fact, there is no direct economic barrier to participation to speak of: yearly dues to enroll at the Woodlawn Boys Club amount to ten dollars; the mandatory license from the Illinois Amateur Boxing Federation costs an additional twelve dollars per annum, and all the equipment necessary for training is graciously lent by the club—only the handwraps and the mouthpiece have to be purchased in one of the few sporting-goods stores that carry them, for a total outlay of less than ten dollars.[3] Youngsters issued from the most disadvantaged families are eliminated because they lack the habits and inclinations demanded by pugilistic practice: to become a boxer requires a regularity of life, a sense of discipline, a physical and mental asceticism that cannot take root in social and economic conditions marked by chronic instability and temporal disorganization. Below a certain threshold of objective personal and family constancy, one is highly unlikely to acquire the corporeal and moral dispositions that are indispensable if one is to successfully endure the learning of this sport.[4]

Preliminary analysis of the profile of the 27 professional boxers (all but two of them African-American, ages ranging from 20 to 37) active in the summer and fall of 1991 in Chicago's three main gyms confirms that prizefighters do, on the whole, stand above the lower tier of the male ghetto population. One third of them grew up in a family receiving public aid and 22 per cent were currently jobless, the remainder being either employed or drawing a "weekly salary" from their manager. Thirteen of them (or 48 per cent) had attended a community college (if only for a brief period and with little if any educational and economic gain to show for it); one had earned an associate degree and another a bachelor of science.[5] Only three (or 11 per cent) had failed to graduate from high school or obtain a GED, and about half held a current

checking account. For comparison, of men ages 18 to 45 living in Chicago's South Side and West Side ghettos, 36 per cent have grown up in a household receiving welfare, 44 per cent do not hold a job, half have not completed their high school education, and only 18 per cent have a current checking account.[6] The educational, employment, and economic status of professional boxers is thus quite a bit higher than that of the average ghetto resident. Most distinctive about their background is that none of their fathers received a high school degree and nearly all held typical blue-collar working-class jobs (with the exception of the son of a wealthy white entrepreneur from the suburbs). And sketchy evidence culled from biographies and native accounts suggests that the social recruitment of fighters tends to rise slightly, rather than descend, as one climbs up the pugilistic ladder. "Most of my boys," says veteran trainer and founder of the world-renowned Kronk gym in Detroit, Emanuel Steward, "contrary to what people think, are not that poor. They come from good areas around the country."[7]

By and large, then, professional boxers do not belong to that disorganized and desocialized "dangerous class" the fear of which fed the recent pseudoscientific discourse on the consolidation of a black "underclass" supposedly cut off from "mainstream society."[8] Everything tends to indicate instead that most of them differ from other ghetto youths by virtue of their stronger social integration relative to their low cultural and economic status, and that they come from traditional working-class backgrounds and are attempting to maintain or recapture this precarious status by entering a profession that they perceive as a skilled manual trade, highly regarded by their immediate entourage, which furthermore offers the prospect—however illusory—of big financial earnings. The great majority of adults at the Woodlawn Boys Club are employed (if only part-time) as a security guard, gas station attendant, bricklayer, janitor, stockman, fireman, messenger, sports instructor for the city's Park District, copy shop clerk, bagger at Jewel's food store, counselor at a youth detention center, and steel mill worker. To be sure, these proletarian attachments are in most cases tenuous, for these jobs are as a rule insecure and low paying, and they do not obviate the chronic need for "hustling" in the street economy to make ends meet at the end of the month.[9] And a contingent of professional fighters does come from the lower fractions of the working class, namely, large female-headed families raised on public aid in stigmatized public housing projects for most of their youth and plagued with endemic and quasi-permanent joblessness. But they are not the majority; nor are they the more successful competitors in the pugilistic field in the medium run.

Furthermore, if their mediocre income and early educational disaffection do not differentiate them clearly from the mass of ghetto residents of their age category, prizefighters come more often from intact families and are much more likely to be married fathers living with their children. And they have the privilege of belonging to a formal organization—the boxing gym—whereas the overwhelming majority of the black residents of the city's poorest neighborhoods belong to none, with the partial exception of their few remaining middle-class members.[10] However, conjugal and familial integration wields its influence in a subtly contradictory manner: a necessary condition for practicing the sport regularly, it must be sufficiently strong to enable the acquisition of the dispositions and motivations necessary for prizefighting but at the same time not so strong as to allow work and household life to compete too intensely with investment in boxing.

"No, Ashante, he don't come ev'ry day, you know that, Louie," ["Louie" is Loïc Wacquant's nickname in the gym. Eds.] explains DeeDee. "It's only them young guys in high school who come regularly ev'ry afternoon. Tha's what's wrong with them grownups: they're married, they got a family, kids, they can't be in d'gym ev'ry day. Rents are high, same with food, an' you gotta go out make some money for all that. They gotta have some job on the side, they gotta find themselves a job that give 'em the money they need for their wife and kids. An' when you got a chance to bring some money home, you gotta go, you ain't gonna come to work out. Tha's Ashante's problem right there. Ashante, he got two kids. He gets jive jobs here an' there. He missed the last event, where he was on the card, cause he had an opportunity to work three–four days in a row and make himself a lil' money. It's a warehouse, when they lookin' for overtime, they call him up [to

work as a stockman on a day-to-day basis]. He ain't no regular employee, but they call him often, yep, soon as they need somebody. He can make more workin' that jive job than he can gettin' in d'ring. [A preliminary fight guarantees a purse of about $150 to $300 to each of the contestants.] And he don't have to get beat up. So he gotta take it."
[Field notes, 13 January 1989]

The conversation turns to Mark—a new guy who has been working as an attendant in a photocopy shop since he left high school without finishing three years ago. He arrived really late but DeeDee let him start his workout anyway. He boxes with fervor, leaning over the sandbag, machine-gunning it with short hooks, which earns him praise from DeeDee. "This dude's good. He move well. *He's a natural.* Look at his moves. He's strong. Good hands. Tha's cause he used to fight in d'streets. He's comin' along quick. But he got stiff legs, he don't know how to bend his legs. An' then he got a job, which mean he can only come in late like this. He's gotta train more than that but he don' have the time. It's a real pity, a real pity, yep, 'cause he could make a good boxer. If only I had had'im earlier, when he was younger ..." "How old is he?" "He's twenty-two. He was tellin' me hisself how he wish he coulda gone to d'gym when he was fifteen-sixteen years old. But there was no gym where he lived, so he didn' do nuthin'. He hung 'round an' spent his time fightin' in his neighborhood. He weighs 127 pounds, he's not big but he's stocky, tha's why. He played football on his high-school team. He can lose some more weight, but it's a shame that he don't have d'time to train more ... Unfortunately, with guys like him, tha's often the case."
[Field notes, 22 March 1989]

DeeDee articulates here in passing one of the factors that differentiate "street fighters" who eventually fall into petty or serious delinquency from those who exercise their skill in the ring and participate, however irregularly, in the wage-labor economy: the same dispositions can lead to one or the other career depending on the space of activities on offer, here deeply rooted gangs that rule a housing project, there a gym that "stays busy" in a comparatively quiet neighborhood.

The enrollment of the Woodlawn Boys Club fluctuates markedly and irregularly from one month to the next. Anywhere from 100 to 150 boys and men sign up over the course of a year, but most of them stay for no more than a few weeks as they soon find out that the workout is too demanding for their taste—an attrition rate in excess of 90 per cent is commonplace for a boxing gym.[11] Attendance is at its highest in winter, just before the Golden Gloves (whose preliminaries take place in early February every year), and in the late spring. A nucleus composed of a score of "regulars," including an inner circle of eight older members who recently turned professional after rising through the amateur ranks together, forms the backbone of this shifting membership. The motivations of participants vary according to their status. Most of the regulars compete officially in the amateur and professional divisions; for them the gym is the locus of an intensive preparation for competition. The others come to the club to get or to keep in shape, sometimes with the explicit design of seducing members of the opposite sex (as does Steve, a massive, twenty-nine-year-old black Puerto Rican who is there "to lose weight, for the chicks. I wanna lose this belly, you know, for the women: that's what they want, man, they're the ones who decide"), to stay in touch with boxing friends (this is the case of several retired "pros" who spend more time talking in the back room than working out on the bags), or to learn techniques of self-defense.[12] In addition to the fighters and trainers, many former pugilists in their old age drop by the gym to chat with DeeDee, spending countless hours in the windowless office reminiscing about the olden days, "when fighters were fighters." For the veteran Woodlawn coach, only competitive boxing really counts. And although he attentively monitors the progress of those who come to the gym only for the sake of exercise, he does not hide his preference for the real pugilists. When the occasion arises, DeeDee does not hesitate to try and entice the "fitness boxers" to the pleasures of the virile embrace of the ring. The following conversation offers a good characterization of this attitude.

6 December 1988. As I'm returning to the back room, a tall black man in his forties, very elegantly dressed in a light brown suit and a matching dark brown tie, graying, hairline receding at the temples, with a curly, well-trimmed beard, a little on the plump side, looking very much like an upper-level manager in the public transportation sector, cranes his neck across the door to ask to see "Mister Armour." DeeDee replies that he's he and invites him to seat himself on the little red stool in front of his desk. I pretend to read that day's *Chicago Sun-Times* in order to discreetly listen in on their conversation.

"I'd like some information about boxing lessons for adults. Do you give them yourself?"
"Yep, it depends on what you wanna do: you jus' wanna keep in shape or you wanna fight? How old 're you?"
"I'm forty-one. No, it wouldn't be to fight, not at forty-one years old. ... It's more for stayin' in shape and also for self-defense on the street."
"Okay, but later you might get interested in fightin', you know. It's quite a few guys who're pretty old, forty-nine, fifty, even fifty-three—we got T-Jay at fifty-three—who come in to keep their selves in shape an' then after three-four months, they wanna do d'Golden Gloves. Of course [in a matter-of-fact tone], they're gonna find themselves squarin' off with these young guys who're gonna cut'em to pieces and bust'em up, but then they lovin' it: they don' care, all they want to do (hissed with an undertow of admiration) is *fight*."
"At forty-nine years old? Isn't that a little old to fight?"
"Yeah, but it depen's, we got young kids as well as adults ..."
The mustachioed executive retorts: "No thanks. What I'm interested in is self-defense, that's all, to fight in the street if I get attacked." He will never be seen in the gym again.

Within the Woodlawn Boys Club, indigenous perception establishes a distinction first, among "serious" boxers, between youth who are still in high school and adults who are free of academic obligations but subject to the more constraining obligation of work and family. The youngest is 13 years old, the oldest 57, with the median age hovering around 22.[13] All members are men, as the gym is *a quintessentially masculine space* into which the trespassing of the female sex is tolerated only so long as it remains incidental. "Boxing is for men, and is about men, and *is* men. ... Men who are fighting men to determine their worth, that is, masculinity, exclude women."[14] While there exists no formal obstacle to their participation—some trainers will even verbally deny having any reticence toward female boxing—women are not welcome in the gym because their presence disrupts if not the smooth material operation of the pugilistic universe then its symbolic organization.

Only under special circumstances, such as the imminence of a big-time fight or the morrow of a decisive victory between the ropes, will the girlfriends and wives of boxers have license to attend their man's training session. When they do so, they are expected to remain quietly seated, motionless, on the chairs that line the flanks of the ring; and they typically move carefully along the walls so as to avoid penetrating the actual training "floor," even when the latter is vacant. It goes without saying that they are not to interfere in any manner with the training, except to help extend its effects into the home by taking full charge of household maintenance and the children, cooking the required foods, and providing unfailing emotional and even financial support. If a woman is present at the Woodlawn Boys Club, boxers are not allowed to walk out of the dressing room bare-chested to come weigh themselves on the scale in the back room—as if men's half-naked bodies could be seen "at work" on the public scene of the ring but not "at rest" in the backstage of the workshop. In another professional gym located near Chicago's Little Italy, the head coach resorts to this heavy-handed method to keep women at a distance: he firmly warns his boxers to not bring their "squeeze" to the gym; if they disobey him, he sends them into the ring to spar with a much stronger partner so that they receive a beating in front of their girlfriend and lose face. At the Windy City Gym, on the edge of the West Side ghetto, a separate area, enclosed by a waist-high wall, is officially reserved for "visitors" to sit in; in practice, it serves only to park the female companions of boxers in training. The famed Top Rank Gym in Las Vegas formally bars entrance to women.

Among regular practitioners, the main division separates amateurs from professionals. These two types of boxing form neighboring universes that, though they are tightly interdependent, are very distant from each other at the level of experience. A pugilist may spend years fighting in the amateur ranks yet know next to nothing about the mores and factors that mold the careers of their "pro" colleagues (especially when it comes to their financial aspects, which all conspire to keep in the dark).[15] Moreover, the rules that govern competition in these two divisions are so different that it would scarcely be an exaggeration to consider them

two different sports. To put it simply, in amateur boxing the goal is to accumulate points by hitting one's opponent as many times as possible in rapid flurries, and the referee enjoys ample latitude to stop the contest as soon as one of the protagonists appears to be in physical difficulty; among professionals, who do not wear protective headgear and whose gloves are notably smaller and lighter, the main objective is to "hurt" one's opponent by landing heavy blows, and the battle continues until one of the fighters is no longer able to carry on. As the head trainer from Sheridan Park puts it, "professional boxers don't screw around, they'll knock you *outa your mind*, you know. It's a rough game, you turn professional, it's a rough game: (abruptly catching himself) it's *not a* game. Amateur, you have your fun. Professional (whispering by way of warning) they're tryin' to kill you." The vast majority of amateur boxers never "turn pro," so that those who do constitute a highly (self-) selected group. Here again, the transition from one category to the other has a better chance of being successful if the fighter can rely on a family environment and social background endowed with a minimum of stability.

Within each of these categories, the other distinctions current in the gym refer to style and tactics in the ring: "boxer" (or "scientific boxer") against "brawler" or "slugger," "counterpuncher," "banger," "animal," and so on. Beyond those differentiations, the gym culture is ostensibly egalitarian in the sense that all participants are treated alike: whatever their status and their ambitions, they all enjoy the same rights and must acquit themselves of the same duties, particularly that of "working" hard at their craft and displaying a modicum of bravery between the ropes when the time comes. To be sure, those who benefit from the services of a personal trainer are in a position to command added attention, and the professionals go through a more demanding and more structured workout. But DeeDee is as keen to teach a sixteen-year-old novice who might never set foot in the gym again after a week of trial how to throw a left jab as he is on polishing the defensive moves of a ring veteran preparing for a televised bout. Whatever their level of pugilistic competency, all those who "pay their dues" are wholeheartedly accepted as full-fledged members of the club.

As he progresses, each apprentice boxer finds his comfort zone: some are content to stick to the role of "gym fighter," one who trains and "gloves up" more or less frequently to spar and enter an occasional tournament; others decide to venture further in competition and launch themselves onto the amateur circuit; still others crown their amateur careers by "turning pro." The differentiation between the mere dabbler boxer and the full-fledged pugilist is made visible by the expenses each consents to acquire his gear and by the use of a permanent locker. Only competitive fighters train with their own gloves (of which they generally own several worn pairs accumulated over the years), their personal head guard and jumprope, which they keep preciously under lock and key in their individual lockers. The purchase of boxing boots (which cost 35 to 60 dollars) and, even more so, sparring headgear (60 dollars minimum) suffices to signal a long-term commitment to fighting for both the boxer and his entourage. Training outfits also provide a good clue as to the degree of involvement in the sport, although this is easier to manipulate and therefore less reliable. The firm Ringside, which supplies boxing equipment by mail order, sells a wide range of custom-made gear (trunks, tank tops, jerseys, and robes), and anyone can order a sweatsuit cut to a unique pattern or emblazoned with the likeness of a great champion. Moreover, professional boxers never wear their fighting apparel during workouts. It nonetheless remains that the amount of money spent on training gear is usually a faithful measure of a boxer's material and moral investment in the pugilistic field.

[...]

We have seen how the ecology of the ghetto environment and its street culture predispose the youths of Woodlawn to conceive of boxing as a meaningful activity that offers them a stage on which to enact the core values of its masculine ethos. Viewed from that angle, the ghetto and the gym stand in a relation of contiguity and continuity. However, once *inside* the gym, this relation is ruptured and reversed by the Spartan discipline that boxers must obey, which harnesses street qualities to the pursuit of different, more astringently structured and distant goals. Thus the first thing that trainers always stress is what one is *not* supposed to do in the gym. Eddie, the coach-in-second at Woodlawn, offers the following enumeration of the prohibitions of the gym: "Cursin'. Smokin'. Loud talkin'. Disrespect for the women, disrespect for the coaches, disrespect for each other. No animosity, no braggin'." To which one could add a host of lesser and often implicit rules that converge to *pacify* the conduct of the gym's members.

Without having to display his severity, DeeDee sees to it that an iron discipline reigns in the Woodlawn gym as regards both behavior and training routines: it is forbidden to bring food or beverages into the club, to drink or talk during workouts, to rest sitting on the edge of a table, to alter the sequence of drills (for instance, to start a session by skipping rope instead of loosening up and shadowboxing) or modify a standard technical figure. There is no using of the equipment in an unconventional fashion, firing punches at objects, or sparring if one is not in full gear for it or, worse yet, faking a fight or tussling outside the ring. (Indeed, such "floor incidents" are so rare that they remain inscribed in the collective memory of the gym, unlike the routine violence of the street.) It is mandatory to wear a jockstrap under one's towel when coming out of the shower room and a dry change of clothes when leaving the gym. Finally, the children from the day-care center or the neighborhood who come in to admire the efforts of their elders must not under any pretext get near the bags. One must even watch closely one's language: DeeDee will not allow the expression "to fight" to be used in lieu of "to box" (or "to spar" for sparring sessions); and neither he nor the club regulars use vulgar language or curse words in their conversations in the gym.

Most clauses of these implicit "internal regulations" of the club are visible only in the deportment and demeanor of the regulars who have gradually internalized them, and they are brought to explicit attention only when violated.[16] Those who do not manage to assimilate this unwritten code of conduct are promptly dismissed by DeeDee or strongly advised to transfer to another gym. [...] The gym functions in the manner of a *quasi-total institution* that purports to regiment the whole existence of the fighter—his use of time and space, the management of his body, his state of mind, and his most intimate desires. So much so that pugilists often compare working out in the gym to entering the military.

BUTCH: In the gym, you learn discipline, self-control. You learn tha' you s'pose to go to bed early, git up early, do your road work, take care of yerself, eat the right foods. Uh, yer body is a *machine*, it's s'pose to be well-tuned. You learn to have some control so far as rippin' an' runnin' the streets, social life. It jus' gives you kin' of like an *army, soldier mentality*, an' [chuckling] tha's real good for folks.

CURTIS: The average guy tha' trains in this gym, kid or man, he *matures*, see, 85 perzent, 85 perzent more than if he was out on d'street. 'Cause it discipline him to try to be a young man, to try to have sportsmanship, ring generalship, you know, uh, I don' know … [stumbles] It's more like, I coul' sit up here an' give you a line of thin's, you know, but [you can] break it down to: it works *like bein' in the military*, it show you how to be *a gentleman* and all, and learn *respect*.

The *boxing gym thus defines itself in and through a relation of symbiotic opposition to the ghetto* that surrounds and enfolds it: at the same time that it recruits from among its youth and draws on its masculine culture of physical toughness, individual honor, and bodily performance, it stands opposed to the street as order is to disorder, as the individual and collective regulation of passions is to their private and public anarchy, as the constructive—at least from the standpoint of the social life and sense of self of the fighter—and controlled violence of a strictly policed and clearly circumscribed agonistic exchange is to the violence, seemingly devoid of rhyme or reason, of the unpredictable and unbounded confrontations symbolized by the rampant crime and drug trafficking that infest the neighborhood.

Notes

1. S.K. Weinberg and Henri Arond, "The Occupational Culture of the Boxer," *American Journal of Sociology* 57, 5 (March 1952): 460–469 (for statistics on the period 1900 to 1950); T.J. Jenkins, "Changes in Ethnic and Racial Representation among Professional Boxers: A Study in Ethnic Succession," M.A. thesis, University of Chicago, 1955; Nathan Hare, "A Study of the Black Fighter," *Black Scholar* 3 (1971): 2–9; John Sugden, "The Exploitation of Disadvantage: The Occupational Subculture of the Boxer," in *Sport,*

Leisure, and Social Relations, eds. John Horne, David Jay, and Andrew Tomlinson (London: Routledge & Kegan Paul, 1987), 187–209; and Sammons, *Beyond the Ring*, chapters 2–6. On the trajectory of American Jews in boxing in the first half of the twentieth century, see Stephen A. Reiss, "A Fighting Chance: The Jewish-American Boxing Experience, 1890–1940," *American Jewish History* 74 (1985): 233–254, and, for the broader context, Benjamin G. Rader, *American Sports: From the Age of Folk Games to the Age of Spectators* (Englewood Cliffs, N.J.: Prentice-Hall, 1983).

2. It would be difficult to overstate the influence of the Tyson phenomenon on boxing in the black ghetto in the late 1980s. The veritable media tidal wave that accompanied his rise (out of the ghetto of Brooklyn and out of prison where, as a teenager, he was initiated into boxing), his conjugal and financial troubles with the African-American actress Robin Givens (featured in several prime-time television specials), his economic ties to the white New York real estate billionaire Donald Trump, his acquaintances in the artistic milieu (via the agency of Spike Lee), and his personal and legal conflicts with his former entourage made him a legendary character who not only fed a continual flood of rumors, stories, and discussions but who was furthermore capable, by the sole virtue of his symbolic value, of stimulating vocations en masse (as did Joe Louis and Muhammad Ali, who were, in their days, the inspirations of thousands of apprentice boxers). The phenomenon has since gone through a spectacular reversal following Tyson's stunning defeat at the hands of James "Buster" Douglas in February 1990, then his sentencing to six years of prison for rape, and the series of bizarre incidents that followed. See Peter Niels Heller, *Bad Intentions: The Mike Tyson Story* (New York: Da Capo Press, 1995), and, on the multiple meanings of Tyson's trajectory as a living emblem of rough masculinity, the stimulating article by Tony Jefferson, "Muscle, 'Hard Men' and 'Iron' Mike Tyson: Reflections on Desire, Anxiety and the Embodiment of Masculinity," *Body and Society* 4, 1 (March 1998): 77–98.

3. The boxing gyms of the city's Park District are even less costly since they levy no dues; one other professional gym in Chicago requires monthly payments of $5 for amateurs and $20 for professionals but allows many waivers. In other cities, some gyms post notably higher dues: for example, $55 per quarter at the Somerville Boxing Club in a working-class suburb of Boston, where I boxed from 1991 to 1993, and $50 a month at a gym in the Tenderloin, a disreputable area in downtown San Francisco.

4. Or else lack of internal government must be compensated by truly exceptional aggressivity, physical prowess, and ring "toughness." Such fighters, however, tend to "burn out" prematurely and rarely fulfill their potential, pugilistic as well as economic. The ring prodigy and three-time world champion Wilfredo Benitez, the son of a Puerto Rican sugar cane cutter, is an exemplary case in point: though he turned "pro" at age fourteen and was world champion by his seventeenth birthday, his irregularity in training and notorious lack of eating discipline quickly cut his career short.

5. Though they are purported to offer a bridge to four-year campuses, community colleges (or junior colleges) function as remedial courses for high school education and deliver degrees that are largely devoid of value on the labor market. Stephen Brint and Jerry Karabel, "Les 'community colleges' américains et la politique de l'inégalité," *Actes de la recherche en sciences sociales* 86–87 (September 1987): 69–84.

6. L.J.D. Wacquant and W.J. Wilson, "The Cost of Racial and Class Exclusion in the Inner City," *Annals of the American Academy of Political and Social Sciences* 501 (Jan. 1989): 17, 19, 22.

7. Cited in David Halpern, "Distance and Embrace," in *Reading the Fights*, eds. Joyce Carol Oates and David Halpern (New York: Prentice-Hall, 1988), 279.

8. For a methodical critique of this bogus concept and its social usages, see Loïc Wacquant, *"L' 'underclass' urbaine dans l'imaginaire social et scientifique américain,"* in *L'Exclusion: l'état des savoirs* (Paris: La Découverte, 1996), 248–262.

9. Betty Lou Valentine, *Hustling and Other Hard Work: Life Styles in the Ghetto* (New York: Free Press, 1978).

10. Wacquant and Wilson, "The Cost of Racial and Class Exclusion in the Inner City," 24.

11. The rate for the Woodlawn Boys Club is comparable to that of the East Harlem gym described by Plummer, *Buttercups and Strong Boys* (New York: Viking, 1989), 57, in which the annual turnover hovers around 80 per cent.

12. I explain to the director of the day-care center adjoining the gym, who is inquiring as to why I got into this "sport for brutes," that I come here mostly to get back in shape. She immediately adds, as if it went without saying: "Oh, yes, and then it can't hurt to know a little bit of self-defense in *this* neighborhood. You also got to keep that in mind" (field notes, 8 October 1988). While I am jumping rope to wind down after a sparring session, Oscar, Little Keith's manager, asks me if I want to turn pro (I reassure him, I'm only a dilettante boxer but I would like to go as far as to have a few amateur fights): "Cuz you box pretty good, you doin' a good job, ya know … And then it give ya confidence in the street 'cuz you can defend yo'self better" (field notes, 17 June 1989).

13. One can obtain an amateur license at age thirteen, and some tournaments allow the participation of children as young as ten, who are called "subnovices." According to Henri Allouch, "Participation in Boxing among Children and Young Adults," *Pediatrics* 72 (1984): 311–312, nearly 30,000 children under fifteen are licensed and tally more than twenty fights a year in North America.

14. Joyce Carol Oates, *On Boxing* (Garden City, N.Y.: Doubleday, 1987), 72. Boxing pundits and commentators sometimes complain about the increasingly constraining regulation of pugilistic violence, which they depict and denounce as a "feminization" of prizefighting apt to pervert it: the reduction from fifteen to twelve rounds for championship bouts, the increased role of physicians, the mandatory 45-day waiting period after suffering a defeat by knockout, and especially the growing latitude given to the referee to stop a fight as soon as one of the protagonists appears unable to defend himself or is at risk of serious injury.

15. Professional boxers never reveal the amount of their purses, even to their regular sparring partners; all monetary negotiations and transactions among fighters, trainers, managers, and promoters take place *sub rosa*. See Loïc Wacquant, "A Flesh Peddler at Work; Power, Pain and Profit in the Prizefighting Economy," *Theory and Society* 27, 1 (February 1998): 1–42.

16. Most of the other gyms I have observed in Chicago and visited in other cities broadcast their rules in the form of a standardized list posted on the entrance door or an a wall, or yet hung from the ceiling for all to see. It appears that the more unstable and socially disparate the membership of a boxing club, the more explicit and conspicuous its regulations.

2.4

Class, ethnicity, and color in the making of Brazilian football

José Sergio Leite Lopes

In this selection, Leite Lopes introduces the myriad roles and functions that sport may perform in both the reinforcement and the contestation of a society's system of social stratification. In particular, this account of the development of football in Brazil details the many ways that the changing nature of competitive sport, especially its professionalization and internationalization, is used by dominant and subordinate groups to vie for resources in given contexts. It is interesting to see how increased competition in sports often pushes previously discriminatory elements toward greater tolerance toward lower classes, different ethnicities, and people of color.

Introduction

The preparations for the 1998 World Cup in France made it possible to envision the strength of Brazilian football as a symbol for the diffusion of world football. The fact that Brazil had won the 1994 World Cup was important, of course. But the value of this victory, obtained for the first time in a final match decided by penalties, is connected to the remarkable victories of 1958, 1962, and 1970 that created Brazil's fame in world football. Because of this glorious past, built between the late 1950s and the early 1970s, excellence in football—the most popular sport in the world—became internationally regarded as a distinctive Brazilian national quality. The 1994 world title indicated that Brazil's excellence was not something of the past, before the great recent transformations connected to the professionalization of this sport, and showed that Brazilian football still had links with that past for which it had become so famous.

In fact, football from the 1980s on distinguishes itself from the past because of the intensification of phenomena that were already present. Many of these factors are related to the live transmission by television of matches and championships from all over the world. Competitions have come, in consequence, to involve larger values, leading to greater commercial interests in the sport. The number of different professionals connected to football (medical staff, trainers, physiotherapists, show business and marketing experts, sports media, security staff, service workers, and so forth) has also grown tremendously. Paradoxically there is also a growth of voluntary activities, such as temporary services for specific championships (as during the World Cup) or permanent organizations like the *torcidas organizadas*. These new fans' associations appeal to a supporter very different from the kind of spectators that went to the stadiums before the 1970s. On the other hand, the international circulation of players has greatly accelerated, leading to a

José Sergio Leite Lopes, "Class, Ethnicity, and Color in the Making of Brazilian Football" from *Daedalus* 129.2 (Spring 2000): 239–270. Reprinted with the permission of MIT Press Journals.

concentration in Europe: among the principal players on the Brazilian team during the 1998 Cup, five were playing for Italian teams, two for Spanish teams, two for Japanese teams, and two for Brazilian teams. The situation was similar in the other important teams at the tournament. There has been a transition from national to multinational professionalism. In the latest World Cups even the transportation of great numbers of Brazilian fans was supported by large state-owned or multinational companies, which paid the fares for their employees or clients as a reward for productivity or sales.

Brazilian football, with its outstanding presence in the history of world football, becomes thus a strategic product to be displayed in the World Cup's marketing strategies. The companies that promoted the Cup or were related to it sought endorsements from Ronaldo, a Brazilian player of poor background from the suburbs of Rio who became an international star after a very early start in the Brazilian national team. By doing so, they focused on Brazilian football as a model for helping poor youngsters—who might thereby not only rid themselves of the dangers of poverty, but also become idols worldwide. Marketing thus aestheticizes poverty, while the large multinational companies express their concern about it—a very paradoxical concern, since it comes from the same enormously wealthy, powerful, and profitable companies that blindly create unemployment and exclude large sectors of the population by means of their internal microeconomic policies and their public demands for liberal macroeconomic policies. [...]

This essay will focus on the formative period of Brazilian football, when no one would have imagined such success. Such a starting point helps to counteract the now-prevailing notion that takes for granted expertise and success in this sport as an inherent national gift. On the other hand, it will show that football is a domain where social conflicts and national dilemmas are clearly brought out.

One way of understanding the peculiarities of the rapid dissemination of football in Brazil is to analyze how early and to what degree blacks and *mestizos* entered the upper echelons of the sport. Football's spread among the Brazilian population was related to the sport's appropriation by the various classes and social groups, but this was not independent of skin color or ethnicity.

In this essay I seek to analyze the social contradictions between the consequences of football's predominantly aristocratic beginnings in Brazil and its appropriation by social groups from below, leading progressively to the transition from amateur to professional football. This transition fostered a huge growth of entry and success by players from the working classes in general, and blacks and mulattos in particular. Yet in the sport's universe there persisted racist beliefs and practices, taking new forms and gaining strength after the defeats Brazil suffered in the 1950 and 1954 World Cups. Only after the 1958 victory in the World Cup (held in Sweden) could the local (Brazilian) public sphere evaluate the success in terms of the historical making of a specific style, reversing an internalized sense of inferiority into a positive self-assessment of Brazilian football.

The football of the Brazilian elites

Following the early growth of football's popularity in Great Britain [...] the sport spread internationally through the previously established network of contacts between local elites and English elites and their institutions. This was no less true in Brazil: the first football games on record in Brazil were played by English sailors [...] and sporadically among employees of English firms. Yet the games played as the outcome of the *missionary* effort by the local British colony, and later by the young elite Brazilians—former students in England, Switzerland, or Germany—upon their return to Brazil were those which depended on the founding of permanent teams in preexisting clubs or a *de novo* founding of football clubs. Although some football initiatives sprang up inside companies, business leaders and company managers soon met in clubs in order to socialize more freely. Thus, many of the major football clubs ended up reproducing (both on the field and in the stands) the social selection practiced by elite families from Rio and São Paulo. The clubs turned into places for urban socializing; by providing participation in or attendance at physical and sporting activities, they prolonged the receptions and soirées bringing together the dominant families from early twentieth-century *sobrados* (town mansions) in those two cities. In addition to cricket (played by the British), until

73

the 1920s the clubs were organized around men's rowing. The rowing contests in Rio attracted the city's population to the beaches and shoreline along Guanabara Bay and were the main source of attraction for the city's budding sports press. Those who practiced rowing felt that football was not a very masculine sport, with what they viewed as chasing and "prancing" around the field. Still, the Fluminense Football Club gradually became the game's benchmark for the "Carioca elites," attracting an elegant public to its stadium—men in suits, ties, and hats, and smartly dressed young girls and women, showing by their clothing that they belonged to Rio's finest families. A little hatband with the team's colors, imported from England and used by the men, was a discrete detail indicating the club's coded, select membership. The cry from the stands when the team entered the field—"*Hip, hip, hurrah!*"—and the team's solemn sideline bow to the fans (especially to the young ladies), were also signs of refinement, imported details from the world metropolises. Such gestures showed the social status of both players and fans, also manifested by the players' frequent visits to the stands during halftime and after the game, when they met up with their own families and those of their peers.

Players also frequented dances at the club; playing football regularly was one of several characteristics of an elite lifestyle. Several football clubs were made up of university students, and access to law, medicine, and to a lesser extent engineering was a form of social reconversion (via schooling) for the declining Brazilian rural aristocracy, or an expanded reproduction of the new scholarized urban elites. Thus, while the original Fluminense team was made up of young businessmen, top employees of factories and major stores, and *rentiers*—the sons of moneyed parents, educated in Europe—from 1910 on it was forced to primarily recruit university students, who were younger, had more time for the game, and were competing with Fluminense on successful rival teams.

[...]

The first football league in Brazil was organized in São Paulo in 1901, and the first championship of football clubs in the country was held there, while in Rio the local league was organized only in 1905 and the first championship only in 1906. Thus, the original football players from Rio de Janeiro's and São Paulo's

elite society in the early twentieth century were *university football majors* as compared to the *primary* players of the working classes, according to a school metaphor used by Mário Filho. Although the equipment needed to play the game was not comparatively sophisticated or exclusive, at that time the leather ball had to be imported from England, as did the football shoes. The grass-covered field was also an attribute of players with higher financial means. Yet the popular substitutes for imitating this leisurely practice were not at all expensive: stocking balls served the purpose for the sandlot games hotly disputed by barefoot players, with goalposts easily improvised from any variety of possible materials. Children and teenagers from the working classes could watch the football matches between the big elite teams (in the neighborhoods frequented by the elites) by either working as ballboys or watching from the cheapest, ground-level places in the stadium, an area used as a ploy to recruit cheering sections for decisive matches.

In São Paulo, the matches between teams of the first division were held at the Velódromo, a former stadium for bicycle races turned into a football stadium in the early years of the century. In this city the popularization of football was facilitated by the many empty, flat areas on the floodplains, where matches and championships between teams of the poor sectors of town could be held. Besides, as more and more factories and companies began promoting football as a form of leisure and integration between their employees and workers, in both São Paulo and Rio there were greater opportunities for the poor population to see matches in the suburbs and popular neighborhoods.

Factory football and company towns

The year 1904 witnessed the founding, in the Rio suburb of Bangú, of the Bangú Athletic Club by English managers, overseers, mechanics, and employees at the Companhia Progresso Industrial textile factory. There, contrary to other Rio clubs in which the English founders were capable of attracting other Englishmen to make up the full complement of a football team, Bangú's geographical isolation from the city proper meant that the English had to include

Brazilian supervisors, overlookers, administrative employees, even shop-floor workers—as well as those of other nationalities. Thus, Bangú's first several lineups included one or two Brazilians among five Englishmen, three Italians, and two Portuguese. The number of Brazilians and factory workers increased over time: the workers stayed at the factory longer, and learning football was a continuous process for them, while managers and overseers tended to return to their native countries or change jobs, and their replacements were not always good at the sport. As the number of workers increased on the team, so did the number of black and mulatto players. In the Bangú stadium there was no distinction between the *gerais* (literally "general [area]," the ground-level area with no seating) and the stands or reserved seating; the community of workers, their families, and other people from the neighborhood made up the team's working-class supporters, the numbers of which grew tremendously when Bangú was incorporated into the Rio de Janeiro football league, the first division in the Carioca championship. The Bangú team was soon more famous than the factory itself and ended up serving as a positive marketing image for the latter.

Bangú inaugurated the figure of the worker-player, a worker less known for his work inside the factory than for his performance as a football player on the factory team. This justified certain relative privileges in the company: time off from the factory for training and games; assignment to light work, for example in the "cloth room" (for quality inspection and recording of each worker's production of fabric). While football was originally introduced by the English for their own delight and socializing, the company soon realized that the sport fit in well with activities and the use of time in a company town. So, too, Bangú was aware of the then-current practice of other European companies of promoting football as a stimulus to workers, increasing the workers' sense of belonging to the company community.

The board of directors at the Bangú factory were quick to discover what would soon lead to one of the watersheds for the spread of football among the various social classes in Brazil, as it already had in other countries in Europe and South America; football could be adopted as a pedagogical and disciplinary technique for "total institutions," a technique invented by

elite English boarding schools but applicable to shaping working-class youth in various types of institutions. Thus, not only schools (catering to the elite in a country with little schooling among the general population), but above all companies, helped make possible direct access to football among the working classes.

Several factories (especially in the textile industry) started promoting football among their workers and administrative employees, founding teams in great numbers all over Brazil in the first three decades of the twentieth century and soon taking the Bangú factory and team as their point of reference. Prime examples of such factories were in the so-called company towns where football fit in well with other recreational activities aimed at maintaining discipline. Thus, in 1908 the English managers of the América Fabril company founded the Sport Club Pau Grande in the rural village of Pau Grande, some 90 kilometers from Rio de Janeiro. Forty years later this factory boasted an outstanding team in the championships between textile factory teams in the Petrópolis region, routinely beating visiting company teams from Rio. The Pau Grande team even outstripped factory teams sponsored by the same company in Rio. And one of the players on this team, Garrincha, was already playing the same basic style that fans would come to love ten years later, when he would be a member of Brazil's 1958 world championship team.

In addition to Bangú, another textile factory club participating in Rio's first-division championship was Andarai, located in the northern-zone neighborhood by the same name. The dominant force in an isolated company town, the Bangú factory formed its team from the little leagues and juniors teams like Esperança, where famous players like Domingos da Guia started their careers. Outstanding young players from these teams could hope to be hired as worker-players in the factory and guaranteed a stable job, even beyond the age at which they could play competitive football. In addition, both Bangú and Andarai allowed players from the working classes—poor whites, mulattos, and blacks—to measure their strength and skills against those of players from the major elite clubs that had introduced football to Brazil, an opportunity denied to the welter of small teams springing up in the main working-class suburban towns, both inside companies and at the initiative of small groups of neighbors. Yet while Bangú was feared when it played on its own field, backed by the home fans, it was no real competitor for the city title: greater available time and resources, together with deeper knowledge of the tactics and training spreading directly from Europe or via Argentina and Uruguay, gave the elite amateurs from the big clubs the upper hand when compared to the limited resources available to the worker-players who (albeit on light work schedules) had to subordinate football to factory production needs.

Social tension and crisis in amateur football

The elite clubs' hegemony, as expressed by successive victories in the Rio de Janeiro city championship, was only broken in 1923 when Vasco da Gama, a team built on support from the burgeoning colony of Portuguese immigrants, vied for the title for the first time and won. The Vasco team, champions in the second division in 1922, had a secret: it had recruited the best players from the working-class suburbs, whether they were white, black, or mulatto, and kept them in a regimen of semiconfinement, financed by the club, where the athletes focused exclusively on football. Vasco's success was a sign of football's growing popularity. The sport was now played in all the working-class neighborhoods and enjoyed enormous popularity, allowing for two seemingly contradictory processes—the intensification of its bourgeois and its proletarian bases of support—simultaneously, much as they had occurred in England. In fact, unlike the aristocratic clubs dominating the first-division championship, the Clube de Regatas Vasco da Gama had no athletes from the same social extraction as its members. In the aristocratic clubs, athletes and member fans socialized during halftime and after the matches—just as they did in daily life, whether at dance parties in the club itself, as family members, family friends, acquaintances, or suitors. The Portuguese club, on the other hand, apparently had no athletes from the same social origins as its members. The Portuguese way of life, immersed in work and tending family businesses, was quite different from that of the sons of the Brazilian aristocracy. Their upbringing, modeled after elite European

schooling, encompassed a long formal education and playing sports, both of which constituted not only a transition period separating one from work and intensive business management but also an educational process preparing one to exercise top-level economic and political domination.

The bourgeois and petit bourgeois sons of the Portuguese colony, with their hands-on approach to family business, played an improvised, haphazard kind of football in neighborhoods that included working-class youth. The only possibility for Vasco da Gama to compete was to "proletarianize" its team by the unrestricted recruitment of the best players from the working-class suburbs, while simultaneously making it bourgeois so as to secure the finances needed to support these players (who had no resources of their own for continuous leisure activity) in a semi-confinement situation where they were fed, housed, and encouraged to train at least as much as the athletes from the major clubs. Vasco's 1923 championship team consisted of white, black, and mulatto players who had already been part of a de facto scratch team in the suburbs, with a taxi driver at the goal and several former factory workers from Bangú, Andaraí, and other minor league teams.

Vasco's victory in the 1923 Carioca championship fueled the defensive stance taken by Brazilian amateur football toward the rise of subordinate social groups in quality football; Dunning has pointed out a similar process that had already occurred in England.[1] From moral qualities associated with the essence of modern football, which in turn was seen as an important part of the way of life characterizing and distinguishing social groups classifying themselves as select, the precepts and practices of amateur play now turned to excluding the "outsiders."

The big clubs were quick in reacting; they set up a new football league that Vasco was not invited to join, allegedly because it had no stadium of its own. The Portuguese colony, in turn, organized itself and funded construction of the city's largest stadium (until the construction of Maracanã in 1950), with a capacity of fifty thousand, inaugurated in 1927. Fluminense's stadium could hold no more than twenty thousand spectators. Yet the unusually large blueprint of Vasco's stadium was not based only on a logic of honor in response to the discrimination the club had suffered. The team played top-quality football; its supporters grew in the wake of mobilization by the Portuguese colony; opposition from other teams' supporters increased; and all the while the fans flocked to see the matches—so much so that the big clubs relented (for economic reasons), allowing Vasco to join the first division even before its stadium was completed.

Yet other measures were taken. The Rio local state team competing for the national championship had not a single player from Vasco's championship team. The new league set up a commission to investigate players' means of survival, to determine the extent to which they were actually playing as amateurs. The very substance and procedures of this investigation expressed a number of class distinctions and prejudices. In fact, in addition to keeping the team in semiconfinement—paying for food, lodging, uniforms, and training equipment—Vasco had a policy of paying them the so-called *bicho*, a bonus based on one's performance in the match, in addition to a "travel allowance" for train fare. Such coverage of athletes' expenses—which assumed, or rather acknowledged, that they had no resources of their own—appeared to be at odds with the prevailing notion of players' social status, at least as expected by the managers and athletes who had introduced football into Brazil. The latter, by contrast, purchased their own sports gear, financed their own free time, and covered their own expenses when the team went to play outside of Rio or outside of Brazil: when the teams traveled to São Paulo, Montevideo, or Buenos Aires, the players never failed to take their dinner jackets along for the hotels and receptions.

Aware of the new league's investigation into the means of support for athletes, Vasco's bourgeois members offered to give the players make-believe jobs, generally in their stores, where they would have many more perks than the worker-players in the factories. Meanwhile, the proletarian worker-players were welcomed by proponents of amateur play—as if the moral shaping provided by the factory, and the fact that a worker-player simultaneously worked and kept up his athletic performance (and thus lacked the time to compete on equal footing with other athletes in the big clubs), were reason enough to regard him as a worthy competitor. So, too, accepting the worker-players

offered the additional merit of not totally excluding the poor from amateur sport at a time when scrutiny was falling on the amateur legitimacy of poor recruits to the game. Even so, some occupations and professions—stevedores, soldiers, and those who habitually received tips (waiters, taxi drivers, and barbers)—were arbitrarily prohibited in written league rules from playing in the first division.

Another step by the new league was to require that players know how to read and write properly. When they entered the field, players had to be able to sign their names on the scorepad and to quickly fill in an "enrollment form" with several items. This implicit test of schooling is characteristic of the indirect, euphemistic exercise of class and color prejudice in Brazil. Entering a game under the eagle eye of league representatives, athletes had to fill in a questionnaire with the following required information: full name, both parents' names, nationality, place of birth, date of birth, and place of study and work. Vasco da Gama and São Cristóvão, another club recruiting players from the suburbs, had their athletes attend specially organized crash literacy courses and remedial primary-school tutoring. Their players from working-class origins, who were almost invariably illiterate or functionally illiterate, managed to scrape by this apparently neutral writing trap, albeit with great difficulty.

Just like this use of writing skills indirectly to block access to first-division football by working-class players, the most famous cases of racial prejudice were also indirect and jocose. Such was the case for the myth behind the origin of the term *"pó de arroz"* ("rice powder") for members and fans of the Fluminense Futebol Clube, the oldest football club in Brazil and the one with the most aristocratic origins. The mulatto player Carlos Alberto, son of a photographer (who took university graduation portraits), was playing on the second team for the América Futebol Clube, where he was friendly with a number of university student players. In 1916 he was called up to the Fluminense starting team. Before entering the field, when the players posed along the sidelines to greet the select public in the stands, Alberto was reported to have been seen in the dressing-room spreading rice powder on his face to lighten his complexion. In a game against América, the group of supporters from his former home team standing in the cheapest area of the stadium refused to forgive their former star athlete and shouted out, "*pó de arroz!*" Alberto paid no heed to their heckling but the stigma of pretentiousness and whitening endured—quite appropriately not only for the team's players but for the aristocratic club as a whole. This episode, supposed to have occurred in the second decade of the twentieth century, was further publicized and immortalized in the chronicles by sports writer Mário Filho in the 1930s to stimulate rivalry between supporters and attract bigger crowds to budding professional football. Thus when Flamengo was becoming the city's most popular club in the late 1930s, the Fluminense fans counterattacked by heckling the Flamengo supporters with *pó de carvão*" ("coal dust"). Originally intended as insults, both cheering sections ended up assimilating the nicknames as self-designating; they have survived to this day.

This episode, with its mythical overtones, denotes not only how mulattos and blacks internalized their inferior social situation (as Carlos Alberto was reported to have done), but also the jocose effect and conciliatory outcome through which much of the ambiguity in racial stereotypes and prejudices in Brazil is expressed. Of the examples cited by Mário Filho, the only case of overt racial prejudice committed against a player involved an athlete nicknamed Manteiga. In 1923 the managers of the América team, motivated by the same spirit of competition that had led Vasco to base its team on players recruited from the working classes, set out on a more timid recruiting search in the docks area of Rio. They recruited a successful local player, a sailor playing right wing and nicknamed Manteiga (or "Butter," because of his slick passes). They proposed that he leave the Brazilian navy and take a job at a business owned by one of the club's board members. But Manteiga was black: as he prepared to enter the field for his first game, other players from the team walked out of the dressing room in a blatant display of prejudice. Next, nine players from the club's first and second teams resigned in protest against the inclusion of this new player. These dissidents were later absorbed by Fluminense. The board members of the club kept Manteiga on despite the crisis, but he felt extremely uncomfortable; his presence made for a greater disturbance in the club's facilities than it had on the playing field itself. During a

tour by América to Salvador (Manteiga's hometown, and where there is a higher concentration of blacks than in Rio), he stayed behind, abandoning the team.

One can thus easily understand the big clubs' reaction to Vasco da Gama's successful entry in 1923, with a team made up of poor whites, *mestizos*, and blacks. Having excluded Vasco from the club league in 1924 and 1925, Fluminense and Flamengo won these two titles respectively, and proper order appeared to have returned to the league: even though "little" São Cristóvão won in 1926 and Vasco (back in the league) took the title in 1929, the 1927, 1928, 1930, 1931, and 1932 titles went to the traditional clubs. Yet the crisis in amateur football, which was already appearing as "yellow amateurism," fueled the faction of players, sportswriters, and even board members of clubs in favor of adopting professional sport.

The events related to the entry of Vasco da Gama into Rio's championship of 1923 and its victory using amateuristic methods with a team formed by players from the working class from the suburbs of the north part of town—some of them black or mulatto—are exemplary of what also happened in other Brazilian states. [...] In São Paulo the reactions from the elite clubs were not caused specifically by the admittance of blacks and mulattos, predominant in the working classes in Rio, as players, but by the additional admittance of immigrant workers, such as Italians and Spaniards. In 1910 one more club, called Corinthians Paulista, appeared in São Paulo, its name an homage to the Corinthians, an amateur team of university students from Oxford and Cambridge that had been in Rio that year at the invitation of the Fluminense and had also played in São Paulo. This appropriation of one of English football's most aristocratic names by a working-class club playing in the floodplain areas of São Paulo is interesting and revealing, and it is ironic that this team was to become the most popular one in São Paulo. Palestra Itália and Corinthians Paulista, both of which had more popular origins than the elite clubs that had created the football league, were admitted to the first division of the city's league after some of the elite clubs had left. The departure of the founding clubs reaffirms their exclusive amateuristic and elitist character, as they preferred to quit football or play out of competition than face the pressure from below exerted by athletes from the lower classes who wanted to participate. Interestingly, once they formally expressed a desire to affiliate with the local league after the retreat of elite clubs, both teams had to wait four years before the final acceptance of a committee judging the "moral values" of newly associating clubs.

The entry of these two new clubs into São Paulo's first division was somewhat less dramatic than the entry of Vasco da Gama into the premier league in Rio. This is perhaps related to the better position in São Paulo of Italian, Spanish, and Syrian immigrants as compared to the slave descendants. Even though many of these immigrants were workers, their communities also had representation in the higher and middle classes, and in general were more broadly accepted by local elites. Palestra Itália, for example, had connections with the higher strata of Italian immigrants. Many Italian immigrant workers, however, were connected to Corinthians, a club with a more universalistic affiliation, which attracted immigrants who had no prospect of associating themselves with an exclusive team like the Palestra Itália. Corinthians became the team of the Spanish, the Syrians, the blacks, and even of the poorer Italians. Palestra Itália, even though it was at first despised by the elite clubs and press, represented the upward mobility of the Italian community—in such a way that in the 1940s it resisted the admittance of black players, allying itself with the traditional elite clubs. It was not until World War II, when Brazil declared war against Italy, that Palestra Itália changed its name to Palmeiras and finally admitted a black player, forced by the circumstances to move toward Brazilian nationalization.

Black players and the emergence of Brazilian professional football

The internal crisis in Brazilian amateur football finally became unbearable due to the outside pressure exerted by the international game. With the beginning of the World Cup, Brazilian players who felt "enslaved" by the traps of amateurism found a way out in the 1930s, as European clubs, particularly the Italians, raised the demand for South American players. Soon after the first World Cup, won by Uruguay, and in light of preparations for the second World

Cup, to be held in Italy, Mussolini began to promote Italian football by promising to build a stadium for the winning team in the Italian Cup. Competition for talent among teams ended up sparking a race for the best players from South America—which in the context of Mussolini's Italy meant the best players of Italian ancestry in Argentina, Uruguay, and Brazil (especially São Paulo). Argentina's football was most threatened by this recruiting: the solution for the Buenos Aires teams was to adopt professionalism, and the Montevideo teams followed soon after. Under these circumstances, professional football would be coming soon to São Paulo and Rio. In both of these cities there were cases of white players who were not *oriundi* (i.e., of Italian ancestry) who adopted Italian names, altering their identification papers with the acquiescence of clubs from Italy. Facing the loss of such players to the European professional teams, factions favoring implementation of professional football gained momentum in Brazil.

White players were exported to Europe, while black players, blocked from playing for the most significant importing country, Mussolini's Italy, and with little stimulus to remain for long in countries where blacks were the exception, became virtually nonexportable. Such was the case of the black player Fausto, a center-half, who was highlighted by international sports coverage during the 1930 World Cup tournament. Rising in the ranks from the Bangú company-town club, recruited into what became Vasco's 1929 championship team, highly rated for his performance in the 1930 World Cup, Fausto, who wanted to live full-time on playing football, had difficulty putting up with the false amateurism in the big Brazilian clubs. During a tour with Vasco to Spain in 1931, Barcelona made Fausto an offer and he stayed behind there. Yet his experience with professional football abroad led him to break off his contract, an episode that he would repeat in Switzerland. When professional football finally came to Brazil, he returned to Vasco in 1933.

The same occurred with Vasco's black goalkeeper, Jaguaré. Recruited by Barcelona along with Fausto, he came back in 1932, even before professional football began in Brazil, offering to play again for his old team. So it was also with Domingos da Guia and Leônidas da Silva, the two of whom had led a victory by the Brazilian national team in 1932, beating the world-champion Uruguayans on their home field in Montevideo. Both players stayed abroad for only a short while. Domingos was hired by Nacional of Montevideo and Leônidas by Peñarol: the former was successful in Uruguay (and later in Argentina) while the latter was not. Both rejoined Brazilian football in 1934, after professional play had begun.

Meanwhile, many white Brazilian players who had gone to Italy ended up integrating into that society, encouraged by the Italian colony in São Paulo, who considered a triumphant return to Italy an ideal to be achieved by Brazilian-born descendents of Italians. Blacks, in turn, appeared to be "condemned" to "local" success, to be great local players—indeed, to be Brazil's greatest players. Significantly, in this sense they became identified as the great initiators of Brazilian national football. Football could not have the same meaning for white and black Brazilians. Between them there was a difference separating "good professionals," prone to exercising their talents on the international football scale, and talented players who—through their athletic success—were seeking ethnic emancipation and were condemned to succeed exclusively within their own homeland. Professional football became a means of emancipation for black athletes—a necessary condition, as it turns out, for establishing football as a "national" sport. Such an undertaking was not just a business strategy (involving money); it established an identity between players and the public, united in their adherence to a common project of social emancipation through sport.

This identity between players and the public was tested soon after the move to professionalism. When Flamengo hired players like Fausto, Domingos da Guia, and Leônidas da Silva, the team—which until then had followed an amateur policy—became the most popular one in the city. By heavily recruiting working-class players (as Vasco da Gama had begun doing twelve years earlier), Flamengo had the advantage of being identified as the prime example of a universally "mixed-race" Brazilian club, in contrast to the nucleus of Portuguese-colony board members and supporters from the equally popular rival club. Flamengo's football club headquarters and field were also moved, in 1935,

from a traditionally elite neighborhood to one characterized at that time by its proximity to factories, company compounds, and a shantytown (all of which have now disappeared, giving way to a middle-class neighborhood). Domingos's and Leônidas's tremendous popularity, which had increased with their participation in the national team competing for the World Cup in 1938, was transferred to and assimilated by Flamengo. Meanwhile, Fluminense, which had begun decisively supporting the implementation of professionalism in 1932, aimed at a policy of separating the athlete-as-professional-employee from its exclusive club membership, expanded its practice of recruiting white players from São Paulo and the interior of Brazil as a whole. Symptomatically, Bangú was able to free its worker-players from their factory jobs and hire a coach who had worked for the big clubs. In 1933, it became the city's first championship team under professionalism.

The 1930s were thus marked by progress in a process of democratization within football, both for the professional definition of players, coaches, and trainers and for the incorporation of a broader, mass public. This process continued into the 1940s: even when Leônidas and Domingos left Flamengo, the team's popularity continued to grow as it won three straight city titles, in 1942, 1943, and 1944. The popularity of some charismatic players who had moved to São Paulo (e.g., Leônidas and Domingos) was transferred to the team as a whole (where mulattos and blacks were the majority) and to the team's shirt, consolidating its image of universalist mixture. Little by little the young mulatto Zizinho occupied the place left by Leônidas. Yet even when he was transferred to Bangú in 1950, the team pulled together without any charismatic players and again won three straight city titles in 1952, 1953, and 1954. Still, in the late 1940s the dominant team was Vasco da Gama; its players were the core of the national team competing in the 1950 World Cup, bringing this club great popularity, splitting between Vasco and Flamengo the loyalties of Rio's lower classes.

Eventually, this process of popularization of formerly elite clubs that used players from working-class backgrounds reached other clubs in Rio, São Paulo, and other cities. In Porto Alegre, it was seen in the development of the great rivalry between two clubs, Grêmio and

Internacional. Grêmio Portoalegrense was founded in 1903 for the practice of football by German associations that promoted gymnastics. It was thus a club of the German community in Porto Alegre, and included sectors of the local business elites. Like the Palestra Itália in São Paulo that began with players of the Italian community, Grêmio also was based at first on players from the German community in Porto Alegre. In contrast with Germania in São Paulo, Grêmio was supported by the large German community that existed in Rio Grande do Sul. But Grêmio did not expect to represent the German community, and was also open to other sectors of the local elites. Internacional, founded in 1909, soon tried to become a rival to Grêmio, but the latter team was dominant until the 1940s. With professionalization, Internacional recruited the best players from the working classes, including blacks and mulattos, while Grêmio sustained its traditional policy, excluding black players.

Without any real chances of being accepted by the main clubs in town, or so they believed, blacks in Porto Alegre decided in the early 1920s to create a separate championship and league in the poor sector of the city, known as the "league of the black legs." It was a successful idea. While Grêmio kept its traditionally exclusive policy, Internacional later incorporated the great black and mulatto players from the second division and dominated the state's championship until the 1950s.

[...]

This late acceptance of professionalism by elite clubs also happened in other states. Thus, São Paulo Futebol Clube was created during the period of professionalism in the 1930s by members of clubs that had desisted playing football because of the end of amateurism—such as Paulistano. But by the early 1940s it was engaged in professional competition and had admitted Leônidas da Silva into the team. The admittance of this great black player from Flamengo, an idol from the World Cup of 1938, opened the way for other players from poor and black sectors of the population, and for the growth of the number of fans. The Corinthians, which had from early times been associated with São Paulo's poor sectors and with the acceptance of black players and fans, answered São Paulo's action by admitting Domingos da Guia in 1944. This was another player from the 1938 Cup who, together with Leônidas, had helped make Flamengo a popular club during the turn to professionalism in the 1930s. The elite clubs in Rio, such as Fluminense and Botafogo, ended up improving their professional policies—for example, by the acceptance of the black player Didi in 1951 by Fluminense and in 1956 by Botafogo.

The resurgence of racist stereotypes after the 1950 World Cup defeat

While such progress in the democratization of football did in fact occur, ambiguous, dissimulated stereotypes and prejudices present in Brazilian society as a whole were also active in sports. Thus, the flow of young, poor, black athletes meant that the greater or lesser faults and threats hovering over the players' careers—lack of discipline, drinking, and taking bribes—were attributed preferentially to blacks, albeit sometimes unconsciously. There was also an ambiguous split between the adoption and idolatry of black athletes by the home fans and the stigmatizing of black athletes from other teams—an expression of the kind of "cordial racism" permeating Brazilian society and oriented by one's own personal relations.

According to this logic, Brazil's defeat by Uruguay in the final game of the 1950 World Cup, held in Brazil, sparked a barrage of accusations against several black ballplayers on Brazil's defense, targeted as the scapegoats for the tragedy. These racial stigma and "common-sense" stereotypes were backed by the pretense of erudite evolutionist and social-Darwinist explanations propounded by physical anthropologists and essayists from various professional backgrounds, which found wide acceptance among Brazilian elites. One result of the confrontation between such evolutionist racial theories—proposing a hierarchy in the various human "races" and belittling racial mixture—and the reality of widespread Brazilian miscegenation was the prediction of a gradual "whitening" of the Brazilian population based on policies to encourage European immigration, and prognoses that the trend in Brazil would be away from miscegenation and toward the predominance of the white "race."

According to such theories, the less "civilized" black and *mestizo* Brazilians were purportedly

81

prone to greater emotional instability relating to achievements and decisions. Although such theories admitted the existence of bodily qualities and skills in blacks and mulattos such as those associated with music and dance, in sports such skills were allegedly linked to a counter-trait of instability and indecisiveness. The result of the 1950 World Cup final thus appeared adequate to illustrate this erudite supposition, and a number of sports directors subscribed to it: the best team in the championship, displaying great beauty and skill in its football technique, succumbed by a score of 2-1 in its own stadium, the biggest in the world with the largest public ever seen, to a technically inferior yet determined and "whiter" team.

Again, when Brazil was eliminated from the 1954 World Cup in Switzerland by the Hungarian team, with the 4-2 defeat ending in a free-for-all, the head of the Brazilian delegation published a report on the team's tour, turning to such theories and justifying Brazil's defeat on the basis of the alleged emotional instability resulting from Brazilian miscegenation.

Reversal of stigmas and new excellence: the 1958 World Cup and the first "multiracial" championship team

The Brazilian national team's victory in the 1958 World Cup in Sweden, tying the English in the second game and beating the Austrians, Russians, Welsh, French, and Swedes, belied the erudite theories and racist stereotypes concerning the alleged weaknesses of *mestizo* Brazilian football. Contradicting the assertion that "only by chance or contingency might we become world football champions and establish hegemony in this sport," virtually the same team won again in the 1962 World Cup in Chile, beating the Mexicans, Spanish, English, Chileans, and Czechoslovakians. It was the first *mestizo* team (blacks, whites, and mulattos) to win a World Cup, at a time when the skin color of European players was universally white.

Indeed, after the defeat in 1950, suffered by the Brazilian population as a national tragedy, and the experience in 1954, the 1958 team had a more seasoned group of managers, the teamwork of a "technical commission" in charge of organizing the entire tour, and above all a group of extraordinary players, combining the experience of left-back Nilton Santos and midfielder Didi with the youth and unnerving style of others like Pelé and Garrincha. These latter three players helped turn physical disadvantages and stigma like skin color into embodiments of excellence in football. Didi was a craftsman of sagacity and elegance, making long-distance, curved passes, and taking foul-shots with his famous "*folha seca*" or "dry leaf" kick (where the ball took an elliptical, semi-boomerang flight, tricking the goalkeeper); he was chosen by the press as the 1958 World Cup's most valuable player. Pelé was the teenage prodigy at seventeen, son of a former football player, aware of the virtues of asceticism to avoid the pitfalls of a professional football career and heir to the synthesis of qualities in his father's generation, which had included Leônidas. Garrincha was the prime example of transforming bodily and social stigmata into physical and athletic capital. Born and raised in a textile-factory company town in the rural village of Pau Grande, some 90 kilometers from Rio, and living there until the eve of the 1962 World Cup, Garrincha embodied the *habitus* of a factory worker deriving the utmost pleasure from the marginal activities of a company town—hunting, fishing, playing as a worker-player for the factory team, dribbling around the work routine, and transferring this hedonistic pleasure to the professional football context. With his crooked legs and total detachment from all things professional in his career (and thus from the nervousness characterizing decisive games), the *mestizo* Garrincha, bearer of the marks and stigma of the Brazilian lower classes, was an extreme case of turning such disadvantages into an unusual, unnerving style, with his dribble down the right wing, fatal to the opponents' defense.

[…]

Brazil's great black and mulatto players, as we have already seen, were "condemned," so to speak, to exercise their talents in their own country; one or another player would spend short periods abroad, generally in Argentina or Uruguay. These players succeeded in making a major contribution to the creation of a national style of football in their own country, beginning in the 1930s. On the other hand, although football had spread throughout Brazil from the 1930s on, and although the public wanted to see exhibition, style, and "art football," there was still a strong belief in the inferiority of Brazilian football as compared to that of Europe (especially England) and Argentina. Factors contributing to this were the stereotypes and erudite racist theories considered natural by the majority of the population and even internalized by blacks and *mestizos* themselves. The latter, in turn, appropriated a certain *functional democratization* in Brazilian society through football, silently constructing their "ethnic" and social liberation through the sport. Brazil's World Cup title in 1958—which had been so close in 1950 in Maracanã—thus in a sense came as a surprise to the country. It took Brazil's international vindication in Sweden to reinforce a positive self-assessment of Brazilian football, reversing the people's sense of inferiority.

Recent trends and final considerations

[...]

After the 1970s, Brazilian players—including *mestizos* and blacks—were coveted by European clubs and frequently moved abroad, participating in a more "globalized" European football. Players of color from Portuguese, French, Dutch, Belgian, and English colonies and former colonies began to circulate through European clubs, especially around Italy and Spain. In the 1970s, Brazilian players, including Pelé, played soccer in the United States; but in the 1980s Japan became the major importer. There was an enormous increase in the wage figures paid by clubs and intermediaries to transfer players. It is worth noting, however, that this high living standard is the privilege of a tiny minority of players acting in the big clubs; the average monthly wage of professional players (in all divisions, not only the first-division clubs) in Brazil is not higher than one or two times the minimum wage (that is, from 80 to 160 dollars per month; the minimum wage was 70 dollars in March of 2000, and in April, a presidential decree raised it to 82 dollars). Unlike the great players of the 1950s and 1960s, who ascended to a relatively modest middle-class standard of living, today's players from the working or lower-middle classes encounter a consumer hedonism that they exploit through their high salaries. Career-management problems are no less complicated than they used to be, given the

rapid leap in the athletes' living standard and harassment by the media and fans.

Unlike the tenuous supporters' groups of the 1940s, 1950s, and 1960s, made up predominantly of adult male factory and office workers, supporters' organizations in the 1970s, 1980s, and 1990s have consisted primarily of young people. While the traditional "carnivalization" of the stands is still present, through the adaptation of old *sambas* or songs from the *escolas de samba* clubs, more recently cheering sections have concentrated on the music and body language of funk, which has spread all over the slums and working-class suburbs in Rio and São Paulo.

Beginning in the 1970s one notes a trend toward relatively greater participation by players from higher social origins and a certain sense of regret over the demise of the sandlot football fields of yesteryear. But in the 1990s one observes considerable effort and initiative in promoting football among the working classes in Brazil's large cities. While previously there had been a spontaneous process of functional democratization through football by which the working classes could achieve real participation and success, there then began an educational process aimed at creating the conditions for team loyalty and discipline among children and youth in these same social classes. The latter, besides no longer having the same access to sandlot or factory football fields, have now often found themselves in neighborhoods where unemployment, a deteriorating school system, and misdemeanors and felonies have become the prospects for a generation of youth no longer incorporated in great numbers as manual or factory labor by the productive system. Even so, in smaller towns in various parts of the country and in the poor suburbs where opportunities still appear for working-class youth to practice football, they continue to appear and renew the regular and the national teams of juniors.

Mestizo football in Brazil thus survives, with its traditions of success and more or less silent conflicts relating to access by and the continued presence of working-class (and thus mulatto and black) ballplayers in an area of activity highly prized in Brazilian national identity—even when the legitimized hierarchy of professions ascribes priority to the more dominant activities in economic, political, and intellectual life. With the

83

vast majority of spectators and ballplayers originating in the working classes, they still take interest in an activity joining the various classes together in a common language—even though living conditions for the lower classes are aggravated by the persistent lack of social sensitivity in the majority of the country's political and economic elite, combining the traditional old kind of masters-and-slaves domination with modern, exclusive neoliberalism. By using a unique body language and inventing an original style for a quasi-universal sport, Brazil's working classes have succeeded in making a silent contribution to their relative social ascent while furnishing an important domain for Brazilian national identity, wherein they have contributed to reverse the elite's racist stereotypes—and an ethnocentrism internalized by society as a whole.

Note

1. See, for example, the article by Dunning in Section 1—Eds.

An unlikely champion

Robert McG. Thomas

Althea Gibson emerged in the tennis world of the 1950s as a most unlikely queen of the lawns of Wimbledon and Forest Hills.

In 1950 she became the first black to compete in the United States nationals. She won 56 tournaments, including five Grand Slam singles titles—the United States nationals and Wimbledon twice, in 1957 and 1958, and the French championship in 1956.

What made that especially remarkable was her background as a rough-hewn product of Harlem, a chronic truant and an eighth-grade dropout.

She had grown up far removed from the two genteel worlds of tennis: the white country club set and the network of black doctors, lawyers and other professionals who pursued tennis on private courts of their own.

Gibson owed much of her success to that very network of black tennis enthusiasts and to a geographic coincidence.

Althea Gibson, born in a sharecropper's shack in Silver, S.C., on Aug. 25, 1927, was brought to New York by her parents when she was a few months old. By chance, the family moved into an apartment on a West 143rd Street block between Lenox and Seventh Avenues that was a designated play street.

When the volunteers from the Police Athletic League closed the block to traffic and set up their recreation equipment, the spot they chose to mark off as a paddle tennis court was right in front of the Gibsons' front stoop.

A natural athlete who excelled in virtually every sport she tried, Gibson took up paddle tennis at 9 and won a citywide championship when she was 12.

In 1941 Buddy Walker, a Harlem bandleader and part-time P.A.L. supervisor, bought her two rackets and introduced her to friends at the Cosmopolitan Tennis Club, a predominantly black club that played on courts on 149th Street just a few blocks away but a world removed from the neighborhood she had known. Gibson was coached there by Fred Johnson, the one-armed club pro, and taken up by the club's members, who taught her some more important lessons.

As she put it in her 1958 autobiography, "I Always Wanted to Be Somebody," the club attracted "the highest class" of Harlem residents, people, she noted, who "had rigid ideas about what was socially acceptable."

Those ideas were alien to her own experience.

"I'm ashamed to say," she wrote, "that I was still living pretty wild."

Gibson would come home late (sometimes the next day) and her father, a garage attendant, would beat her. But Gibson saw her father as merely a stern disciplinarian, not abusive.

Gibson made a lifelong friendship when she approached her idol, the boxing champion Sugar Ray Robinson, in a bowling alley. Sympathetic to her dream of a career in music, he bought her a saxophone.

Finally, to escape her father's wrath, she sought refuge in a Catholic home for girls and eventually received a welfare grant to get her own apartment while she worked at menial jobs.

But it was tennis that gripped her interest. In 1942 she won her first tournament, the New York State girls' championship, sponsored by the American Tennis Association, which had been organized in 1916 by black players as an alternative to the United States Lawn Tennis Association.

In 1946, when she lost in the final of her first A.T.A. women's championship, she caught the eye of two men who changed her life and altered the course of tennis, Hubert A. Eaton of Wilmington, N.C., and R. Walter Johnson of Lynchburg, Va.

These men, both physicians and leaders of a cadre of black enthusiasts determined to crack the racial barriers of mainstream tennis, saw Gibson's potential and became her sponsors.

They arranged for Gibson to live with Eaton and his wife during the school year, practicing on his court and attending high school, and to spend the summer traveling on the A.T.A. circuit with Johnson, who later performed a similar service for Arthur Ashe.

She was 19 when she started at Wilmington Industrial High School, but finished in three years, graduating 10th in her class, and enrolled as a scholarship student at Florida A&M, receiving a degree at 25.

She also flourished on the court, winning the first of her 10 straight A.T.A. national championships in 1947.

In 1949, a year after Dr. Benjamin Weir had become the first black to play in a United States Lawn Tennis Association title event—the 1948 National Indoor Championships—Gibson took her first steps beyond the world of the black tennis circuit, making it to the semifinals of the Eastern Indoor Championships and then to the semifinals of the national championships.

The next step proved harder. Even after she had won the 1950 Eastern Indoor Championship and a clamor had begun to let her play in the National Grass Court Championships at Forest Hills, the precursor of the United States Open, the powers of tennis seemed to close ranks to keep her out.

To qualify for an invitation to the 1950 nationals, she was required to first make a name for herself at one of the major preliminary grass-court events. But no invitations were forthcoming.

Alice Marble, a former champion, rallied support for Gibson. "If tennis is a game for ladies and gentlemen," she wrote in a letter to American Lawn Tennis magazine, "it's time we acted a little more like gentlepeople and less like sanctimonious hypocrites."

Finally, Gibson received an invitation to the Eastern Grass Court Championships at the Orange Lawn Tennis Club in South Orange, N.J. She made it only as far as the second round, but that was enough to win a bid to Forest Hills.

On Aug. 28, 1950, three years after Jackie Robinson had broken the color barrier in major league baseball, Gibson became the first black player to compete in the national tennis championship. Taking her place on a remote court at the West Side Tennis Club in Forest Hills, Queens, she dispatched Barbara Knapp of England, 6-2, 6-2.

The next day, she faced the Wimbledon champion, Louise Brough. After losing the first set, 6-1, Gibson took the second, 6-3, then fell behind by 3-0 in the third before beginning a surge that brought repeated roars from 2,000 hardy spectators who ignored the first peals of thunder and flashes of lightning of a gathering storm.

Gibson took a lead of 7-6 and was on the verge of victory over her visibly spent opponent. But the rains came, the match was suspended, and when it resumed the next day, Brough won three straight games to win the match.

The 5-foot-10½ Gibson gained the attention of the tennis public. A powerful if inconsistent player, the lean and muscular young woman had a dominating serve, and her long, graceful reach often stunned opponents.

Over the next half-dozen years, Gibson became a fixture on the tennis circuit, playing Wimbledon for the first time in 1951 and earning a ranking as high as No. 7 in the United States.

But Gibson became so disenchanted with her failure to break through to the top that she considered abandoning tennis and entering the Army.

In the fall of 1955, the State Department selected her for a goodwill tennis tour of Asia and the Far East, and the experience inspired her game. In 1956 she won 16 of her first 18 tournaments, including the French championship at Roland Garros, her first title at a Grand Slam event.

But once again victory in the singles championships eluded her at Wimbledon and Forest Hills, although she had been favored to win both. Gibson did team with Angela Buxton to win the Wimbledon doubles in 1956. She won in doubles again in 1957, with Darlene Hard, and in 1958, with Maria Bueno.

After losing to Shirley Fry of the United States in the singles final of the Australian Open in 1957, she did not lose another match all year. Passing up the clay court distraction of the French championship to concentrate on tuning up on grass courts in England, she again entered Wimbledon as the favorite and defeated Hard in the final.

"At last," she said, "at last," as she accepted the trophy from Queen Elizabeth II.

She later wrote in her autobiography: "Shaking hands with the Queen of England was a long way from being forced to sit in the colored section of the bus going into downtown Wilmington, N.C."

Upon returning home, Gibson was given a ticker-tape parade up Broadway, a banquet at the Waldorf-Astoria and a celebration on West 143rd Street.

She told friends and supporters, "This victory belongs to you," but she chaffed at efforts to make her a symbol of black achievement.

When a reporter asked if she was proud to be compared to Jackie Robinson as an outstanding representative of her race, Gibson replied: "No. I don't consider myself to be a representative of my people. I am thinking of me and nobody else."

Having won Wimbledon, Gibson rolled through the national championship at Forest Hills. In the final, she defeated Brough, who had eliminated her in her first national seven years before.

After being named the outstanding female athlete of the year in a poll of Associated Press sports editors, Gibson repeated her Wimbledon and Forest Hills singles victories in 1958, and was named the outstanding female athlete again. Then, under pressure from her family to make some money from her talent, she announced her retirement from amateur tennis.

At a time when the professional game was little more than a sideshow, she had little trouble winning the pro title and went on an exhibition tour with the Harlem Globetrotters, playing tennis at halftime.

In the early 1960s she became the first black player to compete on the women's golf tour, but she never won a tournament. Gibson, who was inducted into the International Tennis Hall of Fame at Newport, R.I., later held various athletic posts in New Jersey state government. A resident of East Orange, she had served as its recreation director.

Gibson was married twice, to William Darben and Sidney Llewellyn. She had no children.

When another black woman, Zina Garrison, made it to the Wimbledon final in 1990 before losing to Martina Navratilova, Gibson was there to cheer her on, but she soon receded from the limelight once again with health and financial problems.

"It was truly an inspiration for me to watch her overcome adversity," Billie Jean King, who was 13 when she first saw Gibson play, told The Associated Press yesterday. "Her road to success was a challenging one, but I never saw her back down."

2.6   Journalistic view

Higher, faster, yes. More meritocratic? No

Matthew Syed

Talent doesn't always triumph at the Olympic Games. They are a bastion of elitism where money can buy medals.

The Olympic Games are built on a series of fictions, but one myth towers above all others. It is that the four-yearly festival is a bastion of meritocracy, where success is determined by hard work and talent rather than privilege. This is central to the Games's global appeal and is particularly powerful because it chimes with common sense. Is not sport about the objective measurement of ability, leaving little room for entrenched privilege? Has not the Olympics been the traditional arena for the underdog?

Well, no.

Look beyond the propaganda and you will find that 58 per cent of Great Britain's gold-medal winners at Athens in 2004 went to independent schools. You will also find that in the past three Olympics 45 per cent of medal winners went to the non-state sector. Given that only 7 per cent of children attend independent schools, and assuming that sporting talent is spread evenly, this is a striking demonstration of how Olympic success is driven by wealth as well as by ability. Either way, the 93 per cent who attend state schools are chronically under-represented.

But this is as nothing compared with the global imbalance. India, for example, a country with almost one fifth of the world's population, won less than a fifth of 1 per cent of the medals available in Athens—one out of a total of 826. (Abhinav Bindra's shooting victory this week

was India's first ever individual gold.) Africa, a continent dripping with sporting talent, won only 4 per cent of them. Is there a single global institution that is less equitable?

The reason for this shameful imbalance is not difficult to find—when the French aristocrat Baron Pierre de Coubertin founded the modern Olympic movement he packed it with sports affordable only to his fellow aristocrats, thus excluding the Third World. The legacy of the baron's patrician bias is still with us today: in Beijing, rowing has 14 medal events, sailing 11 and equestrianism 6. If the International Olympic Committee believes that these sports are accessible to anyone beyond a tiny clique in the Western world it is even more deluded than previously thought.

Take the Yngling sailing event for women—at which Great Britain won gold in 2004. Only about four crews at present compete in the UK, with fewer than 100 competitive crews on the planet. Why? Because it costs more than £20,000 to buy a decent boat. You may as well include Formula One in the Olympics. In rowing, sailing and equestrianism there were 186 medals on offer at the last Olympics. Not one was won by an athlete from a low-income nation.

Perhaps the most amusing aspect of all this is how we respond to our success in such sports. Even some of our more intelligent commentators have convinced themselves that Sir Steve Redgrave is the greatest living Olympian for

Matthew Syed, "Higher, Faster, Yes. More Meritocratic? No" from *The Times of London*, Features (August 16, 2008): 18. Reprinted by permission.

winning five successive golds in rowing, not seeming to realise that the sport is so elitist that it is virtually nonexistent across much of the planet. I suggest that Redgrave would not have qualified for a single Olympic final, let alone won any, had rowing been accessible to, say, 1 per cent of the population of Africa—a continent that dominates running, in which the only equipment needed is decent shoes.

It is striking that Britain's medal success generally comes in sports that are not merely expensive but that are also so unpopular that athletes cannot earn enough from prize-money and endorsements to support themselves. Success in these sports—such as rowing, sailing and track cycling—can essentially be bought by siphoning off money from the public purse and handing it to the athletes who are then able to train like professionals.

Indeed, it is a cause for self-congratulation rather than discomfiture in the sporting community that the improved success of British athletes in recent years has been achieved by outspending many of our rivals. That is not to take anything away from the athletes, who are hard-working and talented. It is merely to say that success in sport is easier when it receives huge state subsidies.

We will see this phenomenon once again in Beijing. Get ready for the smugness if we achieve more success in track cycling, with commentators proclaiming that we Brits are endowed with pedalling genius. The reality is that British cycling has been given millions to spend on bike technology, something that is not considered a sensible target for public expenditure by many other rich nations (although not dictatorships such as China, which tend to spend like crazy on elite sport) and is beyond the public finances of the rest.

How does the Government get away with this raid on the public purse? By claiming that Olympic success inspires grassroots participation, which, in turn, has a benign long-term impact on the public finances. It is an argument with everything on its side except evidence. The reality is that elite success has no sustained impact on participation, and, even if it did, the fiscal effects would be ambiguous.

Instead of splurging gargantuan sums on baubles, would we not do better to urge the IOC to alter the medal allocation to include sports that are accessible to all rather than the privileged few? You do not need a vast bank balance or state subsidies to excel in kabbadi or sepak takraw, two wonderful Asian sports. Sure, rich nations might still dominate, but low-income countries would at least have a chance, as they do in sprinting and distance running.

The Olympics should be a global festival, not a rich man's playground.

Section 3

Coloring the game

Race matters in sport

Introduction

Jack Johnson, the first African American to win the heavyweight boxing championship, was so reviled by white Americans that a movement was launched, shortly after he gained the title, to find a white boxer—the putative "great white hope"—who could defeat Johnson and regain the crown for the white race. Jackie Robinson, the first African American to play major league baseball in the modern era, routinely encountered everything from racial epithets from opposing players and fans to blatant discrimination from hotels and restaurants, which refused to admit him when he traveled out of town with his white teammates. The African-American baseball slugger Hank Aaron received death threats and had to be protected by security guards during the season he broke baseball's home run record, because Babe Ruth, the quintessential white male symbol of baseball prowess who had held the record some 60 years, was being supplanted by a black man. These are only a few examples of ways sport can spur racial antagonisms.

Such racial antagonisms are hardly surprising, because in most racially plural societies race exists as a major fault line, typically manifested in a pattern of racial group dominance and subordination, which is supported by ideological rationalizations, ideas and beliefs alleging the dominant group's superiority. Sports contests in such societies become potent symbols that can mobilize racial tensions, especially when the outcomes of these contests challenge the dominant racial group's claim of superiority.

While freighted interactions between sport and race relations can be observed in a wide variety of societies (e.g., South Africa, France, Britain, Germany, and Australia), sport indisputably has had the greatest impact on race relations in the United States. That is because American sports have often led the way, not only in breaking through racial barriers and showcasing exceptional black American talent, but also in revealing the irrationality of racial ancestry as the basis for talent selection.

In contrast to job performances in less visible institutional settings (e.g., business corporations, law firms, and government agencies), work performances in sport are distinguished by one crucial fact: they occur in public spaces, under the gaze of a public who can compare and evaluate the performances for themselves. Augmenting these public observations are the public records of sports performances (e.g., batting averages, runs batted in, touchdowns, yards per carry, rebounds, field goal averages) which are accessible for all to examine. Hence the uniqueness of sport as an institutional site for talent evaluation: whenever blacks had opportunities to participate against whites, some displayed outstanding athletic achievements that had a large hand in eroding the cultural myth of white racial superiority.

African American athletes such as Jack Johnson, Jessie Owens, Joe Louis, Althea Gibson, Wilma Rudolph, and Bill Russell occupy a special place in the history of not only sports and but also American race relations, because they were trailblazers who overcame racial barriers and exemplified images of excellence that transcended sports. By conquering often hostile new frontiers in sports, they and other black athletes both affirmed and expanded the structure of opportunity in American democracy.

Analytical issues

Social scientists have produced various theories of race relations, but those theories have seldom been extended to sports, perhaps because race relations theorists ignored sports as an institutional domain. Our objective here is not to submit a comprehensive summary of race relations theories but to present several examples of theoretical perspectives on race relations that have significant implications for understanding how race matters in sport.

First, there are the concepts of extrinsic and intrinsic racism, concepts developed by the philosopher Anthony Appiah, which focus on the way racism operates on the social psychological level of personal beliefs (Appiah, 1990). Extrinsic racism refers to the most familiar notions of racial bias. It denotes prejudice and discrimination of individuals who believe that they are racially superior and that, therefore, they are entitled to unequal resources and privileges. This concept helps to explain, for example, the attitudes of the average white American fan who supported racial exclusion in sport during much of the nineteenth and twentieth centuries: racial exclusion seemed perfectly reasonable in light of what they believed about racial differences. The same can be said about the attitudes of white South Africans, who supported the racial apartheid sport system well into the 1980s without questioning the exclusion of black South Africans. They believed blacks constituted a lower category of being. Though extrinsic racism has been repudiated in most of the contemporary world (thanks in part to the influence of interracial sport competition), it still exists in covert and subtle forms, which we will consider momentarily.

In contrast, intrinsic racism is a much less familiar way of thinking about discrimination. It denotes in-group tribal sentiments, which are manifested in a preference for people of one's own kind. This is more pervasive than extrinsic

racism in the modern world, because it is much less often perceived as racism. Indeed, most people regard such sentiments as expressions of ancestral loyalty, without realizing that such preferences, when based on beliefs in essentialized biological attributes, foster racial discrimination. Though seldom noted by sports commentators, sports are pervaded by tribal sentiments. We see examples in sports when fans cheer for a boxer, express pride in the performance of a quaterback, or buy the jersey of a basketball star because the athlete shares their racial ancestry. Most people probably view racially chauvinist fan sentiments as trivial. But those sentiments can have significant racial consequences if they influence a team's marketing decisions about player recruitment and position assignments. Prompted by racial sentiments, the St. Louis Hawks basketball team, in 1956, made perhaps the worse trade in the history of the NBA by trading Bill Russell, a newly drafted black college All-American center, to the Boston Celtics for a white player of considerably less talent. Russell, who many observers came to regard as the greatest professional basketball player of his era, went on to lead the Celtics to eleven championships. Meanwhile, the Hawks declined into oblivion and eventually moved the franchise to Atlanta. Similarly, it is hardly a coincidence that white fans have been more reluctant to accept black quarterbacks in NFL football. We also see the effects of intrinsic racism in decisions about position assignments on the playing field in other sports, where central or star roles are reserved for players who fit the preferred racial profile. It is hardly a coincidence that the NBA Pheonix Suns and Utah Jazz, which represent cities with primarily white fan bases, have never fielded all black starting teams, which is not unusual in the NBA where blacks comprise over 80 per cent of the players.

Second, we turn to the implications of theoretical concepts that view racism as an integral part of a society's cultural system. Perhaps best illustrated by the concept of racial hegemony, this perspective, which derives from Antonio Gramsci's writings, highlights the cultural dominance of racist ideas among not only the ruling racial group but also the subjugated racial groups in the society (Gramsci, 1992). Under cultural hegemony, the subordinate racial groups exhibit little—if any—resistance to their racial subjugation. In sport, for example, in the late nineteenth and early twentieth centuries most black athletes (with the exception of Jack Jackson) acquiesced to racial segregation. But this situation changed. Primarily as a result of historical developments, particularly in the 1940s, the grip of the dominant racial hegemony was challenged by counter-hegemonic black resistance in sport. By the 1960s, that resistance expanded into a broad rebellion of black athletes, evidenced in Muhammed Ali's conversion to a radical black nationalist religion and refusal to comply with the military draft, the Olympic boycott movement among black athletes, the protest of Tommy Smith and John Carlos during the Mexico City Olympics, and Curt Flood's challenge to baseball's reserve clause. All manifested counter-hegemonic black resistance which had a large hand in changing the racial dynamics of American sports.

The third, and final, example of theoretical concepts that are useful for understanding the role of race in sport focuses on the changing manifestations of racism. This is illustrated by the distinction between overt and covert manifestations of racism. In the racial caste system in the United States prior to the 1960s and in South Africa prior to the 1990s, racism was overt and visibly manifested in practices of racial exclusion and segregation. Though these overt manifestations of racism later lost their political legitimacy and became subject to criminal sanctions, racism in these societies did not disappear—it simply assumed more covert forms, which the legal system tolerated (Omi and Winant, 1994). For instance, in the United States, by the early 1970s, overt manifestations of racism disappeared in both college and professional sports. Whereas, in the 1950s, college athletic teams such as the University of Kentucky and the University of Mississippi had explicit racial policies excluding blacks, in the 1970s those schools abandoned those policies. But did this mean that race no longer mattered in previously segregated college programs? No, they simply assumed a more covert form. Hence the relative paucity of black head coaches, athletic directors, and other black sports administrative personnel. But, in the post-segregation era, this is accepted because there is no overt evidence of racial bias.

Which brings us onto the terrain of institutional racism, a theoretical perspective which highlights the social processes that have normalized this more subtle (post segregation-era) form of racism (Knowles *et al.* 1969). Focusing on the persisting patterns of exclusion, the institutional racism perspective argues that discrimination has shifted from individually motivated actions to biased impersonal organizational rules and procedures. In sports, for example, if the athletic department of a major university seeks to fill a vacant football coaching position by relying on the athletic director's customary network of white associates, black candidates will be automatically excluded, because they have had no opportunity to work at a Division I-A school or develop a network of white associates, who could vouch for their qualifications. The institutional racism perspective is highly relevant to explanations of current problems of discrimination in hiring black athletic administrators and coaches.

While social scientists have undertaken studies of racial strains and conflicts in sports, they have barely scratched the surface in incorporating paradigms from race relations theories that explain how race affects—and is affected by—sports. Among the analytical questions that need more exploration are the following:

1 What are the links between race relations in the wider society and race relations in sports? Under what conditions are sports likely to reflect race relations in the surrounding society? Under what conditions are they likely to contradict or challenge the society's race relations?

2 What are the specific characteristics of racial barriers in sport? How do they differ from gender and class barriers in sports? To what extent do racial and class barriers in sports overlap? Are racial barriers in sports mitigated by the subordinate racial group's upward class mobility?

3 How do we explain persisting patterns of racial discrimination in sport? What is the role of marketing factors (i.e. catering to a racially biased fan base) versus organizational culture (reflecting racial biases of team owners or sport leagues)? What successful forms of resistance have been used by subordinate racial groups to attack race discrimination in sport? Which patterns of race discrimination are most persistent?

4 Within a particular society such as the United States or Great Britain, what are

the most racially egalitarian sports and what are the least racially egalitarian sports?

5 How is racial exclusivity of a sport maintained where it is not protected by law?

6 How do patterns of race discrimination in sport differ cross nationally? Are sports in less developed, authoritarian societies more racially exclusive than sport in industrial democratic societies? How is race discrimination affected by the racial homogeneity or diversity of the surrounding society?

The articles in this section encompass a broad range of issues focused on the interaction between sport and race relations. In the first article, "Anatomy of Scientific Racism," Patrick B. Miller uses discourse analysis to explain the persistence of extrinsic racism in sports. Presenting an incisive and illuminating historical account of the cultural discourses of race that have served to racialize black American athletic achievements, he suggests that there has been a linkage between pseudo science of racial difference and pernicious social policies. By ascribing superior black sports performance to their group of origin, Miller argues, the prevailing white American racial discourse discounted the efforts of African Americans. Though there has been significant progress in racial discourse, he notes, the older essentialist views of race still persist. He concludes by calling for critical engagement with these entrenched modes of racialist thinking. Also highlighting the role of essentialist ideology in sport, Malcolm Gladwell, in the second article—"The Sports Taboo"—illustrates the fallacy of bio-genetic explanations of black athletic dominance in certain sports. Gladwell's article is especially impressive in its lucid exposition of the logic of statistical variance to dispel the ideological misconceptions about African ancestry and athletic superiority.

Racial ideology frequently surfaces in the form of racial symbolism, the connotative racial meanings people attach to sport performances, which is the focus of the next two articles. In "Manliness and Civilization," Gail Bederman highlights Jack Johnson's dramatic emergence in the American sports world as a symbolic threat to white manhood. The first African American to win the heavyweight championship, he represented an unprecedented challenge to the prevailing ideology of white male superiority. The threat Johnson posed was exacerbated by his romantic relationships with white women. Expanding on this theme of racial symbolism in sport, Gerald Early, in "Hot Spicks and Cool Spades," discusses the "racial tribalism" in fan identification with boxers, a particularly brutal sport that has historically symbolized American racial antagonisms by means of athletic contests. Early explains how these contests, by pitting white and black boxers against each other, stirred intense racial passions among fans.

In contrast to this conception of sports as a source of racial antagonism, sports are sometimes characterized as a force of resistance to racism, a view linked to the assumption that sports inevitably foster progressive racial reform. This is understandable in light of the historical occasions when athletes confronted and prevailed over racial intolerance—e.g., the exploits of Jessie Owens, Joe Louis, and Jackie Robinson come immediately to mind. But, as Doug Hartmann notes, if we take into account the continuing racial discrimination in sport, we must conclude that this idealized conception of sports as a force for progressive social reform, despite its appealing optimism, is simplistic and misleading. In the final article, "Sport as Contested Terrain," Hartmann argues that sports is neither a progressive nor a reactionary social force—but rather that it should be viewed as an institutional site of persisting racial conflict. Because of their popularity, high visibility, and intense competitiveness, Hartmann concludes, major sports constitute institutional settings where racial tensions and strains in the society are most likely to surface.

References

Appiah, A. 1990. "Racisms." In *Anatomy of Racism*. Goldberg, T. Minneapolis: University of Minnesota Press.

Gramsci, A. 1992. *Prison Notebooks*. New York: Columbia University Press.

Knowles, L.L., K. Prewitt, and O. Blank. 1969: *Institutional Racism*. Englewood Cliffs, N.J.: Prentice-Hall.

Omi, M. and Winant, H. 1994. *Racial Formation in the United States*. New York: Routledge.

The anatomy of scientific racism

Racialist responses to black athletic achievement

Patrick B. Miller

In this section, Patrick Miller presents an analysis of racial discourse in sports, highlighting the historical linkage between pseudo-scientific racial discourse and racist social policies.

[...]

When African-American artists and athletes pursued excellence within the boundaries of Western aesthetic and agonistic traditions, they encountered more than customary biases and myriad discriminatory acts. They confronted a discourse of difference, which, inscribed as a set of "racial constants," effectively discounted the efforts of black Americans or denied the cultural significance of their achievements.

Ultimately, this particular dimension of the politics of culture has engaged a vast scholarship that ranges far beyond the history of racial relations in the United States. Within one frame of analysis, the origins and development of the discourse of difference have been examined specifically with regard to the Nazi eugenic theories that finally marked Jews and gypsies, as well as homosexuals, for extermination. Such cultural boundary marking has also been assessed with consideration of the linkages between gender and race in the construction of hierarchies of privilege and subordination over time. As scholars of postcolonial ideology and experience have demonstrated, furthermore, the

ranking of racial traits—especially as it has elaborated the dichotomy between mind and body—continues to serve as a means of suppressing the claims of people of color around the world. What remains is the relationship between the pseudo-science of racial difference and the pernicious social policies it both inspires and informs.[1]

It is significant, then, that even those who endeavor to expose and thus dispose of the cultural hierarchies predicated on the tired old versions of ethnicity and race have lately become involved in earnest and extensive debates over Charles Murray and Richard Herrnstein's *The Bell Curve*, an elaborate ranking of so-called racial and ethnic groups in terms of IQ—with African Americans at the bottom of the list. Scholars have also felt compelled to address the claims made by Dinesh D'Souza, who in *The End of Racism*, has gone so far as to describe the civilizing and Christianizing effects of slavery on the majority of blacks in the United States.[2] In such instances, progressive writers and educators must still regularly engage the persistent stereotypes concerning the "natural" physical abilities of blacks, which are said to explain the

Patrick B. Miller, "The Anatomy of Scientific Racism: Racialist Responses to Black Athletic Achievement" from *Journal of Sport History* 25.1 (Spring 1998): 119–151. Copyright © 1998. Reprinted with the permission of the author and the North American Society for Sport History.

"dominance" of African Americans in sports such as basketball and football.

To account for achievement in biologically essentialist terms effectively discounts the traits identified with "character": discipline, courage, sacrifice. And therein lies the significance of inquiries into racial science when they have been applied to athletics.[3] Ultimately, the questions of who can run faster or jump higher are simplistic, but they are pernicious as well as foolish if conceived as measures of innate racial difference.

[...]

Since "race matters," as the title of one of Cornel West's recent books avows, we need to discuss not only why it should but when it should not—in judgments of individual abilities and accomplishments. With regard to the historical construction of racial categories, we ought to consider that the *body* continues to loom large in many people's thinking about difference. TV sports reports often provide the most obvious marker of distinctions associated with race and ethnicity. In basketball, the trope of the white point guard—court savvy, disciplined, and controlled—has stood in striking contrast to prevailing images of black male athletes, able and all too willing to shatter backboards with their slam dunks. And if that juxtaposition appears too stark and simple—in light of the widespread recognition of what was Michael Jordan's mastery, not just of the mechanics of his game, but also of modern media techniques—we can turn to the lecture hall. "I don't know whether or not most white men can jump," the historian of science Stephen Jay Gould wrote during *The Bell Curve* controversy:

> And I don't much care, although I suppose that the subject bears some interest and marginal legitimacy in an alternate framing that avoids such biologically meaningless categories as white and black. Yet I can never give a speech on the subject of human diversity without attracting some variant of this inquiry in the subsequent question period. I hear the 'sports version,' I suppose, as an acceptable surrogate for what really troubles people of good will (and bad, although for other reasons).[4]

The "sports version" of human diversity, still placing population groups up and down a vertical axis of accomplishment, suggests another significant topic. Without discussing the economic and educational practices that mark "racial" distinctions in the United States, without examining the concepts of whiteness and blackness in cultural terms, and without recognizing the facts of mixed heritage, most racialist formulations have had as their objective the demonstration of African-American inferiority, for example, on intelligence tests. But judgments about culture or ideologies of success also come in response to *black achievement*. Frequently, in reaction to triumphs by African Americans, we hear explanations that qualify excellence fashioned out of the notion of "natural ability."

When African Americans began to register an increasing number of victories on the playing fields during the first decades of the twentieth century, mainstream commentators abandoned the athletic creed that linked physical prowess, manly character, and the best features of American civilization. Although many African Americans had subscribed to the ideal that achievement in sport constituted a proof of equality, a mechanism of assimilation, and a platform for social mobility, the recognition successful black athletes actually received from many educators and journalists explained away their prowess by stressing black anatomical and physiological advantages or legacies from a primitive African past.[5]

Many academicians, beginning in the mid-nineteenth century, thus turned away from the discourse of culture when interpreting the physical talents of blacks—and other Others. As they became engrossed in the "scientific" analysis of racial difference, various anthropologists and anthropometrists reached for their calipers and tape measures in search of a gastrocnemius muscle with a certain diameter or of an elongated heel bone in order to explain the success of certain sprinters or jumpers. In the dominant discourse, an individual's performance was bound to attributes ascribed to the group of his or her origin. Such a racialized view of excellence defined the physical accomplishments of Europeans in terms of diligence and forethought, the application of the mind to the movements of the body, while it framed the achievements of people of color with words such as "natural" and "innate." Ultimately, then, racialized responses to the athletic as well as the artistic accomplishments of blacks have served both to shape and reinforce prevailing stereotypes. In so doing, they have also served to rationalize exclusionary social practices and discriminatory public policies.

The history of racial ranking

The construction of racial typologies can be traced in general terms to Aristotle's attempt to justify slavery. Pictorial representations of Africans dating back to Greek antiquity, as well as the patterns of thought that shaped the characterization of Caliban and Othello, for instance, undergird modern European racism. Such images speak to a lengthy history of racial boundary marking and the color coding of culture. Yet it is in the mid nineteenth-century writings of Joseph Arthur, Comte de Gobineau, that many scholar perceive the racist ideologies that first alluded to measurable distinctions and pretended to scientific objectivity. In *The Inequality of Human Races* (1853–1855), Gobineau asked: "Is there an inequality in physical strength?" His answer, according to the intellectual historian Elazar Barkan, "mixed aristocratic pessimism, romanticism, theology together with biology, all of which became part of a shared European value system based on racial differentiation."[6] "The American savages, like the Hindus, are certainly our inferiors in this respect, as are also the Australians. The Negroes, too, have less muscle power; and all these people are infinitely less able to bear fatigue."[7]

[...]

At the turn of the century, standard reference books continued to include broad generalizations about racial difference based on observations and measurements. Under the subject heading "Negro," the canonical *Encyclopaedia Britannica* of 1895 distinguished between cranial capacities (an average European, 45 ounces; Negro, 35; highest gorilla, 20) and underscored a differential development of the cranial sutures wherein the "premature ossification of the skull" was said to account for the intellectual limitations of blacks. Significantly, such prematurity was said to result in "the inherent mental inferiority of the blacks, an inferiority which is even more marked than their physical differences."[8] Later versions of these notations would accentuate the so-called primitive features of the Negro physiognomy in order to explain the relative failure of

African Americans—in the aggregate—on intelligence tests. Such references would also inform the doctrine of racial eugenics as it was elaborated on both sides of the Atlantic.[9]

By 1900, however, another dimension of scientific racism could be discerned. Rather than simply reinforce prevailing notions of Negro inferiority, experts felt compelled to account for the extraordinary achievements of some black athletes. In the face of an increasing number of victories posted by African Americans, the mainstream culture began to *qualify* the meanings of excellence in sport. The *Encyclopaedia Britannica* had described "the abnormal length of the arm, which in the erect position sometimes reaches the kneepan, and which on an average exceeds that of the Caucasian by about two inches," and "the low instep, divergent and somewhat prehensile great toe, and heel projection backwards ('lark heel')." Increasingly, these specifications would be advanced as reasons for black success in sports. Thus, in 1901 the champion sprint cyclist Marshall "Major" Taylor was X-rayed, as well as measured up and down by a number of French medical anthropologists, in an effort to reveal the source of his triumphs in the velodrome. In similar terms, comment on the speed of the black Olympian John Taylor, and on the prepossessing strength of the heavyweight champion boxer Jack Johnson a few years later, included "scientific" speculation.

Throughout the twentieth century, it would often be the accomplishments of people of color in the realm of sport that particularly vexed and intimidated those who endeavored to defend a long-standing racial hierarchy. The response would not be subtle. Indeed, the Western discourse of racial difference carefully juxtaposed black athletic achievement—assessed in terms of compensation—to the supposed intellectual disabilities or cultural shortcomings of African Americans.

Critically, the initial forays into the anthropometry of athletic difference were expounded against the backdrop of increasing segregation in the United States which involved—beyond the enforcement of Jim Crow in housing, transportation, and education—the exclusion of the vast majority of African-American ballplayers, jockeys, and boxers from mainstream sporting competitions. The cyclist Major Taylor, for instance, competed when he could in Europe and Australia because of the hostility he encountered at home. Hypocrisy was piled upon paradox when those who spoke for the dominant culture began to contrast the alarming vitality of African Americans (as well as immigrant newcomers to the United States) to the alleged degeneration of Anglo-America. Such works as Madison Grant's *The Passing of the Great Race* and Lothrop Stoddard's *The Rising Tide of Color against White World Supremacy* reflected nearly hysterical feelings about the links between demography and democracy. Vaguely informed by statistical data, such discussions of the relative birthrates among the Mayflower descendants, the sons and daughters of the shtetl, and those who were moving from southern farms to northern cities revealed a deep fear about the claims black Americans and "hyphenated" Americans might well make against hallowed ideals such as equality and opportunity.[10]

Black leaders like W. E. B. Du Bois—alongside the guiding lights of the new immigrant groups—did indeed seek full participation in the social, economic, and political mainstream, though they demanded fairness not merely as a measure of their numbers but on the basis of their contributions to American culture. And according to the "muscular assimilationists" among them, there was no better argument for inclusion than success in the "national" pastimes. Major Taylor and Jack Johnson were not the first African Americans to make their mark in sports, and it was clear to racial reformers that they would not be the last to tread "the hard road to glory." Well before the appearance of Joe Louis and Jesse Owens in the 1930s, and a decade later, of Jackie Robinson, black leaders saw in athletics a platform for social change.[11]

Resistance to such assertions was formidable, however. Those who would maintain Jim Crow guarded the portals of the stadium just as they stood at the schoolhouse door. Others reinforced racial hierarchy by constructing elaborate frameworks to distinguish between the laurels won by whites and blacks in sport. During the interwar period, anatomy and physiology were frequently invoked to explain the athletic success of African Americans, circumscribing declarations that prowess in contests of speed, strength, and stamina bespoke fitness for other realms of endeavor. In the idiom of sports, to deny the correspondence between athletics and

other accomplishments (more profound and long-standing), numerous mainstream commentators "moved the goal posts."

By the 1930s, generalizations from individual performances to group characteristics dominated many descriptions of black prizefighters, such as the heavyweight champion Joe Louis. Likewise, to account for the medals won by the sprinters Eddie Tolan and Ralph Metcalfe during the 1932 Olympics and by Jesse Owens, Metcalfe, and many other African-American champions at the Berlin Games of 1936, white commentators insisted that black success derived from innate biological advantages. Early in the decade, E. Albert Kinley—whose claim to expertise was that he was an X-ray specialist—repeated the canard about the elongated heel bone, then predicted more world records for African Americans in events that depended on a certain kind of anatomical leverage. Working from a similar premise, Eleanor Metheny, a well-known physical educator, conducted a number of studies on body proportions. Though somewhat guarded in her conclusions, she asserted that kinesiological differences—in the movements generated by individuals with longer legs and narrower hips, for instance—could account for black dominance in sport. Significantly, and ultimately ironically, Metheny would declare that a different, somehow deficient chest construction, as well as lower breathing capacity among blacks, handicapped them in endurance events such as distance running. In David Wiggins's apt phrase, "great speed but little stamina" became the watchword for many white commentators on black athletics. In formulations repeated both in scholarly journals and the popular press, the science of sport further insinuated itself into the broader history of racism in the United States.[12]

If experiments like those conducted by Metheny were as flawed in their conception as in their conclusions, other writers appeared just as intent on defending myths of Anglo-Saxon or Aryan superiority. "It was not long ago," wrote the track-and-field coach Dean Cromwell in 1941, "that his [the black athlete's] ability to sprint and jump was a life-and-death matter to him in the jungle. His muscles are pliable, and his easygoing disposition is a valuable aid to the mental and physical relaxation that a runner and jumper must have." The attempt thus to "historicize" racial difference in sport revealed a significant strand of popular thought. To invoke an African past, the primitive Other, a state-of-being predicated solely on physical prowess, was literally to denigrate what flowed from it. By extension, it was also to exalt its presumed obverse—civilization and the attributes of the dominant order.[13]

Cromwell's interpretation was a curious notion of nature and culture at odds. It imagined that when blacks in Africa had been off running and hunting, the ancestors of white athletes were composing symphonies and building cathedrals, which placed their descendants at a substantial disadvantage at the modern-day Olympics. If the black athlete's "easy-going disposition" lay at or near the center of his success, then again by contrast, white competitors may have been thwarted from starting blocks to finish line by their particular worries about the fate of Western civilization.

Such luridly imagined observations as Cromwell's never stood alone or without amplification. In the ensuing years, black athleticism fell prey to the Harvard anthropologist Carleton S. Coon, who began his commentary on the inherited advantages of African Americans in sport with a depiction of their slender calves and loose jointedness. But what started with anatomy ended with a striking analogy, as was so often the case with racial scientists. The biological features that suited African Americans for certain sports, Coon declared, were characteristic of "living things (cheetahs, for instance) known for their speed and leaping ability." Two later chroniclers of the history of college football continued to rely on gross stereotype, though they had relocated their analogies from the African jungle to the American palladium. "Because of their tap-dancer sense of rhythm and distinctive leg conformation, blacks excel as sprinters," John McCallum and Charles Pearson averred. "It follows naturally that on the football field they stand out as broken field runners."[14]

After mid-century, racial science often focused on the triumph of black athletes in the track-and-field events of the Olympic Games. The stopwatch and the tape measure seemed to offer a certain validation to the claims of the hereditarians that significant and fixed anatomical and physiological differences accounted for the medals won by black Americans in the sprints and jumps. But then, rather suddenly, racial commentators were confronted by the stellar efforts and world records of African distance runners. On the heels of successive gold medal performances in the marathon, steeplechase, and 10,000-meter race by competitors from Ethiopia and Kenya during the 1960s, the notion of fast-twitch and slow-twitch muscle fibers—which had for a time been used to distinguish between the speed of blacks and stamina of whites—was displaced as a frame of analysis. Substituted for it were assertions that strove to mark differences between East-African and West-African physiques, long and lithe versus compact and muscular. From the vantage not so much of a later era but of a different ideological stance, this swift shift in explanations suggests that the persistence of scientific racism lay not so much in the consistency of the science but in the constancy of its racism.

At odds with such racially essentialist notions, an increasing emphasis on cultural interpretations of African-American success in sports characterized the social science of sport as well as mainstream journalism. A five-part series by Charles Maher in the Los Angeles Times, March 24–29, 1968, that surveyed current biological studies of black athletic performance concluded that hard training and motivational factors accounted for the increasing success of African-American athletes. Mainstream sociological opinion had begun to yield the same conclusions.[15] These were noteworthy developments whose stress on black struggle and triumph within the boundaries marked by the athletic establishment reflected the growing influence of the civil rights movement and its integrationist appeal.

[...]

Responses to the racial "scientists"

References to innate athletic differences between population groups persisted well beyond the era of desegregation in sport. But such ways of thinking have also provoked a variety of reactions, often passionate and profound, from black Americans. From Du Bois at the turn of the century to educators and athletes such as Harry Edwards and Arthur Ashe in our own time, most African-American commentators have objected to the use of stereotype and the misuse of science to distinguish the accomplishments of black and white athletes. Urgently and insistently, many intellectuals and activists in the civil rights movement have asserted that the claims made by excellent black athletes against the mainstream rhetoric of equality and opportunity have stood for the larger aspirations of Afro-America. They have also drawn upon the findings of numerous physical scientists and social scientists, who have disproved the allegations of biodeterminism and dismissed the idea of legacies from a primitive past.

During the early years of the century Du Bois enlisted a new generation of anthropologists led by Franz Boas to refute the tenets of scientific racism. In 1906, at the invitation of Du Bois, Boas delivered a paper titled "The Health and Physique of the Negro American" at the eleventh annual Atlanta University Conference. Emphasizing the significance of culture in perceived racial differences, he was instrumental in prompting young African-American scholars, such as Zora Neale Hurston, to undertake research in black folklore and culture. Through the first half of the century, Boasians were popular speakers on the campuses of historically black colleges. The environmentalism embraced by an increasing number of social scientists in the ensuing years seemed to remove black athletic accomplishment from the shaky anthropometrical foundations first advanced by ideologues like Gobineau and to place excellence in sport, for instance, within the sturdier frames of analysis that address social circumstance and cultural innovation.[16]

At the same time, biological scientists also challenged the generalizations based on anthropometry. Few if any offered findings more emphatic or timely than the African-American scholar W. Montague Cobb. Drawing on his experiments in physiology and anatomy, particularly his biopsies of the muscle tissue of Jesse Owens during the late 1930s, Cobb assailed the proposition that specific biological determinants could account for black athletic success. With reference to the prevailing classification systems, the Howard University professor declared without equivocation that the "Negroid type of calf, foot, and heel bone" could not be found in the Olympic champion; if anything, Cobb asserted, the diameter of Owens's gastrocnemius conformed to "the caucasoid type rather than the negroid."[17]

In professional as well as popular journals, Cobb extended his analysis in important ways.

He was neither the first scientist, nor the last, to underscore the salience of physical variations *within* population groups as well as between them. Nevertheless, he discussed that notion within the context of sporting accomplishment and thus engaged, at an early date, the athletic typologies then in place. What is more, Cobb indicated his clear sense that racial mixing subverted any assertion about fixed and isolated genetic determinants of muscular or mental prowess. Howard Drew had been a co-record holder in the 100-yard-dash and the first black sprinter to be acclaimed "the world's fastest human," Cobb noted in 1936. But Drew was also light-skinned and "usually taken for a white man by those not in the know." Edward Gourdin, the Harvard sprinter and former world-record holder in the broad jump, was similarly light skinned. "There is not one single physical feature, including skin color, which all our Negro champions have in common which would identify them as Negroes," Cobb asserted. A mixed heritage, he concluded, obviously removed such stellar athletes from consideration when rigid racial dichotomies were being cast, thus exposing as arbitrary and contrived the very principles of racial taxonomy.[18]

[...]

The massive resistance to the efforts of the integrationists might begin to explain why other African-American commentators have come to subscribe to essentialist considerations of physical hardihood and athletic prowess. The attempt to strategically appropriate the notion of racial difference—to turn it on its head, as it were— may have been born of frustration. It was clearly sustained by considerations of cultural nationalism and Black Power during the late 1960s and 1970s. But today such racialism is not only manifest in African-centered assertions regarding distinctive patterns of cultural development; it also makes its appeal through the notions of melanin theory, no less weird or pernicious than the pronouncements of coach Cromwell or the journalist Kane. Although the various tenets of Afrocentrism certainly speak to racial pride, it is important not to confuse such a sociological phenomenon with a solidly grounded school of critical analysis; while Afrocentrism may be good therapy, as one prominent scholar has noted, it is not good history.[19]

[...]

Recent developments

[. . .] Al Campanis stated that blacks performed well on the field but lacked "the necessities" to occupy managerial positions or places of responsibility and authority in the front offices of sports organizations. Jimmy "the Greek" Snyder, a bookmaker turned loose on television, linked the heritage of slavery to the modern playing field. "The slave owner would breed his big black with his big woman so that he could have a big black kid," Snyder maintained. The consternation evinced by their respective interviewers and the summary firing of both men indicated a shift of values and standards toward such public declarations and their racist underpinnings. Yet many Americans continue to mark racial differences in the athletic arena in terms both calculated and crude. Toward the end of the 1996–1997 basketball season, a sportscaster was fined by the NBA for his retrograde appraisal of black athletic ability. Commenting on a stellar play by one athlete, David Halberstam, who announced the games for the Miami Heat, remarked that "Thomas Jefferson would have been proud of that pass. When Thomas Jefferson was around basketball was not invented yet, but those slaves working at Thomas Jefferson's farm, I'm sure they would have made good basketball players."[20]

Clearly, such instances draw attention to the prevalence of racialist thinking about athletic accomplishment. Other commentary has been less forthright in addressing the meaning of the success of blacks in sport. In the aftermath of the firing of Jimmy the Greek, the syndicated columnist Richard Cohen vaguely suggested that civil rights activists would want to steer clear of any assessment of the racial dimension of physical attributes for fear of having to engage intellectual and psychological distinctions. Raising the issue of "political correctness," Cohen then shied away from further speculation about racial difference in sport or other endeavors.[21]

Cohen's comments nevertheless made their way into the much more purposive arguments of Dinesh D'Souza in *The End of Racism*, a book that deals with scientific racism principally by repeating its most atrocious pronouncements and ignoring its critics. Thus in a short section concerning athletics, intended to set up his selective digest of IQ statistics, D'Souza not only recapitulated the "categorical imperative"

that has long prevailed among racial scientists, he also reiterated the notion of compensation. "It stands to reason that groups that are unlike each other in some respects may also differ in other respects," D'Souza contends offhandedly. "Why should groups with different skin color, head shape, and other visible characteristics prove identical in reasoning ability or the ability to construct an advanced civilization? If blacks have certain inherited abilities, such as improvisational decision making, that could explain why they predominate in certain fields such as jazz, rap, and basketball, and not in other fields, such as classical music, chess, and astronomy." The end of racism indeed.[22]

The racial essentialism that continues to shadow much of the commentary on sport is confined neither to American culture nor to considerations of the achievements of African Americans. A 1993 article from a popular New Zealand magazine, for example, titled "White Men Can't Jump"—how ironically it is hard to tell—documented the increasing prominence of native peoples in rugby, a sport long identified with British colonialism as a means of toughening those who administered the Empire. Amid a wide-ranging discussion of changing demographics in New Zealand as well as an analysis otherwise sensitive to Maori and Samoan cultural patterns, several white sports figures speculate, first, on the innate abilities vis-a-vis the acquired skills of Polynesian squads. "Polynesian players were naturally superior to us in talent," one former player declared, "but a lot of them aren't there now because they didn't have the discipline for physical conditioning. They lacked the right kind of mental attitude. They'd just turn up and play." Said another, it was once the case that "your typical Polynesian rugby team would have just lost their head in a pressure situation. It was almost as if it was the Polynesian way to do something really stupid that gave the game away." Another passage indicates the malleability of such typologies, however. Polynesians have come to excel at the sport because they are bigger now and play a "more physical and confrontational" brand of the game. Inevitably size will win out in such appraisals: "The Polynesian is basically mesomorphic, tending to be big-boned, muscular, of average height, wide shoulders, thin waist," one trainer asserts. "They have a higher proportion of fast twitch muscle fibre which is the source of their explosive style and the reason they are fast over short distances." Contrasting feats of character to mere physicality, the article offers yet another instance where innatist constructs can be placed in comparative perspective, encouraging us to generalize somewhat about the phenomenon of racial essentialism. In New Zealand as in the United States, athletic competition has offered a way for people of color to fashion significant emblems of identity and pride as well as to challenge the discriminatory practices of old. It is a critical commentary on both social systems that those initiatives are still contested, that racialist thinking continues to qualify such hallowed notions as sportsmanship and fair play, equality and opportunity.[23]

Significantly, taxonomic conventions in the representation of population groups have long stood as the predicate of social authority. That the dominant culture can employ them—and modify them when necessary—to maintain hierarchies of privilege and subordination means that minority cultures cannot use such typologies in the same way. If the strategy of "muscular assimilationism"—a prominent element of the civil rights campaigns of the twentieth century—has not been entirely successful in creating a level playing field, it is more certain still that the separatism manifest in Afrocentrism and melanin theory is patently self-defeating in the long run. Moreover, to the extent that many African-American youth exalt athletic heroes over other role models—spending their formative years in "hoop dreams"—the emphasis on athletic striving has been overplayed. What remains is yet another troubling fact. Even as sociological surveys and a new generation of biographies and memoirs tell us about the increasingly *multiracial* character of U.S. society, the discourse of innate and immutable racial difference still looms large in the popular consciousness. A recent addition to the long shelf of pseudo-scientific racism, Jon Entine's *Taboo: Why Black Athletes Dominate Sports and Why We're Afraid to Talk About It* promises that future genetic research will provide the evidence he begs for—mainly concerning the success of Kenyan runners in the marathon and Steeplechase. Though historians, anthropologists, and sociologists shredded the book, it received a mild reception by most sports columnists, which may reveal the deep-rootedness of racial lore in America.[24]

Ultimately, for intellectual historians, cultural theorists, social scientists, as well as journalists who hope to engage entrenched modes of racialist thought and to create a more expansive conception of culture, it may be well as a first step to adopt a new perspective regarding the texts devoted to innatist thinking. Central to this undertaking would be the compilation of a roster of phrases and pronouncements that clearly links academic racism, past and present. To be sure, as we strive to move beyond category, the idea of an index of racialist literature involves a troubling dimension. Yet it is nevertheless crucial that progressive, or expansive, thinkers on the subject—rather than institute- and foundation-based conservative ideologues—become the cartographers of the contemporary discussion of race. Better still, though from a different interpretive position, we might start erasing racial boundaries altogether.

[...]

Notes

1. See, for example, Stephen Jay Gould, *The Mismeasure of Man* (New York: Norton, 1981); Nancy Stepan, *The Idea of Race in Science: Great Britain, 1800–1860* (London: MacMillan, 1982); Nancy Leys Stepan and Sander Gilman, "Appropriating the Idioms of Science: The Rejection of Scientific Racism," in Dominick LaCapra, ed., *The Bounds of Race: Perspectives on Hegemony and Resistance* (Ithaca: Cornell University Press, 1991), 72–103: Gilman, *Difference and Pathology: Stereotypes of Sexuality, Race, and Madness* (Ithaca: Cornell University Press, 1985); *idem., The Jew's Body* (New York: Routledge, 1991); *idem., Picturing Health and Illness: Images of Identity and Difference* (Baltimore: Johns Hopkins University Press, 1995); *idem., Smart Jews: The Construction of the Image of Jewish Superior Intelligence* (Lincoln: University of Nebraska Press, 1996); William H. Tucker, *The Science and Politics of Racial Research* (Urbana: University of Illinois Press, 1994). See also George Mosse, *Toward the Final Solution: A History of European Racism* (New York: Harper, 1980) and Michael Adas, *Machines as the Measure of Men: Science, Technology, and Ideologies of Western Dominance* (Ithaca: Cornell University Press, 1989); Laura Nader, ed., *Naked Science: Anthropological Inquiries into Boundaries, Power, and Knowledge* (New York: Routledge, 1996); Ivan Hannaford, *Race: The History of an Idea in the West* (Baltimore: Johns Hopkins University Press, 1996).

See also William R. Stanton, *The Leopard's Spots: Scientific Attitudes Toward Race in America, 1815– 1859* (Chicago: University of Chicago Press, I960); Thomas Gossett, *Race: The History of an Idea in America* (New York: Schocken, 1965); John S. Haller, *Outcasts from Evolution: Scientific Attitudes of Racial Inferiority, 1859–1900* (Urbana: University of Illinois Press, 1971); and George Fredrickson, *The Black Image in the White Mind: The Debate on Afro-American Character and Destiny, 1817–1914* (New York: Harper & Row, 1971).

2. See Charles Murray and Richard J. Herrnstein, *The Bell Curve: Intelligence and Class Structure in American Life* (New York: Free Press, 1994); *idem.*, "Race and I.Q.," *The New Republic* (October 31, 1994): 10–37; Russell Jacoby and Naomi Glaubermarn, eds., *The Bell Curve Debate: History, Documents, Opinions* (New York: Times Books, 1995); Steven Fraser, *The Bell Curve Wars: Race, Intelligence, and the Future of America* (New York: Basic Books, 1995); Ashley Montagu, *Race and IQ* (New York: Oxford University Press, 1995); Robert Newby, ed., *The Bell Curve: Laying Bare the Resurgence of Scientific Racism*, special issue of *American Behavioral Scientist* 39 (October 1995); John L. Rury, "IQ Redux," *History of Education Quarterly* 35 (Winter 1995): 423–38; Leon J. Kamen, "Behind the Curve," *Scientific American* 272 (February 1, 1995); 99–103; Claude S. Fischer, Michael Hour, Martin S. Anchez Jankowski, Samuel R. Lucas, Ann Swidler, and Kirm Voss, *Inequality by Design: Cracking the Bell Curve Myth* (Princeton, NJ: Princeton University Press, 1996). See also Marek Kohn, *The Race Gallery: The Return of Racial Science* (London: Jonathan Cope, 1995) and Dinesh D'Souza, *The End of Racism: Principles for a Multiracial Society* (New York: Free Press, 1995).

3. See, for example, "The Black Athlete Revisited," *Sports Illustrated* August 5. 12–19, 1991, pp.38–77, 26–73, 40–51. The prevailing representation of black and white athletes had not changed signifi- cantly, the authors discovered, since 1968, when the magazine published its first expose of racism in the realm of U.S. sport.

4. Gould, "Ghosts of Bell Curves Past," *Natural History* (February 1995): 12.

5. See, for example, Patrick B. Miller, "'To Bring the Race along Rapidly': Sport, Student Culture, and Educational Mission at Historically Black Colleges during the Interwar Years," *History of Education Quarterly* 35 (Summer 1995): 111–33.

6. Elazar Barkan, *The Retreat of Scientific Racism: Changing Concepts of Race in Britain and the United States between the World Wars* (Cambridge, UK; Cambridge University Press, 1992), 16. See Michael D. Biddiss, *Father of Racist Ideology: The Social and Political Thought of Count Gobineau* (London: Weidenfeld and Nicolson, 1970).

7. Gobineau, *The Inequality of Human Races* (London: William Heinemann, 1915), 151–3. I am indebted to Scott Haine for bringing this passage to my attention.

8. *Encyclopaedia Britannica*, American edition, vol. 17 (New York, 1895): 316–20.

9. See, for instance, Thurman B. Rice, *Racial Hygiene: A Practical Discussion of Eugenics and Race Culture* (New York: MacMillan, 1929). For historical assessments of eugenics, see Mark H. Haller, *Eugenics: Hereditarian Attitudes in American Thought* (New Brunswick, NJ: Rutgers University Press, 1963); Gould, *The Mismeasure of Man;* Daniel J. Kevles, *In the Name of Eugenics: Genetics and the Uses of Human Heredity* (New York: Alfred A. Knopf, 1985); Troy Duster, *Backdoor to Eugenics* (New York: Routledge, 1990); Tucker, *The Science and Politics of Racial Research*, 54–137; Joseph Graves, Jr., *The Emperor's New Clothes: Biological Theories of Race at the Millenium* (New Brunswick, NJ: Rutgers University Press, 2001).

10. Madison Grant, *The Passing of the Great Race; or The Racial Basis of European History* (New York: Scribner, 1916); Lothrop Stoddard, *The Rising Tide of Color against White World Supremacy* (New York: Scribner 1920).

11. The "contributionist" writings of George Washington Williams and Carter G. Woodson, for example, closely parallel those of immigrant American authors. With respect to sport, see Edwin Bancroft Henderson, the foremost chronicler of black achievements: *The Negro in Sports* (Washington: Associated Publishers, 1939) and *The Black Athlete: Emergence and Arrival* (New York: Publishers Co., 1968).

12. On Kinley, see the *New York World*, March 14, 1931. Eleanor Metheny, "Some Differences in Bodily Proportions between American Negro and White male college students as Related to Athletic Performance," *Research Quarterly* 10 (December 1939): 41–53; David K. Wiggins, "'Great Speed but Little Stamina': The Historical Debate over Black Athletic Superiority," *Journal of Sport History* 16 (Summer 1989): 162–4.

13. Dean Cromwell and AI Wesson, *Championship Technique in Track and Field* (New York, London: McGraw-Hill, 1941), 6; Wiggins, "Great Speed But Little Stamina," 161.

14. Coon quoted in Marshall Smith, "Giving the Olympics an Anthropological Once-Over," *Life,* October 23, 1964, p. 83; John McCallum and Charles H. Pearson, *College Football, USA, 1869–1973* (New York: Hall of Fame Publishers, 1973), 231.

15. See D. Stanley Eitzen and George Sage, *Sociology of American Sport* (Dubuque, IA: W. C. Brown,

1978), 300; Jay Coakley, *Sport in Society: Issues and Controversies* (St. Louis: Times Mirror/ Mosby College, 1986), 146–50.

16. See David Levering Lewis, *W. E. B. Du Bois: Biography of a Race, 1868–1919* (New York: Holt, 1993), 351–52. See Boas, *The Real Race Problem from the Point of View of Anthropology* (New York: National Association for the Advancement of Colored People, 1912) and *Race and Nationality* (New York: American Association for International Conciliation, 1915).

17. W. Montague Cobb, "Race and Runners," *Journal of Health and Physical Education 7* (January 1936): 3–7, 52–56.

18. *Ibid.* See also W, Montague Cobb, "The Physical Constitution of the American Negro," *Journal of Negro Education* 3 (1934): 340–88, and "Does Science Favor Negro Athletes?" *Negro Digest* 5 (May 1947): 74–7.

19. On African-centered social commentary, see Molefi Kete Asante, *Afrocentricity: The Theory of Social Change* (Buffalo, NY: Amulefi, 1980) and *The Afrocentric Idea* (Philadelphia: Temple University Press, 1987; rev. ed., 1997). See also Cheikh Anta Diop, *Civilization or Barbarism: An Authentic Anthropology* (Brooklyn, NY: Lawrence Hill Books, 1991); Bernal, *Black Athena*. An impressive introduction to the mode of thought can be found in Carl Pedersen, "Between Racial Fundamentalism and Ultimate Reality: The Debate over Afrocentrism," *Odense American Studies International Series,* Working, Paper no. 4 (1993). And, concerning its appeal, see Gerald Early, "Understanding Afrocentrism: Why Blacks Dream of a World Without Whites," *Civilization* (July/August 1995): 31–39. See also Clarence E. Walker, "You Can't Go Home Again: The Problem with Afrocentrism," *Prospects* 18 (1993), 535–43; on "therapy" and "history," see Leon Litwack, "The Two-Edged Suspicion," *American Historical Association Perspectives* 31 (September 1993), 13–14. For a somewhat different view of this strand of black nationalism, see bell hooks, *Black Looks: Race and Representation* (Boston: South End Press, 1992), 30.

20. On these episodes, see Wiggins, "Great Speed but Little Stamina," 179–81; Phillip M. Hoose,

Necessities: Racial Barriers in American Sports (New York: Random House, 1989); *New York Times,* March 27, 1997.

21. See Richard Cohen, "The Greek's Defense," *Washington Post,* January 19, 1988.

22. D'Souza, *The End of Racism,* 440–1.

23. Tom Hyde, "White Men Can't Jump," *Metro: Essentially Auckland,* September 1993, 63–9. I am indebted to Charles Martin for pointing this work out to me. More recently still, the New Zealand anthropologist Phillip Houghton has spoken of the ways Polynesians, such as the great rugby player Jonah Lomu, have finally reached their "genetic potential." Houghton, *People of the Ocean: Aspects of Human Biology of the Early Pacific* (Cambridge, UK: Cambridge University Press, 1996). See also Julia Leilua, "Lomu and the Polynesian Power packs," *New Zealand Fitness* (February/March 1996), 24–7, I am grateful to Douglas Booth for sharing this article with me. In broader terms, Marek Kohn discusses the "race science system" directed at the control of the Romani (gypsy) population that has in recent years been established in parts of Southern and Eastern Europe; see Kohn, *The Race Gallery,* 178–252. On issues of classification and discrimination, see also Saul Dubow, *Scientific Racism in Modern South Africa* (Cambridge, UK: Cambridge University Press, 1995).

24. Entine, *Taboo* (New York: Public Affairs, 2000); Paul Spickard (review), *Journal of Sport History* 27 (Summer 2000), 338–400; Mark Dyreson, "American Ideas About Race and Olympic Races from the 1890s to the 1950s: Shattering Myths or Reinforcing Scientific Racism?" *Journal of Sport History* 28 (Summer 2001), 173–215. The historians of science who have made the most telling rebuttals to the new scientific racists include Jonathan Marks, *Human Biodiversity: Genes, Race, and History* (New York: Aldine De Gruyter, 1995); idem, *What It Means To be 98% Chimpanzee: Apes, People, and Their Genes* (Berkeley: University of California Press, 2002), esp. ch. 6. See also Graves, *The Emperor's New Clothes.*

The sports taboo

Why blacks are like boys and whites are like girls

Malcolm Gladwell

While racial integration has progressed significantly in sports over the past century, racialized thinking, the belief among many people that racial ancestry determines athletic ability, persists. In an eloquent examination of this issue, Malcolm Gladwell exposes the fallacy of racial explanations of black athletic dominance in sports like sprints and marathons.

The education of any athlete begins, in part, with an education in the racial taxonomy of his chosen sport—in the subtle, unwritten rules about what whites are supposed to be good at and what blacks are supposed to be good at. In football, whites play quarterback and blacks play running back; in baseball whites pitch and blacks play the outfield. I grew up in Canada, where my brother Geoffrey and I ran high-school track, and in Canada the rule of running was that anything under the quarter-mile belonged to the West Indians. This didn't mean that white people didn't run the sprints. But the expectation was that they would never win, and, sure enough, they rarely did. There was just a handful of West Indian immigrants in Ontario at that point—clustered in and around Toronto—but they *owned* Canadian sprinting, setting up under the stands at every major championship, cranking up the reggae on their boom boxes, and then humiliating everyone else on the track. My brother and I weren't from Toronto, so we weren't part of that scene. But our West Indian heritage meant that we got to share in the swagger.

Geoffrey was a magnificent runner, with powerful legs and a barrel chest, and when he was warming up he used to do that exaggerated, slow-motion jog that the white guys would try to do and never quite pull off. I was a miler, which was a little outside the West Indian range. But, the way I figured it, the rules meant that no one should ever out-kick me over the final two hundred metres of any race. And in the golden summer of my fourteenth year, when my running career prematurely peaked, no one ever did.

When I started running, there was a quarter-miler just a few years older than I was by the name of Arnold Stotz. He was a bulldog of a runner, hugely talented, and each year that he moved through the sprinting ranks he invariably broke the existing four-hundred-metre record in his age class. Stotz was white, though, and every time I saw the results of a big track meet I'd keep an eye out for his name, because I was convinced that he could not keep winning. It was as if I saw his whiteness as a degenerative disease, which would eventually claim and cripple him. I never asked him whether he felt the same anxiety, but

Malcolm Gladwell, "The Sports Taboo: Why Blacks are like Boys and Whites are like Girls" from *The New Yorker* (May 19, 1997). Reprinted with the permission of the author.

I can't imagine that he didn't. There was only so long that anyone could defy the rules. One day, at the provincial championships, I looked up at the results board and Stotz was gone.

Talking openly about the racial dimension of sports in this way, of course, is considered unseemly. It's all right to say that blacks dominate sports because they lack opportunities elsewhere. That's the "Hoop Dreams" line, which says whites are allowed to acknowledge black athletic success as long as they feel guilty about it. What you're not supposed to say is what we were saying in my track days—that we were better *because* we were black, because of something intrinsic to being black. Nobody said anything like that publicly last month when Tiger Woods won the Masters or when, a week later, African men claimed thirteen out of the top twenty places in the Boston Marathon. Nor is it likely to come up this month, when African-Americans will make up eighty per cent of the players on the floor for the N.B.A. playoffs. When the popular television sports commentator Jimmy (the Greek) Snyder did break this taboo, in 1988—infamously ruminating on the size and significance of black thighs—one prominent N.A.A.C.P. official said that his remarks "could set race relations back a hundred years." The assumption is that the whole project of trying to get us to treat each other the same will be undermined if we don't all agree that under the skin we actually are the same.

The point of this, presumably, is to put our discussion of sports on a par with legal notions of racial equality, which would be a fine idea except that civil-rights law governs matters like housing and employment and the sports taboo covers matters like what can be said about someone's jump shot. In his much heralded new book "Darwin's Athletes," the University of Texas scholar John Hoberman tries to argue that these two things are the same, that it's impossible to speak of black physical superiority without implying intellectual inferiority. But it isn't long before the argument starts to get ridiculous. "The spectacle of black athleticism," he writes, inevitably turns into "a highly public image of black retardation." Oh, really? What, exactly, about Tiger Woods's victory in the Masters resembled "a highly public image of black retardation"? Today's black athletes are multimillion-dollar corporate pitchmen, with talk shows and sneaker deals and publicity machines and almost daily media opportunities

to share their thoughts with the world, and it's very hard to see how all this contrives to make them look stupid. Hoberman spends a lot of time trying to inflate the significance of sports, arguing that how we talk about events on the baseball diamond or the track has grave consequences for how we talk about race in general. Here he is, for example, on Jackie Robinson:

> The sheer volume of sentimental and intellectual energy that has been invested in the mythic saga of Jackie Robinson has discouraged further thinking about what his career did and did not accomplish. ... Black America has paid a high and largely unacknowledged price for the extraordinary prominence given the black athlete rather than other black men of action (such as military pilots and astronauts), who represent modern aptitudes in ways that athletes cannot.

Please. Black America has paid a high and largely unacknowledged price for a long list of things, and having great athletes is far from the top of the list. Sometimes a baseball player is just a baseball player, and sometimes an observation about racial difference is just an observation about racial difference. Few object when medical scientists talk about the significant epidemiological differences between blacks and whites—the fact that blacks have a higher incidence of hypertension than whites and twice as many black males die of diabetes and prostate cancer as white males, that breast tumors appear to grow faster in black women than in white women, that black girls show signs of puberty sooner than white girls. So why aren't we allowed to say that there might be athletically significant differences between blacks and whites?

According to the medical evidence, African-Americans seem to have, on the average, greater bone mass than do white Americans—a difference that suggests greater muscle mass. Black men have slightly higher circulating levels of testosterone and human-growth hormone than their white counterparts, and blacks over all tend to have proportionally slimmer hips, wider shoulders, and longer legs. In one study, the Swedish physiologist Bengt Saltin compared a group of Kenyan distance runners with a group of Swedish distance runners and found interesting differences in muscle composition: Saltin reported that the Africans appeared to have more blood-carrying capillaries and more mitochondria (the body's cellular power plant) in the fibres of their quadriceps. Another study found that, while black South African distance runners ran at the same speed as white South African runners, they were able to use more oxygen—eighty-nine per cent versus eighty-one per cent—over extended periods: somehow, they were able to exert themselves more. Such evidence suggested that there were physical differences in black athletes which have a bearing on activities like running and jumping, which should hardly come as a surprise to anyone who follows competitive sports. To use track as an example—since track is probably the purest measure of athletic ability—Africans recorded fifteen out of the twenty fastest times last year in the men's ten-thousand-metre event. In the five thousand metres, eighteen out of the twenty fastest times were recorded by Africans. In the fifteen hundred metres, thirteen out of the twenty fastest times were African, and in the sprints, in the men's hundred metres, you have to go all the way down to the twenty-third place in the world rankings—to Geir Moen, of Norway—before you find a white face. There is a point at which it becomes foolish to deny the fact of black athletic prowess, and even more foolish to banish speculation on the topic. Clearly, something is going on. The question is what.

If we are to decide what to make of the differences between blacks and whites, we first have to decide what to make of the word "difference," which can mean any number of things. A useful case study is to compare the ability of men and women in math. If you give a large, representative sample of male and female students a standardized math test, their mean scores will come out pretty much the same. But if you look at the margins, at the very best and the very worst students, sharp differences emerge. In the math portion of an achievement test conducted by Project Talent—a nationwide survey of fifteen-year-olds—there were 1.3 boys for every girl in the top ten per cent, 1.5 boys for every girl in the top five per cent, and seven boys for every girl in the top one per cent. In the fifty-six-year history of the Putnam Mathematical Competition, which has been described as the Olympics of college math, all but one of the winners have been male. Conversely, if you look at people with the very lowest math ability, you'll find more boys than girls there, too. In other words, although the average math ability of boys and girls is the same, the distribution isn't: there are more males than females at the bottom of the pile, more males than females at the top of the pile, and fewer males than females in the middle. Statisticians refer to this as a difference in variability.

This pattern, as it turns out, is repeated in almost every conceivable area of gender difference. Boys are more variable than girls on the College Board entrance exam and in routine elementary-school spelling tests. Male mortality patterns are more variable than female patterns; that is, many more men die in early and middle age than women, who tend to die in more of a concentrated clump toward the end of life. The problem is that variability differences are regularly confused with average differences. If men had higher average math scores than women, you could say they were better at the subject. But because they are only more variable the word "better" seems inappropriate.

The same holds true for differences between the races. A racist stereotype is the assertion of average difference—it's the claim that the typical white is superior to the typical black. It allows a white man to assume that the black man he passes on the street is stupider than he is. By contrast, if what racists believed was that black intelligence was simply more variable than white intelligence, then it would be impossible for them to construct a stereotype about black intelligence at all. They wouldn't be able to generalize. If they wanted to believe that there were a lot of blacks dumber than whites, they would also have to believe that there were a lot of blacks smarter than they were. This distinction is critical to understanding the relation between race and athletic performance. What are we seeing when we remark black domination of elite sporting events—an average difference between the races or merely a difference in variability?

This question has been explored by geneticists and physical anthropologists, and some of the most notable work has been conducted over the past few years by Kenneth Kidd, at Yale. Kidd and his colleagues have been taking DNA samples from two African Pygmy tribes in Zaire and the Central African Republic and comparing them with DNA samples taken from populations all over the world. What they have been looking for is variants—subtle differences between the DNA of one person and another—and what they have found is fascinating. "I would say, without a doubt, that in almost any single African population—a tribe or however you want to define it—there is more genetic variation than in all the rest of the world put together," Kidd told me. In a sample of fifty Pygmies, for example, you might find nine variants in one stretch of DNA. In a sample of hundreds of people from around the rest of the world, you might find only a total of six variants in that same stretch of DNA—and probably every one of those six variants would also be found in the Pygmies. If everyone in the world was wiped out except Africans, in other words, almost all the human genetic diversity would be preserved.

The likelihood is that these results reflect Africa's status as the homeland of *Homo sapiens:* since every human population outside Africa is essentially a subset of the original African population, it makes sense that everyone in such a population would be a genetic subset of Africans, too. So you can expect groups of Africans to be more variable in respect to almost anything that has a genetic component. If, for example, your genes control how you react to aspirin, you'd expect to see more Africans than whites for whom one aspirin stops a bad headache, more for whom no amount of aspirin works, more who are allergic to aspirin, and more who need to take, say, four aspirin at a time to get any benefit—but far fewer Africans for whom the standard two-aspirin dose would work well. And to the extent that running is influenced by genetic factors you would expect to see more really fast blacks—and more really slow blacks—than whites but far fewer Africans of merely average speed. Blacks are like boys. Whites are like girls.

There is nothing particularly scary about this fact, and certainly nothing to warrant the kind of gag order on talk of racial differences which is now in place. What it means is that comparing élite athletes of different races tells you very little about the races themselves. A few years ago, for example, a prominent scientist argued for black, athletic supremacy by pointing out that there had never been a white Michael Jordan. True. But, as the Yale anthropologist Jonathan Marks has noted, until recently there was no black Michael Jordan, either. Michael Jordan, like Tiger Woods or Wayne Gretzky or Cal Ripken, is one of the best players in his sport

not because he's like the other members of his own ethnic group but precisely because he's not like them—or like anyone else, for that matter. Élite athletes are élite athletes because, in some sense, they are on the fringes of genetic variability. As it happens, African populations seem to create more of these genetic outliers than white populations do, and this is what underpins the claim that blacks are better athletes than whites. But that's all the claim amounts to. It doesn't say anything at all about the rest of us, of all races, muddling around in the genetic middle.

There is a second consideration to keep in mind when we compare blacks and whites. Take the men's hundred-metre final at the Atlanta Olympics. Every runner in that race was of either Western African or Southern African descent, as you would expect if Africans had some genetic affinity for sprinting. But suppose we forget about skin color and look just at country of origin. The eight-man final was made up of two African-Americans, two Africans (one from Namibia and one from Nigeria), a Trinidadian, a Canadian of Jamaican descent, an Englishman of Jamaican descent, and a Jamaican. The race was won by the Jamaican-Canadian, in world-record time, with the Namibian coming in second and the Trinidadian third. The sprint relay—the 4 x 100—was won by a team from Canada, consisting of the Jamaican-Canadian from the final, a Haitian-Canadian, a Trinidadian-Canadian, and another Jamaican-Canadian. Now it appears that African heritage is important as an initial determinant of sprinting ability, but also that the most important advantage of all is some kind of cultural or environmental factor associated with the Caribbean.

Or consider, in a completely different realm, the problem of hypertension. Black Americans have a higher incidence of hypertension than white Americans, even after you control for every conceivable variable, including income, diet, and weight, so it's tempting to conclude that there is something about being of African descent that makes blacks prone to hypertension. But it turns out that although some Caribbean countries have a problem with hypertension, others—Jamaica, St. Kitts, and the Bahamas—don't. It also turns out that people in Liberia and Nigeria—two countries where many New World slaves came from—have similar and perhaps even lower blood-pressure rates than white North Americans, while studies of Zulus, Indians, and whites in Durban, South Africa, showed that urban white males had the highest hypertension rates and urban white females had the lowest. So it's likely that the disease has nothing at all to do with Africanness.

The same is true for the distinctive muscle characteristic observed when Kenyans were compared with Swedes. Saltin, the Swedish physiologist, subsequently found many of the same characteristics in Nordic skiers who train at high altitudes and Nordic runners who train in very hilly regions—conditions, in other words, that resemble the mountainous regions of Kenya's Rift Valley, where so many of the country's distance runners come from. The key factor seems to be Kenya, not genes.

Lots of things that seem to be genetic in origin, then, actually aren't. Similarly, lots of things that we wouldn't normally think might affect athletic ability actually do. Once again, the social-science literature on male and female math achievement is instructive. Psychologists argue that when it comes to subjects like math, boys tend to engage in what's known as ability attribution. A boy who is doing well will attribute his success to the fact that he's good at math, and if he's doing badly he'll blame his teacher or his own lack of motivation— anything but his ability. That makes it easy for him to bounce back from failure or disappointment, and gives him a lot of confidence in the face of a tough new challenge. After all, if you think you do well in math because you're good at math, what's stopping you from being good at, say, algebra, or advanced calculus? On the other hand, if you ask a girl why she is doing well in math she will say, more often than not, that she succeeds because she works hard. If she's doing poorly, she'll say she isn't smart enough. This, as should be obvious, is a self-defeating attitude. Psychologists call it "learned helplessness"—the state in which failure is perceived as insurmountable. Girls who engage in effort attribution learn helplessness because in the face of a more difficult task like algebra or advanced calculus they can conceive of no solution. They're convinced that they can't work harder, because they think they're working as hard as they can, and that they can't rely on their intelligence, because they never thought they were that smart to begin with. In fact, one of the fascinating findings of attribution research is that the smarter girls are, the more likely they are to fall into this trap. High achievers are sometimes the most helpless. Here, surely, is part of the explanation for greater math variability among males. The female math whizzes, the ones who should be competing in the top one and two per cent with their male counterparts, are the ones most often paralyzed by a lack of confidence in their own aptitude. They think they belong only in the intellectual middle.

The striking thing about these descriptions of male and female stereotyping in math, though, is how similar they are to black and white stereotyping in athletics—to the unwritten rules holding that blacks achieve through natural ability and whites through effort. Here's how *Sports Illustrated* described, in a recent article, the white basketball player Steve Kerr, who plays alongside Michael Jordan for the Chicago Bulls. According to the magazine, Kerr is a "hard-working over-achiever," distinguished by his "work ethic and heady play" and by a shooting style "born of a million practice shots." Bear in mind that Kerr is one of the best shooters in basketball today, and a key player on what is arguably one of the finest basketball teams in history. Bear in mind, too, that there is no evidence that Kerr works any harder than his teammates, least of all Jordan himself, whose work habits are legendary. But you'd never guess that from the article. It concludes, "All over America, whenever quicker, stronger gym rats see Kerr in action, they must wonder, How can that guy be out there instead of me?"

There are real consequences to this stereotyping. As the psychologists Carol Dweck and Barbara Licht write of high-achieving schoolgirls, "[They] may view themselves as so motivated and well disciplined that they cannot entertain the possibility that they did poorly on an academic task because of insufficient effort. Since blaming the teacher would also be out of character, blaming their abilities when they confront difficulty may seem like the most reasonable option." If you substitute the words "white athletes" for "girls" and "coach" for "teacher," I think you have part of the reason that so many white athletes are underrepresented at the highest levels of professional sports. Whites have been saddled with the athletic equivalent of learned helplessness—the idea that it is all but fruitless to try and compete at the highest levels, because they have only effort on their side. The causes of athletic and gender discrimination may be diverse, but its effects are not. Once again, blacks are like boys, and whites are like girls.

When I was in college. I once met an old acquaintance from my high-school running days. Both of us had long since quit track, and we talked about a recurrent fantasy we found we'd both had for getting back into shape. It was that we would go away somewhere remote for a year and do nothing but train, so that when the year was up we might finally know how good we were. Neither of us had any intention of doing this, though, which is why it was a fantasy. In adolescence, athletic excess has a certain appeal—during high school, I happily spent Sunday afternoons running up and down snow-covered sandhills—but with most of us that obsessiveness soon begins to fade. Athletic success depends on having the right genes and on a self-reinforcing belief in one's own ability. But it also depends on a rare form of tunnel vision. To be a great athlete, you have to *care,* and what was obvious to us both was that neither of us cared anymore. This is the last piece of the puzzle about what we mean when we say one group is better at something than another: sometimes different groups care about different things. Of the seven hundred men who play major-league baseball, for example, eighty-six come from either the Dominican Republic or Puerto Rico, even though those two islands have a combined population of only eleven million. But then baseball is something that Dominicans and Puerto Ricans care about—and you can say the same thing about African-Americans and basketball, West Indians and sprinting, Canadians and hockey, and Russians and chess. Desire is the great intangible in performance, and unlike genes or psychological affect we can't measure it and trace its implications. This is the problem, in the end, with the question of whether blacks

are better at sports than whites. It's not that it's offensive, or that it leads to discrimination. It's that, in some sense, it's not a terribly interesting question; "better" promises a tidier explanation than can ever be provided.

I quit competitive running when I was sixteen—just after the summer I had qualified for the Ontario track team in my age class. Late that August, we had travelled to St. John's, Newfoundland, for the Canadian championships. In those days, I was whippet-thin, as milers often are, five feet six and not much more than a hundred pounds, and I could skim along the ground so lightly that I barely needed to catch my breath. I had two white friends on that team, both distance runners, too, and both, improbably, even smaller and lighter than I was. Every morning, the three of us would run through the streets of St. John's, charging up the hills and flying down the other side. One of these friends went on to have a distinguished college running career, the other became a world-class miler; that summer, I myself was the Canadian record holder in the fifteen hundred metres for my age class. We were almost terrifyingly competitive, without a shred of doubt in our ability, and as we raced along we never stopped talking and joking, just to prove how absurdly easy we found running to be. I thought of us all as equals. Then, on the last day of our stay in St. John's, we ran to the bottom of Signal Hill, which is the town's principal geographical landmark—an abrupt outcrop as steep as anything in San Francisco. We stopped at the base, and the two of them turned to me and announced that we were all going to run straight up Signal Hill *backward*. I don't know whether I had more running ability than those two or whether my Africanness gave me any genetic advantage over their whiteness. What I do know is that such questions were irrelevant, because, as I realized, they were willing to go to far greater lengths to develop their talent. They ran up the hill backward. I ran home.

Manliness and civilization

Gail Bederman

The outcomes of sports contests often have social significance beyond the events themselves. This broader significance of sports contests has been often evidenced in American race relations. In this article, Gail Bederman discusses the impact of Jack Johnson, the brash black American heavyweight boxer, whose emergence as the world
champion posed a symbolic threat to the dominant ideology of white male superiority.

Remaking manhood through race and "civilization"

At 2:30 P.M. on July 1, 1910, in Reno, Nevada, as the band played "All Coons Look Alike to Me," Jack Johnson climbed into the ring to defend his title against Jim Jeffries. Johnson was the first African American world heavyweight boxing champion. Jeffries was a popular white former heavyweight champion who had retired undefeated six years before. Although it promised to be a fine match, more than mere pugilism was at stake. Indeed, the Johnson–Jeffries match was the event of the year. Twenty thousand men from across the nation had traveled to Reno to sit in the broiling desert sun and watch the prizefight. Five hundred journalists had been dispatched to Reno to cover it. Every day during the week before the fight, they had wired between 100,000 and 150,000 words of reportage about it to their home offices. Most had assured their white readership that Jeffries would win. On the day of the fight, American men deserted their families' holiday picnics. All across America, they gathered in ballparks, theaters, and auditoriums to hear the wire services' round-by-round reports of the contest. Over thirty thousand men stood outside the *New York Times* offices straining to hear the results; ten thousand men gathered outside the *Atlanta Constitution*. It was, quite simply, a national sensation.

Ever since 1899, when Jeffries first won the heavyweight championship, he had refused to fight any Negro challengers. Jack Johnson first challenged him as early as 1903. Jeffries replied, "When there are no white men left to fight, I will quit the business. … I am determined not to take a chance of losing the championship to a negro." Jeffries' adherence to the color line was not unique. Ever since 1882, when John L. Sullivan had won the title, no white heavyweight champion had fought a black challenger, even though black and white heavyweights had previously competed freely. Sullivan had announced he would fight all contenders—except black ones. "I will not fight a negro. I never have and never shall." It was in this context that Jack Johnson began his career, and eventually defeated every fighter, black or white, who faced him.

For two years Jeffries refused to fight Johnson, but when Jeffries retired in 1905, the remaining field of white contenders was so poor that the public temporarily lost interest in prizefighting. Finally in 1908, the reigning white champion, Tommy Burns, agreed to fight Johnson.

By accepting Johnson's challenge, Burns hoped to raise both interest and prize money. Johnson promptly and decisively thrashed Burns, however, and won the title. Faced with the unthinkable—a black man had been crowned the most powerful man in the world—interest in pugilism rebounded. The white press clamored for Jeffries to return to the ring, "Jeff must emerge from his alfalfa farm and remove that smile from Johnson's face. Jeff, its up to you," implored Jack London in the *New York Herald*. In April 1909, the *Chicago Tribune* printed a drawing of a little blond girl begging the former champion: "Please, Mr. Jeffries, are you going to fight Mr. Johnson?" Across America, white newspapers pleaded with Jeffries to vindicate Anglo-Saxon manhood and save civilization by vanquishing the upstart "Negro."

Eventually the aging, reluctant Jeffries agreed to fight, reportedly explaining, "I am going into this fight for the sole purpose of proving that a white man is better than a negro." From its inception, then, the Johnson-Jeffries fight was framed as a contest to see which race had produced the most powerful, virile man. Jeffries was known as the "Hope of the White Race," while Johnson was dubbed the "Negroes' Deliverer." With few exceptions, predictions of the fight's outcome focused on the relative-manliness of the white and the black races. For example, *Current Literature* predicted Jeffries would win because "the black man ... fights emotionally, whereas the white man can use his brain after twenty rounds." White men were confident that Jeffries's intrinsic Anglo-Saxon manhood would allow him to prevail over the (allegedly) flightier, more emotional Negro.

Thus, when Johnson trounced Jeffries—and it was a bloody rout—the defenders of white male supremacy were very publicly hoist by their own petards. They had insisted upon framing the fight as a contest to demonstrate which race could produce the superior specimen of virile manhood. Johnson's victory was so lopsided that the answer was unwelcome but unmistakable. After the fight, the black *Chicago Defender* exulted that Johnson was "the first negro to be admitted the best man in the world."

The ensuing violence showed what a bitter pill that was for many white American men to swallow. Race riots broke out in every Southern state, as well as in Illinois, Missouri, New York, Ohio, Pennsylvania, Colorado, and the District of Columbia. Occasionally, black men attacked white men who were belittling Johnson. In most of the incidents, however, rampaging white men attacked black men who were celebrating Johnson's victory. In Manhattan, the *New York Herald* reported, "One negro was rescued by the police from white men who had a rope around his neck. ... In Eighth Avenue, between Thirty-Seventh and Thirty-Ninth Streets, more than three thousand whites gathered, and all the negroes that appeared were kicked and beaten, some of them into insensibility. ... Three thousand white men took possession of Eighth Avenue and held against police as they attacked every negro that came into sight." Contemporary reports put the overall national toll at eighteen people dead, hundreds more injured.

Even the United States Congress reacted to the implicit aspersions Johnson's victory cast on white manhood. Before the Johnson-Jeffries fight, Congress had refused even to consider a bill suppressing motion picture films of prize-fights. The prospect of the filmic reenactment of the "Negroes' Deliverer" thrashing the "White Hope" in hundreds of movie theaters across the nation was too much for them, however. Within three weeks, a bill suppressing fight films had passed both houses and was soon signed into law.

Soon after Johnson won the championship, an even more scandalous public controversy arose: the "Negroes' Deliverer" was making no secret of his taste for the company of white women. White men worried: Did Johnson's success with white women prove him a superior specimen of manhood? The spectacle of dozens of white women in pursuit of Johnson's favor pleased Johnson and infuriated many whites. These women were mostly prostitutes, but racial etiquette held all white women were too "pure" for liaisons with black men. It seemed bad enough that Johnson's first wife was white, although antimiscegenist doomsayers felt smugly vindicated when she committed suicide in 1912. But when authorities discovered Johnson was having an affair with an eighteen-year-old blond from Minnesota, Lucille Cameron, they charged him with violating the Mann Act—that is, with engaging in white slavery. The white American public, north and south, was outraged. In Johnson's hometown, Chicago, a man threw an inkwell at him when he made an appearance at his bank. Effigies of Johnson were hung from trolley and electric poles around the city. Wherever Johnson went he was greeted with cries of "Lynch him! Lynch the nigger!" It didn't matter that Lucille Cameron insisted she was in love with Johnson and soon married him. It made no difference that she turned out to have been an established prostitute, not a seduced virgin. It didn't even matter that no violations of the Mann Act had occurred, and the original charges had to be dropped. By winning the heavyweight championship and by flaunting his success with white women, Johnson had crossed the line, and the white public demanded punishment.

The national Bureau of Investigation was ordered to conduct a massive search to find *something* to pin on Johnson. After an expensive and exhaustive inquiry, it dredged up some old incidents in which Johnson had crossed state lines with a long time white mistress. Although the government usually invoked the Mann Act only to combat white slavery and commercial prostitution, officials made an exception for Johnson. He was convicted of crossing state lines with his mistress and of giving her money and presents. For most American men, these were perfectly legal activities. Johnson, however, was sentenced to a year in prison and a thousand-dollar fine. Hoping to get rid of him, government employees tacitly encouraged him to jump bail and leave the country, which he did. For the next seven years, all Johnson's efforts to make a bargain and turn himself in were rebuffed. Only in 1920 was Johnson allowed to return to the United States to serve his sentence, an impoverished and greatly humbled former champion. The photograph of him losing his last championship bout to white fighter Jess Willard in Havana in 1915 was a standard feature in white bars and speakeasies for many years thereafter.

By any standard, white Americans' response to Jack Johnson was excessive. Why should a mere prizefight result in riots and death? What was it about Jack Johnson that inspired the federal government to use the Bureau of Investigation to conduct a vendetta against him? That moved Congress to pass federal legislation to mitigate his impact? That impelled prominent leaders like former President Theodore Roosevelt to condemn him in print? That caused so many respected Americans to describe Johnson's activities as "a blot on our

20th century American Civilization?" That caused American men to celebrate his ultimate defeat in their saloons for decades?

The furor over Jack Johnson was excessive, yet it was not unique. During the decades around the turn of the century, Americans were obsessed with the connection between manhood and racial dominance. This obsession was expressed in a profusion of issues, from debates over lynching, to concern about the white man's imperialistic burden overseas to discussions of child-rearing. The Jack Johnson controversy, then, was only one of a multitude of ways middle-class Americans found to explain male supremacy in terms of white racial dominance and, conversely, to explain white supremacy in terms of male power.

[…] In this context, we can see that Johnson's championship, as well as his self-consciously flamboyant, sexual public persona, was an intolerable—and intentional—challenge to white Americans' widespread beliefs that male power stemmed from white supremacy. Jack Johnson's racial and sexual challenge so upset the ideology of middle-class manhood that both the white press and the United States government were willing to take extraordinary measures in order to completely and utterly annihilate him.

[…]

Johnson's championship was construed by his culture's historically specific way of linking male anatomy, identity, and authority. Late Victorian culture had identified the powerful, large male body of the heavyweight prizefighter (and not the smaller bodies of the middleweight or welterweight) as the epitome of manhood. The heavyweight's male body was so equated with male identity and power that American whites rigidly prevented all men they deemed unable to wield political and social power from asserting any claim to the heavyweight championship. Logically, there was no reason to see a heavyweight fighter's claim to bodily strength as a claim to public power. Yet the metonymic process of turn-of-the-century manhood constructed bodily strength and social authority as identical. Thus, for twenty-seven years African American men, whom whites saw as less manly than themselves, were forbidden to assert any claim to this pugilistic manhood. When Johnson actually won the heavyweight title, white men clamored for Jeffries to ameliorate the situation and restore manhood to what they believed was its proper functioning.

Yet Johnson was not only positioned by these cultural constructs—he also actively used them to position himself. Embittered by years of vainly seeking a title bout, Johnson consciously played upon white Americans' fears of threatened manhood by laying public claim to all three of the metonymic facets of manhood—body, identity, and authority. During his public sparring matches, Johnson actually wrapped his penis in gauze to enhance its size. Clad only in his boxing shorts, he would stroll the ring, flaunting his genital endowments for all to admire, displaying his superior body to demonstrate his superior manhood. In his private life, Johnson also took great pleasure in assuming a more conventional middle-class manly identity, sometimes taking on the persona of a successful self-made man. In 1912, he publicly claimed the right to move into an exclusive white suburb until the horrified residents took steps to prevent him. He also dressed both his beautiful blond wives in jewels and furs and paraded them in front of the press. Johnson, who grew up in Texas, was well aware that throughout the South black men were regularly tortured and lynched for consorting with white women, and that even Northern whites feared that black men lusted irrepressibly after pure white womanhood Therefore, he made certain the public could not view his wives as pathetic victims of Negro lust. Instead, he presented his wives as wealthy, respectable women whose husband was successful and manly enough to support them in comfort and luxury.

Johnson was equally insistent upon his masculine right to wield a man's power and authority. He treated minor brushes with the law—his many speeding tickets and automobile violations—contemptuously, as mere inconveniences which he was man enough to ignore. In his autobiography, he claims (falsely, according to his biographer) to have "mingled … with kings and queens; monarchs and rulers of nations have been my associates." On a more sinister note, he physically beat and emotionally maltreated his wives and mistresses, implicitly claiming a man's right to dominate women. In short he recognized that dominant white usage prevented him from being treated as the epitome of manhood, as a white heavyweight champion would be treated. Nevertheless he scornfully refused to accept this racial slight. Defiantly, Johnson positioned himself as a real man by laying ostentatious claim to a male identity, male body, and male power.

[…]

Hot spicks versus cool spades

Toward a cultural definition of prizefighting

Gerald Early

In this article, Gerald Early discusses the racial passions generated by boxing matches which between opponents of different races symbolizing racial antagonism in American society.

One must have a mind of winter
To regard …
And have been cold a long time
To behold …
—Wallace Stevens, "The Snow Man"

As we enter the eighties and as the sport of boxing spotlights the lighter weight divisions[1] where the Latin fighters tend to congregate, a new variation on the old theme of race begins to emerge. The most important, that is, the most symbolic, battles will no longer be, as in the old days of Jack Johnson, Joe Louis, and Ray Robinson, white versus black, nor, as in the sixties and seventies with Muhammad Ali, Joe Frazier, and Ken Norton, black versus black, but rather black versus Latin. No fight could more appropriately have opened the era of the eighties in boxing than the first Sugar Ray Leonard versus Roberto Duran bout for something called the World Boxing Council's welterweight championship.

No title fight of the seventies, with the exception of the Ali-Frazier clashes and, possibly the Ali-Foreman tilt, received so much publicity as this one, or reached out so far beyond the confines of the sport's enthusiasts to excite the general public. […]

Some said that this fight would be, metaphorically, the matador and the bull—in other words, the classy boxer against the slugger; old-timers talked about its similarity to the Jake LaMotta-Ray Robinson battles; others reminisced about Carmen Basilio and Ray Robinson or Sandy Sadler and Willie Pep; those of more recent memory said the fight was a scaled-down version of Ali versus Frazier. All of these fights were big affairs, and all of them, except Ali-Frazier, were fights between men of different races. Even the Ali-Frazier fight had a deep and bitter intraracial contrast which I will discuss shortly. So in truth the Duran-Leonard fight was, quite properly, placed in this tradition. The fight was the mythical confrontation that was to apotheosize one particular minority as the underground male image of the American collective psyche. The fight was the super-cool nigger versus the hot-blooded greaseball. Here was the monumental encounter between the hot and the cool, between the classical order of technique and the romantic impulse of improvisation; the inner-city warriors at each other for ownership of the night (one as Clark Kent in a Brooks Brothers suit, the other as Chanticleer in a sombrero).

There was Duran, whose style, like that of a jazz musician, relies so much upon the inspiration of the moment that when he is uninterested in a fight he is worse than mediocre; and there was Leonard, so completely absorbed with the intricacies of his talents that with Joycean dispassion he seemed to watch the beautiful nuances his left jab made as it traveled its trajectory through the air. George Benton, once a world-class fighter, and now the trainer of such fighters as the up-and-coming featherweight Rocky Lockridge, also seemed to be just such a combatant, enamored of the artistry of his style. One imagines that Leonard could overwhelm his opponents while not even realizing that they actually existed. Furthermore, Duran represented the old, perhaps dying order of champions, the young kid who learned his art on the street and went straight into the pro ranks at the age of sixteen. Leonard was the product of AAU meets and the extensive amateur programs in this country that threatened to make the old street-corner art of fighting obsolete (just as the old after-hours jam sessions among jazz musicians are a thing of the past; now young musicians learn jazz in the practice rooms of Juilliard).

The question arises why the first Leonard-Duran fight was the symbolic racial showdown of the black and the Latin or, to put it in the vernacular of the average white, between the nigger and the spick, as opposed to the fight between Wilfred Benitez, a Puerto Rican, and Leonard, in which Leonard won the title by a knockout in the fifteenth round. Benitez, who became junior welterweight champ at the age of seventeen by beating Antonio Cervantes and who became welterweight champ before he was twenty-one by beating Carlos Palomino, certainly had credentials that were as impressive as Duran's. Furthermore, while the bookmakers made Benitez an underdog in his fight with Leonard, it must be remembered that Duran was also an underdog. The answer to our question is that Benitez is black. Moreover, he anglicized his first name from Wilfredo to Wilfred, an act for which most New York Latins, among whom Benitez was once considered a young, reckless god, will not forgive him. More important, Benitez does not fight in what we have come to think of as the Latin-macho style of, say, a Duran, or a Pipino Cuevas; Benitez is a slick, polished boxer, a counter-puncher who slips his opponents' blows very well. In short, there seemed to be no real racial contrast between Benitez and Leonard for the press to exploit and the public mind to latch on.

And racial contrast is what the male politics of boxing is all about, and it has a long history. Jack Johnson, the first black heavyweight champion avoided fighting such talented blacks as Sam Langford, Joe Jeanette, and Sam McVey during his championship reign because the ticket-buying public—that is, at that time, the white public—was interested only in seeing him fight a "white hope." Even with Joe Louis, certainly the most beloved of all black boxing champions during the 1930s and 1940s, his most important and most publicized fights were those against Max Schmeling, "Two-Ton" Tony Galento, Billy Conn, and the final bout of his career with Rocky Marciano, all of whom were white. Granted that Louis's fights with black fighters such as Ezzard Charles and Jersey Joe Walcott were certainly major contests, one has only to check the various record books and boxing annuals to discover that only Louis's matches with whites get the pictures. Ray Robinson, the great black welterweight and middleweight champion, also had his most important fights against white opponents: Jake LaMotta, Gene Fullmer, Paul Pender, Bobo Olsen, Carmen Basilio, and for the light heavyweight title, Joey Maxim.

The Patterson-Liston bout changed the racial emphasis and then the most publicized title bouts became intraracial instead of interracial. Most of Ali's important fights, unlike Louis's or Robinson's, were against blacks (e.g., Liston, Frazier, Norton, Foreman, and Spinks). This, of course, was because there were very few white fighters left in the game. Just as the Patterson-Liston bout became in the public mind—and, now, "public" means black and white collectively—a fight between a "punk" and a "bad nigger," the first Ali-Liston match became the "crazy nigger" versus the "bad nigger," and the first Ali-Frazier fight, an encounter so fraught with political overtones that many blacks cried in the streets the day after Ali lost, became the "politically hip" black versus the "homeboy." Ali never really needed to fight white men to create racial contrast for a bout since, with the help of the media, he was able to make over his principal opponents into whites by virtue of their politics or lack of politics; nearly every Ali opponent became a representative of the white establishment. Indeed, by the time of the Foreman fight, Ali had become a sort of Calvinist redeemer of the race and Foreman the pork-eating king of the unelect. [...]

Black fighters captured Ali's easily distracted attention not only because they were better than the corps of white fighters he faced, but quite simply because they were black and were rivals for the attention of white America. And after all, Ali, since winning the gold medal at the 1960 Olympics, wanted the attention of white America, not even its adoration, though to a large degree he got that as well; but its attention was what he and, perhaps secretly in their hearts, most blacks craved. He wanted to make himself so important that whites could not ignore him, to bring the black psyche out from the underground and onto the stage, the very proscenium, of white consciousness. And he felt that he could do this better than other blacks. Ironically, Ali, while playing the role of the militant Muslim, denigrated his black opponents in ways that one would have expected only from a racist white, or a black ill at ease with his collective identity. He called them "stupid," and "ugly," he said that they "couldn't talk" and that they should not be allowed to "represent the race." In short, Ali's black opponents became symbolically that marauding mass of lower-class tricksters and berserkers who made whites flee the cities in fear, and Ali, a roguish combination of Reverend Ike and Ellison's Rinehart, a sort of jive-time, jive-assed shaman, was the middle-class, brown-skinned black who kept them at bay. If on the part of these opponents there was jealousy and envy against Ali, the "crab in the basket" mentality of the poor, then on the part of Ali there was honest abhorrence of blacks who traditionally made things "hard for the race." In some ways, Ali was as much of a striver as a hard-working, light-skinned hero from a Charles Chessnut or Jessie Fauset novel.

Since the retirement of Ali no other black fighter has been able to make an effective contrast between himself and another black fighter. If two black fighters are in the ring, the white public generally ignores it, and the black public, while on a local level supporting such endeavors of black club fighters and novices, tends to feel a bit uneasy when the fight is for higher stakes, obviously thinking that "two brothers shouldn't be beating each other up for entertainment." In effect, the Leonard-Benitez fight was two black men slugging it out. In truth, racial contrast eases the painful realization that boxing is a sort of vicious exploitation of simply being male; racial contrast gives boxing matches symbolism,

a tawdry, cheap, sensational significance that the sportswriter may understate but never leaves unsaid. So with an insufficient white presence in boxing, and lack of general public interest in most black-versus-black fights, the only racial contrast that can be manipulated is black versus Latin. But the Latin must be of a certain sort.

Enter Roberto Duran, the man who, despite or perhaps because of his Indian heritage, looks both so classically and so uniquely Latin, the man with the relentless and uncompromising style—with fifty-five knockouts in seventy fights—who was champion of the lightweights for five and a half years and who exterminated the division's opposition with a degree of fury and disdain that endeared him to the television networks when they decided to recognize the existence of boxing below the heavyweight division. [...]

Very little more needs to be said about either Duran or Leonard; they became the blond and the brunette of the romance of American sports. Duran, we know, was the little tough guy from Panama who knocked out horses as a teenager, quit school at the age of thirteen after having reached the third grade, won the lightweight title in 1972 from Ken Buchanan on a low blow, then refused to honor the return-bout clause of the contract; the man sportswriter Dick Young called "the Animal" (a term he would never dream of using to describe a black fighter) and promoter Don King called "the Little Killer." Duran's bully-boy insouciance brings to mind both the late Bruce Lee and jazz trumpeter Miles Davis, both of whom were also little tough guys, who, at the height of their fame, swaggered and swashbuckled in front of their audiences as if they were preening themselves for some secret fertility rite.

Leonard is the young man who has brought, as Howard Cosell tells us, "class" to boxing. He is articulate and handsome, smiles a lot, never discusses politics, and, aside from having one illegitimate child who was later legitimized through marriage, has very little of the taint of ghetto upon him. He gives talks about good sportsmanship to elementary school kiddies and signs autographs for Jewish ladies vacationing in the Catskills. But in truth Leonard wants so desperately to become a personality, recognizable in the same way that white movie stars and entertainers are, that he seems to be holding himself aloft for the highest bidder. Leonard, in short, wants to end up like such white ex-jocks as Bruce Jenner or Joe Namath. What we are

119

witnessing is not the rise and fall of Sugar Ray Leonard but the selling of "Sugar." Leonard is such a shrewd young man that we can get no real sense of the army of people behind him; he seems to be the only *auteur* of this scenario. He wants to be liked, so he makes himself *likable* in about the only way a black person can in this society, by being inoffensive. (Ali, of course, was terribly offensive to this *Herrenvolk* democracy's taste and values, and he paid a dear price for that.) Leonard is not interested in airing his excesses or becoming, to use the 1920s phrase, "a race man"; he is not mythopoeic material. He is bland and cute, and gives the overwhelming impression of being harmless; his coolness is without subtlety, his manner as polished and chilled as a depthless lake in winter. Unlike other fighters, and most especially unlike Duran, Leonard anesthetizes the general public to the corruption and horrors of boxing because he does not look as if he came from a ghetto and gives the impression that boxing is not the only thing he can do. His presence, unlike, say, that of Leon Spinks, is not a *j'accuse* to the sport of boxing and to the society that supports it.

[…] We have become so accustomed to racial contrast boxing matches that they have become nearly meaningless, just so much shoddy and cheerless brutality, without it. The masks of racial identification that our fighters wear are similar to the masks worn by the actor in ancient Greece; they are not masks that hide, not psychological masks, but rather masks that reveal all, masks of the primitive which are, as it were, giant, lurid images of the ego beneath. Probably boxing comes closest, of all sports, to producing the primitive responses of pity and fear because the sport *is* so primitive—so naked, if you will. It is appropriate that boxing should now be the possession of the cool medium of television (boxers, like other athletes, have become "TV heroes"), where the drama has been modernized to adopt a tone of muted stridency.

So in our cultural hearts racial contrast and what is concomitant with it, racial identification, are important for the completion of ourselves. The cultural weight of the first Duran-Leonard fight is that it reinforced the emotional perception, if not the intellectual idea, that men are different physically and psychologically because they belong to different races. Despite the mass of scientific evidence to the contrary, we still secretly wish to believe that the mask we wear, namely our skin color and our racial background, like the ancient Greek mask, makes us what we are. Duran becomes the stereotypical fiery, macho Latin and Leonard becomes the stereotypical cool, slick boxing black.

Racial contrast awakens the still uglier need of racial identification, something that the ludicrous boxing film *Rocky* exploited in such an obvious, almost embarrassing way. Even today in boxing a cry can be heard that goes back as far as 1910: the cry for a "Great White Hope" who, supposedly, will save boxing for its white fans. As an example of how racial contrast brings about racial identification, consider Gerry Cooney, a promising young Irish heavyweight. Cooney has suddenly been propelled to the position of number-one contender in the official rankings of the World Boxing Council and the World Boxing Association, largely on the basis of beating a very inept white fighter named Dino Dennis. Now according to CBS Sports broadcaster Dick Stockton, the public is "demanding" that Cooney fight for the title (or, since nearly every division has two title-holders, it is more accurate to say "fight for *a* title")—a demand based on his very impressive win over once highly regarded Philadelphia heavyweight Jimmy Young. However, before Young lost to Cooney he was defeated by a young black fighter named Michael Dokes and beaten twice by a black Puerto Rican, Osvaldo Ocasio. The public did not "demand" that either of these fighters should immediately fight for the title. Nor did anyone think that the significance of Cooney's victory was more than slightly diluted by the fact that Young had not won an important fight since his loss to Ken Norton a few years ago. Apparently the catharsis of pity and fear produced by boxing is effected more profoundly when the viewer is of the same race as one, and only one, of the boxers.

World champions from the British Isles such as middleweight Alan Minter and lightweight Jim Watt disguise this urge of racial identification under the cloak of nationalism. Those of us with only a passing acquaintance with the history of Britain are well aware that the British nation is, in truth, the British race and that the British wish to stay as alabaster white as the heroine of an Ann Radcliffe or Jane Austen novel. Besides, when black British junior middleweight champion Maurice Hope has fought over the past few years, no band of brass-playing beefeaters file in the ring before the fight to play national airs and the British fight fans at ringside do not sing "God Save the Queen" with tears in their eyes—which is what actually happened before Minter's most recent defense against Marvin Hagler and Watt's most recent defense against Sean O'Grady of Oklahoma. (Some old-timers might mention Sugar Ray Robinson's black British nemesis, Randy Turpin, as an example that the English love of boxing transcends race. However, Turpin's ghastly suicide several years after his boxing career ended indicates that the love affair between him and his countrymen was short. Turpin died in dire poverty, so his death did not result, certainly, from a surfeit of public esteem.)

And now we must await the article in some leading sports publication such as *Inside Sports* or *Sports Illustrated* or perhaps in *Esquire* or *The Ring* that will ask the asinine question: Are black fighters better than Latin fighters? The article will then offer as possible evidence for an affirmative answer the recent successes blacks have had with Hispanic adversaries: Hilmer Kenty's knockout win over Ernesto España for the lightweight title; Aaron Pryot's knockout win over Antonio Cervantes for the junior welterweight title; Tommy Hearns's devastation of Pipino Cuevas for the WBA's version of the welterweight title; Marvin Johnson's victory over Victor Galindez for the light-heavyweight title[2]; Jessie Burnet's victory over Galindez to become the number-one contender for the newly created cruiserweight crown;[3] Leo Randolph's upset over Ricardo Cardona for the junior featherweight title.[4] But this current trend means nothing. American fighters are coming out of amateur programs better trained than many Latin fighters who fight out of foreign countries. As many of the South American countries improve their amateur athletics, their fighters will generally gain parity with black U.S. fighters. Furthermore, such brilliant Latin fighters as Roberto Duran, Wilfredo Gomez, Alexis Arguello, Wilfred Benitez, and Salvador Sanchez have had a great success against black fighters in the past and probably will continue to be successful in the future. Finally, outside of Muhammad Ali, the two most eminent fighters of the decade 1970–1980 were Duran and now retired middleweight champion Carlos Monzon. No black fighter, aside from Ali, dominated his

division the way these two Latin fighters did, and neither man had, through the decade of the seventies, ever lost a title fight. Let us hope that such an article dies before it is written, since the current *slight* superiority of black fighters has absolutely nothing to do with race and we need no sportswriter to make implications to the contrary in a national publication. [...]

Notes

1. Professional boxing currently has twelve weight divisions: Flyweights (not over 112 pounds), Bantamweights (not over 118 pounds), Junior Featherweights (not over 122 pounds), Featherweights (not over 126 pounds), Junior Lightweights (not over 130 pounds), Lightweights (not over 135 pounds), Junior Welterweights (not over 140 pounds), Welterweights (not over 147 pounds), Junior Middleweights (not over 154 pounds), Middleweights (not over 160 pounds), Light Heavyweights (not over 175 pounds), Heavyweights (over 175 pounds). There are currently twenty-three champions, two for every division except the middleweights, where Marvin Hagler holds the undisputed title. Every other division has a World Boxing Association champion, much to the chagrin of old timers and boxing purists who think that this proliferation of champions has diluted the significance of holding a title, but much to the joy of promoters and television networks who can create twice as many championship fights. The junior weight divisions are less prestigious than their full-weight counterparts. The rules are the same for all divisions, although the scoring of a professional bout may differ slightly in different states. Title bouts are often fifteen rounds, non-title "elimination" bouts between two top contenders are twelve rounds, and other non-title fights are ten rounds. A round is three minutes in length and fighters are given one-minute rest between rounds. Generally, a fighter trains six weeks in preparation for a fight, but in some unimportant non-title fights they may train for as few as three weeks, whereas for very important title fights they may train for nine weeks. Gloves weigh either eight ounces or six ounces.
2. Marvin Johnson subsequently lost the title to Eddie Gregory, who is now known as Eddie Mustafa Muhammad.
3. This division, not officially recognized by all the boxing powers that be, is to accommodate fighters between 175 and 200 pounds. Heavyweights would then be fighters over 200 pounds.
4. Leo Randolph subsequently lost the title to Sergio Palma of Argentina.

3.6

Sport as contested terrain

Douglas Hartmann

Though, historically, sports have often preceded other social institutions in race relations reforms, this article challenges the view that some sports always operate as a progressive social force in race relations. Instead, Douglas Hartmann argues for a more complex view of sports as a major site of race relations conflict.

Introduction

The French sociologist Pierre Bourdieu begins his well-known "Program for a Sociology of Sport" with a parable about African-American athletes in prestigious American universities in the early 1970s. Despite their seeming public prominence and importance, Bourdieu recounts (1988), these student-athletes found themselves in "golden ghettos" of isolation where conservatives were reluctant to talk with them because they were black, while liberals were hesitant to converse with them because they were athletes. This absurd situation and the vivid image Bourdieu uses to capture it serves as an introduction to, and illustration of, the argument about race and sport that I intend to develop in this essay. In many ways, the unparalleled athletic prominence and prowess of African-American athletes is one of the most striking and seemingly progressive features of a society otherwise marked by persistent racial inequalities. Yet, at the same time, it is not clear if success in sport consistently contributes to racial progress and justice. Even more problematic, there are

ways in which this sporting success actually seems to reinforce and reproduce images, ideas and social practices that are thoroughly racialized, if not simply racist.

In the pages that follow I will explore such tensions in the context of a review and critique of existing ways of understanding the relationships between race and sport in American culture.[1] These can be usefully divided into two schools of thought: those which see sport as a positive, progressive racial force and those which see sport as thoroughly implicated in the maintenance and reproduction of existing racial stereotypes and hierarchies. Rather than trying to resolve them completely, I will argue that the tensions between these two camps constitute the defining characteristic of the American sport-race nexus. More specifically, I want to suggest, borrowing from Stuart Hall (1981, see also 1996), that sport is best understood as a "contested racial terrain," a social site where racial images, ideologies, and inequalities are constructed, transformed, and constantly struggled over. It is an exercise which is intended not only to clarify our understanding of the racial

Douglas Hartmann, "Sport as Contested Terrain" from *A Companion to Ethnic and Racial Studies*, edited by David Theo Goldberg and John Solomos. Copyright © 2002. Reprinted with the permission of Blackwell Publishers, Ltd.

significance of sport but also to reiterate the deep and multifaceted ways in which race is implicated in American culture.

My starting point is Bourdieu's insistence that sport be taken seriously *and* treated critically as a social—or in this case, racial—force. The extraordinary and highly visible success of African-American athletes I just mentioned (despite constituting only 12 percent of the American populace, African-Americans comprise 80 percent of the players in professional basketball, 67 percent in football and 18 percent in baseball, Eitzen, 1999: 136–7) is just one of the reasons why it is necessary to begin from this assumption. Another has to do with sport's prominent place in the public culture and the mass media. Large numbers of Americans across racial lines interact with sport and are impacted by its remarkable racial dynamics. Making the sheer demographics of these sport-based interactions even more socially significant is the passion that practices of sport inculcate among those whose lives they touch. Often in very different ways, but to a degree with few correlates in American life, sports fans (especially men[2]) tend to care deeply about sport, and feel free to express strong opinions about sport and the issues they encounter in its social space. That so many sport discussions and debates are not consciously recognized as having broader societal causes, connections, and consequences only, in my view, accentuates sport's racial power and importance further still. Sport, to redeploy Ralph Ellison's classic depiction of the African American, is at once an invisible and hypervisible racial terrain. Finally there are the obvious parallels between dominant liberal democratic ideals (and their optimistic, color-blind vision of racial harmony and justice) and sport's own culture of fairness and meritocracy. All of this is simply to insist that the interesting and important question is not *whether* sport is a significant racial force but *what kind of a racial force is sport?* [...]

Alternative views of sport as a racial force

The popular ideology

The notion that sport is a positive and progressive racial force has a long history in American culture.

Leaders of the sporting establishment have trumpeted such claims at least since the spectacular athletic accomplishments of Joe Louis and Jesse Owens in the 1930s, and the basic empirical-intellectual foundations for the argument were laid in 1939 with the publication of Edwin Bancroft Henderson's seminal study *The Negro in Sports*. But the ideology probably reached its high point in the late 1950s and early 1960s with the fall of the color-line in professional baseball, that self-proclaimed American pastime. It was in the wake of this success that one of the most prominent African-American sportswriters of the day, a man named A. S. "Doc" Young (1963), proclaimed that Willie Mays was as important a figure for civil rights as Martin Luther King, Jr. and that Jackie Robinson ranked next to Jesus Christ among the most important and honorable men ever to have walked the earth.

Today, it is rare to hear bold and unqualified statements about sport's positive racial force (at least in part for a want of supporting empirical verification). But the relative dearth of clearly articulated and empirically supported claims that sport is a positive, progressive racial force does not mean that the notion has fallen out of favor. Quite the contrary, I believe that the absence of empirical investigation and systematic argumentation is actually evidence of how deeply held and commonsensical it has come to be in American culture. The notion that sport is a positive progressive racial force is more than just an idea, it is an ideology, an ideal that has taken on a life of its own. It doesn't need to be restated or defended. It is cultural commonsense, an article of faith held by Americans, black and white, liberal and conservative, even those who don't care about sport in any other way.

A 1996 poll conducted for *U.S. News and World Report* and Bozell Worldwide found that 91 percent of Americans think that "participation in sport" helps a "person's ability to ... get along with different ethnic or racial groups."[3] The popular frenzy that surrounds superstar African-American athletes such as Tiger Woods, or the fact that President Clinton chose to devote one of his three national "town-hall" meetings on race exclusively to sport, are both examples of the prominent and essentially positive racial meanings expressed in and through sport in mainstream American culture. So powerful and widely taken for granted are these ideas that commentators who want to affirm sport's general societal contributions routinely invoke racial examples to make their case. Michael Novak's (1976) and A. Barlett Giamatti's (1989) well-known celebrations of American sport are perfect examples. Despite the fact that neither book has much to say about race, both place Jackie Robinson's integration story prominently in their texts. Perhaps the most powerful illustration of the power of sport's progressive racial ideology came from the 1996 Centennial Olympic Games in Atlanta, Georgia. I am referring here not just to the top performances of African-American athletes such as Carl Lewis, Michael Johnson, or Jackie Joyner Kersee but more to the fact that Atlanta won the right to host the Games because the International Olympic Committee believed it would display for the peoples of the world a model of racial harmony, progress, and prosperity. These connections between sport and racial progress were drawn most forcefully in the pre-Olympic stump speeches of Andrew Young, the former mayor of Atlanta and the cochair of the Atlanta Organizing Committee who touted the Olympic Movement as the secular, global realization of his friend and mentor Martin Luther King, Jr.'s dream for a truly color-blind society.

The scholarly critique

In stark contrast to this sport-as-positive-racial force ideology stand a plethora of empirically grounded scholarly criticisms of the racial form and function of sport. Inspired by athletic activism of the late 1960s and early 1970s,[4] the primary objective and accomplishment of these works has been to demonstrate that racial inequalities and injustices are not so much challenged and overcome in and through sport as they are reproduced and reinforced there. The dominant motif is captured succinctly in the subtitle of one recent (if highly controversial) contribution to the field: "How Sport has Damaged Black America and Preserved the Myth of Race" (Hoberman, 1997).

Two very diffeient strands of research and writing contribute to this critique. One, which I refer to as an institutional approach, analyzes the racial character and organization of the sports world itself. Its primary task and preoccupation has been to demonstrate persistent patterns of racial discrimination, exploitation, and oppression in sport. This case has been made convincingly.

In their 1991 review of sport sociology, the leading disciplinary home of this work, James H. Frey and D. Stanley Eitzen summarized:

> The major conclusion of this work ... is that just as racial discrimination exists in society, [so also] it exists in sport. Blacks do not have equal opportunity; they do not receive similar rewards for equal performance when compared to whites; and their prospects for a lucrative career beyond sport participation are dismal.
> (Frey and Eitzen, 1991:513)

Exposing the deeply racialized character of sport has implications far beyond the world of sport. These are closely connected with the popular ideology that sport is a model of, and institutional symbol for, race relations in the United States. If even sport doesn't live up to liberal-democratic ideals, what does this suggest about their limits as defining standards for racial progress and justice?

Here it is worth noting that one of the most important and controversial claims of recent critical scholarship on whiteness is that liberal-democratic political ideologies are themselves inherently racialized owing to the inevitable social limitations (or contradictions) of their claims to abstract, universal citizenship. Racial categories are, in other words, built into the cultural structure of Western nationalism and liberal democracy. I don't know that we need to go this far. But my own work on the l968 African-American Olympic protest movement (Hartmann, 1996, forthcoming)—the movement most widely associated with the clenched-fist, salute given by two African-American athletes on the Olympic victory stand in Mexico City in 1968—has been directly influenced by such thinking. Indeed, I follow anthropologist John MacAloon (1988) in arguing that these athletes were initially received as villains, extremists, and traitors for doing little more than calling attention to their own blackness precisely because race was not an identity allowed by time-honored Olympic ritual (which itself is directly and self-consciously posited on traditional, Western conceptions of individuals, nations, and humanity and the appropriate relations among them). They were treated this way, that is, because calling attention to race exposed and threatened to disrupt the otherwise comfortable homologies among sport culture, Olympic symbolism, and liberal-democratic ideology. The point here (usually only implicit in most institutional critiques) is that the color-blind, assimilationist values at the root of liberal-democratic theory and much sport culture make it difficult to even recognize racial categories, much less provide mechanisms to address the structural inequalities that typically go along with them.

The second variation on the scholarly critique of sport builds from this notion, attending specifically to the symbolic role that sport plays in American culture with respect to race. This symbolic critique, which has emerged only in the last decade or so but already has some impressive proponents, begins from the undeniable and unparalleled success of African Americans in sport and sport's own widespread public prominence and power. But rather than seeing these social facts as a progressive political development (as the popular ideology would have it) these scholars hold that the powerful presence of African-American athletes in American culture may actually perpetuate and reinforce the racial status quo. This claim derives from a deep, critical conception of the role of mass-mediated, market-based cultural forms such as sport in generating contemporary racial images and ideologies. At the core of this conception is the enormous gap between highly visible and often highly paid African Americans and those of the vast majority of African Americans—and the fact that many mainstream, middle-class Americans are unwilling or unable to recognize this disjuncture. In this context, African-American athletes come to serve as what David Andrews (1996), borrowing from Derrida, calls a "floating racial signifier": dynamic, complex, and contradictory, they can be interpreted virtually any way an audience wants.

Given the persistence of race and racism in American culture, the prominence of African-American athletes thus tends to serve one of three racializing functions. One is that attention to African-American athletic success can deflect attention away from, obscure, or minimize the more general problems of racial inequality and racism. Secondly and even worse, the cultural prominence of African-American atheletes can be used to legitimate existing racial inequalities by making it seem as if there are no racial barriers standing in the way of African-American mobility and assimilation. If in sport, the thinking goes, why not in other social spheres?

The third point has to do with the claim that images of African-American athletes are thoroughly racialized, indelibly linked with the racial stereotypes that permeate the culture.

What is complicated about this final point is that it runs counter to many of our usual social and sociological assumptions about racism and prejudice. We tend to think of these phenomena negatively, in terms of beliefs and behaviors that exclude and privilege one racial group over another. Yet the images of African Americans in sport appear to be quite positive, even flattering and celebratory. The crucial point for critical sport scholars, however, is that what seems to be positive about these images tends to be exaggerated and one-dimensional, thus stripping African-American athletes of agency and working to reinforce imagined racial traits and characteristics. One of the most familiar strains of this argument focuses on the inherent physicality of sporting practices. The claim here, articulated most recently and controversially in John Hoberman's *Darwin's Athletes* (1997), is that because of sport's *de facto* association with bodies, and the mind/body dualisms at the core of Western culture, the athletic success of African-American athletes serves to reinforce racist stereotypes by grounding them in essentialized, biological terms where athletic prowess is believed to be inversely associated with intellectual and/or moral depravity. Cheryl Cole and her associates (Cole and Denny, 1994; Cole and Andrews, 1996) develop this argument in a somewhat different fashion by examining how media portrayals and the cultural commodification of African-American athletes typically exaggerate their social differences, on the one hand, and how quickly the celebration of racial difference can turn into a condemnation of social deviance, on the other. In one of her most provocative papers, in fact, Cole (1996) argues that there is a prevailing cultural logic that links, albeit by inversion, racial images in sport and racial images about crime. Sport's racial imagery thus constitutes and contributes to a rather insidious form of "enlightened racism" (McKay 1995) in which racial stereotypes and hierarchies are reproduced even as mainstream audiences believe they are being subverted.[5] In any case, the point is clear: that racism is a complicated, multifaceted cultural system which often ironically finds expression in the celebration and consumption of racial difference itself.

Criticism and synthesis

As part of public discourse, these scholarly critiques provide a much-needed criticism and deconstruction of the hegemony of the sport-as-positive-racial-force ideology. They expose its empirical limitations with respect to both internal organization and broader symbolic function. Perhaps more importantly, they show how the unqualified acceptance of such an ideology can actually serve to legitimate and reproduce dominant racial meanings, practices, and hierarchies. For all of this, however, I think these critiques have often gone too far. In making these points they have too often simply exchanged one totalization (that sport is a positive force for racial change) for the other (that it is a negative, impeding one). Deconstruction, to put it even stronger, is virtually all these critiques have accomplished. And in failing to do more than deconstruct the popular ideology, these critiques have become (or at least threaten to become) a one-sided ideology of their own, an ideology which fails to appreciate the actual complexity and possibility of sport's place in the American racial order.

Stated differently, the problem with established sociological critiques is that for all the truth they contain, they see the popular ideology that sport is a progressive racial force strictly as a form of false consciousness, as *mere* ideology. The most prominent recent variation on this theme is probably John Hoberman's argument about the supposed "sports fixation" of African-American intellectuals and in the African-American community in general. This cynical, dismissive attitude makes it impossible for academic critics to grasp why popular beliefs appeal so widely, especially among those they are supposed to injure the most. And, as many of Hoberman's critics suggest,[6] there are good, solid empirical reasons for the popular perception of sport as a progressive racial force.

Some are quite familiar and conventional: for example, that sport has provided an avenue of opportunity and mobility for African Americans; that these athletic successes, in turn, have much broader community impacts whether as a space for social interaction and community building or symbol of racial accomplishment and source of pride and collective identification; and that sport provides many Anglo-Americans with some of their most positive and important interactions with people of color. But that doesn't make them any less accurate. While it may not be perfect, sport is also an unparalleled institutional site of accomplishment for African Americans and remains one of the most integrated institutions in American life. In recent years, in fact, a handful of scholars have produced works that are beginning to coalesce into a serious, scholarly defense of these points. For example, Nelson George (1992) describes memorably how in the case of basketball, sport has become a crucial social space for the development of an African-American identity and aesethetic. This distinctive cultural style has obviously been useful in terms of its market value, but it is more significant still, in theoretical terms, for its capacity to inspire productive, creative labor among African-American young people living in otherwise alienating and disadvantaged circumstances (see Wacquant, 1992; Dyson, 1993; and especially Kelley, 1997).

None of this is to now conclude that the scholarly critique of sport is totally wrong and the popular ideology completely correct. Rather, it is to insist that the relationships between sport and race are more complicated and contradictory than sociological critics have usually realized. More than this, it is to suggest that instead of choosing between these one-sided, totalizing perspectives we would do better to blend their insights, to shape them into a broader theoretical synthesis. What we need, in other words, is a theory that is deeply and (once again) properly critical of the popular belief that sport is a pure and perfect arena of racial progress, but which is, at the same time, able to allow that sport may affect positive, progressive racial change under certain conditions, in certain social settings, and for certain kinds of racial concerns.

Sport as contested racial terrain

At the core of such a synthesis is the notion that sport is a kind of "double-edged sword" (Kellner, 1996) or what I will call, extending from Stuart Hall (1981), a "contested racial terrain." That is to say, sport is not just a place (or variable) whereby racial interests and meanings are *either* inhibited *or* advanced but rather a site where racial formations are constantly—and very publicly—struggled on and over. The racial dynamics of sport are both positive and negative, progressive and conservative, defined by both possibilities for agency and resistance as well as systems of domination and constraint.

Thinking of sport as a contested racial terrain requires more than just an abstract balancing act of competing racial forms and forces, much less a simple calculation of "positive" and "negative" outcomes. In addition it must begin from and be grounded in a broad, theoretically informed understanding of the American racial order and the place of sport therein as well as of the paradoxical ways in which racial resistance and change are made in the contemporary, post-Civil Rights moment. A comprehensive treatment of this theoretical framework is obviously beyond the scope of a brief conclusion but two points are crucial.

The first, which I have alluded to already, has to do with social context. It is that the racial form and function of sport cannot be properly understood unless these are situated in the context of a society marked by stark and persistent racial inequalities. If African Americans tend to see sport positively, it is not because they are fixated on sport or even that sport is inherently progressive. (Indeed, there is some evidence—Siegelman, 1998—that African Americans are no more fixated on sport than any other group of Americans.) Rather, it is because sport offers African Americans opportunities and resources rarely found in other institutions in the society. More than this, it helps us appreciate why sport plays a privileged and particularly prominent role in American culture with respect to race.

At the same time, situating sport in the context of racial meanings and practices broadly conceived guards against bringing unrealistic, overly optimistic hopes and expectations to our thinking about the racial form and the racial function of sport in the USA. Seeing sport in context is, in other words, a way to understand the paradoxical "golden ghettos" metaphor from Bourdieu which I used to begin this paper. A similar sensibility is reflected in the title "Glory Bound" which the sports historian David K. Wiggens (1997a) gives to a collection of his seminal essays on African-American sport involvement in the twentieth century. The point for these scholars—Gerald Early's brilliant essays on boxing (1994, 1989 [see Early's essay in this collection. Eds])—must also be included here is that there is tremendous possibility for those who are racially oppressed, but that these

possibilities are always contained within the larger structure of a thoroughly racialized if not simply racist culture.

Thinking of sport as a contested racial terrain also requires a very particular understanding of the relationship between structure and agency. Here the point involves the general theoretical insight, at the core of Bourdieu's general theory of practice; namely, that structure and agency are not opposed or mutually exclusive but in fact deeply interconnected, even mutually constitutive. This is one of the key points of my own (previously cited) work on the 1968 African-American Olympic protest movement: that as much as sport has functioned to structure and reinforce dominant racial formations in the post-Civil Rights era, the dynamics of racial domination have been intimately intertwined with and revealed by attempts at activism, resistance, and challenge. Resistance and domination, as well as opportunity and constraint, thus must be taken together.

[...] It is important to remember that it is precisely because sporting practices are so thoroughly racialized that they present much larger scale opportunities and possibilities for possibilities for social mobilization and change. This is, I think, why many of its most prominent public critics—organizations such as Lapchick's Center for the Study of Sport in Society, the NAACP, or Jesse Jackson's Operation Push—target sport: because of its prominence and the prominence of African-American athletes therein. Sport is not just a site for the reproduction of racial stereotypes and formations but also a site of potential struggle and challenge against them. It is, as I have suggested before in reappropriating Bourdieu's famous phrase, a source (or at least potential source) of cultural capital that can be directed toward larger struggles for racial justice in the USA. Again, it may not be that using sport to deliberate political effect is an easy proposition in the contemporary, post-Civil Rights era (because of the different nature of the racial structures being struggled against). But then again sport's contribution to the movement against racism in the US was never, in any case, automatic or easy. Indeed, as Jeffrey Sammons (1994) makes clear in his excellent review of the still-burgeoning historical literature, racial progress in and through sport never came easily or automatically but rather slowly and unevenly, and almost always only as the result of protracted, deliberate struggles and repressive counterresistance.

So, then, the essence of what it means to think about sport as a contested racial terrain is threefold. First, the relationships between sport and race are more complicated and indeed often contradictory than either popular audiences or sport specialists realize. Second, they are constituted within the structure of a culture that is thoroughly racilized. And third, because of sport's prominence in American culture and sport's own unique racial characteristics, these relationships have meaning and consequence far beyond the usual boundaries of the sporting world itself, meanings and consequences which can reproduce if invested with political intent—transform racial or—especially formations broadly conceived. Thinking of sport as a "contested racial terrain," therefore, not only stands as an alternative to both popular ideologies and scholarly critiques of sport's racial form and function, but is actually a theoretical synthesis of the two.

[...]

Notes

1. I focus on the African-American athletic experience both because this is the case I know best and because it is the one from which most theories of sport and race interactions derive and depart. In any case I hope that it will have much broader applications and generalizable qualities.

2. I might also point out that what I have to say about race and sport is oriented toward, if not centered upon, males and masculinity. There are many reasons for this, but the most important ones are practical and, unfortunately, may obscure many important and consequential intersections (and disruptions) between race and gender in sport and in American culture. Radio stations dedicated almost exclusively to sport talk are perhaps the more recent and most obvious example of the significance of discussions and debates that take place in and around sport. See Goldberg (1998) for a recent discussion and analysis.

3. The poll, which surveyed 1000 people by telephone in a random national sample, was conducted in May of 1996 by the Tarrance Group, Lake Research, and KRC (TARR).

4. For comtemporaneous descriptions of this movement, see Harry Edwards (1969) and Jack Olsen (1968). For more recent and somewhat more critical discussion and analysis see Hartmann (1996, forthcoming); Wiggens (1997b, 1988) and Spivey

(1984). It is also worth recalling that Edwards, widely known as the leader of the movement, was one of the leading practitioners of and spokespersons for the race-based critique of sport. Some of his ideas can be found in *Sociology of Sport* (1973), one of the first widely used sociology of sport textbooks in the country.

5. See also Wonsek (1992); Werner (1995); Boyd (1997); Wilson (1997).

6. For discussions see Sammons (1997). Smith and Shropshire (1998), and the reviews collected in symposia in the *Social Science Quarterly* (December 1998). the *International Journal of the Sociology of Sport* (March 1998), and *Black Issues in Higher Education* (April 1998). I should also note that sports fixation thesis is not inherently liberal or conservative. Indeed, Harry Edwards has long advanced similar claims. The problem with both standard liberal and conservative formulations, in my view, is their failure to situate the African-American experience in sport within the larger context of living in and struggling against a deeply racialized culture (see Edwards, 1984).

References

Andrews, David L. (1996) "The fact(s) of Michael Jordan's blackness: Excavating a floating racial signifier." *Sociology of Sport Journal* 13: 125–58.

Bourdieu, Pierre (1988) "Programme for a sociology of sport." *Sociology of Sport Journal* 5: 153–61.

Boyd, Todd (1997) "... The day the niggaz took over: Basketball, commodity culture, and black masculinity," in Aaron Baker and Todd Boyd (eds.) *Out of Bounds: Sports, Media and the Politics of Identity*. Bloomington: Indiana University Press, pp. 122–42.

Cole, Cheryl L. (1996) "American Jordan: PLAY, consensus and punishment." *Sociology of Sport Journal*. 13: 366–97.

Cole, Cheryl L. and Andrews, David L. (1996) "Look— it's NBA Showtime! Visions of race in the popular imagery." *Cultural Studies Annual* 1: 141–81.

Cole, Cheryl L. and Denny, Harry III (1994) "Visualizing deviance in post-Reagan America: Magic Johnson, AIDS and the promiscuous world of professional sport:" *Critical Sociology*. 20, 3: 123–47.

Dyson, Eric Michael (1993) "Be like Mike? Michael Jordan and the pedagogy of desire," in *Reflecting Black African-American Cultural Criticism*. Minneapolis: University of Minnesota Press, pp. 64–75.

Early, Gerald (1989) *Tuxedo Junction: Essays on American Culture*. Hopewell, NJ: Ecco Press.

Early, Gerald (1994) *The Culture of Bruising: Essays on Prizefighting, Literature and Modern American Culture*. New York: Ecco Press.

Early, Gerald (1998) "Performance and reality: Race, sports and the modern world." *The Nation* August 10/17: 11–20.

Edwards, Harry (1969) *The Revolt of the Black Athlete*. New York: The Free Press.

Edwards, Harry (1973) *Sociology of Sport*. Homewood IL: Dorsey Press.

Edwards, Harry (1984) "The black 'dumb jock': An American sports tragedy." *The College Board Review* 131: 8–13.

Eitzen, D. Stanley (1999) *Fair and Foul: Beyond the Myths and Paradoxes of Sport*. Lanham, MD: Rowman and Littlefield.

Frey, James H. and Eitzen, D. Stanley (1991) "Sport and society." *Annual Review of Sociology* 17: 503–22.

George, Nelson (1992) *Elevating the Game: Black Men and Basketball*. New York: HarperCollins.

Giamatti, A. Bartlett (1989) *Take Time for Paradise: Americans and Their Games*. New York: Summit Books.

Goldberg, David Theo (1998) "Call and response: Sports, talk radio and the death of democracy." *Journal of Sport and Social Issues* 22, 2: 212–23.

Hall, Stuart (1981) "Notes on deconstructing 'the popular,'" in Raphael Samuel (ed.) *People's History and Socialist Theory*. London: Routledge & Kegan Paul, pp. 227–40.

Hall, Stuart (1996) "Gramsci's relevance for the study of race and ethnicity" in David Marley and Kuan-Hsing Chen (eds.) *Stuart Hall: Critical Dialogues in Cultural Studies*. London: Routledge, pp. 411–40.

Hartmann, Douglas (1996) "The politics of race and sport: Resistance and domination in the 1968 African American Olympic protest movement." *Ethnic and Racial Studies*, 19, 3: 548–66.

Hartmann, Douglas (Forthcoming) *Golden Ghettos: Race, Culture and the Politics of the 1968 African American Olympic Protest Movement*. Chicago: University of Chicago Press.

Henderson, Edwin Bancroft ([1939], 1949) *The Negro in Sport*. Washington, DC: The Associated Publishers.

Hoberman, John (1997) *Darwin's Athletes: How Sport Has Damaged Black America and Preserved the Myth of Race*. New York: Houghton Mifflin.

Kelley, Robin D. G. (1997) "Playing for keeps: Pleasure and profit on the post industrial playground," in Wahneema Lubiano (ed.) *The House that Race Built*. New York: Pantheon, pp. 195–231.

Kellner, Douglas (1996) "Sports, media culture, and race—some reflections on Michael Jordan." *Sociology of Sport Journal* 103: 458–67.

MacAloon, John J. (1988) "Double visions: Olympic Games and American Culture," in Jeffrey O. Segrave and Donald Chu (eds.) *The Olympic Games in Transition*. Champaign, IL: Human Kinetics Books, pp. 279–94.

McKay, Jim (1995) "Just do it: Corporate sports slogans and the political economy of 'enlightened racisim.'" *Discourse: Studies in the Cultural Politics of Education* 16, 2: 191–201.

Novak, Michael (1976) *The Joy of Sports: End Zones, Bases, Baskets, Balls and the Consecration of the American Spirit*. New York: Basic Books.

Olsen, Jack (1968) *The Black Athlete: A Shameful Story*. New York: Time-Life Books.

Page, Helan E. (1997) "'Black male' imagery and media containment of African American men." *American Anthropologist* 99, 1: 99–111.

Sammons, Jeffrey T. (1994) "Race and sport: A critical, historical examination." *Journal of Sport History*, 21, Fall: 203–98.

Sammons, Jeffrey T. (1997) "A proportionate and measured response to the provocation that is *Darwin's Athletes*." *Journal of Sport History* 24, 3: 378–88.

Siegelman, Lee (1998) "The American Athletic Fixation." *Social Science Quarterly*, 79, 4: 892–7.

Smith, Earl and Shropshire, Kenneth (1998) "John Hoberman and his quarrels with African American athletes and intellectuals." *Journal of Sport and Social Issues* 22: 103–12.

Spivey, Donald (1984) "Black consciousness and Olympic protest movement," in Donald Spivey (ed.) *Sport in America: New Historical Perspectives*. Westpoint, CT: Greenwood Press, pp. 239–62.

Wacquant, Loïc J. D. (1992) "The social logic of boxing in black Chicago: Toward a sociology of pugilism." *Sociology of Sport Journal* 9: 221–54.

Werner, L. (1995) "The good, the bad and the ugly: Race, sport and the public eye." *Journal of Sport and Social Issues* 18: 27–47.

Wiggens, David K. (1988) "The future of college athletics is at stake: Black athletes and racial turmoil on three predominantly white university campuses, 1968–1972." *Journal of Sport History* 15, Winter: 304–33.

Wiggens, David K. (1997a) *Glory Bound: Black Athletes in White Amercia*. Syracuse, NY: Syracuse University Press.

Wiggens, David K. (1997b) "The year of awakening: Black athletes, racial unrest and the civil rights movement of 1968," in *Glory Bound: Black Athletes in White America*. Syracuse, NY: Syracuse University Press, pp. 104–22.

Wilson, Brian (1997) "good blacks' and 'bad blacks': Media constructions of African-American athletes in Canadian basketball." *International Review for the Sociology of Sport* 32, 2: 177–89.

Wonsek, Pamela L. (1992) "College basketballs on television: A study of racism in the media. *Media, Culture and Society* 14: 449–61.

Young, A. S. (1963) *Negro Firsts in Sports*. Chicago: Johnson Publishing.

129

3.7   Journalistic view

College booster bias is delaying minority hiring

Selena Roberts

The boosters of inequity, the true power brokers of college football, feel safe staring down at a football field and seeing their reflection in the skybox glass.

They take comfort in their "white-like-me" hires as a perk of owning the program with their six-figure donations. They are used-car barons and Fortune 500 executives whose contribution to higher education is not enlightenment but enwhitenment. They tailgate for ignorance.

Nearly 20 football head-coaching vacancies opened on the Division I-A level this past season, but only two were filled by minority coaches: Randy Shannon, an African-American, at Miami; and Mario Cristobal, a Cuban-American, at Florida International.

The total of minority head football coaches jumped to a pitiful 7 out of 119 programs—one fewer than the high of eight in 1998.

"You hate to say it, but so much of change is by force," said University of Washington Coach Tyrone Willingham, an African-American story of resilience. "The N.F.L. had to implement the Rooney Rule."

The lawyer Johnnie Cochran applied the pressure of shame. He helped produce an unsparing report on N.F.L. employment practices in 2002, which prompted a workplace group, led by the Steelers' owner, Dan Rooney, to require teams to include at least one minority candidate per opening, with fines for resistance.

What is good for the N.F.L.—a diverse vision with the Bears' Lovie Smith and the Colts' Tony Dungy on the Super Bowl sidelines for millions to witness next Sunday—is considered a threat to the inner circles of college football.

For years, Richard E. Lapchick has urged the N.C.A.A.'s president, Myles Brand, to adopt a version of the Rooney Rule.

"He has backed away from it big time," said Lapchick, the director of the Institute for Diversity and Ethics in Sport at the University of Central Florida. "He didn't believe the membership would pass it. My position is, test it."

The hazard to Brand is embarrassment. Failure to pass a diversity rule would reveal the sordid power structure of college football, where decisions by presidents and athletic directors are held hostage by booster bias.

To some big-wheel donors, seeking diversity means to risk losing their identity in the secret society of good ol' boys or risk losing influence in the only network they've ever known.

The Nick Sabans soothe them. Minorities make them nervous.

"It's access to power," Willingham said. "It's about asking, Is my access to power diminished because of diversity?"

Comfort level is simply code for bias. Willingham was forced out of Notre Dame in 2004, not by the president or the athletic director, but by four-leaf boosters and trustees who, deep down, craved one of their own.

On the surface, they swore Willingham's dismissal wasn't because he was a Southern Baptist who didn't convert to Irish-olicism or because he didn't protest when "Rudy" was snubbed by Oscar or because he was an African-American who looked different from their base.

Talk of race was malarkey, the Irish cried. Willingham didn't win the big games, they declared. And yet Charlie Weis, sainted by the Touchdown Jesus faithful, has been creamed from Southern California to Michigan in games that matter.

As Jon Wilner of *The San Jose Mercury News* recently noted in a comparison of Weis and Willingham: "Weis is 0–4 in big games in the past 54 weeks. Shouldn't he be held to the same standard?"

Standards are not doomed to a sliding scale. Diversity and fandom can enthusiastically coexist. Mississippi State Coach Sylvester Croom, the only black football coach ever hired in the Southeastern Conference, prepared himself to be accepted.

On Dec. 2, 2003, Croom entered a packed room for his introduction at Mississippi State. He kissed his mother, then stood up to say, "I am the first African-American coach in the SEC, but there is only one color that matters here, and that color is maroon."

He had them, every Bulldogs fan in the state.

"The place just erupted," said Larry Templeton, who as the Bulldogs' athletic director hired Croom, adding: "I'm more confident today that we've hired the right man than I was then, and we haven't won but three games a year for three years. He is going to have every opportunity to succeed. And it's not because he's a minority, it's because of the man."

Progress has moved Starkville, Miss., and yet college football is in racial regression. The better the money in college football, the more white flight there is from the N.F.L. Coaches from Saban to Steve Spurrier have bolted the pros without a cost-of-living hardship on the N.C.A.A. level.

Class barriers and perception obstacles stand like rows of tackling dummies. Keep pushing, keep pounding, say black coaches who dare to hope.

Kansas State Coach Ron Prince is one of them. Before he was hired in 2005, before his team upset Texas last season, he educated himself on the college culture. He knew about the stereotypes—like black coaches can't fund-raise—but he had faith in himself to be all things.

"These are iconic positions," Prince said of coaching." It's mostly the unknown that makes people afraid. I can tell you that Tyrone Willingham and Karl Dorrell at U.C.L.A. and Randy Shannon in Miami—many of these men I know personally—make a great impression.

"I know I have the corporate crowd in Kansas City, and I have the farmers and the ranchers in the western part of the state. And I have to be able to communicate effectively to both."

And, by all accounts, Prince has—one whistle-stop town at a time.

Exposure to diversity can vanquish fear. The Rooney Rule is proof. But what is a sign of progress in the N.F.L. is still a threat to some campus boosters. Comfort, to them, is still a coach who reflects their image in every way.

Section 4

Manning the field

Gender myths and privileges in sports—
constructing masculinity; socialization

Introduction

About one of the greatest female athletes of the twentieth century, Babe Didrikson, it was supposedly written: "It would be much better if she and her ilk stayed at home, got themselves prettied up and waited for the phone to ring." Obviously, the writer did not appreciate female athletes or their accomplishments. Didrikson, who died of cancer in 1956, won gold and silver medals in track and field in the 1932 Olympics and was one of the greatest golfers ever. In addition, she excelled in basketball and baseball. Due to greater opportunities within given sports and the pressures toward specialization and professionalization, it is almost inconceivable that there could be such an athlete—male or female—in this day and age. The closest we get are our track and field decathletes and heptathletes. Can we imagine Annika Sorenstam, the great golfer, winning a gold medal in the hurdles or the javelin? If Michael Jordan *had* been able to hit a curve ball, perhaps we'd be able to put him in Didrikson's league. And yet, as a single woman playing sports that were seen as unladylike, Didrikson had to deal with all sorts of oppressive and marginalizing comments. Once she married and adopted a more acceptable sport, golf, the media and the public seemed to embrace her more keenly. The idea of a great female athlete was accepted during the first half of the twentieth century only if she didn't appear "mannish"—a suspect woman. Even nowadays, as we discuss in the chapter on sexualities, there are issues associated with female athleticism and homosexuality.

Sociologists argue that gender is both socially constructed and constitutive of our social structure, insofar as our major social institutions—family, economy, polity—are patterned consistently and deeply by gender relations. Indeed, certain modes of performing masculinities and femininities are rewarded by the larger social structure and others are marginalized and negatively sanctioned. The most powerful of these modes, dubbed "hegemonic masculinity" by Connell (1987), underscores the dominance of men over women and the domination of a specific kind of masculinity over others. Hegemonic masculinity manifests itself, first and foremost, as heterosexual and, almost derivatively, as homophobic. Images and activities that embody strength, violence, and emotional disengagement are also aspects of hegemonic masculinity and they act as a means of distancing and subordinating other masculinities and more feminine orientations. Insofar as sport serves to reinforce this particular form of masculinity, it naturalizes and normalizes men's participation and engagement with sport and marginalizes women's. When women do participate, they are violating traditionally male-sacred territory and are contesting men's domination in this domain.[1] Women's dominant pattern, which Connell terms "emphasized femininity," acknowledges women's subordination to men and, generally, leaves women outside the athletic sphere. In this chapter, and in the chapter on sexualities, the articles document these patterns of resistance and reinforcement.

Given the dominant gender patterns in contemporary society, one can imagine that there are large numbers of boys who would never participate in sports were it not for the fact that it is *the* social thing for boys to do in many neighborhoods (see the Hartmann article below). If a boy is not particularly athletic, there are strong pressures to participate in sports simply to be "one of the guys." With video games becoming so popular, however, it will be interesting to see if these pressures change. Even nowadays, when Title IX[2] has led to an explosion in women's sports participation, there is still not the same pressure on girls to participate. Needless to say, the professional sports opportunities for men are far greater than those for women, so the incentives, even for elite women athletes, to develop additional expertise in non-athletic domains are extremely strong. For those who have fought for gender equity in sport, one of the most disappointing recent trends has been the declining percentage of women's coaches of women's teams in college sports in the US. As Acosta and Carpenter document (http://www.nacwaa.org/images/pdf/AC_29YearStudy.pdf), there has been a tremendous decline in the percentage of women who coach women's college teams. In 1972, the year that Title IX was enacted, more than nine of every ten women's teams were coached by women; in 2006, fewer than four of every nine women's teams were coached by women. Sociologically, then, the key is to focus on the gendered social structure of opportunity with respect to sport and to understand that this occurs at many levels.

Michael Messner's article on how boys and girls "do gender" in a kids' soccer league wonderfully illustrates how gender is socially constructed in a sports context. Melding interactional, structural, and cultural levels of analysis, Messner provides an excellent example of how, even as adults construct a gendered context for children, adults perceive children as simply "naturally" taking up their "proper" gender roles. As Bourdieu said in another context, "(t)he most successful ideological effects are those which have no need for words, and ask no more than complicitous silence" (Bourdieu, 1977, p. 188). Messner both demonstrates how this happens and elucidates the structural and cultural contexts within which this occurs.

Though their example uses somewhat older men and women, Grindstaff and West also show how gender is both reinforced and contested in their article on co-ed college cheerleading. They demonstrate that the men grapple with being associated with a "girly-girl" activity while literally doing heavy lifting and the women want to be recognized for their athleticism even as they are performing in support of the "real" athletes on the field. Through interesting ethnographic observations, Grindstaff and West describe the ways that men and women relate to each other and to their shared activity (there is much discussion about whether cheerleading is a *sport*) while they engage and re-shape the gender order.

This discussion of gender construction and contestation might lead one to believe that men would slip easily into practices and performances of hegemonic masculinity and that women would slip easily into those of emphasized femininity. Connell's piece on "An Iron Man" reminds us, however, that a variety of individual and social contextual factors are necessary even to reproduce a dominant pattern.

Hartmann's article on "The Sanctity of Sunday Football" also examines how we "do gender" when we play and watch sports. Rather than seeing sport as something that men "naturally" do, he suggests that sport is a place where men and boys learn particular aspects of masculinity, with which they then strongly identify. Since, as noted above, women's sports participation challenges the hegemony of the sport-masculinity equation, it is important to see the relationship between gender and sport as "contested terrain."

In the United States, there has been a revolution in the gender distribution of sports participation. In 1971–72, more than twelve times as many boys as girls participated in high school sports (3.7M to .29M); in 2006–07, the boys' advantage was only 43% (4.3M to 3.0M) (National Federation of State High School Associations, http://www.nfhs.org/core/contentmanager/uploads/2006-07_Participation_Survey.pdf). And yet, as the piece below about University of Michigan athletes illustrates, there are vast differences in the degree to which highly successful male and female college athletes *follow* sports. It appears that, even if women walk the walk, as, increasingly, they do, they do not necessarily talk the talk.

Notes

1. It is important to emphasize that hegemony is never total; even when it is secure, there is almost always resistance. Sometimes, the prominence of that resistance (especially through the media) further legitimates and reinforces the hegemony.
2. Title IX is part of a law passed in 1972 that requires any educational institution receiving federal funds to provide equal opportunities to men and women.

Reference

Bourdieu, P. (1977). *Outline of a Theory of Practice*. Cambridge: Cambridge University Press.

4.2

Sports culture and gender among undergraduates

A study of student-athletes and students at the University of Michigan

Andrei S. Markovits and David T. Smith

In this study, Markovits and Smith examine differences in men's and women's orientations to "follow sports." Using a sample of undergraduates (both athletes and non-athletes) at the athletic powerhouse University of Michigan, the authors explore the degree to which the students are oriented to sports in their daily lives. Using multiple indicators (for example, TV watching, live attendance at sports events, wearing logo clothing, sports knowledge, etc.), the authors show a rather large divide between men's and women's orientations to following sport. At the same time, there's much more overlap than one might expect.

The context

Our project has a well-established intellectual pedigree and forms an essential component of a larger academic concern. Since the late 1980s, Andrei Markovits has worked on what he has called "sports cultures" by which he has meant the large framework wherein people "follow" sports.[1] As such, his work has concentrated more on the consumption of sports—their "followers" or fans or supporters—as opposed to their production, that is their "doers," their participants.

To be sure, there has always existed a major overlap between "followers" and "doers." People follow sports in good part because they also played them at some point in their lives or continue to do so, even on a rudimentary and amateurish level. However, this link has become ever more tenuous, particularly regarding the very few sports that comprise a society's "sports culture." Crudely put, one need not have played one second of football in one's life to have developed into a rabid and highly knowledgeable football fan. Indeed, most American football fans have never played football on any level, let alone the two levels that define football's presence in America's sports culture: the National Football League and college. And this characteristic pertains to all other modern sports that comprise a society's "sports culture." As a major marker of modernity in sports, the followers have gradually—and massively—come to outnumber the doers. More important still, it is the followers that really define what Markovits has called a society's "hegemonic sports culture" that comprises its "sports space."[2]

Hegemonic sports cultures do not only differ by geography and history, but also by factors such as gender, age, class, religion and ethnicity. They may be compared to languages. Just like with languages, the earlier one learns and internalizes these cultures, the better one knows and speaks them, the more one appreciates their nuances, the greater an expert one becomes. Just like languages, these sports cultures create communities which include as well as exclude.

Andrei S. Markovits and David T. Smith, "Sports Culture Among Undergraduates: A Study of Student-Athletes and Students at the University of Michigan" from *Michigan Journal of Political Science* II, no 9 (Spring 2008), www.mjps.org. Reprinted with permission.

American sports languages have remained largely confined to the North American continent and have by and large excluded North Americans from the absolute lingua franca of global sports cultures—the world of soccer. Moreover, these sports cultures—like all other languages—have been massively gendered. Until recently, women were much less advanced and skilled sports speakers than men; and now that they have acquired the cognitive structures of these sports languages and become skillful in them, it seems that they use them quite differently, in their own voice so to speak.[3]

To explore this idea, Markovits surveyed 845 University of Michigan students during Academic Year 2002/3. The questionnaire attempted to tap such questions as: Did male and female Michigan students exhibit marked differences in their respective sports cultures? Did other social characteristics of Michigan students lead to variations in sports cultures? If so, how did they and why? If not, what explained their commonalities?[4]

With the main focus of our study being the real or putative differences in how gender continues to shape the consumption of sports—especially of what we have termed "hegemonic sports culture"—we searched the literature for studies that featured analyses in the perception of sports by male and female fans mainly in the United States, particularly among university-age cohorts. It is to a very brief review of some relevant literature that we now turn.

Literature review

Jeffrey James and Lynn Ridinger undertook a study among sports fans to examine gender differences in the reasons for enjoying sports.[5] In their survey of fans at men's and women's college basketball games at a large Midwestern University, the researchers randomly selected fans to complete a questionnaire regarding their consumption of sports and the reasons for doing so. The main finding from this questionnaire was that men and women define "sport fan" very differently. Whereas men may consider themselves fans of a sport in general and derive part of their social identity in being a fan of that sport (or sports in general), the study suggests that women may think of themselves as fans of a specific team, rather than general sports fans. However, despite these

obvious gender differences in sports consumption, it also appears that men and women consume sports (as observers rather than players) for similar reasons: enjoying the action of games and as an escape from the routine of daily life.

In another study, Dietz-Uhler *et al.*[6] concluded that being a sport fan was more important for the identity of males as individuals and as a collective than it was for females who found sports to be a time and venue for social bonding.

There can be no doubt that Title IX has played an absolutely essential role in the completely changed gender relations that have informed most aspects of college sports in the United States. Studies on this topic are far too numerous and important to be listed cursorily in our context. Still, we would like to mention two particularly relevant ones to our own concern that highlight the advances that women have made in this area but also emphasize the setbacks they have experienced and the continued hurdles they will still need to overcome.

A study conducted by Vivian Acosta and Linda Jean Carpenter investigates the impact of Title IX for female athletes competing in the NCAA.[7] The authors examine the changing levels of female participation, coaching, and sports administrators for women's sports between 1977, the year before Title IX was required to be implemented by all schools, and 1998.

Overall, the researchers find that female participation in intercollegiate athletics has steadily increased over the two decade period that constitutes their study. Yet, over that same period of time, the number of female coaches in women's sports has been decreasing as has the number of female administrators for women's athletic programs. The number of women coaching men's teams has remained the same. However, this phenomenon is less pronounced for Division III schools. These data suggest that as women's sports programs become better funded, better known and socially more acceptable to mainstream sports culture which—of course—remains heavily male, men develop a greater interest in and genuine appreciation of these women's programs possibly to the extent of pushing women out of leadership positions that was formerly their domain prior to the passage of Title IX.

In a fascinating study pertaining to the different (re)presentation and depiction of male and female sports by colleges that belong to the National Collegiate Athletic Association

139

(NCAA), without any doubt *the* leading body of American college sports. Jo Ann Buysse and Melissa Embser-Herbert studied the portrayals of female college athletes on the front covers of media guides published by NCAA-affiliated colleges.[8] The researchers commenced with the premise that the way a college or university portrays athletes on the front cover of its media guides embodies a solid measure as to how that institution in particular—but by dint of college sports' prominent position in American culture the American sports establishment as a whole—perceives athletes and their gender. The authors sought to discover as to whether gender stereotypes existed in these publications. Their analysis of 307 covers from 1990 and 314 from 1997 featured a careful study of the setting, dress, and positioning of the athletes as well as the theme (degree of athleticism) of the cover photograph(s).

Overall, males were more frequently portrayed in uniform and in athletic poses than women in both 1990 and 1997. Pictures of female athletes tended to focus less on their athleticism and more on their beauty and other attributes. The authors regarded this situation as a continuing marginalization of female athleticism and the preservation of "sport as a primary area of ideological legitimation for male superiority through gender differentiation and as represented in the cover photographs of these media guides."[9]

In a detailed review of the literature on leisure sciences (including sports), sociology, marketing, and history from a feminist perspective, Lee McGinnis, Seungwoo Chun and Julia McQuillan demonstrate the unabatedly gendered depiction of virtually all themes in these areas which—needless to say—have not been favorable to women.[10] To be sure, in the world of sports the presence of females as athletes and fans has massively increased in the United States for both live sporting events and those conveyed by the sports media. Advertisers and merchandisers have recognized women as true fans and have begun to market to them accordingly. However, as women begin to "intrude" on traditionally male "turf" by becoming fans of such "male" sports as football and NASCAR, many men resent and resist this intrusion. The authors argue that in the ensuing defense of their domain, men harness seemingly complex "sports talk" to exclude women. Moreover, the researchers submit that the division of participation in sports by gender serves to maintain male resistance to the incorporation of women into the sports domain.

Among female athletes at the collegiate level, Title IX has not yet attained complete equality. McGinnis, Chun, and McQuillan cite the lower salaries of female coaches in NCAA-affiliated institutions and the smaller presence of female involvement with collegiate sports when measured against the percentage of females in the university population, all of which suggest to the authors that the male domination of sports in the media and in society still continues. Lastly, the authors argue that the objectification of women in sports media has led to their continued weakness in the realm of athletics. Objectification includes the posing of female athletes like swimsuit models, the hawking of beauty products in female athletic magazines, and discussion of female athletes in childlike terms (such as the vulnerability of female gymnasts or ice skaters).

The Taylor Research and Consulting Group conducted a study in 2001 tracking the gender differences in sporting habits among children.[11] While older boys (aged 14 to 18) were found to spend the most time on sports, a lot of time revolves around sports for girls aged 9 to 18 as well. Interestingly, young girls and older boys were found to have similar sports habits—enjoying the competition of sports and wanting to be a professional athlete more than older girls or younger boys. The explanation for the similarity in these two groups appears to have a generational or life cycle dimension. The generational aspect accounts for the growth in female athletic role models. The life cycle explanation suggests that as girls grow older, they decrease their interest in all aspects of sports, while as boys age, their interest in sports increases, perhaps due to social factors as suggested by a study of female ice hockey fans in the United Kingdom that corroborates the gendered "language" of sports well beyond the United States and well beyond the sports that comprise a country's "hegemonic sports culture".

Garry Crawford and Victoria Gosling conducted 37 interviews with ice hockey fans in the UK over three years of audience observation at both British and American ice hockey games. Interviewees were attracted and awarded with a signed team jersey. From the respondents, a representative group covering the full range of fans was chosen for interviews.[12]

Female fans were mainly attracted to ice hockey for the safety and accessibility of the games. They tended to be young (in their 20s and 30s) and to bring children to the games. The safety of the events, the lack of hooliganism in the arenas, meant that the sport lacked the fear and hostility found in other mass-spectator sports, particularly football, better known as soccer in the United States. Male fans often viewed female fans as inauthentic, or "puck bunnies," believing that their primary reason to attend the games was to ogle the players rather than appreciate the sport. In the opinion of one male interviewee, "sport's a man-thing, they make it girlie."[13] The authors view the changing composition of sports fans as a process of global bourgeoisification and commercialization; newer sports lack the working-class traditions of the older, more established, sports and thus are more accessible to women and become more middle-class. The authors give soccer in the United States as an example of the phenomenon of newer sports being more accepting of female fans. Indeed, as Markovits has demonstrated in a number of his studies on soccer in the United States and Europe, in both contexts new challengers to the hegemonic sports cultures and established languages are vilified by the insiders (overwhelmingly men) as "feminine," hence inauthentic and undesirable.[14] Soccer, arguably the most macho sport in Europe and much of the world, continues to be derided in the United States as a woman's sport. Conversely, ice hockey, baseball, basketball and even American football are stigmatized by "manly" European "footballers" as effeminate. Thus, the gender ascribed to a sport by the relevant male sport establishment has nothing to do with the sport's purported toughness and everything with its potential challenge to the existing cultural order. The marginalization and delegitimation of a potentially threatening newcomer to the established hegemonic sports culture occurs everywhere via the following well-worn trifecta: it is boring, it is easy, and it is womanly.

We now turn to the presentation of our own study and its findings by commencing with a brief description of our sample.

The sample

In total, 845 students participated in the survey. This included 398 men and 447 women; 434 athletes and 411 non-athletes. Table 4.2.1 shows how our sample fits into four groups, defined by these two dimensions.

Table 4.2.1.

	Male	Female
Athlete	209	225
Non-Athlete	189	222

The athlete sample comprised most members of 24 out of 25 of Michigan's varsity teams (the only team absent was football). Table 4.2.2 shows how our athlete sample is distributed across sports.

Table 4.2.2.

Sport	Number of respondents[15]
Baseball	30
Men's basketball	16
Women's basketball	10
Men's cross-country/track	40
Women's cross-country/track	50
Field hockey	23
Men's golf	8
Women's golf	11
Men's gymnastics	12
Women's gymnastics	24
Ice hockey	41
Women's rowing/crew	28
Men's soccer	19
Women's soccer	19
Softball	19
Men's swim/dive	18
Women's swim/dive	2
Men's tennis	10
Women's tennis	8
Volleyball	13
Water polo	17
Wrestling	21

The non-athlete sample comes from four sources. Three of these were classes in which the survey was distributed to students—a freshman introductory sociology class, Markovits' "Sport and Society" class (Sociology 212), and a German history class. The fourth source was the Excel Copy Center on South University, Ann Arbor, where copies of the survey were deposited for students waiting in line. At the beginning of each semester, many students visit the copy center to obtain course-packs, and frequently they encounter very long lines. To the usual distractions of reading, listening to music and chatting, we added the opportunity to participate in the survey—an opportunity taken by more than one hundred students. Table 4.2.3 shows exactly how many respondents came from each group in our non-athlete sample.

Table 4.2.3.

Group	Number of respondents
Sociology 100—Introduction to Sociology	154
Sociology 212—Sport and Society	120
History 171—German History	25
Excel Copy Center	112

This sample, then, comprises only undergraduates, and is weighted heavily towards students in the College of Literature, Science and Arts—the University of Michigan's main undergraduate liberal arts college—especially the social sciences. All three classes surveyed were undergraduate social science classes, and Excel caters almost exclusively to undergraduates from the College of Literature, Science and Arts. It must also be borne in mind that there exists a large component of students from the sociology of sport class, whom we would expect to be a "self-selecting" group with greater interest in and knowledge of sport than the general student body. We believe that our sizeable sample represents a valuable and telling segment of the University of Michigan's undergraduate student population, but in no way do we claim that it constitutes a representative sample of the general undergraduate student population of this institution.

Our findings

We think it is appropriate to classify our findings into two broad categories:

1 The raw facts about sports culture at the University of Michigan—how often students attend sporting events, how often they watch sports on television, who their favorite professional teams and players are, and how they participate in supporting teams in the state of Michigan. This in itself should be intriguing to anyone interested in how students experience and enjoy sports on one of America's great academic and athletic campuses.

2 The differences between groups of students in the way that they consume and enjoy sports culture. In particular, we are interested in the differences between men and women, between athletes and non-athletes, and between different teams among the athletes.[16] While the pure facts about Michigan's sports culture may be particular to its time and place—such as the prevalence of Detroit-based teams among student favorites, or the fact that male students watch eight hours of sport a week on television—the differences among groups of Michigan students are differences we may expect to find among undergraduates on other college campuses and even in broader American society. Thus the large gap in knowledge about professional sports that we find between men and women, or the greater tendency of athletes to prefer highlights shows to other televised sports, are differences that probably persist beyond the confines of our university. While Michigan students might well be different from the rest of the country's population in any number of ways, there is no particular reason to believe that the differences *among groups* of Michigan students should not be reflective of differences in broader society.

Some of the differences we find raise some intriguing questions. Do women just not like professional sports, or do they think about them and enjoy them in different ways from men? Might sports culture, in the sense of it being the most dedicated and committed form of sports consumption, be better reflected in the following of professional rather than college sports? Put differently, might the involvement with Michigan teams and college sports among Michigan undergraduates not say more about these students' involvement in campus life and college culture than about their knowledge of and involvement with sports? Does the popularity of highlights show—as opposed to the telecast of entire games—among athletes affect the way that they play the game? Complete answers to these questions are beyond the scope of this report, but we are reasonably confident that our investigations allowed us to draw interesting and valid conclusions that—we hope—will lay the foundations for future inquiries along the lines suggested by our research into the nature of sports, and their relationship to American society and culture.

Throughout the study, we employ the well-known and helpful statistical tool of *confidence intervals*. A confidence interval, which will probably be familiar to readers from opinion polls, is a "bracket" that envelops a result such as a mean. For example, around our finding that women on average watch 3.2 hours of sport per week, we have a confidence interval of 2.8 to 3.6 hours. Because we recognize that we may get a different result from a different sample, the confidence interval, set at a "significance level" of 5%, shows us the range in which we would expect to find our answer in 95% of the samples we could take. When we are examining differences among groups, a difference is only *significant* if the confidence intervals for each group do not overlap—in other words, only if we were sure that we would find the same difference in the vast majority of the samples that we would take.

Men and women

On the night of June 8th, 2005, the University of Michigan became the first college east of the Mississippi ever to win the NCAA World Series of college softball. As Jennie Ritter and the Michigan women dueled with two-time defending champions UCLA in a gripping, extra-innings Game 3 in Oklahoma City, back in Ann Arbor a crowd of about twenty gathered at Scorekeepers bar to follow the contest on ESPN. This was not a bad turnout, given that the game occurred on a weeknight during summer vacation. One of the authors of this study, David Smith, was among those present at Scorekeepers, and something struck him as surprising—of the twenty who had come to the bar that night to watch this event in women's sporting event, nineteen were men.

This seemed to be solid and prima facie confirmation of something that is widely known—that men are more "into sport" than women. But this knowledge needs some closer examination. Although most people would probably report from personal experience that men watch more sport, get more excited by it and know much more about it than women, few would be able do so with reference to any hard data to substantiate their anecdotes. Indeed, there is very little data available that contain such information, and we are pleased now to be able to present at least some. Even so, careful examination of these data reveals that the matter is not so clear cut.

Attendance

One of the questions in our survey was how many hours a week students spent attending live sporting events. It may be surprising to see that there is very little difference here between women and men. In fact, the difference is not statistically significant.

Table 4.2.4. Hours of live sport attended

Gender	Mean	95% Confidence interval	Number of respondents
Male	3.0	2.6–3.4	361
Female	2.7	2.3–3.1	400

It seems reasonable to assume that the sporting events most of the students had in mind when responding to this question were college sporting events, as, living in Ann Arbor, these would be the main events that students would have the opportunity to attend (around 40% of students reported that they had no access to a car). Although there are many disparities between men and women in their consumption of sports, these numbers powerfully illustrate that attending college sports—especially, we suggest, attending football games at the University of Michigan—is a vital ceremony for students regardless of gender. Attending Michigan football games is a ritual of college life on campus that very few University of Michigan undergraduates permit themselves to miss, even if they are not particularly interested in football of any sort. Going to a Michigan game thus says very little about any Michigan student's involvement with sports culture of any kind and at any level. Our numbers also suggest that *under the right circumstances*, women enjoy watching sports just as much as men, but the circumstances under which they enjoy it seem to be narrower, on average, than the circumstances under which men enjoy watching sports.

The importance of Michigan's athletic reputation

The ritual of watching college sports, which involves the formation of deep, lifelong loyalties, is something that has to be experienced to be appreciated. As an illustration of this, to gauge how students felt about college sports before they got to college, we asked them on a scale of 1 to 7 how much "the history of Michigan's athletic reputation" influenced their decision to come to Michigan. For non-athletes, the average male score is about 4.1 and the average female score 3; this difference is statistically significant.

Table 4.2.5. Importance of Michigan's athletic reputation to non-athletes

Gender	Mean (on 1–7 scale)	95% Confidence interval	Number of respondents
Male	4.1	3.8–4.4	189
Female	3.0	2.7–3.2	221

For athletes, among whom we would expect more convergence on this question, the difference is still statistically significant.

Table 4.2.6. Importance of Michigan's athletic reputation to athletes

Gender	Mean (on 1–7 scale)	95% Confidence interval	Number of respondents
Male	5.4	5.2–5.6	208
Female	4.7	4.5–4.9	223

The fact that there is a significant gender difference among athletes here is important. We might expect that athletes, regardless of gender, would attach similar levels of importance to the

athletic reputation of the college they choose to attend. This cultural difference between men and women, however, is apparently so strong that we observe it even where we would least expect to find it—among athletes.

Involvement at sporting events

Women tend not to get as noisily involved at sporting events, at least not in their own estimation, as do men. One survey question asked "On a scale from 1–7, how involved are you at a sporting event (i.e. scream with profanity, argue with refs, participate in cheers, etc." 1 was "very quiet" and 7 was "very noisy"). This table gives the complete distribution of answers, and shows that men consider themselves to be noisier at sporting events.

Table 4.2.7. Degree of involvement at live sporting events (numbers of fans)

Gender	1 (very quiet)	2	3	4	5	6	7 (very noisy)	Mean
Male	17	41	51	65	99	61	50	4.48
Female	12	54	73	116	112	51	16	4.11

The difference in means is statistically significant here, and we can also observe that fewer women place themselves in the highest registers.

Watching televised sports

Now we turn our attention to the world of sports beyond the campus. The most typical way in which an American experiences sports is by watching them on television. Although various TV networks cover college sports extensively, the greater overall focus is on professional sports, and even a student who only watched college sports on television would more than likely be watching teams other than those of his or her own college. Students' consumption of televised sports, then, is a measure of their engagement with the broader culture of American sports, over and above the sports experiences of college life. Our data make it obvious that men are much more engaged in this culture than women. On average, men watch about eight hours of sport on television per week, while women watch just over three. This difference is large and significant.

Table 4.2.8. Hours per week watching sports on television

Gender	Mean	95% Confidence interval	Number of respondents
Male	8.0	7.2–8.9	384
Female	3.2	2.0–3.6	418

Discussing sports

Another important feature of the broader sports culture is discussion of sports. One question asked students which level of sports they discussed most—college, professional, high school or other. The overall response is that 67% discuss college sport the most while 33% discuss professional sport the most. As about half the members of our sample are college athletes whom we would naturally expect to spend more time discussing college than professional sport, to make general inferences about college students we should look at the non-athlete sample. Here we find that 51.5% discuss college sports the most and 36.5% discuss professional sports the most. Breaking this group down by gender, we find that more non-athlete males discuss college sports than professional sports (though this lead is not statistically significant), while non-athlete females discuss college sports more than professional sports at a rate of more than two to one. This finding, of course, bespeaks again that, for women, discussing college sports is part of their college experience not of their sports culture. The cultural "space" that female students make for sports in their lives is far more likely, therefore, to be directly related to their college experience than that of men, who show equal or more interest in non-college sports. Once again, it may be useful to look at the athlete sample because we would expect fewer differences among athletes on this question. Overall, athletes are indeed more likely to discuss college sports rather than professional sports the most, at 81% to 27% respectively. Breaking this group down by gender, we find the difference to be more, rather than less, pronounced: over 91% of female athletes discuss college sports the most, while

the figure for male athletes is 70%. This lends some evidence to the notion that women "do" sports whereas men "follow" them. Knowing and following a team such as the Detroit Lions shows a commitment to the broader American sports culture that does not necessarily come with following the University of Michigan's football team. The following table summarizes all of these results, and their relevant confidence intervals.

Table 4.2.9. Level of sports discussed most[17]

Group	% College (with confidence int.)	% Professional (with confidence int.)	Number of respondents
Overall	67.2 (63.9–70.4)	32.8 (28.6–34.9)	822
Non-athletes	51.6 (46.6–56.6)	36.6 (31.8–41.4)	388
Male non-athletes	45.9 (38.5–53.2)	49.7 (42.2–57.2)	181
Female non-athletes	56.3 (49.5–63.1)	25.2 (19.3–31.2)	206
Athletes	81.1 (77.4–84.8)	27.4 (23.2–31.6)	434
Male athletes	69.9 (63.6–76.1)	43.0 (36.3–49.8)	209
Female athletes	91.5 (87.8–95.2)	12.5 (8.1–16.9)	224

Logo clothing

A particularly intriguing aspect of sports culture is the wearing of logo clothing. The importance of logo clothing to the Michigan experience would be obvious to anyone who has been in Ann Arbor on a game day, or who has counted the number of shops in downtown Ann Arbor devoted solely to Michigan merchandise (at least five by our count). Michigan may well have marketed its logo clothing more effectively than any other college nationally—and beyond. David Smith, co-author of this study remembers being bewildered, at the age of thirteen, when Michigan baseball caps arrived in stores in his hometown of Sydney, Australia. Although Australians had long been moderate consumers of the logo clothing of American professional teams, American college teams were unknown in Australia before Michigan merchandise first arrived in the early nineties.

A *USA Today* article (http://www.usatoday.com/sports/college/basketball/men/02tourney/2002-03-27-cover-fab5.htm) documents the heady increase in revenues that the University enjoyed during this period, based largely on the success of Michigan's highly influential basketball team.

It is unsurprising, then, that nearly all Michigan students surveyed should report owning some collegiate logo clothing (the question did not specify which college, but it seems a fair assumption that most would own Michigan clothing). Men and women own collegiate logo clothing in about the same numbers. It is equally predictable that men own professional logo clothing at a substantially greater rate than women—this is consistent with our other data which suggest that men and women participate equally in the campus sports culture, but very differently in the broader sports culture.

Table 4.2.10. Own logo clothing

Gender	% own Collegiate clothing	% own professional clothing	Number of respondents
Male	94.5 (92.2–96.8)	83.2 (79.5–87.0)	382
Female	92.5 (90.1–95.0)	58.8 (54.2–63.5)	430

More surprising are the responses as to when and where students wear their logo clothing. While equally few men and women wear it as ordinary casual clothing (or never wear it at all), significantly more women than men wear logo clothing when watching televised games, and more women than men in our sample also wear logo clothing at live games (this difference is almost, but not quite, statistically significant).

Table 4.2.11. Wear logo clothing

Gender	Never	As ordinary casual wear	To watch televised events	To live events
Male	4.3% (2.3–6.3)	15.1 (11.5–18.6)	28.6 (24.2–33.1)	30.4 (25.9–34.9)
Female	4.7% (2.7–6.7)	10.1 (7.7–13.4)	39.1 (34.5–43.6)	38.2 (33.7–42.7)

What does this mean? Why are women more conspicuous wearers of logo clothing than men, though in nearly every other facet of sports culture they are less involved than men? We cannot make any general conclusions from our sample, but we may hypothesize that logo clothing, for women, with its distinctive team labels and colors, is a way of *visually* identifying themselves as fans. This is all the more important because women participate less than men in other areas of sports culture—especially, as we shall see, in accumulating trivia—and so may be considered "outsiders" within this culture.

Studies have shown that clothing is a crucial marker for out-groups to get accepted by in-groups. Clothing constitutes a very important outward marker of identifying with a group, an event—a culture—and it clearly signifies a sense of belonging. We also know that most out-groups tend to overcompensate when they try to gain access to in-groups precisely because their access is not taken for granted and is always frowned upon and viewed suspiciously by the insiders. Thus, to be accepted as equals by the already present group which, of course, completely defines all the terms of the discourse—to be genuinely regarded as "inside baseball" (to use an appropriate vernacular of American English, in which sports metaphors are more commonly used than in any other major language)—outsiders overcompensate on the terms demanded by insiders. Men's fluency in the language of sports culture needs no outward affirmation. It is assumed by all. For women, however, this is not the case. Women still have to prove to men—and to themselves—that they, too, have acquired fluency in the language of sports culture. One signifier of that language is wearing sports paraphernalia. As is well known from Barry Levinson's film "Diner," in which the main protagonist will only marry his bride if she passes a detailed trivia test about the then still Baltimore Colts, men need constant proof from women that women are really serious about sports; that they pass the audition; that they have mastered the language, so to speak. So women who care about learning the language of sports culture which is totally masculine and male dominated, overcompensate by wearing sports paraphernalia or other items that signify their arrival in this milieu. To make matters even harder for women, once they have in fact mastered this language, men diminish their achievement by labeling it "studied"—which is precisely what it is. But "studied" is not the real thing for any insiders, it is always used to delineate them from newcomers be it in sports or any other realm of social interaction.

Knowledge

A final dimension of sports space is knowledge. Students were asked whether they could name members of the lineups of eight historical and contemporary teams from the four major professional sports: The 1950s and current New York Yankees, the 1960s and current Boston Celtics, the 1970s and current Pittsburgh Steelers, and the 1950s and current Detroit Red Wings. Adding all the answers together, we see that knowledge levels contain the single greatest difference between male and female students in their participation in sports culture: men, on average, could name a total of about eleven players while women on average could name about two. Breaking down the questions into contemporary and historic lineups, we find that men could name three historic players on average, while the female average was .3, and that the male average for contemporary lineups was about 7.2, and for women was 1.7.

Table 4.2.12. Number of players known

Team	Male mean	Female mean	Total mean
1950s Yankees	1.11	0.17	0.61
	(0.99–1.23)	(0.12–0.22)	(0.54–0.68)
1960s Celtics	0.52	0.00	0.25
	(0.43–0.61)	(0.00–0.01)	(0.20–0.29)
1970s Steelers	0.89	0.04	0.44
	(0.77–1.01)	(0.02–0.07)	(0.38–0.51)
1950s Red Wings	0.76	0.14	0.43
	(0.64–0.87)	(0.09–0.18)	(0.37–0.49)
Total historic	**3.28**	**0.35**	**1.73**
	(2.94–3.61)	(0.27–0.44)	(1.54–1.92)
Contemporary Yankees	2.14	0.56	1.30
	(1.96–2.31)	(0.46–0.65)	(1.19–1.40)
Contemporary Celtics	1.25	0.11	0.65
	(1.12–1.39)	(0.07–0.15)	(0.57–0.73)
Contemporary Steelers	1.66	0.15	0.86
	(1.49–1.82)	(0.10–0.21)	(0.76–0.96)
Contemporary Red Wings	2.17	0.88	1.48
	(1.99–2.34)	(0.75–1.00)	(1.37–1.60)
Total Contemporary	**7.17**	**1.69**	**4.27**
	(6.64–7.70)	(1.47–1.92)	(3.93–4.60)
Total	**10.93**	**2.04**	**5.99**
	(9.64–11.22)	(1.76–2.32)	(5.59–6.48)

The lineup that both male and female students knew best was unsurprisingly (given the location) the contemporary Detroit Red Wings, of whom men could name 2.2 on average, and women .9. The least-known lineup was the Boston Celtics of the 1960s, for which the average male and female scores were just .517 and .004 respectively.

Readers who may have been immersed in sports culture their entire lives, who would have no problem reeling off at least five members of each of the four historic teams, and who would consider it a personal failing not to be able to name every starter in the contemporary teams, may be surprised at the apparently low mean scores here. People who are intensely engaged in the broader sports culture are sometimes unaware that much of the population leads satisfied lives without ever knowing the name of a professional athlete. 261 out of our 845 respondents—including 129 athletes—did not give an answer to any of the questions.[18]

Favorite sports

We will conclude this section on gender differences by examining differences in the kinds of sports that men and women like. Students were asked their favorite sport to watch on television, their favorite to attend live, and their favorite to play.

Table 4.2.13. Favorite sport to watch on television

Sport	Men (%)	Women (%)
Baseball	4.2	3.3
Basketball	14	23
Football	44	32
Hockey	15	11
Soccer	4.5	3.5
Track	1.2	3.1
Other	17	24
Total	**99.9**	**99.9**

For both men and women, the overwhelming television favorite is football, though in greater numbers for men than for women (44% to 32%). Football's supremacy is all the more confirmed by the fact that the biggest athlete group at Michigan, the football players, did not even participate in the survey. More women than men list their favorite TV sport as basketball (23% to 14%), while men favor hockey in

147

greater numbers than women (15% to 11%—bear in mind that we are in Michigan!). Baseball, which is not an ideal "television sport," gains 4.2% and 3.3% for men and women respectively. Among women, tennis is a more popular television sport than this (6.2%), though baseball is more popular than tennis for men.

For both sexes, baseball trails (just barely) soccer as a television sport, which finds 4.5% favor with men and 3.5% with women. Our finding about baseball is fascinating since baseball still continues to enjoy the sobriquet of being America's "pastime" and remains—with football and basketball—the third member of the Big Three of America's sports space. Our finding might also corroborate data that demonstrate soccer's immense rise as a major activity among America's youth coinciding with a stagnation, even decline (particularly among African Americans), in the playing and also the following of baseball. America's second-biggest TV sport, NASCAR, gains just one (male) vote as a favorite television sport among Michigan students, putting it behind gymnastics, which gets 3.1% of the female vote and 1.2% of the male vote, and running, which records the same numbers. This would suggest that despite NASCAR's massive nation-wide expansion over at least the last two decades, it remains at core a phenomenon with strong regional links to the South-East, and is geographically limited in the same way that the genuine hockey culture tends to be confined to the North.

These patterns are roughly similar to those that emerge when students are asked their favorite sport to attend live. Football is still number one (41% for men and 31% for women). Hockey remains prominent with both sexes as a live sport, with women listing it as their favorite sport almost in equal numbers to men (17.5% to 18.2%). Baseball also features good numbers as a live sport (8.2% for men and 4.2% for women) which places it slightly ahead of soccer for men and on a par with it for women (6% and 4.2%). There remains a large gap between women and men in favoring basketball as a live sport (20% for women to 11% for men).

Overall, about 61% of respondents list the same sport as their favorite both to watch on television and to attend live. It seems that men

have a greater propensity to favor the same sport in both categories.

Table 4.2.14. Favorite TV sport/favorite live sport

Gender	Same sport	Different sport
Men	64.3%	34.5%
	(249)	(131)
Women	56%	44%
	(224)	(176)
Total	60.7%	39.3%
	(475)	(307)

A different picture emerges when we ask students which are their favorite sports to play. Table 4.2.15 shows these preferences.

Table 4.2.15. Favorite sports to play

Sport	Male Non-Athlete	Female Non-Athlete	All Non-Athlete	Total Sample
Baseball/Softball	11	9	10	10
Basketball	24	13	18	16
Football	16	3	9	7
Hockey	6	2	4	5
Tennis	8	16	12	8
Golf	5	1	3	4
Soccer	16	17	16	15
Track/Running	2	3	3	5
Volleyball	2	9	6	6
Other	10	25	18	22
TOTAL	100	98	99	98

The supremacy of basketball, soccer and tennis are obvious here. Other interesting things to note, however, are the continued high position of football (among men), which is relatively difficult to play as a pick-up game, and the low position of running, which, judging by Ann Arbor's gyms and side walks, may well be the most common form of athletic *activity* (as opposed to sport) among Michigan students. The other notable gender differences are men's stronger preferences for playing basketball, golf, and hockey and women's stronger preferences for tennis and volleyball.

We have seen that about 60% of students named the same sport as their favorite to watch on TV and to watch live; relatively few nominate the same sport as their favorite to play and their favorite to watch, either live or on TV.

In both cases, men are much more likely to name the same sport.

Table 4.2.16. Favorite sport to play/favorite TV sport

Gender	Same sport Percentage (number)	Different sport Percentage (number)
Men	29.4 (109)	71.2 (270)
Women	21.1 (84)	78.9 (314)
Total	75.1 (585)	24.9 (194)

Table 4.2.17. Favorite sport to play/favorite live sport

Gender	Same sport Percentage (number)	Different sport Percentage (number)
Men	31.7 (120)	68.3 (259)
Women	22.9 (73)	319 (81.4)
Total	25.1 (194)	74.9 (579)

A total of 134 students (84 men and 50 women) name the same sport in all three categories.

Conclusion

We are fully aware that any large-scale generalizations emanating from a survey of this kind would be flawed. The instrument itself covered too spotty a ground to allow us to make conclusive comments about American sports culture at the beginning of the 21st century. Moreover, no matter how uncharacteristically—and welcomingly—high the response rate to our survey turned out to be, the fact that it remained restricted to one university considerably limits any generalizations that we can draw from this study. Still, some patterns are well worth noting.

There seems to be little difference as to how members of each varsity team construct their sports culture other than that each team values its own sport as a form of culture that does not pertain to members of other teams—or the non-athletes. In terms of the student-athletes' fluency in the general American sports culture, there seem to be no significant differences among the varsity teams representing the University of Michigan.

Differences between athletes and non-athletes are also surprisingly slender though we noted some fascinating ones such as the preference on the part of athletes for highlight reels on sports shows. We noticed the influence of geography on all our participants—student athletes and non-athletes alike—in terms of their marked preferences for teams and other forms of affective relationships to sports.

Lastly, on the gender dimension, the mere fact that we had more female respondents—both in the athlete and the non-athlete categories—bespeaks a fundamentally altered student topography in the world of American post-secondary education over the past three decades. Title IX really mattered immensely. Furthermore, even though women have come to participate in the world of sports on nearly equal footing with men, it is quite evident that they participate differently. They clearly are equally active producers of sports to men, but very different consumers. Women identify with Michigan sports—and Michigan football—just as enthusiastically as men, but this identification has a very different meaning to them when we look at it in the larger context of football in America. Our study shows how gendered the discourse of sports remains. If in former times, its gendered nature was primarily evident by women's absence from sports, the current genderedness manifests itself by women experiencing sports as activity and culture in their own voice, so to speak. How much, if at all or ever, that might change the fundamental structure of sports culture in the United States, remains to be seen.

Notes

1. See, among other publications, Andrei S. Markovits and Steven L. Hellerman, *Offside: Soccer and American Exceptionalism* (Princeton: Princeton University Press, 2001); and the July 2003 issue of the *American Behavioral Scientist* edited by Andrei S. Markovits, Alan Tomlinson and Christopher Young devoted to the topic "Sport and Cultural Space." See *American Behavioral Scientist (ABS)*, Volume 46, Number 11, July 2003. [Excerpt in this volume–Eds.]
2. Ibid.
3. See, for example, Gillian Lee Warmflash, "In a Different Language: Female Sports Fans in America" (Senior Honors Thesis, The Committee on Degrees in Social Studies, Harvard University, 2004).

4. The current version of the Markovits-Smith article focuses on gender. [Eds.]

5. Jeffrey D. James and Lynn L. Ridinger, "Female and male sports fans: a comparison of sport consumption motives." *Journal of Sport Behavior.* Sept 2002. 25(3): 260–278.

6. Beth Dietz-Uhler, Elizabeth A. Harrick, Christian End, and Lindy Jacquemotte, "Sex differences in sport fan behavior and reasons for being a sport fan." *Journal of Sport Behavior.* Sept 2000. 23(3): 219–231.

7. Vivian R. Acosta and Linda Jean Carpenter, "Women in intercollegiate sport: a longitudinal study—twenty one year update: 1977–1998" (unpublished manuscript, Brooklyn College, Brooklyn, New York). The article is also cited in G.B. Cunningham and M. Sagas, "Occupational Turnover Intent Among Assistant Coaches of Women's Teams: The Role of Organizational Work Experiences," *Sex Roles*, Volume 49, Number ¾, August 2003; 185–190.

8. Jo Ann M. Buysse and Melissa Sheridan Embser-Herbert. "Constructions of gender in sport: An analysis of intercollegiate media guide cover photographs." *Gender & Society.* Feb 2004. 18(1): 66–81.

9. Ibid., p. 80.

10. Lee McGinnis, Seungwoo Chun, and Julia McQuillan, "A review of gendered consumption in sport and leisure." *Academy of Marketing Science Review*, Number 5, 2003; 1–24.

11. Rebecca Gardyn, "A league of their own." *American Demographics.* March 2001. 23(3): 12–13.

12. Garry Crawford and Victoria K. Gosling, "The myth of the 'puck bunny': female fans and men's ice hockey." *Sociology.* 2004. 38(3): 477–493.

13. Ibid. p. 488.

14. Andrei S. Markovits and Steven L. Hellerman, "Women's Soccer in the United States: Another American 'Exceptionalism'" in Fan Hong and J.A. Mangan (eds.), *Soccer, Women, Sexual Liberation: Kicking Off a New Era* (London: Frank Cass, 2004), pp. 14–29; and Andrei S. Markovits, "Parallelen und Divergenzen hegemonialer Sportkulturen in Europa und Nordamerika", Keynote Lecture at the Conference, "Fussball und Globalisierung" at the University of Hamburg, Hamburg, Germany; June 8, 2006.

15. The total is 439; five athlete respondents were not included in the final sample.

16. The current version focuses exclusively on gender issues. For a complete discussion of the other items, see the full article in *The Michigan Journal of Political Science.* [Eds.]

17. Due to the way the question was asked, the percentages may add up to more or less than 100 percent.

18. A similar study of student athletes of Harvard University confirmed these male-female differences. The only major difference in the samples was the greater knowledge of the Red Wings at Michigan and the greater knowledge of the Celtics and Yankees at Harvard.

The sanctity of Sunday football

Why men love sports

Douglas Hartmann

In this clear, elegant, short article, Hartmann discusses the myriad ways in which masculinity and sport seem to achieve a kind of symbiosis. Hartmann demonstrates that this seeming symbiosis is anything but natural; it is socially constructed and dynamically contested.

My father, a no-nonsense grade school principal, had little time for small talk, contemplation, or leisure—with one major exception: sports. He spent Sunday afternoons watching football games on television, passed summer evenings listening to Jack Buck announce St. Louis Cardinals baseball games, and took me to every sporting event in town. He coached all the youth sports his children played, and spent hours calculating team statistics, diagramming new plays, and crafting locker room pep talks. Though never a great athlete, his high school varsity letters were displayed in his basement work area; just about the only surefire way to drag dad out of the house after a long day at work was to play "a little catch." Sports were one of the few topics he ever joked about with other men.

My father's fascination with sports was not unique. Though women are increasingly visible throughout the sporting world, more men than women play sports, watch sports and care about sports. Is it any wonder that corporate advertising campaigns, drinking establishments, and movements such as the Promise Keepers all use sports to appeal to men? Or that sports figures

so prominently in many books and movies dealing with men and masculinity in America? Nevertheless, there is surprisingly little serious reflection about why this is the case. When asked why so many men are so obsessed with sports, most people—regardless of their gender or their attitudes about sports—say something to the effect that men are naturally physical and competitive, and that sports simply provide an outlet for these inherently masculine traits.

To sociologists, however, men love playing, watching, and talking sports because modern, Western sports—dominated as they are by men and by values and behaviors that are traditionally regarded as masculine—provide a unique place for men to think about and develop their masculinity, to make themselves men, or at least one specific kind of man.

Where boys become men

Ask sports enthusiasts why they participate in sports and you are likely to get a wide variety of answers. "Because it is fun and exciting," some respond. Others say it is because they need the exercise and want to stay physically fit. Still others talk about sports providing them a way to relax and unwind, or about the thrill of competition—these responses are especially common for that large percentage of sports lovers whose "participation" mainly takes the form of being a fan or watching sports on television. These are important parts of sports' value, but they do not really explain why men are, on average, more likely to be involved in sports than women.

For many men, the love of sports goes back to childhood. Sports provided them, as young boys and teens, with a reason to get together, to engage with other boys (and men), and in doing so to begin defining what separates boys from girls: how to act like men. Barrie Thorne's study of grammar school playgrounds illustrates the phenomenon. Thorne finds that pre-adolescent boys and girls use recreation on the schoolyard to divide themselves along gender lines. How they play—for example, running around or quiet games—Thorne suggests, distinguishes male and female child behavior. As they get older, kids become more aware of these distinctions and increasingly use sex-segregated athletics to discuss and act out gender differences. Gary Alan Fine, in *With the Boys*, describes how much of the learning that happens in Little League baseball involves being tough and aggressive and dealing with injuries and other setbacks; and in off-the-field conversations young ballplayers learn about sex and about what it means to be a man as opposed to a "dork," a "sissy" or a "fag."

When Michael Messner interviewed retired athletes and asked them how they initially got involved with sports, they told him it had little to do with any immediate or natural attraction to athletics and was really about connecting to other boys and men. "The most important thing was just being out there with the rest of the guys—being friends," said one. Sports, according to Messner, "was something 'fun' to do with fathers, older brothers, uncles and eventually with same-aged peers."

Girls start playing sports for similar reasons, and children of both genders join in other activities, such as choir or community service, for social purposes, too. (Many boys and girls start to drop out of sports at about ages 9 or 10—when the sports they play become increasingly competitive and require them to think of themselves primarily as athletes.) What is distinctive about the experience of boys and young men in sports, however, is that the sporting world is organized and run primarily by men, and that athletic activities require attitudes and behaviors that are typically understood to be masculine.

Of course, not all boys play sports, and boyhood and adolescent experiences in sports are not uniformly positive. A great deal of the sociological research in this area focuses on the downside of youth sports participation. Donald Sabo, for example, has written extensively about the pain and violence, both physical and psychological, experienced by many boys who compete in athletics. And Harry Edwards has long argued that over-investing in sports can divert poor and minority youth from more promising avenues of upward mobility. But, despite the harsh realities, sports remains one of the few socially approved settings in which boys and men, and fathers and sons, can express themselves and bond with each other.

Sport as a masculine enterprise

Once boys and girls separate in physical play, it does not take long for gendered styles of play to emerge. Study after study confirms what most soccer moms and dads already know: boys' athletics tend to be more physical and aggressive and put more emphasis on winning, being tough in the face of adversity, and dealing with injuries and pain. Even in elementary school, Thorne finds boys take up far more of the physical space of the playground with their activities than girls, who tend to play (and talk about their play) in smaller spaces and clusters.

People debate whether there is a physiological component to these differences, but two points are clear. First, parents, coaches, and peers routinely encourage such intensity among boys in youth sports. More than a few single mothers bring their boys to the teams I coach out of concern that their sons are insufficiently tough or physical because they lack a male influence. Messner writes about how he learned—against his inclinations—to throw a ball overhand with his elbow tucked in because his father did not want him to "throw like a girl." Stories about overly competitive, physically abusive coaches may be overplayed in the American media, but in many ways they are the inevitable consequence of the emphases many parents express.

Second, the behaviors and attitudes valued in men's and boys' athletics are not just about sports, but about masculinity more generally. The inherent connection of sports to the body, physical activity and material results, the emphasis on the merit of competing and winning, the attention to rules, sportsmanship and team play, on the one hand, and gamesmanship, outcomes and risk, on the other, are not just the defining aspects of male youth sport culture, but conform to what many men (and women) believe is the essence and value of masculinity. Female reporters, homosexual athletes, and men who challenge the dominant culture of men's sports—especially in the sacred space of the locker room—quickly learn that sports are not just dominated by men but also dominated by thinking and habits understood to be masculine (in opposition to the more nurturing values of compromise, cooperation, sympathy, understanding, and sharing typically associated with femininity). If the military is the quintessential institution of Western masculinity, then sports is surely a close second.

The notion that sports is a masculine enterprise is closely connected with the development of modern Western sports. As historians have detailed, middle- and upper-class men used sports in the 19th and early-20th centuries to present and protect their particular notions of masculinity in both schools and popular culture (the classic literary expression being *Tom Brown's School Days*, a 19th-century English story of boarding school boys' maturation through hard-nosed sports). The media is a critical part of perpetuating sports' masculine ethos today, because most adults participate in sports as spectators and consumers. Not only are female athletes and women's sports downplayed by most sports coverage, but the media accentuates the masculinity of male athletes. For example, Hall of Fame pitcher Nolan Ryan's media coverage, according to a study by Nick Trujillo, consistently described him in terms of the stereotypical American man: powerful, hard-working, family patriarch, a cowboy and a symbol of heterosexual virility. Such images not only define an athlete's personal qualities but legitimate a particular vision of masculinity.

The authority of the masculine ethos is underlined by the fact that so many female athletes believe they can receive no higher compliment than to be told they "play like a man." Many feminists cringe at the irony of such sentiments. But they also realize that, while the explosion of women in sports has challenged their male dominance (2.5 million girls and young women participated in interscholastic sport in 2003, up from 300,000 in 1972—before Title IX's federal mandate for gender equality), women's sports have essentially been based upon the same single-minded, hyper-competitive masculine model. Not surprisingly, they are witnessing the emergence of the same kinds of problems—cheating, physical and emotional stress, homophobia, eating disorders—that have long plagued men's sports.

Sports and maintaining masculinity

As the men Messner interviewed became more committed to being athletes, they began to construct identities and relationships that conformed to—and thus perpetuated—sport's masculine values. Athletes are so bound up with being men that when, in his initial interviews, Messner inadvertently referred to them as "ex-athletes," his interviewees responded as if he were taking away their identities, their very manhood. A professional baseball player expressed a similar sentiment when I asked how he dealt with his time on the disabled list last summer because of a serious arm injury: "I'd throw wiffle balls left-handed to my eight-year-old son—and I had to get him out! Just so I could feel like a man again."

Of course, few men participate in sports with the intensity of professional athletes. Those who cannot move up the competitive ladder can still participate in other ways—in recreational sports, in coaching, and perhaps, most of all, in attending sporting events, watching sports on television, and buying athletic gear and apparel. Indeed, it is in being a fan (derived from *fanatic*) that the male slant of sports is clearest. While women often follow sports, their interest tends to be driven by social ends, such as being with family or friends. Male spectators are far more likely to watch events by themselves, follow sports closely, and be affected by the outcomes of games and the performance of their favored teams and athletes. The basic explanation is similar to the one developed out of sports activity studies: Just as playing sports provides many boys and young men with a space to become men, watching sports serves many men as a way to reinforce, rework, and maintain their masculinity—in these cases, through vicarious identification with masculine pursuits and idealized men. Writing of his obsession with 1950s football star Frank Gifford in *A Fan's Notes*, novelist Fredrick Exley explained: "Where I could not, with syntax, give shape to my fantasies, Gifford could with his superb timing, his uncanny faking, give shape to his." "I cheered for him with inordinate enthusiasm," Exley wrote, because he helped me find "my place in the competitive world of men … each time I heard the roar of the crowd, it roared in my ears as much for me as for him."

It was no accident that Exley chose to write about football. With its explicit appropriation of the rhetoric and tactics of combat, the sport supplanted baseball as the most popular spectator sport in the United States in the 1970s. Football's primary ideological salience, according to Messner, "lies in its ability … to symbolically link men of diverse ages and socioeconomic backgrounds. … Interacting with other men and interacting with them in this male-dominated space … [is] a way to assert and confirm one's own maleness. …" Being with other men allows males to affirm their masculine identity. Listen to today's sports talk radio. These programs are not only sophomorically masculine, many of them serve as little men's communities unto themselves: Tiger fan Jack; Mike from Modesto; Jay the Packer's guy— even teams' announcers have unique personalities and identities, fostering the impression that this is an actual club where all the guys know each other.

The salience of sports as a medium to validate masculinity may be best illustrated when it is taken away. Journalist Susan Faludi reported on what happened when the original Cleveland Browns football team left town to become the Baltimore Ravens. The mostly working-class men who occupied the section of seats in Cleveland called the "Dawg Pound" talked about the team's departure with an overwhelming sense of loss and powerlessness. As it often is for former athletes, it was as if they'd had their manhood taken from them. In tearful media interviews, John "Big Dawg" Thompson compared the team's departure to witnessing his best friend die in the hospital.

Sports as "contested terrain"

Critics of sports' heavy masculinity (most scholars doing work in this area are critics) have focused on its neglect or even exclusion of women. The way that golf outings perpetuate the privileges men enjoy in the corporate world is a frequent example. Others have gone so far as to suggest that the powerful appeal of sports for men arises because sports provide them at least symbolic superiority in a world in which men's real authority is in decline. As columnist and former professional basketball player Mariah Burton Nelson put it in the deliberately provocative title of her popular 1994 book, "The stronger women get, the more men love football."

In recent years, sociologists of sports have also begun to identify tensions within the masculine culture of athletics. Looking at Great Britain's soccer stars, for example, Garry Whannel has studied how the hedonism of the "new lad lifestyle" (as represented by players like David Beckham) rubs up against the disciplined masculinity traditionalists perceive to be necessary for international football success. Messner, for his part, has shown how "high status" men (white and from middle-class backgrounds) and "low status" men differently understood themselves as athletes. The former tended to transfer what they learned in sports about being men to pursuing success in other spheres, such as education and career. Men from lower status backgrounds saw sports as their only hope for success as a man—an accomplishment that the higher status men looked down upon as a narrow, atavistic type of masculinity. Expanding from this, some scholars have demonstrated that in popular culture the masculinity of African-American athletes is often exaggerated and linked to racial stereotypes about violence, risk and threat. Basketball star Dennis Rodman, for example, gained notoriety by playing on his persona as a "bad" ball player. While problematic in many respects, these images of black masculinity can also provide African-American men with unique opportunities for personal advancement and broader political visibility (as I have suggested in my work on the 1968 black Olympics protest movement).

Such research has led many scholars to see sports not only as a place where mainstream masculine culture is perpetuated, but also a place where it is challenged and possibly changed. These issues have played out clearly in the debates over the implementation of Title IX legislation for women's equal access to sports. While still hotly contested (as evidenced by the recent controversy surrounding the all-male Augusta National Golf Club, as well as speculation that the legislation may be challenged in court by the Bush administration), Title IX has transformed men's relationship to sports, to women, and even to masculinity itself. Sports' most vital social function with respect to masculinity is to provide a separate space for men to discuss—often indirectly, through evaluations of favorite players or controversial incidents—what it is to be a real man. And that space is increasingly shared with women.

Some scholars envision new, more humane or even feminine sports—marked less by an emphasis on winning, record-setting and spectatorship, and more by open participation, enjoyment and fitness. Cross-cultural studies of sports show that these are real possibilities, that sports are not "naturally" and inherently masculine as Americans have long assumed. Sexism and homophobia, for example, have never been a real problem in Chinese sports, anthropologist Susan Brownell explains, because sports emerged there as a low-status activity that more powerful men felt no special compulsion to control or participate in. As a consequence, it is widely believed that a skilled female practitioner of kung fu should be able to defeat stronger but less-skilled men. At the same time, Brownell points out, the current proliferation of Western, Olympic-style sports in China seems to be contributing to the redefinition of gender roles there nearer the pattern of Western sports and masculinity.

Playing deeply

In a famous paper on cockfighting in Bali, American anthropologist Clifford Geertz used the term "deep play" to capture the way fans make sense of such competitions as the cockfight, cricket or American football. As passionate and articulate as they may be, these enthusiasts generally do not attempt to justify their pursuits. Instead, they downplay the significance of sports as separate from the serious concerns of real life. We can learn a great deal from such play, Geertz said, if we think about it as an "art form" which helps us figure out who

people really are and what they really care about. Similarly, American men who love sports may not be able to fully articulate and understand how it is part of their being men, but their passion for sports can certainly help us understand them and their masculinity.

This peculiar, "deep play" understanding of sports makes it difficult for most men to recognize or confront the costs and consequences that may come with their sports obsessions. But in many ways isn't this true of masculine culture in general? It makes male advantages and masculine values appear so normal and "natural" that they can hardly be questioned. Therein may lie the key to the puzzle connecting men and the seemingly innocent world of sports: they fit together so tightly, so seamlessly that they achieve their effects—learning to be a man, male bonding, male authority and the like—without seeming to be doing anything more than tossing a ball or watching a Sunday afternoon game.

Recommended resources

Birrell, Susan and Cheryl L. Cole, eds. *Women, Sport and Culture*. Champaign, IL: Human Kinetics, 1994. A collection of feminist critiques of sport that includes several influential contributions on men and masculinity.

Brownell, Susan. *Training the Body for China: Sports in the Moral Order of the People's Republic*. Chicago: University of Chicago Press, 1995. The chapters on sex, gender, and the body offer a fascinating cross-cultural contrast, and provide an introduction to sports in the nation that will host the 2008 Olympics.

Burstyn, Varda. *The Rites of Men: Manhood, Politics and the Culture of Sport*. Toronto: University of Toronto Press, 1999. The most comprehensive treatment of the social, cultural, and historical forces that account for the relationship between men and sports in modern society.

Fine, Gary Alan. *With the Boys: Little League Baseball and Preadolescent Culture*. Chicago: University of Chicago Press, 1987. A pioneering field study from a noted sociologist of culture.

Kelley, Robin D. G. "Playing for Keeps: Pleasure and Profit on the Postindustrial Playground." In *The House that Race Built*, ed. Wahneema Lubiano. New York: Pantheon, 1997. An ethnographically informed treatment of the opportunities basketball presents to inner-city African-American men produced by the country's preeminent historian of black popular culture.

Klein, Alan M. *Little Big Men: Bodybuilding Subculture and Gender Construction*. Albany, NY: State University of New York Press, 1993. A vivid ethnography of competitive body builders on the West Coast that draws upon Robert Connell's seminal critique of the intersection of men's bodies, identities and sexualities in masculine culture.

Messner, Michael. *Taking the Field: Women, Men, and Sports*. Minneapolis, MN: University of Minnesota Press, 2002. The latest book from the leading scholar in the field. It exposes the ways in which men and women together use sports to define gender differences.

Pronger, Brian. *The Arena of Masculinity: Sports, Homosexuality and the Meaning of Sex*. London: St. Martin's Press, 1990. Pronger explores the problematic connections between gender and sexuality in sport, highlighting its libidinal dimensions.

An iron man

R. W. Connell

> In this life-history of an "iron man," Connell elaborates on the concept of hegemonic masculinity and shows how it manifests itself in a particular time and place. Connell's study of Steve Donoghue is important in understanding how we can understand the social construction of a champion athlete, with attention paid both to who Steve is as an individual (his relationships with his parents, girlfriend, etc.) as well as how the structure of sport and its place in the larger society affected who Steve became: as a man and as an athlete.

It is a basic proposition of the current research and political work that masculine character is socially constructed, not inherited with the Y chromosome. But it is now clear that the old understanding of how this construction occurred, a more or less smooth and consensual socialization into a unitary male role, is not adequate.

There are different kinds of masculine character within society that stand in complex relations of dominance over and subordination to each other. What in earlier views of the problem passed for the 'male sex role' is best seen as hegemonic masculinity, the culturally idealized form of masculine character (in a given historical setting), which may not be the usual form of masculinity at all. It is also clear that masculinities are constructed through processes that are often discontinuous or contradictory (and often experienced as such), for which the model of a 'socializing agency' will not work. This has been most clearly seen in psychoanalytic thinking about the formation of masculinity (Connell 1994).

In this chapter I hope to add to the understanding of hegemonic masculinity and its construction in personal life, by a case study of a champion sportsman. The case raises interesting questions about the interplay between the body and social process, and suggests some lines of thought about sport and its commercialization as a phenomenon of gender and class relations.

I hope also to illustrate the usefulness of the life-history method for studying these social processes. [...] Properly handled, the theorized life history can be a powerful tool for the study of social structures and their dynamics as they impinge on personal life and are reconstituted by personal action.

Being a champion

Steve Donoghue is an 'iron man'. This deliberately pretentious phrase is a technical term in surf sports. The iron-man race at surf carnivals is an event involving a combination of swimming, running and surf-craft riding. Both short and long forms of the race exist; the long races may take four and a half hours to complete.

In surf sports, this event occupies a position analogous to a combination of the marathon and the pentathlon in track and field. A champion of the iron-man event holds a great deal of prestige. Steve is one of a very small group of athletes who trade the Australian national championships among themselves.

Steve, in his twenties at the time he was interviewed, lives in a beachfront flat with his girlfriend. He gets up at 4.30 every morning to start his training, which takes four to five hours a day. When it is done he has the rest of the day to himself because he has no job. More exactly, his job is to be an iron man and to market himself as a sports personality.

The training schedule is rigorous and, at his level of performance, essential—as Steve explains in a fascinating passage of the interview:

> The main thing ... is the discipline and motivation side of it. [If] you can't put the five hours in every day, it doesn't matter how old you are—you're not going to win. You've got to have the talent, you've got to have the technique and the ability and everything—and the training is what counts really. Your natural ability only takes you so far, about 60 to 70 per cent of the way, and the rest is where the training comes in, and you've got to be able to. If you are 28 or 30 you have still got to have the time to train. [If you] haven't got business problems, or kids through marriage, or whatever, well, then you'll be right ... just as long as you keep loving it, you can keep backing up and wanting to train and really feeling keen the whole time, you've got no troubles.

Where does the love come from?

> I don't know. I love the beach. And I love the sun and everything to do with the water. The waves, the water. I love the idea—I've always loved this, even when I was at school—of being able to make a living out of sport. I have loved the idea of not having to work, like a strict nine to five set job, you know, like other people, being indoors ... Five hours a day is still a lot but it is something which I enjoy that people are not telling me what to do. And there's not a set wage, if I go well I can really make a lot of money out of it. I just like that. I like everything to do with it really. I like the people I get involved with.

This lyrical picture of pleasure and success in the sun and water is characteristic of Steve's self-presentation in the interview. Though there is ideology here, much of the feeling and tone is genuine enough; Steve has realized a schoolboy dream. It comes as something of a shock, then, to find that he also talks of his regime this way:

> You're up at 4.30 to go training and that goes most of the day. And you are too tired to go out anyway and you've got to get your rest. It is a pretty disciplined sort of life. It's like being in jail.

This sudden douche of cold water comes in the middle of a discussion about girlfriends. Steve notes that 'a lot of the guys don't have girlfriends'. It is just too hard to combine with training: 'The girl wants to go out with you all the time and, you know, party here and there.' This affects the athlete's performance. So Steve's coach 'doesn't like it, tries to put it down, tries to stop anything serious'. (The coach has a financial interest in his athlete's performance, although Steve does not mention this.)

Steve has a girlfriend, who drifts in and out during the interview. And that seems to be her status in Steve's life, too. She is given a clear message about what really counts for him:

> Yes, I've got a girlfriend. I think there is no problem as long as you don't have to go out all the time, [as long as] they understand that, and you've got to take training first, and competition first. That's your living, that's your life. That's what I enjoy the most. It is hard, though ...
>
> It's good if you have a girlfriend that is involved with sport, involved with the same sort of interest that you've got. Not iron man or like that! but the same sort of, doing the training here and there so it can work out. Well, when you're doing some training, well, they'll do something else. And if you have someone who is completely different, which I have had girlfriends in the past like that, it doesn't seem to work. You might start off all right, but you end up splitting up, because you fight all the time. It gets on their nerves when you are training all the time, you won't go out here and here. It's just rat shit.

What would be the attraction for the 'girls' in Steve's life (the slightly childish language is also characteristic) in having a lifestyle not far removed from that of an armchair? In the first place, this is par for the course in the Australian surfing subculture, which is male supremacist to a marked degree (Pearson 1982). If a 'girl' stands up for her own interests, Steve disposes of her and acquires another. As he notes complacently elsewhere in the interview, he has 'never had trouble' with sexual relationships. And in conventional terms, he is a real catch. He is handsome, healthy, easygoing, sexually experienced, famous, and on the verge of becoming rich.

Steve's 'job' of being an iron man nets him prizes, sponsorships, and endorsements which add up to a phenomenal income for a young man recently out of high school. Asked where he would see himself in five years' time, he replies simply, 'A millionaire'. His aim is to be this by the time he retires, at about 30. At present he is expanding his sponsorship deals with several large companies, is buying into surf businesses, and has just signed up with a multi-national marketing company:

> I just want to keep winning, keep winning, and keep rolling the money. So when I do get off I've got something to show for what I've done.

Fame is accepted with the same combination of pleasure and complacency as the cash and the sex. He wanted fame, and now he enjoys it. But there is a problem:

> Well, you can go out at night and you've got to set an example for yourself. You can't go stupid like other people can. Like Joe Blow can get away with drunk-driving charges and no one will know. If it was me it would be on the front page. Things may be not even that serious. Because if I was just mucking around down the street—it's hard really, people think, 'He's got to do this', and they set you in a certain way ... behave in your own limits, you can't go wild or anything. If I go out at night I can't get in a fight. That can happen because people think they can ... say smart comments, and you can hear them, and they try and big-note themselves with friends. And I've had fights before where people have, I have just snapped. But that's only happened once or twice, that's not bad really, considering some of the situations I've had.

This is very much a problem about masculinity. Steve, the exemplar of masculine toughness, finds that his own exemplary status prevents him from doing exactly what his peer group defines as thoroughly masculine behaviour: going wild, showing off, drunk driving, getting into fights, defending his own prestige.

It is also clear in this passage how social the whole business is—the smart-aleck banter among friends, the social pressure that 'sets you in a certain way'. Here we have a vivid glimpse

of the production of an exemplary masculinity as a collective practice. It is an accomplishment not of Steve as an individual (throughout this passage he is kicking against the pricks), but of the whole social network in which Steve finds himself enmeshed.

Soft path, hard goal

How did he get to be an exemplar of masculinity? Steve's own account of his childhood and adolescence portrays a simple progression from active child to schoolboy hero to adult champion. He seems to swim endlessly through a warm bath of admiration from family, teachers and friends. His grandfather was a sporting hero and Steve pictures himself as growing up effortlessly in the same mould.

Without denying the reality of this picture, we may question what it means. Steve's childhood was not a conventional idyll. His parents separated when he was young, and he has few memories of the family together. His clearest childhood memory of his father is in a game of hide-and-seek on the day of the weekly visit, when his father vanished and could not be found for 45 minutes. At the least, this is a memory of anxiety. It is hardly over-interpreting to suggest that this remains a haunting memory because the 'lost father' remained a major emotional issue for Steve.

His mother figures as the main adult in Steve's narrative of growing up. She certainly encouraged and organized his swimming, and paid for his travel to championship meetings. He sees her as having the same qualities as him—'intelligent and strong like I am'—and unwilling to be pushed around. There is some identification here, and she remains an emotional presence for him. Asked near the end of the interview his views on violence, he says the only scene he can imagine that would provoke him to murder would be 'if someone killed my mother'.

Yet Steve also records that she moved to another city after her children had left the nest, and the loss does not seem troubling to him. Indeed, he is now pleased to be re-establishing contact with his father, who is taking an interest in his son's career and helping him negotiate sponsorship deals. Steve has not lacked figures to model himself on.

Thus Steve has been inserted into his career by a close network of family, friends and school. He remembers anxiety about moving up to high school—fear of being physically beaten up by the big boys—but soon formed a group of friends and stuck with them right through school. Physically big as a child, he did well in school sporting events and particularly well in swimming. By age 13 he was far enough advanced in formal competition that he gave up football in order to specialize in swimming—a decision that signals the shift from sport as pleasure to sport as a kind of career.

Sport was a career path that elicited a lot of communal support. Steve was the school swimming champion, and his prowess won the district competition for his school. He was 'a bit of a hero' and a leader among his peers, and was treated with indulgence by his teachers. His mother strongly supported his swimming career, which must have shaped household routine from an early stage. Steve's regime as a teenager involved swimming in the morning, school in the day, then more swimming at night. He didn't much want to study, and he completed high school mainly because his friends were still there. When he left school, the study part simply dropped out of his day and the swimming part went on.

At this point Steve was handed over to a new network, and the transition has been complete. Steve hardly sees the once close-knit group of high-school friends any more. Asked what makes someone decide to take up the iron-man event, Steve describes a social practice rather than a choice:

> There is no decision really. It's just that you've got to be round the beach for starters. And you have got to be involved with the surf club, so that narrows it right down. You've got to have a love of the water. You've got to have a swimming background, pretty well. And you've got to be disciplined and dedicated enough to put the time and work in.

The surf club is a key part of the new network. Steve joined it as a teenager and was thus absorbed into a slightly older peer group, a group of young adult men absorbed in a cult of physical masculinity.

The surf club in Australia is a high-profile voluntary organization with a public-service rationale—it organizes beach lifesaving services—but also with a strong sporting and social flavour.

Its networks merge into competitive sport on one side and consumer capitalism (especially advertising and sporting-goods retailing) on the other. In both directions, Steve was brought into contact with 'older guys' and absorbed some of their sexual, commercial, and technical know-how. His first coital experience was organized at the surf club and witnessed by his friends there, when he was about 17:

> I remember the first time I had sex with a girl; I was at a toga party down at S Surf Club and I was round the rocks and that—pretty funny, yes—all the guys came round and watched ... I ran back and I was the hero.

As his career became focussed and he began to earn big money, Steve's peer group once again narrowed and stabilized, 'My friends are the guys I train with.' The replay is almost conscious: 'All the training you do, and all the time you put in, you are around them nearly as much as you are at school.' With his authoritarian trainer in the role of a schoolmaster, the continuity is striking, though the setting is now different. The peer group travels around the country to the big events, and the classroom furnishings are black leather-upholstered couches, expensive video systems, and live-in girlfriends.

The body and the self

Masculinity is not inherent in the male body; it is a definition given socially, which refers to characteristics of male bodies. If the body is very much at odds with the social definition, there is trouble, as in the situations of transvestites and transsexuals. If the body complies with the social definition it is easier for the meanings to take hold; and sometimes the body cues the social definition. In Steve's case the cue was being tall and strong as a child.

He remembers this with pleasure. The key to the memory is the social meaning of being big. Steve's bodily attributes were appropriated in quite specific social practices. One was the rough-and-tumble atmosphere of an all-boys school, where Steve's group depended on him. The element of nurturance is very interesting: 'We all stuck together; it was really good. I was sort of—I was always bigger than the rest of the guys, I sort of looked after them.'

The other practice was competitive sport organized by adults. Steve's size meant that he won competitive events early on, consistently enough to define him as a champion in the making. His body was certainly given this definition before adolescence, because at 13 he was making the career decision to specialize in swimming.

In Steve's pseudotechnical discussion of the components of success, quoted above, he acknowledges both elements. He calls the bodily cueing 'natural ability', and he theorizes it as inherited from his grandfather. He also acknowledges the highly specific social practice that appropriates the body (training, feeling keen, not having business problems) and turns it into an engine of competitive success.

To call this discussion pseudotechnical is to say that Steve's representation of this process is highly ideological. (I would guess he is quoting his coach, whose relation to sporting ideology is discussed in the next section.) This is not to deny Steve's precise knowledge of his body and its capacities. All top-level sports performers do have this knowledge. Indeed, it is common among adolescent boys engaged in sport, whatever their level of skill. Teenage football players, for instance, develop a detailed knowledge of their own bodies' capacities, and their exact suitability for different positions in the team.

Steve Donoghue is quite eloquent about the particular kind of skill that is involved in top-level performance in his sport. It is far from being pure brawn:

> I can spread my energy over a four-hour race to not die, to not have to start up slowly. I can start at a pace and finish at a pace every time. When I swam, I used to do 200 metres, which is four 50-metre laps. I can start off, and any 50 is pretty well to the tenth of a second the same time each lap, and I wouldn't even be looking at a watch ... It's mental. You've got to be fit to do it, but there are so many guys that are fit and not many are able to do that ... I'm just lucky naturally. But also distance-wise I can measure the distance out without having to think about it and say, 'Right this pace you are going, you will be able to keep going to the end and you will have no energy left at the end—you will have done the best race you can do over that distance.' And I've just done that all the time.

What Steve calls 'being lucky naturally' is in fact a skill developed by ten years of hard practising.

There is more to this than a technical knowledge of skills and capacities. Steve's whole person has become caught up in practices that centre on his body and its performances. Asked 'Where would you like to be as Steve? Nothing to do with business or money, just you?', he fumbles and then starts to grapple with this nexus:

> I haven't even thought about it. I might be just the way I am, but I don't, I never look to the future. Everything is—not day to day—but season to season. I am more interested in winning and racing than anything, and that takes up my whole time, all the preparation and the time I put in. Last winter I was up at T [surf resort]; we were training five hours a day, and the only thing I was thinking about was getting through that day and getting to the next day. Having to make my body, too much energy and not enough rest, to be functional at as good a rate for the next day's training session. That is all I would be thinking about.

In effect, the body becomes the focus of the self in quite a radical way. Social life is drastically curtailed to suit the logic of peak bodily performance. As Steve remarked, 'It's like being in jail.' Even more strikingly for a fit young heterosexual, sexual life is monitored and constricted because of its effect on performance. The kind of regime Steve sustained at school, and sustains now, leaves little room or energy for interests outside his sport. Even his casual peer group life is centred on others in the sport. Despite coming from a bourgeois background, he had little interest in schoolwork, seems to have no cultural interests beyond popular music, and cannot sustain a relationship with a woman who has interests outside of sport.

The picture, then, is of a psychological focus on the body together with a severely constricted social world and an impoverished cultural world. This is confirmed by a series of questions, asked at the end of the interview, about Steve's views on current issues:

Feminists?

> I don't like the ones that dress up in men's clothes and that sort of stuff, but I just think I don't mind women doing that sort of stuff. I'm the sort of guy that opens the car door for a girl all the time.

Gay men?

I've got no gay friends—I don't think I have. I'm not into television and hairdressing and anything like that ... As long as they keep to themselves and away from me I'm happy. I'm against them really. I can't see the reason why they are—I can't understand it—but a lot of people say they are born that way so I don't know. I'm [with a laugh] not into bashing them or anything like that.

Politics?

Nothing to do with it whatsoever. The last vote they had here I didn't even know it was on that day. I was down the beach in the surf.

In this bleached, featureless world centred on the care and maintenance of his body, punctuated by races, it is not surprising that Steve's only tangible goal is to collect dollars: 'Keep winning, keep winning, and keep rolling the money.' He has in view no use for the money except being able to live in comfort, so his only way of defining a purpose is to pick an arbitrary figure. Becoming a millionaire is 'just a goal, just something that I might aim for'; he is almost apologetic about its arbitrariness. The business of winning has consumed his life. With everything subordinated to bodily performance as the means of success, there is nothing very tangible that the success is for. So a goal has to be invented within the mechanism of races and dollars to give Steve the impression that his effort is leading to something worthwhile.

This cycle could, of course, be disrupted. The most likely disruptions are an injury (Steve has had some); a pregnancy (Steve could easily afford an abortion but the girlfriend of the day might insist on marriage and in that case would have a lot of social pressure behind her); or the emergence of a new champion who overshadows Steve and thus undermines his worth to sponsors. The last will certainly happen in time, but Steve has specialized in an event in which champions are good for a relatively long period. He has researched this point and has concluded that an iron man does not peak until 'around 30 or close to ... so in that way I've got at least five years left'.

[...]

Reflections

Steve lives an exemplary version of hegemonic masculinity. To live it does not mean to understand it. Steve has great trouble giving an account of masculinity when directly asked to explain a remark that 'men should be men':

I don't know, I really don't know. I just meant that as— I think just being strong and not—I was talking about gays, I think, don't know. I don't even know why I said it really, just came out.

What do you think it means to be a man, for you?

Not be a gay; I don't know. I've done interviews on that sort of stuff before, people said, 'You're scared of spiders and all that sort of stuff?' Yes I am; I have got fears like any other people. I am scared of heights. So I don't think any of that has got anything to do with being a man.

The best definition he can think of is 'be strong' and 'not be a gay'. Other respondents in our study, less exemplary than Steve, have much more complex and fluent answers to this question.

The exclusion of homosexual desire from the definition of masculinity is, of course, a key feature of modern hegemonic masculinity. It makes sense for Steve to grasp at this straw, especially because his life has long been substantially homo-social (i.e. an all-boys' school, a masculinized surf club and peer group, and a masculinized sport). His consciousness of this pattern is tellingly shown by his specific (and quite unnecessary) exclusion of iron-man events as possible sports for his girlfriends. It is a familiar point that there is a lot of homosexual affect floating around in such milieux. Steve simply blanks this out as we saw in his response to the subject of gay men.

To say that a particular form of masculinity is hegemonic means that it is culturally exalted and that its exaltation stabilizes the gender order as a whole. To be culturally exalted, the pattern of masculinity must have exemplars who are celebrated as heroes. Steve certainly enacts in his own life some of the main patterns of contemporary hegemonic masculinity: the subordination of women, the marginalization of gay men, and the connecting of masculinity to toughness and competitiveness. He has also been celebrated as a hero for much of his life, in school and in adult sport. He is being deliberately constructed now as a media exemplar of masculinity by the advertisers who are sponsoring him.

It is here that the contradictions poke out. Being an exemplar of masculinity actually forbids Steve to do many things that his peer group and culture define as masculine: 'it's like being in jail'. Steve experiences this prohibition as a very tangible pressure. Similarly, sustaining the training regime that yields the bodily supremacy, giving him his status as a champion, is incompatible with the kind of sexual and social life that is expected by affluent young men: 'you end up splitting up'. [...]

At a deeper level, Steve's performance is contradictory. Consider the focussing of both his social and his psychological life on the body, and the inward-turned competitiveness that seems related to his particular sport. There is a definite narcissism here, something often observed about athletes. This is a problem given the dominant cultural construction of masculinity as outward turned and denying the subjective.

Even more of a problem, the narcissism is necessarily unstable, unable to rest in self-admiration or indulgence (which would destroy the performance). In Steve's construction of competition (for instance his remarks about controlling pain), the decisive triumph is over oneself and specifically over one's body.

The magnificent machine of Steve's physique has meaning only when subordinated to the will to win. And the will to win is a curiously hollow construction in Steve's psychological makeup. The will to win does not arise from personal 'drive' (a familiar word in sport talk that Steve, tellingly, does not use at all). It is given to him by the social structure of sporting competition. It is his meaning, as a champion.

So we are returned to the social structures in which masculinities are produced. Indeed, we are led to see masculinity as an aspect of social structure, not just a form of personal character. As a configuration of gender relations, here meshed with consumer capitalism, hegemonic masculinity appropriates Steve's body and gives it a social definition. But it does this in ways that are full of contradiction, visible even behind the euphoria of Steve's tale of pleasure and success.

The long-term effect is hard to judge, but the short-term effect is clear. Steve gets his pleasure and success at the cost of his adulthood. [...] He is, of course, young. But most other men his age are facing the problems of earning a livelihood, constructing long-term relationships, building households, making hard choices, and facing social issues.

Steve has been taken in hand by the institutions of competitive sport and commerce and protected from common issues and problems. Though Steve cannot see it, for he has little experience of the world, his employers genuinely do not want an individual. They want someone to occupy a spot constructed by gender symbolism and the needs of commerce: a handsome, happy, nicely spoken, beach-sport hero who will make no difficulties about advertising their products. (Steve is, for example, sponsored by a beer company, which not everyone would see as a responsible move by a sporting champion.) At the moment he neatly fits the spot, and as long as he keeps up his winning status and his image, the money will keep rolling in and Steve will be preserved in his extended adolescence.

References

Connell, R. W. 1994. "Psychoanalysis on Masculinity." H. Broad and M. Kaufman, eds., *Theorizing Masculinities*, Thousand Oaks: Sage.

Pearson, Kent. 1982. "Conflict, Stereotypes and Masculinity in Australian and New Zealand Surfing." *Journal of Sociology* 18.2: 117–135.

4.5

Cheerleading and the gendered politics of sport

Laura Grindstaff and Emily West

In this article, Grindstaff and West examine how gender is performed by men and women in an activity—cheerleading—that has traditional feminine connotations. Through ethnographic research, the authors explore the different ways that men and women conceptualize the activity and identify its key features. While both genders want cheerleading to be considered a sport, indicating a measure of respect, men, in particular, disdain and try to avoid the sideline/supportive activities that the teams are often required to perform. The article raises the question of how cheerleading articulates with questions about: what is a sport; how gender is performed differently by men and women within a given activity; and how do given activities relate to images of actors' sexuality.

Assumed to exist on the margins of sport (and sport on the margins of "real" life), cheerleading might seem an unlikely subject for academic research. Yet forms of popular culture like cheerleading and sport reveal a great deal about social relations, particularly relations of inequality. Sport has been widely acknowledged as a key institution for examining the production, reproduction, and sometimes contestation of gender inequality. The organization and unfolding of gender relations in a given institution is its "gender regime" (Connell 1987), and, until recently at least, the gender regime of sport tended to buttress notions of male superiority. Scholars generally agree that organized athletics have been central to the construction of what R.W. Connell (1987) calls "hegemonic masculinity," helping to socialize men into business, politics, and war (see Crosset 1990; Kimmel 1990; Messner 1992).

If sport is an arena in which men express and sustain hegemonic masculinity, cheerleading is said to embody the qualities associated with "emphasized femininity" (Connell 1987), notably supportiveness, enthusiasm, and sexual attractiveness (see Kurman 1986). Cast as a feminine auxiliary to sport for the latter half of the twentieth century, cheerleading has served as an icon of normative—meaning white, heterosexual, middle class, and American—girlhood, as well as a ready target for those contesting that ideal (see Adams and Bettis 2003; Hanson 1995). There is a kind of "fit" between emphasized femininity and hegemonic masculinity because the adaptive orientation of one exists in relation to the power of the other (Connell 1987).

While institutions help bring order and stability to social relations, they are not impervious to contradiction and challenge (see Friedland and Alford 1991), and as institutions change, so do their gender regimes. The dramatic entry of women and girls into a wide range of sports since the passage of Title IX is well documented (Festle 1996).[1] Cheerleading also changed. It shifted from a primarily female, sideline activity to a more gender mixed, athletic, competitive activity in recent decades. The 1990s witnessed the rapid rise of what is known as all-star cheerleading—private, for-profit cheer programs devoted exclusively to competition and operating independently of schools. There is much debate, both in the media and in the cheer world itself, about whether or not cheerleading should be recognized as a sport in its own right. At the same time, change is never simple or simply progressive, and the debate over cheerleading and sport is about more than increased athleticism; it is also about the gender regime of sports and the historic status of sport as a male preserve.

Gender is not merely an individual attribute that one has or enacts, it is something accomplished in interaction with others, "an emergent property of social situations" (West and Fenstermaker 1995:9; see also West and Zimmerman 1987). Likewise, people do not simply import their gendered selves into neutral institutions; rather, institutions are themselves gendered (Acker 1990; Connell 1987; Lorber 1994; Messner 2002). Sport has been one of the most masculine of institutions, and despite recent gains by women, it is still largely organized by and for men. This is particularly true at its "institutional core" (Messner 2002), where masculinity—assumed to be heterosexual—is linked to socially sanctioned aggression and physical power (Griffin 1998; McKay, Messner, and Sabo 2000; Messner 1992, 2002; Messner and Sabo 1990; Theberge 1994, 1993; Trujillo 2000).[2]

Historically, women—and middle class white women especially—have found their greatest popular acceptance in the periphery of sport, specifically in "feminine" sports such as gymnastics and figure skating, which are deemed socially acceptable for women but trivialized by the sports establishment (Bryson 1994; Feder 1995). "Feminine" sports mesh neatly with taken-for-granted assumptions that women are "naturally" smaller, slower, and weaker than men but more graceful, flexible, and inclined toward aestheticized or sexualized bodily display—assumptions that work to suppress the actual gender diversity that exists in sport (see Cahn 1994; Kane 1995; Lenskyj 1986). However, sport is far from

coterminous with hetero-masculinity and the "female athlete" is no longer an oxymoron but an increasingly visible cultural icon (see Heywood and Dworkin 2003).

This paper draws upon ethnographic data to argue that cheerleading, particularly coed college cheerleading, provides a powerful lens through which to examine the relational construction of gender and sexuality in both sport and in society at large. The richness of cheerleading for sociological analysis stems less from the way cheerleading "fixes" gendered meanings once and for all than for the way it negotiates contested terrain and transgresses a series of gendered boundaries, notably those between sport and performance, athletics and aesthetics, and competitiveness and supportiveness. These phenomena, like gender itself, exist (and coexist) along a continuum despite being invoked in oppositional terms. As a social phenomenon, cheerleading does not simply express agreed upon definitions of emphasized femininity or hegemonic masculinity in isolation from one another. Rather, it is an activity where the very terms of femininity and masculinity are constructed and worked through side-by-side, and the question of what is "emphasized" (or hegemonic) along the way is a matter of empirical investigation. To draw on Candace West and Don Zimmerman (1987), cheerleading is a space where young women and men "do" (and "undo") gender in the service of producing particular social arrangements. Our goal is to make sense of the *workings* and not just the *existence* of those arrangements.[3]

Methods

Our research is ethnographic, relying on interviews and observations in the field. [...] We examine what male and female cheerleaders say and do in the context of creating and sustaining the contemporary "gender order" (Connell 1987). We focus on coed college teams because we are interested in the construction of masculinity as much as femininity (rates of male participation being highest in college cheerleading) and because, in the coed context, the relational dimension of gender is underscored.

Sustained periods of fieldwork took place in three phases. During the 1998–99 academic year, my co-author Emily West and I observed a 16-member coed squad (5 men and 11 women) at a large northeastern university called "Stanton." We attended biweekly practices and at-home sideline performances during both football and basketball season, and we interviewed the coach and team members. Although the Stanton cheerleaders had competed in the past, at the time they were a non-competitive sideline squad housed under the athletic department—a fairly typical college squad. During the 2002–03 academic year, I observed a 14-member coed squad (5 men and 9 women) at "Fairview College" in Northern California. This team was comparable in skill level to the Stanton group, with a similar practice and game schedule. I conducted interviews with a subset of 12 Fairview cheerleaders (7 women, 5 men).[4]

For the third and most intense phase of fieldwork I shifted my focus to a more highly skilled competitive college team. This was crucial to the study because increasing numbers of college teams in the United States are competing and because competition is central to both legal and lay understandings of sport. During 2004–05, I observed and conducted interviews with a large, 22-member competitive coed team (11 women, 11 men) at "Delta Valley State University" ("Delta State"), also in Northern California. As with most competitive college teams, it has a dual identity, performing on the sidelines of school sports events as well as training for competition.

At all three schools, the racial composition of the squads tended to mirror that of the larger student body, with Fairview and Delta State being more racially diverse than Stanton.[5] However, given that ours is a qualitative study and that the numbers within any one racial group (including white) are small, no clear patterns in the doing of gender by race emerged.[6]

I also engaged in more episodic fieldwork targeting summer training camps and national competitions. In the summer of 2003, I attended three summer training camps for college cheerleaders, one each in Kentucky, Texas, and Southern California. I observed cheerleaders in classes and evaluation sessions, attended daily seminars and informational meetings for coaches, and had many informal conversations with cheerleaders, coaches, and instructional staff.[7] I chose the California camp because it was the one attended by both the Fairview and Delta State squads; I chose the Kentucky and Texas camps because the American South is widely

considered the "heartland" of contemporary cheerleading. The camp in California was hosted by the Universal Cheerleading Association (UCA), the largest and most profitable of the country's many cheerleading companies. Those in the South were run by the National Cheerleading Association (NCA), the oldest and second largest cheerleading company.

As for competitions, my co-author and I attended UCA's national college championship together in January 2003 and I attended NCA's national championship in April of that same year.[8] In February of 2005 I attended a third national competition in Las Vegas hosted by the United Spirit Association (USA), a smaller, regional company that attracts teams primarily from the West and Southwest. I targeted events run by these three companies because, despite being owned by the same parent corporation, each boasts its own cheerleading style based largely on how strongly the roles of men and women are differentiated, and, related to this, how "showy" or "performance oriented" (to use the terms employed by our interviewees) the competition routines are. As we discuss later, these stylistic differences have implications for how participants understand the gender politics of cheerleading.

This more sporadic, event-centered fieldwork not only afforded me the opportunity to converse informally with many people, it gave rise to additional interviews with college cheerleaders and coaches beyond those affiliated with our three core squads, as well as with representatives of the cheerleading companies. In particular, I sought out individuals from the South to help compensate for lack of sustained fieldwork in that region, as well as individuals from teams affiliated with the NCA, to help offset the fact that all three of our core squads were affiliated with UCA and one also with USA. We include as part of our data "supplementary" interviews with 17 cheerleaders, 4 coaches, and 3 industry representatives, with men and women represented in roughly equal proportion.[9] Because members of the same team were sometimes interviewed together, the total number of people interviewed for this paper (72) is greater than the actual number of interviews tape-recorded and transcribed (52).[10] Per ethnographic tradition, we use pseudonyms for our individual participants and the squads we observed on an ongoing basis.

[...] The theme most pertinent to this paper—whether or not cheerleading is a sport—emerged at multiple junctures simultaneously: in interviews when we asked subjects to define cheerleading, to discuss why they got involved, or to defend cheerleading against popular stereotypes; during practices and summer camp sessions as we observed the physical demands on participants; and at national competitions whose very existence is predicated upon a sport model (complete with ESPN television coverage in some cases). As our study progressed, the question of whether cheerleading is a sport was increasingly taken up by the news media as well as by cheerleaders themselves in various online forums, further highlighting the significance and salience of the debate.

We elaborated on the "sport question" in interviews by asking subjects what criteria they applied to sport, whether they saw cheerleading as a sport across all contexts, and whether their private views differed from the public stance they took when discussing cheerleading with outsiders. This latter distinction underlines the importance of "sport" as a marker of legitimacy for those who might resist defining any activity associated with femininity as a sport. That sport and competition are gendered for our participants was revealed in the comparisons they made between cheerleading and "core" sports like football, as well as in the distinctions they imposed between the "sport-like" features of cheerleading and those linked to supportiveness or performativity. The key categories (athleticism, competition, performativity, supportiveness) that drive our analysis of the gender regime of contemporary coed cheerleading emerged out of these conversations.

In search of respect

Although cheerleading was once an all-male activity ("invented" in the late 1800s to increase spectator involvement in collegiate football), it was gradually feminized throughout the nineteenth century and has been female dominated since the 1950s (see Adams and Bettis 2003; Hanson 1995). Female involvement changed the nature of cheerleading, shifting emphasis away from character building and leadership to notions of physical attractiveness and sex appeal,

which led to a white, middle class bias in the selection of female cheerleaders in the aftermath of desegregation (Grundy 2001; Hanson 1995) and the trivialization and devaluation of cheerleading overall (Hanson 1995). Icons of "ideal" femininity notwithstanding, cheerleading is often considered a trivial activity and female cheerleaders have been negatively stereotyped as dumb and/or sexually promiscuous, particularly as traditional gender ideologies underwent significant change in the wake of second wave feminism (Adams and Bettis 2003; Hanson 1995).

In a real if only partial sense, it was the shift toward sport that "saved" cheerleading from obsolescence and secured its contemporary popularity. If cheerleading lost ground in the post-Title IX era with the rise of feminism and women's sports, it was partly because cultural scripts about femininity expanded during this period to incorporate notions of toughness and physical strength.[11] Cheerleading reclaimed its lost status with women by bringing its performance of femininity up-to-date, combining enthusiasm and sex appeal on the one hand with hard-body athleticism on the other (see Adams and Bettis 2003). The transformation of cheerleading has drawn more men to the activity as well. As a UCA executive put it, "the idea of picking the cutest girl to be on the cheerleading team is so far gone now that guys can migrate back into it and feel good about it."

Today, cheerleading routines incorporate advanced tumbling, stunting, and pyramid building as well as cheering and (sometimes) dance. Cheerleaders call themselves "cheer athletes" and the term "team" is used interchangeably with "squad." While the National Collegiate Athletic Association (NCAA) does not recognize cheerleading as a sport, and while only about half of the nation's high school athletic associations do (Dodd 2004), individual schools may classify cheerleading as a varsity sport if they wish. Some—including Delta State—award partial scholarships to cheerleaders. In 2003, to much media fanfare, the University of Maryland used its competitive "all-girl"[12] team to demonstrate Title IX compliance (the legality of this move is pending). Even the slogans on t-shirts and other cheer apparel reflect the bid for sports status: "Girl + Athlete = Cheerleader"; "Hold my weights while I stunt with your girlfriend"; "Other sports use one ball, we use two."

For cheerleaders themselves, the question of whether college cheerleading is a sport, or ought to be classified as a sport, is a complicated one because of the diverse ways that people define sport, the diversity of school cheer squads that exist (coed versus all-girl, competitive versus sideline), the disparate ways that individual schools classify and treat cheerleading,[13] and the difference between believing cheerleading to be a sport and wanting it to be "officially" recognized as such by the NCAA. Regarding this last point, some interviewees were aware of, and supported, the stance of the major cheerleading companies in opposing the classification of school cheerleading as a sport by the NCAA both because of the increased regulation that would ensue and because the sport classification might phase out non-competitive cheerleading altogether.[14] What emerged in the fieldwork and interviews, then, was not a neat calibration of positions for or against the sport designation across all types of cheerleading, much less unanimous support for classifying cheerleading as a sport in a legal sense, but ways of talking about and negotiating the gendered relationship between cheerleading and sport in the search for greater legitimacy. Indeed, the issue of whether or not cheerleading is a "real" sport is a proxy for the issue of respect.

For all the participants in our study, the term "sport" signified high status; cheerleaders knew that playing sports was more prestigious than cheerleading, especially for men, and they complained about being disrespected by the collegiate athletes for whom they cheered. This was true even at Delta State, where the cheer team was the only team in the school's recent history to win a national title. Most of the cheerleaders we interviewed, male and female alike, strongly resented their second class status both in their schools and in the culture at large; recognizing the cultural legitimacy of sport, they wanted that legitimacy for cheerleading. One Delta State cheerleader was quite blunt about this: "I want it to be considered a sport," she said, "so people can't trash it."

Coed college cheerleaders attempt to bring cheerleading under the umbrella of sport in two main ways: by focusing on the competitive nature of cheerleading, and, related to this, by emphasizing the skill or athleticism of cheerleading. The majority of our interviewees, particularly those on competitive teams, drew firm boundaries between competitive and noncompetitive cheer, believing that the former qualifies as a sport but the latter typically does not. The following quote from Jack, a competitive cheerleader on the east coast, is illustrative: "I'm going to say that, for cheerleading to be a sport, it goes from squad to squad. A squad that competes, that has competed in the past, they want to compete in the future, and they're working to compete. I'll say that squad is a sport." Repeatedly we heard phrases such as "a sport is anything where you compete against someone else" (Stanton cheerleader) and "if you're not competing, it's not a sport" (Fairview cheerleader).

At the same time, participants recognize that it is not a competitive orientation alone that puts cheerleading in league with sport, it is also the athleticism and skill presumed to go along with that orientation. Participants routinely characterized competitive cheerleaders as "phenomenal athletes" and emphasized the hard work, dedication, and training required. "If you look at the people who do it, they're not just random people walking in off the street with no ability," said Ruby, a Delta State cheerleader, "they've all been athletes and their bodies are trained. We work hard, it's very dangerous, and we deserve that title [i.e., sport]." Sometimes we heard that cheerleading was *more* demanding athletically than other sports. While interviewees most often compared cheerleading to gymnastics and diving, some also invoked sports in the institutional core. It was Ruby's opinion that "anyone can be a football player, anyone can run with a ball or throw a ball. Not everyone can do a toss-lib" (a type of partner stunt). Her teammate, Lars, said that his "hardest football practice ever" was still easier than a "mediocre" cheer practice. A young man I met at the Kentucky camp compared cheerleading to his experience playing rugby, hockey, and baseball: "each of those sports is tough," he said, "after practices, you are sore for a bit; [but] after an intense cheer workout, your body is sore for two to three days. Every muscle in your body is used." Because of the premium placed on training and athleticism, a minority of participants questioned competition as the litmus test for sports classification, insisting that sideline-only teams were also engaging in sport if they were highly skilled.[15]

The criteria of competition and athleticism were important for distinguishing squads that "deserved" the sport label from those that did not, and for enabling interviewees to distance themselves from the feminine stigma they associate with earlier generations of cheerleading. Interviewees expressed frustration that outdated, 1950s-era stereotypes persisted and were applied indiscriminately to the whole of cheerleading. Manuel, captain of the Delta State team, insisted that assigning the label "sport" would make little difference unless people also stopped thinking of cheerleading as "just a bunch of ditzy girls on the sidelines who jump around and entertain the crowd." He and others in the study believed that greater knowledge of the activity would breed greater respect. Ben, one of Manuel's teammates, said that "ninety-five percent of the people you meet don't know anything about it … as much as cheerleading has changed within the cheer community, for someone on the outside looking in, cheerleading is still the rah-rah skirts and pom-pons kind of thing." Liz, the captain of a competitive Louisiana team, said much the same thing: "People are not willing to accept cheerleading in their brains as a sport. This is based on pure ignorance. They can't accept what they don't know. People think that cheerleading is just a girl's activity or something only girls do."

Cheerleading has had a difficult time gaining recognition and respect not just because people are ignorant of what it is really about but also because certain feminine elements of the cheerleading canon continue to compromise its legitimacy. As much as college cheer has incorporated the traditionally "masculine" qualities of competition and athleticism associated with sport, these qualities have combined with, not replaced, the more traditionally feminine qualities of supportiveness and performativity. That school cheerleading has retained key elements of its feminine legacy complicates the interpretive struggle over the meaning and status of the activity, as cheerleaders construct and deploy "common sense" notions about gender and gender difference in an effort to make sense of their own involvement.

Obstacles to respect: the supportive function of cheerleading

Despite the move toward competition and greater athleticism, cheerleading is still strongly associated with its supportive function, best captured by the image of female cheerleaders on the sidelines of (male) sporting events. This image is not as outdated as the cheerleaders we interviewed liked to think. Industry representatives are quick to point out that the "bread and butter" of the business are sideline squads that do little or no competing; since girls and women dominate cheerleading overall, most of these squads are all-girl.[16] Competitive school squads, both coed and all-girl, also uphold the sideline tradition by cheering at sports events, appearing at pep rallies, and performing at school or community functions. The sideline paradigm suggests that cheerleading is central to doing gender in ways that conflate femininity with emotional supportiveness. Insofar as the role of cheerleaders is to express through ritualized performance support for other athletes, they are doing the same kind of "emotion work" in the context of organized sport that middle class women have traditionally done in the interpersonal context of heterosexual marriage (see Cline and Spender 1987; Hochschild 1983).

The sideline function of cheerleading constitutes a major obstacle to its bid for sports status not only among outsiders but also among cheerleaders themselves. As Tarek, one of the Fairview cheerleaders, observed: "how can a sport be something that encourages other sports? Like, if you're there to supplement sports how can you yourself be a sport?" Tarek, like other sideline-only cheerleaders in our study, did not see sideline cheer as a sport because of its supportive dimension, but he also did not see supportiveness and athleticism as mutually exclusive necessarily. Some of the competitive cheerleaders we interviewed disagreed, making comments like, "sideline cheer is easy," "sideline teams don't train like athletes do for other sports," and "they're just out there looking pretty." While we did meet a few competitive cheerleaders who embraced the "spirit" function of cheerleading whole-heartedly, most downplayed their sideline performances as mere practices, or as obligations to fulfill in order that they might participate in the "real" cheerleading that occurs at competitions. When asked whether her cheerleaders would get rid of their sideline obligations if they could, the Delta State coach said, "Oh yeah. Maybe one or two of 'em would say, 'Aw, we don't get to do that anymore?' But the majority of them … these kids are all here to compete, and do the things on the side that they have to do."

At Stanton and Fairview, where the cheer teams were non-competitive, the denigration of sideline cheer was accomplished more subtly, by arguing that cheerleading was not just—or even primarily—about supporting other athletes, but an opportunity to display one's skills, improve one's skills, and even compete with the opposing cheer squad on the other side of the field or court. They were not alone in employing such arguments. As the coach of a coed squad in Louisiana put it, "when we go to games, there's a whole competition going on that most of the people in the crowd don't even realize. We believe the football game is just a backdrop for our performance." Male cheerleaders also spoke of competing against male teammates when throwing stunts and basket tosses. "We're competitive," said Heiko, a former member of the Fairview squad. "I used to compete with some of the guys on the team, you know, 'if you drop a stunt you owe me a beer.'" Thus cheerleaders can and do distance themselves from the supportive dimension of cheerleading, assumed to embody outdated expectations for women, by interpreting the sideline role in unexpected and even creative ways that cast cheerleading as competitive and athletic in its own right even in a sideline context.

The gender politics of sideline cheer are further manifest in how strongly male cheerleaders chafe against the sideline component compared to their female counterparts. To be sure, some female cheerleaders expressed deep ambivalence about their supportive role, recognizing its links to an outdated and devalued version of femininity, and, as indicated above, most insisted that their sideline performance was as much "for themselves" as for the athletes they supported. But their ambivalence paled in comparison to the men's, for whom supportiveness is not just devalued or outmoded but gender transgressive. The following comment from Forest, a Delta State cheerleader, is illustrative: "What I don't like? I *hate* the games, *so much*. I hate games. I hate games because I hate being out in front of people in uniform. I've gotten better ... like, my first year—trying to get the crowd pumped up for some other guys, it was a little weird." Over and over we heard similar comments, even from the men on side-line-only squads. According to John, a Stanton freshman,

"if it were up to me, I'd come here and practice three times a week and never ever go to games ... they want me to do arm movements, do you know how bad that is? They want me to run with the flag and be happy, and that's just horrible, horrible stuff."

Male cheerleaders communicated discomfort with their sideline role in the way they acted during games, holding back from yelling and expressing less enthusiasm than their female teammates. This was true for the men on all three squads observed as well as on teams at the summer training camps (getting men to embrace the sideline function of cheerleading was one of the topics covered in the coaches' seminars that I attended at the camps). At Delta State, roughly half of the men had been on high school cheer teams where they were excused from cheering games altogether. According to Diego, one of the Delta State cheerleaders and a long time UCA instructor, this arrangement had much to do with the successful retention of male cheerleaders at his school: "all we did was compete. And so that made it a lot easier to retain the guys ... guys hate cheerleading. We hate going to games and standing there and doing motions or yelling. We just want to put the girls up [in stunts]."

Coaches routinely lament the difficulty they face recruiting and retaining boys and men. Some schools, including Fairview, use the term "stunt team" instead of "cheer squad" in an effort to downplay the supportive function and emphasize the athleticism of cheerleading, thereby making it sound more masculine and sport-like. But the part of college cheerleading that involves supporting other teams, whether on the sidelines or when demonstrating crowd skills in a competition setting, undermines its status as a "true" sport, even for participants and coaches who value its athleticism.

More gender trouble: the performative aspects of cheerleading

Also opposed to conventional understandings of sport and closely related to the supportive dimension of cheerleading are its aesthetic, performance demands, which are not unlike those of figure skating (see Baughman 1995; Feder, 1995). As Abigail Feder notes (1995), the theatrical elements of figure skating—costume, makeup, gesture—that provide opportunities for feminine adornment and display also "soften the athletic prowess required for executing triple jumps and flying sit-spins" (p. 24), in effect masking or "apologizing" for the skater's athleticism. The same is true for cheerleading, where the performative elements, undeniably coded as "feminine" by participants, over-determine femininity for the women involved and provide further opportunities for boundary work for the men.

While the term "performance" is arguably gender neutral (as in the phrase "high-performance athlete"), in cheerleading it is used interchangeably with "performativity"—meaning theatrical, energetic, and entertaining—and is understood both as a feminine construct and in contrast to sport. This is evident when cheerleaders speak of performance and sport as opposing tendencies and in the characteristics they associate with performance. According to a Stanton cheerleader, "[the physical training] is similar to what other sports teams do ... but [cheerleading] is hard to define because, at the same time, you're performing ... and I think that's where the question comes in ... I think of cheerleaders as performers as well as athletes." A member of the Fairview squad invoked the same opposition when she compared cheerleading to gymnastics; whereas the latter was "certainly a sport" in her view, she hesitated to characterize cheerleading in the same way because "cheerleading is a spectacle, which is like more performance than sport." Dance figured centrally in these distinctions, with dance representing the performance part of cheerleading and other skills such as a tumbling and stunting representing sport.

The supportive and performative dimensions of cheerleading are closely related, both in fact and in the eyes of cheerleaders. Appearing before a crowd requires that cheerleaders be enthusiastic, energetic, and entertaining. This is accomplished not just through dancing, tumbling, or eye-catching stunts, but also through the bubbly, peppy, performance of "spirit" in cheerleading—what we call "informal cheerleading." Informal cheerleading is what participants do to express enthusiasm and "rally the crowd," whether on the sidelines or competition mat. It includes smiling, "facials" (exaggerated facial expressions), being in constant motion, jumping, and executing dynamic arm, hand, and head motions—all considered

feminine terrain. Performativity is also defined in terms of appearance: how female cheerleaders should look when in front of crowds. In the words of a Stanton cheerleader, "we're told to be in full makeup, to do our hair. Because we're performing. If you're not wearing lipstick, that's the first thing [the coach] will say to you, 'why isn't your lipstick on?'" Being petite is part of the "appearance aspect" for women on coed teams, as is wearing the conventional cheerleader uniform, whose short skirt, tight-fitting shell top (often cropped, exposing the midriff), and hair ribbons suggest a combination of youthfulness and sexual availability. As Connell (1987) so aptly observed: "[emphasized] femininity is performed, performed especially to men" (p. 188).

As a group, the young women we interviewed accepted these feminine accoutrements as "just part of the show," "just for entertainment," and "necessary to please the crowd"—in other words, a taken-for-granted necessity in an activity focused on entertainment and bodily display. While a couple of interviewees expressed discomfort with this state of affairs (as one of the Stanton women put it: "how can it be a varsity sport if you have to have makeup?"), most clearly enjoyed the "girly" aspects of cheerleading and had little interest in trading their short skirts, hair ribbons, and makeup for more gender-neutral attire. Ruby's comment is illustrative: "I think it's fun quite honestly, as a girl I like to do my makeup kind of fun and sparkly and get out there ... I like wearing ribbons in my hair, it's a girly feminine thing and I think it's something that shouldn't be lost." Regarding the "skimpy uniforms," her teammate, Sidney, said, "I guess it goes back to the whole heterosexual thing, the pretty girls ... the skimpy uniforms. The guys enjoy it ... and us looking cute attracts the audience to look at us." She insisted that cheerleading was no different than the rest of popular culture in this regard: "It's the same with being on TV, like, or being a singer. You want them to be cute, you're watching them, you know ... If you gotta wear the short skirts to make people look at you, then I guess that's what you gotta do." Other interviewees pointed out that cheer skirts are no shorter than skirts worn in tennis or field hockey, and that cheerleading uniforms are modest compared to gymnasts' leotards or swimmers' Speedos. "All sports have kinky outfits," observed Sarah, one of the Stanton women, "why pick on cheerleading?"

171

Female cheerleaders are well aware that cheer-leading is trivialized in the larger culture, but they attribute this trivialization not to the short skirts and makeup per se but to people's over-valuation of these elements when assessing the "worth" of cheerleading.

Rather than view the combination of perfor-mativity and athleticism as somehow unique to cheerleading, we suggest that female cheerlead-ers have absorbed the lessons of a culture that strongly emphasizes the display of sexy, athletic bodies (see Heywood and Dworkin 2003) and that this marriage of seemingly contradictory elements is one of the hallmarks of contempo-rary emphasized femininity (see Adams and Bettis 2003). In absorbing this lesson, female cheerleaders may be little different than female athletes in more "legitimate" sports or post-Title IX women more generally. As Leslie Heywood and Shari Dworkin (2003) argue, "for much of the younger demographic, exhibit-ing a hot body is an intense sign of valuation ... not ... devaluation," because being sexualized "no longer carries the social stigma it once did" (p. 89). What makes the femininity of cheer-leaders "emphasized" relative to that of many other female athletes is the fact that, for cheer-leaders, artifice, adornment, and sexual display are not optional characteristics to be adopted off the field or court: they are part of the sport itself. Moreover, the heteronormativity of the girly-girl aspect of coed cheerleading is no small part of the activity's appeal for female partici-pants, as this creates a "safe" outlet for their athleticism—safe because the issue of sexuality appears resolved in the "right" direction. It is telling that while gay men are an acknowledged part of coed cheerleading, lesbians are rarely mentioned and are virtually invisible.

Male cheerleaders are much less sanguine about the performative nature of cheerleading, the increasing sexual commodification of male athletes in the media notwithstanding (see Miller 2001). Commenting on the gender inappropriateness (for men) of cheerleading's "obsession with appearances," Rulond, a Fairview cheerleader, said "never before in my life had I ever been involved in anything where I was so carefully monitored for my [appearance] ... But image is everything in cheerleading. People were 'Rulond, you need to shave. You need to go in there and comb your hair, young man.'" He explained that this was a turnoff for men.

"Usually aesthetics and hygiene and appearance are kind of tertiary and you would rather have your words and actions make your statement about you. I think that's just a nice way of say-ing cheerleading is too fluffy." As further evi-dence of his view, Rulond observed, somewhat disdainfully, that "a game face for a cheerleader is a big smile." Indeed, Rulond was one of sev-eral men in our study who denied the sport label to competitive as well as sideline cheer-leading because the competition is indirect, occurring through the medium of judging, and because the criteria for judging are partly aes-thetic. Significantly, these same objections are also raised by male critics of competitive cheer-leading in the news media (see Dodd 2004; Morrissey 2004). Thus feminine performativity can prevent competitive cheerleading from gaining legitimacy both when people question the presence of performativity in sport and when this performativity necessitates a "subjec-tive" mode of evaluation.

The performance demands of cheerleading not only undermine its status as a "real" sport, they also expose male participants to homo-phobia. Male cheerleaders recognize the tension between conventional notions of performativ-ity, coded as feminine, and conventional notions of heterosexual masculinity (also noted by Davis 1990). This tension makes straight men, as well as gay men invested in maintaining a straight image, initially resistant to the more feminized elements of cheerleading, including dancing and jumping, certain cheer motions, and the repertoire of gestures and facial expressions in the informal performance of spirit. Men on coed teams facilitate the visual spectacle of cheerleading, particularly through stunting, tumbling, and pyramid building, but they gen-erally are not asked to smile constantly, bounce up and down, shake pom-pons, or wiggle their fingers in the air (a gesture known as "spirit fingers"). To do so would risk being labeled gay, a scenario described by one male cheerleader as "the gay cheerleader syndrome."

"Nothing with hips": managing the male cheerleader's "image problem"

According to Connell (1987), hegemonic mas-culinity is constructed in relation to subordinated masculinities as well as in relation to women. The most important feature of contemporary hegemonic masculinity is heterosexuality. Thus a key form of subordinated masculinity is homosexual (or not heterosexual). To the degree that cheerleading is coded as feminine, and to the degree that femininity (for men) is conflated with homosexuality, male cheerleaders are concerned about managing their gender image. *Everyone* we encountered in this study spoke of the gay stereotype for male cheerleaders. As Ben put it: "most people assume, if you say 'I'm a male cheerleader,' they assume you're gay. It happens all the time. That's why I don't even tell people [that I cheer]. People always ask me if I play football, and so I just tell 'em 'yeah.' It's not even worth getting into a conversation about." Mandy, a junior on the Stanton squad, spoke of a teammate who was pledging a "hard core, really masculine" fraternity. She predicted he would "quit before rush" because the existing members would never initiate a cheerleader. When asked why, she replied: "because they look at it like, excuse my language, they think it's such a fag thing to do." Sean, a competitive cheerleader from Texas summed up the reaction he gets when people find out that he cheers, saying, "well um, 'less masculine than most,' 'sissy,' 'fairy'—I've pretty much heard it all."

Male cheerleaders manage the gay cheerleader syndrome in a number of ways, most of which reinforce the notion that being strong and being straight "naturally" go together. For example, some mentioned the importance of throwing impressive stunts as a way to "prove" they weren't gay. "The taunting, I've had it at games," said Jack, a competitive east coast cheerleader. "They call me a fag, and I'm like, 'come on!' and I just shove it in their face. And do a great stunt that they could never do, and shut them up." Others compared themselves to football players—not surprisingly, since football players are widely understood to epitomize hegemonic masculinity. The men on a competitive squad I met at the Kentucky camp lifted weights on the same schedule as their school's football team specifically to impress upon the other athletes their comparable strength. Likewise, Ben, of Delta State, dismissed the assumption that football players were stronger, superior athletes. In his words: "the fact of the matter is, these guys [on the football team] can't do what I do in the gym. Like, I'm more

athletic. I have more strength than these guys. It's just, people look at you differently when they find out you're a cheerleader; it takes away from who you are." Sean provides another variation on the football theme when defending his decision to cheer, in the process displaying what we call "compensatory hypermasculinity"—the explicit assertion of heterosexuality in the face of the "discrediting" fact of being a male cheerleader (see Goffman 1963 on the concept of discreditable identities). "Football players roll around in the grass with other males, shower with each other, and slap each other on the butt," he said, "and then you look at me, I'm hanging around with some of the hottest, in-shape young ladies that the school has to offer. I'm touching them and holding them in places you can only dream about. Now let me ask you, who's gay?"

The male cheerleaders in our study knew what gender appropriate reasons to offer in order to justify taking part in a feminine activity. Unlike female cheerleaders, whose gender identity is confirmed (though not uniformly respected) as a result of their participation, male cheerleaders feel compelled to prove they are "real" men despite being cheerleaders. They do this on as well as off the field by embracing certain parts of the cheerleading repertoire (stunting, pyramid building) and resisting others (smiling, cheering), and in their general demeanor. According to Tom, a freshman on the Stanton squad: "I think if you're a male cheerleader, you tend to try to act more masculine ... You know, you kind of push out your chest, draw up your shoulders a little bit, look like you're big and tough."

Thus it is not that male cheerleaders refuse to be performative at all while on the sidelines or in competitions, but that they seek out gender-appropriate modes of performance. In fact, when male cheerleaders' performance of masculinity is successful, it arguably enhances the image of cheerleading as a tough, athletic activity. Forest described how his attitude toward performativity changed over time, as he came to discover an acceptably masculine approach. He said that in high school he was reluctant to smile and "sell the routine" because he saw that as feminine. "But the more mature I got the more I realized—I saw other [guys] doing it, and you didn't have to do it in a feminine way, you could do it, like, kind of cocky and all pumped up ... you know, [after a great stunt] hit the crowd, show 'em your guns" (lowering his head toward his biceps in a classic muscle man pose). His teammate, Ruby, who was listening, agreed: "I think the guys, they don't play it up physically with makeup, but their job is to look good. Like, you have big, strong guys that are muscular and athletic. And they know how to work it in front of an audience."

These comments reveal a "different but equal" perspective on gender relations (including gender performance) that resonates with the views of the young people in our study generally: that the roles of men and women are equally important but organized differently according to gender appropriateness, understood in relation to common sense notions of what looks good for whom. This is underscored in their assessment of male cheerleaders who violate these common sense notions by adopting a feminine—even hyperfeminine—mode of performativity. Bruce, a Delta State cheerleader, explained that it was "okay to be really showy" and to "make the faces," but "only to a certain extent." "[Cheerleaders] do that stuff to make the routine seem more energetic," he explained, "but then there's some people who take it to another level. I mean, they're so flaming the flames are flying off the stage and hitting you on the head!" These "flaming" cheerleaders are, of course, assumed to be gay, and are sometimes resented by other men for perpetuating the "wrong" image of male cheerleaders. According to Ben, "I don't have a problem with gay people, I know a lot of gay people ... but you get a cheerleader who's, like, flaming, and they take it way too far. Like, the girliest girl I know is not as flaming as guy cheerleaders that are flamboyant about it. It's beyond feminine." When asked why that should bother him, he said, "there's no reason for it, especially if you're going to be in an open forum where it's not just your personal life anymore. Like, this is my life too; this is my cheerleading if you're going to be at a competition I'm at."

At issue here is the *performance of gender* not sexual orientation per se. And the public nature of cheerleading, combined with the fact that cheerleaders are considered ambassadors of their schools, mean that the performance of masculinity is monitored and controlled not just by male cheerleaders but also by coaches, school administrators, and alumni. Diego, of Delta State, said that cheerleading coaches at

the college level were under pressure from alumni to avoid any appearance of homosexuality and that this pressure can lead coaches to pass over men "who don't fit the image of the program." Once a team is constituted, other forms of impression management can occur. Ruth, the veteran coach of a Texas squad, mentioned having a talk every year with the gay men on her team about being too "obvious" with their sexuality during performances, as she believed this to be "a threat to the squad's respect." Lionel, coach of a Louisiana squad, took a similar approach with the gay men on his team and successfully "toned down" their behavior through "conversations about image."

The doing of masculinity in cheerleading is therefore no less a conscious production than the doing of femininity, despite the greater emphasis on artifice and sexual attractiveness for female cheerleaders. What is different is the degree of variation one sees: performances of femininity are far more consistent across squads and across the different cheerleading companies than performances of masculinity, suggesting that within coed cheerleading at least, masculinity is a less coherent, more polyvalent construct. [...]

What version of masculinity a team embraces is shaped by which cheerleading company a team affiliates with. Despite the commitment to hegemonic masculinity expressed by many of the male participants in our study, it was also understood that, because different companies promote different styles of cheerleading at their camps and competitions, "there is something for everyone" when it comes to male participants, although not in equal proportion: the largest and most profitable company, the UCA, is also the most gender conservative. As one long-time UCA instructor from the South explained it: "UCA stipulates no toe touches [for men], no girl motions and moves, nothing with hips, no dancing. At camp, the instructors get yelled at if we're just horsing around and the guys are doing those things." She added: "once you cross that line and let the guys dance like girls you start losing the masculine image you want to project." Participants describe the UCA style as "traditional," "collegiate," and "clean-cut," but also "boring" and "conservative." Dylan, a freshman on the Delta State team, likened the gendered division of labor on UCA squads to a traditional marriage: "In UCA, the guys, they pretty much do the 'men's work.' It's like, the guy goes out and throws the garbage away in a family and the woman cooks dinner. It's like that kind of thing."

This is in contrast to the style of cheerleading promoted by the other two companies, where male cheerleaders do dance and jump, albeit often in a "masculine" way that differentiates them from their female teammates: no twirls, spins, or leaps, no bumping or grinding, "nothing suggestive," was the way the coach of an NCA-affiliated squad at the Texas camp put it. Generally speaking, the NCA style is considered more "performative" than the UCA style, and the USA style is considered the most performative of all. Interviewees used adjectives like "showy," "flashy," "gaudy," and even "cartoony" when describing USA teams, because of the heightened theatricality of the face, head, and hand gestures, as well as the greater attention to choreography.[17]

Within the world of cheerleading, then, the UCA could be said to represent hegemonic masculinity, with the other two companies representing different subordinated masculinities. What image of masculinity a team projects and how male cheerleaders feel as individuals are not always aligned, however, as is implied by the efforts of coaches to either "tone down" or "amp up" the level of performativity of particular men on their squads. Although the majority of the male cheerleaders we met from UCA-affiliated teams strongly supported the company's efforts to "keep male cheerleading a masculine thing" (to quote a Kentucky cheerleader), not all did. Bruce, of Delta State, who earlier we quoted chastising "flaming" male cheerleaders for taking the performativity of cheerleading too far, himself so enjoyed dancing, smiling, and expressing enthusiasm that he declined employment with the UCA. "I'm definitely a performer," he said. "I was in drama before I was ever in cheerleading." Reese was another Delta State cheerleader who didn't shy away from emotional expressiveness: when the team was revamping its UCA routine for the USA national competition, he grew impatient with certain male teammates for resisting the flashier, more expressive USA style. Of course, the reverse was also true: men on teams affiliated with "performance-oriented" companies did not always express gratitude for the opportunity to dance and jump, instead they tolerated

these elements as a necessary part of "what is a predominantly female driven sport" (Texas cheerleader).[18]

What all this suggests is that cheerleading is a contested space for the performance of masculinity. The doing of masculinity in cheerleading is a complicated business both because there is latitude in how masculinity gets expressed and because cheerleading continues to be understood as feminine terrain, an inappropriate activity for "real" men to pursue. This makes cheerleading a welcoming space for men who do not care to prove their heteromasculinity, while at the same time prompting compensatory behavior from men who do. Because cheerleading is a public ritual, staged before an audience, it renders the codes by which gendered identities and practices are constructed particularly visible, both to spectators and to cheerleaders themselves, who otherwise might be less conscious of how, exactly, gender gets done. In this sense, the public "display" of gender (see Goffman 1976) provides the occasion for reflecting on and negotiating the everyday doing of gender in a broader sense.

As West and Zimmerman (1987) note: "to do gender is not always to live up to normative conceptions of femininity and masculinity; it is to engage in behavior at the risk of gender assessment" (p. 136). For the majority of cheerleaders in our study, however, most of whom identified as straight, living up to normative gender expectations played a key role in their attraction to cheerleading. The contrasting appearance of male and female cheerleaders and their different physical performances were necessary both to participants' enjoyment of the activity and to their continued participation. Such differentiation serves to "masculinize" cheerleading for men and to "feminize" it for women. Yet these two tendencies clash when it comes to legitimation as a sport: while masculinization helps cheerleading gain credibility, feminization renders it vulnerable to trivialization and ridicule. Feminization excludes cheerleading from the "institutional core" of sport (Messner 2002) and from getting the kind of respect that cheerleaders desire.

That feminization is an obstacle to legitimacy—and, conversely, that "masculinization" helps secure it—is nothing new (see Feder 1995; Theberge 1993; Williams 1995). Interviewees speak dismissively of all-girl sideline squads (both past and present), while at the most elite levels of competitive college cheerleading coed teams occupy the highest status at camps and competitions. At Delta State, the more prestigious coed squad supported men's sports while the less prestigious all-girl squad supported women's sports, and Stanton had a similar allocation for its varsity (coed) and junior varsity (all-girl) squads. Participants spoke of the ability of coed teams to "build higher and stronger" and "do cooler stuff that girls just sometimes can't do" (Delta State cheerleader) and of the fact that "people take us more seriously" when guys are involved in cheerleading (Fairview cheerleader). Tarek, of the Fairview squad, said that the presence of "big guys" was "a huge part" of the transition to sport, but that the predominance of young girls in cheerleading was sabotaging this effort: "These programs where it's all 12-year-old girls ... I mean, it's understandable, but as long as that's around, I think it's going to be hard to classify ourselves as a sport ... it's got the stigma of an all-girl thing still."

His point is underscored by interviewees who insist that, access to "hot girls" notwithstanding, what really draws men into cheerleading is the presence of other, "masculine" men who send the message "it's okay to be a male cheerleader." According to Diego: "when you have a strong tradition of big guys being on the squad it becomes way easier [to recruit men]. It's hard to break the barrier when you have a guy on the team who's more feminine. Guys kind of shy away from that." Thus the emphasis on big, strong men who make the "cool stuff" possible is part of the gender regime of coed cheerleading and central to its bid for legitimacy at an institutional as well as individual level.

Conclusion

Cheerleading is a space where the doing and displaying of gender are particularly visible, and where the gender regimes represented by hegemonic masculinity and emphasized femininity are being negotiated and resecured in the face of alternative regimes. It is a place where the boundaries of gender difference are crossed as well as preserved. To quote Rulond (ironically, one of the men in our study seemingly most committed to hegemonic masculinity): "[cheerleading] is a way, kind of, of men and women maybe

trying on each other's clothes a little bit." Coed college cheerleading is neither a bastion of gender conservatism nor an unfettered space of gender nonconformity; rather, as a mainstream, "feminine" activity seeking legitimacy as a "serious" sport, it expresses and exposes the gender politics at play in a shifting institutional context. In examining these politics, we have been less invested in demonstrating that cheerleading *is* or *should be* considered a sport than in observing the boundary work of participants as they struggle to "match" their doing of gender in cheerleading with their gendered identities and beliefs.

The process of protecting sport from feminization has been an ongoing one in which masculinity and femininity must be continuously differentiated in order to keep the latter at bay (see Messner 1992). When male cheerleaders distance themselves from the sexualized, performative dimensions of cheerleading, for example, they contribute to the perception that femininity and performativity are "naturally" intertwined and that both are the purview of women (and gay men). Indeed, sport is a powerful site for naturalizing gender difference because it appears to harness "nature" rather than "culture," reflecting biological differences between men and women rather than particular gender regimes. Because gender is defined and performed *relationally* in coed cheerleading, with masculinity and femininity being constructed simultaneously within the same cultural field, the activity warrants special attention for the ways in which it expands gender regimes (e.g., allowing women to embrace athleticism and men to embrace performativity, within limits) while at the same time reinforcing traditional conceptions of gender difference (e.g., assuming that athleticism and performativity differ— and should differ—by gender). While few other sports provide the opportunity for examining gender politics as they play out in this side-by-side manner, sport typically being organized according to separate spheres, the importance of relational analysis for understanding the "gendering" of society more broadly is widely acknowledged (Connell 1987, 2002; Kimmel 2000; Lorber 1994; McKay, Cole, and Messner 1997; Thorne 1993).

The coexistence of gendered opposites—sport and performance, athletics and aesthetics, competitiveness and supportiveness—both captures the relational quality of coed cheerleading as a whole and the gender performance of female cheerleaders specifically. This performance helps to construct and enact a contemporary script for emphasized femininity. Indeed, cheerleading is a key site for the production of emphasized femininity insofar as it allows women to "add" valued, masculine qualities to certain traditionally feminine ones. That the athleticism of cheerleading is packaged in a sexually appealing way and combined with aesthetic or performative demands means that female cheerleaders do not have to exhibit the same degree of "apologetic behavior" (Felshin 1974) as their male counterparts. The apologia for their participation is built into the activity itself—in the grace and flexibility of their athleticism, and in the premium placed on adornment and (hetero)sexual display. At the same time, because the "emphasized" elements of femininity in cheerleading are not selling points in the world of sport, they are not foregrounded by participants invested in garnering for cheerleading greater status and recognition. Female cheerleaders well understand at which end of the gender continuum legitimacy as a "serious" sport lies.

For their part, male cheerleaders generally tolerate the marriage of aesthetics and athleticism for their female teammates, but not for themselves, as the most valued form of masculinity—hegemonic masculinity—is understood to preclude the feminine qualities of supportiveness and performativity. Hence, you have the compensatory behavior of male cheerleaders and the gendered division of labor on many squads, including a separate, masculine mode of performance. The construction of masculinity within cheerleading is contested, however, because the alternatives to hegemonic masculinity, no less a part of cheerleading for being less popular, are so clearly on display. In the feminine world of cheerleading, aesthetics and performativity threaten to (and do) spill over into male terrain, making masculinity a diverse and hotly contested construct that gets institutionalized in different ways. The performance of gender in cheerleading, particularly for men, exists along a continuum that is anchored and secured by the concept of hegemonic masculinity but is not exhausted by it.

Whether cheerleading reflects or helps constitute a change in the status of subordinated masculinities in everyday life is an open question. Connell (1987) argues that actual masculinities in western culture are less diverse than actual femininities because there is greater pressure on men (compared to women) to negate alternative forms, given that men generally hold more social power and there is more at stake to lose. But the rigidity of masculinity in the past may have facilitated an accelerated "opening up" of masculinity now, such that what is considered normative for men is undergoing a significant shift. Toby Miller (2001), for example, argues that the concept of hegemonic masculinity is weakening as men are increasingly subject to the same objectifying media practices formerly associated with women. While our study suggests that hegemonic masculinity is still very much alive, male cheerleaders' efforts to carve out a gender appropriate space for themselves do not simply demonstrate men's allegiance to hegemonic masculinity or secure the dominance of this type of masculinity over and against its alternatives, they also underscore the fragility and tenuousness of the dominance itself.

Of course, no paper is exhaustive, and significant issues remain undeveloped here. One key arena for future analysis is competitive all-girl college teams where, because girls "base" as well as "fly," the division of labor is determined by size and strength rather than gender. Although female bases are subject to the same overdetermined feminine appearance and performance demands as flyers, their more "masculine" role complicates their performance of gender and the public construction of gender difference. Other questions pertain to the impact of "serious" coed cheerleading on younger teams, both scholastic and all-star. Will boys start entering cheerleading at younger ages? Has the rise of coed cheerleading influenced the way younger participants think about the activity?

Another set of questions relate to the impact of cheerleading on other sports, including whether the renewed popularity of cheerleading makes it more difficult for women in traditionally "masculine" sports to define themselves as both athletic and feminine. In other words, do female cheerleaders indirectly reinforce homophobia for other female athletes? And how do the various modes of masculinity performed in cheerleading affect men taking part in other "feminine" sports such as figure skating, diving, and gymnastics? Specifically, does the performance of hegemonic masculinity in cheerleading make it easier for men to participate in such sports or does it simply reinforce heteronormativity?

There are also questions of race. Although the participants in our study insisted that cheerleading is color-blind, the performance of femininity supported by coed cheerleading historically has been associated with middle class whiteness (see Adams and Bettis 2003) and representations of cheerleading in much fictional media reinforce this association (Hanson 1995). Consequently, women of color are not cultural icons of cheerleading the way white women are and outsiders may see their involvement as less "natural" and "authentic."[19] Finally, there is the question of how public and private gender performances influence each other. What are the consequences of "doing gender" in cheerleading for the doing of gender in other realms of life such as school, work, and interpersonal relationships, and vice versa? This last question is significant because forms of popular culture like cheerleading are part of, not separate from, everyday life, helping to reflect, create, and sustain its practices and ideologies.

Notes

1. Title IX, passed in 1972, is a federal law prohibiting gender discrimination in educational institutions that receive federal funds. The law prohibits high schools and colleges that receive federal funds from discriminating on the basis of gender in the provision of any educational activity, including athletics.
2. In the United States, the institutional core of sport, in terms of money, resources, and media coverage, is men's football, basketball, and baseball (Messner 2002).
3. Thanks to Sarah Fenstermaker (personal communication) for helping to articulate this point.
4. The membership of the Fairview team was less stable than the other teams observed. Roughly half of the twelve were on the team the year I observed it, three were on the team the year before I started my observations, and three were on the team the year following.
5. While the Stanton squad had no men of color and only two women of color (one African American and one East Indian), the year that I observed the Fairview squad there were four white women, three Asian American women, and two black women; of the five men, three were white, one was Mexican American, and one was Asian American. Delta State

was similarly diverse, with six white women, five women of color (three Latina and two Asian American), five white men, and six men of color (two black, two Mexican American, one Asian American, and one Arab American).
6. Whenever we asked about race, participants insisted that cheerleading was "color-blind." Nevertheless, college cheerleading was acknowledged to be "whiter" in the South and Midwest than on the two coasts and southern teams dominate the most prestigious national competitions at the college level. As for participants' sexual orientation, we did not ask directly but some cheerleaders volunteered this information and discussions of sexuality—specifically, the visible presence of gay men in cheerleading—surfaced regularly in the interviews.
7. The teams at the camps varied in terms of size, gender composition (some were all-girl, some were coed), racial composition (a few were all-black, most were racially mixed or predominantly white), type of squad (some were competitive, some were not), and type of school (ranging from two year junior colleges to four year universities). Several foreign countries were represented, including Canada, Taiwan, Norway, and Mexico, and a few teams were outside of the college framework altogether, being community-based adult performance squads such as the one I belong to.
8. These two competitions are widely considered the most competitive and prestigious among all those held for college cheerleaders. We were spectators at these events, sitting in the stands watching teams execute their routines alongside thousands of other spectators. In each case, the competitions lasted three days and featured approximately 150 teams (3,000 cheerleaders) from schools across the country.
9. The supplementary interviews are broken down as follows: one with five members of a competitive Georgia team nicknamed "True Grits" (two white women, one Latina, and two white men); a dozen with individual cheerleaders from mostly southern states (three white men, one black man, two black women, one Latina, one Asian American woman, and four white women); four with coaches, one white woman from Texas, one white man from Georgia, and two black men from different regions in Louisiana; and three with representatives of the "cheer industry," all white men, one from UCA, one from NCA, and one from USA.
10. Interviews generally lasted from one to three hours and covered a range of issues in addition to the question of whether cheerleading should be considered a sport. We were interested in why and how participants got involved in cheerleading; the extent and content of their cheerleading

experience; what they liked most and least about the activity; whether they viewed cheerleading as a sport; how friends, family, and peers responded to their involvement in cheerleading; how they perceived and negotiated the sex–gender assumptions of cheerleading; and whether or not cheerleading "fit" with their own views of gender and sexuality. All interviews were tape-recorded and transcribed, and then coded and analyzed for emergent patterns and themes.

11. Thanks to one of the anonymous reviewers for *Social Problems* for helping us to elaborate on this point.

12. The term "all-girl" is commonly used within cheerleading to specify squads that are exclusively female, regardless of participants' ages (that is, little girls, adolescents, and young women are all considered "girls"). At some competitions, the term "all-girl squad" may also be used to describe squads that have one or two male participants.

13. The distinction between cheerleading and "real" sports can be quite pronounced at some schools. Cheer squads may be housed under "activities" rather than "athletics," they may have little or no access to school resources, and they may lack adequate coaching and advising.

14. All three of the cheer company representatives that we interviewed emphasized that, despite the increasing emphasis on competition, sideline cheerleading was still the most ubiquitous form of school cheerleading. If the NCAA were to recognize cheerleading as a sport, not only would squads be forced to compete on a regular basis because the legal definition of sport foregrounds competition, but the competition squads would likely be all-girl rather than coed (further marginalizing men in cheerleading), because only all-girl teams "count" toward Title IX compliance.

15. This minority of interviewees also saw sport designation as hinging on structural similarities between cheerleading and other school sports, such as regular practice and training schedules, getting a varsity letter, being governed by the athletic department, and having scholarship programs. According to Shoshana, one of the Stanton captains: "It's a varsity sport at [Stanton]. It takes a lot of time ... we work just as hard as a sports team. And if you go to the Midwest for college cheerleading, they do recruit. People go to school to be cheerleaders, they get scholarships."

16. Natalie Adams and Pamela Bettis (2003) estimate that school cheerleading is 97 percent female. This figure seems quite high for college cheerleading, however, where men have the highest rates of participation. The major cheerleading companies do not keep gender statistics on college cheerleaders but I estimate that the ratio of women to men at the camps and competitions I observed was roughly 3:2.

17. USA cheerleaders, primarily but not exclusively the women, smile, pout, wink, and blow kisses during routines. Because routines are set to music, participants act out simple scenarios compatible with the lyrics (lassoing a horse, for example, or blowing smoke from the tip of a gun). Also, self-congratulatory gestures are common for men after a tumbling pass or stunt sequence.

18. Coaches may also exert a strong influence on what their male cheerleaders do in routines, despite the norms of the company. One NCA-affiliated coach I interviewed at the Kentucky camp does not incorporate any dancing whatsoever into his competition routines because he considers that "too girly" even for female cheerleaders. Jasper, a coach based in Louisiana, told me that his male cheerleaders "can really perform, can really dance good," but at NCA summer camp they refrain from dancing because "that's not the all-American pie image." Likewise, Monty, a former Texas cheerleader (now an NCA employee) and one of the few openly gay men in our study, spoke of dance in terms of image management: "We did not dance, we were very careful about making that delineation as a matter of fact ... 'cause let's face it, historically there's always the concern on the part of male cheerleaders that 'I'm going to be seen as feminine'... and so they go out of their way not to invite criticism."

19. Our own research suggests that this may be the case for black women but not necessarily other women of color. Two of the five black female cheerleaders we interviewed reported having their participation viewed by others as racially inauthentic; they said it was other African Americans who took this view because members of their black community believed cheerleading to be a "white" activity. The coach of an all-black squad in the South said that his female cheerleaders had a similar experience in that other black women on campus questioned the racial authenticity of their participation. However, none of the black *men* or other women of color (Asian American and Latina) in our study reported having their participation questioned by others on the basis on race.

References

Acker, Joan. 1990. "Hierarchies, Jobs, Bodies: A Theory of Gendered Organizations." *Gender & Society* 4:139–58.

Adams, Natalie and Pamela Bettis. 2003. *Cheerleader! An American Icon*. New York: Palgrave Macmillan.

Baughman, Cynthia, ed. 1995. *Women on Ice: Feminist Essays on the Tonya Harding/Nancy Kerrigan Spectacle*. New York: Routledge.

Bryson, Lois. 1994. "Sport and the Maintenance of Masculine Hegemony." pp. 47–64 in *Women, Sport, and Culture*, edited by Susan Birrell and Cheryl Cole. Champaign, IL: Human Kinetics Books.

Cahn, Susan. 1994. *Coming on Strong: Gender and Sexuality in Twentieth-Century Women's Sport*. New York: Free Press.

Cline, Sally and Dale Spender. 1987. *Reflecting Men at Twice Their Natural Size*. New York: Henry Holt and Company.

Connell, R. W. 1987. *Gender and Power*. Stanford, CA: Stanford University Press.

——. 2002. *Gender: Short Introductions*. Cambridge, UK: Polity Press.

Crosset, Todd. 1990. "Masculinity, Sexuality, and the Development of Early Modern Sport." pp. 45–54 in *Sport, Men, and the Gender Order: Critical Feminist Perspectives*, edited by Michael Messner and Donald Sabo. Champaign, IL: Human Kinetics Books.

Davis, Laurel. 1990. "Male Cheerleaders and the Naturalization of Gender." pp. 153–61 in *Sport, Men, and the Gender Order: Critical Feminist Perspectives*, edited by Michael Messner and Donald Sabo. Champaign, IL: Human Kinetics Books.

Dodd, Dennis. 2004. "Colleges Giving Cheerleading a Sporting Chance." *CBS.Sportsline.com*, June 11. Retrieved June 14, 2004 (http://www.sportsline.com/collegefootball/story/7412313).

Feder, Abigail. 1995. "A Radiant Smile from the Lovely Lady: Overdetermined Femininity in 'Ladies' Figure Skating." pp. 22–46 in *Women on Ice: Feminist Essays on the Tonya Harding/Nancy Kerrigan Spectacle*, edited by Cynthia Baughman. New York: Routledge.

Felshin, Jan. 1974. "The Social View." pp. 179–272 in *The American Woman in Sport*, edited by Ellen Gerber, Jan Felshin, Pearl Berlin, and Waneen Wyrick. Reading, MA: Addison-Wesley.

Festle, Mary Jo. 1996. *Playing Nice: Politics and Apologies in Women's Sports*. New York: Columbia University Press.

Friedland, Roger and Robert Alford. 1991. "Bringing Society Back In: Symbols, Practices, and Institutional Contradictions." pp. 232–63 in *The New Institutionalism in Organizational Analaysis*, edited by Walter Powell and Paul DiMaggio. Chicago: University of Chicago Press.

Goffman, Erving. 1963. *Stigma: Notes on the Management of Spoiled Identity*. New York: Simon and Schuster.

——. 1976. "Gender Display." *Studies in the Anthropology of Visual Communication* 3:69–77.

Griffin, Pat. 1998. *Strong Women, Deep Closets: Lesbians and Homophobia in Sport*. Champaign, IL: Human Kinetics Books.

Grundy, Pamela. 2001. *Learning to Win: Sports, Education, and Social Change in Twentieth-Century North Carolina*. Chapel Hill: University of North Carolina Press.

Hanson, Mary Ellen. 1995. *Go! Fight! Win!: Cheerleading in American Culture*. Bowling Green, OH: Bowling Green State University Popular Press.

Heywood, Leslie and Shari Dworkin. 2003. *Built to Win: The Female Athlete as Cultural Icon*. Minneapolis: University of Minnesota Press.

Hochschild, Arlie Russell. 1983. *The Managed Heart: Commercialization of Human Feeling*. Berkeley: University of California Press.

Kane, Mary Jo. 1995. "Resistance/Transformation of the Oppositional Binary: Exposing Sport as a Continuum." *Journal of Sport and Social Issues* 19:191–218.

Kimmel, Michael. 1990. "Baseball and the Reconstitution of American Masculinity." pp. 55–56 in *Sport, Men, and the Gender Order: Critical Feminist Perspectives*, edited by Michael Messner and Donald Sabo. Champaign, IL: Human Kinetics Books.

——. 2000. *The Gendered Society*. New York and Oxford, UK: Oxford University Press.

Kurman, George. 1986. "What Does Girls' Cheerleading Communicate?" *Journal of Popular Culture* 20:57–64.

Lenskyj, Helen. 1986. *Out of Bounds: Women, Sport, and Sexuality*. Toronto, ON: Women's Press.

Lorber, Judith. 1994. *Paradoxes of Gender*. New Haven, CT: Yale University Press.

McKay, Jim, Cheryl Cole, and Michael Messner, eds. 1997. *Managing Gender: Affirmative Action and Organizational Power in Australian, Canadian, and New Zealand Sport*. New York: State University of New York Press.

McKay, Jim, Michael Messner, and Don Sabo, eds. 2000. *Masculinities, Gender Relations, and Sport*. Thousand Oaks, CA: Sage Publications.

Messner, Michael. 1992. *Power at Play: Sports and the Problem of Masculinity*. Boston: Beacon Press.

——. 2002. *Taking the Field: Women, Men, and Sports*. Minneapolis: University of Minnesota Press.

Messner, Michael and Donald Sabo, eds. 1990. *Sport, Men, and the Gender Order: Critical Feminist Perspectives*. Champaign, IL: Human Kinetics Books.

Miller, Toby. 2001. *Sportsex*. Philadelphia: Temple University Press.

Morrissey, Rick. 2004. "Glitter? Makeup? Cheerleading is Not a Sport." *Duluth News Tribune*, May 4. Retrieved August 6, 2004 (http://www.duluthsuperior.com).

Theberge, Nancy. 1993. "The Construction of Gender in Sport: Women, Coaching, and the Naturalization of Difference." *Social Problems* 40: 301–13.

——. 1994. "Toward a Feminist Alternative to Sport as a Male Preserve." pp. 181–92 in *Women, Sport, and Culture*, edited by Susan Birrell and Cheryl Cole.Champaign, IL: Human Kinetics Books.

Thorne, Barrie. 1993. *Gender Play: Girls and Boys in School*. New Brunswick, NJ: Rutgers University Press.

Trujillo, Nick. 2000. "Hegemonic Masculinity on the Mound: Media Representations of Nolan Ryan and American Sports Culture." pp. 14–39 in *Reading Sport: Critical Essays on Power and Representation*, edited by Susan Birrell and Mary McDonald. Boston: Northeastern University Press.

West, Candace and Sarah Fenstermaker. 1995. "Doing Difference." *Gender & Society* 9:8–37.

West, Candace and Don Zimmerman. 1987. "Doing Gender." *Gender & Society* 1:125–51.

Williams, Christine. 1995. *Still a Man's World: Men Who Do "Women's Work."* Berkeley: University of California Press.

4.6

Barbie Girls versus Sea Monsters

Children constructing gender

Michael A. Messner

In this article about four- and five-year old boys and girls playing soccer, Michael Messner helps us understand how gender is performed in a specific context. He demonstrates that it is critical to analyze the social construction of gender at three, intertwined levels: interactional; social structural; and cultural. Messner not only explains how gender is constructed and contested among these young children but his analysis suggests the role that sport plays in reinforcing "hegemonic masculinity," and its associations with competition and aggression.

[…] The purpose of this article is to use an observation of a highly salient gendered moment of group life among four- and five-year-old children as a point of departure for exploring the conditions under which gender boundaries become activated and enforced. I was privy to this moment as I observed my five-year-old son's first season (including weekly games and practices) in organized soccer. Unlike the long-term, systematic ethnographic studies of children conducted by Thorne (1993) or Adler and Adler (1998), this article takes one moment as its point of departure. I do not present this moment as somehow "representative" of what happened throughout the season; instead, I examine this as an example of what Hochschild (1994, 4) calls "magnified moments," which are "episodes of heightened importance, either epiphanies, moments of intense glee or unusual insight, or moments in which things go intensely but meaningfully wrong. In either case, the moment stands out; it is metaphorically rich, unusually elaborate and often echoes [later]." A magnified

moment in daily life offers a window into the social construction of reality. It presents researchers with an opportunity to excavate gendered meanings and processes through an analysis of institutional and cultural contexts. The single empirical observation that serves as the point of departure for this article was made during a morning. Immediately after the event, I recorded my observations with detailed notes. I later slightly revised the notes after developing the photographs that I took at the event.

I will first describe the observation—an incident that occurred as a boys' four and five-year-old soccer team waited next to a girls' four- and five-year-old soccer team for the beginning of the community's American Youth Soccer League (AYSO) season's opening ceremony. I will then examine this moment using three levels of analysis.

The interactional level: How do children "do gender," and what are the contributions and limits of theories of

Michael A. Messner, "Barbie Girls versus Sea Monsters: Children Constructing Gender" from *Gender and Society* 14.6 (2000): 765–784. Copyright © 2000 by Sociologists for Women in Society. Reprinted with the permission of Sage Publications, Inc.

performativity in understanding these interactions?

The level of structural context: How does the gender regime, particularly the larger organizational level of formal sex segregation of AYSO, and the concrete, momentary situation of the opening ceremony provide a context that variously constrains and enables the children's interactions?

The level of cultural symbol: How does the children's shared immersion in popular culture (and their differently gendered locations in this immersion) provide symbolic resources for the creation, in this situation, of apparently categorical differences between the boys and the girls?

Although I will discuss these three levels of analysis separately, I hope to demonstrate that interaction, structural context, and culture are simultaneous and mutually intertwined processes, none of which supersedes the others.

Barbie Girls versus Sea Monsters

It is a warm, sunny Saturday morning. Summer is coming to a close, and schools will soon reopen. As in many communities, this time of year in this small, middle- and professional-class suburb of Los Angeles is marked by the beginning of another soccer season. This morning, 156 teams, with approximately 1,850 players ranging from 4 to 17 years old, along with another 2,000 to 3,000 parents, siblings, friends, and community dignitaries have gathered at the local high school football and track facility for the annual AYSO opening ceremonies. Parents and children wander around the perimeter of the track to find the assigned station for their respective teams. The coaches muster their teams and chat with parents. Eventually, each team will march around the track, behind their new team banner, as they are announced over the loudspeaker system and are applauded by the crowd. For now though, and for the next 45 minutes to an hour, the kids, coaches, and parents must stand, mill around, talk, and kill time as they await the beginning of the ceremony.

The Sea Monsters is a team of four- and five-year-old boys. Later this day, they will play their first-ever soccer game. A few of the boys already know each other from preschool, but most are still getting acquainted. They are wearing their new uniforms for the first time. Like other teams, they were assigned team colors—in this case, green and blue—and asked to choose their team name at their first team meeting, which occurred a week ago. Although they preferred "Blue Sharks," they found that the name was already taken by another team and settled on "Sea Monsters." A grandmother of one of the boys created the spiffy team banner, which was awarded a prize this morning. As they wait for the ceremony to begin, the boys inspect and then proudly pose for pictures in front of their new award-winning team banner. The parents stand a few feet away—some taking pictures, some just watching. The parents are also getting to know each other, and the common currency of topics is just how darned cute our kids look, and will they start these ceremonies soon before another boy has to be escorted to the bathroom?

Queued up one group away from the Sea Monsters is a team of four- and five-year-old girls in green and white uniforms. They too will play their first game later today, but for now, they are awaiting the beginning of the opening ceremony. They have chosen the name "Barbie Girls," and they also have a spiffy new team banner. But the girls are pretty much ignoring their banner, for they have created another, more powerful symbol around which to rally. In fact, they are the only team among the 156 marching today with a team float—a red Radio Flyer wagon base, on which sits a Sony boom box playing music, and a 3-foot-plus-tall Barbie doll on a rotating pedestal. Barbie is dressed in the team colors—indeed, she sports a custom-made green-and-white cheerleader-style outfit, with the Barbie Girls' names written on the skirt. Her normally all-blonde hair has been streaked with Barbie Girl green and features a green bow, with white polka dots. Several of the girls on the team also have supplemented their uniforms with green bows in their hair.

The volume on the boom box nudges up and four or five girls begin to sing a Barbie song. Barbie is now slowly rotating on her pedestal, and as the girls sing more gleefully and more loudly, some of them begin to hold hands and walk around the float, in sync with Barbie's rotation. Other same-aged girls from other teams are drawn to the celebration and, eventually, perhaps a dozen girls are singing the Barbie song.

183

The girls are intensely focused on Barbie, on the music, and on their mutual pleasure.

As the Sea Monsters mill around their banner, some of them begin to notice, and then begin to watch and listen as the Barbie Girls rally around their float. At first, the boys are watching as individuals, seemingly unaware of each other's shared interest. Some of them stand with arms at their sides, slack-jawed, as though passively watching a television show. I notice slight smiles on a couple of their faces, as though they are drawn to the Barbie Girls' celebratory fun. Then, with side-glances, some of the boys begin to notice each other's attention on the Barbie Girls. Their faces begin to show signs of distaste. One of them yells out, "NO BARBIE!" Suddenly, they all begin to move—jumping up and down, nudging and bumping one other—and join into a group chant: "NO BARBIE! NO BARBIE! NO BARBIE!" They now appear to be every bit as gleeful as the girls, as they laugh, yell, and chant against the Barbie Girls.

The parents watch the whole scene with rapt attention. Smiles light up the faces of the adults, as our glances sweep back and forth, from the sweetly celebrating Barbie Girls to the aggressively protesting Sea Monsters. "They are SO different!" exclaims one smiling mother approvingly. A male coach offers a more in-depth analysis: "When I was in college," he says, "I took these classes from professors who showed us research that showed that boys and girls are the same. I believed it, until I had my own kids and saw how different they are." "Yeah," another dad responds, "Just look at them! They are so different!"

The girls, meanwhile, show no evidence that they hear, see, or are even aware of the presence of the boys who are now so loudly proclaiming their opposition to the Barbie Girls' songs and totem. They continue to sing, dance, laugh, and rally around the Barbie for a few more minutes, before they are called to reassemble in their groups for the beginning of the parade.

After the parade, the teams reassemble on the infield of the track but now in a less organized manner. The Sea Monsters once again find themselves in the general vicinity of the Barbie Girls and take up the "NO BARBIE!" chant again. Perhaps put out by the lack of response to their chant, they begin to dash, in twos and threes, invading the girls' space, and yelling menacingly. With this, the Barbie Girls have little choice but

to recognize the presence of the boys—some look puzzled and shrink back, some engage the boys and chase them off. The chasing seems only to incite more excitement among the boys. Finally, parents intervene and defuse the situation, leading their children off to their cars, homes, and eventually to their soccer games.

The performance of gender

It has become increasingly fashionable among academic feminists to think of gender not as some "thing" that one "has" (or not) but rather as situationally constructed through the performances of active agents. The idea of gender as performance analytically foregrounds the agency of individuals in the construction of gender, thus highlighting the situational fluidity of gender: here, conservative and reproductive, there, transgressive and disruptive. Surely, the Barbie Girls versus Sea Monsters scene described above can be fruitfully analyzed as a moment of crosscutting and mutually constitutive gender performances: The girls—at least at first glance—appear to be performing (for each other?) a conventional four- to five-year-old version of emphasized femininity. At least on the surface, there appears to be nothing terribly transgressive here. They are just "being girls," together. The boys initially are unwittingly constituted as an audience for the girls' performance but quickly begin to perform (for each other?—for the girls, too?) a masculinity that constructs itself in opposition to Barbie, and to the girls, as not feminine. They aggressively confront—first through loud verbal chanting, eventually through bodily invasions—the girls' ritual space of emphasized femininity, apparently with the intention of disrupting its upsetting influence. The adults are simultaneously constituted as an adoring audience for their children's performances and as parents who perform for each other by sharing and mutually affirming their experience-based narratives concerning the natural differences between boys and girls.

In this scene, we see children performing gender in ways that constitute themselves as two separate, opposed groups (boys vs. girls) and parents performing gender in ways that give the stamp of adult approval to the children's performances of difference, while constructing their own ideological narrative that naturalizes this categorical difference. In other words, the parents do not seem to read the children's performances of gender as social constructions of gender. Instead, they interpret them as the inevitable unfolding of natural, internal differences between the sexes. That this moment occurred when it did and where it did is explicable, but not entirely with a theory of performativity. As Walters (1999, 250) argues:

> The performance of gender is never a simple voluntary act. ... Theories of gender as play and performance need to be intimately and systematically connected with the power of gender (really, the power of male power) to constrain, control, violate, and configure. Too often, mere lip service is given to the specific historical, social, and political configurations that make certain conditions possible and others constrained.

Indeed, feminist sociologists operating from the traditions of symbolic interactionism and/or Goffmanian dramaturgical analysis have anticipated the recent interest in looking at gender as a dynamic performance. As early as 1978, Kessler and McKenna developed a sophisticated analysis of gender as an everyday, practical accomplishment of people's interactions. Nearly a decade later, West and Zimmerman (1987) argued that in people's everyday interactions, they were "doing gender" and, in so doing, they were constructing masculine dominance and feminine deference. As these ideas have been taken up in sociology, their tendencies toward a celebration of the "freedom" of agents to transgress and reshape the fluid boundaries of gender have been put into play with theories of social structure (e.g., Lorber 1994; Risman 1998). In these accounts, gender is viewed as enacted or created through everyday interactions, but crucially, as Walters suggested above, within "specific historical, social, and political configurations" that constrain or enable certain interactions.

The parents' response to the Barbie Girls versus Sea Monsters performance suggests one of the main limits and dangers of theories of performativity. Lacking an analysis of structural and cultural context, performances of gender can all too easily be interpreted as free agents' acting out the inevitable surface manifestations of a natural inner essence of sex difference. An examination of structural and cultural contexts, though, reveals that there was nothing inevitable about the girls' choice of Barbie as their totem, nor in the boys' response to it.

The structure of gender

In the entire subsequent season of weekly games and practices, I never once saw adults point to a moment in which boy and girl soccer players were doing the *same* thing and exclaim to each other, "Look at them! They are *so similar!*" The actual similarity of the boys and the girls, evidenced by nearly all of the kids' routine actions throughout a soccer season—playing the game, crying over a skinned knee, scrambling enthusiastically for their snacks after the games, spacing out on a bird or a flower instead of listening to the coach at practice—is a key to understanding the salience of the Barbie Girls versus Sea Monsters moment for gender relations. In the face of a multitude of moments that speak to similarity, it was this anomalous Barbie Girls versus Sea Monsters moment—where the boundaries of gender were so clearly enacted—that the adults seized to affirm their commitment to difference. It is the kind of moment—to use Lorber's (1994, 37) phrase—where "believing is seeing," where we selectively "see" aspects of social reality that tell us a truth that we prefer to believe, such as the belief in categorical sex difference. No matter that our eyes do not see evidence of this truth most of the rest of the time.

In fact, it was not so easy for adults to actually "see" the empirical reality of sex similarity in everyday observations of soccer throughout the season. That is due to one overdetermining factor: an institutional context that is characterized by informally structured sex segregation among the parent coaches and team managers, and by formally structured sex segregation among the children. The structural analysis developed here is indebted to Acker's (1990) observation that organizations, even while appearing "gender neutral," tend to reflect, recreate, and naturalize a hierarchical ordering of gender. Following Connell's (1987, 98–99) method of structural analysis, I will examine the "gender regime"—that is, the current "state of play of sexual politics"—within the local AYSO organization by conducting a "structural inventory" of the formal and informal sexual divisions of labor and power.[1]

185

Adult divisions of labor and power

There was a clear—although not absolute—sexual division of labor and power among the adult volunteers in the AYSO organization. The Board of Directors consisted of 21 men and 9 women, with the top two positions—commissioner and assistant commissioner—held by men. Among the league's head coaches, 133 were men and 23 women. The division among the league's assistant coaches was similarly skewed. Each team also had a team manager who was responsible for organizing snacks, making reminder calls about games and practices, organizing team parties and the end-of-the-year present for the coach. The vast majority of team managers were women. A common slippage in the language of coaches and parents revealed the ideological assumptions underlying this position: I often noticed people describe a team manager as the "team mom." In short, as Table 4.6.1 shows, the vast majority of the time, the formal authority of the head coach and assistant coach was in the hands of a man, while the backup, support role of team manager was in the hands of a woman.

These data illustrate Connell's (1987, 97) assertion that sexual divisions of labor are interwoven with, and mutually supportive of, divisions of power and authority among women and men. They also suggest how people's choices to volunteer for certain positions are shaped and constrained by previous institutional practices. There is no formal AYSO rule that men must be the leaders, women the supportive followers. And there are, after all, *some* women coaches and *some* men team managers.[2] So, it may appear that the division of labor among adult volunteers simply manifests an accumulation of individual choices and preferences. When analyzed structurally, though, individual men's apparently free choices to volunteer disproportionately for coaching jobs, alongside individual women's apparently free choices to volunteer disproportionately for team manager jobs, can be seen as a logical collective result of the ways that the institutional structure of sport has differentially constrained and enabled women's and men's previous options and experiences (Messner 1992). Since boys and men have had far more opportunities to play organized sports and thus to gain skills and knowledge, it subsequently appears rational for adult men to serve in positions of knowledgeable authority, with women serving in a support capacity (Boyle and McKay 1995). Structure—in this case, the historically constituted division of labor and power in sport—constrains current practice. In turn, structure becomes an object of practice, as the choices and actions of today's parents re-create divisions of labor and power similar to those that they experienced in their youth.

The children: formal sex segregation

As adult authority patterns are informally structured along gendered lines, the children's leagues are formally segregated by AYSO along lines of age and sex. In each age-group, there are separate boys' and girls' leagues. The AYSO in this community included 87 boys' teams and 69 girls' teams. Although the four- to five-year-old boys often played their games on a field that was contiguous with games being played by four- to five-year-old girls, there was never a formal opportunity for cross-sex play. Thus, both the girls' and the boys' teams could conceivably proceed through an entire season of games and practices in entirely homosocial contexts.[3] In the all-male contexts that I observed throughout the season, gender never appeared to be overtly salient among the children, coaches, or parents. It is against this backdrop that I might suggest a working hypothesis about structure and the variable salience of gender: The formal sex segregation of children does not, in and of itself, make gender overtly salient. In fact, when children are absolutely segregated, with no opportunity for cross-sex interactions, gender may appear to disappear as an overtly salient organizing principle. However, when formally sex-segregated children are placed into immediately contiguous locations, such as during the opening ceremony, highly charged gendered interactions between the groups

Table 4.6.1. Adult volunteers as coaches and team managers, by gender (in percentages) (*N* = 156 teams)

	Head coaches	Assistant coaches	Team managers
Women	15	21	86
Men	85	79	14

(including invasions and other kinds of border work) become more possible.

Although it might appear to some that formal sex segregation in children's sports is a natural fact, it has not always been so for the youngest age-groups in AYSO. As recently as 1995, when my older son signed up to play as a five-year-old, I had been told that he would play in a coed league. But when he arrived to his first practice and I saw that he was on an all-boys team, I was told by the coach that AYSO had decided this year to begin sex segregating all age-groups, because "during half-times and practices, the boys and girls tend to separate into separate groups. So the league thought it would be better for team unity if we split the boys and girls into separate leagues." I suggested to some coaches that a similar dynamic among racial ethnic groups (say, Latino kids and white kids clustering as separate groups during halftimes) would not similarly result in a decision to create racially segregated leagues. That this comment appeared to fall on deaf ears illustrates the extent to which many adults' belief in the need for sex segregation—at least in the context of sport—is grounded in a mutually agreed-upon notion of boys' and girls' "separate worlds," perhaps based in ideologies of natural sex difference.

The gender regime of AYSO, then, is structured by formal and informal sexual divisions of labor and power. This social structure sets ranges, limits, and possibilities for the children's and parents' interactions and performances of gender, but it does not determine them. Put another way, the formal and informal gender regime of AYSO made the Barbie Girls versus Sea Monsters moment possible, but it did not make it inevitable. It was the agency of the children and the parents within that structure that made the moment happen. But why did this moment take on the symbolic forms that it did? How and why do the girls, boys, and parents construct and derive meanings from this moment, and how can we interpret these meanings? These questions are best grappled within in the realm of cultural analysis.

The culture of gender

The difference between what is "structural" and what is "cultural" is not clear-cut. For instance, the AYSO assignment of team colors and choice of team names (cultural symbols) seem to follow logically from, and in turn reinforce, the sex segregation of the leagues (social structure). These cultural symbols such as team colors, uniforms, songs, team names, and banners often carried encoded gendered meanings that were then available to be taken up by the children in ways that constructed (or potentially contested) gender divisions and boundaries.

Team names

Each team was issued two team colors. It is notable that across the various age-groups, several girls' teams were issued pink uniforms—a color commonly recognized as encoding feminine meanings—while no boys' teams were issued pink uniforms. Children, in consultation with their coaches, were asked to choose their own team names and were encouraged to use their assigned team colors as cues to the theme of the team name (e.g., among the boys, the "Red Flashes," the "Green Pythons," and the blue-and-green "Sea Monsters"). When I analyzed the team names of the 156 teams by age-group and by sex, three categories emerged:

1 Sweet names: These are cutesy team names that communicate small stature, cuteness, and/or vulnerability. These kinds of names would most likely be widely read as encoded with feminine meanings (e.g., "Blue Butterflies," "Beanie Babes," "Sunflowers," "Pink Flamingos," and "Barbie Girls").

2 Neutral or paradoxical names: Neutral names are team names that carry no obvious gendered meaning (e.g., "Blue and Green Lizards," "Team Flubber," "Galaxy," "Blue Ice"). Paradoxical names are girls' team names that carry mixed (simultaneously vulnerable *and* powerful) messages (e.g., "Pink Panthers," "Flower Power," "Little Tigers").

3 Power names: These are team names that invoke images of unambiguous strength, aggression, and raw power (e.g., "Shooting Stars," "Killer Whales," "Shark Attack," "Raptor Attack," and "Sea Monsters").

As Table 4.6.2 illustrates, across all age-groups of boys, there was only one team name coded as

187

Table 4.6.2. Teams names, by age-groups and gender

	4–5	6–7	8–13	14–17	Total
	n %	n %	n %	n %	n %
Girls					
Sweet names	5 42	3 17	2 7	0 0	10 15
Neutral/ paradoxical	5 42	6 33	7 25	5 45	23 32
Power names	2 17	9 50	19 68	6 55	36 52
Boys					
Sweet names	0 0	0 0	1 4	0 0	1 1
Neutral/ paradoxical	1 7	4 15	4 12	4 31	13 15
Power names	13 93	22 85	29 85	9 69	73 82

a sweet name—"The Smurfs," in the 10- to 11-year-old league. Across all age categories, the boys were far more likely to choose a power name than anything else, and this was nowhere more true than in the youngest age-groups, where 35 of 40 (87 percent) of boys' teams in the four-to-five and six-to-seven age-groups took on power names. A different pattern appears in the girls' team name choices, especially among the youngest girls. Only 2 of the 12 four- to five-year-old girls' teams chose power names, while 5 chose sweet names and 5 chose neutral/paradoxical names. At age six to seven, the numbers begin to tip toward the boys' numbers but still remain different, with half of the girls' teams now choosing power names. In the middle and older girls' groups, the sweet names all but disappear, with power names dominating, but still a higher proportion of neutral/paradoxical names than among boys in those age-groups.

Barbie narrative versus warrior narrative

How do we make sense of the obviously powerful spark that Barbie provided in the opening ceremony scene described above? Barbie is likely one of the most immediately identifiable symbols of femininity in the world. More conservatively oriented parents tend to happily buy Barbie dolls for their daughters, while perhaps deflecting their sons' interest in Barbie toward more sex-appropriate "action toys." Feminist parents, on the other hand, have often expressed open contempt—or at least uncomfortable ambivalence—toward Barbie. This is because both conservative and feminist parents see

dominant cultural meanings of emphasized femininity as condensed in Barbie and assume that these meanings will be imitated by their daughters. Recent developments in cultural studies, though, should warn us against simplistic readings of Barbie as simply conveying hegemonic messages about gender to unwitting children (Attfield 1996; Seiter 1995). In addition to critically analyzing the cultural values (or "preferred meanings") that may be encoded in Barbie or other children's toys, feminist scholars of cultural studies point to the necessity of examining "reception, pleasure, and agency," and especially "the fullness of reception contexts" (Walters 1999, 246). The Barbie Girls versus Sea Monsters moment can be analyzed as a "reception context," in which differently situated boys, girls, and parents variously used Barbie to construct pleasurable intergroup bonds, as well as boundaries between groups.

[...]

Recent Third Wave feminist theory sheds light on the different sensibilities of younger generations of girls and women concerning their willingness to display and play with this apparently paradoxical relationship between bodily experience (including "feminine" displays) and public empowerment. In Third Wave feminist texts, displays of feminine physical attractiveness and empowerment are not viewed as mutually exclusive or necessarily opposed realities, but as lived (if often paradoxical) aspects of the same reality (Heywood and Drake 1997). This embracing of the paradoxes of post–Second Wave femininity is manifested in many punk, or Riot Grrrl, subcultures (Klein 1997) and in popular culture in the resounding late 1990s' success of the Spice Girls' mantra of "Girl Power." This generational expression of "girl power" may today be part of "the pleasures of girl culture that Barbie stands for" (Spigel forthcoming). Indeed, as the Barbie Girls rallied around Barbie, their obvious pleasure did not appear to be based on a celebration of quiet passivity (as feminist parents might fear). Rather, it was a statement that they—the Barbie Girls—were here in this public space. They were not silenced by the boys' oppositional chanting. To the contrary, they ignored the boys, who seemed irrelevant to their celebration. And, when the boys later physically invaded their space, some of the girls responded by chasing the boys off. In short, when I pay attention to what the girls *did* (rather than imposing on the situation what I *think* Barbie "should" mean to the girls), I see a public moment of celebratory "girl power."

And this may give us better basis from which to analyze the boys' oppositional response. First, the boys may have been responding to the threat of displacement they may have felt while viewing the girls' moment of celebratory girl power. Second, the boys may simultaneously have been responding to the fears of feminine pollution that Barbie had come to symbolize to them. But why might Barbie symbolize feminine pollution to little boys? A brief example from my older son is instructive. When he was about three, following a fun day of play with the five-year-old girl next door, he enthusiastically asked me to buy him a Barbie like hers. He was gleeful when I took him to the store and bought him one. When we arrived home, his feet had barely hit the pavement getting out of the car before an eight-year-old neighbor boy laughed at and ridiculed him: "A *Barbie*? Don't you know that Barbie is a *girl's toy*?" No amount of parental intervention could counter this devastating peer-induced injunction against boys playing with Barbie. My son's pleasurable desire for Barbie appeared almost overnight to transform itself into shame and rejection. The doll ended up at the bottom of a heap of toys in the closet, and my son soon became infatuated, along with other boys in his preschool, with Ninja Turtles and Power Rangers.

Research indicates that there is widespread agreement as to which toys are appropriate for one sex and polluting, dangerous, or inappropriate for the other sex. When Campenni (1999) asked adults to rate the gender appropriateness of children's toys, the toys considered most appropriate to girls were those pertaining to domestic tasks, beauty enhancement, or child rearing. Of the 206 toys rated, Barbie was rated second only to Makeup Kit as a female-only toy. Toys considered most appropriate to boys were those pertaining to sports gear (football gear was the most masculine-rated toy, while boxing gloves were third), vehicles, action figures (G. I. Joe was rated second only to football gear), and other war-related toys. This research on parents' gender stereotyping of toys reflects similar findings in research on children's toy preferences (Bradbard 1985; Robinson and Morris 1986). Children tend to avoid cross-sex toys,

with boys' avoidance of feminine-coded toys appearing to be stronger than girls' avoidance of masculine-coded toys (Etaugh and Liss 1992). Moreover, preschool-age boys who perceive their fathers to be opposed to cross-gender-typed play are more likely than girls or other boys to think that it is "bad" for boys to play with toys that are labeled as "for girls" (Raag and Rackliff 1998).

By kindergarten, most boys appear to have learned—either through experiences similar to my son's, where other male persons police the boundaries of gender-appropriate play and fantasy and/or by watching the clearly gendered messages of television advertising—that Barbie dolls are not appropriate toys for boys (Rogers 1999, 30). To avoid ridicule, they learn to hide their desire for Barbie, either through denial and oppositional/pollution discourse and/or through sublimation of their desire for Barbie into play with male-appropriate "action figures" (Pope *et al*. 1999). In their study of a kindergarten classroom, Jordan and Cowan (1995, 728) identified "warrior narratives ... that assume that violence is legitimate and justified when it occurs within a struggle between good and evil" to be the most commonly agreed-upon currency for boys' fantasy play. They observe that the boys seem commonly to adapt story lines that they have seen on television. Popular culture—film, video, computer games, television, and comic books—provides boys with a seemingly endless stream of Good Guys versus Bad Guys characters and stories—from cowboy movies, Superman and Spiderman to Ninja Turtles, Star Wars, and Pokémon—that are available for the boys to appropriate as the raw materials for the construction of their own warrior play.

In the kindergarten that Jordan and Cowan studied, the boys initially attempted to import their warrior narratives into the domestic setting of the "Doll Corner." Teachers eventually drove the boys' warrior play outdoors, while the Doll Corner was used by the girls for the "appropriate" domestic play for which it was originally intended. Jordan and Cowan argue that kindergarten teachers' outlawing of boys' warrior narratives inside the classroom contributed to boys' defining schools as a feminine environment, to which they responded with a resistant, underground continuation of masculine warrior play. Eventually though, boys who acquiesce and successfully sublimate warrior play into fantasy or sport are more successful in constructing what Connell (1989, 291) calls "a masculinity organized around themes of rationality and responsibility [that is] closely connected with the 'certification' function of the upper levels of the education system and to a key form of masculinity among professionals."

In contrast to the "rational/professional" masculinity constructed in schools, the institution of sport historically constructs hegemonic masculinity as *bodily superiority* over femininity and non-athletic masculinities (Messner 1992). Here, warrior narratives are allowed to publicly thrive—indeed, are openly celebrated (witness, for instance, the commentary of a televised NFL [National Football League] football game or especially the spectacle of televised professional wrestling). Preschool boys and kindergartners seem already to know this, easily adopting aggressively competitive team names and an us-versus-them attitude. By contrast, many of the youngest girls appear to take two or three years in organized soccer before they adopt, or partially accommodate themselves to, aggressively competitive discourse, indicated by the 10-year-old girls' shifting away from the use of sweet names toward more power names. In short, where the gender regime of preschool and grade school may be experienced as an environment in which mostly women leaders enforce rules that are hostile to masculine fantasy play and physicality, the gender regime of sport is experienced as a place where masculine styles and values of physicality, aggression, and competition are enforced and celebrated by mostly male coaches.

A cultural analysis suggests that the boys' and the girls' previous immersion in differently gendered cultural experiences shaped the likelihood that they would derive and construct different meanings from Barbie—the girls through pleasurable and symbolically empowering identification with "girl power" narratives; the boys through oppositional fears of feminine pollution (and fears of displacement by girl power?) and with aggressively verbal, and eventually physical, invasions of the girls' ritual space. The boys' collective response thus constituted them differently, *as boys*, in opposition to the girls' constitution of themselves *as girls*. An individual girl or boy, in this moment, who may have felt an inclination to dissent from the dominant feelings of the group (say, the Latina Barbie Girl who, her mother later told me, did not want the

group to be identified with Barbie, or a boy whose immediate inner response to the Barbie Girls' joyful celebration might be to join in) is most likely silenced into complicity in this powerful moment of border work.

What meanings did this highly gendered moment carry for the boys' and girls' teams in the ensuing soccer season? Although I did not observe the Barbie Girls after the opening ceremony, I did continue to observe the Sea Monsters' weekly practices and games. During the boys' ensuing season, gender never reached this "magnified" level of salience again—indeed, gender was rarely raised verbally or performed overtly by the boys. On two occasions, though, I observed the coach jokingly chiding the boys during practice that "if you don't watch out, I'm going to get the Barbie Girls here to play against you!" This warning was followed by gleeful screams of agony and fear, and nervous hopping around and hugging by some of the boys. Normally, though, in this sex-segregated, all-male context, if boundaries were invoked, they were not boundaries between boys and girls but boundaries between the Sea Monsters and other boys' teams, or sometimes age boundaries between the Sea Monsters and a small group of dads and older brothers who would engage them in a mock scrimmage during practice. But it was also evident that when the coach was having trouble getting the boys to act together, as a group, his strategic and humorous invocation of the dreaded Barbie Girls once again served symbolically to affirm their group status. They were a team. They were the boys.

Conclusion

The overarching goal of this article has been to take one empirical observation from everyday life and demonstrate how a multilevel (interactionist, structural, cultural) analysis might reveal various layers of meaning that give insight into the everyday social construction of gender. This article builds on observations made by Thorne (1993) concerning ways to approach sociological analyses of children's worlds. The most fruitful approach is not to ask why boys and girls are so different but rather to ask how and under what conditions boys and girls constitute themselves as separate, oppositional groups. Sociologists need not debate whether gender is "there"—clearly, gender is always already there, built as it is into the structures, situations, culture, and consciousness of children and adults. The key issue is under what conditions gender is activated as a salient organizing principle in social life and under what conditions it may be less salient. These are important questions, especially since the social organization of categorical gender difference has always been so clearly tied to gender hierarchy (Acker 1990; Lorber 1994). In the Barbie Girls versus Sea Monsters moment, the performance of gendered boundaries and the construction of boys' and girls' groups as categorically different occurred in the context of a situation systematically structured by sex segregation, sparked by the imposing presence of a shared cultural symbol that is saturated with gendered meanings, and actively supported and applauded by adults who basked in the pleasure of difference, reaffirmed.[6]

I have suggested that a useful approach to the study of such "how" and "under what conditions" questions is to employ multiple levels of analysis. At the most general level, this project supports the following working propositions.

Interactionist theoretical frameworks that emphasize the ways that social agents "perform" or "do" gender are most useful in describing how groups of people actively create (or at times disrupt) the boundaries that delineate seemingly categorical differences between male persons and female persons. In this case, we saw how the children and the parents interactively performed gender in a way that constructed an apparently natural boundary between the two separate worlds of the girls and the boys.

Structural theoretical frameworks that emphasize the ways that gender is built into institutions through hierarchical sexual divisions of labor are most useful in explaining under what conditions social agents mobilize variously to disrupt or to affirm gender differences and inequalities. In this case, we saw how the sexual division of labor among parent volunteers (grounded in their own histories in the gender regime of sport), the formal sex segregation of the children's leagues, and the structured context of the opening ceremony created conditions for possible interactions between girls' teams and boys' teams.

Cultural theoretical perspectives that examine how popular symbols that are injected into circulation by the culture industry are variously taken up by differently situated people are most useful in analyzing how the meanings of cultural symbols, in a given institutional context, might trigger or be taken up by social agents and used as resources to reproduce, disrupt, or contest binary conceptions of sex difference and gendered relations of power. In this case, we saw how a girls' team appropriated a large Barbie around which to construct a pleasurable and empowering sense of group identity and how the boys' team responded with aggressive denunciations of Barbie and invasions.

Utilizing any one of the above theoretical perspectives by itself will lead to a limited, even distorted, analysis of the social construction of gender. Together, they can illuminate the complex, multileveled architecture of the social construction of gender in everyday life. For heuristic reasons, I have falsely separated structure, interaction, and culture. In fact, we need to explore their constant interrelationships, continuities, and contradictions. For instance, we cannot understand the boys' aggressive denunciations and invasions of the girls' space and the eventual clarification of categorical boundaries between the girls and the boys without first understanding how these boys and girls have already internalized four or five years of "gendering" experiences that have shaped their interactional tendencies and how they are already immersed in a culture of gendered symbols, including Barbie and sports media imagery. Although "only" preschoolers, they are already skilled in collectively taking up symbols from popular culture as resources to be used in their own group dynamics—building individual and group identities, sharing the pleasures of play, clarifying boundaries between in-group and out-group members, and constructing hierarchies in their worlds.

Furthermore, we cannot understand the reason that the girls first chose "Barbie Girls" as their team name without first understanding the fact that a particular institutional structure of AYSO soccer preexisted the girls' entrée into the league. The informal sexual division of labor among adults, and the formal sex segregation of children's teams, is a preexisting gender regime that constrains and enables the ways that the children enact gender relations and construct identities. One concrete manifestation of this constraining nature of sex segregated teams is the choice of team names. It is reasonable to speculate that if the four- and five-year-old children were still sex integrated, as in the pre-1995 era, no team would have chosen "Barbie Girls" as its team name, with Barbie as its symbol. In other words, the formal sex segregation created the conditions under which the girls were enabled—perhaps encouraged—to choose a "sweet" team name that is widely read as encoding feminine meanings. The eventual interactions between the boys and the girls were made possible—although by no means fully determined—by the structure of the gender regime and by the cultural resources that the children variously drew on.

On the other hand, the gendered division of labor in youth soccer is not seamless, static, or immune to resistance. One of the few woman head coaches, a very active athlete in her own right, told me that she is "challenging the sexism" in AYSO by becoming the head of her son's league. As post-Title IX women increasingly become mothers and as media images of competent, heroic female athletes become more a part of the cultural landscape for children, the gender regimes of children's sports may be increasingly challenged (Dworkin and Messner 1999). Put another way, the dramatically shifting opportunity structure and cultural imagery of post-Title IX sports have created opportunities for new kinds of interactions, which will inevitably challenge and further shift institutional structures. Social structures simultaneously constrain and enable, while agency is simultaneously reproductive and resistant.

Notes

1. Most of the structural inventory presented here is from a content analysis of the 1998–99 regional American Youth Soccer League (AYSO) yearbook, which features photos and names of all of the teams, coaches, and managers. I counted the number of adult men and women occupying various positions. In the three cases where the sex category of a name was not immediately obvious (e.g., Rene or Terry), or in the five cases where simply a last name was listed, I did not count it. I also used the AYSO yearbook for my analysis of the children's team names. To check for reliability, another sociologist independently read and coded the list of team names. There was disagreement on how to categorize only 2 of the 156 team names.

2. The existence of some women coaches and some men team managers in this AYSO organization manifests a less extreme sexual division of labor than that of the same community's Little League baseball organization, in which there are proportionally far fewer women coaches. Similarly, Saltzman Chafetz and Kotarba's (1999, 52) study of parental labor in support of Little League baseball in a middle-class Houston community revealed an apparently absolute sexual division of labor, where nearly all of the supportive "activities off the field were conducted by the women in the total absence of men, while activities on the field were conducted by men and boys in the absence of women." Perhaps youth soccer, because of its more recent (mostly post-Title IX) history in the United States, is a more contested gender regime than the more patriarchally entrenched youth sports like Little League baseball or youth football.

3. The four- and five-year-old kids' games and practices were absolutely homosocial in terms of the kids, due to the formal structural sex segregation. However, 8 of the 12 girls' teams at this age level had male coaches, and 2 of the 14 boys' teams had female coaches.

4. By 1994, more than 800 million Barbies had been sold worldwide. More than $1 billion was spent on Barbies and accessories in 1992 alone. Two Barbie dolls were purchased every second in 1994, half of which were sold in the United States (DuCille 1994, 49).

5. Rogers (1999, 23) notes that if one extrapolates Barbie's bodily proportions to "real woman ones," she would be "33-18-31.5 and stand five feet nine inches tall, with fully half of her height accounted for by her 'shapely legs.'"

6. My trilevel analysis of structure, interaction, and culture may not be fully adequate to plumb the emotional depths of the magnified Barbie Girls versus Sea Monsters moment. Although it is beyond the purview of this article, an adequate rendering of the depths of pleasure and revulsion, attachment and separation, and commitment to ideologies of categorical sex difference may involve the integration of a fourth level of analysis: gender at the level of personality (Chodorow 1999). Object relations theory has fallen out of vogue in feminist sociology in recent years, but as Williams (1993) has argued, it might be most useful in revealing the mostly hidden social power of gender to shape people's unconscious predispositions to various structural contexts, cultural symbols, and interactional moments.

References

Acker, Joan. 1990. Hierarchies, jobs, bodies: A theory of gendered organizations. *Gender & Society* 4:139–58.

Adler, Patricia A., and Peter Adler. 1998. *Peer power: Preadolescent culture and identity.* New Brunswick, NJ: Rutgers University Press.

Attfield, Judy. 1996. Barbie and Action Man: Adult toys for girls and boys, 1959–93. In *The gendered object*, edited by Pat Kirkham, 80–89. Manchester, UK, and New York: Manchester University Press.

Boyle, Maree, and Jim McKay. 1995. "You leave your troubles at the gate": A case study of the exploitation of older women's labor and "leisure" in sport. *Gender & Society* 9:556–76.

Bradbard, M. 1985. Sex differences in adults' gifts and children's toy requests. *Journal of Genetic Psychology* 145:283–84.

Campenni, C. Estelle. 1999. Gender stereotyping of children's toys: A comparison of parents and non-parents. *Sex Roles* 40:121–38.

Chodorow, Nancy J. 1999. *The power of feelings: Personal meanings in psychoanalysis, gender, and culture.* New Haven, CT, and London: Yale University Press.

Connell, R.W. 1987. *Gender and power.* Stanford, CA: Stanford University Press.

———. 1989. Cool guys, swots and wimps: The interplay of masculinity and education. *Oxford Review of Education* 15:291–303.

DuCille, Anne. 1994. Dyes and dolls: Multicultural Barbie and the merchandising of difference. *Differences: A Journal of Cultural Studies* 6:46–68.

Dworkin, Shari L., and Michael A. Messner. 1999. Just do... what?: Sport, bodies, gender. In *Revisioning gender*, edited by Myra Marx Ferree, Judith Lorber, and Beth B. Hess, 341-61. Thousand Oaks, CA: Sage.

Etaugh, C., and M. B. Liss. 1992. Home, school, and playroom: Training grounds for adult gender roles. *Sex Roles* 26:129–47.

Heywood, Leslie, and Jennifer Drake, Eds. 1997. *Third wave agenda: Being feminist, doing feminism.* Minneapolis: University of Minnesota Press.

Hochschild, Arlie Russell. 1994. The commercial spirit of intimate life and the abduction of feminism: Signs from women's advice books. *Theory, Culture & Society* 11:1–24.

Jordan, Ellen, and Angela Cowan. 1995. Warrior narratives in the kindergarten classroom: Renogotiating the social contract? *Gender & Society* 9:727–43.

Kessler, Suzanne J., and Wendy McKenna. 1978. *Gender: An ethnomethodological approach.* New York: John Wiley.

Klein, Melissa. 1997. Duality and redefinition: Young feminism and the alternative music community. In *Third wave agenda: Being feminist, doing feminism*, edited by Leslie Heywood and Jennifer Drake, 207-25. Minneapolis: University of Minnesota Press.

Lorber, Judith. 1994. *Paradoxes of gender.* New Haven, CT, and London: Yale University Press.

Messner, Michael A. 1992. *Power at play: Sports and the problem of masculinity.* Boston: Beacon.

Pope, Harrison G., Jr., Roberto Olivarda, Amanda Gruber, and John Borowiecki. 1999. Evolving ideals of male body image as seen through action toys. *International Journal of Eating Disorders* 26:65–72.

Raag, Tarja, and Christine L. Rackliff. 1998. Preschoolers' awareness of social expectations of gender: Relationships to toy choices. *Sex Roles* 38:685–700.

Risman, Barbara. 1998. *Gender vertigo: American families in transition.* New Haven and London: Yale University Press.

Robinson, C. C., and J. T. Morris. 1986. The gender-stereotyped nature of Christmas toys received by 36-, 48-, and 60-month-old children: A comparison between nonrequested vs. requested toys. *Sex Roles* 15:21–32.

Rogers, Mary F. 1999. *Barbie culture.* Thousand Oaks, CA: Sage.

Saltzman Chafetz, Janet, and Joseph A. Kotarba. 1999. Little League mothers and the reproduction of gender. In *Inside sports*, edited by Jay Coakley and Peter Donnelly, 46–54. London and New York: Routledge.

Seiter, Ellen. 1995. *Sold separately: Parents and children in consumer culture.* New Brunswick, NJ: Rutgers University Press.

Spigel, Lynn. Forthcoming. Barbies without Ken: Femininity, feminism, and the art-culture system. In *Sitting room only: Television, consumer culture and the suburban home*, edited by Lynn Spigel. Durham, NC: Duke University Press.

Thorne, Barrie. 1993. *Gender play: Girls and boys in school.* New Brunswick, NJ: Rutgers University Press.

Walters, Suzanna Danuta. 1999. Sex, text, and context: (In) between feminism and cultural studies. In *Revisioning gender*, edited by Myra Marx Ferree, Judith Lorber, and Beth B. Hess, 222-57. Thousand Oaks, CA: Sage.

West, Candace, and Don Zimmerman. 1987. Doing gender. *Gender & Society* 1:125–51.

Williams, Christine. 1993. Psychoanalytic theory and the sociology of gender. In *Theory on gender, gender on theory*, edited by Paula England, 131-49. New York: Aldine.

193

4.7   Journalistic view

When tranquillity trumps equality

Selena Roberts

The libbers for lob equality once risked their wood Wilsons so prize purses for women would mean more than a nice clutch bag, so gender equity would include the right to a shared pot.

Amid the estrogen revolution, the women's Tour evolved ahead of society as Billie Jean King made feminism cool, as Martina Navratilova made muscle acceptable, as Chris Evert made an empire out of a playing career.

They were Oprah before Oprah. They were tennis stars who, in their own ways, nurtured the Tour so well, with such a progressive spirit, it is the only women's league where the money measures up to the fellas.

But what happens to the Tour when financial freedom opens an escape hatch?

At age 23, Kim Clijsters doesn't need tennis anymore. She doesn't need waking up with an aching body after another night spent away from her fiance, in a hotel room that looks exactly like the last.

Ranked No. 5 on the WTA Tour, with $14.7 million in career earnings, plus millions more in endorsements, Clijsters chose to retire on Sunday, with an explanation straight off the menu of the "Happy Days" diner.

"Right now, it is time for a new life," Clijsters wrote on her Web site. "Time for marrying. Children? Time for cooking and playing with the dogs."

She would be a lousy bra burner. But Clijsters's decision to opt out of the playing tedium is not an aberration these days; it is a Tour trend. Some high-ranked players have retired—like Clijsters and Lindsay Davenport—while stars from Justine Henin to Amelie Mauresmo, from Martina Hingis to Venus Williams, have alternately disappeared during their careers in a game of "Where's Waldo?"

Injuries, players claim. Lame excuses, the suspicious say.

But what women's tennis may reveal is the same socially sanctioned element that ribbons through every Starbucks, where mommies with M.B.A.'s prefer to run play dates instead of boardroom meetings. In this circle, it's O.K. to jump off the fast track for the mommy track or laugh track. Whatever makes a woman of means happy.

Money hasn't fueled the competition in women's tennis. It has served as a disincentive to play when the ladies reach a point where they have earned enough to buy contentment.

"Money is important, but not the most important in my life," Clijsters wrote in her online diary. "Health and happiness are so much more key to life."

This is the right philosophy, isn't it? And yet, one woman's Zen is another loss for the Tour. Tournaments and majors played without longtime rivals or a consistency of stardom or familiar faces puts women's tennis at risk of vanishing through irrelevance.

Top players on Tour can afford to be ladies of leisure as they parachute in and out of the schedule to indulge in their cultural gender differences with male athletes.

Salary figures and contract numbers define many male pros. To them, wealth is a measure of their self-worth. This is why Roger Clemens needed to be the most ridiculously paid player in the game upon his ego-gratifying return. This is why LeBron James writes down "becoming a billionaire" on his career to-do list, why draft picks hold out, why free agents leave teams, why Tiger Woods has the same goal as James.

Money as a reflection of manhood is not a hard and fast rule. There are exceptions. Bjorn Borg retired early after growing weary of the Tour grind and privacy intrusions. But disillusionment on the women's Tour is a flu bug passing from one star to the next.

In tennis, 23 is the new 40. It's midlife crisis time when players start to ponder the loneliness of the Tour, develop outside interests and realize they have been at the game since age 10, maybe 6. The guys start the game later and enter the scene with less attention. The women experience their first pimple, first love and first breakup, all before the public.

The scrutiny is endless: Is Serena Williams's caboose on the loose? Was Jennifer Capriati's mood too dark? Did Hingis break Sergio Garcia's heart? Just what did the effervescent Clijsters once see in the boorish Lleyton Hewitt?

The constant prying is enough to make a gal run for the exit.

"No more gossip or lies in the newspapers," Clijsters explained.

Mental burnout is nothing new to tennis (as in Andrea Jaeger at age 19) and careers have been cut short by injury before (as in Tracy Austin at 20). Clijsters cited herself as a victim of both. She longed for more time to plan her July wedding to Brian Lynch, an American-born basketball player in Europe. She pined for the days when she could slide on the court into a full split—a trademark of her Silly Putty elasticity—without her back locking up.

Tennis has a history of devouring its youth. But never have so many stars seemed so eager to fade out, whether into retirement or an extended leave.

There is no glass ceiling on the women's Tour—the revolutionists in pleated skirts made sure of it—but there is an open window. Who knew liberation could one day threaten the Tour?

Section 5

Nice guys finish last

Athletes out of bounds and the problem of sports and deviance

Introduction

Deviance in sport

Deviance looms as a persisting and troubling reality in sports. One only needs to read the sports section of major newspapers or watch television sports news to encounter almost daily reports about athletes involved in deviant behavior. Indeed, such reports have become so commonplace that many people stereotype all athletes as misfits. While the stereotype is false, athletic deviance is widespread and varied, as indicated by the following examples.

- The University of Michigan basketball team was forced to forfeit games and a championship because some of its players had received hundreds of thousands of dollars in loans from a team booster.
- An Arizona State basketball captain, in 1999, was sentenced to a prison term after pleading guilty of shaving points in four games in 1994.
- The French superstar, Zinedine Zidane, reacting to an alleged verbal insult in a 2006 soccer World Cup match, brutally head butted an Italian player, which resulted in Zidane's ejection from the game and, ultimately, France's loss of the championship.
- Mike Tyson, the former heavyweight boxing champion, in a desperate effort to reverse a bout he was losing, bear hugged his opponent, Evander Holyfield, and then suddenly bit off the upper part of Holyfield's left ear, prompting the referee to immediately stop the fight and declare Holyfield the winner.
- Floyd Landis, in the summer of 2006, was proclaimed the winner of the Tour de France, only to have his victory nullified by the French race officials, who announced that Landis failed a drug test, which revealed elevated levels of testosterone in his blood.
- Marion Jones, the American winner of several Olympic gold medals in track, lost her medals and was sentenced to prison after a drug test revealed she had taken steroids, about which she lied in grand jury testimony.

Deviance is a ubiquitous and intriguing feature of social life that is defined by sociologists as behavior that violates established normative rules. Typically, it provokes strong public demands that "something be done," that the offender be punished, and that the authority of the rules be restored. Put simply, deviance matters because it unsettles social life.

If allowed to persist and expand unchecked, deviance disrupts social order, which can be sustained only if most of its members adhere to its rules. To elicit high levels of compliance with its normative rules, every social order must develop not only processes of socialization but also effective social controls, which allow it to detect and

199

punish deviations. Each of the above examples, ranging from NCAA basketball to the World Cup and the Olympics, highlights situations where, despite the deviance, the rules governing the social organization of the sport were restored and affirmed by effective social controls.

Leading scholars in the sociology of deviance have tended to ignore the sports world—much like their fellow sociologists in the fields of race relations and politics; they have viewed sports as an insignificant institutional sphere. Hence sociologists have only scratched the surface in addressing the complex causes and consequences of deviance in the sports world. Our aim in this short introduction is not to redress this long history of neglect but rather to present several examples of the type of questions that need to be explored in future research. Beginning with cross national comparisons, we need to ask:

- what is the link between deviance in sport and deviance in the surrounding society? Are societies with high levels of crime likely to evidence higher levels of cheating and deception in sports? Or is deviance in sport affected more by the culture of the specific sports than by the culture of the larger society?
- How do professional sports compare to amateur sports in their levels and types of deviance?
- Are certain sports (e.g. boxing) more susceptible to deviant activities than other sports (e.g. soccer), and if so, why?
- Does the social class status of the sport affect its level and types of deviance?
- What—if any—is the relationship between the rewards for winning and the incidence of cheating?
- To what extent are the prevalence and types of deviance in male and female sports different?
- Are athletes more prone to deviant behavior in their personal lives than non-athletes? How does the punishment of athletes' deviant behavior in their personal lives compare to that of non-athletes? Are athletes more likely to be exempted from punishment or subjected to harsher punishment?

Though some sports scholars have drawn theoretical perspectives from studies of deviance in other institutional sites, most writings about deviance in sports lack a theoretical perspective, which is revealed by their failure to account for how that deviance was influenced by social process. In light of the frequent media reports about sports-related deviance, it would be hardly an exaggeration to say that the sociological study of deviance is more than overdue for significant theoretical development. The following sketches present some of the theoretical perspectives on deviance that have excellent potential to deepen our understanding of deviance as the outcome of social process.

The theoretical perspectives influenced by Emile Durkheim's writings on anomie are particularly relevant to deviant behavior in sports in modern societies, because Durkheim highlighted the effects of modernization for creating social environments characterized by complex social organizations and weak normative constraints (Durkheim, 1993). Following in this Durkheimian tradition, both Robert Merton's "Social Structure and Anomie" and Messner and Rosenfeld's Institutional Anomie Theory provide theoretical perspectives that could advance sociological understanding of the surge in such sports-related deviance as the use of performance enhancing drugs and violations of eligibility rules, as outgrowths of the enormous material rewards for outstanding sports achievements in societies characterized by loose, and increasingly anomic, cultural systems, where materialistic values have assumed dominance (Merton, 1967; Messner and Rosenfeld, 2001). Merton's theoretical perspective is especially applicable to explaining the materialistically motivated deviant behavior of athletes from poor or working class backgrounds; whereas Messner and Rosenfield's perspective, encompassing a broader range of deviant behaviors, is relevant not just to working class athletes but affluent athletes and affluent athletic administrators.

In contrast to the anomie perspective which emphasizes strain on normative behavior created by cultural inducements to wealth and fame, the symbolic interaction perspective focuses on micro-social processes (Manis and Meltzer, 1978). Emphasizing interpersonal and group influences as the source of deviance, it asks—for example—why do some athletes become involved in deviance, such as collaborating with gamblers or engaging in bar fights, whereas others (on the same team or from the same social background) do not? This approach, with its focus on interpersonal inducements to violate official norms, is equally relevant to explaining the behaviors of corrupt coaches and athletic directors, whose deviance is often ignored by the media and scholars.

Related to this social psychological approach, the sub-cultural theoretical perspective also views deviant behavior as being derived from group interpersonal influences, but it focuses explicitly on the position of the group relative to the mainstream social structure (Cohen, 1955; Brymer, 1944). Typically the subculture is a marginalized group which is oriented to alternative, non-mainstream norms. Behaviors such as participating in group rapes or using illegal recreational drugs like cocaine are subcultural insofar as the participants perceive their behavior as being acceptable, from the standpoint of alternative cultural norms.

Related to the subcultural perspective, the cultural conflict perspective is another under-utilized theoretical perspective in studies of sports deviance (Sellin, 1938). However, unlike the subcultural perspective, it focuses on groups whose norms openly contest the legitimacy of the mainstream norms. For example, sport deviance, such as racial epithets or acts of racial violence manifested during European soccer matches, tend to resonate with a cultural conflict perspective rather than sub-cultural deviance because the racial antagonists are often influenced by political groups promoting ideologies that challenge liberal racial norms. The clash between Nazi racial ideology and liberal racial ideology during the 1936 Olympics reflected such a cultural conflict. The banning of South Africa's sports team from the Olympics, in reaction to its apartheid racial practices, also fit within the conflict perspective on deviance. The key question in such situations is determining which social organizations possess authority to label the deviance and enforce the normative rules of the sport. How can sports contests between antagonistic cultural groups be effectively managed?

Without doubt, the most neglected theoretical perspective in studies of sports-related deviance is the perspective on white collar crime. Focusing specifically on elites, this perspective explains the deviant behavior of the powerful and wealthy. This includes not just the deviant acts they commit (i.e. Olympic officials corruption) or accommodate (i.e. assisting athletes to cheat on academic exams, covering up for athletes' crimes); but also the consequences of their deviance. Unlike the deviance of athletes, sports-related deviance by elites (coaches, athletic administrators, and boosters) tend to receive little media attention and weak sanctions, largely due to the respect and deference accorded these elites.

This issue of power and influence is highlighted by labeling theory (though it operates in a different manner), the last theoretical perspective we will consider. Why are some acts of sports deviance more likely to be reported and labeled, while others are ignored? This issue is addressed by the labeling theory. A variant of the symbolic interactionist perspective, labeling theory seeks to explain not the causes of the deviance, but the patterns of bias—e.g. class, racial, gender—in the way deviance is perceived and stigmatized.

The articles in this section cover a diverse range of deviant behavior in sports. The first two articles present explicit theoretical perspectives to explain sports related deviant behaviors. The first, a selection from Michael Messner's article—"Playing Center"—presents an excellent demonstration of the symbolic interactionist perspective to explain off-field group deviance of athletes. Messner explains how inter-personal bonding of male athletes, much like that of juvenile gangs or college fraternities, conduce to group deviance. Taking a different approach, Peter G. Mewett, in this chapter's other theoretically oriented article—"Discourses of Deception"—focuses on cheating in Australian professional running, a working class sport, which he explains from a neo-Marxist theoretical perspective. Highlighting the potential benefits of sports participation for upward social mobility, Mewett argues that cheating in sport can be anticipated as a feature of an acquisitive capitalist society. This argument also resonates with the tenets of Durkheimian anomie theory, which emphasizes the effects of increased individualism and weakening normative integration in modern societies. The next article—"IOC Scandal Part of Sport Corruption Big Picture"—by Joe Pollack, argues that the 1984 Olympic Games scandal was a by-product of business-corporate involvement in sports. This article raises questions about the compatibility of norms underlying competitive sports and free market capitalism. Though Pollack does not explain this corruption from a theoretical perspective on sports related deviance, the argument could easily incorporate the theoretical perspective on white collar crime.

The next article focuses on the use of performance enhancing drugs, a problem of increasing concern in sports. Though reportorial rather than theoretical in objective, the article presents an account of practices and trends that could be framed within the subcultural theoretical perspective. Michael Sokolove—in "In Pursuit of Doped Excellence"—explores the complex world of drug use and drug testing in sports. He discusses the background to the development of drugs such as anabolic steroids. Calling attention to the difficulty of drawing the line between nutritional supplements such as proteins, amino acids, caffeine, and creatine versus steroids, Sokolove highlights the imperfect, arbitrary, and shifting standard distinguishing acceptable from prohibited drug use. Given the role of money in sports and the huge rewards at stake, he foresees no simple resolution of the problem of drug use in sports.

Viewing the problem of deviance in sports from a wholly different angle, Richard Lapchick, in "Crime and Athletes," critically examines the prevailing negative stereotypes of black athletes as deviants. Black athletes, he argues, are routinely portrayed as being unintelligent and violent. He attributes these stereotypes to various factors, ranging from some white males' resentment of star black athletes' wealth and the pervasive racial prejudice in American culture to the role of a predominately white sports media. Noting that most of black athletes do not fit these negative stereotypes, Lapchick argues that the image of black athletic deviance should be placed within its actual social context of racial prejudice. Though Lapchick does not frame his argument within a theoretical perspective, it resonates with key tenets of labeling theory, which would suggest that stereotypes of black athletes simply reflect the more general stereotypes attached to black males in American society.

The final article highlights a closely related but even more complex problem, the double standard in labeling male athlete violence relative to its victims. Theresa Walton, in "The Sprewell/Carlesimo Episode," is concerned with the violence of male sports figures outside of sports contests. Focusing on a single case study, she examines the media's coverage of the violent altercation between Latrell Sprewell and P. J. Carlesimo, in which Sprewell (a black NBA player) attacked Carlesimo (his white coach). Walton argues that the event received extraordinary media coverage because Sprewell violated the normative rules of the white male power structure and the capitalist work place. In contrast, Walton argues that the violence of male coaches or athletes against women receives little or no media coverage because it still has normative legitimacy. Hence it is not labeled deviant. These articles remind us that, ultimately, deviance, as Howard Becker has put it, is not a quality of the act but of societal reactions to the act.

References

Brymer, R. A. 1994. "The Emergence and Maintenance of a Deviant Subculture: The Case of Hunting/Poaching Sub-Culture." In *Symbolic Interaction*. Herman. N. J. and L. T. Reynolds. Dix Hills, N.Y.: General Hall Inc.

Cohen, A. K. *Delinquent Boys: The Culture of the Gang*. Glencoe, Ill.: Free Press.

Durkheim, E. 1933. *The Division of Labor in Society*. New York: The Free Press.

Manis, J. G. and B. N. Meltzer. 1978. *Symbolic Interactionism*. Boston: Allyn and Bacon.

Merton, Robert. 1967. *Social Theory and Social Structure*. New York: The Free Press.

Messner, S. F. and R. Rosenfeld. 2001. "Deviance, The American Dream, and Social Institutions." In *Explaining Criminals and Crime*. R. Paternoster and R. Bachman (eds.). Los Angeles: Roxbury Publishing Company.

Sellin, Thornstein. 1938. *Culture Conflict and Crime*. New York: Social Science Research Council.

Playing center

The triad of violence in men's sports

Michael A. Messner

The media frequently report stories about the flagrant misconduct of athletes in bars and nightclubs or at parties and other places of recreation. In this article, Michael Messner explains the off-field group deviance of male athletes as a by-product of their strong interpersonal bonding.

In November 2000, newspapers reported that six high school football players in Yucca Valley, California, had been arrested on felony charges of, false imprisonment, sexual battery, rape with a foreign object, and conspiracy. The crimes were allegedly perpetrated during a hazing ritiual, when senior members of the football team "initiated" freshmen and sophomore members of the team.[1] These days, we seem to hear story after story describing male athletes' violent acts of ritualized hazing on athletic teams, acquaintance and gang rapes perpetrated against women, and verbal and physical abuse of girlfriends and spouses.[2] Statements of shock and surprise routinely follow these stories. School officials and coaches, backed up by psychologists and other professionals, vow to develop better means of "weeding out the bad apples" in the future. A common working assumption in these cases is that the perpetrators of these kinds of violent acts are deviating from the norms of proper behavior in the school and on the athletic teams. As the Yucca Valley principal put it in the wake of the charges against his students, "Some bad things are alleged to

have happened. It's unfortunate, because these things tend to eclipse all the good things we're doing here."[3]

Are male athletes more likely than non-athletes to engage in acts of violence on the field, or when some athletes assault others are we just more likely to notice it because of their high-profile public status?[4] In this article, I will argue that we should not be surprised when we hear of male athletes committing acts of off-the-field violence, whether sexual or otherwise. Far from being an aberration perpetrated by some marginal deviants, male athletes' off-the-field violence is generated from the normal, everyday dynamics at the center of male athletic culture. Indeed, a number of studies of men's college athletics in recent years have pointed to statistically significant relationships between athletic participation and sexual aggression.[5] In what is widely considered the most reliable study to date, sociologist Todd Crosset and his colleagues surveyed twenty universities with Division I athletic programs and found that male athletes, who in 1995 made up 3.7 per cent of the student population, were 19 per cent of those reported to campus Judicial Affairs offices for sexual assault.[6] In a more recent article, Crosset argues that researchers have more than likely been using far too broad a brush in looking generally at the relationship of "men's sports" to violence against women.[7] Studies that have involved comparisons across various sports have found important differences: the vast majority of reported assaults were perpetrated by athletes in revenue-producing contact sports such as basketball, football, and ice hockey. For instance, in Crosset's study, male football and basketball players made up 30 per cent of the student-athlete population but were responsible for 67 per cent of the reported sexual assaults. These data, according to Crosset, should warn us of the dangers of "lumping all sport environments together under the rubric of 'athletic affiliation.'"[8] More to the point of my argument in this article, the research points to the conclusion that the athletes most likely to engage in sexual and other violent assaults off the field are those participating in the sports that I define as being at the institutional center of sport.

Some activists such as Donald McPherson, of the University of Massachusetts Mentors in Violence program, are wary of pointing the finger at athletes. McPherson argues that athletes are no more or less likely than other men to be engaged in violence against women. Rather, men's violence against women is a broad social problem that is proportionately reflected, like other social problems, in sport.[9] Perhaps fearing that pointing the finger at high-profile athletes will reinforce destructive and oppressive stereotypes of African American males (who make up about 80 per cent of the NBA, for instance) as violent sexual predators, activists like McPherson prefer instead to pull male athletes into positions of responsibility to educate peers to prevent violence against women. This is a real concern. As the media frenzy surrounding the trials of Mike Tyson and O. J. Simpson (for rape and for murder, respectively) illustrated, American culture seems especially obsessed with what Stuart Alan Clarke has called images of "black men misbehaving," especially if the alleged misbehaviors involve a combination of sex and violence.[10] Given the ways that racist stereotypes of black men as violent sexual predators have historically served as a foundation for institutional and personal violence perpetrated against African Americans, we should be wary

of the various ways that these images continue to surface.[11] So, when data reveal that college athletes in revenue-producing sports have higher rates of sexual assault against women, there is a very real danger that the term *athletes in revenue-producing sports* will smuggle in racist stereotypes as a thinly veiled code word for *black male athletes*.[12]

Evidence suggests that the apparent overrepresentation of black male athletes charged with sexual assault in college is due to their dramatic overrepresentation in the central team sports of football and basketball. When we look at high schools, where white males are more evenly represented in the student athlete population, we see that white male athletes perpetrated many of the most egregious examples of sexual assault. And when we look at Canada, where the central sport, ice hockey, is dominated by white men, we see the vast majority of sexual assaults by athletes are committed by white males.[13] Following this logic, I begin with the assumption that it is not their race or ethnicity but their *positions at the center of athletics* that make certain male athletes more likely to engage in sexual assault than other men.

This is not to confuse the "center" with the "majority." In fact, a key to my analysis is the fact that the majority of male athletes do *not* commit acts of off-the-field violence against women or other men. Though in the numerical minority, the men at the center of the athletic peer group are expressing the dominant, hegemonic, most honored form of masculinity. What helps hegemonic masculinity sustain itself as the dominant form in a system of power relations is the *complicity* of other men, some (or many) of whom might be uncomfortable with some of the beliefs and practices that sustain hegemonic masculinity. Intervention strategies must confront the root causes of men's violence against women, and a key way to accomplish this confrontation is to provide a context in which the "silent majority" of men move affirmatively away from being quietly complicit with the culture of misogyny, homophobia, and violence at the center of men's sport culture.

Early experiences in sports commonly divide children into seemingly different and opposed groups of "the boys" and "the girls." In this article I will show how, once separated into all-male homosocial groups, boys and men tend to construct a masculine, athletic center through their everyday peer group interactions. [...] Homosocial sport offers an institutional context in which boys and men learn, largely from each other, to discipline their bodies, attitudes, and feelings within the logic of the triad of men's violence. [...] My level of analysis in this chapter is primarily interactional. That is, I focus mostly on the ways that boys and men perform a particular form of masculinity in their athletic peer groups.

Male athletes' violence against women

In a riveting account of the infamous 1989 Glen Ridge, New Jersey, gang rape case, journalist Bernard Lefkowitz describes how thirteen white male, high-status high school athletes lured a seventeen-year-old "slightly retarded" girl into a basement.[14] The dynamics of the sexual assault that ensued are instructive for my purposes here: First, the boys set up chairs, theater style, in front of a couch. While some boys sat in the chairs to watch, others led the girl to the couch and induced her to begin to give one of the highest-status boys oral sex. When the assault began, one sophomore boy noticed "puzzlement and confusion" in the girl's eyes, turned to his friend, and said, "Let's get out of here." Another senior baseball player felt queasy, thought, "I don't belong here," and climbed the stairs to leave with another baseball player. On the way out, he told another guy, "It's wrong. C'mon with me," but the other guy stayed.[15] In all, six of the young men left the scene, while seven—six seniors and one junior—remained in the basement. While the girl was forced to continue giving oral sex to the boy, other boys laughed, yelled encouragement to their friends, and derisively shouted, "You whore!" at the girl. One boy decided it would be amusing to force a baseball bat up her vagina. When he did this (and followed it with a broomstick), the girl heard one boy's voice say, "Stop. You're hurting her," but another voice prevailed: "Do it more." Later, the girl remembered that the boys were all laughing while she was crying. When they were done, they warned her not to tell anyone and concluded with an athletic ritual of togetherness by standing in a circle and clasping "one hand on top of the other, all their hands together, like a basketball team on the sidelines at the end of a timeout."[16]

In his description of the Glen Ridge community in which the boys and their victim grew up, Lefkowitz points to a number of factors that enabled the gang rape to happen, and these are the very same factors that much of the social scientific literature on men, sexual violence, and sport has pointed to in recent years:

1 the key role of competitive, homophobic, and misogynistic talk and joking as the central, most honored form of dominance bonding in the athletic male peer group
2 the group practice of "voyeuring," whereby boys set up situations where they seduce girls into places and situations in which their friends can watch the sex act and sometimes take an active part in it
3 the suppression of empathy toward others —especially toward the girls who are the objects of their competitive dominance bonding—that the boys learn from each other
4 the enabling of some men's sexual violence against women by a "culture of silence" among peers, in families, and in the community

As I examine these four enabling factors, I will keep in the forefront Lefkowitz's observation that four football players and wrestlers physically perpetrated the assault. Three others apparently sat and watched, sometimes laughing and cheering, but did not actually physically join in the assault.[17] The other six boys left the scene when the assault was beginning. Though these six boys felt uncomfortable enough to leave the scene, they did not do anything at the time to stop their friends, nor did they report the assault to parents, teachers, or the police. And they all refused throughout the subsequent long and painful years of litigation to "turn" on their male friends and provide incriminating evidence. It is the *complicity* of these boys that I take as the centerpiece of my analysis here.

Sexual talk and dominance bonding

In an ethnographic study of eleven- and twelve-year-old Little Leagne baseball players, sociologist Gary Alan Fine found that one of the key ways that these boys connected with each

205

other was through sexually aggressive banter.[18] Reading Fine's descriptions of boys' verbal sparring brought back memories of engaging in what we called cut fights during childhood. I learned in grade school that high-status boys achieved and maintained their centrality in the male peer group not simply through athletic prowess but also through informal, often homophobic and misogynist, banter on the playgrounds, streets, and playing fields. Those who were the most ruthlessly competitive "cut fighters" seemed always capable of one-upping another boy's insults. Following another boy's sharp, cutting insult with silence or with a lame comment like "you too" left one open to derision. I learned this firsthand one day while walking home from fifth grade with a group of boys. Chris, a boy well known for his verbal prowess, and I were in a cut fight. Back and forth we went. I thought I was doing pretty well until Chris hit me with one for which I had no answer: "Messner," he asserted, "blow me!" I didn't know what to say back, and so of course I lost the cut fight. But behind my lack of response was confusion. In my eleven-year-old mind, I knew a few things about sex but was unclear about others. One thing I had recently learned from friends was that there were some men who had sex with other men. They were called homosexuals, and I was told that they were sick and sinful individuals. So, my confused mind spun, if Chris was saying, "blow me," to me, he was in effect asking me to be involved in some homosexual act with him. If homosexuality is such a bad and shameful thing, why then did *he* win the cut fight?

It took me years to figure that one out. Meanwhile, in the short run, I simply added "blow me" to my own cut fight repertoire. Now I can see that insults like "you suck," "blow me," or "fuck you" smuggle into children's and preadolescent groups a powerful pedagogy about sexuality, power, and domination.[19] In short, though children obviously do not intend it, through this sort of banter they teach each other that sex, whether of the homosexual or heterosexual kind, is a relational act of domination and subordination. The "men" are the ones who are on top, in control, doing the penetrating and fucking. Women, or penetrated men, are subordinate, degraded, and dehumanized objects of sexual aggression. This kind of sexual domination is played out most clearly in

cases of rape in men's prisons, where those being raped are symbolically defined as either women or fags.[20] The actual sexual orientation of these men matters little in these cases; it is their vulnerable, subordinate, and degraded status that makes them "women" or "fags." By contrast, those who are doing the raping are not defined as gay. They are "men" who are powerful, in control, and dominant over the symbolically debased "women" or "fags."

A key to the importance of this verbal sparring is the central role it plays in *groups*. Rarely will two boys, alone, engage in a cut fight. But put the same two boys in a group, they will often be compelled to insult each other or to turn on another boy in the group. A cut fight is a group phenomenon that requires an audience. On center stage are the higher-status boys; around the periphery are the lower-status boys, constituted as an admiring audience who, by their very presence, attention, and laughter, validate the higher status of the boys at the center. This dynamic starts early. In their study of first graders, sport scholars Cynthia Hasbrook and Othello Harris observed that "Martin," the highest-status boy in the class, was both athletically tough and socially aggressive. When he refused to hold hands during a relay race, this had an impact on the other boys:

> Other boys fell over themselves trying to be friends with Martin. They mimicked his speech, gestures, and postures; they covered for him so that he would not get in trouble; sought him out as a partner; and wrote stories portraying him as their friend. Martin constantly negotiated a masculine identity that was physically aggressive, tough, distant, and cool, and his refusal to join hands both consolidated his ascendant position and constricted other expressions of masculinity.[21]

These same tendencies are evident among preadolescent children. Patricia Adler and Peter Adler point to patterns of high-status grade school children picking on lower-status kids as well as teasing and "in-group subjugation" as key elements that "served to solidify the group and to assert the power of the strong over the vulnerability of the weak."[22] Similarly, in their study of high school basketball players, Scott Eveslage and Kevin Delaney found that the boys' "trash talking" on the court and their "insult talk" among teammates off the field have common traits: they establish hierarchies, they "involve personal insults or put-downs, often as calls to defend masculinity and honor, and they often degrade objects defined as 'feminine.'"[23] These processes continue into the worlds of young adult men. In a revealing study of talk in a college men's athletic locker room, sociologist Tim Curry observed that there is a dominant mode of conversation that is inclined toward the dual themes of competition and boasting of sexual conquests of women.[24] This dominant conversation is characterized by its high volume—it is clearly intended as a performance for the group—and by its geographic and cultural centrality in the locker room.

But Curry's study also revealed a less obvious dynamic. On the margins of the locker room, other young men were engaged in conversations that were very different from the dominant conversation at the center of the group. These men were speaking in hushed tones, usually in dyads, and were clearly not projecting a performance that was intended to be public. And the topics of their talks were not of competition and sexual conquest of women; rather, they were speaking to each other about personal issues, problems, even insecurities about dating or relationships with girlfriends. These conversations remain marginal, quiet, and private—in contrast with the loud, public, central conversation—partly because boys and young men have had the experience of being (or seeing other boys) humiliated in male groups for expressing vulnerability or for expressing care for a particular girl.[25]

The main policing mechanisms used to enforce consent with the dominant conversation are misogyny and homophobia: boys and men who reveal themselves as vulnerable are subsequently targeted as the symbolic "women," "pussies," and "faggots" on athletic teams (and, indeed, in many other male groups). In fact, it is a key part of the group process of dominance bonding that one or more members of the male group are made into the symbolic debased and degraded feminized "other" through which the group members bond and feel that their status as "men" is safely ensured. Most boys learn early to avoid at all costs offering one's self up as a target for this kind of abuse.[26] The power of this group dynamic was illustrated in an interview I conducted with a former world-class athlete who, during his athletic career, had been a closeted gay man. One of the best ways that he found to keep his sexual identity secret within this aggressively homophobic world was to participate in what he called "locker room garbage" talk about sexual conquests of women.[27]

Curry's descriptions of the dominant, central conversation and the marginal, quiet conversations in the locker room are remarkably similar to Lefkowitz's description of how the Glen Ridge boys set up their gang rape. In both cases, a small minority of high-status young men staged an aggressive, violently misogynist performance at the center of the room. I sketch out this internal dynamic of the athletic male peer group in Figure 5.2.1.

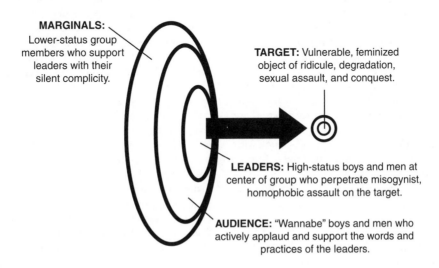

MARGINALS: Lower-status group members who support leaders with their silent complicity.

TARGET: Vulnerable, feminized object of ridicule, degradation, sexual assault, and conquest.

LEADERS: High-status boys and men at center of group who perpetrate misogynist, homophobic assault on the target.

AUDIENCE: "Wannabe" boys and men who actively applaud and support the words and practices of the leaders.

Figure 5.2.1. Dynamics of the athletic male peer group.

1 *Leaders:* At the center of the athletic male peer group are the highest-status boys and young men. They are the members of the group who most actively conform to and directly benefit from hegemonic masculinity. Their performances (from homophobic and misogynist verbal sparring, teasing, or bullying vulnerable boys, to hazing younger athletes, to actual sexual assaults of girls or other boys) involve directing their aggression toward debased feminized objects of sexual conquest.

2 *Audience:* Closely connected to the center, another group of boys constitutes itself as an adoring, cheering audience that directly supports and validates the hegemony of the central performance of the leaders. The gaze of these boys is directed inward, toward the group's center, to which they are erotically attached. They are similar to what Adler and Adler call "wannabes":[28] though not central in the group's status hierarchy, these boys hope desperately to belong, to share in the benefits and pleasures of hegemonic masculinity, and to avoid the pain of becoming the object of the group's putdowns.

3 *Marginals:* Further out, at the margins of the group, are other boys and young men, whispering to each other in quiet dyads. They are perhaps not fully comfortable with the words and actions at the center of the group. They may experience empathy with the victims of the group's jokes and assaults. And they may at times, out of discomfort, opt out of some of the group's more cruel activities. However, they may also feel a powerful, magnetic pull toward the erotic dominance bonding at the group's center. After all, this is the place where these boys have experienced some acceptance and belonging. And their association with this group brings a certain level of respect from outsiders. Moreover, they know that silence will keep them safely in the group.

The active support of the audience and the compliant silence of the marginals make these two groups complicit in constituting the center

as a high-status site of homophobic and misogynist domination. Indeed, the center would not be the center without the active support of the audience and the silent complicity of the outer circle of marginals.

What keeps those at the margins of the peer group silent? Partly, it's fear. One fifth-grade boy told Adler and Adler that he compliantly goes with the flow when high-status kids pick on his friends: "It's a real risk if you want to try to stick up for someone because you could get rejected from the group or whatever."[29] According to Katherine Farr, sexually aggressive banter in groups provides a means of "dominance bonding" for young males.[30] Internal hierarchies are constructed and contested as the boys and young men simultaneously mark the boundaries where the in-group ends and the realm of "outsiders" (women, gay men, non-athlete men, etc.) begins. [...]

But it's not simply fear that keeps marginal boys in silent complicity with the group's practices. It's also pleasure. The bonds of the male peer group often have a decidedly erotic base, as Peter Lyman's research on sexual joking among fraternity members illustrates.[31] To say that male groups' dominance bonding is erotic is not to say necessarily that men's bonds in sports are simply a means of sublimating a desire to have sex with each other. Undoubtedly, that is true with some boys and men, for whom sports are experienced as a "heterosexualization process," in which same-sex desire is repressed, perhaps sublimated into aggression, and eventually converted to sexual desire for women.[32] Some might speculate that this same-sex desire remains submerged in the unconscious of young men who self-define as "100 per cent heterosexual." Whether it does or not, the erotic bond among male athletes tends to be overtly coded as fiercely heterosexual. Boys and men learn to bond with each other through sexually aggressive, erotically exciting talk that serves to forge an aggressive, even violent, hierarchical ordering of bodies, both inside the male peer group and between the male peer group and any other group. To thwart the dominant modes of one's peer group, then, is not simply to risk ridicule and ostracism; it also threatens to undermine the major way that a young male has learned to experience erotic excitement and pleasure with his peers.

"Voyeuring": women as objects of conquest

By the time they were teens, the "jocks" of Glen Ridge used more than talk for their erotic dominance bonding. When parents were away, they would sometimes gather together in a home to watch pornographic films and masturbate together. The next step was the development of a group form of entertainment that they called voyeuring, whereby a plan would be made for one guy at a party to "convince a girl to go upstairs to a bedroom for a sexual encounter." But first, "his buddies would go up and hide in a closet, under the bed, or behind a door," where they could watch. Sex with a girl, for these guys, was less an intimate encounter with a valued human being than it was the use of a woman's body as a sexual performance for one's male buddies. It was, in Lefkowitz's words, "a way for these guys to create their own porn movie."[33] Voyeuring was not invented in Glen Ridge. [...]

Men's use of female bodies to bond with each other is central to the dynamic of gang rape. Anthropologist Peggy Sanday and others who have studied gang rape are careful to argue that, from the point of view of the woman, the rape is not a sexual experience; rather, it is a violent, degrading, and painful assault against one's body. However, from the point of view of perpetrators, there certainly *is* a sexual dynamic at work in gang rapes. But it is not sex with a woman happening here; rather, the male group uses the debased, violated woman's body as an object through which to have sex with each other.[34] In short, the dynamic underlying gang rapes is a statement of group-based male power, expressed through a dual process of misogynist denigration of women and erotic bonding among men, and this process has its roots in the erotic bonding of the misogynist joking culture of athletic teams.

A key to understanding male groups' use of women's bodies through which to erotically bond with each other is that most heterosexual boys and young men go through a period of intense insecurity and even discomfort in learning to establish sexual relations with girls and women. Men who were former athletes reported to me retrospectively that in high school, and even for some in college, talking with girls and women raised intense anxieties and feelings of inadequacy.[35] These young men dealt with their feelings of "lameness" with young women primarily by listening to and watching their male peers deliver a "rap" to women. As the men immersed themselves in this peer pedagogy of heterosexual relations, they learned to put on a performance for girls that, surprisingly for some of them, seemed to "work." The successful utilization of this learned dramaturgy of the heterosexual come-on allowed a young man to mask, even overcome, his sense of insecurity and lameness in his own eyes and, just as important, in the eyes of his male teammates. It also intensified, at a deep psychological level, his adherence to the group process of erotic dominance bonding with other members of his male peer group through collectively constructing women as objects of conquest.

When I was a freshman in college, as a "marginal" member of my community college basketball team, I experienced this peer group dynamic directly.[36] After having been a reasonably good high school player, I found myself at the bottom of the totem pole, thirteenth on a thirteen-player college team. Moreover, off the court, I could not hold my own in the competitive sexual banter. Early in the season, on a road trip, the guys lounged around in a motel room, talking and joking about sex. Drew, our starting center and one of the highest-status guys on the team, noticed that Rob (another marginal player) and I had not been contributing anything to the raucous chronicling of the team's sexual exploits. "Hey, Robby T, hey Mess," Drew asked, "you guys ever had a piece of ass?" A virgin with little to brag about, I tensed up. I knew that Kess, another reserve player on the team, had recently been labeled the team fag after he had refused to jump into the middle of a brawl we had had against another team. I wanted to avoid becoming such a target of joking put-downs, so I employed what I thought was a subtle strategy. "Naw," I replied, but with diverted eyes and a knowing smile that I hoped would suggest that I was simply too cool to brag about sex with my girlfriend, a high school girl. Rob followed the same strategy. Drew, missing the subtleties, clobbered us: "Wow! We got two virgins on this team! We can't have that! Mess, Robby T., we gotta get you laid, and soon! We can't go having any virgins on this team. Havin' Kess is bad enough!"

A couple of weeks later, Drew invited us to a party. Robby T. and I showed up together, with our six-packs of beer. Soon, Drew announced to Rob and me loudly, "Hey, you two virgins ain't gonna be virgins after tonight, eh?" Not knowing what he was talking about, we just agreed and laughed, "Sure, Drew. We're just trying to figure out who we're going to lay tonight." Drew replied, "Man, you don't have to worry about that, because me and the guys have that taken care of. We got a lady comin' over here in a couple of hours. She's real special, and since you guys are the only two virgins on the team, you get to go first." As I felt my palms get sweaty, I knew I was supposed to act grateful. "Wow, Drew. Like, is she some kind of prostitute or something?" Drew smiled. "You could say that. She's kind of a friend of mine, you know?" He laughed loud and hard, and so did we. I took some long pulls on my beer, drained it, and opened another one. I whispered to Robby T., "Let's get the hell out of here," and we escaped out the back door.

Rob and I never did find out whether Drew was serious about his plan to get us laid, or if the guys were just pulling a joke on the two lower-status guys on the team. We felt a bit ashamed of ourselves for leaving the party, and we knew that doing so did nothing to enhance our already marginal status on the team. So we decided that the only way to handle the guys when we next saw them was to tell them a lie: We were now laying our girlfriends and just couldn't do it with someone else because we wanted to be faithful. That's how we escaped being put in the "fag bag" with Kess. We were accepted now; we had learned how to bullshit with the best of them.

But the story did not end there. After this embarrassing incident, I began to step up the pressure on my girlfriend to "put out." Like many young men, I wanted to have sex. But the urgency of my desire was not driven simply by my attraction to my girlfriend. I genuinely and desperately wanted access to the sexual experience and knowledge that would put me on a par with the guys on the team. Fortunately, my girlfriend had a mind of her own and asserted her own timetable on what we would do and when we would do it. However, I can see in retrospect how my experiences with my teammates had created fear, embarrassment, and frustration over my "virgin status" and that this in turn had encouraged a tendency to see and treat my girlfriend more as an object of conquest than as a person with feelings, fears, and desires of her own. More generally, this experience eventually helped me to understand how the athletic male peer groups' voyeuring— their tendencies to bond by watching each other have sex or by listening to each other talk about sex—don't end up only in gang rapes. This group dynamic can also feed the seemingly more private, one-on-one dynamic of date and acquaintance rape, even among young men who are marginal to the athletic peer group.[37]

[...]

Suppression of empathy

A key part of the process of learning to treat a person of a particular group as an object of conquest is the suppression of empathy for such a person. But boys and men have mothers, sisters, female cousins, and friends whom they know as people and whom they are taught to "protect" and care for. How then can they conjure up the emotional distance to be able to sexually assault women? Cross-cultural research on rape has pointed to the importance of the degree and type of contact that boys and men have with girls and women as a variable that correlates with varying rates of rape. Rape rates tend to be higher in societies with rigid divisions of labor and spatial separation between the sexes, especially where these divisions are marked by male dominance and female subordination.[38] Homosocial bonding among men, especially when the bond is of the sort of sexualized dominance bonding that I discussed above, is a very poor.environment for the development of empathy (or respect) for women.

Consistent with this, Lefkowitz notes that the boys who were most central in the actual assault in the Glen Ridge rape grew up without sisters, in families that were headed by domineering male figures. Moreover, their peer group, family, and community experiences taught them that boys' and men's activities were most valued, and girls' and women's were of secondary importance. "The immediate environment," Lefkowitz argues, "did not cultivate great empathy for women."[39] Contrarily, some of the boys who left the scene and felt "uncomfortable" with the assault seemed more open to seeing the pain in the victim's eyes and were thus less able to suppress their empathy for the victim.

Most of these boys, Lefkowitz observes, grew up in homes with sisters.

Male athletes' culture of silence

A question that plagued Lefkowitz in his description of the Glen Ridge rape was why the six boys who left the scene remained complicit in their silence, both the day of the rape and during the subsequent years of litigation. At least some of these young men were very uncomfortable with what happened, even thought it was wrong, but nobody in the group raised a hand or voice to stop it. Two other young men did, however. The case broke when another male athlete, who had not been at the scene of the assault, reported to teachers that he had overheard other guys laughing and bragging about the rape. Significantly, this African American young man who blew the whistle had always felt himself to be excluded from the tightly knit, high-status clique of white athletes. The second boy, who became an activist in the school and community in his quest to see that the jocks did not get away with their crime, was a long-haired "Gigger" (a term used to identify the small minority of radical, artsy, antijock students at the school). Both of these boys—one an athlete, one not—were outsiders to the dominant athletic male peer group. Those inside, even those who were marginal within the group, maintained a complicit silence that enabled the minority to assault their victim.

This culture of silence is built into the dynamics of the group's spoken and unspoken codes and rituals. The eroticized dominance bond has already established that "the guys" are part of a high-status, privileged in-group (and very little during adolescence can solidify this sort of feeling as much as being part of an athletic team). Others—nonathlete boys, racial and ethnic minority boys, girls, parents, teachers, police, and so on—are outsiders. Years of experience within the group have taught these boys that they will be rewarded for remaining complicit with the code of silence and punished for betraying the group. They know that a whistle-blower might be banished from the group and possibly also beaten up. Or he might remain in the group, but now with the status of the degraded, feminized "faggot" who betrayed the "men" in the group.

Notes

1. "Six Football Players Arrested for Hazing."
2. See Benedict, *Athletes and Acquaintance Rape*; and Totten, *Guys, Gangs, and Girlfriend Abuse*. Journalist Laura Robinson offers an especially chilling description of violence and sexual assaults by Canadian hockey players. See Robinson, *Crossing the Line*.
3. "Six Football Players Arrested for Hazing."
4. Jeffrey Benedict and Alan Klein compared national crime data with arrest and conviction rates of male collegiate and professional athletes accused of felony sexual assault; they concluded that when athletes are accused of sexual assault, they are more likely than nonathletes to be arrested or indicted but significantly less likely to be convicted. Benedict and Klein, "Arrest and Conviction Rates for Athletes Accused of Sexual Assault."
5. Boeringer, "Influences of Fraternity Membership, Athletics and Male Living Arrangements on Sexual Aggression"; Fritner and Rubinson, "Acquaintance Rape"; Koss and Gaines, "The Prediction of Sexual Aggression by Alcohol Use, Athletic Participation and Fraternity Affiliation."
6. Crosset and his colleagues also surveyed reports to campus police departments, and although they found that male athletes were more likely to be reported for sexual assault than male nonathletes, the difference was not statistically significant. In their analysis of the two sets of data—Judicial Affairs offices and campus police offices—they argued that there are good reasons to expect that college women are more likely to report assaults to Judicial Affairs than to campus police, and so the (statistically significant) data from the former are a better reflection of reality than the data from the latter. Crosset, Benedict, and McDonald, "Male Student Athletes Reported for Sexual Assault."
7. Crosset, "Athletic Affiliation and Violence against Women."
8. Crosset *et al.*, "Male Student Athletes and Violence against Women."
9. McPherson, "Sport, Youth, Violence and the Media."
10. Clarke, "Fear of a Black Planet."
11. Davis, *Woman, Race and Class*; Staples, *Black Masculinity*.
12. For a thoughtful discussion of this dilemma, see Berry and Smith, "Race, Sport, and Crime."
13. Robinson, *Crossing the Line*.
14. This section of the chapter is a substantially revised version of Messner and Stevens, "Scoring without Consent."
15. Lefkowitz, *Our Guys*, 23–24.
16. Ibid., 25.
17. Lefkowitz's descriptions of the assault are retrospective constructions, based in part on the

victim's descriptions and on subsequent bits of information that came out in the trials. The precise numbers on just how many boys in the basement participated physically in the assault and how many acted as a supportive audience are thus somewhat speculative.

18. Fine, *With the Boys*.
19. Julian Wood argues that this sort of competitive sexual talk among boys is a sort of group pedagogy through which boys are "groping toward sexism" in their attitudes and practices toward girls and women. Wood, "Groping toward Sexism."
20. See Kupers, "Rape and the Prison Code."
21. Hasbrook and Harris, "Wrestling with Gender," 27.
22. Adler and Adler, *Peer Power*, 65.
23. Eveslage and Delaney, "Trash Talkin' at Hardwick High."
24. Curry, "Fraternal Bonding in the Locker Room."
25. Sabo, "The Myth of the Sexual Athlete."
26. Indeed, Hasbrook and Harris, "Wrestling with Gender," 20, report this sort of verbal and physical aggression by higher-status boys toward lower-status boys taking place in their study of first graders.
27. Messner, *Power at Play*, 99.
28. In their study of peer cliques in grade schools, Adler and Adler describe the status hierarchy in this way: "At the high end was the popular clique, comprising the exclusive crowd. Below them were the wannabes, the group of people who hung around the popular clique hoping for inclusion. Next was the middle group, composed of smaller, independent friendship circles. At the bottom were the social isolates, who found playmates only occasionally, spending most of their time by themselves." Adler and Adler, *Peer Power*, 75. Rather than describing the dynamics between differently situated cliques, I am mostly describing here the internal dynamics of an "exclusive crowd" of male athletes.
29. Adler and Adler, *Peer Power*, 67–68.
30. Farr, "Dominance Bonding through the Good Old Boys' Sociability Group."
31. Lyman, "The Fraternal Bond as a Joking Relationship."
32. I develop this argument in Messner, "Studying Up on Sex."
33. Lefkowitz, *Our Guys*, 183–84.
34. Sanday, *Fraternity Gang Rape*.
35. Messner, *Power at Play*, 94–95.
36. I originally wrote of this incident as part of an autobiographical short story. Messner, "Indignities."
37. James Messerschmidt argues that when boys are teased or ridiculed in schools for not being enough of a man, they experience this as a "masculinity challenge." Some boys respond to this subordination among other boys by using sexual

violence against women as a "hegemonic masculine project." Messerschmidt, "Becoming 'Real Men'"; Messerschmidt, *Nine Lives*.
38. Spain, "The Spatial Foundations of Men's Friendships and Men's Power"; Sanday, *Female Power and Male Dominance*.
39. Lefkowitz, *Our Guys*, 280.

References

Benedict, Jeffrey R. *Athletes and Acquaintance Rape*. Thousand Oaks, CA: Sage Publications, 1998.
Benedict, Jeffrey, and Alan Klein. "Arrest and Conviction Rates for Athletes Accused of Sexual Assault." *Sociology of Sport Journal* 14 (1997): 73–85.
Berry, Bonnie, and Earl Smith. "Race, Sport, and Crime: The Misrepresentation of African Americans in Team Sports and Crime." Sociology of Sport Journal 17 (2000): 171–97.
Boeringer, S.D. "Influences of Fraternity Membership, Athletics and Male Living Arrangements on Sexual Aggression." *Violence against Women* 2 (1996): 134–47.
Crosset, Todd. "Athletic Affiliation and Violence against Women: Toward a Structural Prevention Project." In Masculinities, Gender Relations, and Sport, ed. Jim McKay, Michael A. Messner, and Donald F. Sabo, 147–61. Thousand Oaks, CA: Sage Publications, 2000.
Crosset, Todd W., Jeffrey R. Benedict, and Mark McDonald. "Male Student Athletes Reported for Sexual Assault: A Survey of Campus Police Departments and Judicial Affairs Offices." *Journal of Sport and Social Issues* 19 (1995): 126–40.
Crosset, Todd, J. Ptacek, M. MacDonald, and Jeffrey Benedict. "Male Student Athletes and Violence against Women: A Survey of Campus Judicial Affairs Offices." *Violence against Women* 2 (1996): 163–79.
Curry, Timothy. "Fraternal Bonding in the Locker room: Pro-Feminist Analysis of Talk about Competition and Women." *Sociology of Sport Journal* 8 (1991): 119–35.
Davis, Angela. Women, Race and Class. New York: Vintage Books, 1981.
Eveslage, Scott, and Kevin Delaney. "Trash Talkin' at Hardwick High: A Case Study of Insult Talk on a Boys' Basketball Team." *International Review for the Sociology of Sport* 33 (1998): 239–53.
Farr, Katherine A. "Dominance Bonding through the Good Old boys' Sociality Group," *Sex Roles* 18 (1988): 259–77.
Fine, Gary Alan. *With the Boys: Little League Baseball and Preadolescent Culture*. Chicago: University of Chicago Press, 1987.

Fritner, M. P., and L. Rubinson. "Acquaintance Rape: The Influence of Alcohol, Fraternity Membership and Sports Team Membership." *Journal of Sex Education and Therapy* 19 (1993): 272–84.

Hasbrook, Cynthia A., and Othello Harris. "Wrestling with Gender: Physicality and Masculinities among Inner-City First and Second Graders." In *Masculinities, Gender Relations, and Sport*, ed. Jim McKay, Michael A. Messner, and Donald F. Sabo, 13–30. Thousand Oaks, CA: Sage Publications, 2000.

Kaufman, Michael. "The Construction of Masculinity and the Triad of Men's Violence." In *Beyond Patriarchy: Essays by Men on Pleasure, Power, and Change*, ed. Michael Kaufman, 1–29. Toronto: Oxford University Press, 1987.

Koss, Mary, and J. Gaines. "The Prediction of Sexual Aggression by Alcohol Use, Athletic Participation and Fraternity Affiliation." *Journal of Interpersonal Violence* 8 (1993): 94–108.

Kupers, Terry A. "Rape and the Prison Code." In *Prison Masculinities*, ed. Don Sabo, Terry A. Kupers, and Willie London, 111–17. Philadelphia: Temple University Press, 2001.

Lefkowitz, Bernard. *Our Guys*. New York: Vintage, 1997.

Lyman, Peter. "The Fraternal Bond as a Joking Relationship: A Case Study of Sexist Jokes in Male Group Bonding." In *Changing Men: New Directions in Research on Men and Masculinity*, ed. Michael S. Kimmel, 148–63. Newbury Park, CA: Sage Publications, 1987.

McPherson, Donald G. "Sport, Youth, Violence and the Media: An Activist Athlete's Perspective." In *Paradoxes of Youth and Sport*, ed. Margaret Gatz, Sandra Ball Rokeach, and Michael A. Messner, 241–48. Albany: State University of New York Press, 2002.

Messerschmidt, James W. "Becoming 'Real Men': Adolescent Masculinity Challenges and Sexual Violence." *Men and Masculinities* 2 (2000): 286–307.

———. *Nine Lives: Adolescent Masculinities, the Body, and Violence*. Boulder, CO: Westview Press, 2000.

———. "Indignities: A Short Story." In Michael A. Messner and Donald F. Sabo, *Sex, Violence and Power in Sports: Rethinking Masculinity*, 16–27. Freedom, CA: Crossing Press, 1994.

Messner, Michael A., and Mark Stevens. "Scoring without Consent: Confronting Male Athletes' Sexual Violence against Women." In *Paradoxes of Youth and Sport*, ed. Margaret Gatz, Sandra Ball Rokeach, and Michael A. Messner, 225–40. Albany: State University of New York Press, 2002.

Robinson, Laura. *Crossing the Line: Violence and Sexual Assault in Canada's National Sport*. Toronto: McClelland and Steward, 1998.

Sabo, Don. "The Myth of the Sexual Athlete." In Michael A. Messner and Donald F. Sabo, *Sex, Violence and Power in Sport: Rethinking Masculinity*, 36–41. Freedom, CA: Crossing Press, 1994.

Staples, Robert. *Black Masculinity: The Black Male's Role in American Society*. San Francisco, Black Scholar Press, 1982.

Totten, Mark D. *Guys, Gangs, and Girlfriend Abuse*. Peterborough, Canada: Broadview Press, 2000.

Wood, Julian. "Groping toward Sexism: Boys' Sex Talk." In *Gender and Generation*, ed. Angela McRobbie and Mica Nava, 54–84. London: Macmillan, 1984.

5.3

Discourses of deception

Cheating in professional running[1]

Peter G. Mewett

Though cheating is an undeniable reality in many sports, there are few observation-based analyses of this type of deviance. In this article, Mewett presents an ethnographically-grounded analysis of cheating in the working class sport of professional running in Australia. It explains this behavior from a Marxian theoretical perspective.

I stood in the crowd clustered near to the circle races[2] finish line. I could not help but hear the conversation between two men beside me. One man clearly had a deep knowledge of the sport and he was telling the other one about it, including, it seems, about how athletes run dead to secure a lighter handicap. On learning about this, the second man questioned the honesty of the sport, to which the first replied, 'If everybody's a cheat, it's not dishonest'.

(fieldnotes)

Cheating, it seems, occurs in all sports. This is not to claim that all sports players cheat, but rather that each sport contains some who cheat. Revelations about athletics, cricket, cycling, baseball, the football codes, swimming and more have come to light in recent years. There is nothing new about cheating in sport, though: there are numerous historical references to it from the commencement of modern sports over two hundred years ago.[3]

Although cheating may be more widespread than many people suspect, in this paper I examine a sport, professional running, in which it is commonplace. Yet, as with other sports, the public image projected by professional running is that of a sport in which the cheat is weeded-out and dealt with by impartial, vigilant officials. These officials, invariably former professional runners, include people who, it may be assumed, routinely cheated in their running careers, know all the ruses of cheating, are aware that cheating is taking place in the meetings they supervise, but intervene and impose penalties only when it becomes obvious. Competitors then, have to carefully conceal their cheating; successful professional runners seldom lack the art of deception. This form of cheating—'clean' cheating—features in the everyday construction of the sport. The ways of clean cheating form a significant discourse in the sport and serve to underpin its reproduction. The art of the official, to detect and penalise this cheating, forms a second discourse that, although publicly denying clean cheating as constitutive of the sport, implicitly recognises this to be the case. A further discourse centres on the continuing tussle between runners and officials, all knowing what is 'really' occurring but publicly denying the centrality of cheating in their dealings. Another form of

Peter G. Mewett, "Discourses of Deception: Cheating in Professional Running" from *The Australian Journal of Anthropology* 13.3 (2002): 292–308. Copyright © 2002. Reprinted with permission.

cheating, 'dirty' cheating, does not form a part of the officials' discourse. Although the terms clean and dirty cheating are my terminology, they reflect an emic typology used in the sport to distinguish between unconscionable actions and the esoterically expected, accepted ways in which the sport is played out. Dirty cheating usually involves a personal financial gain made from a betrayal of trust or from some form of subterfuge; it is widely condemned and spoken of either in anger or in the guarded terms of the unmentionable.

My concern in this paper is to present the forms of cheating that occur in professional running and to demonstrate how clean cheating promotes discourses central to the reproduction of the sport. This is mostly an exercise in ethnographic description blended with grounded theory; as such, it is based on emic constructions, but I also draw on Bourdieu (1978, 1986) to point to how cheating in this sport may be placed in a wider social context. Methodologically, it is based on two years' observation of the professional running circuit in the Australian State of Victoria, a close association with a 'stable'[4] of runners, approximately 100 semi-structured interviews with runners, trainers and officials, and considerable historical research. Clearly, there are beguiling comparisons to be drawn between professional running and cheating in other sports. Such comparisons go beyond the bounds of this paper, however. Indeed, cheating in sport in all its forms, varieties and significances requires a much larger treatment than can be afforded in one article.

Given the rich rewards afforded top-line runners in 'mainstream athletics',[5] professional running is now perhaps something of a misnomer. As a sport it is the present day version of 'pedestrianism', which originated in eighteenth century Britain and came to Australia in the mid-nineteenth century (Mewett 1999). Today, the sport retains its strongest presence in Australia, particularly in Victoria where Stawell is located—this country town being the site of the sport's most prestigious meeting. Spurned by 'athletics', its amateur offspring, professional running has remained a mostly plebeian sport closely linked with gambling. In Australia it is a sport associated with 'battlers', those for whom each dollar is hard earned and life is a struggle against adversity.

Professional running differs from many other sports—such as soccer, rugby league, cricket, baseball—that are 'professional' in the sense that while the players are waged, they are expected to refrain from betting on the outcome of a game. Professional runners are not paid wages to run, however. Rather, they compete for cash prizes and they routinely bet on the outcome of races in which they are participating:[6] this gambling is a part of the sport for professional runners and, for a few, it has provided the money to 'set them up' for life. Many of the ruses and much of the cheating in professional running derive from the strategies and tactics used to rake in gambling winnings and, as Vamplew (1988:51) has pointed out for horse racing, 'with gambling comes the danger of corruption'. Indeed, the 'unsavoury' nature of gambling to the British higher social orders in the latter half of the nineteenth century was an argument they used to differentiate between their supposedly 'pure' amateur sports, and, to them, the unrespectable, sullied professional sports of the working classes. Although much of the upper class hyperbole served as social markers, an important difference was centred on those who had the financial means to uphold the amateur ethic[7] and those who used sport as a source of income.

Often using sporting metaphors, an ideology of 'fair play' pervades Western-type capitalist societies and perhaps provides a reason for the widely expressed aversion to cheating. In sport, this ideology came from and has been associated most strongly with the ethos of amateurism that emerged from the English 'Greater Public Schools' and Oxford and Cambridge Universities in the second half of the nineteenth century.[8] It is an ideology that remains in many sporting arenas and with it comes the illusion that people compete simply on the basis of their innate, albeit highly trained abilities: the 'best' competitor or team wins. Although in practice numerous cheating tactics may be used and sometimes detected—weeding-out a cheat every now and then gives the appearance that they are an aberrant few and the sport as a whole is honest—the public face of many major sports present an image of fairness and honesty. But this imagery is a throw-back to the amateur fair-play ethos. As an avowedly professional sport closely associated with the working classes, pedestrianism for a long time was shrouded in disrepute, being viewed through the amateur lens as corrupt, 'ungentlemanly' and demeaning. But sport means different things for the working classes than it has for the upper classes, a point made abundantly clear by Bourdieu (1978, 1986). For the lower classes, the opportunity costs of participating in sport are significant, at the time of participation and for their futures. Unlike wealthy amateurs, they cannot afford to support themselves while preparing for competition. They need to make money from the time spent in sport. Pure competition is not an option for them, because the opportunity costs can be too high. Only when the chance involved in sport has been manipulated into an assessable, calculable risk and the promise of financial gain beckons, does the sacrifice of time from alternative income sources in favour of sport become a viable option. Cheating blunts pure competition and permits players to manipulate chance in their favour to increase the probability of a positive outcome. Bourdieu (1978:835) notes that 'class habitus defines the meaning conferred on sporting activity, the profits expected from it'. For the wealthy amateur, the acquisition of social capital, for example, may have constituted the 'profits'. But lower class athletes needed to convert their physical capital into cash. Running and competing supposedly for the thrill of it was not enough: the habitus framing their lives promoted dispositions that supported the manipulation of chance and the minimisation of risk.[9]

While increasing personal incomes over the last half century have lessened the economic imperative associated with participation in professional running, the prospect of the winnings from a big race remains a significant pull for many competitors. Although the really 'big' money now is in mainstream athletics, professional running continues to provide the battler with the chance of a 'kick-on' in life. Over the years, winners of major races have used their winnings to purchase businesses, further careers, buy houses or expensive items that would otherwise bind them in years of debt, and so on. Even though the economic imperative may have lessened—it is now a lifetime away from the Depression years when some men survived from this sport—the ways of succeeding in the sport, including cheating, have remained remarkably similar.

Running dead

[...]

What makes professional running so interesting is that its practitioners, from neophyte runner to peak organisation officials, present a public face of an untainted sport, one in which the cheat is a deviant to be dealt with swiftly by fine and suspension. Yet new runners are taught the tactics of the sport, which involve running in a way to gain a favourable handicap. This is a sport that uses handicaps (also called 'marks') in the form of staggered starts, with the more poorly performed runners starting the race in front of and running a shorter distance than the better performed ones. In theory, handicapping means that differences in ability are levelled by giving the less able an advantage, increasing the uncertainty of a race's outcome thereby making for a more open betting market. But to reduce uncertainty athletes 'run dead', or deliberately lose races while pretending to win, so that by the time that they 'go-off' (that is, attempt to win) they have secured a more favourable handicap than their true ability would warrant. Accordingly, it is common practice for runners to disguise their ability and form and run dead to gain an advantage that they unleash in their targeted races. Such tactics improve the chance of winning a big race, its associated prize money and, hopefully, a princely swag from the betting ring, but this success requires careful concealment of the runners' potential until they go-off. Running dead, a major part of clean cheating, has to be concealed from the watchful eyes of the sport's officials and its followers, the latter factoring into their betting equations any evidence of a runner holding back. Many of the plays in this sport centre on trying to work out what others are doing and planning. Accordingly, to optimise gambling winnings it is important for all players to deceive, to conceal their objectives from others (Mewett 2000; Mewett with Perry 1997).

Runners are in the public gaze when they compete at meetings, which they need to do in order to get the 'lifts'[10] from the handicapper that will give them an advantageous mark. Handicappers and other officials will penalise athletes that they detect running dead. Successful concealment is recognised as that needed to deceive officials into thinking that runners are trying as hard as they can but need a lighter handicap to give them a chance of winning. Perhaps it is more a case, though a generally unspoken one, that the game being played with the officials is not so much one of pretending not to cheat—because runners and officials alike know that cheating is taking place—but rather one of concealing cheating in such a way that it is not obvious to the official and to the public gaze.

Cheating has a self-regulatory quality: a runner will cheat in a way that maintains the officials' face. The consequences of ignoring these self-regulatory practices is to suffer the officials' ire and retribution.

Officials are charged with the responsibility of detecting cheating, punishing it and with keeping the sport free of rogues. But, with very few exceptions, the officials are ex-runners, many of whom had followed the ways of the sport in their own athletic careers. Their job, apart from ensuring the smooth organisation of meets, is to detect instances of running dead, 'inconsistent performances' and so forth, in order that, to the public eye at least, the sport presents as well-regulated, with cheats being detected and the perpetrators punished. Perhaps it is only the poor runner incapable of securing a win who need not cheat. In reality, only those runners with inadequate, readily detectable techniques of cheating are penalised. They, and the officials pulling them up, are well aware that there are others, cheating more effectively, that are not being spotted. Within the sport it is accepted that runners will routinely cheat in order to win; the winners are often those who can cheat most effectively. Handicappers and stewards seek the 'blanket finish', the ideal race of professional running, when all of the competitors cross the winning line very close together.[11] Although this is rarely realised in practice, the officials' nightmare is to be 'embarrassed' by having a winner succeed by a large margin over the next finisher. This makes obvious their failure to detect deception, to weed out the cheat. […]

Deception, then, occurs in multiple ways. Gambling, taken from the wagering closely associated with horse-racing, often lurks behind the deceptive practices. The manipulation of outcomes for pecuniary advantage is hidden from public view, however. The means of cheating change little in a sport, but, when cheating comes to light and creates a scandal, administrators act to impose measures that, in the public eye at least, serve to suppress it. It is important, especially in gambling sports, to deal severely with overt cheating and perpetuate the myth that the probabilities of winning can be calculated from the known performances of the competitors. Cheating only results in large gambling winnings if the bookmakers take in a significant amount of money on a race: winnings are proportional to the total money that is bet.[12] Certainly, those in the sport lay bets

on their own hopefuls and on their evaluations of what others could be doing. But to succeed in gambling, bets need to be laid by other, losing punters. Some of this money will come from a public that may not be fully aware of the deceptions being played out before their eyes. The betting public has to be kept interested in the sport, but it has turned away from professional running on several occasions when cheating became too obvious, to come back to the sport only when the controlling authorities had taken measures designed to demonstrate to spectators that cheating had been stopped. Obvious cases of cheating are dealt with by the sport's officials to avert a drop-off in attendance by spectators, including the loss of gate money (Bull 1959:64–6).

Professional runners do not try to win every event that they enter. Their objective is to win a particular, specified race: in the argot of the sport, the one for which they are 'set'. The set race often is several years away and the athlete's training and running tactics are organised with it in mind. The 'handling' of the runner, typically in the form of the ruses dictated by the trainer, in this long preparatory period is vital to securing a successful outcome. Much of the routine and expected cheating associated with the sport takes place in this lead-up to the runner's set race.

Harry Boyle once said to me that 'handicap is everything' in professional running. Rob Monaghan, a man who ran through the years of the Depression and trained runners for several decades more, had an explicit strategy of letting his runners go-off only when they had achieved a very favourable handicap, even if this meant years of running dead. Rob also went to considerable lengths to ensure that his runners were concealed from the gaze of those who might realise their potential, pick the race in which they were going-off and take the 'cream' of the 'market'.[13]

Running dead is a skill learned from the start of a professional athlete's participation in the sport. The actual techniques can differ between sprinters and distance runners, although runners of all distances commonly put in a very hard training session or run the evening or the morning before a meeting so that carry-over fatigue prevents them from performing to their true ability. Roger Best explained how he managed his running dead:

> I was standing to run well and we were going to a meeting … I went to Monash University on

the way and I ran two flat out four hundreds, one after the other, until I was physically sick and then I went to the meeting. As well as that I was fortunate in that I could run reasonably dead, I mean in ten years I was never picked up.

(taped interview)

Cheating also occurs on the track. Heavier running spikes can be worn, sometimes through the addition of lead; while this is heavily proscribed, lead has been used by runners who were unable to run dead by using the more common tactics. John Whitson was one such runner. An excellent athlete and a good prospect for a major race, his chances of winning were tempered by his inability to run dead without being detected. Whitson told me:

I didn't have the ability, as the term was in those days, 'to run a dead un'. I couldn't run dead and not get caught. And so, what we did ... Wilf [Whitson's trainer] came to training one night with a pair of inner soles and he said, 'Here, put these in your [running] shoes'. He gave them to me and my hand went down like that. He had actually lined the underside of the inner soles with lead and each one weighed about half a pound. So, for all of that season ... I ran ... with these lead weights in ... [T]he only way that you would get caught was if somebody was around when you took your shoes off, and then they had to pick them up because they looked like any other pair of shoes with inner soles ... Didn't let anybody else pick your bag up because it had to [be] the heaviest bag in town. I got right through the whole season without even being spoken to [by the stewards] ...

(taped interview)

More commonly, on-track cheating involves such things as not breathing during a sprint, 'short-striding',[14] the deliberate use of a poor arm action, adjusting blocks to hinder sprint starts, starting a distance race too hard and then fading, and more. The important point is that this has to be done skilfully. As the runner progresses in the sport, skill at cheating becomes increasingly important to avoid being 'picked-up' by a steward. Asinoff (1963:71ff) makes a similar point for baseball when he argues that a very fine line separates effective play from deliberately missed play. A deliberate loss requires great care and considerable expertise.

Race stewards, in Australia appointed by the sport's state-based regulating bodies, know all of the means of cheating that are used to deceive and conceal. Moreover, they know that among the runners who they are carefully watching, many will be running dead. [...]

'The tactics used to run dead and to keep secret runners' abilities involves what I refer to as 'clean' cheating. It is clean because it is anticipated by those in the sport that others will be playing it this way. Harry's acclaim as a 'shifty bastard' refers to his success in effecting successful concealment of his runners. Shifty can refer to the ways of effecting deceptions, but it refers especially to trainers because of their cunning and subterfuge: renowned trainers are often called 'old foxes' or it has been said of some that 'their left hand doesn't know what their right hand is doing'. Used in this context, shifty is a term of praise. To be called a shifty bastard is to be lauded. Over that weekend Harry was a top trickster, the shiftiest of the shifties. There is an aesthetic appreciation of those who succeed in manipulating the ways of the sport to their advantage and it was clear that Harry's achievements won for him considerable kudos. The wins had come from a classic type of professional running strategy and this was recognised as such by others in the sport. In this way these actions were not dishonest because many others had also tried to achieve the same result through cheating, except that they did not cheat as effectively on that occasion. Apart from beating the handicapper, effective clean cheating involves outwitting others who are trying to do the same thing. This is exactly what many consider must be done for a runner to score a significant win. Officials aside, people in the sport frequently openly admire the performer who has outwitted them.

Collusion

Trials are sometimes held between hopefuls from different stables for a major race. For example, a secret trial between contenders for the Stawell Easter Gift, the sport's preeminent race in Australia, saw the losing trialist run last in the final of this race. The deal on this occasion was that the losing trialist would be permitted to lay a predetermined bet at long odds on the winning one, who knew that part of the competition had been eliminated before arriving at the meeting. To be sure, this is collusion and cheating, but it is also a way of minimising risk. Both runners, from different stables, had put considerable work into getting prepared for the Stawell Gift. Much was at stake. They both increased the probability of making a return from their efforts by colluding to control the outcome of the event. As it turned out, the winning trialist went on to take out the major race and, with it, a sackful of money. The losing trialist also scored a hefty reward, from betting on himself to win his heat and semi-final as well as from the money he was allowed to bet on the race winner at long odds.

Collusive practices have been used to fix the outcome of races and have given a means for the better performed, known runners— often handicapped out of any significant chance of winning[15]—to fix races to make certain of a return for their efforts. Morrie Gilson had a good career on the professional track. His uncle, a Stawell Gift winner, had been a noted runner in the tough Depression years. In the following interview Morrie told me some of his deceased uncle's stories about race fixing in that period:

> Gilson: ... he told about the races they fixed and the way they ruined betting, ... he said they would pick a pea as they called it. And they'd, in the Depression days no-one had much money, so they picked one to be the winner, and they'd go and back him ... and in match-races too. 1 think match-races killed off the betting for a while because they'd set up a match race and pick one to win ... He told me many tales of the great Phil Burke and those people.
>
> Mewett: And they were all involved in the fixing of races?
>
> Gilson: Yes.
>
> Mewett: And this was to make money from the bookies during the Depression?
>
> Gilson: Yes, to make sure they didn't gamble with their money and lose their money. ... There's only one winner.
>
> Mewett: How did you make sure that the others didn't win?
>
> Gilson: Well, you'd go and take money off each of those and say right we'll back so and so as the pea. They'd [each] put in a quid.
>
> Mewett: Oh OK. To make sure the bookies kept up a reasonable price ... it had to be staged in such a way that the punters were still putting money on the other runners?
>
> Gilson: Yes, well he had to only win by an inch, and it was a good finish.
>   (taped interview)

Morrie's stories of his uncle's exploits demonstrates the necessity of the 'good finish'. Without this, and the illusion to punters that they lost their bets by the slightest of margins, the money that must be put on the other runners for the 'pea' to realise a good return from gambling winnings, would not be forthcoming: thus Morrie's claim that match-racing, in which cheating can be more difficult to conceal, discouraged punters from laying bets. Achieving a close finish suits all players. The officials, particularly the handicappers, are satisfied because it gives the appearance of them having done a good job in matching the abilities of the runners. The runners need to have the money coming in on other competitors for them to get their bets on at longish odds. And, for this to occur, the punters must think that they have a reasonable chance of placing a winning bet.

Collusion is not restricted to pacts between runners. One ex-runner told me of how he had survived through the Depression by being part of a bookmaker's 'team'. He would do the circuit of meetings with the bookmaker, running to their mutual advantage. Another ex-runner explained how a bookmaker had paid him a considerable sum (£100 in 1935) to 'run out' a competitor on whom he had set inappropriate odds and stood to make massive losses had this man won. Harry Boyle said that bookmakers approached him to let them know when his runners were not going to win. The idea is that the bookmaker then stretches out the odds that he offers on them in order to draw in more bets on known losing runners; the money taken on them is split between the bookmaker and the trainer. But Harry said that he knocked back these approaches, because, had he accepted, it may have become more difficult for him to have concealed from these bookmakers the races when one of his runners was to go-off.

Fixing races is not confined to the collusion between runners or with bookmakers. Allan Goddard is a runner from more recent years and a Stawell Gift winner. He told me of an instance when race organisers in another State were involved in the fixing and manipulation of events:

> Goddard: I went to [another State] one year for a 300 metre race and I was paid to come third.
>
> Mewett: So they [the organisers] actually set it up? Who they wanted to win?
>
> Goddard: It was their own race. They wanted somebody in the final, for instance, like a Stawell Gift winner. I didn't know who was going to win first place, but they didn't want me to win. So they said come third.
>
> (taped interview)

Manipulation of races by organisers can be an unpredictable part of the sport. My guess is that organisers are seldom responsible for the type of occurrence reported by Allan Goddard. It is the predicability of the cheating practice that marks the division between where clean cheating ends and dirty cheating begins. Clean cheating is anticipated and, done well, it can be appreciated. Moreover, getting a return from clean cheating still involves considerable effort, or 'work' as the expenditure of considerable time and effort is called. Work is put into the long hours of training as well as into the strategies devised to effect a win. Dirty cheating is when a relatively unpredictable advantage is gained by someone who has not put in the work.

The unmentionable

The more straightforward instances of dirty cheating include snooping, such as surreptitiously timing a trial, often from a hidden position.[16] Knowledge gained in this way can allow the snooper to take the longest betting odds on a runner and reap a considerable financial benefit without having put in the work. Many stories record how runners, ready to go off in a major race, turn up on the day only to find that they have 'lost the market', which is the term used to refer to someone else getting the best of the betting on them. Faced with a lost market, runners must decide whether to go-off as planned and accept the reduced pay-out if successful, or 'pull-up' and set themselves for another race.

At the heart of dirty cheating is the use of what is seen to be privileged knowledge to one's own advantage. Leo Rumsey did not make the

winnings from the Stawell Gift that he had anticipated. Although he trained full-time in secret, his keep was met by a man who recognised his potential and wanted to make a gambling coup from Rumsey blasting onto the scene and winning this big race as a complete unknown. When this strategy of training hard but seldom competing is in play, it is common for the runner to trial against another who is competing on the circuit, to gauge what the hidden runner's performance might be. Les Michaels, his 'trial-horse', as the other runner is referred to, was a 'known' athlete, having scored some significant wins. According to Leo, this was when the problems for him started:

> Michaels was very, very greedy... he trained with me and he [Rumsey's sponsor] took him into his confidence and that was the worse thing that could ever have happened to us. He just got greedy. As a result of my ability—he had to find out whether I could produce it under pressure—so I used to train with Michaels. Anyway, there wasn't much he [Michaels] could do about me, he couldn't give me starts, and that was when the problem really started. We had blokes ... would be standing there with a bit of paper, watching me run ... Every time we had a trial, a tree moved ... We didn't know how the word was getting out until something happened just before Stawell ... We had to get away from Michaels. What had happened was he went to a place called ... and run about 12 inside[17] with a gale behind him. But then he tried to give me a start and couldn't give me much... so he knew what we was doing. And then we had to drop him off because he was talking too much. This was when the trouble started. Really started. A [State] athletic official... he used to bet on the Stawell Gift a month before and all of a sudden a bet was laid. And the fellow was Eric Connelly ... he laid the bet. ... That in itself started a snowball type of effect so what we had to do then, we had to get away from Michaels. So, we then had to go and train and trial with [another runner] ... in the meantime, the damage had been done. But, I've got to tell you this, Peter: I didn't know until 10 years later who had laid that bet. But we found out in the meantime that Les Michaels was sleeping with his [Connelly's] daughter, he was stopping with Eric Connelly, you know, and he just mentioned to Eric Connelly, 'If there's a world series next year, this bloke'll be in it'. And in the final trial we had, he [Michaels] tried to give me a three yard start and couldn't give it to me. I was equal

to him. ... Then it just snowballed and snow-balled and snowballed. By the time that we got there [to Stawell], the price had gone off ...

(taped interview)

Many successful runners have seen the prospect of sought-after riches—and they are riches for people from the working class backgrounds of most professional runners disappear because others, some 'low down buggers' as one ex-runner referred to them, have made use of privileged information to take the cream of the betting market.

If someone from within the runner's own stable makes use of privileged information for their own advantage the hurt is deeply felt. A stable is supposed to act collectively, its members not revealing to others what takes place within it. The stables constitute professional runners' 'teams'. When a stable's runner goes-off, all members of the stable can benefit through collective betting on their representative. Runners in successful stables can expect a steady trickle of money in this way, with a major prize coming their way should they win a big race. A strong sense of camaraderie characterises the successful stables and with it occurs a reinforcement of the secrecy essential for its triumphs. The reality, however, is that leaks occur from stables, sometimes inadvertently and sometimes by design. Many trainers keep as much as they can to themselves, or share information only with their senior runners, to reduce the risk of a secret slipping out. But when members of a stable use privileged information to their own advantage, the resentment is real and the hurt is deeply felt. Harry Boyle was highly aggrieved that one of his runners had cheated by placing a bet on a fellow runner before the stable had laid its collective stake-money. When a runner is about to go-off, stable members usually pool their stake-money which is bet in the form of a 'plunge'—a well coordinated procedure in which several bookmakers are 'hit' simultaneously. If a member of the stable bets before the plunge, they can get the longest odds and privilege themselves at their stablemates' expense; they can also alert the bookmakers to the runner who is going-off.

Perhaps the most despised form of dirty cheating occurs when trainers cheat their runners. Many runners build close and very fond relationships with their trainers, some claiming that these mentors even changed their lives.

The more prominent and well regarded trainers are known not just for their legendary prowess in preparing athletes and managing brilliant deceptions, but also for their honest dealings with their runners. But some trainers have cheated their wards. Greg Parker did not make as much money from his win of the Stawell Easter Gift as he had anticipated. Parker soon discovered, to his lasting anger, that he had been cheated by his trainer, Dan Gore. Other than the early bets taken by some Melbourne bookmakers, betting on the Stawell Gift opens on Good Friday evening, but some stables will not bet until the following morning, when the running starts, executing their plunge just before or during the running of the Gift heats. This is especially the case for those going into Stawell with a 'dark horse', a runner that others do not think to be a chance for the big race. By delaying the betting plunge, it is hoped that sufficient money will have been laid on other runners for the bookmakers not to shorten their odds too quickly when the stakes go on one's own competitor. Parker, a dark horse for the race, claimed that they had agreed to delay their plunge until the Saturday morning.

Parker: ... We had an agreement not to bet on the Friday night and they organised it so they would hit the betting ring on the Saturday morning before the heats. Unfortunately, the price was only ... it opened at about 15 to 1 or something like that. Subsequently, we found out that Dan and—there was another fellow called Bernie Dawson, he was our punter, he was a professional punter. He had a lot more money than we had and he was going to take the odds and sling back. And Bernie, never saw him back. Unfortunately, Gore and Dawson got into the ring on the Friday night.

Mewett: They took the odds?

Parker: Bloody true. We ... were still at Stawell when we actually found out. We had so many relatives in Stawell. ... and it didn't take long ... it came back to us that they [Gore and Dawson] were peeling off wads of notes and putting the money on on the Friday night. And Bernie Dawson was at the Dandenong trial—that was the final run before Stawell. He wanted to have a look and hold the clock on me.

Mewett: Did he have a good knowledge of professional running?

Parker: Oh yes.

Mewett: Did you feel used?

Parker: I certainly did. ...

Mewett: What [odds] did you open at [on Friday evening]?

Parker: 60s I think.

Mewetti: So there was quite a bit of money laid to take it down to [15s]

Parker: Thousands of pounds. Thousands of pounds. And, of course, when the 'hit the ring' time came about [on Saturday morning], they put money on and the effect of the previous night's betting was well, and truly registered with the bookies at that stage, so it didn't take much money for them to drop it down really low.

(taped interview)

Many years after the rort, Parker remained aggrieved at Gore's treatment of him. Other runners do not know how they lost the market, some surmise dirty cheating but are unwilling to voice their suspicions.

Discourses

As Bourdieu (1978) has pointed out, the sports available for people to take-up result from the history of the activities' emergence and development; an individual cannot change this, he or she must choose between contemporaneous sports. A correlation exists between socio-economic factors and the distribution of sports in a population, moreover. In part this linkage of class and sport arises from differences between people in their availability of spare time, economic capital and cultural capital, but it is essential also to take into account the different meanings given to the practice of their sports by specified sections of the population. These meanings derive from the dispositions born of particular class habituses; upper class sport is a very different thing from that of the lower classes (Bourdieu 1978: 834).

But the hegemonic power of the upper classes ensures that working class sports at least pay lip service to the ideology of fair play, even if, as in professional running, it is turned into a useful masking device for the concealment and deception that necessarily occurs. Publicly, the discourses of clean cheating present an image of a sport that is relatively free from corruption and shady dealings. Beneath the public image, these discourses, from the runners' and their trainers' points of view, are all about how to cheat; about how it is necessary to cheat to win; and about how others are cheating. Their concern is with deception, concealment, beating the handicapper, sowing false leads, and with detecting the subterfuges of others. The officials, from the same habitus as the runners, control the sport and impose penalties when they detect infringements of the rules. But the interesting aspect of the officials' discourse is that they know clean cheating is constitutive of the sport, so they attack the tip of the iceberg while disregarding the submerged mass. The third discourse centres on the tussle between runners and their trainers on one side, and the officials on the other. Tacit understandings about how the sport is constituted underpin an often unspoken complicity between these parties. The sport continues in a well-organised, seemingly amicable manner provided that these games-within-games are played by the unstated, informal rules. This complicity involves keeping the clean cheating to reasonable levels and maintaining the appearance of fair play essential to ensure the participation of a gambling public. Runners are aware that embarrassing the officials by flouting how well they have deceived the handicapper, for instance, will lead to retribution. The revenge may not be limited to the runner but can extend to all of the runners under the same trainer, because these mentors are major players in deception and concealment. Apart from finding a reason to fine or 'rub-out' (suspend) a runner who has embarrassed them, officials may penalise all the athletes in the runner's stable by not giving them expected handicap lifts. A fine line exists between working the sport to one's advantage and offending the officials. The largely unspoken discourse between runners and officials succeeds partly because the latter have come from within the sport, which ensures that all these participants share the same esoteric knowledge. But it is predicated on the shared meanings that all bring to the sport, meanings that derive from a working class habitus.

The participants in professional running bring with them the dispositions of their class habitus. Although this may account for a readiness to embrace this sport—to select it and participate in it from among those available—and for a predisposition towards the ways in which it is played out, it cannot fully explain what goes on within professional running, which has its own subculture, folklore and layers of esoteric knowledge. Although 'sport' as a category may form what Bourdieu (1978:821) refers to as a 'field of competition', professional running produces a field in its own right. Despite their habitus disposing them towards this sport, there is much for neophytes to learn after entering it. That which is learned—and here it is necessary to consider the 'ways' constitutive of the sport, more so, perhaps, than the techniques of acquiring fitness and athletic skills—accords with aspects of the runners' social origins.

Conclusion

An ideology of fair play—a hegemonic imposition of the wealthy upper classes—has little to offer working class people. Fair play insofar as it exists occurs between those in specified alliances for specific ends. Fair play is expected in the dealings between members of the same professional running stable. Trainers sometimes form links to trial their runners against one another. To betray the trust cementing these often labile consociations of individuals and groups is underhand, it is dirty cheating.

Possibly sports people such as professional runners have a more realistic perspective on success than those struggling with ideas of fair play. They see people who have succeeded in business through sharp or shady practice, and they see those possibly using privileged information to strike it rich off the stock market. What is 'fair' about that? How does one succeed in an acquisitive capitalist society, if not by stacking the odds in one's favour? Clean cheating is all in the game—the sporting game that is simply a part of the game of life. This necessitates alliances with others, all of whom can benefit to some greater or lesser extent. When the deceptive ploys are being worked on people outside these alliances, the cheating is an accepted and anticipated part of play. Perhaps an irony of professional running is that the financial returns that may accrue from clean cheating hinge on the exercise of trust between those on the 'inside'. The unacceptable form

of cheating occurs when someone within the alliance uses their privileged knowledge for their personal advantage.

Within professional running, working class athletes have manipulated chance through tactics involving secrecy, deception and the tactical concealment of ability. Done effectively, with the skill that eludes detection by others, it can result in a handsome payout, rewarding the opportunity costs of participation and providing a 'kick-on' for the person's post-sport career. The promise of a reward from the investment of time and effort in the sport justifies the opportunity costs necessarily incurred. The working classes have not been able to afford the dilettantism of amateurism. The model of pure competition is an ideology of the society at large as well of amateurism: embracing it involves more risk than the working classes can allow, it is a luxury that they cannot afford. For the less well off, risk-averse behaviour equates with the avoidance of penury. Cheating is the risk reduction strategy pertinent to the field of professional running. It occurs because the runners bring to the sport the risk-averse dispositions of their social origins.

Notes

1. This research, conducted jointly with John Perry, was supported by grants from the Australian Research Council and from Deakin University.
2. 'Circle races' are those, from 400 metres upwards, that involve one or more full circuits around the running track.
3. See Radford's (2001) biography of Captain Barclay for accounts of cheating in prize-fights in Regency Britain.
4. Professional runners are mostly organised in close-knit groups called 'stables'. A stable usually is under the control of one 'trainer', although the occasional stable is run by two trainers.
5. I use the term 'mainstream athletics' to refer to the relatively recent development from the so-called 'amateur athletics' that dominated global track and field competition for a century. Mainstream athletics has the World Championships and the Olympic Games as its most prestigious meets.
6. I thank an anonymous reviewer for pointing out this difference between professional running and other forms of professional sport. Clearly, as the recent revelations about cricket testify, involvement with gambling may occur as a covert part of any sport. Also see Asinoff (1963) for an account of the infamous 'Black Sox' case in baseball.

223

7. Horse racing certainly continued as a gambling sport significantly supported by the upper classes, but whether these were the same people that condemned plebeian gaming is a matter of conjecture—and an important area for historical research.

8. Amateurism emerged in the second half of the nineteenth century with the 'cult' of upper class athleticism associated with the more prestigious British private schools. Mangan (1981) has described the development of athleticism in these schools.

9. The poolroom 'hustlers' described by Polsky (1971) were also of lower-class origins. It is arguable whether the cheating that occurs in horse-racing (Scott 1968) can be understood in the same way, though.

10. A 'lift' is the term used to describe the acquisition of a lighter handicap. Handicaps are measured from 'scratch', so in a 100 metre race, for example, a person on a handicap of zero starts from scratch and runs the full 100 metres. Another runner, on a handicap of two metres, starts the race in front of the person on scratch and runs 98 metres to complete the race. However, if the runner is re-handicapped to 2.5 metres, which is referred to as getting a 'lift' of 0.5 metre, then 97.5 metres needs to be covered in the race. Conversely, a 'pull' refers to being moved to a harder handicap, so if the handicap was reduced (pulled) by 0.5 metre, to 1.5 metres, the runner would need to run 98.5 metres in the race.

11. The term 'blanket finish' comes from the image of being able to cover all of the close-finishing runners with a blanket.

12. Briefly, the betting on a race is assessed in terms of two variables: the price, or odds that can be obtained or runners and, second, the amount of money, or stake, that can be put on them. Long odds refers to winning more for a specified bet than short odds (for example: a bet laid at 20 to 1 stands to win five times more than one laid at 4 to 1). Bookmakers shorten odds as the bets laid against a runner increase, but the rate at which they shorten depends on the amount of money being laid against the other runners in the same race. If plenty of money is being taken against other runners, then the odds will shorten more slowly against a particular runner. Also, the more money being bet on a race, the more ready that bookmakers are to take larger stakes against runners before, perhaps, refusing to take any further bets against them. The objective in betting is to lay the total stake money at the longest average odds that can be achieved.

13. The 'cream' of the 'market' refers to the longest odds given by the bookmakers against a specified runner in a race. If the betting on a runner opens at 50 to 1, then the betters getting those odds have taken the cream of the market, because the odds will shorten quickly when money is laid against that competitor. The objective of a runner and stable is get the cream for themselves.

14. Short-striding involves putting in shorter than normal steps while moving the legs at the same speed. Done effectively, it gives the appearance of running at full speed.

15. A win involves the re-handicapping of the runner to a tighter mark. Also a different handicapping logic comes into play following a win, because the bigger the monetary value of the race won, the bigger the pull received by the winning runner. Many winners of major races have been handicapped out of further wins.

16. See Mewett (2000) and Mewett with Perry (1997) for some examples of snooping and of the precautions taken by trainers when training their runners.

17. A measure of runners' abilities is how far they can run 'inside' or 'outside' 'evens'. Evens refers to 'even time', which is 10 seconds for the 100 yards, for example. An even-time runner is a good athlete. But the more exceptional athletes—those sprinters capable of running sub-10 seconds over 100 yards, for instance—are referred to as running inside evens, their actual performance being measured as the number of 'yards inside [even-time]'. A similar logic applies to slower runners, those who are 'outside evens'.

References

Anonymous, 1868. Pedestrianism in Britain. *Every Saturday* 6:46–50.

Asinoff, E. 1963. *Eight Men Out: the Black Sox and the 1919 World Series*. New York: Holt Rinehart and Winston.

Bicknell, J.L. 1815. *A Brief Vindication of the Legality of the Late Proceedings against George Wilson, the Blackheath Pedestrian*. London: Clarke.

Bourdieu, P. 1978. Sport and social class. *Social Science Information* 17:819–40.

Bourdieu, P. 1986. *Distinction: A Social Critique of the Judgement of Taste* (transl. R. Nice). London: Routledge.

Bull, J. 1959. *The Spiked Shoe*, Melbourne: National Press Pty. Ltd.

Mangan, J.A. 1981. *Athleticism in the Victorian and Edwardian Public School: The Emergence and Consolidation of an Educational Ideology*. Cambridge: Cambridge University Press.

Mewett, P.G. 1999. The emergence of athletics in colonial Victoria. In R. Hay *et al. Sport in History Reader*. Geelong: Faculty of Arts, Deakin University.

Mewett, P.G. 2000. History in the making and the making of history: stories and the social construction of a sport. *Sporting Traditions* 17:1–17.

Mewett, P.G. with J. Perry, 1997. A sporting chance? The 'dark horse strategy' and winning in professional running. *Sociology of Sport Journal* 14:121–42.

Polsky, N. 1971. *Hustlers. Beats and Others.* Harmondsworth: Penguin.

Radford, P. 2001. *The Celebrated Captain Barclay: Sport, Money and Fame in Regency Britain.* London: Headline.

Scott, M.B. 1968. *The Racing Game.* Chicago: Aldine.

Shaulis, D. 1999. P'edestriennes: newsworthy but controversial women in sporting entertainment. *Journal of Sport History* 26:29–50.

Sinclair, J. 1806. *A Collection of Papers, on the Subject of Athletic Exercises, etc.* London: Blackadder.

Vamplew, W. 1988. Odds against: the punter's lot is not a happy one. *Sporting Traditions* 5:51–60.

Wilson, G. 1815. *Memoirs of the Life and the Exploits of G. Wilson, the Celebrated Pedestrian, who Walked 750 Miles in 15 Days. etc.* London: Dean and Munday.

5.4

In pursuit of doped excellence

The lab animal

Michael Sokolove

Illegal drug use by athletes trying to gain a competitive edge has become one of the most vexing problems confronting contemporary sports. In this article, Michael Sokolove illustrates the complexity of the problem of controlling illegal drug use. He explores the difficulties of devising new tests to keep up with the development of new drugs as well as the ever-changing standards that distinguish acceptable from unacceptable supplements.

On a brisk day last month, I was led through a warren of red brick buildings on the campus of the University of Pennsylvania in West Philadelphia and then up to a fifth-floor molecular physiology laboratory. I had come to visit some mice—and to get a peek at the future of sport.

[…]

The Penn researchers have used gene therapy on mice to produce increased levels of IGF-1, or insulin-like growth factor-1, a protein that promotes muscle growth and repair. They have done this with mice before birth and with mice at four weeks of age. A result has been a sort of rodent fountain of youth. The mice show greater than normal muscle size and strength and do not lose it as they age. Rats altered in the same fashion and then put into physical training— they climb little ladders with weights strapped to their backs—have experienced a 35 per cent strength gain in the targeted muscles and have not lost any of it "detraining," as a human being will when he quits going to the gym.

To the scientists, H. Lee Sweeney, chairman of Penn's department of physiology, and

Elisabeth Barton, an assistant professor, the bizarre musculature of their lab specimens is exciting. This research could eventually be of immense benefit to the elderly and those with various "muscle wasting" diseases.

[…]

But the Penn team has become acutely aware of a population impatient to see its research put into practice—the already strong, seeking to get stronger still. Sweeney gets their e-mail messages. One came from a high-school football coach in western Pennsylvania not long after Sweeney first presented his findings at a meeting of the American Society for Cell Biology. "This coach wanted me to treat his whole team," he said. "I told him it was not available for humans, and it may not be safe, and if I helped him we would all go to jail. I can only assume he didn't understand how investigational this is. Or maybe he wasn't winning, and his job was on the line."

Other calls and e-mail messages have come from weight lifters and bodybuilders. This kind of thing happens often after researchers publish in even the most arcane medical and scientific journals. A whole subculture of athletes and the coaches and chemists who are in the business of improving their performances is eager for the latest medical advances.

Sweeney knows that what he is doing works. The remaining question, the one that will require years of further research to answer, is how safe his methods are. But many athletes don't care about that. They want an edge now. They want money and acclaim. They want a payoff for their years of sweat and sacrifice, at whatever the cost.

[…]

There is a murky, "Casablanca"-like quality to sport at the moment. We are in a time of flux. No one is entirely clean. No one is entirely dirty. The rules are ambiguous. Everyone, and everything, is a little suspect.

Months before the great slugger Barry Bonds was summoned before a grand jury in December to answer questions about his association with the Bay Area Laboratory Co-Operative, known as Balco, which has been at the center of a spreading drug scandal after the discovery of a new "designer steroid," tetrahydrogestrinone (THG), a veteran American sprinter named Kelli White ran the track meet of her dreams at the World Championships in Paris. She captured the gold medal in the 100-meter and 200-meter races, the first American woman ever to win those sprints in tandem at an outdoor world championship. In both events, the 5-foot-4, 135-pound White, a tightly coiled ball of power and speed, exploded to career-best times.

On a celebratory shopping trip on the Champs-Élysées, White, 26, glimpsed her name in a newspaper headline and asked a Parisian to translate. She learned that she had flunked a postrace drug test and that her medals and $120,000 in prize money were in jeopardy. Later, she acknowledged that she had taken the stimulant modafinil, claiming that she needed it to treat narcolepsy but had failed to list it on a disclosure form. What she added after that was revealing, perhaps more so than she intended, "After a competition," she told reporters in Europe, "it's kind of hard to remember everything that you take during the day."

The THG scandal and the attention focused on Balco, which has advised dozens of top athletes (including Kelli White) on the use of dietary supplements, has opened the curtain on a seamy side of sport and on the fascinating cat-and-mouse game played between rogue chemists and the laboratory sleuths who try to police them.

But White's statement exposed another, deeper truth: elite athletes in many different sports routinely consume cocktails of vitamins, extracts and supplements, dozens of pills a day—the only people who routinely ingest more pills are AIDS patients—in the hope that their mixes of accepted drugs will replicate the effects of the banned substances taken by the cheaters. The cheaters and the noncheaters alike are science projects. They are the sum total of their innate athletic abilities and their dedication—and all the compounds and powders they ingest and inject.

A narrow tunnel leads to success at the very top levels of sport. This is especially so in Olympic nonteam events. An athlete who has devoted his life to sprinting, for example, must qualify for one of a handful of slots on his Olympic team. And to become widely known and make real money, he probably has to win one of the gold medals that is available every four years.

The temptation to cheat is human. In the realm of elite international sport, it can be irresistible.

[…]

For athletes, performance-enhancing drugs and techniques raise issues of health, fair play and, in some cases, legality. For sports audiences, the fans, the issues are largely philosophical and aesthetic.

On the most basic level, what are we watching, and why? If we equate achievement with determination and character, and that, after all, has always been part of our attachment to sport—to celebrate the physical expression of the human spirit—how do we recalibrate our thinking about sport when laboratories are partners in athletic success?

Major League Baseball, which came late to drug testing and then instituted a lenient program, seems to have decided that the power generated by bulked-up players is good for the game in the entertainment marketplace. The record-breaking sluggers Mark McGwire and Sammy Sosa have been virtual folk heroes and huge draws at the gate. [As of 2009, MLB's drug testing and penalties have become more serious and McGuire and Sosa have lost some of their popularity. Eds.]

Their runs at the record books became the dominant narratives of individual seasons.

(Barry Bonds has been less popular only because of a sour public persona.) But the sport is much changed. Muscle Baseball is the near opposite of what I and many other fans over 30 were raised on, a game that involved strategy, bunting, stolen bases, the hit-and-run play—what is called Little Ball. [As of 2009, the reputations of suspected steroid users—especially of those who have denied using performance-enhancing drugs—have plummeted. Eds.]

[...]

Even the substances themselves are murky. Because the $18-billion-a-year dietary-supplement industry is (at best) loosely regulated, some of the potions in the vitamin store at your local mall could well be tainted by steroids or growth hormones. The Food and Drug Administration just got around to banning the sale of ephedra last month, long after the herbal stimulant was blamed for numerous serious health problems, along with the sudden death last year of Steve Bechler, a Baltimore Orioles pitcher.

The whole situation cries out for a dose of clarity, but the closer you look, the fuzzier the picture. Start with the line between what's legal and illegal when it comes to enhancing performance. The line, already blurry, is likely over time to disappear entirely.

I visited a U.S. swimmer last September as technicians sealed up his bedroom, after which they installed equipment that reduced the amount of oxygen in his room and turned it into a high-altitude chamber. This is a common and legal training method that Ed Moses, America's best male breaststroker, said he hoped would increase his count of oxygen-carrying red blood cells. A whole team of long-distance runners sponsored by Nike lives in a much more elaborate simulated high-altitude dwelling in Portland, Ore. The desired effect of the so-called "live high, train low" method—sleep at altitude, train at sea level—is the same as you would get from taking erythropoietin, or EPO, which increases red-blood-cell production and is banned in sports.

Two other U.S. swimmers, in the lead-up to the Olympic Games in Sydney, were on a regimen of 25 pills a day, including minerals, proteins, amino acids and the nutritional supplement creatine, an effective but not necessarily safe builder of muscle mass. Much of the mix may well have been useless, but athletes tend to take what's put in front of them for fear of passing up the one magic pill.

"I like to think we're on the cutting edge of what can be done nutritionally and with supplements," the swimmers' coach, Richard Quick, said then as his athletes prepared for the 2000 games. "If you work hard consistently, with a high level of commitment, you can do steroidlike performances." One of his swimmers, Dara Torres, who increased her bench press from 105 pounds to 205 pounds and swam career-best times at the age of 33, said at the time that her goal was to "keep up with the people who are cheating without cheating."

And who are the cheaters? Everyone else. One primary motivation to cheat is the conviction that everyone else is cheating.

To draw the often arbitrary lines between performance enhancing and performance neutral, between health endangering and dicey but take it at your own risk—to ensure that sport remains "pure"—a vast worldwide bureaucracy has been enlisted.

At the lowest level are those who knock on the doors of athletes in their homes and apartments in the United States and Europe and in the mountain villages of Kenya and at the training sites in China and demand "out of competition" urine samples. Higher up on the pyramid are the laboratories around the world chosen to scan the urine (and blood) of elite athletes for the molecular signatures of any of hundreds of banned substances. At the top of the drug-fighting pyramid are the titans of international sport—the same people who cannot see to it that a figure skating competition is fairly judged.

The titans created the World Anti-Doping Agency, which works with governments and designated national organizations, including the United States Anti-Doping Agency. In combination with the urine-sample collectors, the various couriers in the chain of custody and the laboratories, W.A.D.A. is charged with making sure that the world's premier athletes are clean—and additionally that they have not concealed drug use through the use of various "masking agents." (The latest U.S.A.D.A. list specifically prohibits the following brand names: Defend, Test Free, Test Clean, UrinAid and Jamaica Me Clean.)

It is all an immensely complicated endeavor, one that requires W.A.D.A. to keep up with the onrushing science, to disseminate information to thousands of athletes, to navigate in different legal systems so that accused competitors get due process and, lastly, to manage the worldwide trafficking of urine samples. And it is all, in the end, quite possibly pointless.

Despite the hundreds of people and tens of millions of dollars devoted to the effort, international and national sports organizations may just lack the will to catch and sanction cheaters. The United States, specifically, has been singled out as negligent in its oversight. "The real issue is that USA Track and Field has become a complete and utter scofflaw," the W.A.D.A. president, Richard Pound, a Canadian, told me. "They have gone to extraordinary lengths to hide identities and data and to exonerate athletes who have tested positive."

Can you really have a serious antidoping effort without the full cooperation of the world's most powerful nation —and most powerful sports nation? It's hard to see how.

The tougher question is whether it will be scientifically possible to stay ahead of the cheaters. The rogue scientists and coach-gurus have been winning for years, and they have ever more tools available to them. THG, which set off the Balco inquiry, is only a slightly more clever version of an old thing: an anabolic steroid—the kind of blunt builder of muscle mass and strength prevalent in sports since the 1950s. But its discovery required an insider tip and THG is child's play compared with what's coming in the near future (if, in fact, it is not here already): genetic manipulation in order to improve athletic performance.

Ultimately, the debate over athletic doping extends beyond sport. "The current doping agony," says John Hoberman, a University of Texas at Austin professor who has written extensively on performance drugs, "is a kind of very confused referendum on the future of human enhancement."

Pete Rose was the prototypical "self-made" athlete, which is code for a sort of seeming nonathlete who makes the most of his meager abilities. But fans overlooked important genetic traits that made him baseball's all-time hits leader—chiefly, uncommon durability that allowed him to play 24 seasons virtually injury free. And what did Rose do to attain that? Nothing, really. As the son of a semipro athlete who played sandlot baseball and football into his early 40s, he came by that blocky, unbreakable body by way of genetic inheritance. In the off-season, Rose maintained himself by playing

casual basketball a couple of times a week and eating greasy food and heaping bowls of potato chips.

When it comes to elite sport, there is no such thing as self-made. No amount of dedication can turn someone of average ability into a world-class sprinter, an N.B.A. player or a champion marathoner. You can't be an Olympic pistol shooter without some innate steadiness of hand or a Tour de France cyclist without a far-above-average efficiency at moving oxygen to muscles. Even a humdrum, physically unimpressive player on a major-league baseball team has something—usually extraordinary hand-eye coordination—that is not apparent to those who regard athletic gifts only in terms of great size, speed, endurance or power.

The former Olympic track coach Brooks Johnson once told me that sport at its highest level should be viewed as a competition waged among "genetic freaks." He mentioned Carl Lewis and Michael Jordan. But anyone who reaches the top echelon of Olympic competition or draws a paycheck for playing sports professionally should be considered in the same category. You cannot will yourself into an elite athlete, or get there through punishing workouts, without starting out way ahead of the rest of the human race.

You may, through pure dedication, be able to jump one level—from a middle-of-the-pack Olympic sprinter to the final heat, from a marginal N.F.L. prospect to a midround draft pick. Chemical enhancement can produce more significant improvements, but the principle is the same. You've got to start out as a member of the athletic elite.

At the 1996 Summer Olympics in Atlanta, a middling Irish swimmer named Michelle Smith de Bruin raised suspicions when she won three gold medals. She later flunked drug tests. But before the presumed cheating, she was already a competitor on the international swim scene, not a lap swimmer at the Dublin Y.

The use and abuse of performance-enhancing drugs in elite sport, or doping, as it has been called since around 1900, is a mutant form of an exclusive competition. It is an effort by individuals who are already part of a thin slice of humanity—the genetic freaks— to gain an edge against one another, to exceed their physiological limits in a way that they could not through pure training. (The word itself is believed to derive from the Dutch word dop, an alcoholic beverage consumed by Zulu warriors before battle.)

While systematic doping—with the collaboration of chemists, doctors, coaches and trainers—is a modern phenomenon, scientific interest in athletes is not new. The medical establishment once viewed athletes with curiosity and occasionally with alarm. The act of training and pushing yourself to physical limits was considered dangerous or even a form of sickness. Sports science was observational, an opportunity to study the body in motion by looking at individuals at the extremes of human capacity.

The British physiologist A.V. Hill, a Nobel laureate in 1922, went to Cornell to study sprinters because, as he wrote, "matters of very great scientific interest can be found in the performances of that extraordinary machine, the human athlete." John Hoberman, the historian of sports doping, has written that scientists and doctors viewed the high-performance athlete as "a wonder of nature—a marvelous phenomenon that did not require improvement."

Certainly, athletes have long sought their own chemical and nutritional means to enhance performance. The ancient Greeks ran and wrestled in the nude because nothing, not even fabric, was supposed to interfere with the purity of sport, yet they ate mushrooms, sesame seeds, dried figs and herbs that were believed to give a precompetition energy boost. Marathoners and cyclists as recently as a century ago competed under the influence of strychnine, which is both a stimulant and a poison. Cyclists also used caffeine, cocaine, alcohol and even heroin.

What changed everything—what transformed performance-enhancing efforts from the realm of superstition into a true science—was the isolation of the male hormone testosterone in 1935. That led to the development by the late 30s of synthesized testosterone variants, or anabolic steroids. The difference between steroids and all previous performance enhancers was that steroids demonstrably worked—and they worked really well.

Nearly every drug used by athletes to boost performance started out as a therapeutic miracle.

Steroids are still prescribed for men with serious testosterone deficiencies. AIDS patients and others with muscle-wasting conditions are dosed with steroids.

Until the mid-80s, people suffering from severe anemia, as a result of chronic renal failure or other causes, had to undergo frequent blood transfusions. The development of recombinant human erythropoietin was a godsend. Instead of transfusions, anemics could get injections to boost their red-blood-cell count.

But what would the effect of EPO be on a person with a normal or better than normal red blood count? What could it do for an already genetically gifted, highly trained endurance athlete? Just what you would expect: make a super-endurance athlete.

[...]

"In simplest terms, EPO turns on the bone marrow to make more red blood cells," says Gary Wadler, the American delegate to W.A.D.A. "But there's a very delicate balance. You can have too much EPO. The body is a finely tuned instrument. It has feedback mechanisms to keep it in balance. What these athletes are often trying to do is get around the feedback, to trick their own bodies."

Between 1989 and 1992, seven Swedish competitors in orienteering—a mix of running and hiking that is sometimes called "cross country with brains"—died, apparently from heart attacks. Nearly all were in their 20s. As many as 18 Dutch and Belgian cyclists died under similarly mysterious circumstances between 1987 and 1990.

"At first they said it was some kind of virus, a respiratory virus," Wadler says. "But what kind of virus only knocks off the most fit individuals in their country? The autopsies were private. All the deaths were not definitively linked. But it was EPO. That was obvious to a lot of people."

For weight lifters and competitors in the "throwing" sports of shot-put, javelin, discus and hammer, the performance enhancer of choice has long been steroids. Anabolic steroids (anabolic means tissue building) increase muscle mass and enhance the explosiveness needed for a wide range of other athletic endeavors: sprinting, jumping, swimming, serving a tennis ball, swinging a baseball bat, delivering a hit on the football field. They afford an additional benefit in a violent sport like football because one of their side effects is aggressiveness or, in extreme cases, so-called roid rage.

Their use is starkly high risk, high reward. Other side effects include liver tumors, impotence, breast enlargement and shrunken testicles in men and male sexual characteristics in women. (Some of the side effects for women include enlargement of the clitoris, deepening of the voice, facial hair and male-pattern baldness.)

If you want a peek at the future of perform-ance-enhanced sport—at what drug-laced ath-letes can accomplish—look back to the mid-80s, the apex of East Germany's shameful and ruthlessly effective doping program. The East Germans were not the only practitioners of extreme pharmacological sport, only the most flagrant and well organized. (East Germany is the only nation known to have systematically doped athletes, often minors, without their knowledge.)

"Things really got out of hand in the 1970s, 80s and 90s," Richard Pound of the W.A.D.A. says. Even as the science of detection improved, the International Olympic Committee and other global sports bodies were constrained, he says, by a "hesitancy to offend" either side while the world was still divided between East and West. "We looked away, and it snowballed."

Steroid usage works particularly well for women athletes, because they naturally make only a fraction of the testosterone that men pro-duce. John Hoberman says: "In the 80s, what we saw was this new breed of monster athletes, particularly on the female side."

Certain records from this heyday of unpo-liced steroid abuse—particularly in sports in which raw strength is a primary requirement—suggest that performances were achieved then that are unlikely to be matched by a clean com-petitor. The top 14 men's hammer throws in history occurred between 1984 and 1988. In the women's shot-put, you must go all the way down to the 35th farthest throw in history to find one that occurred after 1988.

Until last April, the top 10 men's shot-put throws in history occurred between 1975 and 1990. Then, at a competition in Kansas, the American shot-putter Kevin Toth finally broke into that elite group. His distance, 22.67 meters, was the farthest that anyone had put the shot in 13 years. Six months later, Toth's name was among the first to surface in the Balco scandal. Published reports said he had tested positive for THG, the new designer steroid.

In women's sprinting in the 80s, the star—and still the world-record holder in the 100-and 200-meter dashes—was Florence Griffith Joyner, FloJo. Americans loved her style, her body-hug-

ging track suits, her long and fabulously deco-rated nails, her ebullience. Elsewhere in the world, and even in the United States among those with a knowledge of track and field, FloJo's exploits were viewed with more skepticism.

After Joyner died in 1998, at 38 (the cause was related to a seizure), a strange hybrid of a column appeared in the New York Times sports section. Written by Pat Connolly, who had coached Evelyn Ashford, the woman whose 100-meter record Joyner smashed, it was partly a tribute and partly a posthumous indictment. "Then, almost overnight, Florence's face changed—hardened along with her muscles that now bulged as if she had been born with a barbell in her crib," Connolly wrote. "It was difficult not to wonder if she had found herself an East German coach and was taking some kind of performance-enhancing drugs."

FloJo had been a very good, but never a champion, world-class sprinter. Her 1988 per-formance in Seoul was—in the damning par-lance of international sport—anomalous.

We don't normally think of baseball in the context of hammer throwing, shot-putting or women's sprinting. But in terms of anomalous performance, baseball is East Germany in the 1980s: a frontier.

Just as in the steroid-drenched days of Olympic sport, a deep suspicion has attached itself to some of the latest records in baseball. This accompanies the grotesqueness of the app-earance of some of the players. Curt Schilling, the All-Star pitcher, memorably told Sports Illustrated in 2002, "Guys out there look like Mr. Potato Head, with a head and arms and six or seven body parts that just don't look right."

I'm not sure whom, exactly, Schilling had in mind, but for me, his comment recalls a particu-lar photograph taken in the 2002 season. The subjects are the home-run kings Barry Bonds and Sammy Sosa, sitting together, both of them with thick necks and bloated-looking faces. They look, well, freakish—as well as starkly different from their appearance as young players. Bonds entered baseball lean and wiry strong, much like his late father, the All-Star outfielder Bobby Bonds. Sosa, early in his career, was not particu-larly big and showed little power at the plate.

The question of how many home runs it is possible to hit in one season is more open-ended than, say, the fastest possible time a person can achieve in the 100-meter dash. Factors like the size of the ballpark, liveliness of the ball and skill of opposing pitchers affect the outcome. Nevertheless, a century's worth of experience amounted to a pretty persuasive case that around 60 home runs, for whatever combination of reasons, was about the limit.

In 1927, Babe Ruth slugged 60, which remained the record until 1961, when Roger Maris (in a slightly longer season) hit 61. But in 1998 Mark McGwire of the St. Louis Cardinals obliterated Maris's record by hitting 70 home runs.

Late in that season, a reporter snooping around McGwire's locker spotted a bottle of androstenedione, or andro, a substance usually described as a steroid "precursor" that provides a steroidlike effect (and that is still unregulated in the major leagues). McGwire was forced to acknowledge that his strength was neither entirely "God given" nor acquired solely in the weight room. But at least McGwire entered baseball already big and as a prodigious home-run hitter; he hit 49 in his first big-league season, a record for rookies. Contrast that with the career arcs of Bonds and Sosa, which are unlike any in the game's long history.

Bonds had never hit more than 46 home runs until the 2000 season, and in most years his total was in the 30s. But at age 35, when players normally are on the downside of their production, he hit 49 home runs. The following season he turned into superman, breaking McGwire's record by hitting 73.

Bonds's totals in the next two seasons, 46 and 45, were artificially low because pitchers walked him a staggering 346 times. His new capabilities had thrown the balance between pitcher and hitter completely out of whack: the new Barry Bonds was too good for the game. He needed a league all his own.

Sosa's progression was even more unusual. In his first eight major-league seasons he averaged 22 home runs, although his totals did steadily increase and he hit 40 in 1996, then a career high. He was selected an All-Star exactly once. Unlike Bonds, he was not considered among baseball's elite players.

Then in 1998, McGwire's record-breaking year, Sammy Sosa hit 66 home runs—6 more than the great Babe Ruth had hit in his best season. Sosa wasn't done. The following year he hit 63, followed by seasons of 50, 64

and 49—the best five-year total in baseball history.

That there is rampant steroid use in baseball, at all levels, is undeniable. Ken Caminiti, the 1996 National League M.V.P., admitted his own use in a Sports Illustrated article in 2002 and estimated that at least half the players in the big leagues built strength with steroids. The former slugger Jose Canseco has acknowledged steroid use. In a 2002 USA Today survey of 556 big-league players, 44 per cent said they felt pressure to take steroids.

Last year, The Washington Post published a sad series of stories revealing that teenage prospects in the baseball-rich Dominican Republic, the source of nearly one-fourth of all players signed to U.S. pro contracts, are taking veterinary steroids to try to get strong enough to attract the interest of scouts.

Whether Sosa and Bonds have built home-run power chemically cannot be known definitively. Nobody has presented evidence that they have, and both vehemently deny it. [In June 2009, it was reported that in 2003, Sosa tested positive for performance-enhancing drugs. Eds.] Sosa's name has not surfaced in the Balco case, and he has not testified before the grand jury.

Bonds did testify in December. The home of his personal trainer and boyhood friend, Greg Anderson, has been searched by federal agents. Bonds has acknowledged patronizing Balco, which under Victor Conte, its founder, has specialized in testing athletes' blood to determine the levels of elements like copper, chromium and magnesium and then recommending supplements. Experts I talked to say they consider Conte's theories medical mumbo jumbo, but he consulted with dozens of top athletes, including Marion Jones; Amy Van Dyken, an Olympic champion swimmer; and Bill Romanowski, a linebacker in the N.F.L. Jason Giambi of the Yankees was also a client and also testified before the grand jury.

In an article that appeared last June, Bonds told Muscle and Fitness magazine: "I visit Balco every three to six months. They check my blood to make sure my levels are where they should be. Maybe I need to eat more broccoli than I normally do. Maybe my zinc and magnesium intakes need to increase."

Bob Ryan, a veteran Boston Globe sports columnist, is among the baseball devotees who want to believe all Bonds is taking is broccoli and vitamins. But with both Bonds and Sosa, the presumption of innocence he would like to grant them clashes with the accumulation of circumstantial evidence and his own common sense.

"I knew every baseball benchmark from the time I was 10 or 11 years old," Ryan says. "I knew 60, and I knew 61. I knew 714 (the former career home-run mark held by Babe Ruth). Stats frame who a player is. They're part of the romance of the game, the enjoyment."

[…]

But Ryan is not seeking much new information on this subject. "I'm afraid of what you're going to tell me next," he says at one point in our conversation. "I'm living in some sort of denial. I'm afraid to look under the rock."

The world Anti-Doping Agency, imperfect as it may be, is generally considered an improvement over the patchwork approach to drug enforcement that preceded it. Created in 1999 at the World Conference on Doping in Sport in Lausanne, Switzerland, the agency was intended to bring coherence to antidoping regulations and "harmonization" among all the different nations and sports bodies expected to enforce them. In theory, it is the ultimate authority on matters of drugs and sport—looming over national Olympic committees and the national and international federations of all the individual sports and making it more difficult for those parochial interests to protect athletes caught doping.

W.A.D.A.'s medical committee devoted several years to compiling an impressively voluminous list of banned substances. But the role of W.A.D.A. and its president, Richard Pound, is mainly bureaucratic and political. W.A.D.A. can't slow science down—or influence a culture that hungrily pursues human enhancements of all kinds.

"All of these issues are going to be moot in 20 or 30 years," says Paul Root Wolpe, a professor of psychiatry at Penn and the chief of bioethics at NASA. "We already are seeing a blurring of the line between foods and drugs, so-called nutraceuticals. In the future, it will be more common, accepted. We'll eat certain engineered foods to be sharp for a business meeting, to increase confidence, to enhance endurance before a race or competition."

Currently, in determining whether to put something on its banned list, W.A.D.A. considers whether a substance is performance enhanc-ing, contrary to the spirit of sport or potentially dangerous to health. "If it meets two of the three criteria, we are likely to put it on the list," Pound says.

But the first two criteria are ambiguous. Steroids and EPO are clearly performance enhancing. But so might Gatorade be, if you believe its advertising and all the data on the "science of hydration" disseminated by the Gatorade Sports Science Institute. And plenty of sports drinks claim to do more than Gatorade. "You identify a line and draw it somewhere," Pound says. "Why is it the 100-meter dash and not the 97-meter dash? It just is."

Between Gatorade and anabolic steroids lie all those powders and pills and injectibles that elite athletes put into their bodies, in quantities and combinations that may enhance performance or may prove innocuous. In most cases, no one is quite sure.

Less open to interpretation is "potentially dangerous to health." Any medical or pseudomedical activity that takes place underground or in the black market is, by definition, dangerous. Nearly everyone, regardless of how they feel about abortion, will agree that it's more dangerous when it occurs in a back alley. Steroid use, dicey in most situations, is certainly more so when it takes place in the dark.

So issues of health are the strongest rationale for W.A.D.A. and the whole antidoping effort: to protect athletes from their own worst instincts. (Though the sports world is selective about its concerns for athletes' health. Offensive lineman in the N.F.L. just keep on getting fatter. The typical career of a major-league pitcher usually involves the gradual deterioration of shoulder and elbow.) But safety is going to become less of an issue.

[…]

W.A.D.A. invited geneticists and others involved in the latest medical research to a conference in 2002 on Long Island. The antidoping officials were (and still are) focused on the IGF-1 research at Penn, so Lee Sweeney was there. He listened as Richard Pound tried a very tough sell.

The W.A.D.A. president told the scientists that he certainly appreciated the work they were doing, knew that they approached it with single-minded dedication and understood full well that nothing was more important than seeking cures for dread diseases. He then talked about another "humanistic activity" that he said was already threatened by science of a certain kind—the current science of performance enhancement—and could be ruined by the misuse of their research. As they moved forward, Pound asked, could they somewhere keep in mind the interests of sport?

As Pound recalls, the initial responses he got were somewhat dismissive: "They said we work at the gene level. You can't really tell what was altered from what was there naturally."

Pound, a lawyer, then asked rhetorically: "What if I could assure the Nobel Prize in Medicine would be awarded to the person in this room who figured out how to make a test to determine if a competitor had been genetically enhanced? You could do it, right?"

Pound got an acknowledgment that detection might be possible with enough resources devoted to it.

Lee Sweeney generously consults with W.A.D.A. and other antidoping officials. He's sympathetic to their cause. He just says it's hopeless. "There will come a day when they just have to give up," he says. "It's maybe 20 years away, but it's coming."

There is a parallel from the past for the entire issue of performance-enhancing drugs, one tied to what was once another unwelcome substance in sports: money. Some casual followers of the Olympic movement may still not fully realize that nearly all of the participants are now paid professionals. There never was any big announcement that the cherished concept of amateurism—athletes competing for the pure love of sport—had been discarded. But over time, the changed reality has been accepted. Top athletes profiting from under-the-table payments? The public didn't care, and the ideal of amateurism expired, outdated and unenforceable.

One of the last things Pound said to me indicated that he knows, too, that W.A.D.A.'s mission has an expiration date pending. Maybe genetic enhancements really won't work for athletes, he speculated. "If you strengthen the muscle to three times its normal strength, what happens when you break out of the starting blocks? Do you rip the muscle right off the bone?"

Pound seemed to like the thought of this gruesome image. He paused, then extended the thought. "That would be nice if that happened," he said. "It would be self-regulating."

The Sprewell/Carlesimo episode

Unacceptable violence or unacceptable victim?

Theresa Walton

Why do some types of violence by athletes provoke stronger societal reactions than do others? In this article, Theresa Walton focuses on off-field violence by athletes and argues that the amount of coverage the media gives to a specific episode of violence is directly proportional to the status of the victim. She argues that this is especially evidenced in the different responses to white male and female victims.

Given the extensive amount of violence associated with sport both on and off the playing courts and fields, it is surprising that any one isolated incident of violence between two men would attract much media attention. Yet the amount of mainstream media coverage surrounding men's National Basketball Association (NBA) player Latrell Sprewell's attack on his coach, P.J. Carlesimo, has been quite remarkable. In the 3 months from the altercation (December 1, 1997) to the arbitration decision (March 4, 1998) not a day went by without several media stories about Sprewell in newspapers, magazines, and on television sports channels and news shows. The ways these stories were constructed revealed various meanings of violence within our society. In this paper I examine the way that violence is understood in sport in relation to the Sprewell/Carlesimo altercation and to the normalization of violence against women in American culture. This media analysis reveals how portrayals of the Sprewell/Carlesimo incident differ from descriptions of anti-woman violence committed by male athletes and coaches and what these differences in representation tell us about the cultural valuing of men over women.

A strong belief in capitalist ideology is prevalent within the media coverage of the Sprewell/Carlesimo incident. The threat to capitalism represented by workplace violence is one of the main underlying themes in the media coverage of Sprewell's actions. The discourse of workplace violence that gets taken up creates a space to highlight the economic importance of violence between these two men. The separation between workplace violence and domestic violence works to elevate the violence between Sprewell and Carlesimo above anti-woman violence committed by the same population of men (athletes and coaches). Sprewell's attack on Carlesimo inverts the power relationship between boss and employee. Moreover, this particular incident also inverts the cultural power relationship of black and white. Violence within the workplace, as highlighted with this example, threatens social

Theresa Walton, "The Sprewell/Carlesimo Episode: Unacceptable Violence or Unacceptable Victim?" from *Sociology of Sport Journal* (September 2001). Copyright © 2001 by Human Kinetics Publishers, Inc. Reprinted with the permission of the author and Human Kinetics (Champaign, IL).

order, while violence within the home is not considered as culturally significant. Moreover, with this incident preceding the National Basketball Association players' strike, we witness a foreshadowing of the discomfort surrounding the issue of black basketball players (who are written within a "thug" narrative) making millions of dollars. An examination of Sprewell's vilification in the media reveals inversions of power relations that are presented by media coverage as threats to social order. Violence committed by athletes and coaches against women, on the other hand, are not positioned as the same threat to social order and are therefore more normalized within media. Notably, violence against women does not result in the same harsh economic and judicial consequences called for by the media in the case of Sprewell.

The basics of the incident

On December 1, 1997, Latrell Sprewell reportedly attacked his coach, P.J. Carlesimo, while practicing for the Golden State Warriors. Sprewell allegedly "choked" Carlesimo after the coach ordered him to leave practice. According to Warriors owner Chris Cohan, the incident occurred when Carlesimo criticized Sprewell during a passing drill. Sprewell returned 20 minutes later and said to Carlesimo, "I'll kill you. If you don't get me off of this team, that's what I'll do." Reports conflict as to whether Sprewell again tried to attack Carlesimo. Hours after the attack, the Warriors suspended Sprewell for a minimum of 10 games. Two days later, the Warriors organization fired Sprewell, terminating his $32 million contract. Altogether, this would have cost Sprewell $7.7 million for the remainder of the 1997–1998 season, plus $17.3 million that he was due to receive for the next two seasons (Curiel, 1998; Kelly, 1997; "NBA beyond misbehavin," 1997; Stein, 1997).

According to Sprewell, the tension had been building in his relationship with Carlesimo, and he finally "just had enough" of the way the coach treated him (Curiel, 1998, p. 3D). "All the frustrations had built up to the point where I couldn't take it anymore," Sprewell said in an interview (Curiel, 1998, p. 3D). Carlesimo has an abrasive—some say abusive—coaching style and is well known as a "yeller" (Curiel, 1998; Keown, 1997; Steele, 1997b). From the

beginning and all through the incident, Sprewell is described in media accounts as having the support of most NBA players who voiced an opinion. Players who previously had trouble with Carlesimo, such as Rod Strickland, were not surprised by the incident. Strickland, who was with the Washington Wizards at the time, said in an interview, "[Carlesimo is] annoying, that's the bottom line. We've been face-to-face many occasions, that's for sure, so I can kind of understand Spree" (Steele, 1997b, p. 5B).

On December fourth, 3 days after the episode, the NBA banned Sprewell from the league for one year. Sprewell and the NBA Players Association filed an appeal. Dean of Fordham University Law School John Feerick arbitrated a trial that lasted 2 months. He reduced Sprewell's sentence from 1 year to 7 months and from $22.7 million to $6.4 million, meaning the Warriors had to accept responsibility for the final 2 years of Sprewell's contract. Feerick's decision was met by a media outcry that the penalty was too lenient, despite the fact that it was the "most severe punishment ever meted out for any kind of infraction in NBA history" (CNN/SI, 1998). The next longest sentence was a 26-game suspension of Kermit Washington in the 1977–78 season for punching then Rocket player Rudy Tomjanovich in a fight during the game. In comparison, when Dennis Rodman kicked a court side cameraman during the 1996–97 season he received an 11-game suspension ("The NBA has itself," 1998).

Unacceptable violence?

According to NBA commissioner, David Stern, along with the front office of the Warriors, the severity of the original ban and the termination of Sprewell's contract were merited based on moral grounds. "It was not an economical [sic] decision," according to Garry St. Jean, the Warrior's general manager. "It was about morals and ethics and the right thing to do" ("Ruling elicits," 1998, p. 2D). Carlesimo described the decision as "dramatic and courageous" (Curiel, 1998, p. 3D). Yet, the handling of the incident by the NBA and its construction in the media reveal that it is not simply about violence and what levels of violence are acceptable but rather about social power structures. Many lines of power were crossed. Carlesimo was a white man, Sprewell black. Carlesimo occupies a position of power as coach. Sprewell represents the threat of the insubordinate black man to the control of the white male establishment. While 80% of NBA players are black, less than 15% of the coaches, general managers, and owners are (Stein, 1997).

In the arena of professional male sport where incidents of violence occur on a regular basis, it is instructive to note what types of violence are vilified and which are normalized. Some level of violence, even aggression,[1] is considered integral to popular professional male sports: strategic fouls in basketball, outright fights in hockey, football tackling, and the sport of boxing. Yet violence during play is not the only violence that is normalized. Violence toward women, especially girlfriends and wives, by professional athletes and even coaches is unfortunately prevalent. In understanding this issue, I believe it is important in improving the conditions of women's lives to shed light on instances where (hetero)sexism contributes to dangers women face in our culture. As sociologist Edwin Schur (1984) notes, "To understand or to curb the victimization of women, we must not only determine what 'causes' these behaviors to occur. We must also consider the social responses their occurrence elicits" (p. 133).

Examples of violence by athletes and coaches toward women abound. In November of 2000, former National Football Association player, Rae Carruth, was convicted of conspiring to murder Cherica Adams, who was 8 months pregnant with his son. Carruth was also convicted of being part of the group that committed the murder and shot into an occupied car, attempting to kill the baby. Adams was shot four times by associates hired by Carruth. She died 28 days later. Her baby Chancellor Lee, who survived the shooting, was delivered by Caesarian section that night. Media reports refer to Adams' murder as a "double tragedy," implying that the loss of Carruth's promising football career was nearly as tragic as Adams' death. As one fan of Carruth's said, "I feel he was foolish to let a woman take him out of all the hard work he put into getting into the NFL" (Wright, Frazier, & Whitmire, 2001). The title of a Website dedicated to Rae Carruth and the murder reveals the same sentiment: "Shattered Dreams: Two families suffer a terrible loss." Adams, then, is implicated in Carruth's downfall. Representing Carruth's situation as tragic does little to either vilify Carruth or highlight the social importance of such violence.

One of the most infamous cases involved the late Nicole Brown Simpson and her then husband, O.J. The public did not learn until after Brown Simpson's death that Simpson had pleaded no contest to a charge of assault in 1989, and police were called to their home numerous times to intervene in family disputes involving violence (Connelly, 1994, p. 48). Nor did we hear her statement in the police report with her eye blackened and lip split, "You never do anything about him. You talk to him and then leave" (Paterno, 1994, p. 11). As one editor said of the decision not to investigate the incidences, "He was a hero. He came up from poverty. He had a sweet and fine manner and an unbelievable level of athletic prowess and achievement. And I'm going to tear down a guy's life work because he had a fight with his wife?" (Paterno, 1994, p. 11).

Other high profile cases of domestic violence include charges of Warren Moon hitting, scratching, and choking his wife Felicia Moon at their home in Missouri City, Texas in July of 1995. The charges were brought by the state of Texas against the National Football League quarterback. Yet in February of 1996, Felicia Moon portrayed herself in testimony as a temperamental woman who had provoked her husband ("Moon's wife on stand," 1996). Clearly she defended him at the expense of her own reputation despite having sought a divorce and order of protection in 1986 ("Moon's wife on stand," 1996; "Moon's wife denies abuse," 1996). Later that month after an hour of deliberation the jury found Warren Moon not guilty ("Jury rapidly acquits Moon," 1996). In June of 1996, Moon became the highest paid player in Minnesota Vikings history when he agreed to a 3-year $15 million contract extension ("Moon signs big deal," 1996).

Iowa State University's head football coach Dan McCarney faced no repercussions when the media disclosed that he had been charged with assaulting his estranged wife, Brenda McCarney. Fans given voice in newspapers said the assault did not affect McCarney's job as a coach. Fans were unequivocal: "They didn't hire him to be a marriage counselor, they hired him to be a football coach" (Weeks, 1995a, p. 4A). "The offense was serious but irrelevant," said one fan.

According to another, "We all make mistakes in life" (Weeks, 1995a, p. 4A). Apparently domestic violence is not an issue that should weigh heavily on the public conscious [sic]. As one fan asserts, "I just think there are enough other things we should be concerned about in our society, even right here in Iowa City" (Weeks, 1995a, p. 4A). Perhaps a different (male) victim in a different (public) setting would be one of the "things" that should be of more concern to the public.

Many college athletes, perhaps learning from their role models, have assaulted the women in their lives. A University of Nebraska scholarship basketball player, Kate McEwen, was assaulted by her former boyfriend and classmate, football player Lawrence Phillips in September of 1995. Yet he was suspended from playing for only 6 days and was later drafted by the St. Louis Rams in the first round ("Husker rebuff," 1996). Early in March of 1998, University of Iowa football player Eric Thigpen was arrested for assaulting his girlfriend. He spent the night in jail but was neither suspended nor expelled from either the football team or the university.

Violence against women by male athletes does not receive the same media outcry as the Sprewell case. Professional boxer Mike Tyson was convicted of rape in February of 1992, yet an article in the *New York Times* suggests that he was a victim of a corrupt system that took advantage of him. Tyson was said to be "out of control" since Don King took over his management. His victim was implicated as part of the cause of his downfall in boxing (Berkow, 1992; Shipp, 1992). A week after the trial, a group of ministers gathered where the trial was held with 10,000 signatures on a petition seeking a suspended sentence (Vecsey, 1992). A change in coverage occurred after Tyson twice bit Evandar Holyfield's ears in a heavy weight title fight in 1997. This behavior was deemed unacceptable violence, arguably because it was against a man and in the "work" environment of the boxing ring. One boxing analyst said after the biting incident, "Tyson is a menace to himself and to boxing" ("A bite out of boxing," 1997, p. 20A).

One of the more heinous cases occurred in 1989 and involved four male high school athletes from Glen Ridge, New Jersey, who used a broom and a full sized baseball bat to sexually assault a female classmate with mental disabilities. According to Bernard Lefkowitz, journalism professor at Columbia University, the male athletes at Glen Ridge High School were often destructive and "treated female teachers and students with contempt. Repeatedly, the boys of the class of '89 found, there was little or no reprimand—not from teachers or from parents. ... For them, sports was a means of gaining supremacy" (Lefkowitz, 1997, pp. 84 and 94). Moreover, "these Ridgers were taught that women's main purpose was to be decorative and to please and to praise men. A girl who resisted this role was treated as one more opponent to be bullied into submission" (Lefkowitz, 1997, p. 98). The boys' defense was that their victim had encouraged them with her sexual provocation. Their victim remembered it much differently: "Everyone was laughing. I was crying to myself, but I had tears coming out of my eyes" (Lefkowitz, 1997, p. 83). Unfortunately, these boys were typical gang rapists. They were part of the "popular," "jock" crowd—leaders on sports fields and courts, as well as in school and town. Partly these boys were "regarded as above suspicion on campus, but their elevated status also discouraged them from moral reflection; it made them feel entitled" (Lefkowitz, 1997, p. 97). Four years after the attack, three of the boys were finally convicted of aggravated sexual assault in March of 1993. In a controversial decision, they were released on bail until their appeals were heard and did not go to prison until 1997. While Lefkowitz wrote a very sensitive and critical article, the Glen Ridge boys and others like them were not vilified relentlessly by the media in the way that Sprewell was for his attack on Carlesimo.

Unfortunately, violence against women is so prevalent that these examples barely begin to outline the list of violent acts committed by male athletes and coaches. In part we hear about these particular incidents because they are committed by public figures. According to Marian Meyers in her book, *News Coverage of Violence Against Women* (1997), one of the main guiding principles of reporters and editors choosing one story over another is the "unusualness" of the case. To be reported, a crime must be "quirky, out of the ordinary, rare, and uncommon. Because cases of domestic violence and rape are all too common, they can be dismissed by reporters unless they have an unusual twist" (Meyers, 1997, p. 98), such as being committed by a well-known athlete or against someone who is perceived as a defenseless victim, as with the Glen Ridge case. Yet as Ann Marie Lapinski, editor of the *Chicago Tribune,* said, "We should pay attention to women not as famous as Nicole Simpson who are just as dead" (Paterno, 1994, p. 33). The message being portrayed makes it clear that violence against women, while unfortunate, is not villainized and comes closer to being normalized. Columnist Larry Stewart of the *Los Angeles Times* defended not covering the domestic violence of O.J. Simpson by stating, "What man in this country hasn't yelled at his wife?" (Paterno, 1994, p. 11). Value judgements are made in reporting and editing, which determine the importance and meaning of violence—often according to whether the victim is female or male as well as the prestige of the attacker. According to Meyers (1997), when reporters' decisions of "newsworthiness" are based on ideas of "unusualness," "the complexity and interlocking nature of oppression" (p. 98) is revealed. Thus, she argues a sentiment that critical cultural studies scholars[2] share:

> Patriarchy does not operate independent of racial or class interests; these forms of oppression work together to support, maintain and reproduce dominant ideology, which is reflected within journalists' collective understandings and beliefs concerning newsworthiness and the nature of news.
>
> (1997, p. 98)

Male athletes are neither banned from their sports for attacking women, nor are they daily villainized in the news, as Sprewell was.

In attempting to answer the basic who, what, when, where, how, and why, many journalists miss the mark. According to Meyers (1997), when journalists attempt to determine the "why" of a story of violence against a woman they often look to the abuser's psyche or the actions of the victim. She argues that in our patriarchal culture, the "real why behind the violence is that men believe that they have the right to control women" (p. 123). Thus, the pathology of anti-woman violence is "reflective of a society that devalues and hates women, that views women as an appropriate repository for male rage and blame" (p. 123). A lack of control is sometimes excused as the result of some foreign substance in the abuser's system such as alcohol, steroids, or illegal recreational drugs. Sugar Ray Leonard's assault on his wife, Juanita, was attributed to his admitted use and addiction to cocaine. Moon also talked of the pressure of professional athletics sending him over the edge. Reporters also explore the question of "why" by examining the role of the victim to determine her guilt or innocence provoking the attack. Felicia Moon blamed herself when she testified that she was a "temperamental woman." These examinations often lead to a blaming of the victim and an absolution of the attacker. Had reporters been more sympathetic to the "why" of Sprewell's case, they would have produced much different stories about the incident.

Unlike the great outcry by the media calling for strict punishment of Sprewell, media sources continually downplay violence against women and excuse this violence by male athletes. In fact, these acts of violence, according to Schur (1984), are "closely tied to our society's scenarios of approved male behavior" (p. 135). As Schur points out, "The persistence and the relative tolerance of such victimization represents, therefore, a price we pay for maintaining a dehumanizing and exploitative gender system" (p. 135).

[...]

The acceptance of violence toward women comes from the low value placed on "womanhood" and the associated domestic sphere as constructed by our culture. Moreover, there is a failure to effectively stigmatize male offenders for their violent actions toward women. While Sprewell was daily stigmatized after his attack on Carlesimo by the Warriors organization, the NBA, and the sports media, perpetrators of anti-woman violence get much less attention. The successful vilification of Sprewell may work to reduce actions similar to his in the future. This clearly sends the message that an attack on Carlesimo, a white male in a position of power, is more consequential than an attack of a female "domestic" partner. He is important enough that the man who attacked him was publicly criticized every day for 3 months.

The constant portrayal of women as victims in the media works to control women and heightens feelings of disempowerment of female viewers (Reid & Finchilescu, 1995; Walkowitz, 1997). Violence against women functions to control women with the constant fear of the threat of violence. Yet in a paternalistic capitalistic society like the United States, the very idea of "domestic" violence being a "private" matter contributes to the subordination of women. In 1994, two-thirds of victims of completed rapes did not report being assaulted to the police. Among victims who chose not to report a violent crime to the police, many indicated that they felt the matter was private or personal in nature (Perkins & Klaus, 1994). Violence, such as that committed by Sprewell against an authority figure in the "public sphere" of work, is considered more deplorable than violence committed against a "subordinate" woman in the "private sphere" of home because it threatens social order. Thus, the hierarchizing of the "public" sphere as male and the "private" sphere as female is strengthened and perpetuated, with the public/male sphere being more important than the "other," private/female sphere.

Alternative understandings of the incident

The work environment of professional sports is not like other work environments, although it is clearly in the public sphere. Sprewell used the pressure of his situation to defend his attack of Carlesimo, thus taking on the role of victim. Professional male athletes are in a work environment over which they have little control. Sprewell had wanted to leave the Warriors, but as a professional player he has little control over his work environment. He has little control over where he works or who works with him. In return, professional athletes are highly paid. One of the underlying tensions hidden within the narratives surrounding Sprewell is a sentiment that he is paid enough to play a game to be expected to deal without complaint with whatever style his coach uses. This may also show uneasiness over the amount of money black players such as Sprewell make to play basketball. According to sportswriters, problems between coaches and players in part occur because players often make more than their coaches. Again this threatens to invert the hierarchy of the social order.

[...]

Within sport the role of the coach has been cast as a patriarchal figure. Sprewell is apparently rejecting his resulting casting in the "child-like" role. Rather, Sprewell sees Carlesimo as a professional equal and wants to be treated accordingly—"like a man." This works to again support the public/work sphere as male but inverts the traditional coach/athlete power relationship. Sprewell stepped over the line

within the public sphere and attacked a representative of authority, the organization, and by extension the white male power structure.

I contend that it is precisely this threat to (white male) authority that fueled the unprecedentedly harsh ban and fine as well as both the (large) amount of media coverage of the Sprewell "incident" and the vilification of Sprewell by the media. Sprewell's punishment exceeded the total of all suspensions imposed on all players for physical altercations during the 1995–96 and 1996–97 seasons combined as well as all suspensions imposed for altercations during the 1992–93, 1993–94, and 1994–95 seasons combined. In spite of this, most sports writers were not sympathetic to Sprewell. Michael Kelly (1997) described Sprewell as a "millionaire ballplayer and recent attempted strangler" (p. 27A). Tim Keown (1998) of the *San Francisco Chronicle* called him "spoiled and disturbed" (p. 1B). And *Time* magazine's Joel Stein (1997) reports, "As a talk-radio villain Spree has virtually replaced Saddam" (p. 91).

Not only were many journalists not sympathetic to Sprewell, the consensus was that the sentence was too lenient. David Steele (1997f) of the *San Francisco Chronicle* called Feerick's ruling "a surprising arbitration decision" (p. 1A), revealing his belief that the original sentence was fair. Deputy NBA commissioner Russ Granik said, "I have some concern that fans, and perhaps even players, might unfortunately get the message that no matter what you do, your contract can't be terminated" (Curiel, 1998, p. 3D). NBA commissioner Stern said, "The arbitrator is a very charitable man, and he made a charitable decision in respects to Mr. Sprewell in this decision" (Steele, 1998b, p. 1A).

Despite the fact that Carlesimo did not press charges, many sports writers expressed the opinion that Sprewell should have been imprisoned for his actions. In these instances writers lean heavily on ideas of appropriate behaviors in the work place but do not consider how professional sports differ from other job situations. Michael Kelly (1997) of the *Washington Post* wrote,

> Sprewell was not arrested, despite the fact that the acts he had committed certainly seemed to constitute assault and battery. ... If I had tried to strangle my boss in front of a dozen witnesses, I would expect to lose not merely my job but my freedom.

(p. 27A)

Anastasia Hendrix (1998) of the *San Francisco Examiner* quotes a labor lawyer who says, "Even when an employee so much as shoves a superior, the verdict results in 'industrial capital punishment'… a term synonymous with firing" (p. 1A). According to Tim Keown (1998) of the *San Francisco Chronicle*, "The man choked his boss, took a shower, returned to the court, fought his way through assistant coaches and players, took another shot at his boss and still didn't lose his job" (p. 1B). Stern said, "I think the fundamental point is whether you can strike your boss and still hold your job. The answer is that you cannot strike your boss and still hold your job—unless you play in the NBA and are subject to arbitrator Feerick's decision" (Keown, 1998, p. 1B).

Stern and many of the sports writers also questioned Feerick's ability to arbitrate. Ray Ratto (1998) of the *San Francisco Examiner* wrote of the arbitrator's decision:

Most people see this decision as the latest example of permissiveness gone mad. They look at the facts, they look at Feerick, and they decide a ferret with a GED could have done better, and more sensibly. It's hard to tell them that they're wrong, largely because they are right.

(p. 1D)

Keown (1998) calls Feerick's decision an "irrational act" saying his "lengthy and addle-brained decision… has the reek of random guesswork to it. … He decided to uphold an employee's right to drag the boss across the key by his vertebrae. He decided to preserve the sanctity of sociopathic behavior in the workplace" (p. 1D).

The emphasis on the work place also brings to light the economic ramifications of Sprewell's sentence. The issue is racially charged and underscores basic class issues. According to Michael Kelly, the NBA is afraid to punish Sprewell harshly because they need him for the income he provides for them. Thus, they are exploiting Sprewell for their commercial benefit. He contends that the incident is mostly about "thuggism" but does not acknowledge how racially charged the idea of "thuggism" is. He writes that the Sprewell attack stemmed from the fact that

The white men who run pro and college sports value athletes like Sprewell too much, in the commercial sense, to care that, by tolerating the rise of a culture of thuggism in their business

they are encouraging boys and young men to believe in a world where to be a success means not having to obey the rules.

(1997, p. 27A)

Bruce Jenkins (1997) agrees: "There's a deep-seated anger among athletes from hard backgrounds, an anger stemming from racism, injustice and the constant specter of violence. Players will continue to bring that anger into the professional ranks" (p. 2E).

Yet Kelly goes on with some rather racist remarks claiming that it is acceptable to let white athletes get away with preferential treatment because "white society" will save them if they step over the vague boundaries and become drug addicts or get in trouble for violence. "But for black kids, [stepping over the line is] the passport to a life where the best job they will ever get involves a bicycle or a burger or a Xerox machine" (1997, p. 27A). Kelly manages in one paragraph to perpetuate racial stereotypes, blame "black" society for not stepping in to save "their" kids, and offer the usual paternalistic solution of organizations controlled by white men as the saviors. Within the narrative of "thuggism," acts of violence, such as Sprewell's attack on Carlesimo, as well as domestic violence are seen as a "natural" consequence of black anger and oppression.

Conclusion

The power the media has to influence public sentiment can be powerfully witnessed with the coverage of the Sprewell/Carlesimo incident. Media coverage does not offer the same intense and prolonged vilification of perpetrators of anti-woman violence. Apparently, violence committed by the same population (athletes and coaches) upon the bodies of women does not disrupt culturally established lines of power or threaten social order. By establishing "domestic" violence as a "private" matter, media coverage contributes to women's social subordination. Perhaps violence against women would not continue to be so prevalent if it were treated as more serious and significant within media coverage. Couching Sprewell's "choking" of Carlesimo within the language of work place violence, clearly placing it within the public sphere, works to mark it as culturally significant.

241

Representing Carlesimo as the "boss" and Sprewell as the worker positions Sprewell's violence as a threat not just to Carlesimo, but to the social order of capitalism. Carlesimo has the doubly privileged position in our culture of being white and male. Furthermore, he is in a position of power over others—a role often reserved for white men. Sprewell not only attacked the man, Carlesimo, but also then threatened the very privilege that Carlesimo represents. It is not a simple case of violence being unacceptable. Violence is a very accepted aspect of sport, especially male sport. What is unacceptable in this case is the threat to white male privilege as represented by Carlesimo in a position of power. Sprewell's attack on Carlesimo crosses the line and threatens to invert long-standing traditional lines of power.

Notes

1. A significant amount of sport psychology research deals with the issue of aggression in sport (e.g., Silva & Conroy, 1995; Silva & Husman, 1995; and Thirer, 1993). For the purposes of this paper, I consider aggression to be use of physical force with the intention of causing harm. Violence then is a more general term that can include acts of aggression, such as anti-woman violence, as well as accepted aspects of sport, such as football tackling, which do not necessarily carry with them the intention of causing physical harm. Social psychologists refer to aggressive and violent acts that are expected role-playing behavior, such as football tackling, as institutional aggression.
2. Analysis of unequal power relations unifies critical cultural studies work, especially out of the British tradition. For a useful sport studies discussion dealing with relationships of power along intersecting axes, see Birrell and McDonald (2000).

References

A bite out of boxing. (1997, July 1). *New York Times*, p. 20A.

Anderson, D. (1996, July 14). The New York State Athletic Omission. *New York Times*. p. 8:3.

Berkow, L. (1992, February 11). The 'animal' in Mike Tyson. *New York Times*, p. 11B.

Birrell, S. & McDonald, M. (2000). *Reading sport: Critical essays on power and representation*. Boston: Northeastern University Press.

CNN/SL (1998, March 9). *Press Conference*. Time Warner Broadcasting.

Connelly, R. (1994, September 3). Domestic violence and the press. *Editor and Publisher*, 127, 48.

Curiel, J. (1998, March 5). Sprewell's 3-month odyssey. *San Francisco Chronicle*. p. 3D.

Hendrix, A. (1998, March 5). Did Sprewell get off easy? *San Francisco Examiner*, p. 1A.

Husker rebuff for Phillip's assault victim (1996, April 19). *New York Times*, pp. 11B &16B.

Jenkins, B. (1997, December 6). Warriors' wasteland gets deeper. *San Francisco Chronicle*, p. 2E.

Jury rapidly acquits Moon of spousal abuse charges (1996, February 23). *New York Times*, p. 12B.

Kelly, M. (1997. December 11). The Sprewell saga. *Washington Post*, p. 27A.

Keown, T. (1997, December 3). Incident puts Carlesimo out of criticism's way. *San Francisco Chronicle*, p. IB.

Keown, T. (1998, March 5). Irrational act follows another. *San Francisco Chronicle*, p. ID.

Lefkowitz, B. (1997, June 23). Our guys. *Sports Illustrated*, 83–98.

Marinucci, C. (1997, December 6). Brown's shift on Sprewell: He wants to focus on violence, kids. *San Francisco Chronicle*, p. 1A.

Marinucci, C. and D. Steele. (1997, December 5). NBA suspends Sprewell for a year. Angry S.F., Oakland mayors call for investigation. *San Francisco Chronicle*, p. 1A.

McCallum, J. (1997. December 15). Foul trouble. *Sports Illustrated*, 68–69.

McCarney apologizes; ISU weighs his future (1995, March 21). *Iowa City Press Citizen*, p. 4A.

Meyers, M. (1997). *News coverage of violence against women, engendering blame*. Thousand Oaks, CA: Sage.

Moon signs big deal (1996, June 4). *New York Times*, p. 12B.

Moon's wife denies abuse (1996, February 20). *New York Times*, p. 8B.

Moon's wife on stand, blames her temper (1996, February 17). *New York Tunes*, p. 34.

The NBA: Beyond misbehavin' (1997, December 8). *Washington Post* [On-line]: Levey Live. Available: http://discuss.washingtonpost.com/wp-srv/zforum/97/levey.htm

The NBA has itself to blame for condoning violence and other misbehavior (1998, March 5). *San Francisco Examiner*, p. 18A.

Ortiz, J. (1998, March 5). Spree's pals cheer victory for player 'family.' *San Francisco Examiner*, p. 4D.

Paterno, S. (1994, July 23). Covering sports heroes: Sports editors discuss why the 1989 wife abuse arrest of O.J. Simpson was not taken seriously by the media. *Editor and Publisher*, 127, 11, 33.

Perkins, C., & Klaus, B. (1994). *Violent crime. National crime victimization survey.* Government Documents: United States Department of Justice.

Ratto, R. (1998, March 5). Deeper into darkness, my old friend. *San Francisco Examiner,* p. 1D.

Records contradict Moons' statements (1996, February 16). *New York Times,* p. 10B.

Reid, P., & Finchilescu, G. (1995). The disempowering effects of media violence against women on college women. *Psychology of Women Quarterly,* 19, 397–411.

Schur, E. (1984). *Labeling women deviant: Gender, stigma, and social control.* New York: McGraw-Hill.

Score one for bad sportsmanship (1998, March 5). *San Francisco Chronicle,* p. 22A.

Shipp, E. (1992, February 11). Tyson found guilty on 3 counts as Indianapolis rape trial ends. *New York Times,* p. 1A, 15B.

Silva, J., & Conroy, D. (1995). Understanding aggressive behavior and its effects upon athletic performance. In: K. Henschen and W. Straub (Eds.), *Sport psychology: An analysis of athlete behavior* (pp. 149–159). Ithaca, NY: Movement.

Silva, J., & Husman, B. (1995). Aggression: An historical perspective. In: K. Henschen and W. Straub (Eds.), *Sport psychology: An analysis of athlete behavior* (pp. 149–159). Ithaca, NY: Movement.

Sprewell wins his case; Warriors contract reinstated (1998, March 5). *San Francisco Chronicle,* p. 1D.

Steele, D. (1997a, December 3). Warriors may void Sprewell's contract: 'Conduct clauses' could be invoked. *San Francisco Chronicle,* p. 1B.

Steele, D. (1997b, December 3). Strickland says be can relate to Spree. *San Francisco Chronicle,* p. 5B.

Steele, D. (1997c, December 4). Warriors' losing Spree continues: Teammates stunned by news after Cavs roll to victory. *San Francisco Chronicle,* p. 1D.

Steele, D. (1997d, December 4). Warriors notebook: Tight-lipped Sprewell opens up to media. *San Francisco Chronicle,* p. 4D.

Steele, D. (1997e, December 6). The many moods of complex Sprewell. *San Francisco Chronicle,* p. 1E.

Steele, D. (1997f, December 9). Sprewell, Coach tell each other they're sorry: Player apologizes for attack, Carlesimo for his role in it. *San Francisco Chronicle,* p. 1A.

Steele, D. (1998a, March 5). Ruling elicits new questions: Decision sets divisive tone around league. *San Francisco Chronicle,* p. 1D.

Steele, D. (1998b, March 5). Sprewell back with the Warriors: Arbitrator reduces suspension. *San Francisco Chronicle,* p. 1A.

Stein, J. (1997, December 15). Tall men behaving badly. *Time,* 91–92.

Taylor, P. (1997a, December 15). Center of the storm. *Sports Illustrated,* 60–67.

Taylor, P. (1997b, December 15). The race card. *Sports Illustrated,* 70–71.

Thirer, J. (1993). Aggression. In: R. Singer, M. Murphey, & L. Tennant (Eds.). *Handbook of research in sport psychology* (pp. 365–387). New York: Macmillan.

Thomas's troubled history (1996, July 14). *New York Times,* Sec. 8, p. 4.

Tjaden, P., & Thoennes, N. (1998). *'Prevalence, incidence, and consequences of violence against women,' national violence against women survey.* Government Documents: United States Department of Justice.

Tong, R. (1989). *Feminist thought.* Boulder, CO: Westview Press.

Transcript of Sprewell's public statement (1997, December 2). *ESPN Sportszone.com* [On-line]. Available: http://espnsportszone.com/nba/news/971209/0048874.html.

Vecsey, G. (1992, February 18). A petition for Tyson. *New York Tunes,* p. 17B.

Walkowitz, J. (1997). *City of dreadful delight: Narratives of sexual danger in late-Victorian London.* Chicago: University of Chicago Press.

Warriors' Sprewell suspended for attacking, choking coach (1998, December 3). *San Francisco Chronicle,* p. 5B.

Weeks, S. (1995a, March 21). Coach's home life not key to job success, fans say. *Iowa City Press Citizen,* p. 4A.

Weeks, S. (1995b, March 21). Sports not cause of violence off field, experts say. *Iowa City Press Citizen,* p. 1A.

What they're saying (1998, March 5). *San Francisco Chronicle,* p. 2D.

Why women-only self defense? (1998). *Women defending ourselves* [On-line]. Available: http://www.wdo.org/women.html.

Wright, G., Frazier, E., & Whitmire, T. (2001, January 19). Carruth convicted, but not of murder. *Charlotte Observer* [On-line]. Available; http://www.charlotte.com/observer/special/carruth/docs/ 0120carruth.htm

5.6

Crime and athletes

New racial stereotypes

Richard E. Lapchick

Exaggerated media focus on athletes who commit crimes has fostered pervasive myths about the criminal pro-clivities of athletes. In this article, Richard Lapchick discusses the negative stereotypes of athletes (and black athletes in particular), which persist despite considerable evidence of their inaccuracy.

It is ironic that as we begin a new millennium, hopeful that change will end the ills such as racism that have plagued our society throughout past centuries, more subtle forms of racism in sport may be infecting American culture.

Polite white society can no longer safely express the stereotypes that so many believe about African Americans. Nonetheless, surveys show that the majority of whites still believe that most African-Americans are less intelligent, are more likely to use drugs, be violent, and are more inclined to be violent against women.

However, sport as it is currently being interpreted, now provides whites with the chance to talk about athletes in a way that reinforces those stereotypes about African-Americans. With African-Americans dominating the sports we watch most often (77 per cent of the players in the National Basketball Association, 65 per cent in the National Football League, 15 per cent in Major League Baseball—another 25 per cent are Latino). African Americans comprise 57 per cent of the students playing National Collegiate Athletic Association (NCAA) Division I basketball and 47 per cent of those playing NCAA

Division lA football. Whites tend to "think black" when they think about the major sports.

Many athletes and community leaders believe that the public has been unfairly stereotyping athletes all across America. The latest, and perhaps most dangerous, stereotype, is that playing sport makes athletes more prone to being violent and, especially, gender violent.

Rosalyn Dunlap, an eight-time All-American sprinter who now works on social issues involving athletes, including gender violence prevention, said, "perpetrators are not limited to any category or occupation. The difference is that athletes who rape or batter will end up on TV or in the newspapers. Such images of athletes in trouble create a false and dangerous mindset with heavy racial overtones. Most other perpetrators will be known only to the victims, their families, the police and the courts."

On our predominantly white college campuses, student-athletes are being characterized by overwhelmingly white student bodies and faculties while they are being written about by a mostly white male media for a preponderance of white fans.

At an elite academic institution, I asked members of the audience to write down five words they would use to describe American athletes. In addition to listing positive adjectives, not one missed including one of the following words: dumb, violent, rapist, or drug-user!

In the past two years, I have met with NBA and NFL players as well as college student-athletes on more than a dozen campuses. There are a lot of angry athletes who are convinced the public is characterizing them because of the criminal acts of a few.

Tom "Satch" Sanders helped the Boston Celtics win eight world championships. Sanders noted, "If they aren't angry about their broad brush depiction, they should be. The spotlight is extremely bright on athletes; their skills have made them both famous and vulnerable. Their prominence means they will take much more heat from the media and the public for similar situations that befall other people with normal lives."

[...]

Many American men have grown to dislike athletes. Given the choice, a typical man might want the money and the fame but knows it is unattainable for him. After reading all the negative stories about athletes, he doesn't want to read about Mike Tyson complaining about being treated unfairly when Tyson has made a reported $100 million in his post-release rehabilitation program; or about the large number of professional athletes signing contracts worth more than $10 million a year.

The anger of some white men extends to people who look or act differently than themselves. They are a mini-thought away from making egregious stereotypes about the "other groups" they perceive as stealing their part of the American pie.

Big time athletes fit the "other groups." Whether it is an African-American athlete or coach, or a white coach of African-American athletes, when something goes wrong with a player, the national consequences are likely to be immediate.

[...]

Here is the equation we are dealing with as stereotypes of our athletes are built. Fans, who are mostly white, observe sport through a media filter which is overwhelmingly made up of white men. There are 1,600 daily newspapers in America. There are only four African American sports editors in a city where there are

professional franchises and 19 African American columnists. Both numbers, as reported at the recent conference of the National Association of Black Journalists, have almost doubled since 1998 and represent a positive sign. Nonetheless, there are no African American sports writers on 90 per cent of the 1,600 papers!

I do not, nor would I ever, suggest that most or even many of the white writers are racist. However, they were raised in a culture in which many white people have strong beliefs about what it means to be African American.

The obvious result is the reinforcement of white stereotypes of athletes, who are mostly African American in our major sports.

According to the National Opinion Research Center Survey, sponsored by the National Science Foundation for the University of Chicago, whites share the following attitudes:

- 56 per cent of whites think African-Americans are more violent;
- 62 per cent think African-Americans are not as hard working as whites;
- 77 per cent of whites think most African-Americans live off welfare;
- 53 per cent think African-Americans are less intelligent.

It can be expected that some white writers learned these stereotypes in their own upbringing. When they read about an individual or several athletes who have a problem, it becomes easy to leap to the conclusion that fits the stereotype. Sanders said, "Blacks in general have been stereotyped for having drugs in the community as well as for being more prone to violence. However, now more than ever before, young black athletes are more individualistic and they resist the 'broad brush.' They insist on being judged as individuals for everything." But even that resistance can be misinterpreted by the public and writers as merely being off-the-court trash-talking.

Sports specific problems

There are, of course, problems in college and professional sports. For the purposes of this article, I will only deal with those that involve problems and perceptions of athletes.

[...]

We are recruiting athletes:

[...]

- who have seen friends or family members devastated by drugs.
- who have seen battering in their home.
- who were victims of racism in school. Three quarters (75 percent) of all students surveyed by Lou Harris reported seeing or hearing about racially or religiously motivated confrontations with overtones of violence very or somewhat often.
- who come home alone: 57 per cent of all American families, black and white alike, are headed by either a single parent or two working parents.

We desperately need professionals on our campuses who can deal with these nightmarish factors. The reality is that few campuses or athletic departments have the right people to help guide these young men and women into the 21st century. So what are our problems?

Academic issues in college sport

Academically, we get athletes who have literacy problems. The press discusses that student-athletes have literacy problems extensively throughout the year as if it was a problem unique to athletes. However, it is rarely reported—and never in the sports pages—that 30 per cent of all entering freshmen must take remedial English or math.

Academically, we get athletes who will not graduate. It is—and always should be—an issue for college athletics to increase the percentages of those who graduate from our colleges. However, the demographics of college have now changed to the point where only 14 per cent of entering freshmen graduate in four years. If an athlete does not graduate in four years, some call him dumb; others say the school failed him. Few note that he may be typical of college students.

Don McPherson nearly led Syracuse to a national championship when he was their quarterback in the 1980s. After seven years in the NFL and CFL, McPherson worked until recently directing the Mentors in Violence Prevention (MVP) Program. MVP is the nation's biggest program using athletes as leaders to address the issue of men's violence against women.

McPherson reflected on the image of intelligence and athletes. "When whites meet an uneducated black athlete who blew opportunities in college or high school, they think he is dumb. They don't question what kind of school he may have had to attend if he was poor, or how time pressures from sport may have affected him. If they don't make it as a professional athlete, they're through without a miracle.

[...]

There is a common belief that student-athletes, especially those in the revenue sports, have lower graduation rates than students who are not athletes. The facts do not bear this out. Yet it is difficult to get accurate reporting.

- Irrespective of color or gender, student-athletes graduate at higher rate than non student-athletes.
- White male Division I student-athletes graduate at a rate of 58 per cent vs. 57 per cent for white male non-athletes. African-American male Division I student—athletes graduate at a rate of 42 per cent vs. 34 per cent for African American male non-athletes.
- White female Division I student-athletes graduate at a rate of 70 per cent while 61 per cent of white female non-athletes graduate. African American female Division I student-athletes graduate at a rate of 58 vs. only 43 per cent of the African-American female non-athletes.

The disparities, however, remain when we compare white to African-American student athletes:

- White male Division I basketball student-athletes graduate at a rate of 52 per cent versus a 38 per cent graduation rate for African-American male Division I basketball student-athletes, still higher than the 34 per cent grad rate for African-American male non-athletes.
- White female Division I basketball student athletes graduate at a rate of 71 per cent while only 57 per cent of African-American female Division I basketball student-athletes graduate.

College sport does not own these problems. They belong to higher education in general and

246

its inheritance of the near bankruptcy of secondary education in some communities. The publication of graduation rates, long feared by athletic administrators, at once revealed those scandalous rates, but also showed what poor graduation rates there were for all students of color. It turned out that our predominantly white campuses were unwelcoming environments for all people of color.

African-American student-athletes arrive on most campuses and see that only seven per cent of the student body, three per cent of the faculty and less than five per cent of top athletics administrators and coaches look like them. Unless there is a Martin Luther King Center or Boulevard, all of the buildings and streets are named after white people.

In many ways, the publication of graduation rates for student-athletes helped to push the issue of diversity to the forefront of campus-wide discussions of issues of race, ethnicity and gender. Educators finally recognized what a poor job they were doing at graduating all students of color.

Drugs and alcohol in sport

We will get athletes who use drugs. CNN Headline News will understandably run footage of every name athlete who is arrested with drugs. It has become a common belief that athletes have a particular problem with drug and alcohol abuse. Reoccurring problems of athletes like Darryl Strawberry reinforce this image but facts do not bear this out.

According to an extensive *Los Angeles Times* survey of athletes and crime committed in 1995, a total of 22 athletes and three coaches were accused of a drug-related crime in 1995. That means that, on average, we read about a new sports figure with a drug problem every two weeks! Anecdotally, those numbers have seemed to continue in succeeding years. Each new story reinforces the image from the last one.

Their stories are and surely should be disturbing. But those stories are rarely, if ever, put in the context of the 1.9 million Americans who use cocaine each month or the 2.1 million who use heroin throughout their lives. A total of 13 million people (or a staggering 6 per cent of the American population) use some illicit drug each month! When you look at the 18–25 male

age group in general, the percentage leaps to 17 percent. Twenty–two athletes represent a small fraction of a single per cent of the more than 400,000 who play college and professional sports in America.

[...]

In the same *Los Angeles Times* survey, 28 athletes and 4 coaches had charges related to alcohol. None of these 32 cases were put in the context of the 13 million Americans who engage in binge drinking at least 5 times per month. Yet we read about a new athlete with an alcohol problem every 11 days. Such images can surely create a building sense of problems in athletics if they are not viewed in the context of society.

McPherson remembered being "shocked" when he arrived on Syracuse's campus to see how much drinking went on each night among students in general. He felt compelled to call football players he knew on other campuses. "It was the same everywhere. Now when I go to speak on college campuses I always ask. It is worse today. Athletes are also part of that culture, but insist that practice and academics crowd their schedules too much to be in bars as often as other students."

Athletes and violence

We are getting athletes who have fights during games, in bars and on campus. Is there a link between the violence of a sport and one's actions away from that sport? There is certainly a growing body of public opinion that assumes that there is. Media reports regularly imply that the violence of sport makes its participants more violent in society.

Are sports any more violent today than 20 years ago when no one would have made such an assertion? Or is it the fact that our streets and our schools surely are more violent. According to the National Education Association, there are 2,000 assaults in our schools every hour of every day! It is an ugly phenomenon that is neither bound by race, class, geography, nor by athlete vs. non-athlete.

We do have athletes who are the perpetrators in cases of gender violence. In the wake of the O.J. Simpson case, any incident involving an athlete assaulting a woman has received extraordinary publicity. The individual cases add up to the mindset stereotype of 1999: athletes, especially basketball and football players, are more inclined to be violent towards women than non-athletes.

Joyce Williams-Mitchell is the executive director of the Massachusetts Coalition of Battered Women's Service Groups. As an African American woman, she abhors the imagery of athletes being more prone to be violent against women. "It is a myth. The facts do not bear this out. All the studies of patterns of batterers defined by occupation point to men who control women through their profession. We hear about police, clergy, dentists, and judges. I only hear about athletes as batterers when I read the paper. They are in the public's eye. Men from every profession have the potential to batterers."

There have been, of course, too many cases of athletes committing assaults on girls and women.

However, there has never been a thorough, scientific study conclusively showing that athletes are more inclined than others to commit assaults. The only study that comes close was written by Jeffrey Benedict, Todd Crossett and Mark McDonald. It was based on 65 cases of assault against women over three years on 10 Division 1 campuses. Thirteen (13) of the cases involved athletes; 7 were basketball or football players.

In spite of the authors pointing out the limitations of both the small numbers and the fact that they did not control for use of alcohol, tobacco and the man's attitude toward women (the three main predictors of a mate's inclination to gender violence), the press regularly quote their study without qualification. Media reports never state that it is a study that came up with 13 athletes over three years. They simply say that the study concluded that nearly 20 per cent of all campus assaults are committed by student-athletes and most are committed by basketball or football players. Rosalyn Dunlap underlines that "This is a racially loaded conclusion. When I was a student-athlete at the University of Missouri, I never thought of keeping myself safe from a 260-pound football player anymore than any other man on the street. In fact, male athletes on campus protected me."

Here is some critical data usually missing in the debate about athletes and violence against women.

- In 1994, 1,400 men killed their significant others. O.J. Simpson was the only athlete accused of murder.

- In 1998, an estimated three million women were battered and close to one million were raped. According to various reports in the press over the past five years, between 70 and 100 athletes and coaches have been accused of assault against a woman each year.
- In data released in 1999 in The Chronicle of Higher Education's annual campus crime survey, there were 1,053 forcible sex offenses in 1997. Less than 35 student-athletes were arrested.

Gender violence is a serious problem of men in America. The cost of crime to America is pegged at $500 billion per year according to a National Institute for Justice research report for the Justice Department released in March 1996. Gender assault and child abuse account for $165 billion—more than one-third of that total! Men who beat their significant others are statistically also likely to beat their children.

Dunlap, who works with McPherson to create more awareness about the issue, said, "There are no men who should be exempted from being educated about the issue of gender violence although many believe they are. It is a problem for naval commanders, day care providers, fraternities, guys at a bar, in corporations, in halls of higher education and, yes, on athletic teams. But no more so on athletic teams."

There have been numerous cases in corporations in which women brought suits against the corporation for harassment and/or assault. The Boston Globe gave extensive coverage to the case in which there were 16 formal legal complaints for incidents from sexual harassment to rape at Astra USA, Inc., a chemical company. Mitsubishi had a suit against it placed by 29 women for the same reasons. No stories about Astra suggested that working in a chemical company produced this climate. At Mitsubishi, no one suggested any relationship to the manufacturing process is a link to gender assault. So why do stories about athletes imply such a linkage to athletics? Does it fit white America's racial imagery?

McPherson believes it does. "Football and basketball mean black. When the public talks about gender violence and athletes, it talks black. No one discusses the problems of golfer John Dailey or Braves manager Bobby Cox. Warren Moon was another story altogether."

"Problems about athletes hit the papers and people think they detect a pattern because of the seeming frequency. But no one else's problems get in the papers. How do we make legitimate comparisons?

"With Astra and Mitsubishi, we look at the corporate climate and don't generalize about individuals. But with athletes, especially black athletes, we look at players and look for patterns to add up."

Some observers say athletes are trained to be violent and we can expect that to carry over into our homes. If this is true about training, then what about the training we give to police, the Army, Air Force, Navy and Marines to use lethal force. Will they come home and kill? McPherson adds, "There is no logic to connect these cases but we do fit our stereotypes of African-Americans with such images when we carry through the implication for athletes."

With all the recent publicity about the horrors of gender violence, it would be easy to forget that it was America's big, dirty secret until the notoriety surrounding the O.J. Simpson case. Few were willing to talk about gender violence. But we can never change if we do not confront this disease that is devouring our communities. The same unwillingness to confront racism diminishes society's ability to eradicate it.

Neither were being realistically discussed on college campuses nor in corporate board rooms. We are paying a horrible human price as we realize that society rarely told men that their dominating and controlling actions against women have helped create a climate in which there is a seemingly uncontrollable tidal wave of men's brutality against women.

Athletes should take a leadership role on this, just as they have on drug abuse and educational opportunities. In 1990, Louis Harris completed a landmark study which showed that our children desire to participate in changing their society and viewed athletes as their first choice in terms of who they wanted to hear socially relevant messages.

The MVP Program, organized in 1992 by Northeastern University's Center for the Study of Sport in Society, has been on more than 55 campuses over the last seven years training male athletes to be spokespeople on the issue of gender violence. Each of those schools has become proactive on an issue that has hurt so many women and their families. Don McPherson worked full-time for MVP for several years.

Our society is unraveling at a breakneck pace and McPherson insists "we have to do more to help our youth survive by including our athletes rather than excluding them in helping our youth. The stereotyping of our athletes does not help. We need to be ready with facts to dispute the easy labels."

McPherson and Sanders both argue vigorously that America's athletes not only don't fit the emerging stereotypes about athletes and crime but that the vast majority of professional athletes are extremely positive individuals. Sanders said, "when I look at the many NBA players who have their own foundations and who are very involved with giving back to the communities where they play and where they came from, I know they are hurt by the stereotypes." McPherson asserts that "most of the players in the NFL are deeply religious, family-centered men who are constantly giving back to their communities with time and money." […]

The distortions about our athletes and the crimes that a few of them commit need to be put in their real social context. The misleading perceptions need to be corrected so we can focus on the truth and what is really necessary. In that way, we can help America live up to the dream that Jackie Robinson created for us more than 50 years ago.

5.7 Journalistic view

IOC scandal part of sports corruption big picture

Joe Pollack

Perhaps all the corruption began with Peter Ueberroth, and the fact that the 1984 Olympic games made money and, more important, made Olympic organizers greedy. More logically, the problems of the Olympians are the same ones that have bedeviled men and women since they have been able to walk upright. Modem times and high technology merely made things worse.

Many years ago, the late Phog Allen, long-time basketball coach at Kansas, described—and dismissed—Olympic committee members as "quadrennial international hitchhikers." Allen spoke even before 1981 when Juan Antonio Samaranch was anointed president, with powers far greater than those of an absolute monarch who rules by divine right.

The Olympics, however, are just one example of greed and corruption and money and favors in the sports business, and believe me, all sports are a business of some sort. Little kids who play for prizes, or even for medals, are into the business of sports. If money for uniforms is raised by selling candy to neighbors, relatives and friends, the seller is in business. If money to pay players' salaries is raised by selling beer to strangers, it's the same thing. The difference is only in degree.

Therefore, on one level, why all the flap about Salt Lake City or Sydney or Nagano giving money to International Olympic Committee members, buying votes to be a game host?

Is that different from St. Louis and St. Louisans building the world's ugliest stadium and giving millions to Georgia Frontiere to bring the Rams? Or from the mayor of Hartford, Conn., spending millions to build a stadium to attract the New England Patriots?

If the members of the IOC shake hands with palms up—and open—as they are introduced to the representatives of Salt Lake City (using this city as an example), they merely are doing what their predecessors on the committee did, and what they have been advised to do.

"When you get to the bidding city," the retiring, or dying, member tells his successor, "Keep your eyes shut and your hands open. Someone will fill the hands with all sorts of good things."

In many respects, the United States is merely reaping what it has sowed. For more years than we can remember, the nation has solved every problem in a simple manner—throw money at it. Want to keep a country from adopting Communism? Pay it off; just call it aid. Want to make sure your friends get elected? Pay them off; just call it retraining.

The reason for blaming Ueberroth is that once the IOC discovered money could be made with sponsors, or from sponsors, well, the door opened wide and remains that way. And sponsors from Anheuser-Busch to Nike to Dr. Pepper are used to paying for what they want. They boast about how much they spend and what they will get for it. A-B has happily announced the spending of many millions to be the "official beer" of darn near everything. Big deal!

I don't know whether new stadiums or new teams really bring money to a city or whether they just give the head of the Chamber of Commerce or RCGA [Regional Chamber and Growth Association—Eds.] some extra bragging rights. Economists argue in both directions. But cities pay off NCAA officials to insure being the site for a Final Four, or kowtow to the NFL to be a Super Bowl site. I wonder how much St. Louisans paid under the table-or in the form of gifts-to bring basketball finals here. Or did we just accept a women's tournament in order to get the men, the way we had to buy two packs of Raleigh cigarettes in order to get one of Lucky Strikes during the shortages of World War II?

Payoffs and *sub rosa* payments have been part of the Olympics since the first laurel wreath was draped upon the first Athenian forehead. Why, then, does everyone jump up and down and scream that the sky is falling when Salt Lake City does it?

Elections are sold to the highest bidder just as paintings are, and influence is sold in the same manner. I guess what is insulting is the way both buyers and sellers treat us, the ultimate payers, as if we were retarded.

Over the last month or so, I've been told that this person was being polite and that one didn't know there was anything wrong and the other thought this was the usual custom. I've also been told that the money was given to the country's delegates to improve all sports, and that the presence of girls was just to give everything a little gender balance, and that the kid of this rich businessman needed a job and the kid of that one needed a college education and the kid of the other one needed surgery.

Admit you bought the election. Admit you bought the team or the stadium. Don't take me for a fool. Do it, don't apologize for it and go on about your business. If I like what you're making, I may buy it. If I like the sports or the theater you present maybe I'll buy a ticket.

As always, there are humorous spots, often when some Olympic committee person or politician shows a track record of stupidity and corruption but is convinced he or she is bulletproof. Take Deedee Corradini, recently resigned mayor of Salt Lake City, which deals in greed and corruption while the Mormon Tabernacle Choir sings in the background. I remember Salt Lake City very well. The Big Red played the 49ers in an exhibition game in 1962. My suite at the Hotel Utah displayed a red sitting room with a white piano. In those days, with the Catholic proscription against meat on Fridays still in force, one of my jobs while serving as advance man was to call the local bishop and request a dispensation so the players could eat meat at a pregame meal.

In exchange, there were tickets for the bishop, though this one declined.

Anyway, when I finished getting clearance for the players, the priest asked if there was anything else he could do for me.

"Well, father," I said, thinking fast and remembering my employers, "our traveling party includes a number of Catholics (two sports writers, a doctor, some assistant coaches and the club owners, to name a few). What about them?"

"Young man," he said, "you give a dispensation to anyone you like."

And that's how Stormy and Bill Bidwill ate steaks and I ate ham in our pregame meal in Salt Lake City.

But back to Deedee the Democrat. When she was first elected in 1992 she was embroiled in the collapse of the Bonneville Pacific Corporation. Several corporate executives went to jail and Deedee, on the board of a related company, agreed to an $800,000 settlement. After her re-election in 1996, it was revealed that she had paid some of the settlement with $231,000 she had solicited from prominent Salt Lakers. Half of the 24 people who gave or lent the money also did business with the city. The district attorney, a friend of hers, decided against filing charges because, he claimed, Utah conflict of interest laws are too vague. When she was not indicted she claimed she was vindicated.

By the way, the D.A. was defeated for reelection last fall and the victor says he will reopen the case. Don't heap all the blame on the Olympics. There's plenty to go around, and don't forget that in any competition greed wins.

Section 6

Certain kinds of people

Sexuality and sports

Introduction

No issue in the sports world ignites more controversy than does that of homosexuality. This was evidenced recently in an interview of a former NBA star player—Tim Hardaway. When asked his opinion about another former NBA player, who had just published a book professing his homosexuality, Hardaway snapped: "I hate gay people, so I let it be known. I don't like gay people. I don't like to be around gay people." With specific reference to the former NBA player, John Amaechi, Hardaway said: "First of all, I wouldn't want him on my team. And second of all, if he was on my team, I would, you know, really distance myself from him because, uh, I don't think that is right. I don't think he should be in the locker room while we are in the locker room."[1] Hardaway, at the time of the interview, was employed by the NBA as a community relations representative. But soon after his statement was publicized by the media, the NBA dismissed him, and issued a press release denouncing his statement.

This episode was curious because it revealed not just the prevailing homophobic norm in sport but also the hypocrisy of league officials who were quick to dissociate themselves from Hardaway's statement. Hardaway's comments, though crudely expressed, actually reflected the general attitude about homosexuality, not only in the NBA, but also in other major American male sports. In the culture of male sports, the issue of homosexuality is a minefield that is simply avoided. Though seldom stated openly, male sports, historically, have served the functions of cultivating and affirming the virtues of heterosexual masculinity. In fact, male sports have operated as major vehicles for male gender socialization, much like military service; they supported and reinforced sharp differentiation between male and female genders. This has been addressed by scholarly writings on sports from the theoretical perspective of hegemonic masculinity.

More pertinent to the concerns of this chapter, however, are the major consequences of hegemonic masculinity, which helps to nurture homophobia and the stigmatization of homosexuals. By establishing rigid heterosexual normative boundaries through practices of sexual discrimination, that ideology has fostered a climate of fear, shame, and secrecy that has preserved sports as a strategic site for legitimizing a male-dominated gender order. The ways in which this was achieved, at the level of both the attitudes of individual athletes and sports organization norms, has been explained perhaps best by studies of homophobia in sports from the perspective of deviance labeling theory. That theory highlights the way social imputation creates negative social sanctions and stigmas that operate as powerful mechanisms of social control.

The readings in this chapter can be viewed as responses to the analytical question: what are the effects on athletes of the stigma of sexual deviance? The power of homophobic labeling in sports is pervasive. Women athletes face an especially unsettling predicament. Because sports are perceived as a masculine domain, they often find themselves suspected of being lesbians. Blinde and Taub, in "Women As Falsely Accused Deviants," study how a group of women college athletes deal with the stigma of being labeled lesbians. The authors argue that these athletes, due to their lack of power, seldom challenge the homophobic norm but generally rely on passive stigma management techniques of silence and denial, which ironically enhance the overall power of the stigma. The response to the stigma of being labeled homosexual is not, however, always passive stigma management. Some lesbian athletes apparently have responded differently. Susan K. Cahn, in "From The 'Muscle Moll' To The 'Butch' Ballplayer," traces the historical development of the stereotype of the "mannish lesbian athlete" and examines its relationship to the experiences of mid-twentieth century lesbian athletes. The stigma, notes Cahn, had a paradoxical effect. The very cultural climate that produced the pejorative image also created possibilities for lesbian affirmation, because sports, like women's softball, provided the social and psychic space for some lesbians to validate their identity and build a subculture.

The sexuality norms in sports—like those in the larger society—are hardly static. In the last article, Peter Dreier, in "Is Baseball Ready For A Gay Jackie Robinson," presents a provocative argument that, by the end of the first decade of the twenty-first century, we are likely to see an openly gay major league baseball player and that this will have an impact on sports similar to the historic breakthrough by Jackie Robinson, the first black to play major league baseball in the modern era. In the last several decades, signs of resistance to homophobia and increasing tolerance of alternative sexual orientations have resulted from the gay liberation movement and subsequent changing public attitudes. These are evidenced perhaps most clearly in the expanding legal rights for sexual minorities, and the greater acceptance of diverse sexualities in the media, higher education, and the occupational structure. The most significant of these changes in sports have occurred in women's professional sports, where several major athletes—Billy Jean King (tennis), Martina Navratilova (tennis), and Sheryl Swoopes (basketball)–have come out as lesbians. The changes in men's sports, by contrast, have been far more modest. A few minor male professional athletes in major sports—e.g. David Kopay (football), Esera Tuaolo (football), Billy Bean (baseball), and John Amaechi (basketball)—have come out as homosexuals after they retired. But, thus far, no high profile male athlete in any of the four major American professional sports has done so. This is no doubt a measure of the persisting power of the ideology of hegemonic masculinity in male sports. The opinions about homosexual professional athletes expressed by Tim Hardaway, noted above, simply reflected that ideological reality.

While public attitudes have changed over the past several years, there still exist considerable public misgivings about gay athletes in sports. As indicated by the following findings of a 2005 *Sports Illustrated* survey (http://sportsillustrated. cnn.com/2005/magazine/04/12/survey. expanded/):

- 62 per cent agree the reason there is so little coverage of gays in sports is because America is not ready to accept gay athletes
- 68 per cent agree it would hurt an athlete's career to be openly gay
- 64 per cent agree that brands and products are unlikely to select athletes as endorsers if the athletes are gay or ever have been accused of being gay
- 65 per cent agree society is more accepting of gays playing sports like golf and tennis and less accepting of gay participating in more contact sports like wrestling and boxing.

The last finding in the *Sports Illustrated* survey provided part of an answer to one particular analytical question: Which sports are most associated with homophobia and which are least? Apparently contact sports such as boxing, football, wrestling, and hockey are most associated with homophobia—at least in the opinions of sports fans. This view seems plausible. Because these sports feature the attributes of idealized masculinity, they probably perform more important functions for maintaining the gender order than do less physical noncontact sports such as tennis, swimming, and gymnastics. This is of course only speculative and will need more research before we can reach a conclusion.

Among the analytical questions for research on sexuality and sports are the following:

1 Which sports are the most and the least homophobic? What characteristics of those sports account for those differences?
2 How do men's and women's sports compare in their levels of homophobia?
3 What are the specific characteristics of sexuality barriers in sports? How do they differ from the barriers of race and class?
4 What are the links between homophobia in the wider society and homophobia in sports? Under what conditions is sport likely to reflect *or* contradict homophobic attitudes in the wider society?
5 How do patterns of homophobia in sport differ cross-nationally? Which societies are most tolerant of sexual minorities in sport and which are least?

Note

1. Both Hardaway quotes are from an Associated Press story in *USA Today* (http://www.usatoday. com/sports/basketball/nba/2007-02-15-hardaway_ x.htm?POE=SPOISVA).

Women athletes as falsely accused deviants

Managing the lesbian stigma

Elaine M. Blinde and Diane E. Taub

Sterotyped views of women athletes as unfeminine often discourage women from playing sports. In this article, Blinde and Taub focus on the stigma management techniques of women athletes who find themselves suspected of being lesbians.

Gender represents a powerful normative system that both evaluates and controls the behavior of men and women (Schur 1984). This system entails socially constructed conceptualizations of behavior intricately tied to societal perceptions of "masculinity" and "femininity" (Keller 1978).

[...] Stigmatization represents a means of social control as it preserves the traditional gender system. Fear of being labeled deviant keeps women "in their place" and reduces challenges to prevailing gender norms (Schur 1984). Not surprisingly, individuals who occupy positions of power or privilege, the "deviance-definers," benefit from continued subordination or suppression of the less powerful (Becker 1963).

Although all women experience devaluation and stigmatization by virtue of being female (Schur 1984), some women occupy roles or engage in behaviors that make them even more susceptible to deviant labeling. This labeling is particularly indicative of women who violate multiple categories of gender norms, including (1) presentation of self (e.g., emotions, nonverbal communication, appearance,

speech), (2) marriage and maternity, (3) sexuality (e.g., sexual behavior/orientation), and (4) occupational choice (Schur 1984).

One group of women judged to violate multiple categories of gender norms and thus subjected to various forms of deviance labeling and stigmatization is athletes. Women athletes are frequently perceived to cross or extend the boundaries of socially constructed definitions of "femininity" (Theberge 1985; Willis 1982). In a culture that traditionally equates athleticism with masculinity, women who participate in sport are often viewed as masculine, unladylike, or manly (Willis 1982). Such descriptors imply that women athletes violate presentation of self and occupational gender norms (Schur 1984). Moreover, both the popular press and research literature have examined the assumed conflict between athleticism and femininity (Colker and Widom 1980; Griffin 1987; Hall 1988). This presumed incompatibility, along with equating sport and masculinity, results in a belief system linking women athletes with lesbianism (Lenskyj 1991).

The lesbian label, representing a violation of sexuality norms (Schur 1984), is based on the idea that women who challenge traditional gender-role behavior cannot be "real" women (Lenskyj 1991),

The lesbian label as applied to women athletes is particularly significant given the assumed threat of lesbianism (as well as male homosexuality) to the prevailing gender system (Goodman 1977; Lenskyj 1991; Schur 1984). Stigmatization of lesbians is common as the phenomena of "heterosexual assumption" and "heterosexual privilege" ensure that lesbians realize they are indeed norm violators, deviants, and subjects of oppression (Schur 1984; Wolfe 1988). Such stigmatization reflects contempt for those who strectch the boundaries of culturally defined gender roles.

Since the behavior of women athletes is often interpreted to challenge gender norrms they may be subject to various forms of devaluation and stigmatization. Although athleticism represents the initial discrediting attribute, its linkage with lesbianism magnifies the devaluation and stigmatization associated with female athletes. The present study examines the manner in which such forms of devaluation and stigmatization impact on women athletes and how they manage the lesbian label (and accompanying masculine image) attached to their sport participation. Not only has there been a paucity of research investigating the specific topic of the stigmatization of women athletes as lesbians, but the entire issue of the perceived presence of lesbianism in women's sport has been neglected (Griffin 1987).

Methodology

Sample

[…]

Three universities (two Midwestern and one Southern) provided names and addresses of all women athletes with at least one year of completed athletic eligibility who were participating in the school's sport programs during the 1990–1991 school year. All sport programs offered by the universities were represented. Varsity women athletes, rather than intramural or informal sport participants, were the focus of this study because of the salience of their athletic identities and their greater sport commitment. […]

These 24 athletes were currently participating in a variety of intercollegiate sports—basketball (5), track and field (4), volleyball (3), swimming (3), softball (3), tennis (2), diving (2), and gymnastics (2). With an average age of 20.2 years and predominantly white (92%), the sample consisted of 2 freshmen, 9 sophomores, 5 juniors, and 8 seniors. The majority (22) were receiving athletic scholarships.

Procedures

Two trained interviewers conducted in-depth and semi-structured tape-recorded telephone interviews that lasted 50–90 minutes The interview schedule focused on several aspects of the intercollegiate sport experience, one of which related to societal perceptions of women's sport and female athletes. The lesbian topic usually surfaced in responses to questions regarding (1) positive and negative connotations associated with women's sport and female athletes, and (2) stereotypes associated with women athletes. In response to these two questions, 17 of the 24 athletes initiated discussion of the lesbian topic. When asked whether they were aware of the lesbian label being associated with women athletes, 6 of the 7 remaining athletes indicated strong familiarity with this association.

Further, several questions explored how athletes dealt with the lesbian label, for example (1) why they felt women athletes are labeled lesbian, (2) which athletes or teams are most likely to be labeled, (3) who applies this label, (4) how this label affects athletes, and (5) the degree to which athletes discuss this topic among themselves. Questions were open-ended to allow athletes to discuss the most relevant aspects of their own experiences.

[…]

Overall, the design of the study allowed for the emergence of concepts from the data rather than imposing preconceived conceptual or theoretical frameworks on the interview protocol and data. Such an approach utilizes the voices of athletes to identify and develop emerging concepts and themes.

In analyzing and reporting the comments of athletes, the intent was not to construct a single profile characterizing the majority of respondents. Rather, realizing that athletes differ and that all comments are important, both similarities and variations in responses are explored.

Results and discussion

[...]

This article focuses on Becker's (1963) construction of the "falsely accused deviant" and Goffman's (1963) conceptualization of "stigma management." Not only do these two concepts enhance our knowledge of the experiences of women athletes, but the athletes' experiences add further understanding and validation to the conceptualizations of the "falsely accused deviant" and "stigma management."

Falsely accused deviant

The vast majority of respondents thought that labeling women athletes lesbian (or at least questioning sexual preference) was quite common. One athlete referred to it as a "societal blanket covering all of collegiate female athletes."

Despite athletes' perception that the lesbian label is prevalent in women's sport and often indiscriminately applied to women athletes, it would be unreasonable to assume all women athletes are lesbian. Although our intent was not to ascertain the sexual orientation of respondents, it was clear that a large majority responded to questions as to suggest that they were not lesbians. For example, phrases like "lesbians don't bother me as long as they don't hit on me," "I have a boyfriend," "the label does not pertain to me," "I'm not really the person to ask about lesbianism because I don't really see enough of it," "people know how I am" (suggesting heterosexuality), or "it's not a problem I'm faced with" were common.

Another way athletes implied distance from lesbianism was through out-group (e.g., "they" or "them") and in-group (e.g., "those of us who aren't" or "we joke about them") terminology. Even though women athletes as a whole frequently are viewed as the out-group in terms of social deviance, a secondary level of deviance exists within the athletic group. That is, within this deviant group, athletes use in-group and out-group terminology to distinguish between the nonlesbian and lesbian athlete.

Given this widespread disassociation from lesbianism, it was assumed that the majority of athletes interviewed were not lesbians. However, since the label is indiscriminately applied to women athletes, many are incorrectly labeled lesbian, typifying what Becker (1963) terms the "falsely accused deviant." One difficulty noted by Klemke and Tiedeman (1990) in the study of false accusations is documenting that accusations are indeed false. Relative to our research, the need of respondents to mislead interviewers should have been substantially reduced as the interviews were anonymous and conducted by strangers over the telephone.

The concept of the "falsely accused deviant" derives from Becker's (1963) original classification scheme of deviant behavior. Basic to Becker's typology are two factors: whether an individual (1) is a rule violator and (2) has been labeled deviant. In contrast to the "pure deviant," correctly labeled a rule violator; the "conformist," correctly labeled a rule abider; and the "secret deviant," a rule violator not labeled as such, the "falsely accused deviant" is incorrectly labeled deviant.

Unfortunately, Becker (1963) does not systematically examine or discuss the "falsely accused deviant." In fact, this category of deviant is underresearched compared to the other three types. Neglect of the category exists despite its potential to enhance understanding of labeling, especially in terms of conditions and social processes involved in creating false conceptions of social reality (Klemke and Tiedeman 1990). Conceptualizations surrounding the "falsely accused deviant" are particularly useful in understanding why the lesbian label permeates women's sport.

[...]

Societal preconditions for false accusation. There are general societal preconditions or organizational factors that increase the probability false accusations will occur (Klemke and Tiedeman 1990). Three factors in particular may account for why female athletes and women's sport, compared to other individuals and domains, are more often targets of lesbian accusations: (1) the growth of women's sport and its perceived threat to the male sport structure, (2) women athletes' lack of power and outsider status, and (3) stereotype adoption.

260

As the growth of women's sport challenges the male-controlled sport structure, attempts to devalue women's sport by dominant groups can be anticipated. Lenskyj (1986) argues that efforts to preserve sport as a stronghold of male supremacy positively relate to the movement of women into sport. The expansion of women's sport in the past 20 years (due in part to Title IX legislation promoting equal gender opportunity in educational institutions) has been perceived as a threat to men's sport, thus triggering an increased interest in preserving male sport (Blinde 1987). The generalization of the lesbian label to female athletes seeks to discredit and devalue women's sport and ultimately works to keep women "in their place" (Lenskyj 1986).

Second, since women as a group possess relatively little power in the larger society, they are not only more likely to suffer false accusations but also be unable to challenge or disprove the label. [...] Support for this latter contention was found when athletes indicated that men, especially male athletes, were the most common group labeling women athletes lesbian.

Third, confounding this situation are long-standing stereotypes directed toward women who violate traditional gender norms. In the current example, the societal linkage of athleticism and masculinity increases the likelihood that women in sport will be the target of false charges of lesbianism.

Given the factors that lead to the indiscriminate stigmatization of women athletes, both lesbian and nonlesbian athletes adopt strategies to manage the lesbian stigma. As discussed in the following section, a variety of stigma management mechanisms are utilized by athletes to manage these labels.

Stigma management

According to Goffman (1963), stigmas represent discrediting attributes that reflect a discrepancy between individuals' virtual (assumed) and actual (real) social identities These attributes fall outside the range of what is considered ordinary or natural and generally "spoil" the social identity of the stigma possessor. Since the stigma taints and discredits the individual, attempts are generally undertaken to control and manage the discrediting attribute. The need for such

management mechanisms is not necessarily limited to individuals who possess the discrediting attribute; stigma management is arguably the domain of the "falsely accused" as well.

As noted previously, sport participation (especially elite competition) is often considered outside the range of what is ordinary or normal for women. Moreover, given the widespread labeling of women athletes as lesbian and the corresponding stigmatization, women athletes must manage these discrediting attributes.

The particular strategy utilized to manage a stigma largely depends on the degree to which the attribute is visible or perceivable to others. Goffman (1963) distinguishes between individuals possessing attributes easily identifiable (i.e., discredited individuals) and not immediately perceivable (i.e., discreditable individuals). Techniques designed to manage the impact of these two types of attributes differ; the discredited individual manages tension while the discreditable manages information. Although the degree to which others can identify women as athletes varies, athletic status (and the accompanying lesbian label) is generally not immediately perceivable, thus resulting in a discreditable stigma. As Goffman (1963) suggests, such a stigma is associated with the control and management of information.

Concealment. One basic stigma management mechanism noted by athletes was concealment. As an information management technique to prevent association with the lesbian label, women athletes sometimes simply conceal information about their athleticism. Elliott, Ziegler, Altman, and Scott (1990) and Goffman (1963) identify several forms of concealment, including self-segregation, passing, and use of disidentifiers.

Common in the responses of athletes was *self-segregation,* a condition where the stigmatized interact primarily with those sharing a similar affliction or those considered "wise." Wise individuals are familiar and comfortable with the stigmatized but do not have the stigma (Goffman 1963). Athletes frequently indicated that most of their friends are athletes and interaction with the general student body is limited. This compressed social network reduces athletes' interactions with those most likely to react negatively toward their athletic participation. Such avoidance limits disruption in the pursuit of athletic goals (Elliott *et al.* 1990). Although the reason for self-segregation is not exclusively stigma management (e.g., some indicated they relate better to other athletes or that time prohibits developing friendships outside of sport), the comfortable, nonthreatening environment other athletes provide may enhance the prevalence of self-segregation. As one athlete indicated, those outside the women's sport community most commonly initiate the lesbian labeling.

Self-segregation, however, is not without its complications. As Adler and Adler (1987) suggest, self-segregation often isolates athletes both socially and culturally from the university student body. The protective environment of self-segregation is offset by the sometimes narrow and limited athletic subculture.

Since self-segregation is not always practical, women athletes also conceal their athletic identity by *passing*. As information management, passing involves controlling the disclosure of discrediting information about oneself to conceal the stigma entirely (Elliott *et al.* 1990). Several women described techniques they (or other athletes) use so others will not know they are athletes. For example, some simply withhold information about their athletic status in conversations with outsiders. Alternatively, one individual stated athletes sometimes "over-talk" the lesbian topic to disassociate the label from themselves.

Other athletes relied on what Goffman (1963) terms *disidentifiers* to separate themselves from things most stereotypical associated with lesbianism. For example, to contradict the masculine image identified with lesbianism, athletes sometimes consciously accentuated their femininity by wearing dresses, skirts, makeup, and earrings or by letting their hair grow. Others indicated that being seen with men or having a boyfriend is a common technique to reaffirm their heterosexuality. In a few instances this need to identify with men fosters more extreme behaviors including "hanging on men" in public or establishing a reputation as promiscuous with men. Some women athletes take care not to constantly be seen in public with groups of women; others were cautious about the nature of physical contact publicly displayed with women. In all cases, the athlete's presentation of self is consciously monitored or altered to conform to appropriate gender roles.

Although effective in controlling information, passing behaviors and disidentifiers can negatively affect individuals' psychological well-being, as well as alienate them from their personal identities (Goffman 1963). Goffman's work suggests that athletes who engage in passing may experience feelings of disloyalty and self-contempt as they disassociate themselves not only from their athletic identities but from qualities representing their personal essence.

In another form of disidentification, some athletes distanced themselves from athletes more seriously "contaminated" or stigmatized. This mechanism is accomplished through techniques such as making "rude comments" about a suspected lesbian team-mate, establishing team cliques on the basis of sexual orientation, and being "very critical and mean" to lesbian team-mates behind their backs.

Since the lesbian label is not equally applied to all athletes or teams, association with "certain" athletes increases the chance of stigmatization. In response to the question why women athletes are labeled lesbian, athletes identified three categories—appearance, personality characteristics, and nature of the sport activity.

Relative to appearance or externally identifiable characteristics, factors such as dress, hair style, body build, body posture/carriage, muscularity, and mannerisms were mentioned as underlying usage of the labels "dyke," "butch," or "lesbian." Athletes with personality characteristics such as being assertive, outgoing, strong, independent, aggressive, and hard-nosed are most likely to be labeled lesbian.

Regarding the nature of the sport activity, participants in team sports such as softball, basketball, and field hockey are more often recipients of the lesbian label. When asked why team sports are a more likely target, athletes indicated that such activities require more athleticism and strength, involve more physical contact, and are more commonly viewed as sports played by men. These qualities associated with team sports reflect traits socially defined as masculine (Bern 1974). Stigmatization of these team sports may discourage women from both engaging in "masculine sports" and participating in activities with potential to develop cooperation, teamwork, and solidarity among women (Lenskyj 1986). Self-distancing from those more seriously "contaminated," although effective for controlling information, may at the same time prevent women athletes from bonding together as a collective.

In a few instances athletes disassociate themselves from the lesbian label by publicly making fun of lesbian athletes or criticizing homosexuality. This disparaging behavior frequently occurs in the course of conversations with "outsiders" when the topic of women athletes is discussed. As Goffman (1963) suggests, a discreditable individual often finds it dangerous to refrain from joining in the vilification of one's own group. Such a strategy may protect the social identity of the individual athlete but impede the development and maintenance of the collective identity of women athletes.

When concealment is not possible, a stigmatized individual may adopt other stigma management strategies. Included are salience reduction through deflection and direct confrontation through normalization (Elliott *et al.* 1990).

Deflection. Individuals may use deflection to reduce the importance or salience of a discrediting attribute. Representing the original source of stigmatization, the athlete's role is publicly downplayed by athletes. Not only do women athletes use disidentifiers to distance themselves from this role, but they attempt to accentuate the significance of nonsport roles and attributes. It is thus important to many to be viewed as more than an athlete; efforts to demonstrate mastery in other areas (e.g., student role, social role) are common. For example, several athletes mentioned they want to do well in the classroom so that others will not identify them exclusively as athletes. Moreover, some athletes highlighted their social role by mentioning dating and party activities.

Normalization. In some situations it is difficult to reduce the visibility of the discrediting attribute (i.e., athletic status) when it is salient and relevant. This difficulty is particularly true of athletes who are visible on campus or the focus of media and where athletic status frequently impacts on the dynamics of social interaction. Rather than conceal or deflect, the individual has no choice but to directly confront the stigma. The ideal outcome for the athlete is a state of normalization where the discrediting attribute loses its stigmatizing capability. To accomplish normalization, strategies attempt to

redefine the stigma and re-educate "normals" (Elliott *et al.* 1990). Although not widespread, redefinition efforts generally emphasize the positive characteristics or contributions of female athletes while re-education consists of athletes informing outsiders that lesbianism is not prevalent in women's sport or that sexual preference should be a non-issue.

Even though most respondents thought the lesbian label is unfairly applied to women athletes, attempts at normalization are difficult given their assumed violation of multiple gender norms. Although some athletes indicated the label did not bother them and that people could "think what they wanted," little evidence existed to suggest that the discrediting attribute of lesbian has lost its stigmatizing capability. Efforts to redefine or reeducate are generally futile since the vast majority of women athletes do not directly confront these labels, preferring to engage in other stigma coping strategies.

This refusal to confront the lesbian label resembles what Elliott and colleagues (1990) term capitulation. Even if false or inaccurate, the lesbian label assumes a master status for the individual (Becker 1963; Schur 1979) and becomes central to her identity and interactions. The stigmatized accept both the stereotypes placed upon them and the accompanying stigmatization. Athletes were generally not proactive in fighting the stereotypes; resistance to these stereotypes and labels usually emerges after a direct confrontation or challenge from an outsider. For example, one respondent stated "I am not an activist," while another indicated she "would not bring up the topic unless something negative was said."

Acceptance of the normative definition of deviance is often true of socially marginalized groups as they (1) rely on others for self-definition, (2) engage in self-hate, and (3) identify with the aggressor (Kitzinger 1987; Nobles 1973; Sarnoff 1951; Thomas 1971). Interestingly, several remarks from respondents demonstrate that women athletes accept and internalize societal stereotypes about themselves and incorporate these images into their identity accounts and personal interactions. For example, internalization of societal beliefs about appearance norms was evident in such comments as "I don't look like an athlete so I rarely am labeled a lesbian" and "I've never seen somebody that looks like a girl called a dyke or lesbian." One athlete dismissed lesbianism as a problem on her team since her "teammates were pretty." This same athlete implied, however, that lesbianism might be more prevalent on other teams since "most of the athletes on these teams looked like guys."

Self-hate was occasionally noted in responses as well. Although generally indicating the lesbian label angers them, athletes also mentioned that it makes them feel "unattractive" and "less desirable to men" and leads some to "always worry about how I look." Identification with aggressors was also evident in that some nonlesbian athletes engage in negative conversations that criticize or mock lesbian athletes.

Nevertheless, the presence of the deviant label does not necessarily garner negative outcomes (Elliott *et al.* 1990; Goffman 1963). As a few athletes' responses indicated, being labeled lesbian makes them stronger individuals and less dependent on what outsiders think of them. For example, learning to cope with the lesbian label helped one athlete "find confidence" in herself and encouraged another to learn more about homosexuality through reading and coursework. Moreover, some athletes claimed exposure to the issue of homosexuality makes them less judgmental and more accepting/respectful of dissimilar others.

Women athletes thus utilize a variety of stigma management techniques to control and manage information about their athleticism. This effort is somewhat paradoxical since most respondents were generally proud to be athletes and viewed their athletic experience as positive. The prevailing negative societal linkage of female athleticism with masculinity and lesbianism often overrides positive self-definitions of their athleticism.

Conclusion

[...]

The role of labeling is undeniably central to understanding the experiences of women athletes forced to resort to stigma management strategies in the absence of deviant behavior. Female athletes acquire the deviant label because more powerful groups impose their definition of morality on the athletic act (Erikson 1962; Kitsuse 1962). Critical in this labeling are the stigma-laden meanings female athleticism evokes and the processes by which these ideas

are perceived and applied. Such meanings are relayed to women, reminding them of "their place" in the gender system (Henley and Freeman 1979).

Overall lack of power confounds the ability of women athletes to actively challenge deviant labels. Not only do women in general lack power, but the discrediting attributes of athlete and lesbian diminish the power position of women athletes even further. Generally lacking organizational backing and viewed as outsiders, women athletes, rather than actively challenge the stigma, rely on stigma management. This passivity not only has negative social and psychological outcomes for the athlete, but enhances the overall power of the label itself. Since athletes resort to actions where silence and denial are central and internalization of deviant labels is frequent, the likelihood of resistance to these labels is significantly reduced.

References

Adler, Peter, and Patricia A. Adler. 1987. "Role Conflict and Identity Salience: College Athletics and the Academic Role." *Social Science Journal* 24: 443–455.

Anderson, Margaret L. 1988. *Thinking About Women; Sociological Perspectives on Sex and Gender.* 2nd ed. New York: Macmillan.

Becker, Howard S. 1963. *Outsiders: Studies in the Sociology of Deviance.* New York; Free Press.

Bern, Sandra L. 1974. "The Measurement of Psychological Androgyny." *Journal of Consulting and Clinical Psychology* 42: 155–162.

Birenbaum, Arnold. 1970. "On Managing a Courtesy Stigma." *Journal of Health and Social Behavior* 11: 196–206.

Blinde, Elaine M. 1987. "Contrasting Models of Sport and the Intercollegiate Sport Experience of Female Athletes." Ph.D. dissertation, Department of Physical Education, University of Illinois, Urbana-Champaign.

Bogdan, Robert C., and Sari Knopp Biklen. 1982. *Qualitative Research for Education.* Boston: Allyn and Bacon.

Colker, Ruth, and Cathy S. Widom. 1980. "Correlates of Female Athletic Participation: Masculinity, Femininity, Self-Esteem, and Attitudes Toward Women." *Sex Roles* 6: 47–58.

Elliott, Gregory C., Herbert L. Ziegler, Barbara M. Altrman, and Deborah R. Scott. 1990. "Understanding Stigma: Dimensions of Deviance and Coping." pp. 423–443 in *Deviant Behavior,* edited by Clifton D. Bryant. New York: Hemisphere.

Erikson, Kai T. 1962. "Notes on the Sociology of Deviance." *Social Problems* 9: 307–314.

Goffman, Erving. 1963. *Stigma: Notes on the Management of Spoiled Identity.* Englewood Cliffs, NJ: Prentice Hall.

Goodman, Bernice. 1977. *The Lesbian: A Celebration of Difference.* New York: Out and Out Books.

Griffin, Patricia S. 1987. "Homophobia, Lesbians, and Women's Sports: An Exploratory Analysis." Paper presented at the annual meetings of the American Psychological Association, New York.

Hall, M. Ann. 1988. "The Discourse of Gender and Sport: From Femininity to Feminism." *Sociology of Sport Journal* 5: 330–340.

Henley, Nancy, and Jo Freeman. 1979. "The Sexual Politics of Interpersonal Behavior." Pp. 391–401 in *Women: A Feminist Perspective,* edited by Jo Freeman. Palo Alto: Mayfield.

Keller, Evelyn F. 1978. "Gender and Science." *Psychoanalysis and Contemporary Thought* 1: 409–433.

Kitsuse, John I. 1962. "Societal Reaction to Deviant Behavior: Problems of Theory and Method." *Social Problems* 9: 247–256.

Kitzinger, Celia. 1987. *The Social Construction of Lesbianism.* London: Sage.

Klemke, Lloyd W., and Gary H. Tiedeman. 1990. "Toward an Understanding of False Accusation: The Pure Case of Deviant Labeling." Pp. 266–286 in *Deviant Behavior,* edited by Clifton D. Bryant. New York; Hemisphere.

Lemert, Edwin M. 1972. *Human Deviance, Social Problems, and Social Control,* 2nd ed. Englewood Cliffs, NJ: Prentice Hall.

Lenskyj, Helen. 1986. *Out of Bounds: Women, Sport and Sexuality.* Toronto: Women's Press.

——. 1991. "Combating Homophobia in Sport and Physical Education." *Sociology of Sport Journal* 8: 61–69.

Nobles, Wade W. 1973. "Psychological Research and the Black Seif-Concept: A Critical Review." *Journal of Social Issues* 29: 11–31.

Pollak, Otto. 1952. "The Errors of Justice." *The Annals of the American Academy of Political and Social Science* 284: 115–123.

Sarnoff, Irving. 1951. "Identification with the Aggressor: Some Personality Correlates of Anti-Semitism Among Jews." *Journal of Personality* 20: 199–218.

Scheff, Thomas J. 1964. "The Societal Reaction to Deviance: Ascriptive Elements in the Psychiatric Screening of Mental Patients in a Midwestern State." *Social Problems* 11: 401–413.

Schur, Edwin M. 1979. *Interpreting Deviance: A Sociological Introduction.* New York: Harper and Row.

——. 1984. *Labeling Women Deviant: Gender, Stigma, and Social Control.* New York: Random House.

Smith, Dorothy E. 1978. "A Peculiar Eclipsing: Women's Exclusion from Man's Culture." *Women's Studies International Quarterly* 1: 281–295.

Theberge, Nancy. 1985. "Toward a Feminist Alternative to Sport as a Male Preserve." *Quest* 37: 193–202.

Thomas. Charles W. 1971. *Boys No More.* Beverly Hills: Glencoe.

Willis, Paul. 1982. "Women in Sport in Ideology." Pp. 117–135 in *Sport, Culture and Ideology,* edited by Jennifer Hargreaves. London: Routledge & Kegan Paul.

Wolfe, Susan J. 1988. "The Rhetoric of Heterosexism." Pp. 199–224 in *Gender and Discourse: The Power of Talk,* vol. 30, edited by Alexandra Dundas Todd and Sue Fisher, Norwood, NJ: Ablex.

6.3

From the "muscle moll" to the "butch" ballplayer

Mannishness, lesbianism, and homophobia in US women's sport

Susan K. Cahn

Stigmatization of lesbian athletes, as a mechanism of social control, sometimes had unintended consequences. In this sweeping historical account, Susan Cahn discusses the experiences of mid-twentieth century lesbian athletes in coping with demeaning stereotypes, which paradoxically had the effect of attracting these women to sports and strengthening the lesbian subculture.

In 1934, *Literary Digest* subtitled an article on women's sports, "Will the Playing Fields One Day Be Ruled by Amazons?" The author, Fred Wittner, answered the question affirmatively and concluded that as an "inevitable consequence" of sport's masculinizing effect, "girls trained in physical education today may find it more difficult to attract the most worthy fathers for their children."[1] The image of women athletes as mannish, failed heterosexuals represents a thinly veiled reference to lesbianism in sport. At times, the homosexual allusion has been indisputable, as in a journalist's description of the great athlete Babe Didrikson as a "Sapphic, Broddingnagian woman" or in television comedian Arsenio Hall's more recent witticism, "If we can put a man on the moon, why can't we get one on Martina Navratilova?"[2] More frequently, however, popular commentary on lesbians in sport has taken the form of indirect references, surfacing through denials and refutations rather than open acknowledgment. When in 1955 an *Ebony* magazine article on African American track stars insisted that "off track, girls are entirely feminine. Most of

them like boys, dances, club affairs," the reporter answered the implicit but unspoken charge that athletes, especially Black women in a "manly" sport, were masculine manhaters, or lesbians.[3]

The figure of the mannish lesbian athlete has acted as a powerful but unarticulated "bogey woman" of sport, forming a silent foil for more positive corrective images that attempt to rehabilitate the image of women athletes and resolve the cultural contradiction between athletic prowess and femininity. As a stereotyped figure in U.S. society, the lesbian athlete forms part of everyday cultural knowledge. Yet historians have paid scant attention to the connection between female sexuality and sport.[4] This essay explores the historical relationship between lesbianism and sport by tracing the development of the stereotyped "mannish lesbian athlete" and examining its relation to the lived experience of mid-twentieth-century lesbian athletes.

I argue that fears of mannish female sexuality in sport initially centered on the prospect of unbridled heterosexual desire. By the 1930s, however, female athletic mannishness began to

Susan K. Cahn, "From the Muscle Moll to the Butch Ballplayer: Mannishness, Lesbianism, and Homophobia in US Women's Sport" from *Feminist Studies* 19.2 (Summer 1993): 343–368. Reprinted by permission of the publisher, Feminist Studies, Inc.

connote heterosexual failure, usually couched in terms of unattractiveness to men, but also suggesting the possible absence of heterosexual interest. In the years following World War II, the stereotype of the lesbian athlete emerged full blown. The extreme homophobia and the gender conservatism of the postwar era created a context in which longstanding linkages among mannishness, female homosexuality, and athletics cohered around the figure of the mannish lesbian athlete. Paradoxically, the association between masculinity, lesbianism, and sport had a positive outcome for some women. The very cultural matrix that produced the pejorative image also created possibilities for lesbian affirmation. Sport provided social and psychic space for some lesbians to validate themselves and to build a collective culture. Thus, the lesbian athlete was not only a figure of discourse but a living product of women's sexual struggle and cultural innovation.

Amazons, muscle molls, and the question of sexual (im)mortality

The athletic woman sparked interest and controversy in the early decades of the twentieth century. In the United States and other Western societies, sport functioned as a male preserve, an all-male domain in which men not only played games together but also demonstrated and affirmed their manhood.[5] The "maleness" of sport derived from a gender ideology which labeled aggression, physicality, competitive spirit, and athletic skill as masculine attributes necessary for achieving true manliness. This notion found unquestioned support in the dualistic, polarized concepts of gender which prevailed in Victorian America. However, by the turn of the century, women had begun to challenge Victorian gender arrangements, breaking down barriers to female participation in previously male arenas of public work, politics, and urban nightlife. Some of these "New Women" sought entry into the world of athletics as well. On college campuses students enjoyed a wide range of intramural sports through newly formed Women's Athletic Associations. Off-campus women took up games like golf, tennis, basketball, swimming, and occasionally even wrestling, car racing, or boxing. As challengers to one of the defining

arenas of manhood, skilled female athletes became symbols of the broader march of womanhood out of the Victorian domestic sphere into once prohibited male realms.

The woman athlete represented both the appealing and threatening aspects of modern womanhood. In a positive light, she captured the exuberant spirit, physical vigor, and brazenness of the New Woman. The University of Minnesota student newspaper proclaimed in 1904 that the athletic girl was the "truest type of All-American coed."[6] Several years later, *Harper's Bazaar* labeled the unsportive girl as "not strictly up to date," and *Good Housekeeping* noted that the "tomboy" had come to symbolize "a new type of American girl, new not only physically, but mentally and morally."[7]

Yet, women athletes invoked condemnation as often as praise. Critics ranged from physicians and physical educators to sportswriters, male athletic officials, and casual observers. In their view, strenuous athletic pursuits endangered women and threatened the stability of society. They maintained that women athletes would become manlike, adopting masculine dress, talk, and mannerisms. In addition, they contended, too much exercise would damage female reproductive capacity. And worse yet, the excitement of sport would cause women to lose control, conjuring up images of frenzied, distraught co-eds on the verge of moral, physical, and emotional breakdown. These fears collapsed into an all-encompassing concept of "mannishness," a term signifying female masculinity.

The public debate over the merits of women's athletic participation remained lively throughout the 1910s and 1920s. Implicit in the dispute over "mannishness" was a long-standing disagreement over the effect of women's athletic activities on their sexuality. Controversy centered around two issues—damage to female reproductive capacity and the unleashing of heterosexual passion. Medical experts and exercise specialists disagreed among themselves about the effects of athletic activity on women's reproductive cycles and organs. Some claimed that athletic training interfered with menstruation and caused reproductive organs to harden or atrophy; others insisted that rigorous exercise endowed women with strength and energy which would make them more fit for bearing and rearing children. Similarly, experts vehemently debated whether competition unleashed nonprocreative, erotic desires identified with male sexuality and unrespectable women, or, conversely, whether invigorating sport enhanced a woman's feminine charm and sexual appeal. channeling sexual energy into wholesome activity.

Conflicting opinion on sexual matters followed closely along the lines of a larger dispute which divided the world of women's sport into warring camps. Beginning in the 1910s, female physical educators and male sport promoters squared off in a decades-long struggle over the appropriate nature of female competition and the right to govern women's athletics. The conflict was a complicated one, involving competing class and gender interests played out in organizational as well as philosophical battles. It was extremely important in shaping women's sports for more than fifty years. Although historians of sport have examined the broad parameters of the conflict, they have paid less attention to the competing sexual perspectives advanced by each side.[8]

Physical educators took a cautious approach on all matters of sexuality, one designed to safeguard vulnerable young athletes and to secure their own professional status as respectable women in the male-dominated worlds of academia and sport. Heeding dire warnings about menstrual dysfunction, sterility, and inferior offspring, educators created policies to curtail strenuous competition and prohibit play during menstruation. They worried equally about the impact of sport on sexual morality. Alleging that competition would induce "powerful impulses" leading girls into a "temptation to excess" and the "pitfall of overindulgence," educators and their allies pressured popular sport promoters to reduce the competitive stimulation, publicity, and physical strain thought to endanger the sexuality of their female charges.[9]

Popular sport organizations like the Amateur Athletic Union agreed that unregulated female competition posed physiological and moral dangers. But AAU officials countered protectionist physical education policies with a nationalist, eugenic stance which argued that strenuous activity under proper guidance would actually strengthen reproductive organs, creating a vigorous cadre of mothers to produce a generation of stalwart American sons.[10] Although making some concessions to demands for modesty and female supervision, in the long run AAU leaders and commercial sport promoters also

rejected educators' emphasis on sexual control. Sponsors of popular sport found that sexual hype, much more than caution, helped to attract customers and mute charges of mannishness. In working-class settings and in more elite sports like swimming, an ideal of the "athlete as beauty queen" emerged. Efforts to present the female athlete as sexually attractive and available mirrored the playful, erotic sensibility present in the broader commercial leisure culture of the early twentieth century.[11]

The class and gender lines in this dispute were complicated by overlapping constituencies. Female educators adhered closely to middle-class, even Victorian, notions of respectability and modesty. But their influence spread beyond elite private and middle-class schools into working-class public schools and industrial recreation programs. And male promoters, often themselves of the middle-class, continued to control some school sport and, outside the schools, influenced both working-class and elite sports. Moreover, Black physical educators advanced a third point of view. Although few in number, early-twentieth-century African American physical education instructors generally aligned themselves with popular promoters in favor of competition and interscholastic sports. Yet their strong concern with maintaining respectability created some sympathy for the positions advanced by white leaders of women's physical education.[12]

On all sides of the debate, however, the controversy about sport and female sexuality presumed heterosexuality. Neither critics nor supporters suggested that "masculine" athleticism might indicate or induce same-sex love. When experts warned of the amazonian athlete's possible sexual transgressions, they linked the physical release of sport with a loss of heterosexual *control*, not *inclination*. The most frequently used derogatory term for women athletes was "Muscle Moll." In its only other usages, the word "moll" referred to either the female lovers of male gangsters or to prostitutes. Both represented disreputable, heterosexually deviant womanhood.

By contrast, medical studies of sexual "deviance" from the late nineteenth and early twentieth centuries quite clearly linked "mannishness" to lesbianism, and in at least two cases explicitly connected female homosexuality with boyish athleticism.[13] It is curious then that in answering charges against the mannish Muscle

Moll, educators and sport promoters of this period did not refer to or deny lesbianism. However, the "mannish lesbian" made little sense in the heterosocial milieu of popular sports. Promoters encouraged mixed audiences for women's athletic events, often combining them with men's games, postgame dances and musical entertainment, or even beauty contests. The image of the athlete as beauty queen and the commercial atmosphere that characterized much of working-class sport ensured that the sexual debate surrounding the modern female athlete would focus on her heterosexual charm, daring, or disrepute. The homosocial environment of women's physical education left educators more vulnerable to insinuations that their profession was populated by "mannish" types who preferred the love of women. However, the feminine respectability and decorum cultivated by the profession provided an initial shield from associations with either the mannish lesbian or her more familiar counterpart, the heterosexual Muscle Moll.

The muscle moll as heterosexual failure: emerging lesbian stereotypes

In the 1930s, however, the heterosexual understanding of the mannish "amazon" began to give way to a new interpretation which educators and promoters could not long ignore. To the familiar charge that female athletes resembled men, critics added the newer accusation that sport-induced mannishness disqualified them as candidates for heterosexual romance. In 1930, an *American Mercury* medical reporter decried the decline of romantic love, pinning the blame on women who entered sport, business, and politics. He claimed that such women "act like men, talk like men, and think like men." The author explained that "women have come closer and closer to men's level," and, consequently, "the purple allure of distance has vamoosed."[14] Four years later, the *Ladies Home Journal* printed a "Manual on the More or Less Subtle Art of Getting a Man" which listed vitality, gaiety, vivacity, and good sportsmanship–qualities typically associated with women athletes and formerly linked to the athletic flapper's heterosexual appeal-as "the very qualities that are likely to make him consider anything but

marriage."[15] Although the charges didn't exclusively focus on athletes, they implied that female athleticism was contrary to heterosexual appeal, which appeared to rest on women's difference from and deference to men.

The concern with heterosexual appeal reflected broader sexual transformations in U.S. society. Historians of sexuality have examined the multiple forces which reshaped gender and sexual relations in the first few decades of the twentieth century. Victorian sexual codes crumbled under pressure from an assertive, boldly sexual working-class youth culture, a women's movement which defied prohibitions against public female activism, and the growth of a new pleasure-oriented consumer economy. In the wake of these changes, modern ideals of womanhood embraced an overtly erotic heterosexual sensibility. At the same time, medical fascination with sexual "deviance" created a growing awareness of lesbianism, now understood as a form of congenital or psychological pathology. The medicalization of homosexuality in combination with an antifeminist backlash in the 1920s against female autonomy and power contributed to a more fully articulated taboo against lesbianism. The modern heterosexual woman stood in stark opposition to her threatening sexual counterpart, the "mannish" lesbian.[16]

By the late 1920s and early 1930s, with a modern lesbian taboo and an eroticized definition of heterosexual femininity in place, the assertive, muscular female competitor roused increasing suspicion. It was at this moment that both subtle and direct references to the lesbian athlete emerged in physical education and popular sport. Uncensored discussions of intimate female companionship and harmless athletic "crushes" disappear from the record, pushed underground by the increasingly hostile tone of public discourse about female sexuality and athleticism. Fueled by the gender antagonisms and anxieties of the Depression, the public began scrutinizing women athletes—known for their appropriation of masculine games and styles—for signs of deviance.

Where earlier references to "amazons" had signaled heterosexual ardor, journalists now used the term to mean unattractive, failed heterosexuals. Occasionally, the media made direct mention of athletes' presumed lesbian tendencies. A 1933 *Redbook* article, for example, casually mentioned that track and golf star Babe Didrikson liked men just to horse around

269

with her and not "make love," adding that Babe's fondness for her best girlfriends far surpassed her affection for any man.[17] The direct reference was unusual; the lesbian connotation of mannishness was forged primarily through indirect links of association. The preponderance of evidence appears in public exchanges between opponents and advocates of women's sport.

After two decades of celebrating the female collegiate athlete, yearbooks at co-ed colleges began to ridicule physical education majors and Women's Athletic Association (WAA) members, portraying them as hefty, disheveled, and ugly. A 1937 Minnesota yearbook sarcastically titled its presentation on the WAA "Over in No Man's Land."[18] Finding themselves cast as unattractive prudes or mannish misfits, physical educators struggled to revise their image. They declared the muscle-bound, manhating athlete a relic of the past, supplanted by "lovely, feminine charming girls" whose fitness, suppleness, and grace merely made them "more beautiful on the dance floor that evening."[19]

Similar exchanges appeared in popular magazines. After *Literary Digest* published Fred Wittner's assertion that "worthy fathers" would not find trained women athletes attractive mates, AAU official Ada Taylor Sackett issued a rebuttal which reassured readers that because athletic muscles resembled "those of women who dance all night," women in sport could no doubt "still attract a worthy mate."[20] When critics maligned athletic femininity, they suggested that athletes were literally un-becoming women: unattractive females who abdicated their womanhood and fell under sexual suspicion. When defenders responded with ardent assertions that women athletes did indeed exhibit interest in men, marriage, and motherhood, it suggested that they understood "mannish" to mean "not-heterosexual."

The butch ballplayer: midcentury stereotypes of the lesbian athlete

Tentatively voiced in the 1930s, these accusations became harsher and more explicit under the impact of wartime changes in gender and sexuality and the subsequent panic over the "homosexual menace." In a post-World War II climate markedly hostile to nontraditional women and lesbians, women in physical education and

in working-class popular sports became convenient targets of homophobic indictment.

World War II opened up significant economic and social possibilities for gay men and women. Embryonic prewar homosexual subcultures blossomed during the war and spread across the midcentury urban landscape. Bars, nightclubs, public cruising spots, and informal social networks facilitated the development of gay and lesbian enclaves. But the permissive atmosphere did not survive the war's end. Waving the banner of Cold War political and social conservatism, government leaders acted at the federal, state, and local levels to purge gays and lesbians from government and military posts, to initiate legal investigations and prosecutions of gay individuals and institutions, and to encourage local police crackdowns on gay bars and street life. The perceived need to safeguard national security and to reestablish social order in the wake of wartime disruption sparked a "homosexual panic" which promoted the fear, loathing, and persecution of homosexuals.[21]

Lesbians suffered condemnation for their violation of gender as well as sexual codes. The tremendous emphasis on family, domesticity, and "traditional" femininity in the late 1940s and 1950s reflected postwar anxieties about the reconsolidation of a gender order shaken by two decades of depression and war. As symbols of women's refusal to conform, lesbians endured intense scrutiny by experts who regularly focused on their subjects' presumed masculinity. Sexologists attributed lesbianism to masculine tendencies and freedoms encouraged by the war, linking it to a general collapsing of gender distinctions which, in their view, destabilized marital and family relations.[21]

Lesbians remained shadowy figures to most Americans, but women athletes—noted for their masculine bodies, interests, and attributes—were visible representatives of the gender inversion often associated with homosexuality. Physical education majors, formerly accused of being unappealing to men, were increasingly charged with being uninterested in them as well. The 1952 University of Minnesota yearbook snidely reported: "Believe it or not, members of the Women's Athletic Association are normal" and found conclusive evidence in the fact that "at least one ... of WAA's 300 members is engaged."[23] And in 1956, a newspaper account of the University of Texas Sports Association (UTSA) women's sports banquet led off with the head-line, "UTSA Gives Awards," followed by a sub-heading "Gayness Necessary." The second headline referred to a guest speaker's talk on positive attitudes, entitled "The Importance of Being Debonair," but the lesbian allusion was unmistakable and I believe fully intentional.[24]

The lesbian stigma began to plague popular athletics too, especially working-class sports noted for their masculine toughness. The pall of suspicion did not completely override older associations with heterosexual deviance. When *Collier's* 1947 article on the Red Heads, a barn-storming women's basketball team, exclaimed "It's basketball—not a strip tease!" the author alluded to both the heterosexual appeal and the hint of disrepute long associated with working-class women athletes.[25] But the dominant postwar voice intimated a different type of dis-repute. Journalists continued to attack the man-nish athlete as ugly and sexually unappealing, implying that this image could only be altered through proof of heterosexual "success."

The career of Babe Didrikson, which spanned the 1920s to the 1950s, illustrates the shift. In the early 1930s the press had ridiculed the tom-boyish track star for her "hatchet face," "door-stop jaw," and "button-breasted" chest. After quitting track, Didrikson dropped out of the national limelight, married professional wrestler George Zaharias in 1938, and then staged a spectacular athletic comeback as a golfer in the late 1940s and 1950s. Fascinated by her per-sonal transformation and then, in the 1950s, moved by her battle with cancer, journalists gave Didrikson's comeback extensive coverage and helped make her a much-loved popular fig-ure. In reflecting on her success, however, sportswriters spent at least as much time on Didrikson's love life as her golf stroke. Headlines blared, "Babe Is a Lady Now: The World's Most Amazing Athlete Has Learned to Wear Nylons and Cook for Her Huge Husband," and reporters gleefully described how "along came a great big he-man wrestler and the Babe forgot all her man-hating chatter."[26]

Postwar sport discourse consistently focused on women's sexual as well as their athletic achievements. As late as 1960, a *New York Times Magazine* headline asked, "Do men make passes at athletic lasses?" Columnist William B. Furlong answered no for most activities, concluding that except for a few "yes" sports like swimming,

women athletes "surrendered" their sex.[27] The challenge for women athletes was not to conquer new athletic feats, which would only further reduce their sexual appeal, but to regain their womanhood through sexual surrender to men.

Media coverage in national magazines and metropolitan newspapers typically focused on the sexual accomplishments of white female athletes, but postwar observers and promoters of African American woman's sport also con-fronted the issue of sexual normalcy. In earlier decades, neither Black nor White commentary on African American athletes expressed a concern with "mannish" lesbianism. The white media generally ignored Black athletes. Implicitly, however, stereotypes of Black females as highly sexual, promiscuous, and unrestrained in their heterosexual passions discouraged the linkage between mannishness and lesbianism. Racist gender ideologies further complicated the meaning of mannishness. Historically, European American racial thought characterized African American women as aggressive, coarse, passion-ate, and physical—the same qualities assigned to manliness and sport.[28] Excluded from domi-nant ideals of womanhood, Black women's suc-cess in sport could be interpreted not as an unnatural deviation but, rather, as the natural result of their reputed closeness to nature, animals, and masculinity.[29]

Within Black communities, strong local sup-port for women's sport may also have weakened the association between sport and lesbianism. Athletes from Tuskegee Institute's national championship track teams of the late 1930s and 1940s described an atmosphere of campuswide enthusiastic support. They noted that although a male student might accuse an athlete of being "funny" if she turned him down for a date, in general lesbianism was not a subject of concern in Black sport circles.[30] Similarly, Gloria Wilson found that she encountered far less uneasiness about lesbianism on her Black semipro softball team in the late 1950s and 1960s than she did in the predominantly white college physical education departments she joined later. She explained that the expectation of heterosexual-ity was ingrained in Black women to the point that "anything outside of that realm is just out of the question." While recalling that her team-mates "had no time or patience for 'funnies,'" Wilson noted that the issue rarely came up, in large part because most team members were married and therefore "didn't have to prove it because then too, their men were always at those games. They were very supportive."[31]

Although Black athletes may have encountered few lesbian stereotypes at the local level, circumstances in the broader society eventually pressed African American sport promoters and journalists to address the issue of mannish sexuality. The strong association of sports with lesbianism developed at the same time as Black athletes became a dominant presence in American sport culture. Midcentury images of sport, Blackness, masculinity, and lesbianism circulated in the same orbit in various combinations. There was no particular correlation between Black women and lesbianism; however, the association of each with mannishness and sexual aggression potentially linked the two. In the late 1950s, Black sport promoters and journalists joined others in taking up the question of sexual "normalcy." One Black newspaper in 1957 described tennis star Althea Gibson as a childhood "tomboy" who "in later life ... finds herself victimized by complexes."[32] The article did not elaborate on the nature of Gibson's "complex," but lesbianism is inferred in the linkage between "tomboys" and psychological illness. [...]

Constant attempts to shore up the heterosexual reputation of athletes can be read as evidence that the longstanding reputation of female athletes as mannish women had become a covert reference to lesbianism. By midcentury, a fundamental reorientation of sexual meanings fused notions of femininity, female eroticism, and heterosexual attractiveness into a single ideal. Mannishness, once primarily a sign of gender crossing, assumed a specifically lesbian-sexual connotation. In the wake of this change, the strong cultural association between sport and masculinity made women's athletics ripe for emerging lesbian stereotypes. This meaning of athletic mannishness raises further questions. What impact did the stereotype have on women's sport? And was the image merely an erroneous stereotype, or did lesbians in fact form a significant presence in sport?

Sport and the heterosexual imperative

The image of the mannish lesbian athlete had a direct effect on women competitors, on

strategies of athletic organizations, and on the overall popularity of women's sport. The lesbian stereotype exerted pressure on athletes to demonstrate their femininity and heterosexuality, viewed as one and the same. Many women adopted an apologetic stance toward their athletic skill. Even as they competed to win, they made sure to display outward signs of femininity in dress and demeanor. They took special care in contact with the media to reveal "feminine" hobbies like cooking and sewing, to mention current boyfriends, and to discuss future marriage plans.[33]

Leaders of women's sport took the same approach at the institutional level. In answer to portrayals of physical education majors and teachers as social rejects and prudes, physical educators revised their philosophy to place heterosexuality at the center of professional objectives. In the late 1930s, they invited psychologists to speak at national professional meetings about problems of sexual adjustment. Such experts described the "types of people who are unadjusted to heterosexual cooperative activity" and warned women in physical education to "develop a prejudice *against* segregation of the sexes."[34] Told that exclusively female environments caused failed heterosexual development, physical educators who had long advocated female separatism in sport were pressed to promote mixed-sex groups and heterosexual "adjustment."

Curricular changes implemented between the mid-1930s and mid-1950s institutionalized the new philosophy. In a paper on postwar objectives, Mildred A. Schaeffer explained that physical education classes should help women "develop an interest in school dances and mixers and a desire to voluntarily attend them."[35] To this end, administrators revised coursework to emphasize beauty and social charm over rigorous exercise and health. They exchanged old rationales of fitness and fun for promises of trimmer waistlines, slimmer hips, and prettier complexions. At Radcliffe, for example, faculty redesigned health classes to include "advice on dress, carriage, hair, skin, voice, or any factor that would tend to improve personal appearance and thus contribute to social and economic success."[36] Intramural programs replaced interclass basketball tournaments and weekend campouts for women with mixed-sex "co-recreational" activities like bowling, volleyball, and "fun nights" of ping-pong and shuffleboard. Some departments also added co-educational classes to foster "broader, keener, more sympathetic understanding of the opposite sex."[37] Department heads cracked down on "mannish" students and faculty, issuing warnings against "casual styles" which might "lead us back into some dangerous channels."[38] They implemented dress codes which forbade slacks and men's shirts or socks, adding as well a ban on "boyish hair cuts" and unshaven legs.[39]

Popular sport promoters adopted similar tactics. Marshalling sexual data like they were athletic statistics, a 1954 AAU poll sought to sway a skeptical public with numerical proof of heterosexuality—the fact that 91 percent of former female athletes surveyed had married.[40] Publicity for the midwestern All-American Girls Baseball League included statistics on the number of married players in the league. In the same vein, the women's golf tour announced that one-third of the pros were married, and the rest were keeping an eye peeled for prospects who might "lure them from the circuit to the altar."[41]

The fear of lesbianism was greatest where a sport had a particularly masculine image and where promoters needed to attract a paying audience. Professional and semipro basketball and softball fit the bill on both accounts. Athletic leaders tried to resolve the problem by "proving" the attractive femininity of athletes. Softball and basketball tournaments continued to feature beauty pageants. Although in earlier times such events celebrated the "sexiness" of the emancipated modern woman, in later decades they seemed to serve a more defensive function. The AAU's magazine, the *Amateur Athlete*, made sure that at least one photograph of the national basketball tournament's beauty "queen and her court" accompanied the photo of each year's championship team. Behind the scenes, teams passed dress and conduct codes. For example, the All-American Girls Baseball League prohibited players from wearing men's clothing or getting "severe" haircuts.[42] That this was an attempt to secure the heterosexual image of athletes was made even clearer when league officials announced that AAGBL policy prohibited the recruitment of "freaks" and "Amazons."[43]

In the end, the strategic emphasis on heterosexuality and the suppression of "mannishness" did little to alter the image of women in sport.

The stereotype of the mannish lesbian athlete grew out of the persistent commonsense equation of sport with masculinity. Opponents of women's sport reinforced this belief when they denigrated women's athletic efforts and ridiculed skilled athletes as "grotesque," "mannish," or "unnatural." Leaders of women's sport unwittingly contributed to the same set of ideas when they began to orient their programs around the new feminine heterosexual ideal. As physical education policies and media campaigns worked to suppress lesbianism and marginalize athletes who didn't conform to dominant standards of femininity, sport officials embedded heterosexism into the institutional and ideological framework of sport. The effect extended beyond sport to the wider culture, where the figure of the mannish lesbian athlete announced that competitiveness, strength, independence, aggression, and physical intimacy among women fell outside the bounds of womanhood. As a symbol of female deviance, she served as a powerful reminder to all women to tow [sic] the line of heterosexuality and femininity or risk falling into a despised category of mannish (not-women) women.

Beyond the stereotype: "mannish" athletes and lesbian subculture

Changes in American sexual practices, politics, and beliefs help account for the emerging lesbian stereotype and its impact. However, that explanation alone fails to consider lesbian agency. Was the mannish lesbian athlete merely a figure of homophobic imagination, or was there in fact a strong lesbian presence in sport? When the All-American Girls Baseball League adamantly specified, "*Always appear in feminine attire ...* MASCULINE HAIR STYLING? SHOES? COATS? SHIRTS? SOCKS, T-SHIRTS ARE BARRED AT ALL TIMES," and when physical education departments threatened to expel students for overly masculine appearance, were administrators merely responding to external pressure?[44] Or were they cracking down on women who may have indeed enjoyed the feel and look of a tough swagger, a short haircut, and men's clothing? And if so, did mannishness among athletes correspond to lesbianism, as the stereotype suggested? In spite of the public stigmatization, some women may have found the activities, attributes, and emotions of sport con-ducive to lesbian self-expression and commu-nity formation.

As part of a larger investigation of women's athletic experience, I conducted oral histories with women who played competitive amateur, semiprofessional, and professional sports between 1930 and 1970. The interviews included only six openly lesbian narrators and thirty-six other women who either declared their heterosexuality or left their identity unstated.[45] Although the sample is too small to stand as a representative study, the interviews offered a rich source of information about popular sexual theories, the association of lesbianism with sport, and lesbian experience in sport. The oral histories and scat-tered other sources indicate that sport, particu-larly softball, provided an important site for the development of lesbian subculture and identity in the United States.[46] Gay and straight infor-mants alike confirmed the lesbian presence in popular sport and physical education. Their tes-timony suggests that from at least the 1940s on, sport provided space for lesbian activity and social networks and served as a path into lesbian culture for young lesbians coming out and searching for companions and community.

Lesbian athletes explained that sport had been integral to their search for sexual identity and lesbian companionship. Ann Maguire, a softball player, physical education major, and top amateur bowler from New England, recalled that as a teenager in the late 1950s,

> I had been trying to figure out who I was and couldn't put a name to it. I mean it was very— no gay groups, no literature, no characters on "Dynasty"—I mean there was just nothing at that time. And trying to put a name to it. ... I went to a bowling tournament, met two women there [and] for some reason something clicked and it clicked in a way that I was not totally aware of.

She introduced herself to the women, who later invited her to a gay bar. Maguire described her experience at age seventeen:

> I was being served and I was totally fascinated by the fact that, oh god, here I am being served and I'm not twenty-one. And it didn't occur to me until after a while when I relaxed and started realizing that I was at a gay bar. I just became fascinated. ... And I was back there the

next night. ... I really felt a sense of knowing who I was and feeling very happy. Very happy that I had been able to through some miracle put this into place.[47]

Loraine Sumner, a physical education teacher who for several decades also played, coached, and refereed sports in the Boston area, recalled: "We didn't have anybody to talk to. We figured it out for ourselves you know." In sport she found others like herself, estimating that as many as 75 percent of the women she played with were lesbian. In such a setting Sumner put a name to her own feelings and found others to support her: "There was a lot of bonding, there's a lot of unity. You've got that closeness."[48] For these women, sport provided a point of entry into lesbian culture.

The question arises of whether lesbians sim-ply congregated in athletic settings or whether a sports environment could actually "create" or "produce" lesbians. Some women fit the first scenario, describing how, in their struggle to accept and make sense out of lesbian desire, sport offered a kind of home that put feelings and identities into place. For other women, it appears that the lesbian presence in sport encouraged them to explore or act on feelings that they might not have had or responded to in other settings. Midwestern baseball player Nora Cross remembered that "it was my first expo-sure to gay people. ... I was pursued by the one I was rooming with, that's how I found out." She got involved with her roommate and lived "a gay lifestyle" as long as she stayed in sport. Dorothy Ferguson Key also noticed that sport changed some women, recalling that "there were girls that came in the league like this ... yeah, gay," but that at other times "a girl come in, and I mean they just change. ... When they've been in a year they're completely changed. ... They lived together."[49]

The athletic setting provided public space for lesbian sociability without naming it as such or excluding women who were not lesbians. This environment could facilitate the coming-out process, allowing women who were unsure about or just beginning to explore their sexual identity to socialize with gay and straight women without having to make immediate decisions or declarations. Gradually and primar-ily through unspoken communication, lesbians in sport recognized each other and created social networks. Gloria Wilson, who played softball in a mid-sized mid-western city, described her entry into lesbian social circles as a gradual process in which older lesbians slowly opened up their world to her and she grew more sure of her own identity and place in the group.

> A lot was assumed. And I don't think they felt comfortable with me talking until they knew me better. Then I think more was revealed. And we had little beer gatherings after a game at somebody's house. So then it was even more clear who was doing what when. And then I felt more comfortable too, fitting in, talking about my relationship too—and exploring more of the lesbian lifestyle, I guess.[50]

Like Wilson, other narrators stated that after playing together, lesbian teammates frequently went out to eat and drink or joined each other for parties at private homes. In addition, they recalled that lesbian fans regularly attended softball games and occasionally socialized with athletes over postgame meals and drinks. Outside sources confirm the interview testimony. Lisa Ben, founder of the first known U.S. lesbian magazine *Vice Versa*, moved to wartime Los Angeles thinking she was the only "girl" who preferred to "go out strictly with girls." After meeting some women in her apartment building who admitted to the same desires, she recalled, "Then they took me to a girls' softball game; of course I wasn't the least interested in sports, but it gave me a chance to meet other gay girls."[51] Women's softball provided public space for lesbians to gather when there were few gay bars or other social institutions. Lesbian activist Barbara Grier stated the point succinctly: "It was a place to go where you knew there would be dykes."[52]

Gay narrators also reported encountering lesbians in physical education, but their accounts suggest that the level of professional and personal fear in physical education circles created an intense pressure to conceal and even deny the lesbian presence among faculty and majors. As professionals concerned with propriety and reputation, many lesbian physical educators may have avoided gay bars or other public gatherings, choosing to build more secretive, privatized lesbian networks which protected them against exposure.

In an era when women did not dare announce their lesbianism in public, the social world of popular sport allowed women to find each other as teammates, friends, and lovers. Loraine Sumner explained. "Well it was very nice because you see you developed your friendships. You didn't have to go out looking for women; they were all right there." Among amateur and semipro sports, softball had the most notorious lesbian reputation, but informants noted that other sports offered similar possibilities. They also theorized that both the personal networks and the public validation gained through these sports were especially important for working-class women with limited job and educational opportunities. Sumner recalled her own options as an unmarried, working-class Catholic in Boston: "Back then you either had to go into the convent or you had to get married and that was about it. Nobody ever thought that there was anything else for women back then. So it was—Thank God we had the sports!"[53]

While lesbian narrators underscored the significance of sport in their own lives, many other former athletes concurred that lesbians were indeed recognizably present in sport. A few women remained unaware of lesbians or even the stereotype. But others recalled that although they rarely or never heard lesbianism openly discussed, all but the most naive figured it out. Some kept their comments brief, as in the case of a physical educator and star softball pitcher who curtly replied, "as far as that existing, *affirmative*." Others elaborated, explaining that over time they became aware of women "pairing off," "getting clannish" with each other, or joining others who appeared to be "on the masculine side." A Chicago softball player recalled that gay athletes, "didn't expound that they were, like they do today on television and all over. It was more of a secretive thing." Nevertheless, she concluded that "you'd have to have been pretty naive not to have known. And I was naive, too. But not that naive!"[54]

If athletics provided a public arena and social activity in which lesbians could recognize and affirm each other, what exactly was it that they recognized? This is where the issue of mannishness arises. Women athletes consistently explained the lesbian reputation of sport by reference to the mannishness of some athletes. Nebraska softball player Jessie Steinkuhler suggested that the lesbian image of sportswomen came from the fact that "they tried to act like a man, you know the way they walked, the way they talked and the things they did."[55] Rarely did informants specify whether they were referring to known lesbians or just to "mannish athletes" who might give the impression of lesbianism. The distinction was not marked, indicating a substantial overlap in how the two categories of "deviant" women were perceived.[56]

When narrators did speak specifically of lesbians, they also remarked upon hairstyles. dress, and an overall mannish appearance. Whether from personal contact or hearsay, women who came of age at midcentury had become familiar with lesbian stereotypes and fashions, and they used gender cues to assess and describe sexual identity. All-American league baseball player Dorothy Ferguson Key recalled that "tomboyish girls" who "wanted to go with other girls" signaled their mannishness "in the shoes they bought. You know, it was how they dressed. ... In some way you could just tell they were mannish."[57] Another softball and baseball player echoed Key's claim: "I think that when people were lesbians, or whatever you want to call them, they wanted short haircuts, they wanted to wear pants, they wanted to, you know, *be* like a boy. ... Somebody had a short haircut then, they might as well have had a sign on their back."[58]

These comments could merely indicate the pervasiveness of the masculine reputation of athletes and lesbians. However, lesbian narrators also suggested connections, although more complicated and nuanced, between athletics, lesbianism, and the "mannish or "butchy" style which some lesbians manifested None reported any doubt about their own gender identification as girls and women, but they indicated that they had often felt uncomfortable with the activities and attributes associated with the female gender. They preferred boyish clothes and activities to the conventional styles and manners of femininity. For example, track and softball competitor Audrey Goldberg Hull recalled her attraction to "masculine" dress and style, a preference which she experienced as being related to her sexual attraction to women. As the youngest member of a semi-pro softball team, she met older women whose "masculine" style made her feel she was not alone, even if she could not yet articulate her feelings or make contact with others who shared them. She had no knowledge of these women as lesbians, but described "a subjective idea that yes, these

two women were masculine. They had that definite—the dress. ... Well you know, the more masculine ones, I would think, wouldn't it be nice to know these girls. But I was so much younger. ... Gosh, here 1 am, I'm playing softball with these older nice looking women."[59]

The pejorative image of the masculine lesbian has a long and harmful history. We obviously need to reject the onerous characterization of lesbians as unwomanly females who tend toward manly sexual desires and activities. However, statements like Hull's suggest that it is important to consider how gendered identities, activities, and sensibilities inform sexual identities and experiences. Societies employ gender to organize emotional experience as well as activities and physical traits. Along with Hull, other lesbian narrators confirmed a connection, although a complex one, between sexual identity and gendered structures of feeling. Several spoke of their own attraction to styles deemed masculine by the dominant culture and their relief upon finding athletic comrades who shared this sensibility. Josephine D'Angelo recalled that as a lesbian participating in sport, "you brought your culture with you. You brought your arm swinging ..., the swagger, the way you tilted or cocked your head or whatever. You brought that with you." She explained that this style was acceptable in sports: "First thing you did was to kind of imitate the boys because you know, you're not supposed to throw like a girl." Although her rejection of femininity made her conspicuous in other settings, D'Angelo found that in sport "it was overlooked, see. You weren't different than the other kids. ... Same likeness, people of a kind."[60]

These athletes were clearly women playing women's sports. But in the gender system of U.S. society, the skills, movements, clothing, and competition of sport were laden with impressions of masculinity. Lesbianism too crossed over the bounds of acceptable femininity. Consequently, sport could relocate girls or women with lesbian identities or feelings in an alternative nexus of gender meanings, allowing them to "be themselves"—or to express their gender and sexuality in an unconventional way. This applied to heterosexual women as well, many of whom also described themselves as "tomboys" attracted to boyish games and styles. As an activity that incorporated prescribed "masculine" physical activity into a way of being in the female body, athletics provided a social space and practice for reorganizing conventional meanings of embodied masculinity and femininity. *All* women in sport gained access to activities and expressive styles labeled masculine by the dominant culture. However, because lesbians were excluded from a concept of "real womanhood" defined around heterosexual appeal and desire, sport formed a milieu in which they could redefine womanhood on their own terms.

Moreover, in sport, lesbian athletes found a social practice compatible with midcentury lesbian culture. By the 1940s many lesbians participated in an urban lesbian subculture which articulated sexual identity through gendered butch/femme styles and sexual roles.[61] Although lesbians cultivated a public presence that encompassed elements of masculinity and femininity, in the wider culture it was the "masculine" style that stood out as the sign for lesbianism. The "tough," "boyish," "swaggering" style some athletes adopted resonated with butch styles in the broader lesbian community. It was this sensibility that narrators referred to when they spoke vaguely of "the way they walked, the way they dressed, and the things they did."[62] Athletic lesbians who embraced a "tough" posture, "mannish" dress, and short hair drew upon a visual and emotional vocabulary of masculinity to create a recognizable style and positive female identity. Narrator Loraine Sumner made this point when she described sport as particularly well-suited for lesbian recognition. "Well, I shouldn't say you surmise, but there's something there that you recognize in others that are in the same lifestyle you are. More so than if you saw a woman walking down the street. Some you can tell and some you can't. But in sports I think there's just a way that you can pick it out."[63]

However, the connections among lesbianism, masculinity, and sport require qualification. Many lesbians in and out of sport did not adopt "masculine" markers. And even among those who did, narrators indicated that butch styles did not occlude more traditionally "feminine" qualities of affection and tenderness valued by women athletes. Sport allowed women to combine activities and attributes perceived as masculine with more conventionally feminine qualities of friendship, cooperation, nurturance, and affection. Lesbians particularly benefited

from this gender configuration, finding that in the athletic setting, qualities otherwise viewed as manifestations of homosexual deviance were understood as inherent, positive aspects of sport.[64] Aggressiveness, toughness, passionate intensity, expanded use of motion and space, strength, and competitiveness contributed to athletic excellence. With such qualities defined as athletic attributes rather than psychological abnormalities, the culture of sport permitted lesbians to express the full range of their gendered sensibilities while sidestepping the stigma of psychological deviance. For these reasons, athletics, in the words of Josephine D'Angelo, formed a "comforting" and "comfortable" place.[65]

Yet lesbians found sport hospitable only under certain conditions. Societal hostility toward homosexuality made lesbianism unspeakable in any realm of culture, but the sexual suspicions that surrounded sport made athletics an especially dangerous place in which to speak out. Physical educators and sport officials vigilantly guarded against signs of "mannishness," and teams occasionally expelled women who wore their hair in a "boyish bob" or engaged in obvious lesbian relationships. Consequently, gay athletes avoided naming or verbally acknowledging their sexuality. Loraine Sumner explained that "you never talked about it. ... You never saw anything in public amongst the group of us. But you knew right darn well that this one was going with that one. But yet it just wasn't a topic of conversation. Never."[66] Instead, lesbian athletes signaled their identity through dress, posture, and look, reserving spoken communication for private gatherings among women who were acknowledged and accepted members of concealed communities.

Although in hindsight the underground nature of midcentury lesbian communities may seem extremely repressive, it may also have had a positive side. Unlike the bars where women's very presence declared their status as sexual outlaws, in sport athletes could enjoy the public company of lesbians while retaining their membership in local communities where neighbors, kin, and coworkers respected and sometimes even celebrated their athletic abilities. The unacknowledged, indefinite presence of lesbians in sport may have allowed for a wider range of lesbian experience and identity than is currently acknowledged in most scholarship.

For women who did not identify as lesbian but were sexually drawn to other women, sport provided a venue in which they could express their desires without necessarily having articulated their feelings regarding their sexual identity. It is possible that even as they started "going around" with other women some athletes may have participated in lesbian sexual relationships and friendship networks without ever privately or publicly claiming a lesbian identity. My evidence supports only speculative conclusions but suggests that the culture of sport provided social space for some women to create clearly delineated lesbian identities and communities, at the same time allowing other women to move along the fringes of this world, operating across sexual and community lines without a firmly differentiated lesbian identity.

[...]

The paradox of women's sport history is that the mannish athlete was not only a figure of homophobic discourse but also a human actor engaged in sexual innovation and struggle. Lesbian athletes used the social and psychic space of sport to create a collective culture and affirmative identity. The pride, pleasure, companionship, and dignity lesbians found in the athletic world helped them survive in a hostile society. The challenge posed by their collective existence and their creative reconstruction of womanhood formed a precondition for more overt, political challenges to lesbian oppression which have occured largely outside the realm of sport.

Notes

I would like to thank Birgitte Soland, Maureen Honish, Kath Weston, George Chauncey, Jr., and Nan Enstad for their criticisms, encouragement, and editorial advice on earlier versions of this essay.

1. Fred Wittner, "Shall the ladies Join Us?" *Literary Digest* 117 (19 May 1934): 43.
2. Jim Murray, on impressions of Didrikson as a young woman, from 1970s' column in *Austin American Statesman* (n.d.), Zaharias scrapbook. Barker Texas History Center (hereafter, BTHC), University of Texas, Austin; Arsenio Hall Show, 1988.
3. "Fastest Women in the World," *Ebony* 10 (June 1955): 28.
4. Among the works that do consider the issue of homosexuality are Helen Lenskyj, *Out of Bounds:*

Women, Sport, and Sexuality (Toronto: Women's Press, 1986); Yvonne Zipter, *Diamonds Are a Dyke's Best Friend* (Ithaca, N.Y.: Firebrand Books, 1988); Roberta Bennett, "Sexual Labeling as Social Control: Some Political Effects of Being Female in the Gym," *Perspective* (Fresno, Calif.: Western Society for Physical Education of College Women) 4 (1982): 40–50. On the relationship between male homosexuality and sport, see Brian Pronger, *The Arena of Masculinity: Sport, Homosexuality, and the Meaning of Sex* (New York: St. Martin's Press, 1990).
5. There is a large literature on sport as a male preserve. See J.A. Mangan and Roberta Park, eds., *From "Fair Sex" Feminism: Sport and the Socialization of Women in the Industrial and Post-Industrial Eras* (London: Frank Cass, 1987); Donald J. Mrozek, *Sport and the American Mentality, 1880–1910* (Knoxville: Univesity of Tennessee Press, 1983); Michael S. Kimmel, "The Contemporary 'Crisis' of Masculinity in Historical Perspective," in *The Making of Masculinities: The New Men's Studies*, ed. Harry Brod (Boston: Allen & Unwin, 1987), 137–53; and Eric Dunning, "Sport as a Male Preserve: Notes on the Social Sources of Masculine Identity and Its Transformation," in *Quest for Excitement: Sport and Leisure in the Civilizing Process*, ed. Eric Dunning and Norbert Elias (New York: Basil Blackwell, 1986), 267–83.
6. 1904–5 Scrapbooks of Anne Maude Butner, Butner Papers, University of Minnesota Archives, Minneapolis.
7. Violet W. Mange, "Field Hockey for Women," *Harper's Bazaar* 44 (April 1910): 246; Anna de Koven, "The Athletic Woman," *Good Housekeeping* 55 (August 1912): 150.
8. On the philosophy and policies of women physical educators and their conflict with male sport promoters, see Ellen W. Gerber, "The Controlled Development of Collegiate Sport for Women, 1923–1936," *Journal of Sport History* 2 (Spring 1975): 1–28; Cindy L. Himes, "The Female Athlete in American Society, 1860–1940" (Ph.D. diss., University of Pennsylvania, 1986), chaps. 2–4; and Joan Hult, "The Governance of Athletics for Girls and Women," *Research Quarterly for Exercise and Sport* (April 1985): 64–77.
9. Dudley A. Sargent, "Are Athletics Making Girls Masculine?" *Ladies Home Journal* 29 (March 1913): 71–73; William Inglis, "Exercise for Girls" *Harper's Bazaar* 44 (March 1910): 183; J. Parmley Paret, "Basketball for Young Women," ibid. 33 (October 1900): 1567.
10. See, for example, Bernard MacFadden, "Athletics for Women Will Help Save the Nation," *Amateur Athlete* 4 (February–July 1929): 7; Fred Steers, "Spirit," ibid. (October 1932); 7.

11. On eroticism and early-twentieth-century popular culture, see Kathy Peiss, *Cheap Amusements; Working Women and Leisure in Turn-of-the-Century New York* (Philadelphia: Temple University Press, 1986); Lewis Erenberg, *Steppin' Out: New York Nightlife and the Transformation of American Culture, 1890–1930* (Westport, Conn.: Greenwood Press, 1981); Estelle Freedman and John D'Emilio, *Intimate Matters: A History of Sexuality in America* (New York: Harper & Row, 1988), chaps. 10–12.

12. On Black physical education, see Ruth Arnett, "Girls Need Physical Education," *Chicago Defender*, 10 Dec. 1921; Amelia Roberts, letter to *Chicago Defender*, 12 Mar. 1927, sec. 2, p. 7; Elizabeth Dunham, "Physical Education for Women at Hampton Institute," *Southern Workman* 53 (April 1924): 167; and A.W. Ellis, "The Status of Health and Physical Education for Women in Negro Colleges and Universities," Journal *of Negro Education* 8 (January 1939): 58–63.

13. In his 1883 article, "Case of Sexual Perversion," P. M. Wise described the "peculiar girlhood" of a lesbian who had "preferred masculine sports and labor, had an aversion to attentions from young men and sought the society of her own sex" (*Alienist and Neurologist* 4 [1883]): 88. Sexologist Havelock Ellis commented as well that among lesbians "there is often some capacity for athletics." See Havelock Ellis, *Sexual Inversion*, vol. 2 of *Studies in the Psychology of Sex*, 3d rev. ed. (Philadelphia: F.A. Davis, 1915), 250; Wise and Ellis, quoted in George Chauncey, Jr., "From Sexual Inversion to Homosexuality: Medicine and the Changing Conceptualization of Female Deviance," in *Passion and Power: Sexuality in History,* ed. Kathy Peiss and Christina Simmons (Philadelphia: Temple University Press, 1989), 90, 91. Chauncey argues that sexologists were in the process of separating gender inversion from lesbianism, but his evidence indicates that the phenomena remained linked even as they became more differentiated.

14. George Nathan, "Once There Was a Princess," *American Mercury* 19 (February 1930): 242.

15. A. Moats, "He Hasn't a Chance," *Ladies Home Journal* 51 (December 1934): 12.

16. This is an extremely brief and simplified summary of an extensive literature. For a good synthesis, see Freedman and D'Emilio, chaps. 8–10. On antifeminism and the lesbian threat, see Christina Simmons, "Modern Sexuality and the Myth of Victorian Repression," in *Passion and Power*, 157–77.

17. William Marston, "How Can a Woman Do It?" *Redbook*, September 1933, 60.

18. *Gopher* Yearbook (1937), Univenity of Minnesota Archives.

19. Gertrude Mooney, "The Benefits and Dangers of Athletics for the High School Girl" 1937, Department of Physical Training for Women Records (Health Ed. folder), box 3R251, BTHC; Alice Allene Sefton, "Must Women in Sports Look Beautiful?" *Journal of Health and Physical Education* 8 (October 1937): 481.

20. Wittner, 42; and Ada T. Sackett, "Beauty Survives Sport," *Literary Digest* 117 (19 May 1934): 43.

21. John D'Emilio, *Sexual Politics, Sexual Communities; The Making of a Homosexual Minority in the United State, 1940–1970* {Chicago: University of Chicago Press, 1983), 9–53; Freedman and D'Emilio, chap. 12; and Alan Bérubé, *Coming Out under Fire: The History of Gay Men and Women in World War Two* (New York: Free Press, 1990).

22. On the relation between postwar gender dynamics and studies of the "masculine" lesbian, see Donna Penn, "The Meanings of Lesbianism in Post-War America," *Gender and History* 3 (Summer 1991): 190–203. On postwar gender anxieties and social science, see Wini Breines, "The 1950s: Gender and Some Social Science," *Sociological Inquiry* 56 (Winter 1986): 69–92.

23. *Gopher* Yearbook (1952), 257, University of Minnesota Archives.

24. *Texan*, 10 May 1956, from the *Texan* scrapbook, box 3R212, Department of Physical Training for Women Records, BTHC. Although the term "gay" as a reference to homosexuals occurred only sporadically in the mass media before the 1960s, it was in use as a slang term among some homosexual men and lesbians as early as the 1920s and quite commonly by the 1940s.

25. John Kord Lagemann, "Red Heads You Kill Me!" *Collier's* 119 (8 Feb. 1947): 64.

26. Paul Gallico, *Houston Post*, 22 Mar. 1960; Pete Martin, "Babe Didrikson Takes Off Her Mask," *Saturday Evening Post*, 20 (Sept. 1947): 26–27; *Life*, 23 (June 1947): 90; and Roxy Andersen, "Fashions in Feminine Sport," *Amateur Athlete*, (March 1945): 39.

27. William B. Furlong, "Venus Wasn't a Shotputter," *New York Times Magazine*, 29 Aug. 1960, 14.

28. This ideology has been discussed by many scholars of African American women. See, for example, Paula Giddings, *When and Where I Enter: The Impact of Black Women on Race and Sex in America* (New York: William & Morrow, 1984), chaps. 1, 2, 4; Patricia Hill Collins, *Black Feminist Thought: Knowledge, Consciousness, and the Politics of Empowerment* (Boston: Unwin Hyman, 1990), chaps. 4, 8; Hazel V. Carby, *Reconstructing Womanhood: The Emergence of the Afro-American*

279

Woman Novelist (New York: Oxford University Press, 1987).

29. Elizabeth Lonbeck notes a similar pattern in her discussion of medical theories of the "hypersexual" white female. Because psychiatrists assumed that Black women were naturally "oversexed," when defining the medical condition of hypersexuality, they included only young white working-class women whose sexual ardor struck physicians and social workers as unnaturally excessive. See her, "A New Generation of Women': Progressive Psychiatrists and the Hypersexual Female," *Feminist Studies* 13 (Fall 1987): 513–43.

30. Alice Coachman Davis and Lula Hymes Glenn, interviews with the author, Tuskegee, Alabama, 7 May 1992; Leila Perry Glover, interview with the author, Atlanta, Georgia, 8 May 1992.

31. Gloria Wilson (pseudonym), interview with the author, 11 May 1988.

32. *Baltimore Afro-American,* Magazine Section, 29 June 1957; 1.

33. On the "female apologetic," see Patricia Del Rey, "The Apologetic and Women in Sport," in *Women and Sport,* ed. Carole Oglesby (Philadelphia: Lea & Febiger, 1978), 107–11.

34. National Amateur Athletic Federation-Women's Division, Newsletter, no, 79 (1 June 1938), from Department of Women's Physical Education, University of Wisconsin Archives.

35. Mildred A. Schaeffer, "Desirable Objectives in Post-war Physical Education," *Journal of Health and Physical Education* 16 (October 1945): 446–47.

36. Physical Education Director, Official Reports, Kristin Powell's collected materials on Radcliffe Athletics, Radcliffe College Archives, acc. no. R87.

37. "Coeducational Classes," *Journal of Health, Physical Education, and Recreation* 26 (February 1955): 18. For curricular changes, I examined physical education records at the universities of Wisconsin, Texas, and Minnesota, Radcliffe College, Smith College, Tennessee State University, and Hampton University.

38. Dudley Ashton, "Recruiting Future Teachers," *Journal of Health, Physical Education, and Recreation* 28 (October 1957): 49.

39. The 1949–50 Physical Training Staff Handbook at the University of Texas stated (p. 16), "Legs should be kept shaved." Box 3R213 of Department of Physical Training for Women Records, BTHC. Restrictions on hair and dress are spelled out in the staff minutes and physical education handbooks for majors at the universities of Wisconsin, Texas, and Minnesota.

40. Roxy Andersen, "Statistical Survey of Former Women Athletes," *Amateur Athlete,* September 1954, 10–11.

41. All-American Girls Baseball League (AAGBL) Records, on microfilm at Pennsylvania State University Libiaries; and "Next to Marriage, We'll Take Golf," *Saturday Evening Post,* 23 Jan. 1954, 92.

42. AAGBL 1951 Constitution, AAGBL Records.

43. Morris Markey, "Hey Ma, You're Out!" undated publication reproduced in the 1951 Records of the AAGBL; and "Feminine Sluggers," *People and Places* 8, no. 12 (1952), reproduced in 1952 AAGBL Records.

44. AAGBL 1951 Constitution, AAGBL Records. On physical education rules, see Ashton, 49; and records from universities of Texas, Wisconsin, and Minnesota.

45. The sample included forty-two women, ranging in age from their forties to their seventies, who had played a variety of sports in a range of athletic settings in the West, Midwest, Southeast, and Northeast. The majority were white women from urban working-class and rural backgrounds. Researching lesbian experience, which has been silenced, suppressed, and made invisible, raises many methodological problems. Because the fear of discussing such a sensitive topic made finding openly lesbian narrators extremely difficult, I had to rely on supporting evidence from women who did not claim to be lesbians (although observation and indirect comments led me to believe that many of the narrators are or have been lesbian-identified but chose not to reveal it to a relative stranger in the interview setting). Except when I knew in advance that the narrator was willing to discuss her lesbian experience, I raised the subject by asking about lesbian stereotypes in sport. From there, many narrators went on to tell me what they knew about actual lesbianism as well as stereotypes in sport.

46. On softball, see Zipter. Lillian Faderman also mentions the popularity of lesbian softball teams in the 1950s; see *Odd Girls and Twilight Lovers: A History of Lesbian Life in Twentieth-Century America* (New York: Columbia University Press, 1991), 154, 161–62.

47. Ann Maguire, interview with the author, Boston, 18 Feb. 1988.

48. Loraine Sumner, interview with the author, West Roxbury, Massachusetts, 18 Feb. 1988.

49. Nora Cross (pseudonym), interview with the author, 20 May 1988; Dorothy Ferguson Key, interview with the author, Rockford, Illinois, 19 Dec. 1988.

50. Wilson interview.

51. Lisa Ben, interview in Jonathan Ned Katz, *Gay/Lesbian Almanac* (New York: Harper & Row, 1983), 619.

52. Barbara Grier, quoted in Zipter, 48.

53. Sumner interview.

54. Anonymous. In a few cases I have left quotes unattributed when I believed they might involve more self-disclosure than the narrator intended.

55. Jessie Steinkuhler, interview with the author, Douglas, Nebraska, 10 Oct. 1987.

56. The concept of lesbian masculinity was so deeply entrenched that when asked to explain the lesbian-athlete stereotype narrators uniformly reported that the association between sport and lesbianism derived from the masculine reputation of sport, but none continued the line of thought by stating explicitly that people also thought lesbians were masculine. The masculinity of lesbians was the social "fact" that did not even have to be mentioned for the explanation to make sense.

57. Key interview.

58. Anonymous.

59. Audrey Goldberg Hull, interview with the author, Santa Cruz, California, 18 Nov. 1988.

60. Josephine D'Angelo, interview with the author, Chicago, 21 Dec. 1988.

61. On lesbian culture, see Madeline Davis and Elizabeth Lapovsaky Kennedy, "The Reproduction of Butch-Fem Roles," in *Passion and Power,* 241–56, and "Oral History and the Study of Sexuality in the Lesbian Community: Buffalo, New York, 1940–1960," *Feminist Studies* 12 (Spring 1986): 7–26; Joan Nestle, "Butch-Fem Relationships: Sexual Courage in the 1950s," in Joan Nestle, *A. Restricted Country* (Ithaca, N.Y.: Firebrand Books, 1987), 100–109; and D'Emilio, chaps. 2–3.

62. Steinkuhler interview.

63. Sumner interview.

64. The notion of gay subculture turning stigmatized qualities into valued attributes is discussed by Joseph P. Goodwin in *More Man Than You'll Ever Be! Gay Folklore and Acculturation in Middle America* (Bloomington: Indiana University Press, 1989), 62.

65. D'Angelo interview.

66. Sumner interview.

6.4

Is baseball ready for a gay Jackie Robinson?

Peter Dreier

In this probing selection, Peter Dreier speculates that, by the end of the first decade of the twenty-first century, we are likely to see an openly gay baseball player. What are the barriers? How do they differ from other patterns of exclusion? Will baseball see these barriers disappear once one gay ballplayer comes out? Or, will it be like the WNBA, where Sheryl Swoopes' announcement that she was gay has not ushered in an entirely new ballgame?

Richard Greenberg's *Take Me Out*, which won this year's Tony award for best Broadway play, tells the story of a celebrated New York City baseball hero who announces that he's gay. In reality, no gay major league player has ever publicly acknowledged his homosexuality while still in uniform. How close are we to real life imitating art?

The U.S. Supreme Court's June ruling in *Lawrence v. Texas* is one indication that Americans are increasingly accepting of homosexuals. Out-of-the-closet gays and lesbians have been elected to Congress and are prominent in the entertainment industry, business, journalism, and the clergy. Many big cities and suburbs have openly gay schoolteachers. TV sitcoms have openly gay characters and the *New York Times* now includes same-sex wedding announcements.

Certain spheres of American life, however, have resisted change. The military has infamously clung to its code of "don't ask, don't tell." Professional sports leagues may not enforce such a policy overtly, but in practice its force is equally felt, especially for male athletes.

It is easier for athletes in individual sports—like tennis star Martina Navratilova and diver Greg Louganis—to come out of the closet than players in team sports. According to conventional wisdom, a gay teammate would threaten the macho camaraderie that involves constant butt-slapping and the close physical proximity of the locker room. So while there are no doubt homosexuals currently playing in the National Football League, National Basketball Association, and Major League Baseball, they are deep in the closet.

Three former NFL players have come out after they retired. David Kopay, who hid his homosexuality while playing as an NFL running back for nine years in the '60s and '70s, came out in 1975 and was the first major athlete to do so. Roy Simmons, an offensive guard for the Giants and the Redskins from 1979 to 1983, revealed his sexual orientation during an appearance on *The Phil Donahue Show* in 1992. Esera Tuaolo, a 280-pound defensive lineman who played nine years in the NFL, came out last year, three years after he retired. Revealing his secret on HBO's *Real Sports* and in *ESPN Magazine*, he

Peter Dreier, "Is Baseball Ready for a Gay Jackie Robinson?" from *In These Times* (August 15, 2003). Reprinted by permission.

acknowledged that while playing in the NFL he lived with his partner, with whom he now has two adopted children, but felt compelled to keep it a secret. His teammates routinely told gay jokes in the locker room, he explained. "They made me go further and further into depression, further and further into shame."

Only two gay former major league baseball players, Glenn Burke and Billy Bean (not to be confused with former player and current Oakland A's General Manager Billy Beane), have come out of the closet. Burke, who played for the Dodgers and Oakland A's from 1976 to 1979, came out to family and friends in 1975 but lived in fear that his teammates and managers would discover his sexual orientation.

In his autobiography, *Out at Home*, published posthumously, Burke revealed that the Dodgers' management offered to pay for a luxurious honeymoon if he would agree to a "marriage of convenience" to conceal his homosexuality. When he refused, he was traded to the A's. The A's manager Billy Martin made public statements about not wanting a homosexual in his clubhouse, a clear reference to Burke.

Frustrated, Burke retired and kept his homosexuality secret until he cooperated for a 1982 article in *Inside Sports* magazine. Burke continued to play competitive sports. He won medals in the 100- and 200-meter sprints in the 1982 Gay Games and played basketball in the 1986 Gay Games. Later, Burke struggled with drug abuse, homelessness, and AIDS, from which he eventually died in 1995.

While Bean played for the Tigers, Dodgers, and Padres from 1987 to 1995, he pretended to date women, furtively went to gay bars, and hid his gay lover from teammates and fans. In his recently published memoir, *Going the Other Way*, Bean recounts how Dodgers manager Tommy Lasorda constantly made homophobic jokes, even as Lasorda's gay son was dying from AIDS.

Bean quit when he could no longer stand living a double life. When he came out publicly in 1999, his story made front-page news in the *New York Times*. Like Kopay, since coming out, he has become active in gay rights causes.

In his autobiography, *Behind the Mask*, Dave Pallone—a major league umpire who was quietly fired in 1988 after rumors about his sexual orientation circulated in the baseball world—contends that there are enough gay major league players to create an All Star team. Indeed, because everyone assumes that there are gay ballplayers, the game of trying to identify them sometimes leads to bizarre rumors and denials. Last year, for example, *Details* magazine quoted New York Mets manager Bobby Valentine as saying that professional baseball is "probably ready for an openly gay player," adding, "the players are diverse enough now that I think they could handle it."

Then, *New York Post* gossip columnist Neal Travis speculated that Valentine's comments were a "pre-emptory strike" meant to pave the way for one of his players to come out. "There is a persistent rumor around town," Travis wrote, "that one Mets star who spends a lot of time with pretty models in clubs is actually gay and has started to think about declaring his sexual orientation."

The rumors focused on the Mets' star catcher Mike Piazza, who felt compelled to hold an impromptu press conference. "I'm not gay," Piazza announced. "I'm heterosexual." But he also said he believed that players were ready to accept an openly gay teammate. "In this day and age," Piazza told reporters, "it's irrelevant. I don't think it would be a problem at all."

Perhaps not. But at least one team and one player has to be willing to break the barrier, just as the Brooklyn Dodgers and Jackie Robinson did more the 50 years ago.

The breaking of baseball's color line was not simply an act of individual heroism on Robinson's part. As historian Jules Tygiel recounts in *Baseball's Great Experiment*, it took an interracial protest movement among liberal and progressive activists, as well as the Negro press, who had agitated for years to integrate major league baseball before Dodgers General Manager Branch Rickey signed Robinson to a contract in 1945, then brought him up to the majors two years later.

Rickey, aware of the many great black ballplayers in the Negro Leagues, believed that the integration of baseball would improve the overall level of play. He also believed—correctly, it turned out—that black baseball fans would flock to Ebbets Field to watch black athletes play on the same field as whites.

Robinson did more than integrate major league baseball. The dignity with which he handled his encounters with racism among fellow players and fans—on the diamond as well as in hotels, restaurants, trains, and other public places—drew public attention to the issue, stirred the consciences of many whites, and gave black Americans a tremendous boost of pride, paving the way for the civil rights movement a decade later. Indeed, Martin Luther King once told pitcher Don Newcombe—who along with Roy Campanella followed Robinson from the Negro Leagues to the Brooklyn Dodgers—"You'll never known what you and Jackie and Roy did to make it possible for me to do my job."

Major league sports and the military were two of the first national institutions to be racially integrated, but they are among the last to openly accept gays into their ranks. Some managers, fellow players and sportswriters know the identity of at least a few gay major leaguers, but so far no gay player has been involuntarily outed.

No doubt a few of MLB's gay players have considered coming out publicly while still in uniform. Certainly there are gay players in college or in the minor leagues who fantasize about being the gay Jackie Robinson. But so far they have calculated that the personal or financial costs outweigh the benefits. They fear being ostracized by fellow players, harassed by fans, and perhaps traded—or dropped entirely—by their team's management. There is a strong fundamentalist Christian current within major league baseball, which could make life uncomfortable for the first "out" player. That, in turn, could affect his ability to play to his potential.

And, initially at least, an openly gay player might lose some of his commercial endorsements.

Of course, if several gay ballplayers came out simultaneously, no single player would have to confront the abuse (as well as bask in the cheers) on his own, as Robinson did.

In 1947, Rickey feared that if Robinson turned out to be a bust as a major league player, it would set back the cause of ending baseball apartheid for at least several years. The same may be true today in terms of the first out-of-the-closet ballplayer. A player of All Star stature would make things easier for everyone who followed.

Asked about the likelihood of a gay player coming out of the closet, Philadelphia Phillies manager Larry Bowa told the Associated Press: "If it was me, I'd probably wait until my career was over. I'm sure it would depend on who the player was. If he hits .340, it probably would be easier than if he hits .220."

Baseball executives certainly recognize that there are plenty of gay—or otherwise sympathetic—baseball fans who would spin the turnstiles to cheer for a homosexual player. Lesbians now constitute a significant segment of the audience for women's pro basketball.

In 2001, ESPN conducted a poll, asking: "If a player on your favorite professional sports team announced he or she was gay or lesbian, how would this affect your attitude towards that player?" Only 17 per cent said they would turn against the player, 63 per cent said it would make no difference, and 20 per cent said they would become a bigger fan.

Although baseball no longer has the monopoly on fans' affections that it did in Robinson's day, it still plays a central role in our culture. As Robinson showed, once that barrier is shattered, it will have profound ripple effects, not only in sports but in many aspects of American society.

However it happens, expect to see an openly gay major league baseball player by the end of the first decade of the 21st century.

An off-field obituary

The death of Reggie White

Dave Zirin

NFL legend Reggie White passed away in his sleep at the age of forty-three. The 6-foot, 5-inch, 300-pound "Minister of Defense" was a football immortal. He played in thirteen consecutive pro bowls and retired as the all-time NFL leader in sacks. In 1997, White led the hapless Green Bay Packers to their first Super Bowl victory in more than thirty years. Packers QB Brett Favre said that White was "the best football player I ever played with or against."

White's premature death unleashed a torrent of testimonials about his off-field work as well. He set up countless charities and got his hands dirty in the lives of gang members, drug addicts, and convicts. As former NFL great Cris Carter said, "Reggie made a far greater impact off the field than he did on it."

But there is another side to White that deserves exploration—and certainly more exposure than it has received. White's political ideas spanned the gamut from the noble to the wretched, and were rooted in the best and worst of his deep evangelical Christian faith. Religion is never static, either in its beliefs or uses. Black slaves in the U.S. transformed the religion that was at first imposed upon them into a weapon against oppression, while slave owners used what was ostensibly the same religion to justify their barbarism. "The religion of the slave" and "the religion of the slave owner" are two entirely separate belief systems, even when they use the same book as a reference. One set of beliefs

helped to forge Martin Luther King Jr., a moral giant, and the other helps to sustain the cruel small-mindedness of George W. Bush. Reggie White embodied and voiced both sets of beliefs. And it is wrong to celebrate either his on-field successes or his off-field works of charity without denouncing his homophobic bigotry.

Burn

During the epidemic of Black church burnings that swept the South in 1995, Reggie White brought the issue national attention after one of his own Tennessee parishes was torched. "I think it's time for the country to take this stuff seriously," White told the *Boston Globe*. "It's time to stop sweeping this stuff under the rug because progress in race relations has not been made."

He then stood up to authorities shamefully trying to blame African Americans for torching their own churches. White put the focus squarely on the white supremacist hate groups everyone outside southern law enforcement could see were responsible. "When is America going to stop tolerating these groups?" White asked the *New York Times*.

It is time for us to come together and to fight it. One of the problems is that the people financing and providing the resources for this type of activity are popular people with money who are hiding under the rug. Some of them may be policemen, doctors, lawyers, prominent people who speak out of both sides of their mouths. That makes it difficult to stop but not impossible. Not when we come together as one force against hate.

There was a joy in hearing someone like Reggie White speak the truth and make it plain in his signature raspy voice. When this mountain of a man sifted through the wreckage of his church, shaking with anger, we seethed alongside him. Maybe in another era, White would have embarked on a path of antiracist struggle, fighting the tide of oppression. But in the absence of a mass movement, the ugly side of Reggie White's politics and beliefs found voice. He became a confident and proud voice for an anti-gay agenda, and in the process became a spokesperson for organizations fanning the flames of the very bigotry that gutted his church.

The wheel turns

White's journey began in 1998 when he was invited to address the Wisconsin state legislature. White was expected to speak for roughly five minutes about his charity work. Instead he delivered a rambling hour-long rant in which he said the U.S. had "turned away from God" by allowing "homosexuality—one of the biggest sins—to run rampant." He also said, "People from all different ethnic backgrounds live in this lifestyle. But people from all different ethnic backgrounds also are liars and cheaters and malicious and back-stabbing."

He pointedly rejected the idea of civil rights protections for gays and lesbians (first enacted by the state of Wisconsin), claiming to be "offended" by any comparison between the struggle for gay rights and the Civil Rights movement. Afterwards, White was utterly unapologetic, saying that if anyone found his remarks offensive, "that was their problem."

In the commotion that followed, *CBS Sports* withdrew their contract offer to White to become a pre-game show announcer after his retirement. White and his wife Sara, on the television show *20/20*, blamed this on "sodomites" within and outside the network.

White continued to speak out against gays and lesbians, and in doing so, allied himself with a rogue's gallery of bigots and hatemongers. He hired a "family spokesman" named Bill Horn, president of the vociferously antigay organization "Straight from the Heart Ministries." Soon White was getting support, well wishes, and speaking engagements from the likes of the Reverend Donald Wildmon's American Family Association (AFA), Gary Bauer's Family Research Council, and the Christian Coalition. Unlike Bauer, who resembles a Kermit the Frog Shrinky Dink, White could successfully articulate the "Pro-Family agenda"—equating gays with child molesters and drug addicts—to a Black audience. His Blackness was also a plus for the nearly all-white groups trying to shake accusations that their antigay, "pro-family" agenda had kissing cousins in both racist and white supremacist ideas.

White spoke at one rally in Iowa protesting Governor Tom Vilsack's executive order banning antigay discrimination in state agencies. "Straight from the Heart's" Horn said the order "is a big political payoff to the governor's transvestite and cross-dresser supporters." At the rally, Horn wept as he introduced White to the crowd, saying "Reggie doesn't hate homosexuals; he loves them so much he is going to be honest with them and tell them that what they are doing is destructive." White followed Horn by preaching, "Every black person in America should be offended that a group of people should want the same civil rights because of their sexual orientation." When several gay rights advocates attempted to question the speakers, they were escorted out by force. "They were promoting anger and violence tonight," expelled activist Tina Perry told the *Des Moines Register*. "They slammed anyone who did not agree with their agenda."

According to the Minnesota Family Council, White became someone who "defends the family the same way he defended the goal line." This is a lie. As a player, Reggie White never ran away from a battle and worked to inspire his teammates to greater heights, liberating the Green Bay organization from decades of futility. As a "defender" of family values, he stood for bigoted ideas that keep humanity in chains. He supported the vilification of gays and lesbians instead of bringing people "together as one force against hate," as White himself so eloquently put it as he sorted through the burnt remains of his church.

I will miss Reggie White. He was a force of nature who changed the game with an unholy combination of speed, strength, and smarts. But more than that I will miss seeing if there would have been another chapter in his life down the road, in which he would have devoted his body and soul to standing against the moneyed bigots of this country instead of alongside them.

Section 7

Growth of global community or neo-imperialism?

National cultures and the internationalization of sports

Introduction

Globalization is arguably the most dynamic, far reaching, and unpredictable development in the contemporary world. Though the analytical emphases of scholarly writings about globalization differ, most regard it as the process that increases the levels of economic, technological, political and cultural interdependence among nations and peoples throughout the world. Sports have definitely been drawn into this globalization process—indeed, it could argued that sports are among the vanguard globalizing institutions—which is evidenced by their international expansion in both recruiting players and attracting fans.

Take the example of the San Antonio Spurs, the 2007 National Basketball Association (NBA) champions. Three of its five starting players were non-US citizens, marking the first time in NBA history that the majority of a championship team's starters were foreign born. Also, almost half (five) of the Spurs' twelve man roster were from abroad (Receiveur. 2007. "Foreign Players Help San Antonio Win." http://www. America.gov.st/peopleplace-english/2007/ June/20070619155528btreuv). This reflects a growing trend toward globalization in the NBA, as 20 percent of the league's players, in 2007, were foreign born (85 players from 37 countries)— up from only six foreign players in 1979 (http://www.npa.com/global/nba-host-offseason-070827.html).

Other evidence of the increased globalization of the NBA: it now maintains an international web site; fans from more than 200 countries and territories watched its finals in 46 languages; 128 broadcasters provided coverage of its finals for a world wide audience; the countries where it has scheduled exhibition games, in the summer of 2008, extend literally around the world—from Canada, Spain, France, England, France, and Turkey to the Philippines, South Korea, China, India, and South Africa—all countries where NBA's fan bases are expanding (http://aol.nba.com/global/—June 29, 2008). If its current plan for the next several years goes as anticipated, the league will expand beyond the United States and Canada and add teams based in Europe.

Though its global reach is not as extensive as that of the NBA, major league baseball (MLB) is manifesting a similar trend. Once regarded as the quintessential American sport, inextricably linked to America's national identity, MLB now draws approximately one-third of its players from outside the United States. No doubt a major by-product of this development, it is attracting growing numbers of foreign fans, reflected by its current schedule of pre-season games in such countries as Mexico, Japan, and England (http://www.sportsticketdepot.com/mlb_sport_news_archive-July31-2008.html).

While globalization is beginning to surface in American professional sports, it has already become an established structural reality in professional sports such as soccer in European nations. As one observer has noted, "[E]ver since European clubs loosened restrictions on the number of foreign players, the game has become truly global. African players, in particular, have become ubiquitous on the scene, supplementing the usual presence in soccer of Brazilians and Argentines. Indeed, the foreign presence in soccer surpasses anything that we see in other areas of commerce ... If you put together all the English players on the roster of the four English clubs which recently advanced to the final 16 of the UEFA Champions' League, you would hardly be able to field a single team" (http://ksghome.Harvard.edu/~drodrik/ps—March%2008.doc). The extent to which European professional soccer leagues' player recruitment has been globalized is readily apparent from the percentages of foreign players in various European countries: Italy (30%); France (34%); Spain (38%); Netherlands (39%); Germany (50%); England (59%) (http://Soccer-europe.com/Statistics/Players/Foreign Players.html).

We must make a distinction between the international diffusion of sports (such as soccer, cricket and tennis) and the other dimensions of globalization. The international diffusion of sports, it is important to note, began under colonialism, which was characterized by European political control and economic exploitation of non-western societies. This early diffusion of sports was merely a by-product rather than a major goal of colonial cultural hegemony. There was no consumer market and profit motive driving this diffusion; these sports remained non-commercial, provincial and undeveloped. In contrast, the globalization of sports, following the demise of colonialism and the cold war, has facilitated not only the diffusion of sports but also the international recruitment of players, the international attraction of fans, and the expansion of sports leagues across national boundaries.

Though its current stage of development constitutes a looser social formation, with less clearly defined power relations than colonialism, globalization is characterized by certain distinct social and economic developments that have encouraged the internationalization of sports.

1 widespread immigration
2 new multi-cultural forms of identity
3 weakening national bonds
4 transnational economic and political institutions
5 new global media
6 new patterns of corporate ownership

Documenting the empirical reality of sports globalization is of course far easier than explaining its causes and consequences for both sports and society. Our aim here is to identify some of the analytical issues pertaining to sports globalization that need to be explored.

- First, does the globalization of sports portend the emergence of a more tolerant and cosmopolitan world community or merely a new and more insidious form of western cultural hegemony?
- Second, what impact is globalization having on local sports institutions in poor nations? Is globalization creating a pattern of sports stratification similar to the economic stratification between nations?
- Third, what is the impact of globalization on fan loyalties? Are these loyalties changing? If so, are these changes related to changes in national or local identities?
- Fourth, what is the relationship between sports globalization and new patterns of ownership in sports—such as that of corporate conglomerates like Murdoch's News Corporation—which may use sports as a means to expand the consumer markets for their other business products? To what extent is sports globalization a by-product of corporate marketing strategies?
- Fifth, what is the role of the global media in sports globalization? Is sports globalization feasible without global media? To what extent have global media fundamentally altered the relationship between the sports' teams and their fans' territorial location?
- Sixth, and finally, what are the effects of sports globalization for social and cultural changes in recipient societies, which have been historically isolated from global media and commercial influences? What forms of resistance have these societies mobilized? Where has resistance been most successful? Where has resistance failed?

The articles in this chapter provide insights into these analytical issues as they explore different dimensions of sports globalization. In "Sport and Globalization," Barrie Houlihan attempts to clarify the concept of globalization by drawing a distinction between its meaning as a process and its meaning as an outcome. Through its careful interrogation of the concept and its various applications, this article provides valuable leads for empirical research. Also addressing the meanings of globalization of sport, but from a different angle, Joseph Maguire, in "Theorizing The Global Process," discusses the major sociological theories of globalization and their implications for sports. By highlighting the alternative theoretical lens through which social scientists have viewed the globalization process, Maguire illuminates key issues about how sports have changed in the context of global cultural and economic flows. Rather than focusing on one theory (e.g. cultural imperialism) or one global process (e.g. "Americanization") as the key explanations or source of change, he calls attention to the contexts within which specific theories or processes are most pertinent.

Viewing globalization from a different dimension, Raffaele Poli, in "The Denationalization of Sport," suggests that sports are undergoing denationalizing processes, as evidenced in international flows of players and global mass media across national boundaries. These processes have in turn changed the relationships of State/country/nation to national culture and ethnicity. Presenting many examples of athletes who compete in or for countries to which they have emigrated, Poli suggests that denationalization of sport leads to a de-territorialization of identity (e.g. French fans of San Antonio Spurs,

Chinese fans of the Houston Rockets) and a deethnicization of nations (e.g. Africans playing for German teams, Italians playing for Swedish teams).

Both the article by Kaufman and Patterson and the article by Markovits and Hellerman move onto new terrain as they analyze the social conditions under which a particular sport succeeded or failed to gain acceptance in other societies. In effect, these articles problematize the process of diffusion. In "Cross National Diffusion," Kaufman and Patterson explain why cricket, which was transplanted successfully into India, Pakistan, and the West Indies, failed to become established in the United States and Canada. This article superbly demonstrates the value of a cross national comparative methodology for studying the differential receptivity of societies to particular sports. Similarly taking a comparative approach, Markovits and Hellerman address one of the most intriguing questions in sports: why did soccer fail to gain widespread acceptance in the United States, despite its popularity in much of the world? Moving beyond the easy but erroneous answers to this question, they present an insightful explanation by reference to what they term "American Execptionalism."

Finally, presenting a very different perspective on globalization, Silk and Andrews, in "Beyond the Boundary?", focus on the ways sports have been used by corporate advertising campaigns to draw provincial societies into the nexus of global consumer taste.

7.2

Sport and globalisation

Barrie Houlihan

The meanings of the term globalisation in media and scholarly publications are ambiguous and contradictory. In this article, Barrie Houlihan critically examines the concept of globalisation and its varied applications in order to clarify its analytical implications for sports.

In a humorous guide to revision for chemistry examinations, school students were told 'When in doubt say it's "osmosis". If osmosis is the default explanation of chemical processes, then it has a lot in common with much of the use of the concept of globalisation. Whether the focus of discussion is the spread of Olympic sports, or changes in eating habits, intergenerational relationships, welfare policy or manufacturing work practices, the default explanation is a reference to the often poorly specified concept of globalisation. Globalisation has established itself across the social sciences to the extent that Featherstone and Lash were moved to suggest that globalisation had become the 'central thematic for social theory' (1995: 1). However, paralleling the growing dominance of globalisation as an explanation within the social sciences was a sceptical reaction against the paradigmatic status that the concept seemed to be assuming. Unease focused on the utility of the concept, its descriptive accuracy and its explanatory potential. [...]

The overextension and casual use of the concept will add little to our understanding of global change and its implications for sport.

There are three aspects of the concept of globalisation in the study of sport that require consideration before the concept can be used with confidence. The first is the need to distinguish between different dimensions of globalisation such as the political, economic and cultural, and consider their interrelation and relative significance as well as distinguishing between globalisation as a process and globalisation as an outcome. Second, there is a need to specify how that outcome of globalisation would be recognised and specify the criteria that would have to be fulfilled before we could confidently state that we now live in a globalised world. The third aspect concerns exploring the reach of globalising forces and the response of the 'receiving' nation/community.

Globalisation as a process: dimensions and flows

Political scientists make the important distinction between *democratisation*, which is the process of making progress towards democracy,

---

and *democracy* itself, which is the outcome of the process. There is a need to be aware of a similar distinction between process and outcome when considering globalisation and sport. If we use the term 'globalisation' primarily to refer to the *process* of movement away from a world of discrete nation states and their social systems, cultural patterns, political systems and economies, then there is still the problem of defining the outcome of the process. More will be said about the outcome of globalisation in the next section with the focus in this section remaining on an examination of globalisation as a process.

Scholte (2000) identifies five common uses of the term globalisation, namely as internationalisation, liberalisation, universalisation, Westernisation/Americanisation and deterritorialisation (see Box 7.2.1). Each usage of the term is based on a different balance between economic, political and cultural processes. Some definitions give priority to one process: liberalisation gives clear priority to economic forces whereas universalisation focuses more on the role of culture in globalisation. Other conceptualisations of globalisation, such as Westernisation/Americanisation, reflect a combined emphasis on economic, political and cultural factors.

Because so much of the discussion of sports globalization focuses on sport as an element of culture, it is important to consider, if only briefly, the relative importance of the various dimensions of globalisation. For most Marxists

---

Box 7.2.1. Varieties of globalisation

Globalisation as a process of	Examples from sport
Internationalisation, reflecting greater cross-border exchanges, especially trade, but also people and ideas, between countries	Trade in athletes, an increase in the number of international competition circuits
Liberalisation, whereby government restrictions on cross-border business are removed and to a large extent reflect the efforts of the World Trade Organisation and at a regional level the European Union and the North American Free Trade Area	The impact of the European Union ruling regarding the transfer of players and the number of non-national players that a team may field (Bosman ruling), and also the liberalisation of cross-border, TV media ownership and broadcasting
Universalisation of culture, a synthesis of existing cultures producing a homogeneous cultural experience	The global coverage of the Olympic Games both in terms of the number of countries participating (more countries than are members of the United Nations) and the number of countries receiving television broadcasts, contributing to an increasingly homogeneous sports diet
Westernisation/Americanisation whereby the social structures of modernity, capitalism, rational-bureaucracy, industrialism and representative democracy, are spread throughout the world	Rational-bureaucratic sports structures (written rules, leagues and records of achievement), a scientific approach to talent identification and development, specialisation both on and off the field of play (physiotherapists, psychologists and dieticians, etc.), and commercialisation
Deterritorialisation whereby the spatial organisation of social relations is altered as a result of a dramatic change in our perception of space, location and distance	The development of large fan groups for English and Scottish football teams not just outside the locality but outside the national state boundaries; the live transmission of international sports events

Source: adapted from Scholte, 2000

the answer is fairly clear: economic factors dominate with cultural practices being broadly a reflection of the underlying mode of production. In relation to sport, Marxists would emphasise the comodification of sport and athletes, the domination of sport by powerful media interests which increasingly determine what sport is practised, especially at the elite level, and what sport will reach a global television market. Thus media interests, especially television, and the major international federations (football, cricket, Rugby Union/League and athletics) share a common concern to produce a marketable global product. Sport is no different from any other product in the capitalist economy where markets are carefully managed and where labour is exploited as the primary source of profit. The spectacular wages of footballers such as Figo, Beckham and Veron, detract attention from the more modest wages and short careers of most footballers and the ruthless exploitation of footballing talent of many poorer nations, particularly in Africa (Darby, 2001). Support for this argument comes from the work of Klein (1991), who demonstrated how the United States Major League baseball teams undertook a crude form of asset-stripping of talent in the Dominican Republic. Although a number of players from the Republic became major stars in the United States, most of the talented young players who were exported to the US were abandoned when they did not 'make the grade', However, such was the exodus of talent that the domestic Dominican Republic league was systematically undermined.

For Marxists and others who prioritise economic processes, culture is either a tool for incorporating economies through the manipulation of values and attitudes—cultural imperialism—or it is mere froth and not worthy of serious consideration. Examples of the former include Hamelink, who refers to a process of worldwide 'cultural synchronisation' (1983: 3), and Levitt who refers to the world's preference structure becoming relentlessly homogenised (1983). Scholte summarises the arguments as follows: 'Globalisation introduces a single world culture centred on consumerism, mass media, Americana, and the English language' (2000: 23) and one might add a diet of Olympic sport and Western-defined world championships in sports such as soccer, Formula One, athletics and swimming. Rather more bluntly, Brohm argues that global sport

ideologically reproduces bourgeois social relations ... spreads an organisational ideology specific to the institutions of sport and ... transmits on a huge scale the general themes of the ruling bourgeois ideology like the myth of the superman, individualism, social advancement, success, efficiency etc. (1978: 77).

According to Brohm, the value of sport to capitalism is not just as a source of profit but also as a subtle vehicle for infiltrating capitalist values into a society because awareness of the manipulative capacity of sport is so low.

Priority to the economic dimension draws attention to the commodification of sport, the creation and management of global markets for sports products, and the increasing vertical integration between television media companies and the sports they broadcast. Christian Aid (Brookes and Madden, 1995) provided a powerful indictment of the practices of sports goods companies: They found that the manufacture of sports shoes was located in the lowest labour cost countries where employment conditions, especially for children, were very poor and, perhaps most damning of all, that less than 5 per cent of the final retail price was received by the factory workers in South East Asia (see also Maguire; 1999: Ch. 6; Sage, 1996; Katz, 1994). As regards the role of sports media in furthering the vertical integration within the industry, companies such as BSkyB, Canalt and NTL have all sought to purchase football clubs or at least a shareholding (Brown, 2000), thus enabling them to exercise greater control over their key product.

Events such as the Olympic Games are also examples of the careful development of sports products and more importantly the extent to which even an event as profitable as the Olympics is so heavily dependent on American corporations. Around 60 per cent of all income to the Olympic movement comes from US businesses either in the form of sponsorship (eight of the ten largest sponsors are US based) or in the income generated from the sale of broadcasting rights. It is no wonder that the Games have been awarded to US cities three times in the last 18 years and that a recurring preoccupation for the local organising committee for the Games is how best to schedule events to meet the requirements of US east coast television viewers.

Such is the interconnection between economic power and sport that it should come as no surprise that, with a small number of notable exceptions, the same countries that dominate the world economy also dominate international sport. The G8 countries (USA, UK, France, Germany, Canada, Italy, Russia and Japan) share 65 per cent of world trade with the remaining 200 or so other national economies, accounting for the remaining 35 per cent. As in world trade so in Olympic medals where the same G8 countries dominate, accounting for just under half of all gold medals and 44 per cent of all medals at the Sydney Olympics. The figures would undoubtedly have been closer to the G8 level had it not been for the residual effect of the prominence of sport in the former socialist countries of Central Europe and the continuing high political status of sport in the remaining socialist countries such as China and Cuba. In a study of a range of structural factors that might account for success in Olympic competition, Stamm and Lamprecht (2001) concluded that the structural factors of population size and level of economic development were the primary indicators of Olympic success and were becoming more pronounced.

In the study of the globalisation of sport, economic processes are clearly of central importance. However, this does not mean that culture should be written off as a mere cipher for more significant economic processes. There are a number of students of globalisation who are willing to grant the cultural sphere a substantial degree of autonomy. Hall (1983), for example, arguing from a broadly Marxist position, suggests that despite the clear power of business interests, there is still scope for a reconstruction of everyday practices and a rearticulation of cultural practices, such as in the area of sport. For Hall, capitalist power determines culture in the first, rather than the last, instance. Hannerz (1990) provides a useful attempt to disaggregate dimensions of globalisation and to investigate their interrelationship. He identifies three cultural 'flows', namely: (a) that of cultural commodities which circulate within the marketplace to include sports fashionwear and individual sports or competitions; (b) that which concerns the actions of the state, to include decisions about funding for sport; and (c) that which concerns the 'form of life', which refers to deeply embedded patterns of behaviour,

attitudes and values. What is especially significant about this conceptualisation is, first, that it does not suggest that cultural phenomena are only to be found at the superficial or superstructural level and, second, that in order to ask significant questions about global sport, we need to be able to disaggregate culture and distinguish between levels or depths of embeddedness.

For example, within the realm of social relations, we could ask whether sport globalisation is evident 'merely' at the commodity level or has penetrated to the level of deep structural values and practices. A number of the major European football clubs have extensive worldwide networks of supporters' clubs with their own local fan magazines and club products. While such a phenomenon is evidence of some form of globalisation, we might be tempted to dismiss it as functioning only at the surface of society as a fashion. Like all fashions, it will exhaust itself and be supplanted by a new passion for a different team, sport or other cultural product and remembered in later years with a degree of fond embarrassment. However, if the support for European clubs were to be extended through the emulation of some of the less attractive patterns of fan behaviour such as hooliganism and racism, it might prompt the government to regulate fan behaviour. The intervention of the state would indicate that the degree of cultural change was of a more significant kind. If the growing popularity of football led to the establishment not only of national men's leagues, but also of leagues for women and, more significantly, to a decline in local or regional sports, then we might have evidence of cultural change of a far more profound kind.

Similarly, if we were to focus on the political dimension of culture, we would be rightly sceptical of bestowing too much significance on the attendance of politicians, even from countries with a strong football tradition, at major football matches, as this is likely to be an aspect of the froth of electioneering and cheap populist politics rather than an indication of deeply rooted state commitment. However, if the popularity of football were to prompt the government to reorder its funding properties for sport with the intention of establishing a national professional league or strengthening the chances of the national team qualifying for the World Cup, we would be right to see this as a change of deeper significance. Furthermore, if the state began to undermine the traditional autonomy of sports clubs in order to pursue its policies, then the degree of cultural change would be far more significant. As should now be clear, there is a danger of reading too much significance into the fact that such a high proportion of the world's population watch some part of the Olympic Games or the soccer World Cup. What is more significant is when the state intervenes to manipulate, support or impose emergent cultural trends. More significant still is when there is evidence of changes to long-established sporting traditions or to deeply embedded societal attitudes and values in relation to patterns of social deference, gender roles or intergenerational relations, such as a move closer to the rational-bureaucratic model of sports organisation or an acceptance of women's participation in the same elite competitive sports as men.

There are two conclusions that emerge from the discussion of globalisation as a process. The first is an acknowledgement that the significance of cultural change must be conceptualised in terms of depth of social embeddedness and that we must be wary of granting too much importance to shifts in the popularity of particular teams, sports or events. The second conclusion is that while the political and cultural dimensions have a degree of autonomy from economic processes, it is economic interests that have become much more prominent in sport in the last 25 years as major sports and sports events have become increasingly a focus for private profit rather than state subsidy.

Globalisation as an outcome

In the opening section of this chapter an analogy was drawn between democratisation and democracy on the one hand and globalisation as process and globalisation as outcome on the other. What was not made clear at the time is that while there is a reasonable degree of agreement about what might constitute evidence of democratisation, there is far less agreement about the grounds for declaring that a country qualifies as a democracy. There is disagreement about the criteria for democracy and the relative weight each criterion should be given. It should come as no surprise that there is an equal degree of uncertainty regarding the threshold for a

globalised world and the form that that world would take.

The contemporary complex mix of globalising pressures and their ebb and flow over time make it extremely difficult to predict the precise trajectory of the process of globalisation. From the point of view of sport globalisation, there are at least three fairly clearly observable trajectories of globalisation in visible contemporary sport (see Table 7.2.1). The first is a globalised sporting world where nation and nationality mean little in tems of defining identity, the provision of funding or the regulatory framework within which sport takes place. Sports teams, leagues and events are deterritorialised and no longer defined primarily by national affiliation but structured according to some other principle such as commercial opportunity, religion, sexuality or ideology. Professional road cycling, where multinational teams compete in a global competition circuit, is probably the best example of organisation around a commercial principle, although it is interesting to note the extent to which regional and national communities adopt teams as their own, even though the link with the territory is often tenuous.

The second trajectory of globalisation leads to an outcome which is characterised by a pattern of intense inter *national* sporting competition. In other words the inter *nationalised* sporting world is defined by the volume of competition between athletes, squads and teams drawn from clearly defined nation states and where these international competitions are considered, by regional and national communities, to be more important competitions. Whether Liverpool FC beat Everton FC and whether Liverpool FC win the Premier League would be clearly of less interest to their fans than whether Liverpool FC won the European Champions League. A third possible outcome is best described as multinationalised sport, where the nation is still an important reference point for identity and the state a key source of resources for sports development, but the pattern of sports participation and identification reflects the increasingly "common multiple or nested identities that a growing proportion of the world's population experience, especially in the industrialised countries. In the UK, for example, there has long been a capacity among Rugby Union supporters to support the England team in the Six Nations championships and also the British and

Table 7.2.1. Sport, and the outcomes of globalisation

Characteristic	Globalised sport	Internationalised sport	Multinationalised sport
Nation as the defining unit of international sport and nationality as the defining characteristic of sportsmen and sportswomen	Multinational/ nationally ambiguous teams the norm, as in Formula One motor-racing and professional road cycling	Teams defined by their country of origin, e.g. as in the Olympic Games, and international soccer club competitions	The nation is an important, and perhaps primary, reference point for team/athlete definition. However, athletes/teams will represent their nations, but also other politically defined units whether sub-national (Quebec's participation in the Francophone Games or the participation of Scotland in the World Cup) or supranational (a European team in the World Athletics Championships or the Irish rugby or hockey teams which comprise players from Northern Ireland and the Irish Republic)
Extent of global diversity in sport	Diminishing diversity and/or the overlaying of regionally/nationally distinctive sporting traditions with an increasingly uniform pattern of Olympic and major international team/ individual sports	Maintenance of a vigorous national/ regional sporting culture which exists alongside or takes precedence over Olympic and major international team/ individual sports	Increasing diversity in terms of opportunities for competitions, although there may be a decline in diversity among sports themselves with those without an international stage being especially vulnerable to marginalisation through the adoption by governments of selective funding policies
Extent of state patronage of elite sport	Minimal, sports are either financially self-sufficient or attract commercial patronage	Substantial, most Olympic and major international sports depend on state subsidy	Substantial, although some wariness regarding the allocation of national funds to support supranational teams
Extent to which sports businesses and organisations operate within a national framework of regulation	Self-regulaton by the industry or no regulation	National framework of regulation, e.g. licensing of clubs, coaches, sports venues and television broadcasting or supranational framework of regulation, for example, by the European Union	National regulatory frameworks important but both businesses and sports organisations operate within multiple regulatory frameworks, especially within the European Union
Extent to which international sports federations and the IOC are subject to domestic control	Immune from domestic regulatory and legal systems or in countries where the legal system is 'protective' of corporate/ organisational interests	Subject to legal challenge and regulatory oversight at state level, but also at supranational level	Subject to legal challenge and regulation at both national and supranational levels

Source: Adapted from Hirst and Thompson, 1999

Irish Lions (a team drawn from the four home countries plus Ireland, a foreign country) who compete against Australia and New Zealand. England supporters seem quite able to cheer on the Irishman Keith Wood when he is playing for the Lions a few weeks after he was playing for Ireland against England at Twickenham. Furthermore English football supporters of Irish descent seem quite capable of supporting both England and Ireland in international matches and coping with the split loyalty when the two teams have to play each other.

Split, hybrid, multiple or nested loyalty in sport is not the only dimension of an increasingly fragmented identity. Previous generations in the early and mid-twentieth century inhabited societies, in Western Europe in particular, in which identity was subject to powerful homogenising forces of class, religion and nationality. Since then identity has become more multifaceted with an increasing range of dimensions which now include gender, sexuality, ethnic origin and education, and a fragmentation and decline in significance of traditional homogenising forces. The rapid decline of the industrial working class, the rise of new Christian churches and the import of eastern religions through immigration, and the effect of European Union membership on national identity have all contributed to a much more complex and heterogeneous social fabric which is reflected in sport. When the Conservative Party MP Norman Tebbit questioned the 'Britishness' of Asian immigrants who supported touring Indian or Pakistani cricket teams, he not only failed to appreciate the extent to which the concept of 'Britishness' had changed, but also failed to appreciate the long-established capacity of Britons to manage multiple/nested identities. Norman Tebbit did not apply his 'test' to Scots or Welsh who cheered for their countries when playing football and who, it appears, can cope quite adequately with being both British and Scottish or Welsh without running the risk of becoming the 'lost souls' described by Scholte (2000: 161).

Taking each criterion identified in Table 7.2.1 in turn, the first is the role and significance of the nation as the defining factor or reference point in international sport. The extent to which a nation was ever a clear and unambiguous concept is often exaggerated, but it is undoubtedly the case that the reality underpinning the 'imagined community' of the nation is often both frail and pragmatic. On the one hand governments have frequently been enthusiastic in allowing applications for naturalisation from elite athletes and have, on occasion, actively 'bought' elite athletes from other countries. For example, the South African, Zola Budd, was awarded British citizenship remarkably rapidly so that she could compete for her new country. Fiona May, the British-born long-jumper, was granted Italian nationality and subsequently went on to win a world title in 1995. When May lost her title four years later, she lost it to an athlete, Niurka Montalvo, whose nationality was equally complex. Montalvo originally competed for Cuba but when she took May's title she was a Spaniard. There are also examples of Ethiopian-born athletes competing as naturalised Turks and Sudanese-born athletes competing as naturalised Qataris. Finally, Mohammed Mourhit, previously of Morocco, won bronze in the world 5000 m cross-country event in 2000 in Seville for Belgium and then posed wrapped in a Moroccan flag with his former teammate Salah Hissou.

On the other hand, there are many examples of athletes who have sought to maximise their opportunity to compete at the highest level by changing sporting nationality. Athletes can thus retain legal nationality with one country while adopting the sporting nationality of another by virtue of ancestry or even residence. For example, the Canadian tennis player Greg Rusedski adopted British sporting nationality; many British-born footballers have opted to represent the Republic of Ireland; and at one time there were more non-English-born members of the England cricket team as players from Wales, Zimbabwe, Australia and South Africa joined the squad.

Merged, blurred and ambiguous national identities would be expected in truly globalised sport. By contrast, under conditions of internationalised sport, the nation would be protected as the defining unit of international sport. The status of the nation as an organising concept for sport is intimately linked to the significance of the state with which it has, in the vast majority of cases, a mutually dependent if not symbiotic relationship (see Houlihan, 1997). Under conditions of multinational sport, the state would retain a central role as a reference point for the organisation of international sport and for the identity of athletes, but it would lose a degree of exclusivity. Increasingly, other geo-political reference points would emerge either based on supranational organisations (such as the European Union) or on geography, with the increasing construction of 'continental' teams (e.g. the European team that competes against the USA in golf's Ryder Cup; the presence of a European team, alongside other national and continental teams, in the IAAF Athletics World Championships).

The second characteristic is the extent of sports diversity throughout the world. Maguire (1999) refers to 'diminishing contrasts and increasing varieties' with regard to sport, while Hannerz (1990: 237) identifies a major impact of globalisation as producing the 'organisation of diversity'. An illustration of Maguire's conclusion would be the increase in the variety of running events (new distances, new contexts, or new combination of running with other sports, e.g. triathlon) but the decline or exclusion of events and sports that are more sharply differentiated from the dominant Olympic programme, such as dog-fighting, bear-baiting and bare-knuckle fighting.

Though Maguire's conclusion is a compelling one, the measurement of diversity is problematic; indeed, determining when a variation becomes a contrast is far from easy. Nevertheless, the conclusions of both Maguire and Hannerz suggest that under conditions of globalised sport, one might expect to find that local/regional sporting forms were retreating in the face of a largely European diet of Olympic sports and major commercial sports and the rational-bureaucratic form of organisation with which they are underpinned. At the very least, one would expect to find evidence of a 'third culture' (Featherstone, 1991) which overlays more localised sports cultures. In essence it would be the anational holders of power, such as the international federations and transnational sports businesses, that would provide the direction and momentum for change at the domestic level. By contrast, under conditions of internationalised sport, the dynamics of change in sporting culture would be substantially national. Moreover, while engagement with, and adoption of, non-traditional sports might be common, it would be the result of choice rather than imposition or coercion. Multinationalist sport would result in an increasing diversity of competition opportunities with, for example,

the European Union providing a context for new competitions, but not necessarily any increase in the diversity of sports available at the elite level.

Third, under conditions of globalised sport, one would expect the role of the state as a patron of, and organisational focus for, elite sport to be slight, by comparison with commercial patrons for example. The influence of the state in determining the pattern of engagement with global sport would be minimal. Internationalised sport would be characterised by a key role for the state, which would play a central role in funding and organising elite sport, reflecting a situation where engagement with global sport is determined significantly by nationally set priorities. Under conditions of multinational sport, state patronage would remain important, although supranational state organisations would provide both an additional source of patronage and a further set of constraints on the decision-making freedom of sports governing bodies.

The fourth characteristic refers to the degree to which commercial sports organisations, including professional soccer clubs, broadcasting companies, and event organising bodies, operate within national frameworks regulation. Globalised sport would be typified by minimal regulation or a pattern of self-regulation while under conditions of internationalised sport national or regional (e.g. European Union) systems of licensing, certification and training would create a mosaic of distinctive regulatory systems and consequently of sports practices. The conditions of multi-nationalised sport would be similar to those of internationalised sport, except that there would be clear evidence of dual regulation from the domestic and the supranational levels.

The final characteristic is the degree to which international sports organisations, such as the Commonwealth Games Federation, the IOC and the international federations, are subject to control by the domestic political/administrative/legal system. Under conditions of globalised sport, one would expect these engines of globalisation to be substantially immune from domestic systems of regulation or to be located in countries traditionally protective of corporate interests, such as Switzerland and Monaco. Within an internationalised system, international federations and the IOC would be open to legal challenge and interest group lobbying and enjoy no privileges arising solely from their status as global sports organisations. Multinationalised sport would be characterised, in Europe at least, by dual-level oversight and regulation.

A cursory reflection on the pattern of engagement between sport in the UK and international sport would quickly indicate that it corresponds neatly to none of the three ideal types, but rather exhibits a hybrid profile. The nation clearly remains the primary reference point for sports identity, but paradoxes and ambiguities abound. Chelsea FC still attracts passionate support from over 35,000 fans for each home game as well as from the many thousands who are not able to attend matches. Yet Chelsea regularly field eight or nine non-English players and on one occasion fielded a team that had no English players. Moreover its current and two previous managers have been foreigners. The lack of any depth of association between the team members and England, let alone West London, has done nothing to undermine the intensity of support. In marked contrast to this apparent embrace of cosmopolitanism and globalisation, the proposals to merge Oxford FC with a neighbouring club or to move Wimbledon FC out of London to Milton Keynes was met with passionate parochial opposition. In tennis and boxing there is the strong impression that the British public is more at ease supporting Tim Henman and Frank Bruno than Greg Rusedski and Lennox Lewis. Similarly, in Formula One motor racing the fact that many of the top teams are based in Britain is given little weight if the driver is not British. Thus it appears that for some sports (e.g. football), place is important in affecting the public's sense of identity, while for others (Formula One) it is not; for some sports the nationality of the players does not prevent strong identification while for other sports (e.g. tennis and boxing), nationality, or at least accent, remains important.

In considering the extent of sports diversity in the UK, the role of the state becomes sharply apparent. The Conservative government of John Major reshaped the National Curriculum for physical education to ensure that traditional British sports were embedded in the education system and it initiated the reorientation of elite funding policy to prioritise the major traditional team sports and Olympic sports. Given the relative poverty of most sports governing bodies, the power of state patronage is of considerable if not defining importance. The importance of the state and supranational state organisations in shaping the UK's engagement with globalisation is further emphasised by an examination of the regulatory framework within which sport operates. While at the national level state regulation is still modest, it is undoubtedly growing in areas such as the vetting of coaches who work with children, the licensing of major sports grounds, and the integration of coach training into the national system of vocational qualifications. At the European Union level where a regulaltory culture is more deeply entrenched, the impact on sport has been substantial particularly in relation to the movement of players and the control of sports broadcasting.

If the evidence so far seems to be indicating that the current trajectory of globalisation is toward internationalised or multinationalised sport, the relative immunity of international federations and the IOC from domestic state or supranational state regulation and oversight provides contrary evidence. However, the capacity of the United States to call the IOC to account over the Salt Lake City bribery allegations and the role of countries such as Canada, Australia and the UK along with the European Union in forcing the IOC to agree to an independent anti-doping agency (the World Anti-Doping Agency) both demonstrate the capacity of states to challenge the transnational status of international federations and the Olympic movement.

From the foregoing discussion of the three-fold ideal typology, it should be clear that, as in the discussion of the process of globalisation, the state commands a central position in any discussion of the outcome of globalising processes. Whichever exampes of globalisation are selected, anti-doping efforts, the development of sports broadcasting, the movement of sportsmen and women between clubs and countries, or the response to soccer hooliganism, the state is of central significance in determining the pattern of engagement between national and global sport and is far from the residual institution that is sometimes suggested (see Houlihan, 2003). This is not to argue that the state is a natural adversary of globalisation. Indeed some states, especially those with an ideological commitment to liberal economics, may well be the primary source of momentum for the intensification of flows between the national and the international. Moreover, it is argued that the capacity of the state to adapt to a changing global environment should not be underestimated. Any cursory review of the nature of globalisation in sport will provide ample examples of the close relationship between globalisation and regulation by the state or by international governmental bodies. As Vogel (1996: 2) argues, 'the rhetoric of globalisation ... serves only to obscure what is really going on ... [L]iberalism requires reregulation.'

In summary, it can be argued that sport globalisation as a process has no predetermined outcome. Indeed there are a variety of possible outcomes which would conform to the conventional definitions of globalisation, which stress the more extensive and intensive connections between people and places due to the increasing transnational flow of people, ideas, information, commodities and capital. However, a significant determinant of the trajectory of globalisation in general and sport globalisation in particular is the behaviour of states.

Reach and response

In the wake of the US-led invasion of Afghanistan and the defeat of the Taliban following the 11 September attack on the World Trade Center and the Pentagon, the Western press was keen to produce stories and pictures of the return to 'normal' life within the country. Two stories that received wide coverage were, first, the contact between the Afghan sports authorities and the IOC concerning the future involvement of the country in the Olympic Games and, second, the revival of a local sport (involving a headless goat and teams of horsemen) previously banned by the Taliban. The celebration of local sporting culture and the conscious embrace of global sport is by no means unusual. Many, perhaps most, countries can provide examples of dual sporting cultures sitting comfortably alongside one another. The Irish have various Gaelic sports yet participate enthusiastically in the soccer World Cup and the Olympic Games; Australia has its parochial sport of Australian Rules Football, but is also active across a wide range of Western team and individual sports; and the USA seems unconcerned that few other countries play American football or baseball.

Just at the time when we are coming to terms with the impact of globalisation, there appears to be a contradictory phenomenon emerging, namely that of localisation. If globalisation reflects the power of universalistic socio-cultural flows, then localisation emphasises spatial definition and socio-cultural specificity. This phenomenon is evident in politics, especially in Europe, where the enlargement of the European Union has been paralleled by the creation of 16 new states since 1989. For Rosenau (1994) the relationship between the two processes is described as 'fragmegration aiming to capture, if not very elegantly, the dual processes of fragmentation and integration. Robertson (1995) identified a similar phenomenon which he referred to as 'glocalisation'. For Robertson global culture is contested terrain where 'what is taken to be a worthy direction of societal aspiration—is something which is constructed in the global arena in relation to the constraints upon (most) societies to maintain their own identities and senses of community' (1987: 38). Globalisation involves the reconciliation of a paradox which is the 'particularization of universalism (the rendering of the world as a single place) and the universaiization of particularism (the globalised expectation that societies ... should have distinct identities)' (Robertson, 1989: 9).

The capacity of globalisation to reach into every community is not denied, but what is less clear is the impact of that 'reach'. As mentioned above, for a number of writers, the impact of globalisation on culture is to lead to synchronisation, Americanisation or homogenisation and, as Scholte observes, 'Depending on one's perspective, this homogenisation entails either progressive cosmopolitanism or oppressive imperialism' (2000: 23). However, there is little evidence of a consensus on the impact of globalisation on culture generally or on sports culture in particular. In contrast to those who see only cultural homogeneity and the 'end of the national project' (Brown, 1995), there is an equally strong view that globalisation is not only compatible with continuing cultural heterogeneity but may even stimulate greater heterogeneity.

Underlying much of the discussion of the impact of globalisation is an appreciation that the basis on which national identity is defined has subtly shifted. It has long been accepted that defining national/regional identity is a mutually constitutive process in so far as identity is defined

301

in relation to contrasts with 'foreigners'. More recently, it can be argued that there is a set of globally recognised reference points which are now also important in establishing identity and against which each nation or community has to position itself. These reference points range from the relatively mundane, such as distinctive postage stamps, military uniforms, national flags and anthems, to the more significant such as membership of the World Trade Organisation and the United Nations, participation in UN peacekeeping/ making activities, and attitudes towards global 'principles' of human rights, state sovereignty and internal democracy. One of these reference points is clearly participation in international sport and the Olympic Games in particular. Sport is thus an example of the common paradox of utilising a uniform vehicle for the demonstration of difference.

On one level therefore the reach of globalisation should not he equated with homogeneity, as its 'arrival' may be a welcome opportunity to demonstrate community/national distinctiveness. At another level, the capacity of communities to modify and adapt global culture should not be underestimated. Jensen, in a study of the local response to television news program-mes in a range of countries, noted how 'respondents consistently redefined and reinterpreted the agenda offered by journalists and political actors appearing on the news' and emphasised the extent to which 'the varied local cultures manifest themselves in the interpretation of foreign as well as domestic news. Culture shines through' (Jensen 1998: 194, 195). Hannerz reinforces Jensen's conclusion and observes that peripheral cultures have a clear capacity to absorb 'the influx of meanings and symbolic forms from the centre [and] transform them to make them in some considerable degree their own' (1990: 127). For Hannerz engagement with global culture is an active process according to which cimmunities/groups appropriate selectively global cultural commodities and use them to refine and reform their own distinctive cultural identity.

Hannerz's marketplace model of globalization overemphasizes the element of choice and discretion in peripheral communities but it does have a resonance in developed countries, where engagement with global culture is on more equal terms. Warde (2000) demonstrates the capacity of communities to adapt global culture in his study of eating habits in the UK. He

illustrates a number of responses to non-traditional food, including the domestication of the exotic whereby previously exotic ingredients are incorporated into traditional British dishes and where foreign recipes are modified to suit British taste. These closely related processes can be seen in many British sports in recent years, where sports such as tennis, football, cricket, swimming and hockey have imported 'foreign' training methods and playing strategies. Similarly, the influx of foreign players into the Premier League has required an adaptation on their part to aspects of the traditional English game, such as the pace and aggression.

There are a number of parallel examples to the British experience. In his study of baseball and the relationship between the Dominican Republic and the United States, Klein (1991) argues strongly that the game of baseball has been metamorphosed and that far from simply reflecting American cultural hegemony, it has become a vehicle for demonstrating Dominican excellence. Baseball has been reshaped to infuse it with distinctive Dominican characteristics and qualities, suggesting a clear capacity for a community to import, redefine and re-export a sports cultural product. Similar conclusions were reached by a number of writers in relation to the impact of cricket in the West Indies. James (1963) argued that cricket was significant in establishing a West Indian identity, while St Pierre suggests that cricket 'has been reshaped in sympathy with the cultural ethos of the West Indies [and] has been used as a tool to foster and further nationalist sentiment and racial pride' (1990: 23). For Burton the form of cricket might remain English but it has been 'injected with a new, specifically West Indian content and meaning' (1991: 8). The use of four fast bowlers and the panache and flamboyance of play are considered to be in marked contrast to the English playing norms of seriousness, respectability and moderation.

Just as it was difficult to pin down the particularities of the process of globalisation, so it is equally difficult to be precise regarding the process by which outcomes are determined. Table 7.2.2 suggests a model for investigating the mediation of global culture at the community level (see Houlihan, 1994).

Passivity generally implies an inability to challenge the external culture and would come close to descriptions of cultural imperialism with the

Table 7.2.2. Global reach and local response in sport

Reach of global culture	Response of the local community		
	Passive	Participative	Conflictual
Commodities	Unmediated reception of satellite television sports broadcasts	Gradual widening of participation in major international sports events such as the soccer World Cup and the Olympic Games through the formation/action of non-governmental sports bodies	The manufacturing of high retail value football kit and equipment in low-wage countries
Actions of the state	Ignoring the issue of doping by national athletes	Shifts in public funding to protect/promote particular sports	Olympic boycotts
Deep structure of societal processes	The gradual marginalisation of local sports or their repackaging for global consumption	The arranging of specific sports events for women, e.g. in Iran	Banning of female athletes in Olympic squads in many Islamic countries

relationship between the United States and the Dominican Republic being a good example. By contrast, the development of sport in much of Western Europe and in English settler states such as Canada and Australia suggests not only a deep penetration by external culture, but more significantly, a strongly participative relationship in shaping and mediating external culture through control over media businesses or through influence within international sports bodies such as the IOC. Further examples of participative relationships between the domestic and the external culture include Japan and many of the countries of South East Asia, where the depth of penetration might be lower and where cultural adaptation and reinterpretation are greater. A conflictual response to external sports culture was seen briefly in both Russia and China in the immediate post-revolutionary period and more recently in the 1960s, when a group of mainly Asian states organised GANEFO (Games of the New Emerging Forces) as a challenge to the perceived dominance by Western capitalist and pro-Israeli states of the Olympic movement and the major federations.

Conclusion

There can be no doubting the importance of current debates concerning globalisation in aiding our understanding of a number of key issues in sport, including: the significance of sport in the cultural fabric of a community; the interpenetration of sport with business in general and the international media in particular; and the significance of sport to governments and supranational governmental organisations. Yet, as this chapter has demonstrated, the analysis of globalisation and the consequent refinement of the concept is still in its infancy. As a result there is a need for caution both in the use of the concept and in the conclusions drawn about the nature and consequences of globalising trends.

This chapter has touched on three key debates over the nature of globalisation: globalisation as process; globalisation as outcome; and the reach of globalisation and the response of local communities. In all three of these areas there is a notable lack of consensus which reflects not only the shortage of empirical study, but also the complexity and multifaceted character of the processes under consideration. As regards the process of globalisation, the significance of economic power in sport must be acknowledged, but simply to treat global sport as a cipher for, or a tool of, economic interests is an overextension of the limited evidence available. Moreover, claims that sport is capable of penetrating and altering deeply rooted local cultural practices must also await more substantial evidence. This scepticism is not to deny the possibility that sport may be a leading factor in, for example, bringing about greater equality for women, but rather to suggest that while sport may indeed be in the vanguard of cultural change, it may also be simply a highly visible reflection of change which has originated elsewhere—in the workplace for example.

The discussion of globalisation as an outcome highlighted the importance of treating globalisation as an open-ended set of processes which do not necessarily lead to a fixed destination. Globalisation is a complex and contingent set of processes within which the state plays a key role in shaping their pace, character and trajectory. The state is still the primary reference point for international sport and a central actor in determining the pattern of engagement between domestic sport and international sport. The final discussion concerned the need to appreciate the resilience, dynamism and interpretive capacity of local cultures. The language of sport may be universal but the meaning it carries is as much determined locally as it is in the boardrooms of multinational sports corporations.

References

Bauman, Z. 1999. *Globalization: the Human Consequences.* Cambridge: Polity Press.

Brohm, J.M. 1978. *Sport: A Prison of Measured Time.* London: Pluto Press.

Brookes, B. and Madden, P. 1995. *The Globetrotting Sports Shoe.* London: Christain Aid.

Brown, A. 2000. "Sneaking in through the back door? Media company interests and dual ownership of clubs', in S. Hamil *et al.* (eds), *Football in the Digital Age: Whose Game Is It Anyway?* London: Mainstream Publishing.

Burton, R.D.E. 1991. "Cricket, Carnival and Street Culture in the Caribbean", in *Sport, Racism and Ethnicity.* G. Jarvie (ed.) London: Falmer Press.

Darby, P. 2001. *Africa and Football's Global Order.* London: Frank Cass.

Featherstone, M. 1991. "Global culture: an introduction", in M. Featherstone (ed.), *Global Culture: Nationalism, Globalisation and Modernity,* London: Sage.

Featherstone, M. and Lash, S. 1995. "Globalisation, modernity and the spatialisation of social theory: an introduction", in M. Featherstone, S. Lash and R. Robertson (eds), *Global Modernities.* 10th Anniversary Conference. London: Sage.

Fitch, R. 1996. *The Assassination of New York.* London: Verso.

Hall, S. 1983. "The problem of ideology—Marxism without guarantees", in B. Matthews (ed.), *Marx: A Hundred Years On.* London: Lawrence and Wishart.

Hamelink, C.J. 1983. *Cultural Autonomy in Global Communications: Planning National Information Policy.* London: Longman.

Hannerz, U. 1990. "Cosmopolitans and Locals in World Culture". *Theory, Culture, and Society.* 7: 237–51.

Harvey, D. 1989. *The Condition of Postmodernity.* Oxford: Blackwell.

Hirst, P. and G. Thompson. 1999. *Globalization in Question: The International Economy and the Possibilities of Governance.* Cambridge: Polity Press.

Houlihan, B. 1997. "Sport, National Identity and Public Policy", *Nations and Nationalism,* 3(1): 113–37.

——. 2003. "Sports Globalisation, the State and the Problems of Governance", in T. Slack (ed.) The *Commercialisation of Sport.* London: Frank Cass.

James, C.L.R. 1977. *The Future in the Past.* New York: Lawrence Hill.

Jensen, C.B. 1998. "Conclusion", in C.B. Jensen (ed.), *News of the World.* London: Routledge.

Katz, D. 1994. *Just Do It: the Nike Spirit in the Corporate World.* New York: Random House.

Levitt, T. 1983. *The Marketing Imagination.* London: Collier-Macmillian.

Maguire, J. 1999. *Global Sport: Identities, Societies, Civilizations.* Oxford, England. Polity.

Robertson, R. 1987. "Globalization and Societal Modernization: A Note on Japan and Japanese Religion", *Sociological Analysis,* 47 (Summer): 35–43.

——. 1989. 'Globalization, Politics and Religion', in J.A. Beckford and T. Luckman (eds), *The Changing Face of Religion.* London: Sage, pp. 10–23.

——. 1995. "Globalization: Time-Space and Homogeneity-Heterogeneity", in M. Featherstone, S. Lash and R. Robertson (eds), *Global Modernities.* 10th Anniversary Conference. London: Sage.

Rosenau, J.N. 1994. "New Dimensions of Security: The Interaction of Globalizing and Localizing Dynamics", *Security Dialogue,* 25(3): 255–81.

Sage, G.H. 1996. "Patriotic Images and Capitalist Profit: Contradictions of Professional Team Sports Licensed Merchandise', *Sociology of Sport Journal,* 13: 1–11.

——. 1998. *Power and Ideology in American Sport: A Critical Perspective.* Champaign, Ill.: Human Kinetics.

Scholte, J.A. 2000. *Globalization: A Critical Introduction*. Basingstoke, U.K: Palgrave.

St. Pierre, M. 1990. "West Indian cricket: A cultural contradiction?" *Arena Review*, 14 (1): 13–24.

Stamm, H. and Lamprecht, M. 2001. "Sydney 2000—The Best Games Ever? World Sport and Relationships of Structural Dependency". Paper presented at the First World Congress of Sociology of Sport, Seoul, July.

Vogel, S.K. 1996. *Freer Markets, More Rules: Regulartory Reform in Advanced Industrial Countries*. Ithaca, N.Y.: Cornell University Press.

Wallerstein, I. 1991. "Culture as the Ideological Battleground," in M. Featherstone (ed.), *Modernity*. London: Sage.

Warde, A. 2000. "Eating Globally: Cultural Flows and the Spread of Ethnic Restaurants", in D. Kalb *et al.* (eds), *The Ends of Globalization*: Rowman and Littlefield Publishers.

7.3

Theorizing sport in the global process

Joseph Maguire

In this article, Joseph Maguire discusses the major sociological theories of globalization and illuminates key issues about how sports have changed in the context of global cultural and economic flows.

Let us export our oarsmen, our fencers, our runners into other lands. That is the true free trade of the future; and the day it is introduced into Europe the cause of Peace will have received a new and strong ally.

> Pierre de Coubertin, paper presented at the Union des Sports Athlétiques, Sorbonne, 25 November 1892

That the representatives of cultures communicate, compete, emulate and/or distinguish themselves from others across a range of global networks has seemingly become so much part of the lives of late twentieth-century Westerners that it is viewed as 'second nature' and treated in an unproblematic way. Clearly, the export of the Olympics, that de Coubertin called for, has proved to be so successful that people do not question its history, though George Orwell's comments about international sport being, 'war minus the shooting', should make people more circumspect about whether the Olympics add to global peace and harmony.

[...] Here, I will examine the broad debate concerning globalization processes and then consider how the study of global sport reflects the general issues and questions that characterize this debate. In doing so, a broad review of the existing pool of social scientific knowledge regarding the global sport process will be provided.

Making sense of the globalization debate

Use of the term *globalization* has become, as noted, widespread in academic and media discourse over the past two decades. The meaning and usage of the term has been, however, marked by confusion, misinterpretation and contentious debate. Perhaps because the term diffused so rapidly into 'everyday' use, commentators, politicians and academics have taken fairly rigid positions over its precise meaning. In addition, the term appears to provoke a degree of moral judgement, as if its use, in itself, implies support for or criticism of the existing world order. The following remarks offered by Tony Mason, a historian, are symptomatic of this kind of thinking when applied to the study of sport.

Comparing Brazilian and European soccer, Mason observes:

> In 1994 it could be argued that this footballing dichotomy of styles no longer exists. All teams now play in a similar fashion with teamwork and organization paramount ... Caution is the watchword; the game is not to lose. Perhaps this is an aspect of that globalization or homogenization of the sporting world about which sociologists excitedly chatter ... But if the homogenization theory is true something which made football vital and attractive will have been lost.
>
> (Mason, 1995: pp. 156–7)

In these observations, globalization is unequivocally equated with homogenization and is seen as a 'threat' to some idealized notion of what football was or is. Yet, the local meanings and patterning of sport in general and of football in particular, were influenced by global diffusion processes in quite complex ways. The contrasts between playing styles may have diminished but new varieties of playing formations have emerged. Equally, the perspective offered by sociologists on globalization is, ironically, not as homogeneous as Mason's observations suggest.

Indeed, several traditions have sought to compare and contrast the development of different societies. These traditions include: the modernization perspective, theories of imperialism, dependency theory, world-system theory, hegemony theory and 'globalization' research. [...] My aim is to identify several key issues and themes that characterize the debates, within and between these traditions, regarding globalization. In turn, when consideration is given to the emergence and diffusion of sport cultures, a number of these issues and themes are also evident.

Several key features associated with the term globalization can be detected in the literature. Reference is repeatedly made to the idea that globalization involves some form of greater interdependence between the local and the global.[1] A series of local—global nexuses can be identified. These include: local responses to economic practices; local resistance to ideological processes; local revivals of traditional customs; local celebrations of diversity and local initiatives to combat global pollution. [...] It is clear that every aspect of social reality, our activities, conditions of living, belief systems, knowledge base and responses, is affected by interconnections with other groups, both 'near' and 'far' away. For Anthony Giddens, globalization entails 'the intensification of world-wide social relations which link distinct localities in such a way that local happenings are shaped by events occurring miles and miles away and vice versa' (Giddens, 1990: p. 64).

These interconnections are seen to have deepened and also to have stretched across the globe. The world becomes 'compressed' as the scope and intensity of global interconnectedness has increased. Central in this regard have been the emergence of a world economy, an international nation-state system, a global diffusion of technology and division of labour, and a system of military alliances and treaties (Giddens, 1990: pp. 63–77). Hand in hand with these interconnections, the scale, velocity and volume of globalization processes gathered momentum.

This much is clear. Understood in this light, we can see that a series of interconnections also characterize global sport. Consider the example of basketball. Citizens of countries spread across the globe regularly tune in by satellite broadcasts to National Basketball Association (NBA) games. In these games perform the best male players drawn from North America and Europe. The players use equipment—balls, shoes, uniform, etc.—that is designed in a range of European and North American locations, financed in the USA and assembled in the Pacific Rim. This equipment is then sold on to a mass market across the globe. This equipment, basketball boots for example, is made out of raw materials from 'developing countries', the molecular structure of which was researched and patented, in the case of Nike, in Washington State (USA) and fabricated in Taiwan. Several other transnational corporations are also involved in the production and consumption phases of this global cultural product. The product is itself provided by a global media sport production complex and is viewed on a television that was itself manufactured as part of a global telecommunications network. The beguiling appeal of the slogan 'Just Do It', and of the transnational cultural icon Michael Jordan, hides the stark reality of the global sports industry complex.

Several writers have sought to discern a pattern, or structure, to these interconnections. Appadurai (1990), for example, refers to a series of diverse, fluid and unpredictable global flows.

These 'scapes' include the movement of capital, technologies, people and mediated images. As a consequence of the diverse and unpredictable nature of these movements, a series of 'disjunctures' marks these 'scapes'. Hannerz (1990) also views globalization in terms of 'cultural flows'. These flows include: cultural commodities, the actions of the state in organizing and managing meanings, the dissemination of habitual perspectives and dispositions and the activities of social movements. Though he emphasizes diversity as opposed to uniformity, Hannerz observes that, 'the world has become one network of social relationships, and between its different regions there is a flow of meanings as well as of people and goods' (Hannerz, 1990: p. 237).

The idea that the world 'has become one network' has been taken up by several writers (Giddens, 1990; Robertson, 1992; Wallerstein, 1974). In this connection it is useful to highlight Robertson's notion of a global field. In mapping what he terms the 'global human condition', Robertson stresses four aspects of the global field. These are: nations/societies; individuals or selves; relations between nations/societies; and humankind as a whole. The pattern of this global field stems from the interweaving of these aspects (Robertson, 1992). People have become aware of the global condition, and of the 'finitude and boundedness of the planet and humanity' (Featherstone, 1991a). For Featherstone and Lash, an understanding of this 'global human condition' requires new types of thinking, and for them, 'the global *problematique* represents the *spatialization* of social theory' (1995: p. 1). In this endeavour, sociologists have been joined by geographers who examine the geography of global change, focusing on place, space, 'power geometry' and identity politics; the local/global scales of economic processes and the interconnections between human activities and ecological sustainability (Dickens, 1992; Harvey, 1989; Johnson *et al.*, 1995; Massey, 1994; Yearley, 1996). Some of these concerns, as will be noted later, have also surfaced in the geography of sport (Bale, 1994).

If these are some of the broad themes and issues where a degree of consensus is evident, when it comes to understanding the periodization of globalization, the main dynamics involved, and the impact that such processes have, then what emerges is a sharp division of opinion and position. Let me try to illustrate some of the

tensions and major fault lines that characterize these debates. A series of binary oppositions can be detected. Are globalization processes unidimensional or multidimensional? Are monocausal or multicausal factors the main dynamic of global processes? Do globalization processes lead to a form of 'unity', or perception of 'unity' or of fragmentation? Are globalization processes the intended or the unintended result of intended social actions? Do globalization processes lead to homogenization or heterogenization? At this stage, it is appropriate to examine the claims of the various contributors to these debates.

Making sense of cross-cultural processes: competing traditions

Several traditions of sociological thought have, as noted, sought to examine trans-societal development. The modernization approach, closely linked to functionalism, was the dominant paradigm in this research area until the early 1970s. Essentially concerned with how traditional societies reach modernity, this approach has focused on the political, cultural, economic and social aspects of this process.

Consideration is given to the development of political institutions that support participatory decision-making. The growth and development of secular and nationalist ideologies is also examined. The emergence of a division of labour, the use of management techniques, technological innovations and commercial activities have been the subject of attention. These changes are seen to be accompanied by urbanization and the decline of traditional authorities. The modernization approach also tends to assert that the 'effects' of these trends leads to homogenization. Societies in different parts of the globe 'eventually' follow the Western model of development.[2]

Some or all of these themes have surfaced in 'comparative' studies of sport where a 'critical' approach has failed to take hold (Baker, 1982; Jokl & Simon, 1964; Pooley, 1981; Seppanen, 1970). This, of course, relates to a major criticism that other traditions have of the modernization approach: issues of conflict, exploitation and underdevelopment are ignored (Hettne, 1990). Cultural imperialist analyses have proved more popular in accounts provided by sport historians and sociologists of sport (Klein, 1989; Mangan, 1986). Ironically, though cultural imperialist accounts stress issues of conflict and exploitation, they share an important feature in common with the modernization approach, that is, an emphasis on the alleged homogenizing impact of these processes. Equally, these approaches tend to stress the unidirectional character of these global developments—from the West to the 'rest'—and deploy a mono-causal explanation, technological or economic, to explain these changes.

In cultural imperialism accounts, terms such as 'Westernization' or 'Americanization' are used to capture the homogenizing tendencies said to be involved in cross-cultural processes. Cultural flows are identified with the activities of representatives of nation-states and/or multinational corporations. These activities entail a form of domination of one culture over another. Issues of power, control and the ability of 'indigenous' people to interpret, understand and/or resist cultural manipulation and domination arise in evaluating these types of studies. The idea of the 'invasion' of an indigenous culture by a foreign one is the usual way of understanding the processes involved (Tomlinson, 1991).

Two main emphases in cultural imperialism accounts of global cultural flows can be identified. In one, the focus is placed on a 'world' made up of a collection of nation-states in competition with each other. One manifestation of this is 'Yankee imperialism'. The 'hearts and minds' of foreign people are said to be at stake. Another approach views the 'world' as an integrated political-economic system of global capitalism. Here the focus is on the activities of multi- or transnational corporations. Whether attention focuses on the imperatives of multinational capitalism, or on the spread of a specific nation's 'value-system', an alleged homogenizing trend is identified. While the scale and pace of the process are disputed, the general drift towards the convergence of cultures is accepted.

Studies within this Marxist tradition explain the colonialism of specific nation-states, especially Western nation-states, in terms of the necessity for capitalist expansion. At least three dimensions of these colonial ventures have been noted. These include the search for new markets in which to sell products, the search for new sources of raw materials and the search for new sources of 'cheap' or 'skilled' labour power.

This process is seen to help Western economic development while impoverishing the rest of the world. Large business corporations, as well as state organizations, have played and continue to play a leading role in these developments. While the formal possession of empires has largely disappeared, with the concomitant rise in self-governing countries a form of economic neo-imperialism has developed. Western countries are thus able to maintain their position of ascendancy by ensuring control over the terms upon which world trade is conducted. Ideas of this kind have surfaced, as will be developed shortly, in the literature on sport.

In several respects dependency theory links with neo-imperialist accounts. Dependency theorists argue that the global economy cannot be conceived as a system of equal trading partners and relations (Frank, 1967; Larrain, 1989). The superior military, economic and political power of the 'centre' imposes conditions of unequal exchange on the 'periphery'. Former colonial countries remain dependent on the West. Concerned with the uneven manner and form of global development, advocates of dependency theory also stress the integrated and systematic nature of modern global capitalism. Though the origins and nature of the dependency of specific nations vary according to how far a country was colonized, and by whom, those countries located at the 'periphery' experience unequal access to markets and unequal exchange for their raw materials. These materials include cash crops, such as sugar, or 'human crops', such as athletes.

There are, however, several strands, including dependent underdevelopment, dependent development and dependency reversal, that are evident in this tradition. In the first strand, it is argued that the global capitalist system operates actively to underdevelop the 'third world'. This is done largely, but not exclusively, through multinational corporate activity. The impoverishment of third world countries is the direct result of their subordinate position compared with the industrialized countries. The wealth of the industrialized countries is at the expense of third world countries, the latter being economically dependent on the former. Exponents of this strand argue that no genuine development is possible if this system is in place. Western ownership and control of the major governing bodies, the media sport complex and the sports equipment manufacturing and services nexus ensure that this is also the case in world sport.

Yet, this dependent underdevelopment strand appears unable to account for the growth of some 'third world' countries. Hence, advocates of this approach coined the idea of dependent development. That is, the growth of some third world countries is acknowledged, but this is viewed as limited in nature. Examples include South Korea and Taiwan—both nations which have become bases for the manufacture of sports goods such as tennis racquets and shoes. While dependent development is conceived of as possible, such an approach still does not appear to grasp that certain countries can break out of the 'double bind' of dependent development. In this context, a further revision of the basic approach is evident in which reference is made to dependency reversal. In this approach, it is viewed as possible that certain third world countries, and/or institutional sectors of third world countries, can escape and reverse the previous disadvantageous relations with developed countries. Successful individual or team performances by representatives of third world countries could be considered as evidence of such an 'escape', but these countries remain locked into a structure of world sport controlled by the West. Despite the fruitfulness of the dependency perspective, attention has increasingly been given, if not in the study of sport, then certainly in other fields of social science, to 'world-system theory'.

Associated with the work of Wallerstein (1974), the main theme of world-system theory centres on the historical dynamics of capitalism. The logic of capitalism permeates global processes. Several key elements of this approach can be identified. Dating from the sixteenth century onwards, a 'world system' of commerce and communication has developed. Based on the expansion of a capitalist world economy, this world system has produced a series of economic and political connections. For Wallerstein, the world capitalist economy is orientated around four sectors. The core states dominate and control the exploitation of resources and production. Their wealth derives from their control over manufacturing and agriculture, and is characterized by centralized forms of government. Those states that are linked in various kinds of dependent trading are referred to by Wallerstein as being semi-peripheral to the core. Peripheral states are those that depend on selling cash crops directly to the core states, and are seen as at the outer edge of the world economy. For Wallerstein, however, there were states that were, until colonial expansion, relatively untouched by commercial development. Their dependency, and indeed that of those states at the periphery of the world economy, has been established and maintained by the legacy of colonialism. These nations are enmeshed in a set of economic relations that enrich the industrial areas and impoverish the periphery. The driving force of globalization is seen to be located in the logic of the capitalist world economy. As yet, this latter approach has not been taken up extensively by scholars studying global sports and leisure development. It is not difficult, however, to view the trade of sports talent from 'peripheral' countries to 'core' countries from this perspective. Think of the recruitment of African athletes to American college sport programmes (Bale & Sang, 1996).

This approach alerts us to the extent to which hegemonic powers exploit other nations in their search for new markets to sell sport forms, leisure products, equipment and cultural merchandise. Further, in the context of sports and arts labour migration, the activities of hegemonic states centre on the search for new sources of 'skilled' labour whose early development was resourced by these former colonial countries. From this perspective, the global sports and leisure system can be seen to operate largely but not exclusively through multinationals or organizations dominated by first world nations. This system operates actively to underdevelop the third world by excluding third world countries from the centre of the global political decision-making process and from the economic rewards derived from the world sports/leisure economy.

Indeed, it could be argued that the core states dominate and control the exploitation of resources and production. A deskilling of semi-peripheral and peripheral states occurs on the terms and conditions set by core states. The most talented workers, in which peripheral or semi-peripheral states have invested time and resources, are lured away to the core states whose wealth derives from their control over athletic and artistic labour and the media-sport/ leisure production complex. Non-core states are thus in a position of dependent trading, their athletic or artistic labour being the equivalent of the cash crops that they sell in other sectors of the world economy.

While the existence of these relatively autonomous transnational practices must be recognized, it is also important not to overlook another key feature of the global media-sport complex. In seeking to avoid slipping into a homogenization thesis, the analysis must not overlook how transnational practices are subject to control and manipulation. This can involve the actions of transnational agencies or individuals from the 'transnational capitalist class' (Sklair, 1991). Transnational agencies such as the International Olympic Committee (IOC), the International Amateur Athletic Federation (IAAF), the International Marketing Group (IMG) or International Sport and Leisure (ISL) seek to regulate access to cultural flows. Individuals who belong to the 'transnational capitalist class' (such as, Juan Antonio Samaranch, Primo Nebiolo, Mark McCormack and the late Horst Dassler) are also centrally involved as these are some of the key players whose plans and actions interweave in attempting to develop a global media–sport complex. Such interventions cause cultural struggles of various kinds and at different levels.[3]

Several of these themes, as will be emphasized later, have been fruitfully employed by scholars in sport history and the sociology of sport. Any account of global sport that does not consider the issues of power, exploitation and cultural control that such work highlights would be deficient. Yet, it has also to be noted that there are several problems associated with cultural imperialist and world-system theory accounts. These can best be summarized as several 'sensitizing' questions that need to be asked about these accounts. What constitutes Westernization and/or Americanization? Is it simply a question of the presence of a cultural product from a 'foreign' culture or does it involve a shift in the conscious and subconscious make-up of people? How 'intended' is the process described? How complete does the process have to be for domination to be said to have occurred? What ability have people to understand, embrace and/or resist these processes? What constitutes the 'indigenous/authentic' culture that the foreign culture threatens? The problems associated with a modernization account of convergence have already been noted. Ironically, by emphasizing a unidirectional and monocausal explanation, evident in some cultural imperialism accounts, the contested and contradictory nature of global change is overlooked.

Writers such as Featherstone (1991a), Nederveen Pieterse (1995), Robertson (1990b) and Tomlinson (1991) have concluded that this is a non-productive line of thinking, and have sought to reconceptualize the debate, suggesting that the globalization concept helps reorientate the analysis. Several objections to variants of dependency theory are thus raised by exponents of globalization research. Whereas dependency theories use monocausal explanations, for example Americanization, to explain the global condition, some globalization research emphasizes the need for a multicausal analysis. Globalization research also disputes whether there is a trend towards homogenization. In contrast, Robertson and Featherstone maintain that the unity of nation-states is being dissolved, identity pluralized and partial mixing of global cultures is occurring. Indeed, in some globalization accounts, emphasis is placed on the emergence of global diversity (Nederveen Pieterse, 1995). Citizens of different nations are becoming aware of 'otherness' and recognizing difference. Polyculturalism, not homogenization, is said to be one of the main features of global processes.

A feature that reinforces these processes is the reassertiveness of 'local' identities. Global cultural products are also seen to be actively interpreted and used by those who consume them. From this, some observers have concluded that the dynamics of globalization are powered by an 'infinitely varied mutual contest of sameness and difference' (Appadurai, 1990: p. 308). Globalization is viewed as a far less coherent or culturally directed process and occurs as a result of the complex dynamics of political, economic and cultural practices. These do not, of themselves, aim at global integration, but nonetheless produce it. The effects, then, of globalization are to weaken the cultural coherence of nation-states. This includes those nations who are more powerful within the interdependent world order (Tomlinson, 1991).

In stressing the formation of a global culture, the danger is thus to overstate the case for homogeneity and integration (Featherstone, 1990). This tendency is due to associating the idea of a global culture with the culture of any one nation-state. The tendency towards dichotomous thinking regarding global culture reinforces this weakness. Instead of endlessly arguing about whether homogeneity or heterogeneity, integration or disintegration, unity or diversity are evident, it is more adequate to see these processes as interwoven (Nederveen Pieterse, 1995; Robertson, 1992). Moving the analysis to an examination of what Sklair (1991) describes as transnational practices, the observer is better placed to note that there is something more at work than solely flows between nation-states. Transnational practices, which take a variety of cultural forms, gain a degree of *relative autonomy* on a global level.

Referring to what he terms trans-societal processes, Robertson (1990) maintains that it is these that sustain the exchange and flow of goods, people, information, knowledge and images. By utilizing terms such as *transnational* and *trans-societal*, both Sklair and Robertson are seeking to move beyond the nation-state as the sole reference point for understanding the 'integration' of the world. It is not difficult to conceive how the media-sport production complex is an integral part of this general process. Think of the technological advances involved in the media coverage of the modern Olympics and how satellites now relay powerful images across the globe in an instant. For Real (1989b), these images, however briefly and superficially, reflect and help sustain the emergence of a global culture.

How then to navigate a route round or through these competing explanations? Robertson tries to steer a middle course. Others, as will be noted, seek to move away from a homogeneity thesis altogether. Though Robertson sees globalization as referring, 'in its most general sense, to the process whereby the world becomes a single place' (Robertson, 1992: p. 135), he is also keen to avoid the suggestion that this notion of a 'single place' entails a crystallization of a cohesive system. Yet, he maintains, globalization does involve the development of a global culture. This culture, he argues, is not a homogeneous, binding whole, but refers to a 'general mode of discourse about the world as a whole and its variety' (Robertson, 1992: p. 133). Concerned to trace the way in which the world is ordered, Robertson maps out, as noted earlier, what he refers to as the 'global field'. In tracing the pattern of this global field, Robertson maintains that reference to a single causal process must be avoided. Globalization is not the direct outcome of inter-state processes. Rather, these processes need to be understood as operating relatively independently of conventionally designated societal and socio-cultural processes. He stresses the relative autonomy and 'logic', and the long-term nature of the processes involved. While he refers to the development of a global culture, Robertson also stresses, as noted, that globalization processes do not lead to homogeneity. For Robertson, global processes involve both the particularization of universalism and the universalization of particularism (Robertson, 1992: p. 130). That is, these processes are marked by heterogeneous tendencies and characteristics. In sum, 'globalization is ... best understood as indicating the problem of the form in terms of which the world becomes "united" but by no means integrated' (Robertson, 1992: p. 51).

The process by which people have come to understand the world-system as a whole has a long history. In mapping out the global condition, Robertson identifies five main phases (germinal, incipient, take-off, struggle for hegemony and uncertainty phase) in this long process (Robertson, 1992). Lasting from around the 1870s until the mid-1920s, the third phase involves the process through which the 'increasingly manifest globalizing tendencies of previous periods and places gave way to a single, inexorable form' (Robertson, 1992: p. 59). These globalization processes are evident in several areas: the growth of agencies that straddle the globe; the establishment of global awards and prizes; the emergence of a global ccmmunications system; and the emergence of a standardized notion of human rights. As part of this general framework, Robertson is also keen to explore how standardized notions of 'civilization' emerged during this period. Robertson does not view ethnic reassertiveness as running counter to globalization processes. These processes are not mutually exclusive. Indeed, he suggests that 'the contemporary concern with civilizational and societal (as well as ethnic) uniqueness—as expressed via such motifs as identity, tradition and indigenization—largely rests on globally diffused ideas' (Robertson, 1992: p. 130). Roudometof and Robertson have recently further developed these ideas. Rejecting the idea that the process of globalization is a phase of capitalist development, and that economic integration necessarily leads to cultural convergence, they conclude:

> Cultural homogeneity and heterogeneity are consequences of the globalization process. Although cultural diffusion can transform a locale, the recurrent 'invention of tradition' makes it possible to preserve, create or recreate cultural heterogeneity at the local level.
> (Roudometof & Robertson, 1995: p. 284)

Significantly, it was in the third phase identified by Robertson that contemporary notions of national/ethnic identity and culture were formed. During the period of intense globalization (roughly 1880 to 1920), Featherstone (1991b) suggests that more nations were drawn together in a tighter global interdependency and set of power balances. Representatives of national cultures sought both to reinvent traditions of the nation and to marginalize local ethnic and regional differences. For Featherstone, this entailed the invoking of a collective memory. This was done through the performance of ritual, bodily practices and commemorative ceremonies. Royal Jubilees, the Olympic Games, international competitions and national days all performed this function. These practices became 'echoes of the sacred' where the fundamental elements of national culture and identity were revealed. Leisure events came to express myths, invoke memories, emphasize heroes and embody traditions. These tied popular consciousness together (Featherstone, 1991b).

In this earlier phase of globalization, leisure practices functioned to bind nations together around *specific* invented traditions. In contrast, the more recent phase of globalization, dating from the 1960s, is forcing nation-states to reconstitute their collective identities along more pluralistic and multicultural lines. Significantly, leisure practices also take on new meanings. Featherstone notes in this connection:

> ... festive moments [such as Woodstock] in which the everyday routine world becomes transformed into an extraordinary sacred world enabled people to temporarily live in unison, near to the ideal. Subsequent gatherings often incorporate rituals which reinvoke the aura of the sacred. ... Televised rock festivals such as the Band Aid, Food Aid, the Nelson Mandela concert and other transnational link-ups may also invoke a

more direct sense of emotional solidarity which may reawaken and reinforce moral concerns such as the sense of common humanity, the sacredness of the person, human rights, and more recently the sacredness of nature and non-human species.
> (Featherstone, 1991b: p. 122)

Although global consumer culture can be perceived to be destroying local culture, Featherstone argues that it can also be used for reconstituting a sense of locality. Given the moral concerns about humanity, human rights and environmentalism, identified by Featherstone as permeating some leisure events, it is not surprising that he believes that global consumer culture is leading to polyculturalism and a sense of otherness. Global leisure practices do not automatically involve a homogenization on process. In contrast, for Featherstone, 'the tendency ... within consumer culture to reproduce an overload of information and signs would also work against any coherent integrated universal global belief on the level of content' (Featherstone, 1991b: p. 127). More recently, Featherstone and Lash developed this argument further, and noted that analyses must 'become attuned to the nuances of the process of globalization and seek to develop theories which are sensitive to the different power potentials of the different players participating in the various global struggles' (Featherstone & Lash, 1995: p. 3). The very prevalence of images of the 'other' contained in global sport and leisure practices may both decentre the West and put other cultures more centre stage. Sport practices, such as the Olympic movement, will also be part of this global cultural contest. An even more robust case for viewing globalization as involving hybridization of the kind noted comes from the work of Nederveen Pieterse (1995).

For Nederveen Pieterse, there are many modes and forms of globalization. Seeking to avoid the potential Eurocentric and modernization connotations that can be associated with the concept, he stresses the plural, multidimensional and open-ended nature of the process. His approach is primarily a critique of essentialism. Advocating a geographically 'wide' and historically 'deep' analysis, Nederveen Pieterse emphasizes the flows between the West and the non-West and how globalization processes precede the recent 'rise of the west' to relative predominance. For Nederveen Pieterse, the problem of globalization involves a diverse

313

range of currents and counter-currents, entails an active and critical reception by 'locals', and is leading to creolization of cultural forms and a hybridization of people's identities. For Nederveen Pieterse, cultural experiences have not been moving in the direction of cultural uniformity and standardization, but rather towards a global *mélange*. As he concludes:

> How do we come to terms with phenomena such as Thai boxing by Moroccan girls in Amsterdam, Asian rap in London, Irish bagels, Chinese tacos and Mardi Gras Indians in the United States? ... Cultural experiences, past or present, have not been simply moving in the direction of cultural uniformity and standardization. This is not to say that the notion of global cultural synchronization is irrelevant—on the contrary—but it is fundamentally incomplete.
>
> (Nederveen Pieterse, 1995: p. 53)

In reaching this conclusion, Nederveen Pieterse argues that the global cultural synchronization thesis fails to note the influence that non-Western cultures exercise on each other, leaves no room to explore cross-over cultures, overstates the homogeneity of the West and overlooks the fact that many of the standards and cultural forms exported by the West and its cultural industries turn out to be of a culturally mixed character. Adopting a long-term perspective allows him to stress that 'Europe', until the late fourteenth century, was the recipient of cultural influences from the Orient. While such observations provide a powerful corrective to the excesses of the homogenization thesis, in either its modernization or cultural imperialist guise, there is a danger that the analysis veers too far in the opposite direction.

[...] It is important to push the globalization process time-frame back beyond the so-called 'modern' period and also to accont for the influence of non-Western cultures on the West. Likewise, as it is important to probe the hybridization of cultural identities. Equally, the creolization of sport cultures does, to some degree, parallel similar processes at work in the areas of music, art and food. Nevertheless, the analysis must not lose sight of the need to account for interrelated processes; that the contrasts between cultures have also diminished over time and that powerful groups do operate to construct, produce and provide global sport processes. This much is clear from the dependency

and world-systems theorists. An uncritical deployment of concepts like hybridization and creolization can lead to a position where the individual is assumed to be sovereign and where people freely choose from the global sport *mélange*. The insights of scholars of cultural imperialism, dependency or world-system theory would thus be overlooked. That is too high a price to pay. At this juncture, it is appropriate therefore to see how the themes, questions and issues raised above have found expression in the cross-cultural study of sport.

Studying sport in the global order: the state of play

[...] Though the use of globalization concepts is a relatively new feature of research studying sport processes, cross-cultural analyses have been attempted for some time.[4] Johan Huizinga's 1949 work, for example, developed a cross-cultural account of the origins of modern sport and remains compelling reading. This is what Huizinga concluded.

> The great ball-games in particular require the existence of permanent teams, and herein lies the starting-point of modern sport. The process arises quite spontaneously in the meeting of village against village, school against school, one part of a town against the rest, etc. That the process started in nineteenth-century England is understandable up to a point, though how far the specifically Anglo-Saxon bent of mind can be deemed an efficient cause is less certain. But it cannot be doubted that the structure of English life had much to do with it. Local self-government encouraged the spirit of association and solidarity. The absence of obligatory military training favoured the occasion for, and the need of, physical exercise. The peculiar form of education tended to work in the same direction, and finally the geography of the country and the nature of the terrain, on the whole flat and, in the ubiquitous commons, offering the most perfect playing-fields that could be desired, were of the greatest importance. Thus England became the cradle and focus of modern sporting life.
>
> (Huizinga, 1949/1970: p. 223)

[...] At this stage, it is sufficient to note that scholars accept the basic premise that 'England became the cradle and focus of modern sporting life'

(Dunning & Sheard, 1979; Gruneau, 1988; Guttmann, 1991). Here the consensus breaks down. Different interpretations exist with regard to the dynamics underpinning the emergence and subsequent diffusion of modern sport (Dunning & Sheard, 1979; Gorn & Goldstein, 1993; Hargreaves, 1986; Hargreaves, 1994; Mandell, 1984). Similar themes, issues and questions that characterize the broader debate regarding global cultural flows also surface in discussing modern sport. Not surprisingly, similar fault-lines regarding homogeneity/heterogeneity, monocausal/multicausal, unidimensional/multi-dimensional, unity/fragmentation, universalism/particularism are also evident. I identify key research, and outline where such work is positioned along these fault-lines.

The clearest exposition of the modernization thesis as it applies to sport can be found in the work of Eric Wagner. Reviewing a diverse set of trends that are said to characterize global sport, Wagner correctly observes that 'Americanization is part of these trends but it is only one part of much broader processes; it is not by itself the key process' (Wagner, 1990: p. 400). [...] Yet, Wagner mistakenly then assigns central status to what he terms 'international modernization' (Wagner, 1990: p. 402). While he acknowledges important caveats, such as 'sport culture flowing in all directions', and a 'blending of many sport traditions', Wagner does appear to downplay the conflictual nature of these processes, to overemphasize the ability of people to pick and choose as they wish from global sport cultures, and to see such development as a sign of progress. His concluding comments echo many of the features, and weaknesses, of the modernization perspective outlined earlier in this chapter. This is what he had to say:

> I think we make too much of cultural dependency in sports when in fact it is people themselves who generally determine what they do and do not want, and it is the people who modify and adapt the cultural imports, the sports, to fit their own needs and values. Bringing sports into a new cultural context probably serves more as examples available for people to pick up or trade if they wish, rather than any imposed or forced cultural change. ... The long-term trend has to be, I think, towards greater homogenization, and I don't think there is anything bad or imperialistic about

this; rather, these sports trends ultimately must reflect the will of the people.
> (Wagner, 1990: p. 402)

Though modernization was one of the first approaches within the field, ideas of this kind still surface in the literature on sport. Consider Baker and Mangan's collection of papers on sport in Africa (1987), Cashman's exploration of the phenomenon of Indian cricket (1988), Arbena's evaluation of literature relating to Latin America (1988) and papers published in comparative sport studies edited by Wilcox (1995). In his early writing on this subject, Allen Guttmann supported this position, arguing that Wagner was 'correct to insist that we are witnessing a homogenization of world sports rather than an Americanization', and that 'the concept of modernization is preferable because it also implies something about the nature of the global transformation' (Guttmann, 1991: pp. 187–8). Though he acknowledges that terms like 'Gemeinschaft and Gesellschaft, the traditional and the modern, the particularistic and the universalistic' employ an 'admittedly simplified dichotomy', Guttmann still works within a modernization time frame, and overlooks what Robertson describes as the 'universalization of particularism' and not just the 'particularization of universalism' (Robertson, 1992). This is odd. In other work by Guttmann, important lines of enquiry are opened up when he refers to the diffusion of game forms in the ancient world and to the influence of the Orient on the West (Guttmann, 1993). Guttmann's solution has been to adopt a cultural hegemony position and to concentrate on more recent events.

While advocates of a cultural imperialist and dependency theory approach would reject several, if not all of the premises outlined by Wagner and Guttmann, these perspectives do share a common assumption that we are witnessing the homogenization of world sports. Within sport history research, informed by a cultural imperialist perspective, several insightful case studies of the connection between the diffusion of sport and imperialism have been provided (Mangan, 1986; Stoddart, 1989). The diffusion of sport, out of its European heartland, moved along the formal and the informal lines of Empire—particularly, though not exclusively, the British. But it was not just the diffusion of specific sports, such as cricket,

315

that reflected this broader process (James, 1963). From a cultural imperialist perspective, what was also at stake was the diffusion of a cultural/sporting ideology and a form of Western cosmology. This argument can be highlighted with reference to the work of Henning Eichberg, John Bale and Johan Galtung.

Eichberg's study probes several of the issues identified. He suggests that Olympism is a 'social pattern' that reflects the 'everyday culture of the western (and east European) industrial society' (Eichberg, 1984: p. 97). He emphasizes several negative consequences of Olympism, including drugs, violence and the scientification of sport. Eichberg maintains that these excesses are not accidental or marginal, but logically related to the configuration of Western Olympic sport, with its emphasis on 'faster, higher, stronger'. Olympism is seen to reflect the colonial dominance of the West, and its spread across the globe has been remarkably successful. While it is possible to agree with Eichberg on this, Wilson overstates this case when he suggests that 'the major impetus for the globalization of sport was the Olympic movement' (Wilson, 1994: p. 356). The dynamics underpinning the globalization of sport are more multifaceted than this. Indeed, as Eichberg argues, Western domination is increasingly subject to resistance. Alternatives to Olympism are emerging. These alternatives include a resurgence of national cultural games, open-air movements, expressive activities and meditative exercises. He concludes that 'the age of Western colonial dominance is coming to an end—and with it the predominance of Olympic sports', and that, 'new physical cultures will arise … from the different cultural traditions of the world' (Eichberg, 1984: p. 102). Not all, share Eichberg's optimism.

Tackling these issues within the subdiscipline of sports geography, John Bale paints a more conflict-ridden and destructive picture of the impact of the diffusion of sport along the lines of Empire. As Bale records, 'western sports did not simply take root in virgin soil; they were firmly implanted—sometimes ruthlessly—by imperialists' (Bale, 1994: p. 8). For Bale, such 'sports colonisation' marginalized, or destroyed, indigenous movement cultures and, 'as cultural imperialism swept the globe, sports played their part in westernising the landscapes of the

colonies' (Bale, 1994: p. 8). There is much in this latter argument and Bale's pioneering study raises our understanding of sport landscapes to a new level. There are, however, grounds for suggesting that the homogenization process is not as complete as these observations appear to indicate. This reservation is not, however, shared by Galtung. In similar vein to Bale and Eichberg, Galtung sets up his analysis with the following question: 'What happens when there is massive export of sports, radiating from Western centers, following old colonial trade and control lines, into the last little corner of the world, leaving cricket bats, soccer fields, racing tracks, courts of all sorts and what not behind?' (Galtung, 1991: p. 150). For Galtung, the answer is clear. Sports carry the sociocultural code of the senders, and those from the West 'serve as fully fledged carriers of the combination typical for expansionist occidental cosmology' (Galtung, 1991: p. 150). Unlike Eichberg, however, Galtung detects no hopeful alternatives. Whatever the merits of his overall argument, Galtung rightly points to the role of the body in these processes, and insightfully observes that, as people learn these body cultures at an early stage in their lives, they leave 'imprints that may well be indelible' (Galtung, 1991: p. 150).

Although the research highlighted above emphasizes a cultural imperialist perspective, variants of dependency theory have been used in the study of sport. Several studies have also examined Latin and South America (Arbena, 1993; Mandle & Mandle, 1988). Alan Klein's study of Dominican and Mexican baseball are examples of dependency research at its very best (Klein, 1991; 1997). Grounded in a careful and sophisticated anthropological approach, he probes the contradictory status and role of baseball in relations between the Dominican Republic and the USA. Klein skilfully observes:

> Because baseball is the only area in which Dominicans come up against Americans and demonstrate superiority, it fosters national pride and keeps foreign influence at bay. But the resistance is incomplete. At an organizational level American baseball interests have gained power and are now unwittingly dismantling Dominican baseball. Therefore, just when the Dominicans are in a position to resist the influence of foreigners, the core of their resistance

is slipping away into the hands of the foreigners themselves.

(Klein, 1991: p. 3)

Despite noting, in similar fashion to Eichberg's interpretation of the Olympic movement, that 'Caribbean baseball is rooted in colonialism', Klein does not convey the sense of uniformity, or of total domination, that Galtung does. On the contrary, while pointing to the unequal nature of power relations, Klein remarks, 'having struggled in obscurity to refine the game Dominicans have made it their own, a game marked by their cadence and color' (Klein, 1991: p. 156). Local responses to broader processes are acknowledged. Klein goes further, and argues that 'the Dominicans are a beleaguered people who may someday rebel; to predict when the flash point will occur, look first to the firefights being waged in a game that has inspired their confidence. Look first at Sugarball' (Klein, 1991: p. 156). In studying the US–Mexican border, baseball and forms of nationalism Klein makes the same incisive case. As he remarks, 'an examination of the sport and the subculture of baseball in this region illustrates these nationalisms as well or better than other kinds of studies' (Klein, 1997: p. 13).

Other scholars working within this broad cultural imperialist/dependency theory and cultural hegemony tradition either straddle these perspectives or downplay the role of Americanization and, instead, stress the role of global capitalism. Sugden and Tomlinson, for example, appear to draw on aspects of these traditions. Take, for example, their following remarks, 'although on the one hand FIFA has served as a forum for Third World resistance, on the other hand it has undoubtedly aided and abetted neocolonialist forms of economic and cultural exploitation' (Sugden & Tomlinson, 1998b: p. 314). In studies that Donnelly (1996) refers to as being located within a cultural hegemony position, the contested nature of global capitalism is highlighted. Guttmann, for example, argues that 'cultural imperialism is not ... the most accurate term to characterize what happens during the process of ludic diffusion. Cultural hegemony comes closer' (Guttmann, 1994: p. 178). For Donnelly, the advantage of this cultural hegemony perspective lies in avoiding an overdeterministic view of Americanization: the transfer of cultural products is not one way, the ideological messages are not fixed and those who are exposed to such products have a degree of freedom to interpret and reinterpret these messages and products. As Donnelly concludes, 'cultural hegemony may be seen as a two-way but imbalanced process of cultural exchange, interpenetration, and interpretation' (Donnelly, 1996: p. 243). There is much in this that figurational sociology would share. Yet, interestingly, while Guttmann (1994: p. 179) also sees merit in this perspective, he argues that cultural hegemonists overstate the intentionality involved in ludic diffusion processes. Perhaps this is so, but equally important is the fact that the unintentional dynamics involved in global processes are overlooked. In addition, non-occidental influences on the West and the linkages between non-occidental societies and their impact on each other are still not accounted for. Civilizational struggles of a quite complex kind are the key to unlocking aspects of global processes.

Bruce Kidd's study of sport in Canada, located within a broader analysis of the development of Canadian national culture, insightfully explores the role of global capitalism (Kidd, 1981). Noting the potential importance of sport in the strengthening and enunciation of national identity, Kidd observes that the commodification of Canadian sport has served to undermine this potential. Focusing on the National Hockey League (NHL) as a 'critical case' in this regard, he highlights how both the ideological marketing strategy of the NHL and the general process of commodification between the two world wars served to 'accelerate the disintegration of beliefs and practices that had once supported and nurtured autonomous Canadian institutions' (Kidd, 1981: p. 713). For him, an explanation of these processes lies not in Americanization *per se* but in a critique of capitalism Kidd observes:

> Explanation lies neither in U.S. expansion nor national betrayal, but in the dynamics of capital. Once sport became a sphere of commodity production ... then it was almost inevitable that the best Canadian hockey would be controlled by the richest and most powerful aggregates of capital and sold in the richer and more populous markets of the U.S. The disappearance of community control over Canadian hockey strengthened a much larger process—the centralization of all popular forms of culture.
>
> (Kidd, 1981: p. 714)

317

Whereas Kidd deals with issues between 'core' economies, George Sage (1995) draws on the work of Wallerstein and adopts a more 'world-system model' to explain the global sporting goods industry. Surveying the social and environmental costs associated with the relocation strategies of multinational corporations such as Nike, Sage concludes that such companies have been 'following a model which places exports over domestic needs, profits over worker rights, growth over the environment', and that a 'neocolonial system of unequal economic and political relationships among the First and Third World countries envisioned by Wallerstein's world-system model of global development becomes abundantly evident to even a casual observer' (Sage, 1995: p. 48). [...]

While noting the obvious American influences on Australian popular culture, McKay and Miller (1991) adopt a similar stance to Sage. They view the concept of Americanization to be of limited help in explaining the form and content of Australian sport. For them, the political economy of Australian sport can best be analysed by concepts such as post-Fordism, the globalization of consumerism and the cultural logic of late capitalism. Though McKay and Miller (1991) and McKay, Lawrence, Miller and Rowe (1993) prefer the term 'corporate sport', Donnelly has argued that the 'notion of corporate sport may easily be extended to indicate the Americanization of sport, given that most of the conditions for corporate sport are either American in origin, or have been more fully developed in the United States' (Donnelly, 1996: p. 246). It would seem, however, that neither Sage, nor McKay and his fellow researchers, would accept this interpretation. As McKay and Miller remark, 'in the discourse of the daily report from the stock exchange, the Americans are not the only players in the cultural game' (McKay & Miller, 1991: p. 93).

Yet, Donnelly (1996) would have much in common with these writers. In certain respects his position, as noted, represents a modified and more sophisticated form of the Americanization thesis. Eschewing the excesses of the Americanization as imperialism argument, Donnelly views Americanization as a form of cultural hegemony with resistance and accommodation evident and also with other imperialist influences at work. There is some common ground with this approach and the figurational perspective and

the conclusion that the American corporate model of sport is the dominant form at present would be accepted by both. While differences with regard to the dynamics of socio-historical processes remain, in the area of globalization a more fruitful dialogue is opening up between hegemony theory and figurational sociology than has previously been the case. [...]

Although McKay and Miller de-emphasize the pervasiveness of American control, and concentrate on the dynamics of global capitalism *per se*, the work by David Andrews would, at first sight, appear to be more in keeping with the position adopted by Donnelly. Andrews, for example, examines the 'global structure and local influence of the National Basketball Association (NBA) as a transnational corporation, whose global ubiquity inevitably contributes to the hyperreal remaking of local identities' (Andrews, 1997: p. 72). Andrews goes on to argue that the NBA has been turned 'into one of the popular commodity-signs which had usurped the material economic commodity as the dynamic force and structuring principle of everyday American existence' (Andrews, 1997: p. 74). In language sometimes akin to.that used by Adorno and his fellow contributors to the Frankfurt School, Andrews argues that during the 1980s, 'the NBA became a hyperreal circus whose simulated, and hence self-perpetuating, popularity seduced the American masses' (Andrews, 1997: p. 74). This 'success' is not confined to the USA. Though it may be unwise to overestimate the knowledge of the powerful and underestimate the ability of 'locals' to reshape, resist, or simply ignore, the marketing strategies of multinationals, Andrews is correct to observe that the NBA does 'have a vivid global presence' (Andrews, 1997: p. 77). The source of debate, however, as he himself acknowledges, is 'the extent to which the circulation of universal American commodity-signs has resulted in the convergence of global markets, lifestyles and identities' (Andrews, 1997: p. 77). [...] Despite the manner in which he formulates the early part of his argument, Andrews stresses the 'built-in particularity (or heterogeneity) in terms of the ways that products and images are consumed', and that, products, images and services from other societies 'to some extent ... inalienably become indigenized' (Andrews, 1997: p. 77). As with the broader globalization literature, sociology of sport research is divided over the precise form and blend of homogeneity and heterogeneity characteristic of the global sport process.

What kind of assessment can be made regarding the state of play of the sociological study of global sport? Several writers have attempted some overall review (Donnelly, 1996; Harvey & Houle, 1994; Houlihan, 1994). While there are clear fault-lines along which the literature lies, reflecting the more general globalization debate, there is also some overlap. Research from both a modernization and a cultural imperialism perspective concludes that a homogenization process is occurring. This common ground can be seen in Guttmann's work. While his early work endorsed a modernization perspective, his more recent contribution has swung in favour of a form of cultural imperialism (Guttmann, 1991, 1994). While issues of cultural struggle and contestation are much more to the fore in this latter work, and in the work stemming from a cultural hegemony perspective, the common denominator is still a continued emphasis on homogenization.

Within the broad 'Marxist' tradition (cultural imperialism, dependency theory, world-system theory and hegemony theory), common emphasis is placed on power, exploitation and the role that multinationals play in local markets. While the relative role of Americanization and/or global capitalism is disputed, what is agreed upon is that modern sport is structured by a political economy in which multinationals play a decisive part. In some instances, as we have seen, a particularly unidirectional and monocausal focus is used to explain these processes. More recently, work by Andrews and Klein illustrates, to a greater extent, issues of local resistance, reinterpretation and indigenization. In this, they are in keeping with a trend in the more general globalization literature that emphasizes heterogeneity (Nederveen Pieterse, 1995). Harvey and Houle summarize aspects of this debate that have surfaced in the sociology of sport when they conclude:

> Thus, linking sport to globalization leads to an analysis of sport as part of an emergent global culture, as contributing to the definition of new identities, and to the development of a world economy. Therefore, the debate between globalization and Americanization is more than a question of vocabulary. Indeed, it is a question of paradigmatic choice, which leads to completely different interpretations of a series of phenomena.
>
> (Harvey & Houle, 1994: p. 346)

While the observations made here would endorse these writers when they argue that different interpretations of globalization more broadly, and global sport processes in particular, are 'a question of paradigmatic choice,' there is room to doubt whether such interpretations are as polarized as they suggest. This chapter reveals a degree of common ground and a basis on which to build future work. It is not necessary to discard research from other traditions simply because we do not have all assumptions and concepts in common. That is not a sound strategy from which to develop a reality-congruent social scientific knowledge base (Elias, 1987). [...] What is clear from the literature reviewed here is that the study of global sport processes is a vibrant area, and that narrow, natiocentric analyses do not capture the complexity of modern sport in the late twentieth century.

Notes

1. Globalization research has taken various forms and has been subjected to extensive debate. For further discussion, see Beyer, 1994; Chase Dunn, 1989; Featherstone, 1990, 1991a, 1991b; Featherstone, Lash & Robertson, 1995; Friedman, 1994; Giddens, 1990; Gilpin, 1987; Hall, 1991; Hall et al., 1992; King, 1991; McGrew, 1992; Robertson, 1990a; Rosenau, 1980; Sanderson, 1995; Sklair, 1991; Waters, 1995; Wolfe, 1991.
2. For further discussion of this, see Blomstrom & Hettne, 1984; Frank, 1967; Hettne, 1990; Larrain, 1989. For consideration of how this approach has been applied to the development of sport, see Gruneau, 1988.
3. For examples of how this cultural imperialism approach has been applied to the media more generally, see Emanuel, 1992; Mattelart, 1977; Rollin, 1989; Schiller, 1969; Tunstall, 1977.
4. Examples of these cross-cultural studies include Bale, 1985; Clignet & Stark, 1974; Jokl & Simon, 1964; Krotee, 1979; Mandell, 1984; Wagner, 1989.

References

Andrews, D. (1997) "The transnational basketball association: American commodity-sign culture and global-local conjuncturalism" in Cvetkovich, A. and D. Keller (eds), *Articulating the Global and the local: globalization and cultural studies*. Boulder, Colo: Westview Press. Pp. 72–101.

Appadurai, A. (1990) "Disjuncture and difference in the global cultural economy", *Theory, Culture and Society* 7, pp. 295–31.

Arbena, J. (1988) Sport and Society in Latin America. Westport, CT: Greenwood Press.

Arbena, J. (1993) "Sport and nationalism in Latin Ameica, 1880–1970: the paradox of promoting and performing 'European' sports." *History of European Ideas* 16, pp. 837–44.

Baker, W. (1982) *Sports in the Western World*. Rowman and Littlefield: Totowa, N.J.

Baker, W. and J. Mangan (eds.) (1987) *Sport in Africa: essays in social history*. New York: Africana.

Bale, J. (1994) *Landscapes of Modern Sport*. Leicester: Leicester University Press.

Bale, J. and J. Sang (1996) *Kenyan Running : movement culture, geography and global change*. London: Frank Cass.

Cashman, R. (1988) "Cricket and colonialism: colonial hegemony and indigenous subversion?" in Mangan, J. A. (ed.) *Pleasure, Profit and Proslelytism: British culture at home and abroad 1700–1914*. London: Frank Cass. Pp. 258–72.

Dickens, P. (1992) *Global Shift: the internationalization of economic activity*. 2nd ed. London: Paul Chapman.

Donnelly, P. (1996) "The local and the global: globalization in the sociology of sport", *Journal of Sport and Social Issues* 20, pp. 239–57.

Dunning, E. and K. Sheard (1979) *Barbarians, Gentlemen and Players: a sociological study of the development of rugby football*. Oxford: Martin Robertson.

Elias, N. (1987) Involvement and Detachment. Oxford: Blackwell.

Eichberg, H. (1984) "Olympic sport: neocolonialism and alternatives", *International Review for Sociology of Sport* 19, pp. 97–105.

Featherstone, M. (1990) "Global culture: an introduction", *Theory, Culture and Society*. 7, pp. 1–14.

Featherstone, M. (1991a) "Local and global cultures", *Vrijetijd en Samenleving* 3/4, pp. 43–58.

Featherstone, M. (1991b.) *Consumer Culture and Postmoderism*. London: Sage.

Featherstone, M. and S. Lash (1995) "Globalisation, modernity and the spatialisation of social theory: an introduction," in M. Featherstone, S. Lash and R. Robertson (eds), *Global Modernities. 10th Anniversary Conference*. London: Sage.

Frank, G. (1967) *Capitalism and Under-development in Latin America*. New York: Monthly Review Press.

Galtung, J. (1991) "The sport system as a metaphor for the world system", in Landry, F., Landry, M. and Yeles, M. (eds) *Sport ... the third millennium*. Quebec: University of Laval Press. Pp. 147–56.

Giddens, A. (1990) The Consequences of Modernity. Cambridge: Polity Press.

Gorn E.J. and W. Goldstein. (1993) *A Brief History of American Sports*. New York.: Hill and Wang.

Gruneau, R. (1988) "Modernization or hegemony: two view on sport and social development", in Harvey, J. and Cantelon, H. (eds.) *Not Just a Game*. Ottawa: University of Ottawa Press. pp. 9–32.

Guttman, A. (1991) "Sports diffusion: a response to Maguire and the Americanization commentaries", *Society and Leisure* 11, pp. 185–90.

Guttman, A. (1994) *Games and Empires: modern sports and cultural imperialism*. New York: Columbia University Press.

Hargreaves, J. (1986) *Sport, Power, and Culture*. Cambridge: Polity Press.

Hargreaves, J. (1994) *Sporting Females*. London: Routledge.

Harvey, D. (1989) *The Condition of Postmodernity*. Oxford: Blackwell.

Harvey, J. and F. Houle (1994) "Sport, world economy, global culture and new social movements", *Sociology of Sport Journal* 11, pp. 337–55.

Hettne, B. (1990) *Development Theory and the Three Worlds*. London: Longman.

Houlihan, B. (1994) "Homogenization, Americanization, and creolization of sport: varieties of globalization", *Sociology of Sport Journal* 11, pp. 356–75.

Huizinga, J. (1949/70) *Homo Ludens: a study of the play element in culture*. London: Temple Smith.

James, C.L.R. (1963) *Beyond the Boundary*. London: Stanley Paul.

Johnson, R.J. *et al.* (1995) *Geographies of Global Change: remapping the world in the late twentieth century*. Oxford: Blackwell.

Jokl, E. and E. Simon (1964) *International Research in Sport and Physical Education*. Springfield, IL: Thomas.

Kidd, B. (1981) "Sport, dependency and the Canadian state", in Hart, M. and Birrell, S. (eds.) *Sport in the Sociocultural Process*. Dubuque, Ia: Wm. C. Brown. Pp. 707–21.

Klein, A.M. (1989) "Baseball in the Dominican Republic." *Sociology of Sport Journal* 6, pp. 95–112.

Klein, A.M. (1991) *Sugarball: The American Game, The Dominican Dream*. New Haven: Yale University Press.

Klein, A.M. (1997) *Baseball on the Border: a tale of two Laredos*. Princeton, N.J.: Princeton University Press.

Larrain, J. (1989) *Theories of Development*. Cambridge: Polity Press.

McKay, J. and T. Miller (1991) "From old boys to men and women of the corporation: the Americanization and commodification of Australian sport." *Sociology of Sport Journal* 8, pp. 86–94.

McKay, J., G. Lawrence, T. Miller, and D. Rowe (1993) "Globalizations and Australian sport", *Sport Science Review* 2, pp. 10–28.

Mandell, R. (1984) *Sport: a cultural history*. Columbia University Press.

Mandle, J. and J. Mandle (1988) *Grass Roots Commitment: basketball and society in Trinidad and Tobago*. Parkesburg, Ia.: Caribbean Books.

Mangan, J.A. (1986) *The Games Ethic and Imperialism*. London: Viking Press.

Mason, T. (1995) *Passion of the People": Football in South America*. London: Verso.

Massey, D. (1994) *Space, Place and Gender*. Cambridge: Polity Press.

Nederveen Pieterse, J. (1995) "Globalization as hybridization", in Featherstone, M., Lash, S. and Robertson, R. (eds) *Global Modernities*. London: Sage. Pp. 45–68.

Pooley, J.C. (1981) "Ethnic soccer clubs in Milwaukee: a study in assimilation", in Hart, M. and Birrell, S. (eds.) *Sport in the Sociocultural Process*. Dubuque, Ia: Wm. C. Brown. Pp. 430–47.

Real, M. (1989) "Super bowl football versus world cup soccer: a cultural-structural comparison." in Wenner, L. (ed,) *Media, Sports and Society*. Newbury Park, Calif: Sage. Pp. 180–203.

Robertson, R. (1990) "Mapping the global condition: globalization as the central concept." *Theory, Culture and Society* 7, pp. 15–30.

Robertson, R. (1992) Globalization: social theory and global culture.

Roudometof, V. and R. Robertson (1995) "Globalization, world-system theory, and the comparative study of civilizations: issues of theoretical logic in world-historical sociology", in Sanderson, S.K. (ed) *Civilizations and World Systems*. Walnut Creek, Calif.: Alta Mira. Pp. 273–300.

Sage, G. (1995) "Deindustrialization and the American sporting goods industry", in Wilcox, R.C. (ed) *Sport in the Global Village*. Morgantown, W. Va.: Fitness Information Technology, Inc.

Seppanen, P. (1970) "The role of competitive sports in different societies." Paper presented at the 7th World Congess of Sociology, Varna, Bulgaria, September.

Sklair, L. (1991) *Sociology of the Global System*. London: Harvester.

Stoddard, B. (1989) "Cricket's impersonal crisis: the 1932–33 MCC tour of Australia." In Cashman, R.M. and McKernan, M. (eds) *Sport in History*. St. Lucia: University of Qeensland Press. Pp. 124–47.

Sugden, J. and A. Tomlinson (1998) *FIFA and the Contest for World Football: who rules the people's game?* Cambridge: Polity Press.

Tomlinson, A. (1991) *Cultural Imperialism*. London: Printer Publishers.

Wagner, E. (1990) "Sport in Africa and Asia: Americanization or mondialization?" *Sociology of Sport Journal* 7, pp. 300–402.

Wallerstein, I. (1974) *The Modern World System*. New York: The Academic Press.

Wilcox, R.C. (1995) *Sport in the Global Village*. Morgantown: W. Va.: Fitness Information Technology, Inc.

Wilson, J. (1994) *Playing by the Rules: sport, society, and the state*. Detroit: Wayne State Press.

Yearley, S. (1996) *Sociology, Environmentalism, Globalization and the World-system*. London: Sage.

7.4

The denationalization of sport

De-ethnicization of the nation and identity de-territorialization

Raffaele Poli

In this challenging and provocative essay, Raffaele Poli suggests that "denationalization" processes in sport – an international flow of players across boundaries and global mass media presentations – have changed the relationships among State, identity, and territory. Essentially, Poli argues, sport has made problematic the link between a state/country/nation and a specific national culture and ethnicity. Providing many examples of athletes who compete *in* and/or *for* countries to which they emigrated, Poli suggests that with the denationalization of sport come a de-territorialization of identity (e.g. French fans of the San Antonio Spurs) and a de-ethnicization of nations (e.g. Africans playing for German teams).

Introduction

The concept of denationalization was first used in the 1970s in economic studies as a synonym for privatization. For two decades, most of the articles in which the notion has been employed referred to the sale of State-owned companies. More recently, the concept has come to be used among others, such as deterritorialization, transnationalism, post-national, etc., as a means to circumvent 'methodological nationalism' or 'state-centrism' which has been dominant in the social sciences for many years.[1] Neil Brenner has defined the latter approach as the tendency to conceptualize 'space as a static platform of social action that is not itself constituted or modified socially' and state territoriality 'as a preconstituted, naturalized, or unchanged scale of analysis'.[2] The increasing importance of phenomena such as the development of transnational corporations, the intensified deployment of information technologies, the advent of 'a consciousness of the world as a whole',[3] the formation of transnational communities of migrants, etc., has encouraged researchers to develop concepts allowing them to transcend the limits of state-centric based theories. As in the case of deterritorialization, latent in the notion of denationalization, there is the idea that the territoriality of state is an historical construction that is not the 'natural' container of economic, political or social life.

From a spatial point of view, Brenner defines the 'denationalization of the State' as the process by which 'the role of the national scale both as a self-enclosed container of socio-economic relations and an organizational interface between sub- and supra-national scales' declines.[4] According to Saskia Sassen, denationalization can be defined as the filtering and embeddedness of

Raffaele Poli, "The Denationalization of Sport: De-Ethnicization of the Nation and Identity Deterritorialization" from *Sport in Society* 10.4 (July 2007): 646–661. Copyright © 2007. Reprinted with the permission of Routledge.

the global in what has historically been thought, represented, constructed and institutionalized as national. Thus, one central task of contemporary social sciences is 'to decode particular aspects of what is still represented or experienced as "national", which may in fact have shifted away from what had historically been considered or constituted as national'.[5]

From this standpoint, the aim of the essay is to test under what conditions and under which forms it is possible to speak of a denationalization process taking place in sport. Without careful analysis, it may seem to the causal observer that sport is not affected by any form of denationalization. Sportsmen continue to compete for nation states and every international competition is preceded or followed by a national anthem. Media and spectators also play an active role in the (re)production of this national semantic. This is noticeable in collective sports, where TV audiences are generally greater when a national team or club is competing. In 2004, for example, in France, the four biggest recorded sport audiences were during matches of the national football team.

The particular way in which sporting competitions are organized also tends to perpetuate the geopolitical division of the world in nation states, reproducing a spatial fetishism where blocks of territory, thought as homogeneous, are juxtaposed and never superimposed. In the contemporary globalized world, as Pascal Boniface suggests, the elite sports worldwide spectacle seems primarily to be an activity by which nations find new meaning and homelands are glorified.[6] While in the context of European unification, nationalist feelings and sentiments are rekindled through international sporting competitions.[7] As a consequence, the idea according to which state territories are the natural physical container for identity is reactualized. Nationalist feelings reinforced through sport tend also to justify the existence of borders and hide the imagined nature of national communities.[8] In this respect, Duke and Crolley underline that 'football captures the notion of an imagined community perfectly. It is much easier to imagine the nation and conform national identity, when eleven players are representing the nation in a match against another nation'.[9]

Without neglecting these aspects of sport, the goal of this essay is to show that sport also plays a role in the deterritorialization and reterritorialization of identities. The first form of denationalization on which this essay is centred is linked to increasing migratory movements, partially provoked by professional sport itself, and the increasing tendency towards naturalizations of sportsmen and nationality changes. The second form is linked to the global broadcasting of images and information and to the increasing possibilities to identify with teams and sportsmen representing geographical entities on different scales (from the town to nation-state's), located thousands of miles away from the supporter's place of residence. While these two forms of denationalization may appear as marginal when compared to the importance of the state-national basis on which international sports events are still grounded, the author considers it of major importance to take them into account.

If these two distinct forms of contemporary sport denationalization cannot be considered as dominant trends from a historical perspective, it is possible to understand them as incipient changes, intervening in the broader context of globalization, of which researchers—sociologists above all—have to be aware. The results of further investigation of these two phenomena could thus be interpreted as premises to bigger changes that may progressively lead to a redefinition of both sports' organizational structure and the popular understanding of sporting events on a greater scale than is actually the case. The essay's intention is neither to judge negatively the interpretation of sport according to a state national grid, nor to propose radical changes to eligibility conditions for international competitions. The goal is rather to stimulate a debate in the academic field on a topic—identities—that has predominantly been treated from a state-centric perspective. This has, up till now, prevented many researchers from taking into account processes such as the changing character of nations and the new expressions of identity occurring both in and through sport. Thus, the purpose of the essay is to draw attention to the impact on the playing field of processes that have been discussed abundantly in other domains.[10]

The essay is divided into three parts. First of all, the author has considered it useful to take a step back and examine how elite sport became nationalized and some of the reasons for this. Indeed, some aspects that can appear as being naturally nation-based in today's organization of sport are in reality historical constructs. The first section furnishes the elements that allow us to understand why we can speak of a new trend towards denationalization. The second and third sections focus on the analytical description of two sets of processes causing denationalization, which either stimulate a de-ethnicization of the nation or lead to a deterritorialization of identity. If these two forms of denationalization are different both in terms of their origin and in their consequences, the author considers that they are intrinsically linked and have thus to be analyzed in conjunction with each other. Even if international migratory flows and changes of nationality do not directly bring about a deterritorialization of identity, and the global broadcasting of sports events does not necessarily provoke a de-ethnicization of the nation, both sets of processes in different ways result in a denationalization in sport in which the 'natural' correspondence between a State, an identity and a territory is called into question.

The nationalization of sport

At their very beginning, modern sports in England stimulated more the competition between members of upper classes (university students, aristocrats) than competition between territorial groups.[11] The advent of national and global diffusion of modern sports was then accompanied by the appearance of a strong territorial significance, according to which clubs and players did not symbolically represent social classes but geographical areas. This was followed in the early years of the twentieth century by the emergence of national football teams outside of Great Britain.[12] The Fédération Internationale de Football Association (FIFA) was founded in 1904 and the international fixtures organized between teams representing nation states helped to 'dramatize senses of national difference and cultural opposition'.[13] Nevertheless, the idea of having only players with a national passport in national teams was not yet completely integrated. For example, in April 1900, nine foreigners played for Italy against Switzerland in Turin. According to Papa and Panico, 'the concept of "national" was understood by football pioneers in a purely residential way'.[14] This was a reflection of the over-representation of expatriates in football clubs

and, more generally, proof of the early internationalism of modern sports.[15]

With the growth of nationalism that preceded the First World War, elite sport was imbued with strong political meaning. Between the two World Wars, two European countries in particular used sport for political ends: Italy and Germany. According to Holt and Mason, sport in these countries was considered as 'a device of the strength of the State' and 'has been used as a weapon of foreign policy'.[16] Arnaud underlines that in France too, since the beginning of the 1920s, sport has become a State matter. Indeed, a national Office of Physical Education and Sport was created. The goal of this office, placed under the aegis of the Ministry of Public Instruction, was to 'promote (the) sport at a high level in order to restore France's image in the world'.[17]

Inside national borders, sport has become instrumental in the construction of a national consciousness. According to the ideological project that dominated for many years the building of nation states, this construction had to be realized through an uniformization of the citizens living inside national borders. In fact, instead of taking into account the variety of its populations, the internal logic of the nation-state was to encompass the cultural unity of all, as this was considered as the only means of creating a national identity.[18] According to Lefebvre's view, 'the modern state is grounded intrinsically on the drive to rationalize, unify, and homogenize social relations within its territorial space'.[19]

The direct consequence in sport of this ideological project has been the exclusion of non-national sportsmen in national teams, followed by the introduction of quotas limiting the presence of foreign sportsmen in national clubs. From the 1920s onwards, all major national federations of collective sports had introduced these kinds of restrictions. Having become accustomed to thinking not only in national but also in nationalist terms, sport federations up until this day continue to act to maintain these limitations, even at the risk of infringing rights such as the EU one regarding free movement of workers. Thus, it is not by chance that the free movement of communitarian sportsmen in European Union countries resulted from a juridical decision, the 'Bosman' decree of December 1995, rather than from an internal choice taken by sport bodies.

Sports federations have been intrinsically linked to the project that creates a correspondence between national territories and national societies, and have helped states to attain the objective of building a nationalism grounded in ethnic and cultural homogenization. On an international level, federations worked also to both create and preserve a nation-based reading grid. In 1932, in reaction to the employment of former Argentinean football players in the Italian team, such as Raimundo Orsi and Julio Libonatti, FIFA introduced a new rule according to which each player had to wait at least three years before playing for another national team. In the 1950s, after having been confronted by Laszlo Kubala's case,[20] FIFA introduced a rule, still in force, according to which a player, even if he has dual nationality, cannot play for more than one national team at a senior level. On 17 March 2004, FIFA's Urgency committee decided to forbid the employment in national teams of players that, even if they have received the passport of their host country, have not lived at least two years consecutively in the territory of the football association concerned. This decision followed rumours about a possible recruitment of the Brazilian forward Ailton by the Qatari selection. After different cases of nationality changes through naturalization, the International Olympic Committee in turn decided in 2000 to introduce a period of three years before which a sportsman can compete for his new country.

These examples show that in sport, nationalization is inscribed in an historical trend, which tends towards the preservation of the concept of a nation based on cultural homogeneity rather than pluralism. More recently, apart from ideological convictions according to which a national consciousness is only possible where there exists an ethnic and cultural uniformity, governing bodies of sport also act to preserve national identities for commercial reasons. UEFA's former president Lennart Johansson, for example, declared, 'our game is founded on traditional values, such as the pride in the jersey, national or regional identity and other mixes of social-cultural phenomena that are not financially related. And if television is so interested in football as a product today, it is thanks to these factors. Thus they have to be preserved with care if we want to guarantee a sustainable future for it.'[21]

Migrations, naturalizations and the de-ethnicization of the nation

The 'label of origin'[22] is omnipresent in modern sports. This label, which is usually represented in the media via the inscription of the code of the nation-state for which sportsmen compete, is largely employed not only for collective sports, but also for individual ones, such as, among others, cycling.

Table 7.4.1 is one example of the media's tendency to 'label' sportsmen's results by referring to the national code of the country that they symbolically represent.

Medias [sic] and state officials also encourage the reading of sporting performances on a nation-based grid. Every four years, during the Olympic Games, the total number of the medals won by national teams and athletes serve to elaborate a ranking in which some of the most powerful states in the world usually occupy the top positions. In 2004, this special ranking classified consecutively the United States, China,

Table 7.4.1. Overall standing of the Tour de France 2005, after the 15th stage (http://www.letour.fr)

Pos	No.	Name Surname	Team	Nat.	Gaps
1	001	ARMSTRONG Lance	DSC	USA	
2	021	BASSO Ivan	CSC	ITA	02′ 46″
3	057	RASMUSSEN Mickael	RAB	DEN	03′ 09″
4	011	ULLRICH Jan	TMO	GER	05′ 58″
5	031	MANCEBO Francisco	IBA	ESP	06′ 31″
6	164	LEIPHEIMER Levi	GST	USA	07′ 35″
7	066	LANDIS Floyd	PHO	USA	09′ 33″
8	019	VINOKOUROV Alexandre	TMO	KAZ	09′ 38″
9	101	MOREAU Christophe	C.A	FRA	11′ 47″
10	014	KLÖDEN Andréas	TMO	GER	12′ 01″

Russia, Australia, Germany, Japan, France, Italy, South Korea and Great Britain. If the sportsman has dual nationality, the medals he wins cannot be attributed to more than one state. This illustrates sports organizations' incapacity to take into account dual nationalities. The negative perceptions associated with dual nationality are linked to elite sports' ethno-nationalization process described above and, more generally, to the crucial role played by sport in competition between nation-states. According to Saskia Sassen: 'the aggressive nationalism and territorial competition among European states in the eighteenth, nineteenth and twentieth centuries made the concept of dual nationality generally undesirable, incompatible with individual loyalties and destabilizing of the international order'.[23] This is also the case in sport. As a consequence, a considerable number of sportsmen have to choose whether they want to compete for their native country or whether they prefer to compete for their adoptive one. As in a state of war, simultaneous loyalty to two countries is simply unthinkable in sport.

Due to the acceleration of migratory flows occurring in the context of globalization, the inability of sports organizations to take into account dual nationalities is rendered problematic.[24] On the one hand, sport is often a means by which young immigrants participate in local societies, which favour their integration. On the other hand, sports organizations do not accept plural identities and oblige dual nationals to choose one nationality over another. States' citizenship models play a crucial role in the management of migratory flows. The waiting period that applicants must adhere to before obtaining the right to be naturalized varies considerably from one country to another. This is true also at a European level. The shortest delay is in Belgium (three years of uninterrupted stay) and the longest is in Liechtenstein (30 years).[25] Similar to the latter country, the right to nationality in Switzerland is based on *ius sanguinis*.[26] Foreign people, even if they are born on national soil, have to wait 12 years before being eligible to apply for nationality. Despite this, in the under 20-year-old Swiss national football team that participated in the 2005 World Cup in the Netherlands, nine players out of 11 had foreign origins. National coach Bernard Challandes declared that 'instead of discriminating against players with foreign origins, we must promote them and do everything that we can do to convince them to choose to play for the Swiss team'.[27] Germany, another country where the right to nationality is grounded in *ius sanguinis*, tends also to employ a growing number of foreign-born sportsmen. In 2001, Gerald Asamaoah, a Ghanaian-born forward, became the first black player to play for a German football team. In June 2005, during the Confederation Cup, the German national trainer Jürgen Klinsmann asserted that 'to open national teams to immigrants' sons is important. It gives a better image of our country.'[28] These changes in the conception of who can be part of the 'national' indicate the existence of a trend towards a de-ethnicization of the nation. This process is accelerated by the fact that professional sport itself stimulates migrations, sometimes on a global scale.[29] A considerable number of sportsmen migrating for sport-related reasons are confronted with the dilemma of changing nationality, such as in the well-documented Wilson Kipketer case.[30]

During major sporting competitions, States' and national federations' authorities try to reinforce their selection by naturalizing athletes. In France's case, every four years, before the Olympic Games, a special department of the national Olympic and sport committee select and submit to the international Olympic executive committee a list of sportsmen that France wishes to naturalize. For the 2004 Olympic Games, 270 naturalized athletes were present (2.7 per cent of the total). Detailed statistics show that most of them have grown up in less well off countries and actually compete for more powerful States. Indeed, the balance in naturalizations on a continental or subcontinental scale is positive for Western Europe (+67), America (+22) and Oceania (+12) and negative for Eastern Europe (−47), Africa (−36) and Asia (−18).[31]

In football, the final example of an instrumentalized naturalization attempt occurred shortly before the 2006 World Cup, in the case of Salomon Kalou. The Dutch national trainer Marco Van Basten, wishing to convoke the Ivorian forward of Feyenoord Rotterdam, encouraged him to ask for a new passport. Finally, after a long juridical battle, the Immigration minister Rita Verdonk refused his request. This is not always the case. Indeed, some countries have allowed exceptions for sportsmen regarding the right to nationality. In Slovenia, for example, a special law has been passed in order to make possible naturalizations of celebrities such as artists or sportsmen. Since then, 93 persons have obtained a Slovenian passport. Most of them did not have any Slovenian origins, as in the case of the former Jamaican sprinter Marlene Ottey or the former Austrian skier Josef Strobl. Speaking about the latter example, the head of Slovenian international cooperation, Zoran Verovnik, maintained that 'ski professionals supported his candidacy for Slovenian citizenship. We trust the opinion of the individual sport branch. If the sportsman wins several times, this is a good promotion for the State.'[32]

A much better known case in comparison with the examples cited above has been that of the nationality change of the former Kenyan runner, Stephen Cherono. In 2003, just before the World championships, the pre-eminent specialist of the 3,000 meters steeple agreed to become Qatari and to change his name to Saif Saïd Shaheen. He admitted having made this choice for financial reasons. Qatari officials promised him a life pension of 1,000 dollars per month. Shortly after the naturalization, his agent, the Briton Ricky Simms, confirmed that Cherono 'will continue to live between London and Kenya, even if the Qatari federation puts a house at his disposal'.[33] Another East African runner, the former Ethiopian Zanebech Tola, who first unsuccessfully sought asylum in Switzerland, finally decided to accept the proposal of adopting Bahrain nationality. On 26 January 2005, a messenger from the Bahrain National Youth and Sport's Ministry came to Geneva to reach an agreement with her. She finally flew to Bahrain after being promised 1,100 euros per month and a special award of 80,000 euros. She actually lives in Switzerland and runs for Bahrain under the name of Mariam Jamal.

These brief examples show that there is an increasing tendency in modern sport competitions to include in the 'national body' sportsmen who, because of their origins, do not correspond to the historical ethnic composition of the citizens of the state for which they compete. These instrumental and commercial naturalizations occurring without sportsmen putting down roots in their new homeland challenge the traditional vision of the nation as a group of people belonging to the same culture and having the same ethnic origin. If in the past sport has contributed to the historical construction of a correspondence between the State and a specific 'national culture', nowadays, the study of sport helps to highlight the historical character of this construction. While it is undeniable that football still 'offers the possibility for nationhood to be represented through (...) fixed archetypes', it can also be considered as a platform from 'which the circumscriptions of the national body politic—particularly in terms of race—can be breached'.[34] The 'Black-Blanc-Beur' French football national team is perhaps the best example to illustrate this.

The case of rugby is an excellent instance that reveals an incipient process consisting of a progressive dissociation between nationality and citizenship in sport. Many authors have underlined that the historical project of the nation state in most European countries has been to link the rights granted to citizens with the holding of the requisite nationality. Thus, nationality has become a key component of citizenship and the two concepts tend to converge.[35] In the cases of the above-mentioned naturalization of sportsmen, the acquisition of nationality remains a prerequisite condition to have the right to represent a State, but this is no longer the case in rugby. The international rugby board now permits the employment of up to three foreign players at any one time. Even if their employment is conditional on them having played for at least three years in their 'country of adoption' and not having already played for the national team of their country of origin, these new rugby rules on nationality could prefigure a revolution in the world of sport. In fact, the incorporation into the national team is here partially disconnected from the nationality of the sportsman, giving rise to a sport citizenship, which in not based on nationality.

[...]

Worldwide sporting stars, transnational adoption and identity deterritorialization

This essay evokes the relationship between the global mediatization of sporting events arising from developments in telecommunications and the resulting changes in identification processes. Competitions can be viewed worldwide much more easily than in the past. For example, the most important football matches of European clubs are regularly broadcast live on all continents. As a consequence, sportsmen have become worldwide stars. Because sport is an activity in which the identification process has a very important emotional aspect,[36] the possibility to follow a competition or a match live throughout the world is a major factor in increasing the geographical areas of people affected by the event. Thus, identification appears to become less subject to state borders and territorial criteria. In an article based on the example of Norwegian fans of English clubs, Hognestad suggests that, 'as a hugely popular phenomenon in Norway, football becomes interesting as a possible generator of identities that are liberated from the role of carrying its key national symbols', and that 'the attraction of English football provides a possible creative space of hybridization, in which the geographical distance itself generates options for a more liberated and imaginative playing with identities'.[37] Bourgeois and Whitson explain the identification with geographically distant clubs by the growing overlap between sport events and promotional activity: 'the owners of teams look for bigger markets and woo rich consumers and corporate bodies'. There is a resulting deterritorialization of identities that is closely linked to the capitalist system. Within this type of society, 'the identity is expressed by the choices available to consumers' and no longer by 'a feeling of belonging to a place' or by 'any implication in a collective destiny'.[38] Following a similar train of thought, Giulianotti and Robertson draw an analogy between big European football teams and transnational corporations (TNCs), and evoke the existence of 'deterritorialized communities of global consumers' underlining that 'transnational clubs like Manchester United, Juventus and Bayern Munich have global communities of supporters and merchandise consumers that are similar in size, if not patterns of identification, with the citizenry of nations'. In their view, these football communities, that they call 'self-invented virtual diasporas', 'are forged from the global dispersal of club-focused images and products, and from the voluntaristic identification of individuals with club-related symbols and practices'.[39]

From the points of view of the authors cited above, the identification of Japanese supporters with European clubs, for example, is primarily linked to the marketing politics pursued by these clubs. Players are transformed into commercial products and are called upon to play the role of mediators between the supporter and the team for which they play, in order to encourage the allegiance of the former to the latter. As a consequence, the resulting identification with the club is not inscribed in a territorial reading grid. The identity that emerges does not operate through clubs representing cities, regions or countries, but by the personal identification with stars that are part of a global star system. For example, supporters do not follow Real Madrid because it is a Spanish club, but because the team had strongly publicized players such as David Beckham in the squad. Because of this, before his move from Manchester United to Real Madrid, Reuter's correspondent in Asia, Jason Szep, asserted, 'the allegiance of millions of Asian fans is likely to move with him'.[40]

The increasing spatial reach of sports broadcasting gives rise to a pluralization of the ways in which people identify with modern sporting heroes. Besides the label of origin, other criteria of identification appear, such as, among others, aesthetic, lifestyle, biographical or behavioural ones. By stating this, the objective is not to deny the importance of territorial aspects in the identification processes to sportsmen and teams, but to show that these aspects are less and less important when taken into account. Concepts such as deterritorialization and denationalization allow us to shed light upon phenomena that have been ignored in the past. For example, if the transnational adoption of foreigners is inscribed in football's history, these players having very often represented the best expression of talent and fantasy, only a few studies exist on the cultural meaning of this acceptance.

In 2005, the Argentinean Diego Armando Maradona returned to Naples almost 15 years after his departure. More than 70,000 hysterical people attended the match in which he participated in the San Paolo stadium. More than any Neapolitan player, Maradona has been adopted and adored by Neapolitan fans who have elevated him to cult status. This devotion dates back to the 1980s, when Maradona enabled SSC Naples to win two Italian championships and, above all, to take an historical revenge against the well-off clubs of the wealthy northern cities of the Peninsula, Milan and Turin. During the semi-final of the 1990 World Cup played between Italy and Argentina in Naples, many Neapolitans preferred to support Argentina instead of Italy, which resulted in an increase in the historical tensions existing between the Southern and Northern parts of the country. Maradona's case merits particular attention because it shows that, in the context of a growing migratory circulation of sportsmen, the geographical origin of the latter is not a hindrance to identification. On the contrary, the individual identification with a foreign sporting star can sometimes surpass the criterion of national belonging when it comes to choosing which team to support.

[...] In terms of identities, denationalization can be defined as the loss of importance of the label of origin in the identification process with sportsmen and teams. The decreasing impact of the label of origin reflects the growing disconnection between identities and territories. This disjuncture[41] is linked to the migratory movements of people, both inside and outside professional sport, and to the development of global media. Occurring at every geographical level, from the national to the local, this disconnection induces deterritorialization.

Conclusion

Even if they continue to support ethnic nationalisms and the division of the world into nation states, sporting competitions can also play an opposite role by promoting a double movement of denationalization. Firstly, the integration of sportsmen of foreign origin in the national selections of their host countries, coupled with the global circulation of sports workers and the naturalizations linked to these migrations, favour the acknowledgement of a cultural pluralism within countries and encourage a de-ethnicization of the nation through sport. The appearance of a sporting citizenship in rugby not directly related to nationality shows that sport could even play an avant-garde role regarding denationalization. While leading sport authorities are still accustomed to thinking in state-national reading grid terms, they are also concerned with issues linked to nationality that occur outside of this framework. [...] The idea of creating a 'special independent commission' that could allow athletes to compete for a country without having the national passport would go some way towards dealing with the intensification of mobility of professional sportsmen.

Secondly, the worldwide diffusion of the sports spectacle heralded by the development of global media has stimulated a new playing with identities, resulting in spectators becoming interested in countries or areas that are sometimes very distant from their home. This also makes possible the transnational allegiance of supporters to global stars whose label of national origin doesn't play a key role in the process of identification. As an activity that is part of a worldwide popular culture, sport assumes here the role of precursor in the identity deterritorialization process challenging the postulate according to which there exists a perfect correspondence between a state, a territory and an individual identity. [...] By resituating the state-national reading grid of sport, which is often regarded as a given, into its historical context of genesis and development, its socially constructed nature becomes apparent. This should enable us to consider contemporary changes in the representation of the nation through sport as part of an evolution occurring within a broader, nonlinear historical process, which previously had the tendency to ethnicize the nation and to territorialize identities and which actually tends to de-ethnicize the first and deterritorialize the second.

Notes

1. Wimmer and Glick Schiller, 'Methodological Nationalism and Beyond. Nation-State Building. Migration, and the Social Sciences'.
2. Brenner, 'Beyond State-Centrism? Space, Territoriality, and Geographical Scale in Globalization Studies', 45.
3. Robertson, *Globalization: Social Theory and Global Culture*.
4. Brenner, 'Beyond State-Centrism?', 52.
5. Sassen, 'Globalization or Denationalization?', 15.
6. Boniface, *La terre est ronde comme un ballon. Geopolitique du football.*
7. Maguire *et al.*, 'The War of the Words? Identity Politics in Anglo-German Press Coverage of EURO 96'.
8. Anderson, *Imagined Communities: Reflections on the Origin and Spread of Nationalism.*
9. Duke and Crolley, *Football, Nationality and the State,* 4.

10. Habermas, *Apres l'Etat-nation: une nouvelle constellation politique;* Appadurai, 'Global Ethnoscopes. Notes and Queries for a Transnational Anthroplogy'; Soysal, *Limits of Citizenship; Migrants and Postnational Membership in Europe; Beck, What is Globalization?;* Sassen, 'The Repositioning of Citizenship: Toward New Types of Subjects and Spaces for Polities',

11. Armstrong and Giulianotti, 'Introducing Global Football Oppositions'.

12. The first international match recorded was played between England and Scotland in 1872.

13. Armstrong and Giulianotti, 'Introducing Global Football Oppositions', 2.

14. Papa and Panico, *Storia sociale del ealcio in Italia,* 73.

15. Lanfranchi, 'Football, cosmopolitisme et nationalisme'.

16. Holt and Mason, 'Le football, le fascisme et la politique étrangère britannique: l'Angleterre, l'Italic et l'Allemagne (1934–1935)', 79 and 89.

17. Arnaud, 'Des jeux de la victoire aux jeux de la paix? (1919–1924)', 135.

18. Schnapper, 'De l'Etat-nation au monde transnational. Du sens et de l'utilité du concept de diaspora'.

19. In Brenner, 'Beyond State-Centrism?, 49.

20. Laszlo Kubala was born in 1927 in Hungary to a Hungarian father and a Czech mother. He first played for the Hungarian national team. During the Second World War he moved to Czechoslovakia and played for the Czech national team. In 1949, he moved to Spain, where he received political asylum. He obtained Spanish nationality in 1952 and he also played for the national team. However, FIFA did not allow him to play for Spain in the qualifiers for the 1954 World Cup.

21. *I Quaderni del calcio,* 3, Second trimester 1999.

22. Calmat, 'Sport et nationalisme'.

23. Sassen,' The Repositioning of Citizenship', 3.

24. Papastergiadis, *The Turbulence of Migration, Globalization, Deterritorialization and Hybridity.*

25. Clarke *et al.,* 'New Europeans: Naturalisation and Citizenship in Europe', 49; Weil, 'L'accès à la citoyenneté. Unc comparaison de vingt-cinq lois sur la nationalité'.

26. Piguet, *L'immigration ans Suisse. 50 ans d'entrouverture.*

27. Personal interview, February 2003.

28. *Guerin Sportivo,* 27 (1554), 5–11 July 2005.

29. Lanfranchi and Taylor, *Moving with the Ball. The Migration of Professional Footballers;* Poli, *Lesmigrations internationales des footballeurs;* Bale and Maguire (eds), *The Global Sports Arena: Athletic Talent Migration in an Interdependent World.*

30. Poli, 'Conflit de couleurs. Enjeux géopolitiques autour de la naturalisation de sportifs africains'.

31. Gillon and Poli, 'Naturalisation de sportifs et fruite des muscles. Le cas des Jeux Olympiques de 2004'.

32. *Courrier des Balkans,* 9 January 2005 (www.balkans.eu.org).

33. *Le Monde,* 17–18 August 2003.

34. Back *et al. The Changing Face of Football. 270.*

35. Sassen, 'The Participation of States and Citizens in Global Governance'; Sassen, 'The Repositioning of Citizenship'; Courtois, 'Habermas et la question du nationalisme: le cas du Québec'; Déloye, 'Le débat contemporain sur la citoyenneté au prisme de la construction européenne'.

36. Bromberger, 'Se poser en s'opposant. Variations sur les antagonismes footballistiques de Marseille a Téhéran'.

37. Hognestad, 'Long-distance Football Support and Liminal Identities among Norwegian Fans', 97 and 108.

38. Bourgeois and Whitson, 'Le sport, les médias et la marchandisation des identities', 157 and 160.

39. Giulianotti and Robertson, 'The Globalization of Football: A Study in the Glocalization of the "Serious Life"', 551.

40. Reuters, 13 June 2003.

41. Appadurai, 'Disjuncture and Difference in the Global Culture Economy'.

References

Anderson, B. *Imagined Communities: Reflections on the Origin and Spread of Nationalism.* London: Verso, 1983.

Appadurai, A. 'Disjuncture and Difference in the Global Culture Economy'. *Theory. Culture, and Society 7* (1990): 295–310.

Appadurai, A. "Global Ethnoscapes. Notes and Queries for a Transnational Anthroplogy." In *Recapturing Anthropology. Working in the Present,* edited by R. G. Fox. Santa Fe: School of American Research Pr., 1991: 191–210.

Armstrong, G. and R. Giulianotti. "Introducing Global Football Oppositions." In *Fear and Loathing in World Football,* edited by G. Armstrong and R. Giulianotti. Oxford: Berg, 2001: 1–5.

Arnaud, P. "Des jeux de la victoire aux jeux de la paix? (1919–1924)." In *Sport et relations Internationales,* edited by P. Arnaud and A. Wahl. Metz: Universite de Metz, 1994: 133–55.

Back, I., T. Crabbe and J. Solomos. *The Changing Face of Football. Racism, Identity and Multiculture in the English Game.* Oxford: Berg, 2001.

Bale, I. and J. Maguire (eds). *The Global Sports Arena: Athletic Talent Migration in an Interdependent World.* London: Frank Cass, 1994.

Beck, U. *What is Globalization?* Cambridge: Polity Press, 2001.

Boniface, P. *La terre est ronde comme un ballon. Géopolitique du football.* Paris: Seuil, 2002.

Bourgeois, N. and D. Whitson. 'Le sport, les médias et la marchandisation des identitiés', *Sociologie et sociétés* 27, no, 1 (1999): 151–63.

Brenner, N. 'Beyond State-Centrism? Space, Territoriality, and Geographical Scale in Globalization Studies'. *Theory and Society* 28, no. 1 (1999): 39–78.

Bromberger, C. 'Se poser en s'opposant. Variations sur les antagonismes footballistiques de Marseille à Téhéran'. In *Football et identités. Les sentiments' appartenance en question,* edited by R. Poli. Neuchâtel: CIES, 2005: 35–55.

Calmat, A. 'Sport et nationalisme'. *Pouvoirs,* 61 (1992): 51–6.

Clarke, J., E. van Dam and L. Gooster. 'New Europeans: Naturalisation and Citizenship in Europe'. *Citizenship Studies 2,* no. 1 (1998): 43–54.

Courtois, S. "Habermas et la question du nationalisme: le cas du Québec." *Philosophiques* 27, no. 2 (2000): 377–401.

Déloye, Y. 'Le débat contemporain sur la citoyenneté au prisme de la construction européenne'. *Etudes européennes* (http://www.etudes-europennes.fr), (2004): 1–9.

Duke, V. and L. Crolley. *Football, Nationality and the State.* London: Addison Wesley Longman, 1996.

Gillon, P. and R. Poli. 'Naturalisation de sportifs et fuite des muscles. Le cas des Jeux Olympiques de 2004'. In *Sport et nationalité. Enjeux et problèmes,* edited by D. Oswald. Neuchâtel: CIES Editions (2007): 47–72.

Giulianotti, R. and R. Robertson. "The Globalization of Football: A Study in the Glocalization of the "Serious Life"." *British Journal of Sociology* 55, no. 4 (2004): 545–568.

Habermas, J. *Aprés l'Etat-nation: une nouvelle constellation politique.* Paris: Fayard, 2000.

Hognestad, H. "Long-distance Football Support and Liminal Identities among Norwegian Fans." In *Sport, Dance and Embodied Identities,* edited by N. Dyck and E. Archetti. Oxford: Berg, 2003, pp. 97–113.

Holt, R. and T. Mason. 'Le football, le fascisme et la politique étrangère britannique: l'Angleterre, l'Italie et l'Allemagne (1934–1935)'. In *Sport et relations internationales,* edited by P. Arnaud and A. Wahl. Metz: Université de Metz, 1994: 73–95.

Lanfranchi, P. "Football, cosmopolitisme et nationalisme." *Pouvoir* 10 (2002): 15–25.

Lanfranchi, P. and M. Taylor. *Moving with the Ball. The Migration of Professional Footballers,* Oxford: Berg, 2001.

Maguire, J., E. Poulton and C. Possamai. 'The War of the Words? Identity Politics in Anglo-German Press Coverage of EURO 96'. *European Journal of Communication* 14, no. 1 (1999): 61–89 Berg, 2001.

Papa, A. and G. Panico. *Storia sociale del calcio in Italia.* Bologna: II Mulino, 2002.

Papastergiadis, N. *The Turbulence of Migration. Globalization, Deterritorialization and Hybridity.* Cambridge: Polity Press, 2000.

Piguet, E. *L'immigration en Suisse. 50 ans d'entrouverture.* Lausanne: Presses polytechnique; et universitaires romandes, 2004.

Poli, R. *Les migrations internationales des footballeurs. Trajectoires de joueurs camerounais en Suisse.* Neuchâtel: CIES, 2004.

Poli, R. 'Conflit de couleurs. Enjeux géopolitiques autour de la naturalisation de sportifs africains'. *Auirepart,* 37 (2006): 149–61.

Robertson, R. *Globalization: Social Theory and Global Culture.* London: Sage, 2002.

Sassen, S. "Globalization or Denationalization?" *Review of International Political Economy* 10, no. 1 (2003): 1–22.

Sassen, S. 'The Participation of States and Citizens in Global Governance'. *Indiana Journal of Global Legal Studies* 10, no. 5 (2003): 5–28.

Sassen, S. 'The Repositioning of Citizenship: Toward New Types of Subjects and Spaces for Politics'. *Campbell Public. Affairs Institute* (http://www.campbellinstitute.org), (2004): 1–15.

Schnapper, D. 'De l'Etat-nation au monde transnational. Du sens et de lutilité du concept de diaspora'. *Revue Européenne des Migrations Internationales* 17, no. 2 (2001): 9–36.

Smith, A. *La passion du sport. Le football, le rugby et les appartenances en Europe.* Rennes: PUR, 2001.

Soysal, Y. *Limits of Citizenship: Migrants and Postnational Membership in Europe,* Chicago: The University of Chicago, 1994.

Weil, P. "L'accés à la citoyenneté, Unc comparaison de vingt-cinq lois sur la nationalité." *Travaux du centre d'études et de prévision du Ministre de l'Intérieur* (2002): 9–28.

Wimmer, A. and N. Glick Schiller. "Methodological Nationalism and Beyond. Nation-State Building, Migration, and the Social Sciences." *Global Networks* 2, no. 4 (2002): 301–34.

7.5

Cross-national cultural diffusion

The global spread of cricket

Jason Kaufman and Orlando Patterson

Why do some foreign practices take root while others either arrive dead in the water or take hold only to wither and die? Modern diffusion studies have focused primarily on the structural aspects of diffusion, or the existence of tangible points of contact between adopters and adoptees, as well as the environmental contexts that modulate such interactions. But as Strang and Soule (1998: 276) note, "[S]tructural opportunities for meaningful contact cannot tell us what sorts of practices are likely to diffuse," whereas an "analysis of the cultural bases of diffusion speaks more directly to what spreads, replacing a theory of connections with a theory of connecting." According to this more culturally minded approach, diffusing practices are more likely to be adopted when they are first made congruent with local cultural frames or understandings, and are thus "rendered salient, familiar and compelling" (Strang and Soule 1998: 276; see also Gottdiener 1985; Rogers 1995). In other cases, however, more than just "congruence" is needed for successful adoption; institutional support, repeated exposure, and/or active instruction in the new practice are required for it to "take hold" in new settings. The original cultural profile of that practice is often transformed in the process (e.g., Appadurai 1996; Bhabha 1994; Guillén 2001;

Watson 2002). Sometimes, moreover, it is the very difference in social, cultural, and political power between change agents and adopters that accounts for successful long-term diffusion.

One case that encompasses all of these factors is the cross-national diffusion of cricket. Cricket originated in England as an informal rural game, though it quickly emerged into a highly competitive sport. Over time, cricket evolved into an English national pastime, along with soccer, rugby, and horse racing (Allen 1990). Cricket began diffusing to other countries when British soldiers and settlers brought it with them to the various colonies of the empire, and today, most Commonwealth countries support active cricket cultures, though not all.

The case of Canada is particularly striking in this regard. Cricket was popular in Canada and the United States in the mid-nineteenth century—in fact, the first official international cricket match in the world took place between American and Canadian "elevens" in 1844 (Boiler 1994a: 23). The game's popularity rivaled that of baseball until the late nineteenth century, after which interest declined sharply. The game languished in both countries until quite recently, when new immigrants from the Caribbean and South Asia began arriving in North America in significant numbers

Jason Kaufman and Orlando Patterson, "Cross-National Cultural Diffusion: The Global Spread of Cricket" from *American Sociological Review* 70.1 (February 2005): 82–110. Copyright © 2005 by the American Sociological Association. Reprinted with the permission of the author and the American Sociological Association.

(Gunaratnam 1993; Steen 1999). This pattern of adoption-then-rejection poses important substantive and theoretical issues regarding the cross-national diffusion of cultural practices. Given Canada's—and to a lesser degree, America's—demographic, cultural, and socio-political connections to Britain, the game's unexpected demise there is puzzling, especially in contrast to its successful diffusion in far less "British" parts of the Commonwealth. At the same time, this disjuncture also seems at odds with several important perspectives in the socio-logical study of diffusion.

[...]

Cricket's universe: the study population

As noted earlier, our primary concern here is the transmission of a complex innovation between very complex collective units.[1] This presents formidable problems of verification, made more difficult by the fact that there are limited data sources on sports during our period of focus—the mid-nineteenth through early twentieth centuries. We are concerned with uncovering those covariates that explain ulti-mately successful or unsuccessful cases of diffu-sion among the population of societies exposed to the game of cricket. It will thus be enough for us to define, first, the population of British-influenced societies that were exposed to and that initially played the game (the population of potential long-term adoptees); and second, the success or failure of adoption in each case within that population, including cases where discon-tinuation followed successful adoption. Please note that the focus of our inquiry is on the early period when cricket was first being institution-alized in England and spread throughout its colonies (i.e., the 19th and early 20th centu-ries). Much happened in the cricket world after World War II (when many of these colonies gained independence) that we cannot account for here. Wherever possible, we try to account for late-twentieth-century manifestations of the game, but our empirical focus is on the earlier period in which the game was either successfully or unsuccessfully transplanted to the various British settlements considered here.

One reason the global diffusion of cricket is of particular sociological interest is that it is so strongly associated with a specific country of origin. Cricket was first played in England, and since its earliest years, global diffusion of the game has been controlled by Englishmen and their cricket clubs. C.L.R. James (1963: 164), the great West Indian social analyst, once wrote, for example, "Cricket was one of the most com-plete products of that previous age to which a man like Dickens always looked back with such nostalgia. ... It is the only contribution of the English educational system of the nineteenth century to the general education of Western civilization." Similarly, J. A. Mangan (1986: 153), author of *The Games Ethic and Imperialism*, wrote, "Cricket was the umbilical cord of Empire linking the mother country with her children."

Moreover, the game was deliberately "exported" to the British colonies as part of British colonial policy. According to one histo-rian of the game, Brian Stoddart (1988: 658), "Cricket was considered the main vehicle for transferring the appropriate British moral code from the messengers of empire to the local populations."

International cricket has long since been dominated by ten core constituencies, each of which is officially recognized by the International Cricket Council (ICC) as "qualified to play offi-cial Test matches." The ICC was founded in England in 1909 and originally comprised just three member countries: England, Australia, and South Africa. (South Africa was expelled from the Commonwealth, and thus the ICC, in 1961 but was reappointed to the ICC as a "full member" nation in 1991.) In 1926, India, New Zealand, and a conglomeration of British Caribbean islands (the West Indies) were added to the ICC's membership, allowing them to compete in global competition at the highest level. The remaining four full-member nations are Bangladesh, Pakistan, Sri Lanka, and Zimbabwe. These ten countries thus make up what one might view as those parts of the world in which cricket has in fact attained the status of "hegemonic sports culture." Note the con-spicuous absence of Canada, itself a major Commonwealth country. The United States is excluded as well. These twelve nations—the world's ten major cricketing countries plus the United States and Canada—constitute the pri-mary set of cases analyzed here (see Table 7.5.1).

All of the foregoing reaffirms that the global diffusion of cricket is more than just a case of a popular sporting activity being adopted by societies around the world. Cricket has never been an Olympic sport, and its main international body, the ICC, was originally an appendage of the British colonial state. Until 1965, in fact, it was the express policy of the ICC to admit only Commonwealth countries as members—the International Cricket Council was actually named the *Imperial* Cricket Council until 1965, further evidence of its distinct ties to the British colonial system. At the same time, it is rather ironic that so many countries with painful colonial histories—India and the West Indies, for example—dominate the sport today. We will explore in detail all of the questions raised so far, but first, we must outline more specifically how we determine "successful" diffusion.

Hegemonic sports culture: definition and application

By what criteria do we designate some countries as "cricket-playing countries" and others as merely countries where cricket is played, or not played at all? In trying to define what exactly constitutes a national sports culture we borrow Markovits and Hellerman's (2001) concept of "hegemonic sports culture." In their timely monograph, *Offside: Soccer and American Exceptionalism,* Markovits and Hellerman ask why soccer (i.e., "football" in international parlance) is not more popular in the United States. Americans play soccer, field an increasingly competitive World Cup squad, and have supported professional soccer leagues of varying success, but, argue Markovits and Hellerman, soccer is still not a national pastime in America. By this they mean that there is not a large audience for soccer among American sports fans. Soccer matches are not major events in America, players are not idolized, and the sport is not a common topic of conversation as are football, baseball, and basketball. In other words, a hegemonic sports culture is one that "dominates a country's emotional attachments" (Markovits and Hellerman 2001: 10).

Nevertheless, measuring comparative levels of "emotional attachment" to sport is extremely difficult. Should emotional attachment be measured relative to those who are self-reported sports fans? Or should we more properly consider what percentage of the total population is committed to, or at least interested in, a given sport? There is no clear answer to this question, nor do Markovits and Hellerman attempt to provide one. They argue for a more qualitative, impressionistic approach: Are the local sports

Table 7.5.1. The study population in brief

Potential Adopter Nations	Key Period of "Popularization"	"Successful" Adopters	"Failed" Adopters	References
Australia	1850s–70s	****		Cashman 1998a; Mandle 1973; Pollard 1987
British Caribbean (West Indies)	1830s–60s	****		Beckles 1998a, 1998b; James 1963; Stoddart 1998a;
Canada	1860s-90s		****	Boller 1994b; Hall and McCulloch 1895; Metcalfe 1987
England	17th–18th centuries	****		Allen 1990; Brookes 1978; Dunning and Sheard 1979; Mandle 1973; Sandiford 1998a
India (including Bangladesh & Pakistan)	1880s–1900s	****		Appadurai 1996; Bose 1990; Cashman 1980, 1998b; Nandy 2000
New Zealand	1860s–90s	****		Ryan 1998; Reese 1927
South Africa	1860s–80s	****		Merritt and Nauright 1998; Stoddart 1998b
Sri Lanka	1880s–90s	****		Cashman 1998b; Perera 1998, 1999
United States	1860s–90s		****	Boller 1994b; Kirsch 1989, 1991; Mrozek 1983
Zimbabwe	1890s–1900s	****		Stoddart 1998b; Winch 1983

pages filled with soccer news? Do patrons at bars and cafes talk soccer with any frequency? Does one see soccer stars endorsing major products on TV and in print media? How is soccer represented in the media relative to other sports?

To give but two brief examples, we searched the sports pages of one major Canadian and one major Australian newspaper (both with free Internet editions) for the day July 17, 2002. The *Sydney Morning Herald*, a major daily newspaper from Sydney, Australia, contained an entire section devoted to cricket news (www. smh.com.au/sport/cricket). On this particular day, it included 10 articles on cricket, spanning the range from "Wanted: Australian all-rounder" (i.e., a player who can pitch, field, and bat equally well) to news of the birth of cricketeer Adam Holioake's son. This is exactly the kind of minutiae that constitutes a hegemonic sports culture. Fans are interested not only in the latest standings and scores but in the future prospects of leading teams and even the daily ups and downs of players' lives. In contrast, the *Toronto Globe and Mail* (www.globeandmail. ca), one of Canada's leading daily newspapers, did not post a single article about cricket on this day at the height of the warm-weather season in Canada. If this is any testament to the local

salience of cricket, Canadians regard it as a marginal practice indeed.

Figure 7.5.1 illustrates a more systematic comparison of cricket coverage in the sports pages of online newspapers from 12 relevant countries at four points in time (one day in each season of the year).[2] Of the 12 articles surveyed, the United States, Canada, and Zimbabwe contained the fewest articles on cricket. Shortly, we will recount the history of cricket in the United States and Canada in detail. We do not attempt to deal with the case of contemporary Zimbabwe owing to the vast disruptions experienced in its political and economic systems of late. We suspect that expressing an interest in anything as "British" as cricket in contemporary Zimbabwe could in fact be quite dangerous. This was not the case in earlier decades, however, as evidenced by Zimbabwe's admission into the top tier of "test match" cricket. Note, too, that England has the next lowest number of cricket stories—an average of only about 8 per cent of the sports coverage on these particular days, though 17 per cent of the sports coverage was dedicated to cricket in the one "summer" edition we investigated. (There was no such summer "bounce" in the Canadian and American newspapers that we examined.) Naturally, these percentages reflect not only local interest in

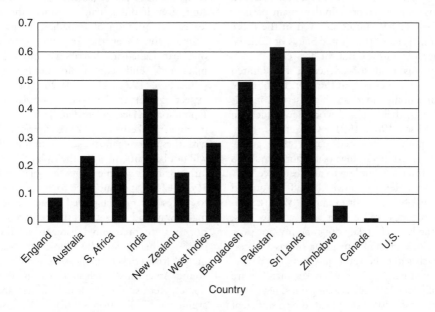

Figure 7.5.1. Average percentage of sports stories about cricket in select national newspapers.
Note: Online editions: October 15, 2003; January 6, April 15, July 5, 2004

335

cricket but also the prevalence of newsworthy events in other local sports. Our concern here is not on the exact distribution of coverage, however, but on the popularity of cricket more generally. From what we found in these newspapers, we can tentatively conclude that cricket has become a "hegemonic sports culture" in much but not all of the Commonwealth. Our endeavor is to explain this variance in the diffusion of the sport.

Traditional explanations of the failure of cricket in Canada and the United States

In trying to explain the virtual absence of popular interest in cricket in the US and Canada, we encountered several common arguments. The most obvious, having to do with climate, is tempting but ultimately unsatisfactory. True, Canadians are fanatical about ice hockey, a decidedly cold-weather sport; and true, most of the leading cricket-playing nations do not suffer particularly cold winters. On the other hand, Canadians enjoy a wide variety of warm-weather sports, including not only baseball but also field hockey, football, and lacrosse. Furthermore, England, where the game was invented, is hardly a "warm" country itself. Indeed, the game is played there only in the summer season, which is subject to more rain than many parts of Canada. Nor has cricket survived in the more temperate parts of the United States or Canada. Weather, obviously, is not the answer.

Some historians of cricket in the United States have suggested that the sport is not more popular among Americans because it is inconsistent with their cultural worldview (Adelman 1986; Kirsch 1989, 1991). Cricket is a long, slow, tightly regimented game, they argue, whereas Americans are always in a hurry and anxious for results. According to nineteenth-century sportswriter Henry Chadwick (1868: 52, quoted in Kirsch 1991: 12), for example, "We fast people of America, call cricket slow and tedious; while the leisurely, take-your-time-my-boy people of England think our game of baseball too fast. Each game, however, just suits the people of the two nations." True, cricket matches are generally longer than baseball games; nevertheless, time itself does not appear to be a sufficient explanation. While international test matches can last up to five days, many local matches are only one day in duration. In Australia, for example, an abbreviated, "limited overs" version of cricket is popular with television audiences (Cashman 1998a). Anthropologist Arjun Appadurai (1996: 101) even argues that, "Cricket is perfectly suited for television, with its many pauses, its spatial concentration of action, and its extended format. ... It is the perfect television sport." Moreover, when played by amateurs, among whom wickets fall quickly, the game easily adapts to a spirited afternoon "knock" no longer than amateur soccer or baseball games. Note, too, that such perceptions are as much an effect of the differential status of sports as a cause thereof: Americans' pejorative descriptions of cricket are a product, as well as a cause of, the sport's wider failure to reach "hegemonic" status in the United States.

Similarly, cricket has been described by some as a sport that requires too much submission (i.e., orderly behavior) for Americans. Neither spitting nor swearing are officially condoned on the cricket field, for example, and disagreement with match officials is strictly forbidden.[3]

Nonetheless, while some might criticize Americans for their ungainly habits, this would hardly appear to constitute a satisfactory sociological explanation, particularly when Americans are so attracted to other sports that make similar demands of players, such as tennis and golf. And, even if this is true of Americans, it still leaves the question of Canadian habits unaccounted for. Given the frequency with which one hears Canadians described as modest, well-mannered, and community-minded people (e.g., Frye 1971; Lipset 1996), one would expect cricket to be wildly popular in the Dominion. In fact, a Canadian, James Naismith, invented basketball (in Massachusetts, USA) with these very characteristics in mind: "If men will not be gentlemanly in their play," he said in introducing the game to its first players (Wise 1989: 124), "it is our place to encourage them to games that may be played by gentlemen in a manly way, and show them that science is superior to brute force with a disregard for the feelings of others." So why didn't Dr. Naismith merely foist cricket on these "ungentlemanly" young Americans? Such explanations echo, in homely terms, the "cultural understanding" argument of diffusion scholars. We discount such explanations as overly simplistic and, in some cases, patently biased.

This brings us to another popular explanation of "Americo-Canadian Exceptionalism"—Anglophobia. This perspective focuses on Canadians and Americans' (presumably negative) disposition toward England and the English. True, a significant minority of Canadians claim French, not English heritage, and a large percentage of Canada's Anglo-population also trace their heritage back to Scotland and Ireland—all possible reasons for Canadian antipathy toward a cultural practice as English as cricket. On the other hand, one can easily refute such arguments with reference to other cricket-playing countries: Australia was populated by many people of Scottish and Irish heritage, for example, and a large portion of its Anglo-population can actually blame the cruelties of the English penal system for sending their ancestors to Australia in the first place. The white population of South Africa, another cricketing nation, is also comprised of rival English and Dutch, as well as indigenous African, peoples. Why would Canadians be any more resistant to an English cultural practice like cricket than their counterparts in these other former colonies? Why, moreover, would Canadians be more hostile to English culture than the descendants of peoples cruelly subjugated by the English in places like Jamaica, Barbados, India, Bangladesh, Pakistan, and Sri Lanka? Finally, why would Americans be so enamored with tennis and golf, both sports with British origins, but not cricket?[4] While we will argue that nationalism did play a significant role in American and Canadian attitudes toward cricket, we do not accept so facile an explanation as their contempt for all things British. Cricket was widely perceived by American and Canadian audiences to be a British "affectation" for reasons particular to the game's history in their respective countries. Explaining how this came to be is a major part of this project.

One related thesis about the decline of American and Canadian interest focuses on changes in the rate of English immigration to both countries (e.g., Metcalfe 1987). It is true that many early adherents of the game were British immigrants, civil servants, and military personnel, particularly in Canada, where British troops were garrisoned until 1867. In the United States, moreover, some cricket clubs, such as the famous St. George Club of New York, were largely peopled by British residents. Such ethno-national social clubs were exceedingly popular in the United States in the late nineteenth century (Kaufman 2002). Nonetheless, there is clear evidence that many "native-born" Americans and Canadians participated in cricket alongside their British-born counterparts in the late nineteenth century. Consider, for example, the following observation made in the 1895 book, *Sixty Years of Canadian Cricket* (Patteson quoted in Hall and McCulloch 1895: 258): "The so-called American eleven in 1859 contained [only] one native-born American. ... In 1860 the number of Americans had slightly increased. And now, in 1894, all are native Americans 'bar one.'" Furthermore, many of today's dominant cricketing countries have scarcely any population of direct British descent, and in the cases of Australia and New Zealand, one must still grapple with the question of how a British sport like cricket survived and flourished in the face of declining immigration flows and the declining influence of British culture and identity on their own national cultures. In other words, we must go beyond the question of cricket's *transmission* to the foregoing countries and ask how and why the sport was actually *adopted* by locals and reconstructed as a persistent national pastime (the final, *acculturation* phase of cultural diffusion).

One final "common" explanation of the failure of cricket in British North America is the rising popularity of baseball, an American sport with similar origins and style of play. There is some truth to this argument, at least to the extent that the rise of baseball and the decline of cricket do seem temporally related. Why this is so is hard to explain, however. Few Canadians would willingly admit that they prefer American to British culture. In fact, a large part of Canadian national identity is focused around their very distaste for Americans and American cultural hegemony (Frye 1971). Why would Canadians replace English cricket with a sport from a country to which they are so poorly disposed? We take seriously the need to explain the rise of baseball and decline of cricket in two countries with distinctive cultural ties to cricket's motherland, England. We turn first, however, to the initial invention and diffusion of cricket in the British Empire.

Analysis: network-building and class competition in the global diffusion of sport

The invention of cricket and its original transmission throughout the British Empire

Despite its stodgy reputation in America, cricket was not originally an aristocratic game. In its earliest incarnation cricket was, in fact, an agrarian pastime for modest farmers and craftsmen. Though historical precedents exist as far back as the twelfth century, English cricket is commonly thought to have come into its own in the seventeenth century (Allen 1990: 16–17; also Brookes 1978; James 1963: 164). According to most historical accounts, it was gambling that truly inspired enthusiasm for cricket among England's upper classes (e.g., Allen 1990; James 1963; Sandiford 1994). Country gentlemen found that they could field highly competitive teams by hiring skilled "players" (i.e., professionals) to work on their estates, thus inaugurating a long tradition of collaboration between "gentlemen and players," in which elites and commoners played cricket side-by-side (Warner 1950).

At the same time, English elites encouraged their colonial subjects to play cricket because of the game's professed ability to discipline and civilize men, English and native alike.[5] The literature on colonial cricket is rather explicit in this regard. After touring India and Burma with an amateur team from Oxford University, author Cecil Headlam (1903: 168–69) commented, "[C]ricket unites, as in India, the rulers and the ruled. It also provides a moral training, an education in pluck, and nerve, and self-restraint, far more valuable to the character of the ordinary native than the mere learning by heart of a play of Shakespeare." Interestingly, Indian cricket was originally supported by British and Indian elites alike. Britons like Lord Harris, governor of Bombay from 1890–95, sponsored tournaments between Indian and English teams. Similarly, cricket-playing was endorsed and encouraged by local elites as "an aristocratic game which upheld traditional notions of social hierarchy and patronage" (Cashman 1979: 197; also Bose 1990), Thus, it was a win-win situation for everyone concerned: cricket reaffirmed the authority of English and

Indian elites over their respective constituencies while providing a forum for social interaction between them.

The same was true elsewhere in the colonies. Cricket was promoted as an English sport for both Englishmen and natives. In 1868, a famous all-Aborigine squad of Australian cricketers toured England. Parsi teams from India came in 1886 and 1888. Even in South Africa, non-whites were encouraged to play cricket, though on rigidly segregated terms (Merrett and Nauright 1998: 55–57). The British colonies in the Caribbean are particularly well known for their legacy of interracial play (Beckles 1998a, 1998b; Beckles and Stoddart 1995; Cozier 1978; James 1963; Sandiford 1998c). "From as early as the 1860s the secondary schools and churches in Barbados deliberately began to use cricket as a socializing and civilizing agent," writes historian Keith Sandiford (1998c: 1–2). "In those days the schools were dominated by headmasters who had come from Victorian Britain steeped in the public school ethos which then placed great store in team sports."

Indeed, the popularity of cricket in England itself owes much to its secondary education system. Cricket was regarded as an important right of passage for young British males, particularly those schooled in the elite "public schools" erected to train the future aristocrats of the empire (Mangan 1986; Penn 1999; Sandiford 1994; Stoddart and Sandiford 1998; Williams 2001).

> [British] educators encouraged cricket participation among their students in the profound conviction that it produced better citizens as well as scholars. ... [They] argued that organized sports could bring order and discipline to aggressive groups of rich, spoilt and rebellious brats. ... The public schools established the cricketing cult from about 1830 onwards. By 1860 it was an essential feature of their curriculum.
>
> (Sandiford 1998a:14)

So central did cricket become to British elite education that by the mid-nineteenth century, headmasters began hiring professional cricketers to coach their boys to victory over rival schools.

The creation of distinctly British secondary schools throughout the colonies of the British Empire also helped expose indigenous populations to the game. In Jamaica, for example, the educational system strongly promoted cricket in the secondary schools where, because of the merit principle in admissions, a substantial minority of darker lads of working-class background could be found. The same was true in the Asian Subcontinent, where promising young lads from low-status households were sometimes sent to English-style boarding schools and thus introduced to cricket. The importance of these schools in the cultivation of national cricket cultures is particularly evident in places where the educational system followed a different model. As Sandiford (1998b: 4) points out, cricket languished in Anglo-African colonies like Kenya, Nigeria, and Uganda, where, in the nineteenth century, "European communities remained only minute fractions of the overall population and where the Victorian public school ethos never really took root." British-run secondary schools there were more committed to religious education than to competition and sport. This attitude was likely a result of the fact that British colonization began in these countries rather late, by which time the goals of imperialism had become somewhat more modest.[6] The virtual absence of a dedicated white settler population contributed to a garrison mentality in which the English sought to mollify, rather than civilize, their central African subjects. Similarly, the British did not encourage indigenous participation in cricket in the Far East (Stoddart 1998b: 136–37).

Several unique features of the game itself appear to have facilitated its cross-national adoption and acculturation in many parts of the Commonwealth. That cricket requires no physical contact between players explains in part its diffusion to mixed-race and deeply class-divided colonies where "contact" sports like rugby and soccer/football were either ignored, practiced only among whites, or played along strictly segregated lines (meaning that white teams only played white teams, and so forth [Stoddart 1988]). Interracial play was permissible as long as it did not involve close contact, as with cricket. The formal attire of official cricket matches also helped smooth the way for integrated play—even in the searing heat of India and the Caribbean, players were expected to wear white or cream flannel trousers and long-sleeved white shirts. It is significant, too, that even the most minor of games required two umpires dressed in authoritative white overcoats

and that a cardinal principle of the game was that the umpires' decisions were always final. (The umpires were also invariably members of the elite class in interclass games.) These arrangements effectively curtailed any rabble-rousing or arguments that would demean the "masters" or undermine the pervasive atmosphere of *noblesse oblige* in the colonial milieu. Thus, even in England, non-whites were permitted to play on local cricket teams. In fact, one of the most famous batsmen in all of English cricket history is a man known by the name of Ranjitsinhji, a native of India who originally learned the game at Rajkumar College and later played at the University of Cambridge before going on to become an English sports celebrity (Williams 2001: 22–32).

Another important feature of the game that facilitated interracial play was "stacking," or "positional segregation," within teams. From its earliest period in Britain, we find stacking along class lines in cricket: bowling and wicket-keeping were performed by low-status "players" while the roles of star batsmen and captain were mainly reserved for high-status "gentlemen." The practice of stacking thus allowed elite Englishmen to recruit nonwhite and lower-class players without compromising the social segregation prevalent in English society more generally. Gentlemen and players were allocated separate changing rooms and entrances to the field of play; and separate accommodations were arranged for team travel; team captains were exclusively drawn from the amateur (i.e., high-status) ranks; and "professionals were expected, independently of relativities of age and skill, to call amateurs, 'Sir,' and, particularly when young, to perform menial duties around the ground" (Dunning and Sheard 1979: 181). Stacking was even more important in multiracial British colonies, such as Jamaica, Barbados, and India, where "natives" were generally expected to specialize in bowling, thus leaving captaining, umpiring, and batting to their colonial overseers. Malcolm (2001) has shown that this pattern was not only transferred to the colonies but persists to this day in British cricket clubs where, as late as 1990, 70 per cent of the bowlers were of West Indian and other colonial ancestry. Until fairly recently, even the most superlative nonwhite players were barred from captaining their clubs or national teams (Coakley 1998).

Nonetheless, enthusiasm for and participation in cricket became a national pastime in every former major colony of the British Empire *except* Canada and the United States. In the cricketing colonies, elite enthusiasm for the game was transferred to the population at large. In the United States and Canada, on the other hand, cricket remained largely a sport for country club members and elite boarding school students (Kirsch 1989, 1991; Lester 1951; Melville 1998; Metcalfe 1987; Redmond 1979). In other words, cricket culture had been transmitted to, and adopted by, some portion of the American and Canadian populations, but it failed to persist or develop as a popular pastime in both cases. Understanding variance in the global diffusion of cricket thus requires further investigation of the *acculturation* process, or the way the meaning and cultural significance of the game was transformed in the process of diffusion. As mentioned earlier, we do not find explanations based on "national values" or "cultural resonance" useful in this regard. Instead, we look carefully at the social systems of each country, as well as actual histories of the game (and related games) in them.

Adoption followed by failed acculturation: elite versus popular sports in Canada and the United States

The most distinctive feature of the history of cricket in both the United States and Canada is its elevation to a pastime for elites only. [...]

The dismal fate of cricket in Canada. As fewer Canadian elite schools devoted time to training young men in the finer points of cricket, the quantity and quality of play declined. Without fresh infusions of talent or widespread networks of league play, the game gradually took on the air of a marginal, old-fashioned pastime for antiquarians and Anglophiles. [...]

The central feature of the Canadian story is thus the isolation of cricket as a class-specific pastime. The clubby "Britishness" of Canadian elites may be one reason for this split, but the key causal factor remains the exclusivity of the sport, not its association with Britain per se. In looking at Canadian sports history of the late nineteenth and early twentieth centuries, one

sees substantial evidence that cricket was an increasingly insular pastime, practiced only by those with the time and money to join exclusive clubs. Contributors to an 1895 volume, *Sixty Years of Canadian Cricket* (Hall and McCulloch, eds.), refer frequently to the gentlemanly, amateurish nature of the Canadian game, as compared to its quasi-professional English variant. In addition, Canadian sports historian Richard Gruneau (1983: 108–9) notes that elite sports teams in Canada actually began avoiding competition with non-elite teams in the mid-to-late nineteenth century. Gruneau (1983: 109) hypothesizes that "as the Canadian class structure began to elaborate, and as meritocratic liberal values began to develop widespread support, members of the dominant class apparently became unable to tolerate the possibility of defeat at the hands of those they considered to be their social inferiors. They also may have become progressively more alarmed at the prospect that commercialism in sport could very easily get out of hand under such conditions and vulgarize traditional upper-class views of 'the nobility of play.'" Cricket had become for them something precious, part of their heritage, an elite pastime more akin to ancestor worship than play. In England, by contrast, cricket remained something spirited and boisterous, as well as highly competitive, thus facilitating the incorporation of low-status "players" into the game.

Counterfactual: the rise of baseball in the United States. This last observation points to a second facet of cricket's ultimate rejection in North America: its failure to cultivate mass appeal through frequent matches in which large crowds, intense rivalries, and spirited fans might bring the sport to the attention of major portions of the population. The history of American baseball provides a telling comparison with that of cricket in both the United States and Canada. Though baseball and cricket both began as relatively informal leisure games in the United States, baseball was later blessed by a cadre of brilliant entrepreneurs, determined to make it the "nation's pastime." One such person was A. G. Spalding, star player, manager, league organizer, and sports manufacturer. To call Spalding an impresario or a marketing genius would be a bit of an understatement. He engaged in every part of the game, from promoting star players and intercity rivalries to squelching nascent efforts at labor organization among players (Levine 1985).

In addition to cricket, baseball had other rivals for people's time and money in the United States—crew regattas were major business for some time, for example, as were bicycle races, track meets, and college football games (Smith 1988). Spalding helped secure baseball's place in American national culture through a two-part strategy: On the one hand, he promoted the highest possible level of play with the widest possible audience by creating and managing a system of professional league play throughout North America. On the other hand, he built a manufacturing and marketing empire devoted to selling youngsters the accoutrements of the game—the Spalding name still stands prominent in the world of sporting goods. In the late 1870s, after a successful career as player and manager, Spalding published an official rulebook for the game and also licensed official merchandise for play. Spalding also produced bats and balls of different sizes and shapes for players of various abilities and backgrounds. Noting that American educators were increasingly interested in finding healthy leisure pursuits for students, Spalding donated equipment and trophies to groups like the Public School Athletic League (Levine 1985: 110–12).[7] Spalding is even credited with inventing the now widely discredited "Cooperstown myth," by which the origins of baseball were explained in a compelling story of its humble but ingenious small-town roots (see Spalding [1911] 1992).

[...]

At the same time, Spalding contributed to the emerging American consensus that cricket was an effeminate game for men too precious to play baseball. In his best-selling 1911 book, *America's National Game,* Spalding boasts ([1911] 1992: 7), "I have declared that Cricket is a genteel game. It is. Our British Cricketer, having finished his day's labor at noon, may don his negligee shirt, his white trousers, his gorgeous hosiery and his canvas shoes, and sally forth to the field of sport, with his sweetheart on one arm and his Cricket bat under the other, knowing that he may engage in his national pastime without soiling his linen or neglecting his lady. ... Not so the American Ball Player. He may be a veritable Beau Brummel in social life. He may be the Swellest Swell of the Smart Set

in Swelldom; but when he dons his Base Ball suit, he says good-bye to society, doffs his gentility, and becomes—just a Ball Player! He knows that his business now is to play ball, and that first of all he is expected to attend to business. ... Cricket is a gentle pastime. Base Ball is War! Cricket is an Athletic Sociable [sic], played and applauded in a conventional, decorous and English manner. Base Ball is an Athletic Turmoil, played and applauded in an unconventional, enthusiastic and American manner."

[...] Many of the wealthy sons of American and Canadian society eschewed cricket for baseball, perhaps, in part, because of late-nineteenth-century rhetoric about the manliness of American culture. The 1875 *Harvard Book* does not include reference to a college baseball team, for example, but the *1887–88 Annual Report* (Harvard College 1889: 29) proudly reports a gift of $25,000 from Mr. Henry Reginald Astor Carey to build appropriate facilities for "the Baseball Nine." In fact, beginning in the 1860s and 70s, baseball became an intensely popular sport at the nation's most prestigious colleges. America's first recorded intercollegiate game took place in 1859 between Amherst and Williams. Bowdoin, Middlebury, Dartmouth, Brown, Trinity, Hamilton, Princeton, and Kenyon all had organized teams by 1862. "By the end of the 1870s, a group of eastern colleges, consisting of Amherst, Brown, Dartmouth, Harvard, Princeton, and Yale, were playing regular home and away series of games" (Smith 1988: 59). College teams also regularly played professional teams, and play was extremely competitive; so much so that the colleges began offering "financial incentives" to especially talented players (Smith 1988: 62–66).

The incipient professionalization of college athletics presented America's elite college presidents with something of a conundrum, another key to understanding the trajectories of cricket and baseball in the United States and Canada. Baseball's popularity grew through the result of excessive promotion, intense competition, and a do-anything-for-victory mentality among coaches and players. Aspiring athletes at America's elite colleges were clearly attracted by the glamour and notoriety of the game. (Posh summer jobs playing exhibition baseball at resort hotels and other financial "perks" for playing were probably also attractions.) At the same time, college masters and alumni objected

341

strongly to this development; they preferred a sports ethic closer to Spalding's stereotype of English cricket—leisurely, good-natured, and safe. College presidents had previously tried to ban excessively violent sports to no avail— American-style tackle football was first developed at Harvard College, where it was repeatedly and unsuccessfully banned by the president. American college presidents responded to the emergence of pay-for-play with equal reproach. Even the notion of hiring professional, full-time coaches for college teams was originally considered anathema by college boards (Mrozek 1983; Smith 1988; Townsend 1996).

American college masters eventually managed to minimize financial incentives for student-athletes, but the wider "professionalization" of certain sports continued nonetheless. Crew, football, baseball, and track and field attracted enormous audiences, particularly when rival schools, such as Harvard and Yale, had their annual meetings. Winning teams often received valuable cash prizes. Competition became increasingly defined around key dates and rivalries. Thanksgiving Day became a focal point of the college football season, for example, and competitive schools could bring in tens of thousands of dollars at the gate. Major crew regattas and track meets could also bring in crowds of 10,000 or more (Smith 1988: 30–34). By this time, therefore any college athlete still devoted to cricket would had to have asked himself why he was willing to forego the glory and gammon of the era's more popular sports— especially baseball, which essentially requires the same skill-set as cricket.

Whereas football, crew, and track and field all remained more or less confined to the collegiate arena, baseball supported a number of professional leagues in addition to the college teams. An 1888 *New York Times* story ("The Game Was Stopped") reports a crowd of 40,000 spectators at a professional baseball game outside of Philadelphia; so many, in fact, that the game was "called" after a mob of unseated fans surged onto the field at the end of the first inning. Pro-am baseball games were also a common occurrence, which surely contributed to the sport's popularity on college campuses. American baseball, in sum, increasingly resembled English cricket: a sport in which elites and commoners shared a passion for the game, one in which gambling, professionalism, and a willingness to do anything to win were fundamental.

Cricket in the United States. The place of cricket in late-nineteenth-century American society could hardly be more different: Though cricket was originally popularized in the United States by working-class immigrants from the British Isles, it later became a sport practiced by only a select few Americans (Melville 1998: 16–17, 25). Note, moreover, that while the increasing popularity of baseball did present a formidable challenge to American cricket, the two games existed comfortably side-by-side throughout the 1850s and 60s. It was not uncommon, in fact, for cricket and baseball teams to challenge one another to matches in their rival's sport (Melville 1998: 67). In truth, it was American elites' exclusivist attitude toward cricket that led to the sport's decline among the population at large. As in Canada, American cricket players increasingly retreated to small, elite clubs, and competition with rival "elevens" was quickly restricted to a small coterie of suitable teams (Kirsch 1989: 221–22).

Over time, the sport's snooty image took a toll on the popularity of cricket among Americans at large, an image that elites sought to cultivate. In contrast to the robust English tradition of "gentlemen and players," American cricket clubs strictly forbade professionals from play, even if it meant bitter defeat at the hands of traveling English and Australian teams. Melville (1998: 77; also 120–22) notes that, "As the old-line [American] competitive cricket clubs went into decline, their roles were assumed by cricket organizations dedicated to providing an environment of more socially selective participation upon strictly amateur lines." A 1907 *New York Times* story ("Cricket") quips, "Once more the game of cricket has been shown to be a languishing exotic in New York." It noted, "A visiting team of Englishmen have worked their will upon the local cricketers. ... In the West, New York is supposed to be the seat and centre of Anglomania. But the West ought to be softened when it sees how very badly New York plays the Anglican national game. Cricketally [sic] speaking, Philadelphia is the Anglomaniacal town." Indeed, with the exception of a few New England college teams, cricket thrived only in Philadelphia by the end of the nineteenth century. As early as 1884, a *New York Times* story ("Philadelphia Cricketers") joked, "Residents of American cities where cricket is not played, except by a few homesick

Englishmen, assert that it is played in Philadelphia because cricket is the slowest of games and Philadelphia the slowest of cities."

Regardless of the Philadelphians' supposed motives, it is true that a handful of Philadelphia-based teams provided the bulk of American training and participation in the sport during the late nineteenth and early twentieth centuries. One finds little evidence, furthermore, that the Philadelphians were concerned about the overall decline of interest in American cricket; in fact, they appear to have encouraged it. They confined the game to prestigious country clubs like the Merion and Belmont Cricket Clubs, founded in 1865 and 1874 respectively. Sports historian George Kirsch (1991: 15) sums up the Philadelphia scene, and the American milieu more generally, by saying:

> The upper-class "Proper Philadelphians" who patronized the sport after the Civil War did not wish to convert the masses. They preferred their leisurely game because they were amateur sportsmen who had plenty of time for recreation. They supported the English game until the early twentieth century, when tennis and golf became more popular amusements for the upper class. Elite Boston cricketers and working-class English immigrants also kept the game going into the 1900s. But by the eve of the First World War very few were still alive who could recall the days when cricket had a chance to become America's national pastime.

Approximately 120 cricket clubs are said to have existed in the Philadelphia area at one time or another, at least ten of which still exist today. One might hypothesize that cricket thrived there in part because of the nature of elite Philadelphian society in the late nineteenth century. Says E. Digby Baltzell, a sociologist who has studied the American elite in detail, "[T]he flowering of New England was the product of an aristocratic social structure led by men with deep roots in the governing class of the society, going back to the glacial age; Philadelphia's Golden Age, on the other hand, was the product of a heterogeneous and democratic social structure whose leadership elites came largely from elsewhere and from all classes within the city" (Baltzell [1979] 1996: 54). By our thinking, then, social mobility in Philadelphia might have prompted its "old-money" elite to look

for ways to segregate themselves from the city's nouveau riche and upwardly mobile populations. Boston Brahmins had no such cause for status anxiety, given their long-standing dominance of the city's cultural and urban affairs, though they did establish other forms of elite cultural institution in their midst (DiMaggio 1982). Nor were social mobility and status anxiety unique to Philadelphia at this time. Thus, we think that there is a more salient explanation of the Philadelphia-phenomenon in American cricket, one that mirrors the success of American baseball at the national level.

Cricket seems to have survived in Philadelphia primarily because there was a critical mass of clubs ready to field competitive teams. [...] It would appear that the popularity of cricket in both the United States and Canada suffered primarily from the exclusionism of its elite practitioners. North American cricket prevailed, though weakly, in places where status anxiety was high among wealthy families and where these families established and maintained multiple dense networks of rival cricket clubs. In both Canada and the United States, an egalitarian ethos encouraged economic elites to cultivate exclusive status-based activities with which to maintain their superior position in the social system. Cricket was not an inevitable response to this status anxiety, but it was one viable option.

At the same time, however, even elite tastes began changing in the early twentieth century. Increasingly, America's wealthiest families "placed maximum importance on the pleasuring of the individual sportsman taken as a consumer, albeit a wealthy one, and on gratification as a suitable goal in his life" (Mrozek 1983: 106). Country clubs, though still popular, increasingly built their reputations on the quality of their clubhouses, tennis tournaments, and golf courses. According to the sporting news of the day, even long-standing cricket clubs began hosting tennis and golf tournaments on their grounds. Cricket was languishing.

The obvious irony here is that elitism spelled the death of a once-popular pastime in two countries known for their exceptional egalitarianism. Thus we ask: why would elites in other countries not have done the same? How did cricket become so popular in these societies? Answering these questions requires that we look back at the cases in which cricket was successfully adopted and espoused by wide segments of the population, places like Australia, New Zealand, India, South Africa, and the West Indies. Despite their vast social and political differences, what do all these countries have in common beside their British colonial roots?

Adoption and successful acculturation: cricket elsewhere in the Commonwealth

It would appear that, in part, it was the very lack of a rigid social system that encouraged elitist attitudes toward cricket in the United States and Canada. Cricket became a marker of high social status, and the game was thus not promoted among the population at large. Conversely, rigid social stratification systems in other British colonial societies appear to have nurtured segregated but inclusive cricket cultures. In India, for example, love for the game was spread through the organization of matches between rival ethno-religious groups, each of which welcomed talented players from within their communities regardless of rank (Bose 1990). C. L. R. James's autobiographical accounts of Trinidadian cricket culture support similar conclusions. In Trinidad, as in Jamaica and Barbados, blacks and whites sometimes played cricket together (though not as equals). Individual cricket clubs were established at each rung of the social hierarchy, from the lowest-caste blacks to lighter skinned "browns" and whites. "I haven't the slightest doubt that the clash of race, caste and class did not retard but stimulated West Indian cricket," writes James (1963: 72). Thus we see that the specific criteria of social stratification are less important than the existence of a cohesive vertical hierarchy in the receiver nation. Racial, socioeconomic, and/or ethno-religious differences could provide the basis of stratification with the same result: elites' decision either to actively promote or at least passively to permit the acculturation of cricket among lower social strata.

There are three mechanisms underlying this process in the case of cricket: First, colonial elites, comfortable in their place atop the social hierarchy, had little reason to discourage those beneath them from playing a game that paid symbolic homage to British cultural and political hegemony; in fact, elites tended to regard cricket as a good means of "civilizing" natives in their own image. Given a rigid social system, furthermore, emulation of those at the top had benefits for those at the upper-middle and lower-middle rungs, particularly among non-whites seeking "entry" into a white-dominant world. With opportunities for upward mobility so severely limited, moreover, cricket provided those of the lower castes some means of symbolic competence—that is, by competing against those of other castes, races, and classes, low-caste cricketers could assert themselves in ways not permitted in ordinary society (Malcolm 2001).

Thus cricket was attractive to all major strata in these colonial societies. Even in Australia and New Zealand, where class mobility was relatively more common, yearning for status in the eyes of England created opportunities for "liberation cricket." Having been settled largely by working-class British immigrants, many of them "transported" to Australia as criminals, the Antipodes have long had a sense of cultural inferiority to England. British culture thus had an elevated status for Australians and New Zealanders of all classes. Understanding the Australian and New Zealand cases nonetheless requires a bit of extra background information, to which we now turn.

Australia and New Zealand. Though contemporary Australia and New Zealand are egalitarian, socially mobile societies much like the United States and Canada, matters were significantly different in the nineteenth century, the key years in the global diffusion of cricket. Socioeconomically, early Australian society was stratified into three classes: an upper-crust of absentee (mostly English) landlords; a middle class of émigré soldiers, artisans, and professionals; and a lower class of emancipated prisoners, their offspring, and the vast hordes of freemen tending sheep and sharecropping on other people's land (Clark 1995; Hughes 1986; Stone and Garden 1978). The key point about late-nineteenth-century Australia for our concerns is that its wealthiest citizens did not attempt to build strong institutional barriers between themselves and the rest of society. This may be the result of the elite's relative sense of security atop the Australian status hierarchy, though we suspect that it stems more directly from the fact that Australia was still a relatively new settlement at the time. Its richest citizens had yet to accumulate wealth or exclusive social networks comparable to those in the eastern United States and Canada. The separate classes desperately needed one another in the struggle to settle this vast, isolated continent. In the continent's burgeoning cities, for example, where Australian cricket truly thrived, the mercantile elite actively embraced the working classes, both socially and politically (Connell and Irving 1980). The presence of many British military men, moreover, coupled with the colony's distance from England, made English pastimes particularly valuable to Australians, particularly those activities that did not require fancy concert halls or awareness of the latest fads and fashions. Thus, Australia's various social strata cooperated in a nationwide effort to cultivate British ideals and social practices, cricket foremost among them (Clark 1995; Hughes 1986). The Sydney *Gazette,* according to one account (Pollard 1987: 10), stated in 1832 that "cricket was now the prevailing amusement of the colony and that no gentleman could expect to 'dangle at a lady's apron strings' unless he could boast of his cricket prowess."

Nonetheless, urban elites did establish some fairly exclusive cricket clubs in Australia—the Melbourne Cricket Club was founded in 1838 on such grounds, thus prompting the formation in 1839 of a rival middle-class club, the Melbourne Union Cricket Club (Pollard 1987: 40–2). In this way, Australian cricket resembled the stratified game in other British colonies, such as India and the Caribbean. The key to the widespread popularity of cricket in Australia was, again, the decision of its wealth-iest citizens to "share" the game with those of lower strata. Competitiveness trumped exclusivity in the minds of Australia's socioeconomic elite, in other words, much as it had done in eighteenth-century England. Having issued a challenge of one thousand pounds to any team in Australia that could beat it, the prestigious Melbourne Cricket Club signed a contract with a professional English cricketer to bolster its competitiveness with rival clubs. The MCC also hired a groundskeeper to eject nonmembers from club grounds. Both practices resembled the English cricket tradition in full flower—assiduously maintaining status-group distinctions while facilitating whatever integration was necessary to maintain the highest possible level of play (Pollard 1987: 46–7; Dunning and Sheard

1979: 181). This competitiveness also helped cultivate large audiences for the game: Match organizers for the MCC insisted that "spectators would not attend cricket unless the best players were on view." (Pollard 1987: 143). They were clearly interested in popularizing the game among the widest possible audience. In only a few instances, such as distant Tasmania (originally known as Van Dieman's Land), did anything like the American and Canadian elites-only attitude manifest itself. Pollard (1987: 37) refers, tellingly, to the fact that Tasmanian cricket did not thrive owing to "the strange reluctance of the strong, prestigious clubs in Hobart and Launceston to hire professional players to coach and strengthen their teams."

Over time, Australian cricket remained a national pastime despite the democratization of its social, political, and economic systems. In the late nineteenth century, teams were often stratified by class and ethnic background, while a spirit of inclusive competition prevailed nonetheless (Cashman 1984). The widespread role of publicans in promoting Australian cricket personifies its popular nature: "[P]ublicans quickly realised that the promotion of cricket stimulated their business," notes one historian (Pollard 1987: 10). Creation of neighborhood and trade-based cricket clubs was, moreover, a source of tremendous pride for urban boosters in cities like Sydney and Melbourne (Cashman 1998a; Pollard 1987). Sydney, in particular, struggled to distance itself from its origins as an English penal colony. Excellence at cricket appeared early on as a way for locals to make a statement about "the character of colonial society and the nature of the imperial relationship." "Thrashing the mother-land" was an indirect expression of "the love-hate relationship of a youthful colonial society attempting to define its identity and a greater sense of nationhood" (Cashman 1998a: 36, 39; see also Mandle 1973: 525–26). Hence, a long Australo-English rivalry began early on, and it is still a source of tremendous interest to Australian sports fans, particularly given their long-standing dominance over increasingly weak English teams. More important still is the fact that intra- and inter-provincial leagues were actively promoted early on in Australia, thus stimulating the creation of adequate playing grounds and competitive teams throughout the country.[8]

345

Cricket evolved along similar lines in New Zealand. Though New Zealand was never home to any English penal colonies, its wealthier citizens shared with those of Australia the sense that they needed to prove themselves in the eyes of the British. New Zealand cricket has its longest and strongest legacy of play in the province of Canterbury, "the most English of New Zealand provinces" and one founded upon economic principles designed to perpetuate the rigid social order of the English countryside (minus the truly poor). Here, class stratification and inclusive Anglophilia promoted cricket as a healthy pastime for all, excepting the native Maoris (Ryan 1998).[9] Christchurch was home to both exclusive and "open" clubs. Elite schools began early on to train young men in the game, and the hiring of professional coaches from England was also common beginning in the 1890s (Reese 1927: 41, 49). A steady stream of English and Australian immigrants provided ready instruction and talent. Interprovincial play was also quite popular—when an annual match was first arranged between the neighboring provinces of Canterbury and Otago, "it was agreed that the teams should wear the great English university colours," Canterbury in Oxford's dark blue, Otago in the light blue of Cambridge (Reese 1927: 36). The creation of several annual prizes—the Plunket Shield for best "major" team (generally those from major cities) and the Hawke Cup for best "minor association," as well as the Heathcote Williams Shield for best secondary school team—helped create the kinds of well-anticipated sports rivalries vital to the creation of a "hegemonic sports culture."

Promotion of the game in minor population centers through the Hawke Cup competition was clearly important to the long-term survival of the game in New Zealand. Emphasis among New Zealand cricketers was not on the social status generated by membership in elite clubs but on the prestige gained by winning. This was so much the case that a visiting Australian star, Warwick Armstrong, reportedly advised that the "various [Kiwi] associations are too inclined to pick the coach who can help his province to win matches. What is really wanted is the coach who can impart knowledge and keenness to the boy" (quoted in Reese 1927: 76). In sum, New Zealand, like Australia, followed a somewhat different path to "hegemonic" cricket than

British colonies in which a minority white elite dominated a majority colored population. Cricket helped Antipodean elites cultivate their Englishness, but the size and isolation of their European settlements limited the extent to which they could be truly exclusive. Everyone involved in the game aspired to gentility but none was excluded on the grounds of wealth or social standing. "Proper conduct, rather more than heredity, was the mark of an amateur gentleman," comments one history of Australian cricket (Pollard 1987: 65).

The Asian subcontinent. Interestingly, it was not originally the intent of the British to popularize cricket in the subcontinent of Asia. British soldiers are said to have played the game in India as early as 1721, but it was not until the mid-nineteenth century that Indians actually began to play. Then, too, it was primarily the "middle-man" Parsi population that first cultivated the game. The Parsis were an ancient immigrant community in India known for their wealth and success at business. "It was no accident that the first community [in India] to take up the game were the Parsis," comments one historian (Cashman 1979: 190–91). They were "a wealthy entrepreneurial group who acted as cultural brokers between the British and Indian society. ... In the tradition of colonial elites, the Parsis took up the game of cricket, along with other imperial customs, partly to demonstrate their fitness for the role of collaboration." Parsi success at the game also prompted India's elite Hindu and Muslim populations to take an active interest in it (Bose 1990: 32).

From the start, indigenous participation in Indian cricket was centered around elites: Princes would build ornate cricket grounds and invite guests to watch them play. The princes would rarely even bowl or field the ball, relying on hired players to provide them easily hit balls. This provided valuable opportunities for Indians of lower social strata to get involved in the game. Audiences, too, were carefully segregated; Europeans from Indians, commoners from elite, men from women, and so on (Cashman 1998b: 126–67; Cashman 1980). "So cricket prospered," comments Bose (1990: 36), "not because the different communities mixed but because they did not. Competition, not cooperation, was the spur." Thus, elite members of India's vastly segregated social system embraced the game as a way of distinguishing themselves vis-à-vis the British and one another. Important for our purposes is the fact that talented nonelites were encouraged to play the game. The relative security of elites within their own communities, as well as their competitiveness with elites in rival ethno-religious communities, allowed for this kind of segregated-integration.

"By the 1930s," writes Cashman (1998b: 123), "there were many cricketing princes, players and patrons, who lavished great sums of money and energy to secure the top prizes in cricket, control of the game and captaincy of the side. ... Cricket prominence provided the princes with more clout in the Chamber of Princes and enhanced their status with the British." Rivalry between Indian and English sides developed from this, which subsequently helped cultivate further talent and interest among the public at large (Appadurai 1996; Bose 1990). The widespread incorporation of Indians into the British civil service system in India also exposed many indigenous men to the game. By 1947, when India became independent, cricket was a national passion, if not yet *the* national passion. Jawaharlal Nehru, first prime minister of India, further encouraged participation in the sport, himself having been educated at Harrow in England. In Bombay, where cricket has, perhaps, its longest history on the subcontinent, and where the Indian television and film industries are centered, star cricketers are given all the adulation and fame of their Bollywood counterparts (Cashman 1998b: 130). Televised matches in indigenous languages have also helped build and maintain a wide fan base, as has the transference of regional political tensions onto the wicket—international test matches between India, Pakistan, Bangladesh, and Sri Lanka are, today, rabidly nationalistic events replete with hooliganism, jingoism, and sometimes outright violence (Appardurai 1996; Nandy 2000).

The West Indies. The historic status hierarchies that nurtured passion for cricket in Indian society have a close parallel in the West Indies, where the game is equally popular today. Though originally cultivated by and for white elites in the British Caribbean, high-status blacks and Indians were provided some training in the game early on, thus leading to the eventual formation of cricket clubs for nonwhites. Clubs were rigidly stratified on color and class lines. Nonetheless, the status hierarchy was

sufficiently rigid that space could be created for interaction and competition among them—just so long as it remained on the field. Beating a team from an adjacent status position was a feat worthy of respect, and though it did not ultimately change the social order, it did at least provide an outlet for status emulation and achievement. The possibility of being recruited to play professionally in England was further incentive for talented athletes from poor families to devote time and energy to the game. Because the symbolic stakes were high, moreover, large audiences would often turn out to watch and successful players would receive great acclaim. "Supporters of the respective sides had invested considerable amounts of emotional capital in the outcome," notes Stoddart (1998a: 84), a development that later extended to international matches with sometimes violent consequences (Patterson 1995).

Thus we see another case where the relative stability of the status hierarchy within a society promoted a segregated but inclusive cricketing culture, one that gained valuable momentum from the muted tension of competition among status groups. Unique to the West Indies is the nature of their international "test" match status: rather than play as separate national teams, the "Windies" have traditionally comprised top players from throughout the Caribbean. The contemporary game in the Caribbean is thus less oriented around national pride than around racial and ethno-Caribbean solidarity (Beckles 1998b).

Southern Africa. The case of South African and Zimbabwean cricket is a bit more complicated and follows lines distinct from, though comparable to, those already described. The large presence of British military personnel provided a ready pool of talent for the game in southern Africa, but its diffusion to indigenous and Afrikaner populations was somewhat erratic. Some Afrikaners openly played cricket before the onset of the Boer War, and they gladly joined the British in a white unity movement during the Apartheid era, but the early twentieth century was a less active period for Afrikaner cricketers in the aftermath of the war. British whites, meanwhile, staked the very reputation of their settlements on the game. The small size of the Anglo-white population in South Africa meant that class distinctions among them were muted; cricket became a focal point of

347

colonial life. Indeed, British South Africans and Rhodesians were in some ways more "British" than the British (Winch 1983). In colonial Rhodesia, for example, one memoirist noted, "Where previously one had to be a member of the la-di-da class to get a job in the Civil Service, now you had to beat the hide off a ball," meaning that prowess at cricket was sufficient means of attaining status and respect in the British community (G. H. Tanser quoted in Winch 1983).

Vitally important to the long-term success of cricket in southern Africa is the fact that the British allowed nonwhites to play the game there. Before the early 1900s, when government-sponsored race policies began their long descent toward apartheid, British settlers actually encouraged segregated play among middle-class blacks and Asians, "Because the ideology of respectability was crucial for the aspirations of middle-class blacks," they not only aspired to play the game well but also provided an example for less "respectable" blacks (Stoddart 1998b: 56). Again, the relative stability of the status hierarchy in these societies allowed for the diffusion of the game from the top-down. Blacks were excluded from white cricket clubs, as well as the national teams, but they learned to play and to watch the game nonetheless. In the ensuing years, politics have been the greatest barrier to "hegemonic" cricket in South Africa and Zimbabwe. Opposition to apartheid limited South African participation in international test matches for a good part of the twentieth century, and the political turmoil in contemporary Zimbabwe may mean the permanent demise of cricket there.

Though the particulars motivating cricket adoption thus varied from one British colony to another, the development and perpetuation of a hegemonic cricket culture required in each case that members of high-status groups remained interested not only in cultivating their own cricket skills but also in sharing the game with those of lower orders. This did not occur in the United States or Canada.

Discussion: cricket and sociological models of cultural diffusion

Our analysis suggests an important extension of current diffusion theory. It is widely accepted among scholars in the field that diffusion is most likely to succeed where change agents and adoptees share the same culture and social category (especially the same socioeconomic status). Thus Rogers (1995: 7) asserts as "an obvious principle of human communication that the transfer of ideas occurs most frequently between two individuals who are similar or homopholous," this being "the degree to which two or more individuals who interact are similar in certain attributes such as beliefs, education, social class, and the like. ..." Rogers contrasts this with situations where relations are heterophilous (i.e., the social position of the change agent is different from that of the adopters) and notes that this can present a major obstacle to successful diffusion. The ideal situation in the initial adoption phase, he argues, is thus one in which change agents and potential adopters "would be homophilous on all other variables (education and social status, for example) even though they are heterophilous regarding the innovation" (Rogers 1995, 7; for similar views see Strang and Meyer 1993; Wejnert 2002).

We are inclined to agree that homophilous diffusion is indeed true in many, perhaps most, cases, especially those involving the intra-societal transfer of simple innovations among individuals. Our study, however, indicates that there is an important class of diffusion processes in which just the opposite might occur—i.e., cases in which a distinctly heterophilous relationship between change agents and would-be change-adopters promotes diffusion. In the case of cricket, it is precisely the stable status-inequality between those who brought the game from England and the lower-status colonial populations that adopted it that accounts for the successful diffusion of cricket. In such cases (i.e., top-down, or heterophilous, diffusion), it is the authority and high social status of change agents, combined with their willingness not simply to transmit but actively to participate in the promotion of the innovation, *and* their desire to continue their engagement with it even after it has begun to spread down and across the social hierarchy, that accounts for successful diffusion.

As shown in the case of cricket, all three elements are necessary for this kind of top-down diffusion to work: It is not enough for elites simply to introduce the innovation; they are required to promote it actively and to persist in lending it their prestige by continuing to practice it themselves. Where they do not, one of two outcomes, both fatal for the long-term acculturation of the innovation, is likely: One possibility is that the innovation becomes a fad, thereby enjoying a brief period of widespread popularity because of its upper-class origins, but later being abandoned by the elite transmitters because of this very popularity, thereby trig-gering a decline in overall popularity. The history of fashion is replete with examples of this (e.g., Crane 2000). Another possible "negative" outcome is that status-insecure first-adopters "capture" the innovation, thus preventing its diffusion into the population at large. Precisely this happened to cricket in Canada and the United States, as we have seen.

Naturally, the nature of social stratification in these Commonwealth countries is not sufficient to explain the success or failure of cricket in each country; nor does it fully explain the failed cases of Canada and the United States. Our earlier discussion of the rising popularity of baseball in the United States offers several keys to refining our explanation. Baseball was aggressively promoted throughout the United States by league-owners, sporting goods manufacturers, and "star" players. Inter-urban play helped promote widespread audiences. Youths were encouraged to play in and out of school, and the necessary equipment and playing grounds were made widely available. Similar efforts were made for football and basketball in the United States, and for cricket throughout much of the Commonwealth. Cross-class participation in such sports was supplemented, in other words, by intense efforts to recruit spectators, as well as new talent, to the games. At some point, such self-promotion seems to cross a threshold at which the game's popularity fuels itself: baseball was so popular and baseball rivalries so intense that even American elites flocked to it, thus leaving cricket virtually no following whatsoever. Absent celebrity players and careful marketing, crew and track and field, in contrast, lost momentum and popularity among American audiences.

The lessons here are rather simple: On the supply side, would-be audiences must be offered a steady stream of well-publicized events between evenly matched, talented teams. Annual matches, such as Thanksgiving Day college football games or "The Ashes," a biennial cricket match between England and Australia, help solidify a sport's place in the public mind (cf. Schudson 1989). On the demand side, a surfeit of opportunities whereby talented athletes can find selective incentives to devote time and effort to one sport over another also appears to make a difference. Such factors, it should be noted, can also erode support for a sport even after it has been successfully adopted. The popularity of professional rugby in the Antipodes, for example, and the spread of basketball to the Caribbean, both potentially represent threats to their nations' hegemonic cricket cultures.

The evolution of the game in each country, then, is the result not only of the relative status position of interested parties but also such intangibles as the rise of sports entrepreneurs devoted to the promotion of a specific sport; the rise of competitive league play, which helps draw regular 'fans' from different strata of society; and the rise (or demise) of other seasonal sports competing for the same talent and audience base. Nonetheless, we feel that of these multiple factors, it is social stratification that lies most fundamentally at the heart of the matter. The extent to which an elite cultural practice like cricket was shared with or shielded from the general population was a direct result of elites' own sense of their place atop the social hierarchy. Had American elite cricketers felt less anxious about their social position, for example, they might have popularized the sport along the same lines as baseball (or golf and tennis).

Conclusion: what might we learn from the global diffusion of cricket?

[...] Substantively speaking, we wondered why Canadians were not more enthusiastic about cricket given their strong cultural and political connections to England. This case seemed especially compelling in light of all the recent attention put on globalization and the would-be homogenization of world culture. What might the global history of cricket tell us about other potentially diffusible phenomena, particularly those that bear with them such strong relations to their country of origin?

With regard to cricket, we have identified several factors that seem closely related to variance in the success or failure of the sport in countries connected to the former British Empire. Beyond merely being exposed to the sport, settler societies needed to dedicate time and resource to nurturing indigenous support for the game. In other words, some portion of the population needed to devote itself to playing cricket (*adoption*), and some larger portion needed to be persuaded to care about it (*acculturation*). We note, too, that in the final, acculturation phase, the game appears to take on cultural valence unique to its people; in other words, it becomes part of the national patrimony, as opposed to a simple cultural import. In some colonial societies, for example, cricket developed as a way for settlers to prove their "Britishness," whereas in others, excellence at the game offered an opportunity for natives literally to beat the British at their own game. In the unique case of Australia, moreover, both elements combined into a fiercely nationalist but ultimately anglophilic love of the game.

More specifically, cricket was elevated to a national sporting pastime in societies where players and audiences were recruited from an array of social class backgrounds. In the United States and Canada, elites literally took cricket from the public sphere and confined it to their own social circles. This contrasts sharply with the history of cricket in the other colonies of the British Empire, where racial inequality, selective access to secondary education, and quasifeudal land allocation systems limited socioeconomic mobility. Those at the top of the economic system felt comfortable sharing their pastimes with the masses. Elites actively promoted and stuck with the game even after it became a sport practiced by low-status members of society. Thus, cricket became a popular sport played and enjoyed by all.

The very nature of the game itself, we have argued, was also an important part of the diffusion process: Cricket's strong identification with English imperialism made it attractive to both those who cherished the "mother country" and those who wished for nothing more than symbolically to defeat it. The sport's absence of physical contact, its strictures on rowdiness, and its low costs when played informally— bats, balls, and stumps can all be handmade—also contributed to its diffusion throughout much of the British Commonwealth.

We argue, furthermore, that it was the relative social mobility of mid-nineteenth-century American and Canadian society that prompted elites there to protect their cultural patrimony from the masses. This reasoning is comparable to that offered in explanation of the development of other forms of exclusionary cultural practice. According to Elias ([1939] 2000), for example, economic elites in late medieval Europe responded to the status pressures of defeudalization by promoting specific repertoires of etiquette by which they might differentiate themselves from the masses. In a more modern context, social elites in late-nineteenth-century Boston responded to similar status pressure by cultivating tastes for European music, art, and theater, as well as creating exclusive social venues in which to partake of them (DiMaggio 1982; Levine 1983; see Dunae 1981 and Gruneau 1983 for comparable analyses of Canada). Seen from this perspective, equality of *economic* opportunity promoted elite efforts to limit equality of *cultural* opportunity.

In the big picture, the history of cricket highlights an important feature of global culture more generally. Global cultural diffusion relies not simply on the transmission of cultural "signals" from place to place, but also on: (1) The relationship among different categories of recipients in host societies, particularly with respect to the distribution of social status among them, as well as the equality of opportunity to gain such status; and (2) the ability of some groups of recipients to dominate or otherwise limit access to cultural imports, thereby "capturing" such imports for themselves. While limiting access to high-status goods might only make them more attractive to lower-status consumers, there is a point of diminishing returns at which popular interest will peak and subsequently subside. Thus, for example, ownership of raw commodities like diamonds and pearls may become more prevalent as their price increases; not so for cultural practices that are more easily "protected."

Access to cricket in the United States and Canada was "overprotected," so to speak, thus forestalling its acculturation as a "hegemonic sports culture." In point of fact, any cultural good or practice can be so protected if it requires: (a) *repeated points of contact*, as in the case of anything that must be learned, replenished, or maintained; (b) *extensive gatekeeping*, as with cultural practices that are sufficiently sophisticated, esoteric, or non-obvious as to require explanation, instruction, or prior evaluation by specialists; and/or (c) *widespread collaboration,* as with "social" goods such as musical performances or team sports that require interaction with groups of competitors and/or co-participants. While nearly anything can be had for the right price, some cultural commodities are simply too "social" to be assimilated without ready and consistent support. Thus, the global diffusion of cultural practices requires not only that those in "receiver" societies show interest in these practices, but that the resources necessary to adopt them are widely available. This access often hinges on indigenous elites' desire and ability to keep such resources to themselves.

We see here an important dimension of the cross-cultural diffusion process otherwise overlooked; something we have called, borrowing a term from Rogers (1995), *heterophilous,* or top-down, diffusion. While popular tastes and consumer agency play a large role in the reception and adoption of easily accessible foreign cultural goods and practices—so-called *homophilous* paths to successful diffusion—indigenous elites sometimes play an even more important role in casting imported cultural goods or practices as high- or low-brow items. Elites' ability to control access to such goods has significant ramifications for popular retention thereof. Presumably, cross-national variation in the diffusion of many such items can be explained in exactly this fashion. Thus, it may be that future studies of cross-national cultural diffusion should pay as much attention to elite as to popular tastes. So, too, should the institutionalization of such tastes across public and private venues be of increasing concern to those interested in the topic. Neither value nor venue are a priori features of cultural imports, we argue. Diffusion scholars must then strive for renewed sensitivity toward the culturally specific meanings of the items or practices being diffused, as well as toward the social strata associated with and/or in control of access to their use.

Notes

1. Admittedly, one shortcoming of this particular case study is that it pertains primarily to male athletes and sports fans in the countries in question. Nonetheless, we have no reason to expect that our findings would be different were we to study a sport or other "national" cultural practice with greater cross-gender appeal.

2. Actual newspapers searched were the *Evening Standard* (London, England—January) and the *Times Online* (London, England—October, April, and July); the *Sydney Morning Herald* (Sydney, Australia); the *Mail and Guardian* (Johannesburg, South Africa); the *Times of India* (Delhi, India); the *New Zealand Herald* (Auckland, NZ); the *Jamaica Observer* (Kingston, Jamaica); *The Independent* (Dhaka, Bangladesh); the *News International* (Islamabad, Pakistan); the *Daily News* (Colombo, Sri Lanka); the *Standard* (Harare, Zimbabwe); the *Globe and Mail* (Toronto, Canada); and *USA Today* (United States).

3. We are told by an anonymous reviewer familiar with English cricket, however, that "county" cricket is rife with swearing arid disputes with officials.

4. It should be noted, moreover, that the popular North American sports of baseball and football have direct ties to the English games of "rounders" and rugby respectively (Dunning and Sheard 1979: 7). In the nineteenth century, two other British "public school" sports, rowing and track and field, were directly incorporated into American collegiate life as well (Smith 1988).

5. Again, we regret the fact that women are not an especially relevant part of this case study. The question of English colonial attitudes toward the moral "improvement" of women is certainly a topic worth further consideration, though it is far beyond the purview of this particular study.

6. Note, however, that English colonial policy in places like India did not originally embrace the anglicanization of their native populations either— this was an innovation of the mid-nineteenth century in India (Cashman 1998b: 118).

7. PSAL was founded in New York City in 1900 with the support of Andrew Carnegie, John D. Rockefeller, and J. Pierpont Morgan. It soon spread to other cities around the United States (Levine 1985: 110–12).

8. Interestingly, rugby was first promoted in Australia as a way for local cricketers to keep in shape over the winter months (Hickie 1993).

9. It is not clear to us why white New Zealanders did not work to promote the game among Maoris in the same way that Australians did among the Aborigines. It may be related to the Maoris' fierce resistance to white settlement in the early years of the colony, but we were not able to confirm this.

References

Adelman, Melvin L. 1986. *A Sporting Time: New York City and the Rise of Modern Athletics, 1820–1870.* Urbana, IL: University of Illinois Press.

351

Allen, David Rayvern. 1990. *Cricket: An Illustrated History.* Oxford, England: Phaidon Press.

Appadurai, Arjun. 1996. *Modernity at Large: Cultural Dimensions of Globalization.* Minneapolis, MN: University of Minnesota Press.

Baltzell, E. Digby. [1979] 1996. *Puritan Boston and Quaker Philadelphia.* New Brunswick, NJ: Transaction Publishers.

Barney, Robert. 1992. "In Search of a Canadian Cooperstown: The Future of the Canadian Baseball Hall of Fame." *Nine: A Journal of Baseball History and Social Policy* 1.

Barney, Robert. 1989. "Diamond Rituals: Baseball in Canadian Culture." Pp. 1–21 in *Baseball History 2: An Annual of Original Baseball Research,* edited by Peter Levine. Westport, CT: Meckler.

Beckles, Hilary McD. 1998a. *The Development of West Indies Cricket, vol. 1 The Age of Nationalism.* Barbados: Press of the University of the West Indies.

——, ed. 1998b. *A Spirit of Dominance: Cricket and Nationalism in the West Indies.* Barbados: Canoe Press.

Beckles, Hilary McD and Brian Stoddart, eds, 1995. *Liberation Cricket: West Indies Cricket Culture.* Manchester, England: Manchester University Press.

Bhabha, Homi. 1994. *The Location of Culture.* London, England: Routledge Press.

Boller, Kevin. 1994a. "International Cricket: Launched by a Hoax." *The Canadian Cricketer* 22:23.

——. 1994b. "The 49th Parallel Divide: The Story of Canada and the United States at Cricket." *The Canadian Cricketer* 22:24–25.

Bose, Mihir. 1990. *A History of Indian Cricket.* London, England: Deutsch.

Bouchier, Nancy and Robert Barney. 1988. "A Critical Examination of a Source on Early Ontario Baseball: The Reminiscence of Adam E. Ford." *Journal of Sport History* 15:75–90.

Bourdieu, Pierre. 1978. "Sport and Social Class." *Social Science Information* 17:819–40.

Brookes, Christopher. 1978. *English Cricket: The Game and Its Players Throughout the Ages.* London, England: Weidenfeld and Nicholson.

Burt, Ronald. 1987. "Social Contagion and Innovation: Cohesion vs. Structural Equivalence." *American Journal of Sociology* 92:1287–335.

Buskens, Vincent and Kazuo Yamaguchi. 1999. "A New Model for Information Diffusion in Heterogeneous Social Networks." *Sociological Methodology* 29:281–325.

Cashman, Richard. 1979. "The Phenomenon of Indian Cricket." Pp. 180–204 in *Sport in History: The Making of Modern Sporting History,* edited by Richard Cashman and Michael McKernan. Queensland, Australia: University of Queensland Press.

——. 1980. *Patrons, Players and the Crowd: The Phenomenon of Indian Cricket.* New Delhi, India: Orient Longman.

——. 1984. '*Ave a Go, Yer Mug! Australian Cricket Crowds from Larrikin to Ocker.* Sydney, Australia: Collins.

——. 1998a. "Australia." *The Imperial Game: Cricket, Culture and Society,* edited by Brian Stoddart and Keith A. P. Sandiford. Manchester, England: Manchester University Press.

——. 1998b. "The Subcontinent." *The Imperial Game: Cricket, Culture and Society,* edited by Brian Stoddart and Keith A. P. Sandiford. Manchester, England: Manchester University Press.

Chadwick, Henry. 1868. *American Chronicle of Sports and Pastimes* 1:52.

Clark, Manning. 1995. *A Short History of Australia.* 4th rev. ed. Victoria, Australia: Penguin Books.

Clemens, Elisabeth S. and James M. Cook. 1999. "Politics and Institutionalism: Explaining Durability and Change." *Annual Review of Sociology* 25: 441–66.

Coakley, J. J. 1998. *Sport in Society.* St. Louis, MO: Mosby.

Cole, Robert E. 1989. *Strategies for Learning: Small-Group Activities in American, Japanese, and Swedish Industry.* Berkeley, CA: University of California Press.

Coleman, James S., Elihu Katz, and Herbert Menzel. 1966. *Medical Innovation; A Diffusion Study.* Indianapolis, IN: Bobbs-Merrill.

Connell, R. W. and T. H. Irving. 1980. *Class Structure in Australian History: Documents, Narrative and Argument.* Melbourne, Australia: Longman Cheshire.

Cozier, Tony. 1978. *The West Indies: Fifty Years of Test Cricket.* Brighton, England: Angus and Robertson.

Crane, Diana. 2000. *Fashion and Its Social Agendas: Class, Gender, and Identity in Clothing.* Chicago, IL: University of Chicago Press.

"Cricket." 1907. *New York Times,* Sept. 21.

DiMaggio, Paul J. 1982. "Cultural Entrepreneurship in Nineteenth-Century Boston." *Media, Culture, and Society* 4:33–50.

DiMaggio, Paul J. and Walter W. Powell. 1983. "The Iron Cage Revisited: Institutional Isomorphism and Collective Rationality in Organizational Fields." *American Sociological Review* 48:147–60.

Dobbin, Frank and John R. Sutton. 1998. "The Strength of a Weak State: The Rights Revolution and the Rise of Human Resources Management Divisions." *American Journal of Sociology* 104: 441–76.

Dunae, P. A. 1981. *Gentlemen Emigrants: From the British Public Schools to the Canadian Frontier.* Vancouver, Canada: Douglas and McIntyre.

Dunning, Eric and Kenneth Sheard. 1979. *Barbarians, Gentlemen and Players: A Sociological Study of the*

Development of Rugby Football. New York: New York University Press.

Elias, Norbert. [1939] 2000. *The Civilizing Process.* Rev. ed. Oxford, England: Blackwell.

Frye, Northrop. 1971. *The Bush Garden: Essays on the Canadian Imagination.* Toronto, Canada: Anansi.

"The Game Was Stopped." 1888. *New York Times,* May 21.

Gottdiener, M. 1985. "Hegemony and Mass Culture: A Semiotic Approach." *American Journal of Sociology* 90:979–1001.

Granovetter, Mark and Roland Soong. 1983. "Threshold Models of Diffusion and Collective Behavior." *Journal of Mathematical Sociology* 9:165–79.

Gruneau, Richard. 1983. *Class, Sports, and Social Development.* Amherst, MA: University of Massachusetts Press.

Guillén, Mauro F. 1994. *Models of Management: Work, Authority, and Organization in a Comparative Perspective.* Chicago, IL: University of Chicago Press.

———. 2001. *The Limits of Convergence: Globalization and Organizational Change in Argentina, South Korea, and Spain,* Princeton, NJ; Princeton University Press.

Gunaratnam, Visva. 1993. "I Have a Dream." *The Canadian Cricketer* 21:11.

Hall, John E. and R. O. McCulloch. 1895. *Sixty Years of Canadian Cricket.* Toronto, Canada: Bryant.

Harvard College. 1889. *Annual Reports of the President and Treasurer of Harvard College, 1887–1888.* Cambridge, MA: Harvard College.

Headlam, Cecil. 1903. *Ten Thousand Miles Through India and Burma: An Account of the Oxford University Authentics' Cricket Tour with Mr. K. J. Key in the Year of the Durbar.* London, England: Dent.

Hickie, Thomas V. 1993. *They Ran with the Ball: How Rugby Football Began in Australia.* Melbourne, Australia: Longman Cheshire.

Hughes, Robert. 1986. *The Fatal Shore: The Epic of Australia's Founding.* New York: Vintage.

Humber, William. 1995. *Diamonds of the North: A Concise History of Baseball in Canada.* Toronto, Canada: Oxford University Press.

James, C.L.R. 1963. *Beyond a Boundary.* London, England: Hutchinson.

Kaufman, Jason. 2002. *For the Common Good? American Civic Life and the Golden Age of Fraternity.* New York: Oxford University Press.

Kirsch, George. 1991. "Massachusetts Baseball and Cricket, 1840–1870." Pp. 1–15 in *Sports in Massachusetts: Historical Essays,* edited by Ronald Story. Westfield, MA: Institute for Massachusetts Studies, Westfield State College.

Kirsch, George. 1989. *The Creation of American Team Sports: Baseball and Cricket, 1838–72.* Urbana, IL: University of Illinois Press.

Lester, John A., ed. 1951. *A Century of Philadelphia Cricket.* Philadelphia, PA: University of Pennsylvania Press.

Levine, Lawrence W. 1988. *Highbrow/Lowbrow: The Emergence of Cultural Hierarchy in America.* Cambridge, MA: Harvard University Press.

Levine, Peter. 1985. *A. G. Spalding and the Rise of Baseball: The Promise of American Sport.* New York: Oxford University Press.

Lillrank, Paul. 1995, "The Transfer of Management Innovations from Japan." *Organization Studies* 16:971–89.

Lipset, Seymour Martin. 1996. *American Exceptionalism: A Double-Edged Sword.* New York: Norton.

Maguire, Joseph. 1999. *Global Sport: Identities, Societies, Civilizations.* Oxford, England: Polity Press.

Malcolm, Dominic. 2001. "'It's Not Cricket': Colonial Legacies and Contemporary Inequalities." *Journal of Historical Sociology* 14:253–75.

Mandle, W. F. 1973. "Games People Played: Cricket and Football in England and Victoria in the Late Nineteenth Century." *Historical Studies* 15(60): 511–535.

Mangan, J. A. 1986. *The Games Ethic and Imperialism: Aspects of the Diffusion of an Ideal.* London, England: Frank Cass.

Markovits, Andrei S. and Steven L. Hellerman. 2001. *Offside: Soccer and American Exceptionalism.* Princeton, NJ: Princeton University Press.

Marsden, Peter and Joel Podolny. 1990. "Dynamic Analysis of Network Diffusion Processes." *Social Networks Through Time,* edited by J. Weesie and H. Flap. Utrecht, Netherlands: ISOR.

Melville, Tom. 1998. *The Tented Field: A History of Cricket in America.* Bowling Green, IN: Bowling Green State University Popular Press.

Merrett, Christopher and John Nauright. 1998. "South Africa." Pp. 55–78 in *The Imperial Game: Cricket, Culture and Society,* edited by Brian Stoddart and Keith A. P. Sandiford. Manchester, England: Manchester University Press.

Metcalfe, Alan. 1987. *Canada Learns to Play: The Emergence of Organized Sport, 1807–1914.* Toronto, Canada: McClelland and Stewart.

Meyer, John and Michael Hannan, eds. 1979. *National Development and the World System: Educational, Economic and Political Change, 1950–1970.* Chicago, IL: University of Chicago Press.

Miller, Toby, Geoffrey Lawrence, Jim McKay, and David Rowe. 2001. *Globalization and Sport.* London, England: Sage Publications.

Mizruchi, Mark S. and Lisa C. Fein. 1999. "The Social Construction of Organizational Knowledge: A Study of the Uses of Coercive, Mimetic, and Normative Isomorphism." *Administrative Science Quarterly* 44:653–83.

Molotch, Harvey, William Freudenburg, and Krista E. Paulsen. 2000. "History Repeats Itself, but How? City Character, Urban Tradition, and the Accomplishment of Place." *American Sociological Review* 65:791–823.

Mrozek, Donald J. 1983. *Sport and American Mentality, 1880–1910*. Knoxville, TN: University of Tennessee Press.

Nandy, Ashis. 2000. *The Tao of Cricket: On Games of Destiny and Destiny of Games*. New Delhi, India: Oxford University Press.

Palloni, Alberto. 2001. "Diffusion in Sociological Analysis." Pp. 67–114 in *Diffusion Processes and Fertility Transition: Selected Perspectives*, edited by John B. Casterline. Washington D.C.: National Academy Press.

Patterson, Orlando. 1994. "Ecumenical America: Global Culture and the American Cosmos." *World Policy Journal* 11:103–17.

——. 1995. "The Ritual of Cricket." Pp. 141–47 in *Liberation Cricket*, edited by Hilary McD Beckles and Brian Stoddart. Kingston, Jamaica: Ian Randle Publishers.

Penn, Alan. 1999. *Targeting Schools: Drill, Militarism and Imperialism*. London, England: Woburn Press.

Perera, S. S. 1998a. *The. Janashakthi Book of Sri Lanka Cricket, 1832–1996*. Colombo: Janashakthi Insurance.

——. 1998b. "Notes on Sri Lanka's Cricket Heritage." *Crosscurrents: Sri Lanka and Australia at Cricket*, edited by Michael Roberts and Alfred James. Petersham, Australia: Walla Walla Press.

"The Philadelphia Cricketers." 1884. *New York Times*, July 15.

Pollard, Jack. 1987. *The Formative Years of Australian Cricket, 1803–1893*. North Ryde, Australia: Angus and Robertson.

Redmond, Gerald. 1979. "Some Aspects of Organized Sport and Leisure in Nineteenth-Century Canada." *Loisir et société/Society and Leisure* 2:73–100.

Reese, T. W. 1927. *New Zealand Cricket. 1814–1914*. Christchurch, New Zealand Simpson and Williams.

Robertson, R. 1992. *Globalization: Social Theory and Global Culture*. London: Sage Publications.

Rogers, Everett M. 1995. *Diffusion of Innovations*. 4th ed. New York: Free Press.

Ryan, Greg. 1998. "New Zealand." Pp. 93–115 in *The Imperial Game: Cricket, Culture and Society*, edited by Brian Stoddart and Keith A. P. Sandiford. Manchester, England: Manchester University Press.

Sandiford, Keith A. P. 1994. *Cricket and the Victorians*. Aldershot, England: Scholar Press.

——. 1998a. "England," Pp. 9–33 in *The Imperial Game: Cricket, Culture and Society*, edited by Brian Stoddart and Keith A. P. Sandiford. Manchester, England: Manchester University Press.

——. 1998b. "Introduction." Pp. 1–8 in *The Imperial Game: Cricket, Culture and Society*, edited by Brian Stoddart and Keith A. P. Sandiford. Manchester, England: Manchester University Press.

——. 1998c. *Cricket Nurseries of Colonial Barbados: The Elite Schools, 1865–1966*. Barbados: Press of the University of the West Indies.

Sayen, Henry. 1956. *A Yankee Looks At Cricket*. London, England: Putnam.

Schudson, Michael. 1989. "How Culture Works: Perspectives from Media Studies on the Efficacy of Symbols." *Theory and Society* 18:153–80.

Smith, Ronald A. 1988. *Sports and Freedom: The Rise of Big-Time College Athletics*. New York: Oxford University Press.

Spalding, Albert G. [1911] 1992. *America's National Game*. Lincoln, NE: University of Nebraska Press.

Starr, Paul. 1989. "The Meaning of Privatization." Pp. 15–48 in *Privatization and the Welfare State*, edited by Sheila Kamerman and Alfred Kahn. Princeton, NJ: Princeton University Press.

Steen, Rob. 1999. *The Official Companion to the 1999 Cricket World Cup*. London: Boxtree.

Stoddart, Brian. 1988. "Sport, Cultural Imperialism, and Colonial Response in the British Empire." *Comparative Studies in Society and History* 30: 649–73.

——. 1998a. "West Indies." *The Imperial Game: Cricket, Culture and Society*, edited by Brian Stoddart and Keith A. P. Sandiford. Manchester, England: Manchester University Press.

——. 1998b. "Other Cultures." *The Imperial Game: Cricket, Culture and Society*, edited by Brian Stoddart and Keith A. P. Sandiford. Manchester.

Stoddart, Brian and Keith A. P. Sandiford, eds. 1998. *The Imperial Game: Cricket, Culture and Society*. Manchester, England: Manchester University Press.

Stone, Derrick I. and Donald S. Garden. 1978. *Squatters and Settlers*. Sydney, Australia: Reed.

Strang, David. 1990, "From Dependency to Sovereignty: An Event History Analysis of Decolonization 1870–1987." *American Sociological Review* 55:846–60.

Strang, David and John Meyer. 1993. "Institutional Conditions for Diffusion." *Theory and Society* 22:487–511.

Strang, David and Sarah Soule. 1998. "Diffusion in Organizations and Social Movements: From Hybrid Corn to Poison Pills." *Annual Review of Sociology* 24:265–90.

Townsend, Kim. 1996. *Manhood at Harvard: William James and Others*. Cambridge, MA: Harvard University Press.

Vaille, F. O. and H. A. Clark, eds. 1875. *The Harvard Book: A Series of Historical, Biographical, and Descriptive Sketches.* Cambridge: Welch, Bigelow.

Van den Bulte, Christophe and Gary L. Lilien. 2001. "Medical Innovation Revisited: Social Contagion versus Marketing Effort." *American Journal of Sociology* 106:1409–35.

Warner, Sir Pelham. 1950. *Gentlemen v. Players, 1806–1949.* London: George G. Harrap.

Watson, James L. 2002. "Transnationalism, Localization, and Fast Foods in East Asia." pp. 222–32 *McDonaldization: The Reader,* edited by George Ritzer. Thousand Oaks, CA: Pine Forge Press.

Wejnert, Barbara. 2002. "Integrating Models of Diffusion of Innovations: A Conceptual Framework." *Annual Review of Sociology* 28:297–326.

Williams, Jack. 2001. *Cricket and Race.* Oxford, England: Berg.

Winch, Jonty. 1983. *Cricket's Rich Heritage: A History of Rhodesian and Zimbabwean Cricket, 1890–1982.* (Bulawayo, Zimbabwe: Books of Zimbabwe).

Wise, S. F. 1989. "Sport and Class Values in Old Ontario and Quebec." Pp. 107–129 in *Sports in Canada: Historical Readings,* edited by Morris Mott. Toronto, Canada: Copp, Clark, Pitman.

7.6

Offside

Soccer and American exceptionalism

Andrei S. Markovits and Steven L. Hellerman

What makes a society more receptive to certain sports rather than to others is one of the most intriguing socio-logical questions in the study of sports. In this article, Markovits and Hellerman explain why soccer, which enjoys popularity in most of the world, never became a major sport in the United States.

The argument: sports as culture in industrial societies

Eric Hobsbawm brilliantly argued that through-out the twentieth century in "the field of popular culture the world was American or it was provin-cial" with one unique exception: that of sport. Hobsbawm credits soccer as the universalizing agent for sport in the twentieth century the way American culture was for much of everything else. Hobsbawm states: "The sport the world made its own was association football, the child of Britain's global presence. ... This simple and elegant game, unhampered by complex rules and equipment, and which could be practiced on any more or less flat open space of the required size, made its way through the world entirely on its merits."[1] But not in the United States. Our study is to shed light on this matter. In particular, we harness the classics of modern and contemporary political sociology as well as comparative politics and polit-ical economy to gain a conceptual understanding of this major difference between the United States (and Canada) on the one hand, and Europe, indeed much of the world, on the other. [...]

Hegemonic sports culture

Our study offers yet another dimension to the comparative analysis that sees the United States as an integral, yet at the same time "exceptional," representative of advanced industrial societies. Indeed, we argue that America's sports excep-tionalism is deeply rooted in other exceptional-isms that constitute essential features of modern American life. But before we embark on a detailed discussion of these exceptionalisms, of what makes the United States different from the rest of the world, we would first like to present a few overall points differentiating the sports cul-tures of *all* modern industrial societies, includ-ing that of the United States. In this context, it is important to emphasize that what we mean by *sports culture* is what people breathe, read, dis-cuss, analyze, compare, and historicize; what they talk about at length before and after games on sports radio; what they discuss at the office watercooler; and what comprises a significant quantity of barroom (or pub) talk; in short, what people *follow* as opposed to what people *do*. In other words, while activity (doing) and culture (following) overlap to a certain crucial degree (as will become evident in this study), they are separate entities in which we view the "following" as more essential for our conceptualization of a society's sports culture. To be more precise, we are interested in what we call "hegemonic sports culture," meaning the sports culture that dominates a country's emotional attachments rather than its calisthenic activities. This domination need not be exclusive or total; indeed, it never is. Rather, it is hegemonic in the sense that Raymond Williams has used this concept so fruitfully in his pathbreaking studies on culture: "The reality of any hegemon, in the extended political and cultural sense, is that, while by definition it is always dominant, it is never either total or exclusive. At any time, forms of alternative or directly oppositional politics and culture exist as significant elements in society."[2] Put differently, this [study] is less about the world of athletes than it is about that of couch potatoes. Indicators of what we mean by hegemonic sports culture occur with greater frequency on sports radio call-in programs than on the sports fields, arenas, and courts themselves.

Thus, to stay with the United States as an example, we are much less interested in the fact that there are currently 19 million (largely youthful and upper-middle-class) soccer players in the country than we are with the fact that the *Boston Globe*—very typical for any comparable daily paper in a city with major sports teams—ran a minimum of six articles every day on the New England Patriots during the last three weeks of the 1997 football season, a number that regularly ballooned to ten on the Monday following an important game, and that such coverage of a local football, baseball, basketball, and—in some parts of the United States— hockey team is nothing unusual.[3] Yet another example of sports culture as opposed to activity would be the immense prominence accorded to the annual drafts for new players in the National Basketball Association (NBA) and the National Football League (NFL), which have been televised live and nationally for years and are always subject to passionate debates among fans all over the country. This book focuses on those sports that garner as much—in certain cases more—public attention off the field (court, rink) as in their actual performance. It views the lengthy pre-game analyses and post-game assessments in the media, especially on the hundreds of sports radio shows dotting the

land, as perhaps more salient for hegemonic sports culture than the actual contests themselves. Sport culture need not comprise atheletes themselves (although they are certainly involved). Instead, it features anyone with a love of sports, regardless of whether they ever participated in them in their own lives. Again, following is much more central to our argument than doing; culture supersedes activity.

To clarify further: There are 30 million pool and billiards players in the United States and 45 million engaged in fishing on a regular basis. Even though both these numbers far exceed the number of basketball, football, and baseball players, we would not classify billiard playing or fishing as part of American sports culture. Instead, what we mean by sports culture is an intense, frequent, perhaps even constant, preoccupation of a large public on at least a national—but also often on an international—scale that reaches well beyond the activities of the (professional) actors and the (amateur) spectators concerning the sports themselves, thereby rendering the "following" much more important than the actual "doing." Of course, all activities entail "culture": Recreational fishermen exist in a culture wherein they swap stories; discuss where, when, and how to fish; and the merits of bait, lures, or flies. Billiard players might meet a few nights a week in the bar or pool hall to play (engaging in both friendly and serious competition) and discuss their game. Indeed, in this sense, stamp collectors have a culture of their own, which also entails interest, passion, and know-how. However, the key to our premise and interpretation is this: These cultures (e.g., of fishing, pool playing, or stamp collecting) are inextricably tied to the activists/practitioners and their immediate entourages, whereas the culture of what we have defined as hegemonic sports is much more diffuse, and elicits passions and interest far beyond those of the participants and their physical space.

Hegemonic sports culture receives ample representation in other outlets of popular culture such as films, television shows, and, of course, literature. For example, Suzanne Wise, a specialist on American literature with sport themes, has compiled a bibliography of 4,500 adult works on baseball, 4,100 on football, 2,800 on basketball and—tellingly—only 15 on soccer.[4] There have been many films, television shows, musicals, novels, and short stories that feature baseball, football, basketball and hockey, boxing and even golf. Such staples of American culture as *The Boys of Summer, Field of Dreams, Damn Yankees, Brian's Song, Hoosiers, The Natural, Bull Durham, Cobb, White Men Can't Jump, Flubber, Hoop Dreams, North Dallas Forty, The Eighty-Yard Run, End Zone, A Fan's Notes,* and *Tin Cup*—to mention just a few at random—have become part of the American vernacular. Everybody knows them, including people who are not sport fans by any stretch of the imagination. To be sure, here too exists a hierarchy in which baseball—"the national pastime"—receives the greatest and perhaps the best representation in American literature and film. As framed by author George Plimpton: "The smaller the ball, the better the literature."[5] In contrast, we could only find a few American films in which soccer was featured. Sure enough one was set outside the United States, in a German prisoner-of-war camp during World War II: in *Victory,* released in 1981, Allied prisoners led by Michael Caine, Sylvester Stallone, and Pelé manage to escape from their German captors by using their formidable soccer skills. Revealingly, Hollywood had to use Pele—the only truly recognizable soccer star to a wide American audience—to give the movie any chance for commercial success; moreover, the only American actor, Sylvester Stallone, played goalie (naturally). Another American film on soccer was *Lady Bugs,* a Rodney Dangerfield vehicle aimed toward adolescents wherein the plot—tellingly—revolves around a *girls'* soccer team. Films such as *The Big Green, Manny's Orphans, Hotshot, Soccer Dog,* and *The Boys in Company C* featured soccer in some fashion but have remained obscure to the American public.

These phenomena about the cultural representation of hegemonic sports in the United States have their counterparts in other cultures and countries with the parallel representation of their own hegemonic sports. Be it cricket in the West Indies, India, and Pakistan, or soccer in Argentina, Austria, or Romania, these team sports have attained a cultural representation over the years that renders them social forces in their countries well beyond the actual playing fields on which they occur as a mere physical activity.[6] To use an example from the world of soccer: What we mean by hegemonic sports culture is not so much that Brazil has sent a team to every one of the sixteen World Cups thus far contested, but that the team's departure from the Rio de Janeiro airport has been televised, that its practice sessions are broadcast live back to Brazil, and that over one thousand journalists cover the team's every move on and off the field for a country of 140 million self-professed soccer coaches. Similar situations of sports culture in the guise of "following" pertain to virtually all countries in the world during the quadrennially held World Cup, except the United States, of course, where equivalent passions emerge around baseball's World Series, football's playoffs and Superbowl, and the championship games in basketball.

To be sure: there *is* an overlap between what people do—and have done since childhood—and what they follow. Sport as a topic for our book is a Durkheimian construct of a collective experience subject to formalities, norms, and agreements but whose main attribute lies in its inherently cohesive and solidaristic nature. Few social phenomena embody Durkheim's "conscience collective" better than modern hegemonic sports.[7] This pertains to team sports to a far greater extent than to individual sports. For example, nobody would argue that cycling was not immensely popular in France throughout the twentieth century and that the Tour de France, particularly, had not attained near iconic dimensions in France's sport space. French Tour de France winners such as Louison Bobet, Jacques Anquetil, and Bernard Hinault became national heroes after repeatedly winning this grueling contest, undoubtedly the world's premier bicycle race. And still, none of them once brought 1 million people out into the streets of Paris in celebration of their amazing feats, let alone three times within five days, as was the case with the two final victories of the French soccer team during the 1998 World Cup.[8] Celebrating crowds of similar quantities welcomed the French team in July 2000 after it had just won the European Championship in Holland, thereby becoming the sole national side ever to hold the two most prestigious crowns in international soccer at the same time: World and European champions. Lending additional support to our argument that team sports exercise much greater emotional power and collective cohesion than individual sports is that such unprecedented celebrations occurred in a country where soccer had allegedly enjoyed much less public enthusiasm and cultural hegemony than in neighboring Germany, Italy, Spain, and England. The sport may differ, but the phenomenon does not. With their shared belief system, common sentiment, mutually intelligible rules and norms, sports—particularly team sports—create a culture that varies by country and society in its empirical manifestations but appears compellingly similar in its analytic construct (as culture). And here we see some fascinating features common to all industrial societies. It is to a discussion of these that we now turn before embarking on a presentation of the "exceptions" informing the American experience.

Common features of industrial societies

Modern sports as culture are inextricably tied to the development of mass societies. Sport in its organized form of regulated leisure and, subsequently, of commodified culture, has proceeded hand in hand with such major components of "modernization" as urbanization, industrialization, education, and the perpetually expanding participation of a steadily growing number of citizens in the public spheres of politics, production, and consumption. Modern sports everywhere became inextricably linked to the most fundamental aspects of modernization: discipline exacted by regulated industrial life, the strict separation of leisure and work, the necessity of organized and regularized recreation for the masses, cheap and efficient public transport by train, later airplane (intercity) and bus as well as trolley (intracity), prompt and widely available mass communication via the press (introduction of the sport pages in newspapers and the establishment of sport journalism) followed by telegrams (crucial for the development and proliferation of betting), radio and then television, and the development and rapid expansion of modern education. Nobody has written more insightfully than Allen Guttmann about the inextricable link between societal modernization and modern sports the way both came to be understood throughout the twentieth century. In adopting concepts from Max Weber, Emile Durkheim, Ferdinand Toennies, and Talcott Parsons, Guttmann convincingly demonstrates how mechanisms as decisive as secularism, equality of opportunity to compete and the conditions of competition, specialization of roles, rationalization,

bureaucratization, quantification, and the quest for records transformed "premodern" games, play, and contests into "modern" sports.[9] The creation and—perhaps more important—dissemination of modern sports as culture are thus part and parcel of a public life defined by the (often conflicting) interaction between modernization's two most important social agents: the bourgeoisie and the working class. Modern sports have also become a major forum as well as a replica of the contradictions of modern life. Concretely, modern sports are totally achievement oriented, hence egalitarian, yet at the same time also inherently unequal, thus elitist. They are liberal and decidedly not collectivist in one essential way: Their equality of opportunity is accompanied by a singularity of results. All can participate and start, but only one emerges as winner. Vince Lombardi's famous dictum that "winning is not everything, but the only thing" comes closer to being a superb characterization of the essential quality of modern sports than he likely cared to realize.

[...]

The story is pretty much the same in all advanced industrial societies. Once a nation's "sport space" is filled, there are very few changes in this space.[10] To be sure, the notion of "space" is twofold. It refers first to a sheer logic of quantity. So, as in a popular restaurant where tables are full and there is a waiting list for patrons, who can only be seated once space has become available by departing guests, sport space also describes a finite entity of entrants, a limited capacity to give all participants equal prominence and presence. Thus, the concept of "sport space" is indeed physically determined and quantitatively defined, since the capacities of all such spaces are limited. Above all, timing matters immensely. The sequence as to which sport came first, which managed to modernize most efficiently, and how this modernization process related sequentially to the particular society's overall modernization all represent crucial ingredients in the formation of a society's sport space.[11] But more important, sport space denotes a qualitative dimension of cultural construction and group contestation that reflects power relationships in society at large, and in sport in particular. Sport space is not "filled" simply on a first-come, first-served basis, but rather disputed and contested by social groups and actors with particular sets of interests.

359

Positions within any society's sport space can thus be denied by dominant groups and alliances of interests.[12] This sense of sport space as contested cultural territory, as well as a sphere of established institutional interests, complements—rather than contradicts—the previously mentioned notion of sport space as merely a physical entity, a quantity that once filled, remains so forever.[13]

However, one thing is clear: Whichever sport entered a country's sport space first and managed to do so in the key period between 1870 and 1930, the crucial decades of industrial proliferation and the establishment of modern mass societies, continues to possess a major advantage to this day. Put differently, the contingent trajectory of sport culture—what social scientists would call its "path dependence"—is very high. Early arrival does not guarantee late survival, but it most certainly helps, because choices are very rapidly narrowed once sport spaces become filled both quantitatively and spatially, and qualitatively in that any newcomer must exert a great deal of power and expend major resources to be given, using the previous example, a seat at the restaurant's increasingly limited tables from which few want to depart. The "liability of newness" becomes increasingly burdensome once the topography of a country's sport space has been established.[14] Tellingly, the window of arranging the sport spaces of virtually all industrial democracies roughly occurs in that crucial period between 1870 and 1930. Once the occupants have settled in, they are virtually impossible to dislodge. The continually reinforcing feedback of escalating success provide them a cultural and institutional presence that render them virtually invincible.[15] Exit options as well as entrance possibilities become severely limited, relative costs increase considerably, and the whole compact is driven by loyalties that are constantly reproduced. Moreover, their reproduction in turn helps enhance the staying power of the existing arrangements.[16] A "mechanism of reproduction" develops that creates a self-reinforcing and positive feedback process that strengthens those that are already present and weakens the entrance options for all newcomers.[17] This led to a situation that permitted substantial shifts *within* many a country's sport spaces over the past century, although few entrants were accorded the status of cultural importance and popular following accorded to

that enjoyed by the early arrivals. In other words, once the window of opportunity between 1870 and 1930 was missed, it was virtually impossible to break into a country's sport space successfully for the ensuing seven decades. The "barriers to entry" remain exceedingly high, since the existing occupants enjoy significant cost advantages vis-à-vis all newcomers, have a fine and widely appreciated product differentiation, and benefit from substantial economies of scale.[18] Factor in that newcomers will inevitably suffer from an inadequate demand for their product, and it is clear that a belated entrance into this virtually closed world is almost prohibitive.[19] Newcomers, in effect, remain "crowded out."

While markets differ immensely, it is clear that in situations with few but very powerful players—that is oligopolies, indeed virtual monopolies in cases with only one dominant sport occupying a country's sport space—factors that deter entry also forestall exit, and elements that impede exit restrict entry.[20] This deterrence need not be part of a manifest or conscious strategy on the part of the incumbents to keep out newcomers; the structural power of incumbency is sufficient.[21] One way to alter entrance requirements and exit options is through unexpected exogenous influences or shocks that change the playing field in a major way. Whatever these exogenous factors may be—new technologies, new discoveries, new channels of communication, major social shifts, political upheavals, or a combination of some or all of these—they certainly reorder and reorient the existing structures of incumbency and might indeed threaten it with potential newcomers and even some departures from the old order. As to the sport space of the United States and other advanced industrial societies, it is possible that just such a period of restructuring and realignment is taking place that might perhaps make the current era a potential "critical juncture" somewhat analogous to the situation one century ago—though we doubt it, at least as far as the short run is concerned.[22]

If the path dependence just described pertains to the macrolevel of sport space and the collective dimension of the social, there is an equally significant—and profoundly related—path dependence on the microlevel of the individual that is crucial to the establishment of hegemonic sports cultures. It is mostly when one is a child that the lifelong attachment to a sport takes root. A potent mixture of the roles

360

of spectator, participant, and then of fan creates an allegiance to a sport at a young age that seems almost irrevocable for life. Here we have noticed the pre-dominance of teams, and thus of team sports, as opposed to individual sports, in the perpetuation of such dominant cultures in all advanced industrial societies. Teams have the modern power of continuity; they are institutions whose presence continues regardless of the individuals on the team. Teams are modern complex entities that exhibit "organic solidarity" in the best Durkheimian sense, meaning that the entity itself is far more important and lasting than any individual in it (no matter how prominent the individual). Additionally, individual sports do not exact solidarity in the act of performing, in the process of production. They are thus of a less complex and modern order than team sports. To cite Durkheim once again, individual sports remain stuck in the world of "mechanical solidarity" in which the collective is incidental. In team sports, the collective is essential, the whole always more than the sum of its individual parts.

This is not to say that success is meaningless and the affective equivalent to failure, as there are plenty of "fair weather fans" who support a team only when it is victorious. But it is to say that teams—as continuous institutions with clear identities apart from those of their individual players—are particularly powerful vehicles for establishing affective relationships with their fans very early in life. Individual sports are different: When a boxer, tennis player, figure skater wins a major following and becomes an icon clearly enjoying mass appeal—be it for achievement of style, as a "hometown favorite" (i.e., for patriotic reasons), or as a "personality"—the attraction and loyalty remain ephemeral because they are totally tied to this particular individual's persona, character, charisma. Once the boxer, tennis player, figure skater loses his or her charisma through decline, defeat, and/or retirement, fans are left in a void, in need of finding a new icon. Teams, on the other hand, endure. To be sure, Celtics fans mourned the departure of Larry "Legend" Bird just like Bayern Munich fans still invoke the days when Franz "Kaiser" Beckenbauer graced their team's uniform. And nobody in the world bemoaned the departure of Michael Jordan more emphatically than Chicago Bulls fans. But even without Michael Jordan's charisma, the Chicago Bulls continue as an institution. Very few fans of these respective teams—indeed of all other team sports—desert their team or lose their love for the sport because of the loss of a spectacular player's charisma. As such, team sports are more modern and enduring entities than individual sports; they not only capture our imagination at an earlier age, but they do a much better job of shackling our affect for life. And these affective feelings and deep-seated partisanships are non-transferable. Once an Arsenal fan, always an Arsenal fan, even when one's fate leads to a move far away from Highbury.

The same pertains to team sports in America, where it is not only the fans who have been mobile but—unlike anywhere in Europe—also the teams. Notice the continued loyalty of many Brooklynites after the Dodgers moved to Los Angeles in 1958,[23] or of the denizens of Oakland, whose allegiance to the Raiders was so powerful that it was one of the main reasons for the team's return to Oakland after a fifteen-year "desertion" to Los Angeles. Moreover, team allegiances and affect supersede that which is directed at individual players regardless of the power of the individual's particular charisma. [...] Marriages fail, relationships end, jobs disappear, anything can happen; only one red thread remains reliably through life: team loyalty."[24]

[...] Marketers are fully aware of this early path dependence and the ensuing increasing returns that a lifelong allegiance to a team and its sport entails. In its attempt to woo youngsters from their increasing attraction toward rival team sports, the National Football League hired a former MTV executive who clearly recognized that "it's all about getting a football ... into a kid's hands as soon as you can. Six years old, if possible. You want to get a football in their hands before someone puts a basketball in their hands, or a hockey stick."[25]

"Frozen spaces" and the dialogue with history

Following the pioneering work of Seymour Martin Lipset and Stein Rokkan in terms of their historical explanation of the contemporary topography of party spaces in advanced industrial democracies, we adapt the concept of the "freezing" of party spaces to the world of sport.[26] In a comparative analysis of the party landscape in the advanced industrial democracies of Europe, Lipset and Rokkan conclude that it was largely four major cleavages that—by their prominence and acerbity—gave rise to voter alignments that continue to define the party system that these countries exhibit to this day. In particular, Lipset and Rokkan argue that with the last—and most pronounced—of these cleavages (that between capital and labor, which they label the "owner-worker" cleavage) well established following the Great War, the cleavage system and its reflection in a nation's party topography was by and large in place by 1920. Indeed, it became so ensconced, Lipset and Rokkan aver, that it remained "frozen" well into the 1960s and beyond. While there are clearly flaws in this scheme (for example, the failure to account for fascism in a number of the countries critical to Lipset and Rokkan's analysis and the ensuing major alteration of the party landscape in the countries concerned), we remain impressed by how accurate the analysis has proven over time and how the cleavages that defined the party topography of industrial democracies at the early part of the twentieth century remarkably still pertained at its end. Some edges frayed, as newcomers entered the party space, and there were a few exits, but on the whole, the landscape that was frozen after World War I is still intact and quite recognizable.

We believe that such an analogy to the situation in sports is apt and strong, as it appears that sport spaces in virtually all of the advanced industrial countries were frozen by the end of World War I and virtually no significant thawing occurred until, perhaps, the current period. Whatever sport (or sports) managed to become culturally dominant—or hegemonic—by 1930 remained so through the end of the twentieth century. Of course, changes occurred in sport—its institutions, rules, and venues—over the years. Just like political parties adapted to—and in turn co-opted—political change, these "frozen" sports proved to be highly adaptable, malleable, and energetic.

Conclusion

The United States has played a preeminent role in the twentieth century and it has done so in most facets of human endeavor, be it in science and politics, the arts and economics, social organization and culture. What rendered the United States such an original, dynamic, valuable—but also controversial—contributor to all these aspects of the human condition in the twentieth century was the fact that its very own history and existence were part of a larger whole, yet separate from it. In particular, America's intimate, yet also conflicting, relations with its European progenitors has been the source of wonderful creativity and attraction, as well as of much misunderstanding and angst on both sides of the Atlantic. From the days of Alexis de Tocqueville and Harriet Martineau to our jet age, when millions of European tourists flock to all parts of the United States on a yearly basis, America has been a complex and puzzling entity to most Europeans precisely for being so similar to Europe, yet at the same time so different from it.

These commonalities and differences have been the source of many a fruitful comparison of the United States with Europe as a whole (or with a few select countries as its representatives) in virtually every field of the social sciences as well as in many of the humanities, cultural studies perhaps the most prominent among them. We see the essence of our [study] precisely in this vein, as yet another attempt to look at a particular aspect of American culture in light of its exception vis-à-vis a European—and in our case, even global—commonality. In our study, too, the mixture of similarities and differences renders the comparison fruitful but also complex. On the one hand, the United States is no exception at all in our story. Like all industrial countries, it developed what we have termed "hegemonic sports culture," that is, a structure wherein team sports played with some kind of a ball or puck attained such societal importance that they became part of popular culture in every industrial nation throughout most of the twentieth century. This hegemonic sports culture began in the latter quarter of the nineteenth century and had solidified by the 1930s. Its adherents and protagonists were almost exclusively male, among whom the working classes and the commercial middle classes played a leading and decisive, if not necessarily exclusive, role. This culture proliferated in a commodified manner and became an intrinsic feature of modern industrial and urban life. As such, it shared a deep affinity with nationalism, one of the most ubiquitous expressions of modern industrial culture. Similarities—better still, commonalities—defined this part of our story.

However, when we look at the actual form and content of this hegemonic sports culture as it manifests itself in the United States and its family of industrial democracies, our story shifts away from the similarities and focuses on the differences. Here we realize that the very similar male industrial and white-collar workers (in terms of class position, age, social milieu, cultural consumption, to mention but a few key sociological markers) in Europe and the United States spend their days (and nights) thinking, talking, dreaming, hoping, worrying, and perhaps even playing different sports, the former most likely soccer and the latter most likely baseball, football, basketball, hockey—or perhaps all four—of the sports that we identified as comprising the American sport space.

The central task of our [study] has been to explain this difference. We believe that this difference and its explanation matter for one simple reason: a better understanding of American culture in the comparative context of industrial modernity. And no matter how globalized this culture became in the course of the twentieth century, key aspects of it remain local and apart from that of the norm elsewhere. They remain exceptional, not in a normative sense but in an empirical one.

Studies of this kind are by necessity historical. They have little, if any, predictive power and value. Hence, we have no idea whether the story we have presented in this book will continue, and if it does, for how long. We have no way of knowing whether America's hegemonic sports culture will remain the same during the twenty-first century as it is at its outset. Soccer seems to be in a much better position at the beginning of the twenty-first century than it was at the beginning of the twentieth in terms of entering America's sport space. Then again, this space itself has drastically changed. Just because America's soccer exceptionalism remained a staple of American culture for more than one hundred years is no reason to assume that this will continue into the indefinite future. Indeed, changes may be afoot that could possibly herald a new development in terms of soccer's entry into America's hegemonic sports

culture. To be sure, this will take generations. But the beginning may be more auspicious this time than at any previous point in the history of soccer in America.

To wit, pronouncements such as the following would have been unthinkable one hundred years ago: "U.S. Soccer's mission statement is very simple and clear: to make soccer, in all its forms, a preeminent sport in the United States and to win the FIFA World Cup (men's) by the year 2010."[27] Is this a realistic project or a chimera? Might the indestructible optimism so characteristic of American pragmatism prevail in reaching such a seemingly hopeless goal? Will American "can-doism" succeed yet again, as it did with the Apollo project (a task that—to be sure—was a good deal more important than winning a soccer world championship, but also much more calculable)? In short, will soccer finally become ingrained in America's main culture and not remain the subculture it continues to be despite the major advances the sport experienced in the 1980s and 1990s? Will soccer become a major topic on sports-talk radio, or will it remain for most Americans a pleasant recreational activity for families, young people, and children?

We believe that our study offers powerful arguments for both scenarios: For soccer's continued marginalization in American sports culture and American life, and for its becoming a solid fifth team sport in America's sport space on the level of ice hockey, perhaps even a tad closer to the Big Three. We would like to conclude by delineating the trajectories and possibilities that might create either of the two scenarios, thereby reprising some of the key themes developed in our study.

The pessimistic scenario of soccer's continued marginalization in America's sport space relies on the observation that all team sports that attained cultural power in America, as elsewhere, succeeded in gaining a decisive foothold in the respective country's sport space between 1870 and 1930, a crucial era in the political, economic, and cultural modernization of industrial societies. By having the advantage of first-comers, these sports then reproduced themselves by establishing histories and affective ties with a large number of the population that then developed into an integral part of the respective country's mass culture, meaning baseball, football, and basketball in the United States, with hockey assuming enough of a hybrid status to qualify in our definition of culture. Soccer—so our argument—fulfilled a commensurate function in virtually all European and Latin American countries. These sports cultures—rendered popular by the commercial middle and working classes—became mass sports or "the people's games" in their respective countries and have remained so to this day. Despite the immense political, economic, and cultural changes that affected modern industrial societies in the course of the twentieth century, their sports cultures, in notable contrast to their sport activities, remained surprisingly resilient. The countries in Europe and Latin America, where soccer became king by the 1920s, still revere it as their premier sport despite the advent of various other sport activities since the late 1960s, including American sports such as baseball, basketball, and football.[28] To be sure, basketball and (to a lesser extent) American football have eked out a nice little niche in Germany's sport space, just like baseball has established a cultlike following with its own leagues and complete infrastructure in Holland and Italy. Basketball has indeed developed into a rather well-received popular game in countries such as Spain, Italy, Greece, Croatia, Yugoslavia, and Israel; yet it still does not come close to soccer's popularity by any measure. Using the immense power of television and other forms of modern communication, these hegemonic sports succeed in augmenting their already dominant position in a country's sport space by constantly reproducing their hegemony to the direct detriment of newcomers. Add in the power of habit, familiarity, knowledge, emotional attachment—to name but a few key ingredients in identity formation—and the task for any newcomer becomes perhaps more than formidable.

As a necessary but certainly not a sufficient condition, all sports cultures emerge through a complex interaction of grassroots activity "from below" and the setting of institutional parameters "from above." While these two dimensions are absolutely indispensable for the creation of any sports culture, they far from guaranteed its successful and continued existence throughout such a turbulent century as the twentieth. Once a symbiotic relationship between these two mechanisms has evolved, it then assumes a life of its own and becomes a successful new entity, in our case a hegemonic sports culture.

As we have discussed, soccer in America (until the 1980s) lacked both necessary prerequisites—grassroots activity from below and appropriate institution building from above—to warrant consideration as a viable candidate in a country in which it could never become part of the sports culture. During the course of the last two decades of the twentieth century, American soccer made tremendous strides on both dimensions: From below, it has become one of the nation's main recreational and physical activities since the early 1980s; with the formation of MLS and the concomitant streamlining of soccer's organizational framework, more important strides to establish soccer's institutional setting from above were achieved in the late 1990s than in the preceding one hundred years. But will this be enough? Can one establish culture by fiat, by following a blueprint? Here are some voices from unnamed American soccer experts, the gist of which would lead one to a pessimistic view of soccer becoming part of American sports culture in the foreseeable future.

> Nigerians play in the street. Latin Americans play in the street. Also, those who have had fathers who played will play. In the United States of America, we have no street soccer and fathers who did not play soccer.
>
> Soccer is not ingrained in the main culture. It is still a sub culture sport in the USA.
>
> The reason we can't compete and win at the international level, is we do not have a soccer culture on a daily basis.
>
> USA soccer is, in fact, still a feel good arena. Look at the folks who swarm around the game, and too many of them are simply participating in a fad. I often wonder how many U.S. youth, high school or college coaches could name a real world eleven and the clubs they play for.[29]

The pessimistic scenario is that sports cultures cannot be established in an "in vitro" fashion. And, after all, Project 2010 will be a kind of in vitro soccer creation from above designed to forge a World Cup winning team out of two- to three-dozen exceptionally talented athletes chosen from the millions of soccer-playing children and youth across the United States. This French-style planning approach—perhaps even more appropriately labeled East German-style strategy—to winning a major international tournament might work well in individual disciplines like track and field or lugeing, for example. But this is very hard to accomplish in team sports that are deeply anchored in complex cultural webs reinforced by structural networks of organizations and leagues on all levels of the game. Further complicating matters is that among team sports, soccer in particular—in notable contrast to American football and baseball, and to a lesser degree even basketball and ice hockey—relies much more on improvisation and an ephemeral, but all the more decisive, "feel" for the game that emanates from the sport's culture, rather than from learned strategies and set plays that can be conveyed at the level of activity but leave the game's overall quality far below the threshold of excellence required to be considered world class. Indeed, such top-down, blueprint style approaches to forging a winning soccer team at the highest level of global competition are exceedingly hard—perhaps impossible—to implement, as best demonstrated by East Germany's conscious decision not to pursue such a plan for its soccer teams (national or club) even though soccer assumed a much more prominent place in East Germany's sports culture than it ever has in the United States, including the game's boom period beginning in the early 1980s.[30] Put differently, a Project 2010–style approach to creating world-class excellence is much more controllable, confined, and thus realistic in sports such as gymnastics and bicycling than it is in a very fluid and culture-bound team sport such as soccer.

To be sure, even though a successfully accomplished Project 2010—unlikely as it may seem at this juncture—would be a necessary condition to catapult soccer onto the level of hegemonic sports culture in America, it would most definitely not be a sufficient one. A winning national team will still be no guarantee for the sustained articulation of a quotidian culture, which is ultimately the only way to make any sport part of the social fabric and create the "organic" basis for continued excellence in quality of play and competitive success. As long as little boys—and it is doubtful that little girls could carry this burden all by themselves, barring a fundamental change in the ways in which the vast majority of women and girls approach sport as culture—do not start playing one-on-one or two-on-two soccer with anything

resembling a ball on any surface that masquerades as a playing field, as long as they rely on their soccer moms to drive them to organized soccer practice on well-appointed grassy grounds supervised by coaches (who have learned much of their trade by reading the myriad publications on the techniques of coaching soccer), soccer will not be "the people's game" in the United States, and thus will never escape the levels of mediocrity on the global scene. Lastly, soccer continues to bear one further burden that impedes its development as culture in America's sport space: its virtual absence in the African American community with few, if any, signs of this lacuna abating in the foreseeable future.[31] The essence of the pessimistic scenario is simply that the shadows of American soccer's sad history have been far too dark and gloomy to have a ray of sunlight alter the fundamental presence of darkness. The continuity of soccer's marginalization in American culture will prevail despite a few sporadic successes.

But let us close this book by delineating the optimistic scenario for soccer's development in the United States during the first two decades of the third millennium. With MLS establishing a steady presence, soccer will gradually become a regular fixture in America's crowded sport space, not at its center, to be sure, but also far from the exotic fringes where it had barely subsisted for one century. The quality of its product—its games, its coaching, its players—will significantly improve, raising the level of competition on the field, establishing team rivalries, and developing into a solid summer sport that will become a respectable second to baseball. This will in turn improve the quality of the American national soccer team, thus making impressive victories such as the two consecutive ones against Germany and the one against Argentina in 1999 much more common and meaningful than in these largely inconsequential games. If such victories against comparable soccer powers increase in their frequency, if, in short, the American national team develops a consistency in its quality of play on an international level that will garner the soccer world's steady respect and lead to further wins in significant tournaments, then these victories will ignite a national pride, which—as we have argued—serves like virtually no other catalyst to ignite a sport's popularity and to catapult it from the realm of activity to that of culture. Consider how the success of the U.S. women during the World Cup tournament in 1999 developed into a national celebration. To be sure, women's soccer has been more popular in the United States than anywhere else in the world, constituting yet another of the many American exceptionalisms. But the power of national allegiance, if not necessarily nationalist fervor, proved far more important in the vast popular accolades that the women's team received than the love for the game in which it attained its success. For let us be clear: Had the final been contested between, say, Brazil and China, or Norway and Germany—teams with virtually equal playing skills to those of the Americans—very few people outside the narrow confines of the American soccer community proper would have noticed, let alone cared. As we argued [above] the power of nationalism in popularizing a sport cannot be overstated. Here, the United States constitutes absolutely no exception and conforms to the norm that so forcefully governed the sports world throughout the twentieth century. One can discern no signs that this trend might abate, let alone disappear, during the first decades of the twenty-first. If anything, quite the opposite seems to be the case.

As a consequence of soccer's growing visibility and respectability in America's sports culture, triggered by the success of its national teams in international competitions, the game will gain a greater presence than ever before in America's inner cities and among its economically less advantaged social groups. With soccer thus becoming a viable means of earning good money, thereby offering a genuine venue for escaping the blight of poverty for a talented athlete and his family, the sport will for the first time become a serious option for athletes who previously would have had to act against their best interest had they chosen a career in professional soccer instead of one of America's Big Three and One-Half. Sooner or later this confluence of positive forces will give rise to a genuine American soccer star—if not quite at the superstar level of Michael Jordan, Joe Montana, Ken Griffey Jr., and Wayne Gretzky, to pick appropriate representatives of the four team sports currently comprising America's sports culture—who will create the necessary buzz in his wake that every successful professional sport in America has always exacted and received.

There is a possible variation to this scenario, a "positive offshoot," as it were: The success of a women's league might fully utilize the institutions of primary competition and global excellence coupled to a concurrent change in the ways in which girls and women relate to sports and sports culture. As discussed [elsewhere],[32] the creation and proliferation of following and affect on the part of women for women's sports, specifically soccer—the one sport not a part of American hegemonic sports culture and not claimed by American men—is necessary for a women's league in the United States to elevate soccer to a position approaching at least that of ice hockey. In such a hypothetical case, interest in MLS and the U.S. men's national team might piggyback on the popularity of the women's game and engender a wide proliferation of interest in soccer for many American sports fans, male and female alike. This would be sacrilege and/or farce to most of the millions of (male) soccer aficionados in Europe, Latin America, and elsewhere, but well in tune with the American exceptionalism in sport. However, we once again reiterate that fundamental changes in the relationship of women to sports must occur for this "offshoot" of the positive scenario to become a reality. Put starkly, as long as women continue to confine their involvement with sports to the realm of activity (doing) and do not let it expand to that of culture (following), as long as "talking sports" remains strictly a "guy thing" and does not become part of "girl talk," the transformative power of women's activities in sports will remain culturally limited.

America, like the rest of the advanced industrial world, has become much more varied in the taste of its consumers. Concomitant with an obvious trend toward uniformity in culture in the wake of what is now called globalization, we also observe the exact obverse: a definite process of segmentation and fragmentation. These two opposing, yet also mutually reinforcing, social and cultural trends inform contemporary life in the United States. Certain aspects of American culture have become uniform across this vast continent as never before. Yet, an equally impressive array of identity-forming experiences have undergone processes of fragmentation and segmentation that are new. Indeed, America's new uniformity lies precisely in the motley variety that is widely enjoyed by millions of citizens coast to coast. The proliferation of Starbucks and of local micro-breweries represent but two examples of the nationalization of diversity, multiplicity, and variety that for decades remained confined to the ethnic enclaves of big cities and the country's cosmopolitan centers mainly, though certainly not exclusively, arrayed on its two coasts. To be sure, this new culture of diversity has not displaced the more conventional culture of standardized American conformity; rather, the two exist side by side with their own publics, which, however, are increasingly overlapping in all areas of consumption. Bagels, café latte and microbrewed beers have not replaced doughnuts, Maxwell House instant coffee, and Budweiser beer in contemporary America; rather, these products and their cultures have found a relatively comfortable way of coexisting in America's consumption space. However, this space either got larger or much more diverse—or most likely both—in the course of the last two decades of the twentieth century. The world of sports mirrors both of these processes. On the one hand, advances in technology and developments in media ownership have rendered local clubs such as the Chicago Cubs, Chicago Bulls, and Atlanta Braves nationally observable phenomena. Yet, on the other hand, the very same technological and media-related forces are in the process of creating a world where fans of a particular local team will be able to watch their team from anywhere in the country—indeed the world. American sports, just like American society, exist in toto; but they also exist in discrete and separate niches. Until the late 1970s and early 1980s, there existed very few outlets apart from the three national networks and their local affiliates to impart sports culture to the vast American public. This handful of channels has now been supplemented by well over fifty in most areas of the United States. This has led to a niched sports world in which hitherto obscure and marginalized sports have been able to develop and retain their specialized audiences apart from, as well as in addition to, the national audiences of the Big Three and One-Half, which succeeded in developing their audiences in an earlier age with far fewer options. Hence, soccer in America—like wrestling, bowling, car racing, curling, skateboarding, and any number of sports and activities—has its very own well-defined world of experts, activists, participants, and followers with its newspapers, magazines, web sites, mailing lists, and all other accoutrements that render it a legitimate culture. However, we feel that only through a major triggering event associated with a surge in popularity—caused by national pride and affect—can we expect this culture to depart from its enclave and emerge as a force on the national scale.

This is the optimistic scenario that we feel is not unreasonable to envision for soccer's future in the United States. Given the demographic changes that will occur in the United States in the course of the next twenty years and given the country's astounding economic and cultural dynamism, which has always characterized it and shows no signs of abating, it seems plausible to argue that America's sport space—just like its consumer space—will increase. In so doing, it will allow a certain growth in diversity, since we believe that the already entrenched actors will not be replaced or even substantially weakened; the immense staying power that they have attained over more than a century's worth of tradition and institutional presence will continue. Try as the involved actors might, through lengthy strikes, lockouts, or other actions that most certainly do not serve the image and cause of their sports, the Big Three and hockey will remain indestructible staples of America's sports culture. But there may well be possibilities for new members by virtue of the increasing diversification of this culture and the growth of America's sport space. If this scenario occurs in the next decade or two, we believe that soccer in America is in a fine position to join the club. The necessary groundwork was successfully laid in the last two decades of the twentieth century. It would be a terrible shame for soccer in the world, and for sports culture in the United States, were this—like in other instances with soccer in America—to have yet again been for naught.

Notes

1. See Hobsbawm, *The Age of Extremes,* p. 198.
2. Williams, *Marxism and Literature,* p. 113.
3. While the *Boston Globe* is known for the quality of its sports journalism and the extensive coverage it gives to many sports, in addition to the hegemonic team sports comprising much of the American

367

sport space, the point can be generalized to other American newspapers covering any of these papers' home teams in the dominant American sports of football, baseball, basketball, and even hockey where pertinent.

4. Wise, *Sports Fiction for Adults*.

5. As quoted in Samuel G. Freedman, "Of Those Boys of Autumn, Neither Beloved Nor Lauded," the *New York Times*, 5 September 1998, p. 15. This is a wonderful piece analyzing why baseball and the "Boys of Summer" have held a decided preferential edge in American literature and culture over football and the Boys of Autumn."

6. Thus, for example, in a virtual mirror image to the prominence of the Big Three in American literature, soccer's presence as a subject of study and literature in Britain is overwhelming. So, a compendium lists 5,629 sources on soccer. Sedon, *A Football Compendium*.

7. Durkheim, *The Division of Labor in Society; Sociology and Philosophy;* and Nisbet, *The Sociology of Emile Durkheim*.

8. For a detailed study of the World Cup in France and its singular effects on French public life, see Andrei S. Markovits, "Reflections on the World Cup '98" in *French Politics and Society*.

9. See Guttmann, *A Whole New Ball Game*, pp. 1–12, esp. p. 6; and *From Ritual to Record*, p. 16. We agree with Guttmann that all industrial societies— that is "modern" societies—created modern sports in a very similar way; in this the United States is not an exception at all, precisely the point of the first part of our analytical discussion presented here. However, we disagree with Guttmann that the United States was no exception at all. Guttmann angrily rejects the notion of States was no exception at all. Guttmann angrily rejects the notion of American exceptionalism, attributing to it only the normative notion of "exceptional" in the sense of being "better," of Americans feeling superior to others, of an "Only in America" belief and faith. What makes Guttmann's argument particularly weak on this important point is that he not only fails to mention, let alone engage, the huge body of scholarly literature discussing American exceptionalism in a serious empirical manner, but that he subsequently devotes entire chapters discussing precisely the different—and very unique—nature of American sports, American sports organization, and American sports culture. Sentences such as "Here, the United States is once again exceptional in that we have no Minister of Sports, nor, it must be added, are our amateur athletes governed by a single voluntary association" bespeak this contradiction (ibid., p. 46) We mean the term "exceptionalism" in an analytic sense, *not* in a normative manner, as Guttmann seems to (mis)interpret it.

10. Pierre Bourdieu uses the term "space of sports" which he sees as the methodological and conceptual equivalent of the field of power. See Bourdieu, *In Other Words*, pp. 156–67. We use the term "sport space" in its Bourdieuian sense, but also borrow it conceptually from the literature on political parties where the notion of "party space" has been advanced.

11. On sequence theory in political development, see Rustow, *A World of Nations*. Even though critical of modernization theorists, Moore also rested his analysis of modern political rule on sequences. His classic *Social Origins of Dictatorship and Democracy* is a brilliant expose of comparative sequence theory at its best.

12. For a superb presentation of this nuanced view of sports space, see the fine article by Tomlinson and Sugden, "What's Left When the Circus Leaves Town?, pp. 238–58. See also Sugden and Tomlinson, *FIFA and the Contest for World Football*.

13. The concept of "sports space," developed independently by Markovits and the eminent British football historian Tony Mason, came under criticism by Waddington and Broderick for representing in their view "an implicit—and therefore unexamined—assumption that in each society there is a limited amount of 'space' for sports, and that once this 'space' has been 'filled' by one sport, there is no room for other sports." For Markovits, see "The other 'American exceptionalism,' "pp. 230–64. For Mason, see his book *Passion of the People?;* and for Waddington and Roderick, see their article "American Exceptionalism."

14. On the concept of the "liability of newness," see Stinchcombe, *Constructing Social Theories;* pp. 108–18.

15. For a cogently written argument on the power of feedback in reinforcing already existing conditions, see Pierson, "When Effect Becomes Cause," pp. 595–628.

16. On the concepts of "exit" and "loyalty" as options for social action, see Hirschmann, *Exit, Voice and Loyalty*.

17. On the concept of the "mechanisms of reproduction," see Collier and Collier. *Shaping the Political Arena*.

18. We are grateful to Paul Pierson for referring us to the literature on "barriers to entry" as relevant to our project at hand. According to Joe Bain, who did pioneering work in this field, the three mentioned factors are the most salient in defining barriers to entry into a market by newcomers. See Bain, *Barriers to New Competition*.

19. George Stigler identifies "inadequate demand" rather than "economies of scale" as a barrier to entry by new firms into a market. See Stigler,

The Organization of Industry. For a nice comparison to Bain's and Stigler's analysis, see Nahata and Olson, "On the Definition of Barriers to Entry," pp. 236–39.

20. See Chapter 8, entitled "The Dynamics of Monopoly and Oligopoly Pricing" in Scherer, *Industrial Market Structure and Economic Performance,* pp. 229–56.

21. Rosenbaum and Lamort, "Entry Barriers, Exit, and Sunk Costs," pp. 297–304. See also Weizsäcker, *Barriers to Entry.*

22. On the concept *of* "critical junctures," see the superb article by Pierson, Path Dependence, Increasing Returns, and the Study of Politics"; on the concept of realignments and de-alignments in electoral politics and the topography of a society's party system, particularly that of the United States, see Burnham *Critical Elections and the Mainsprings of American Politics;* "Party Systems and the Political Process."

23. See, for example, Goodwin *Wait until Next Year,* as an example of the devotion and loyalty that a team—in this case the Brooklyn Dodgers—developed with its fans.

24. Roman Horak, as quoted in Demmel, "Ballfieber," p. 22.

25. Seabrook, "Tackling the Competition." pp. 42–51.

26. Lipset and Rokkan, "Cleavage Structures, Party Systems and Voter Alignment," pp. 1–64.

27. United States Soccer Federation, *U.S. Soccer Yearbook 1998,* p. 6.

28. According to Christiane Eisenberg, one of Germany's foremost sports scholars and soccer historians, the German Sports Federation listed 189 sport categories in which Germans engaged in 1998.

29. All of these voices hail from the third part of the so-called Queiroz Report, called "We can fly 2010." Carlos Queiroz, a Portuguese soccer coach with extensive American experience, was asked by the United States Soccer Federation to write a detailed report on the state of American soccer following the national team's awful showing in the World Cup of 1998. In this report, Queiroz delineates Steps that, in his view, need to be taken in order to improve the quality of soccer in America and—ultimately—make the game part of America's sports space. In the course of his research Queiroz interviewed many American soccer experts from the most diverse parts of the American soccer constituency. Queiroz's report was posted on the Internet on the U.S. Soccer web page.

30. As is well known, East Germany's strategy to excel in international sports targeted the "amateur" Olympics and consciously excluded the "professional" soccer World Cup. It designated individual sports as targets of opportunity precisely because they were much more easily implemented in a top-down manner than team sports (which required a much greater network of grass-roots activity and a larger pool of potential candidates for excellence). With the state's prime aim to gain as many Olympic medals as possible, simple calculation showed it much cheaper and easier to attain medals in single sport disciplines than in team competition. After all, a country was awarded one medal for individual swimmers and track-and-field athletes and one medal for a successful soccer team with a 22-member roster. Team sports, in short, were a good deal less efficient and much too costly in terms of human resources when compared to individual sports. Hence, soccer in the East Germans' grand sports plan was surrendered to the capitalist West. Basketball was briefly considered as a possible target by the state authorities, only to be abandoned when it became obvious that the brotherly Soviet Union already had a top-notch team that was always in contention for an Olympic medal. As a result, there was exactly one basketball court in all of East Germany.

31. When a reporter for the *New York Times* asked black teenagers at Polo Grounds Towers in New York City to rank their favorite sports, he received the following unanimous reply: "Basketball, football, baseball, and hockey." "And Soccer?" queried the reporter. To which the telling answer: "You've got to interview some Australians about that." Jesse McKinley, "On Baseball's Hallowed Grounds Young Worship Basketball," the *New York Times,* 10 October 1999.

32. In Chapter 5 of *Offside* by Markovits and Hellerman.

REFERENCES

Bain, J. (1956) *Barriers to New Competition.* Cambridge, Mass: Harvard University Press.

Bourdieu, P. (1990) *In Other Worlds.* Standford: Standford University Press.

Burnham, W.D. (1970) *Critical Elections and the Mainsrpings of American Politics.* New York: W.W. Norton.

Collier, R. and D. Collier (1991) *Shaping The Political Arena.* Princeton, N.J.: Princeton University Press.

Durkheim, E. (1950) *The Division of Labor in Society.* New York: The Free Press.

——(1974) *Sociology and Philosophy.* New York: The Free Press.

Freedman, S.G. (1998) *New York Times,* 5 September.

Goodwin, D.K. (1997) *Wait until Next Year.* New York: Simon and Schuster.

Guttman, A. (1988) *A Whole New Ball Game*. Chapel Hill, N.C.: University North Carolina Press.

Hirschman, A.O. (1970) *Exit, Voice and Loyalty*. Cambridge, Mass.: Harvard University Press.

Horak, R. (1997) in D. Demmel, "Ballfieber." *Werkstattblatter* 9(4) Sept.

Howbsawm, E. (1994) *The Age of Extremes*. New York: Pantheon.

Lipset, S.M. and S. Rokkan (1967) "Cleavage Structures, Party Systems and Voter Alignment: An Introduction," in S. Lipset and S. Rokkan (eds.) *Party Systems and Voter Alignments: Cross National Perspectives*. New York: The Free Press.

Markovits, A. (1998) "Reflections on the World Cup '98," in *French Politics and Society*.

Mason, T. (1995) *Passion of the People*. London: Verso.

Moore, B. (1966) *The Social Origins of Dictatorship and Democracy*. Boston: Beacon Press.

Nisbet, R. A. (1974) *The Sociology of Emile Durkheim*. New York: Oxford.

Pierson, P. (1997) "Path Dependence, Increasing Returns, and the Study of Politics." (paper, Harvard University, Center for European Studies).

Pierson, P. (1993) "When Effect Becomes Cause," *World Politics*. July.

Rosenbaum, D. and F. Lamort (1992) "Entry Barriers, Exit, and Sunk Costs," Applied Economics. 24 (3).

Rostow, D. (1967) *A World of Nations*. Washington, D.C.: Brookings Institution.

Scherer, F.M. (1980) *Industrial Market Structure and Economic Performance*, 2nd ed. Chicago: Rand McNally.

Seabrook, J. (1997) "Tackling the Competition." *The New Yorker*. 8 August.

Seddon, P. J. (1995) *A Football Compendium*. Boston: The British Library.

Stigler, G. (1968) *The Organization of Industry*. Chicago: University Chicago Press.

Stinchcombe, A. (1968) *Constructing Social Theories*. New York: Harcourt, Brace, and World.

Sudgen, J. and A. Tomlinson. (1998) FIFA and the Contest for World Football. Cambridge, U.K.: Polity Press.

Waddington, I. and M. Roderick (1996) "American Exceptionalism," in Sports Historian, British *Society of Sports History*, v.16 May.

Williams, R. (1977) *Marxism and Literature*. New York: Oxford.

Wise, S. (1986) *Sports Fiction for Adults*. New York: Garland Publishing.

Beyond a boundary?

Sport, transnational advertising, and the reimagining of national culture

Michael Silk and David L. Andrews

The increasing international interests in sports such as professional basketball and golf are typically viewed as the driving force behind sports globalization. But that view of sports, particularly in the contemporary world, is often inaccurate, because it ignores the role of sports' appeal as a resource that is used by other institutions to achieve non-sports objectives. In this article, Silk and Andrews explain the varied ways corporate advertising has used sports to penetrate provincial societies and draw them into global consumer culture.

[...]

Within the contemporary advertising industry, it is possible to discern indifferent and enthusiastic engagements with the concepts of nation and national identity. In terms of the former, and perhaps prompted by the hegemonic "borderless world" (Ohmae, 1990) rhetoric of the global marketplace, many advertising agency account directors eschew the utility of national cultures in providing the basis for profitable consumer segmentation and targeting. Instead, they focus on developing what are deemed to be more cost-effective global campaigns that circumvent national borders by creating more expansive global consumer tribes linked by lifestyle values or preferences rather than spatial location. Numerous corporations possessing the technological wherewithal (in terms of networks facilitating the instantaneous global flow of capital and information), political approval (derived from the major Western democracies' perception of market globalization as an unavoidable force of nature), and economic structure (in regard to the deregulationist initiatives that have lowered trade and tariff barriers) have sought to rationalize their products and promotional strategies into single, globally focused directives. In seeking to transcend national boundaries, these corporations look to benefit from the massive economies of scale derived from the establishment of a truly global market. By way of illustration, this notion of postnational geographies of consumption (Leslie, 1995) clearly underpins the work of 180, the innovative Amsterdam agency founded by defectors from Wieden and Kennedy (the agency responsible for most of Nike's advertising).

180's corporate mission speaks to universal traits, experiences, and emotions in a manner designed to appeal beyond the specificities of national cultural boundaries. With this

Michael Silk and David Andrews, "Beyond a Boundary: Sport, Transnational Advertising, and the Reimagining of National Culture" from *Journal of Sport & Social Issues* 25.2 (May 2001): 180–201. Copyright © 2001 by Sage Publications, Inc. Reprinted with the permission of Sage Publications, Inc.

objective in mind, 180's creative director, Larry Frey, outlined the following:

> When we execute things we work very hard to make sure it doesn't look like it's from one specific place and we are really picky about directors. We like international looks that make it difficult to pin down where this director makes their [*sic*] home. We use this checks and balances system on the music we select, on the editing techniques we use, on casting and on all of the directors. ... We ask, is this thing too American, too German, too Spanish. We identify what are the styles that tend to emerge out of those countries and make a conscious effort to avoid them.
>
> (Hunter, 2000)

180's placeless universality is perhaps most graphically exemplified within their recent global "Adidas makes you do better" campaign for the sports footwear and apparel giant. In four separate television commercials, English soccer player David Beckham (clearing the streets of litter), Trinidadian sprinter Ato Boldon (returning a stolen television), Russian tennis starlet Anna Kournikova (countering cheating at an arcade game), and New Zealand rugby player Jona Lomu (rescuing a suffocating fish) all utilize their sporting or physical skills for the good of humanity as a whole. By focusing on such seemingly universal moralistic and heroic traits, the campaign thus transcends the nationality of the athlete in question and the national cultural context within which the advert is consumed. As Frey opined, "I think the Adidas we've done prove we can create and cross borders effectively" (Hunter, 2000).

In contrast to the aforementioned cultural globalism, the global-local element within the ranks of the culture industries actively affirms the continued relevance of national cultures. [...]

Clearly, the commercially inspired reinvigoration of the nation within the context of an increasingly global economy represents a telling economic, political, cultural, and technological issue, yet is one that has thus far received little intellectual interrogation within the broader field of sport studies (for two analyses that consider sport in relation to the transnational, corporation-inspired reimagining of national communities, see Cole, 1996; Cole & Andrews, 2000). Moreover, such a project is of particular interest to the sociology of sport community, because sport (either in terms of sporting

practices, spectacles, or celebrities) is frequently used within advertising campaigns as de facto cultural shorthand delineating particular national contexts. As such, this discussion problematizes the "end of the nation" rhetoric that punctuates the globalization debate by demonstrating the apparent contradiction exposed by the continued presence and importance of the nation as a cultural entity, within what Albrow (1996) describes as the "global age." This article examines the role played by transnational corporations and their promotional armatures in reimagining national cultures, introduces the concept of cultural Toyotism as a means of understanding the manner in which transnational entities negotiate the global-local nexus, and explicates empirical examples of the contrasting processes whereby sport has been used as a means of constituting the nation within the advertising discourses of transnational corporate entities.

[...]

In the remainder of this article, we aim to unearth these two primary strands of cultural Toyotism, particularly in relation to the ways that sport practices, celebrities, and spectacles have been appropriated by transnational corporate capitalism as culturally resonant vehicles used in the commercially motivated process of national reimagining. According to Bell and Campbell (1999), sport has become one of the "world's biggest obsessions" (p. 22). Clearly, advertising and promotional innovators have operated under the assumption that, and indeed capitalized on, the stylized excitement and glamour that characterizes most contemporary, consumer-oriented sporting forms. As leading sport marketing agency ISL's Daniel Beavois has indicated, "Sport is probably the only thing that fascinates everyone in the world. ... Many people now feel more concerned by sport than almost anything else in their lives" (quoted in Bell & Campbell, 1999, p. 22). Although clearly an overexaggeration—what else would one expect from an employee of one of the world's largest and most influential sport marketing agencies—this quote does suggest the way in which the corporate world has come to view sport and its potential as a means of engaging and mobilizing consumers around the globe. It is argued, then, that prefigured within the logic of cultural Toyotism, sport is mobilized as a major cultural signifier of a nation that can engage national sensibilities, identities, and experiences. As such, sport is used as de facto cultural shorthand delineating particular national sentiments. That is, within the logics of transnational corporate capitalism, sport is seen as a globally present cultural form, but one that is heavily accented by local dialects. It is this notion of sport as a globally present but locally resonant cultural practice that advertisers seek to mobilize within this process of cultural Toyotism.

Multivocal transnationalism I: acting globally, thinking locally

During earlier phases in the process of globalizing consumer capitalism, the aspiring giants within the global marketplace—most, if not all, of whom originated in the United States—treated the international market as a uniform and homogenous entity. Hence (and here one is thinking of Coca-Cola, Disney, and McDonald's, in particular), globalizing corporations routinely adopted standardized advertising campaigns regardless of the national context within which consumption was being encouraged. This frequently meant the indiscriminate running of advertising campaigns originally produced for the "home" American market. Whether intentionally or otherwise, this inevitably led to charges of a cultural imperialism being waged by American corporations. This is perhaps better expressed as an America-flavored Coca-Colonization; a bringing of "America to the world" through Coca-Cola, Disney, McDonald's, and so forth (Leslie, 1995). Although the hawking of Americana (the symbols and products readily associated with American culture) continues to be a profitable strategy (especially in efforts targeted at engaging the global youth market), many mature global corporations have acknowledged the pitfalls associated with such blanket strategizing and have modified their approaches accordingly. In this vein, Coca-Cola began to soften its American edge, initially by producing nationally ambiguous and thereby globally inclusive advertising campaigns such as the "I'd like to buy the world a Coke" television commercial that first aired in 1971 (Prendergrast, 1998). In an attempt to further distance its brand image from its storied American roots, certain

Coca-Cola campaigns provided an even narrower focus on specific regional and national cultures. In terms of the former, the "Eat Football, Sleep Football, Drink Coca-Cola" campaign is of most relevance to this article. In separate pan-North American (American football), pan-European (Association football), and pan-Australian (Australian Rules football) television advertisements, Coca-Cola was unselfconsciously conjugated with regional sporting cultures through commercial narratives that focused on the passion, intensity, and excitement of the various football codes and, by inference, drinking Coca-Cola itself.

Coca-Cola's subsequent incursion into the realm of national cultures is most graphically, and indeed beautifully, illustrated in the 1996 "Red" commercial developed by Wieden and Kennedy, Portland, as a means of furthering Coca-Cola's presence on the Indian subcontinent. The very real poverty experienced by much of India's vast populace would suggest little consumer interest in a carbonated soft drink that to many would represent an unattainable luxury. Nevertheless, the sheer volume of the Indian population (approaching 1 billion) means that—although small in percentage terms of the total populace—the potential market for Coca-Cola (India's middle and upper classes) is sizeable enough to encourage global corporations into the Indian market. Such was the rationale behind Coca-Cola's recent foray into Indian popular consciousness, as realized through the "Red" commercial. This 60-second depiction of the vibrancy and complexity of Indian culture keyed on the byline "Passion has a colour"—the color in this instance being red: the red of chili drying in fields, the red of a Rajasthani man's turban, the red of the *bindis* adorning women's foreheads, the red of the *dupata* drying on river banks, the red of the cricket balls that regularly punctuate the visual narrative, and the red of the Coca-Cola brand symbolism so subtly and seamlessly inserted into this panoramic sweep of Indian culture. With the backdrop of the late Nusrat Fateh Ali Khan's hypnotic Sufi-inspired devotional "Mustt Mustt" (himself a Pakistani but with a considerable following in India), the commercial brazenly synthesizes India's passion for cricket (red ball) with a desired passion for Coca-Cola (red logo). Through this association with the cricket thematic, Coca-Cola sought to

373

thrust itself into the mainstream of Indian culture by providing itself with a seemingly natural place within local culture and experience. To be sure, this stunning commercial warrants article-length analysis in its own right (something we are presently working on). However, for our present purpose, it is sufficient to state that Coca-Cola's "Red" represents a vivid example of the way in which national sporting practices have been mobilized by the symbolic processes, and through the mediated products, associated with the transnational corporate modus operandi that we have characterized as cultural Toyotism.

As well as mobilizing the sporting practices associated with particular nation cultures, corporations adopting the cultural Toyotist approach regularly appropriate sporting celebrities as mechanisms of identification with a particular locality. Nike, now also seeking to shed its overt American demeanor, has been noticeably promiscuous in forming relations with national sporting heroes. As an exemplar of this type of initiative, Nike developed a television advertisement in which the Australian cricketer Shane Warne bowled a chainsaw rather than a cricket ball toward a cowering batsman. In this example, Nike selected a national sporting hero and a national sporting pastime, and attached their commodity sign (brand identity) to these potent national cultural signifiers. Through its liaison with Warne, Nike sought to nurture an authentic sense of national affiliation (Hobsbawm & Ranger, 1983) for the company, which still could be perceived as something of an interloper into Australian culture. Utilizing a widely acknowledged aspect of Australian cricket culture, namely the aggressive style of Warne's spin bowling, the advert illustrates the precise way in which transnational entities seek to ingratiate a global brand (Nike) within a local context (Australia). In doing so, and in the true spirit of cultural Toyotism, Nike crafted a highly engaging yet superficial and depthless representation of Australian national sporting identity—effectively, a construction of Nike designed to fit unself-consciously into Australian culture. Of course, Warne is by no means Nike's only nationally bounded sport celebrity, as evidenced by the considerable promotional work the company has put into nurturing such national sporting icons as Ian Wright (the English footballer), Jeff Wilson (the New Zealand rugby player), Christian Vieri (the Italian footballer), and Americans Tiger Woods (golf) and Michael Jordan (basketball).

McDonald's is perhaps the most common signifier of transnational capitalist expansion, as well as being among the most (along with Nike) targeted recipient of anticapitalist demonstrations. Having long nurtured its explicitly American demeanor, in recent times, like both Toyota and Nike, McDonald's appears more concerned with melding its brand identity into the superficial vagaries of the local culture. In Britain, perhaps unsurprisingly, McDonald's has regularly drawn on British footballing heroes to cement its place within the British national imaginary. In one noted television commercial, Alan Shearer, then England's football captain, embarks on a nostalgic journey through his native Newcastle, visiting, among other places, his old school, football boys club, and a McDonald's restaurant. Significantly, the advert draws on what are perhaps the best-known cultural signifiers of Newcastle: Shearer himself, the football club for which Shearer plays, and the evocative Tyne Bridges. Hence, McDonald's invokes the cultural specificities of an English locale as it embeds itself ever deeper within the experience of everyday British life. A more recent promotional offering operates more explicitly at the national level. McDonald's revises and resites, as an element in the commercial production process, the 1966 Soccer World Cup final between England and Germany. The advert commodifies history and reinvents a reality that could never have existed—a simulacrum of the nonexistent, a place in which space, time, and place boundaries have been collapsed and fact fused with fiction (Harvey, 1993). The advert depicts Geoff Hurst, mythologized in English history for his three goals in the 1966 World Cup final, scoring his third goal in the game, a goal made even more immortal in English consciousness by the accompanying commentary from Kenneth Wolstenholme: "There's some people on the pitch, they think it's all over, it is now!" Rather than the ball entering the net for Hurst's third goal, the advert revises history by showing a streaker running onto the pitch and causing Hurst to miss the shot. The advert concludes with Hurst consuming the new product in McDonald's range (the McDonald's Triple Burger with twisty fries), with the narrative defining the revised footage as "a triple with a twist." The Shearer and Hurst campaigns, however parodically, are attempts to insert the global brand (McDonald's) into the imaged recollections of the national psyche. Specifically, the adverts use selected imagery, both concrete signifiers and sporting celebrities, to nurture the distinctly local (national) demeanor of the global brand.

Multivocal transnationalism II: global anthems/local sensibilities

Thus far, we have proposed that cultural Toyotism is characterized by the local being incorporated and reflected in the promotional processes of global capitalism. Extending Castells (1996), we suggested that cultural Toyotism could point to the degree to which transnational corporate forces, rather than internal or regional politico-economic forces, have begun to reconstitute the tenor of popular national sensibilities and imaginings. To this point, we have addressed the ways in which transnational corporations have inserted brands within specific local cultures, initiatives that thus fuse the global with the local. However, the advertising and promotional denizens of transnational corporations, who actively endorse the implausibility of a global culture conclusively extinguishing national difference, have also constructed initiatives that seek to engage a multitude of markets at one and the same time. Specifically, these campaigns rationalize the escalating costs implicit in reaching the maximum market base by producing single, multivocal, multinationally oriented texts. These texts appeal to a number of different local markets and thus simultaneously exhibit the global reach and the local resonance of the brand in question. Despite the globalizing cosmopolitan logic underpinning such campaigns, the producers of these initiatives are aware that the particularities of place and culture can never be absolutely transcended. Rather, they recognize that

> globalization is, in fact, also associated with new dynamics of re-localization. It is about the achievement of a new global-local nexus, about new and intricate relations between global space and local space. Globalization is like putting together a jigsaw puzzle: it is a matter of

inserting a multiplicity of localities into the overall picture of a new global system.
> (Morley & Robins, 1995, p. 116)

Following Dirlik (1996), these campaigns reflect the ability of transnational corporations to operate within the language of the local simultaneously in multiple locations. For example, the Ford "Just Wave Hello" advert provides a set of global products (some tailored specifically for local markets) that are appropriated within a number of different physical places (complete with national cultural referents, such as a homecoming parade).

Through its transnational advertising agency, Wieden and Kennedy (which has offices in Portland, New York, London, Amsterdam, and Tokyo), Nike has produced a series of global, multivocal promotional campaigns that select various authentic national traditions (in the form of sporting heroes) and combine them to exhibit the global ubiquity and the local pertinence of the brand. This trend is most evident within Nike's insurgence into the nationally charged, global football marketplace—an initiative prompted by Nike's recognition that if it were to become a truly global sport corporation it would need to secure a global presence within what is unquestionably the global game (Giulianotti, 1999). Initially, Nike's multivocal football campaigns selected specific physical locales and corroborated them with images of complementary national football heroes as they sought to engage the national sensibilities and affiliations of multiple and dislocated consumers. Nike's first incursion into global football was realized in their 1994 Wall campaign, created within Wieden and Kennedy's main office in Portland. Within this spot, Nike selected a series of football heroes, hijacked from the cultural memory of particular localities, and positioned them as representatives of their respective nations. Significantly, the advert depicted these celebrities within their own localities, and it was a football that orbited a time-space compressed "Nikeworld." The advert highlighted various footballing celebrities who were moored, quite literally, in the bricks and mortar of their own locales while kicking a ball around a compressed globe. The advert depicts Eric Cantona, a former French international and Manchester United player on a billboard next to Paris' Eiffel Tower. Cantona, adorning a Manchester United

375

shirt, perhaps to engage the French and the global Manchester United marketplace at one and the same time, beats a nondescript opponent, also moored on the billboard, and kicks the ball over the English Channel, past the Houses of Parliament and into a billboard in London's Leicester Square. Here, Ian Wright, then of Arsenal and England, controls the ball and fires it past Tower Bridge. The ball continues its flight around the world, passing between various national symbols and heroes, such as a Rio de Janeiro beach and the Brazilian player Romario, and finally ending up in Mexico City, where the ball is saved by the Mexican goalkeeper, Jorge Campos.

As Nike's global football strategizing evolved, explicit representations of place would appear to have been discarded in preference for a sole focus on football heroes as signifiers of national cultural difference. In 1996, Wieden and Kennedy's Amsterdam office produced the direct successor of the Wall campaign. According to Nike's U.K. spokesperson, Graham Anderson, the 1996 advertisement, titled "Good versus Evil," highlighted football stars from a whole range of countries demonstrating how the game can unite the planet against the forces of evil (www.auto-server.com/newsroom/sports). "Good versus Evil" did not define the other (opponents) as place bound; rather, the selected heroes were pitted against opponents that were temporally and spatially ambiguous. Set in a Roman amphitheater, the advert depicted the selected celebrities (good) playing, and ultimately beating, a team lead by a representation of the devil and his underlings (evil). Nike complicated local affiliation: Some players adorned their national team uniforms, whereas others wore their club uniforms. Paolo Maldini and Ronaldo, for example, wore their Italian and Brazilian national team shirts, respectively. However, Ian Wright (Arsenal), Patrick Kluivert (Ajax), Luis Figo (Barcelona), and Eric Cantona (Manchester United) adorned their club shirts not only to appeal to a multitude of markets but also as an attempt to capitalize on the market within which the player was best known. Cantona, resplendent in Manchester United livery, proved the central figure in the ad by destroying evil with his deadly penalty kick. At the time of the advert, Cantona was better known for his exploits with Manchester United than with the French national team. Nike capitalized on the

global appeal of Manchester United (and indeed Barcelona, Ajax, and Arsenal) as symbols that would better engage a multitude of markets than the national team uniforms of most of the assembled players. And yet, given Italy and Brazil's globally acknowledged (and indeed celebrated) football heritage, Maldini and Ronaldo (wearing national team uniforms) could be seen as an attempt by Nike to constitute a global (as well as an implicitly national) market for these universally admired national football dynasties.

Like Nike, Adidas have produced transnational campaigns that are multivocal in nature through selecting particular national heroes and events with which audiences in different localities can affiliate. The futuristic "Soccer Reinvented" campaign revealed Team Adidas, made up of (among others) the Italian Alessandor Del Piero, the Argentinian Fernando Redondo, the Dutchman Edwin Van de Saar, the Englishman Paul Gascoigne, and the American John Harkes. The advert depicts two teams of identical clones, each outfitted in bland Adidas uniforms, with the only difference being that the one team who dons Adidas Predator boots has names on the backs of their uniforms. Not surprisingly, the predator team plays the more inventive, exhilarating, and ultimately successful football. Like Nike's "Good versus Evil," the game is played in a nonplace (Auge, 1995), a vacuous neostadium resembling an immense bank vault devoid of any signs, symbols, or color. The only spectators present within the stadium are depthless simulations of spectators (Baudrillard, 1983), for the fans in this campaign are surface representations spatially constrained in television screens adorning a small area of the vast stadium. The advert thus eliminates physical place and replaces it with a spatial ambiguity—or placelessness—that removes any relational or historical attachment that the consumer may have to a particular sport stadium (Bale, 1998, p. 268). By removing all referents to place yet selecting national football heroes, Nike and Adidas are able to promote their brands transnationally, effectively engaging and invoking national sensibilities and experiences within a multitude of markets at one and the same time.

The direct successor to Nike's "Good versus Evil" campaign once again emanated from Wieden and Kennedy, Amsterdam, and was timed to coincide with the 1998 World Cup. "Nike Beach" rendered a new assemblage of burgeoning football celebrities (Ronaldo, Ariel Ortega, Christian Vieri, Nankwo Kanu, Ibrahim Ba, Roberto Carlos, Luis Enrique, and Hernan Crespo). Like Adidas's "Soccer Reinvented" commercial, these players were located in a distinctly ambiguous space: A remarkably indistinct beach idyll could quite easily have been located anywhere from the Brazilian beach to the French Riviera or Australia's Gold Coast. The transnational thematic has been transposed subsequently to Nike's latest band of football celebrities (now christened the Nike Geoforce) in the 2000 television commercial "The Mission." Within this highly stylized commercial, the Nike Geoforce set out to reclaim the new GeoMerlin soccer ball stolen from Nike by Uri, a fictional character who sought to impose a defensive approach to the game. The GeoMerlin soccer ball was seen as a threat to Uri's dour football—a game dominated by standardized and mechanized robots that replaced human players and thus eliminated irrational and risk-taking individuals from the game (www.nikefootball.com). "The Mission" advert and its accompanying promotional mechanisms depict how Nike's Geoforce used their inventive football skills to storm the defensive fortress, destroy the robotic leader of Uri's operation, blow up Uri's headquarters and his soccer-playing robots, and return the prototype ball to Nike. The Geoforce was made up of Edgar Davids (Holland), Oliver Bierhoff (Germany), Francesco Totti (Germany), Guardiola (Spain), Figo (Portugal), Lilian Thuram (France), Andy Cole (England), Dwight Yorke (Trinidad and Tobago), and Hidetoshi Nakata (Japan), all of them wearing the latest range of Nike Mercurial apparel. According to Nike, these agents were selected for this particular mission given their demonstrated courage, aggression, determination, deadliness, and natural athletic ability. In selecting these agents and their concomitant skills, Nike are involved in the transnational reconstitution of the cultural experiences of football, yet at the same time they retain elements of particular localities through the selection of sporting heroes whose distinctly different skills evoke distinctly different national (football) cultures. For example, the German, Bierhoff, is defined as a natural leader who brings creativity, intelligence, and determination, whereas the Japanese Nakata is composed, consistent, and instinctive. As such, Nike are incorporating within their transnational campaign the very local differences that global capitalism

has attempted to overcome (Hall, 1991). However, rather than romanticize or celebrate the sophistication of such campaigns, it is important to outline that these campaigns point to the ways in which transnational corporations are providing commercially inspired representations of locality. In this case, Nike have done little more than select celebrities who represent a superficial and depthless caricature of national cultural differences, sensibilities, and experiences—modern nation-statehood effectively being replaced by late capitalist corporate-nationhood.

Coda

Clearly, the cultural innovators responsible for the marketing and promotional strategies of transnational corporations are keenly attuned to the continued resonance of the nation within the logics of transnational corporate capitalism. In this article, we have attempted to highlight the enthusiastic engagements with national sensibilities and experiences within specific advertising campaigns. In exposing the durability and resilience of the nation as a cultural entity—thus problematizing the "end of the nation" rhetoric rooted in the global panic brought about by the instantiation of a globally homogenous commercial culture—we proposed that the nation is of central and prefigurative importance in global promotional imperatives. Moreover, we have suggested that sport is a globally present, but locally resonant, cultural practice that transnational advertisers mobilize to negotiate the global-local nexus. This strategy, which we have termed cultural Toyotism, points to the ways in which the reproduction of the nation has become exteriorized through and internalized within the promotional strategies of transnational corporations.

Our initial investigations suggest that these commercially inspired reflections are likely to be depthless caricatures of nation that delineate particular national contexts through drawing out, or selecting, stylized signifiers of (sporting) traditions, pastimes, and celebrities. Of interest here is the centrality of sporting forms and sporting celebrities in what Hannerz (1996, p. 89) described as a changing of the nation under the logics of transnational corporate capitalism. Sporting spectacles and celebrities— or perhaps more accurately, a commercially inspired reflection of sport that emphasizes entertainment, glamour, and at times violence—are increasingly being incorporated into these transnational campaigns. Of course, this is merely an observation; however, it does point to the problematic nature for sporting and national cultures of a climate increasingly dictated by an external and commercial locus of control. These corporate reflections of nation are not necessarily any more false, imagined, or inauthentic than those constituted internally through the political and economic realm. However, significant questions remain to be answered in respect to the problems posed when national identity becomes externally and commercially constituted.

Our subsequent research intends to extend our initial observations through addressing the professional and intellectual practices of the new class of cultural intermediaries (Du Gay *et al.*, 1997) who inhabit the corridors of transnational corporations. That is, to better understand the practices that motivate and shape these expressions of cultural Toyotism, we need empirically based investigations that concentrate on the nature of the symbolic analytic workforce, their training, values, and their global-local cultural literacy. Clearly, there are differences within the philosophies of individual advertising agencies in respect to the relevance of the nation as a source of identity and differentiation. As we outlined in the introduction, the global campaigns of ISO transcend the nation and create a more expansive global tribe based more on lifestyle values, taste, and consumer choice than on spatial location. However, others, such as Bensimon Byrne D'Arcy and Wieden and Kennedy, recognize the implausibility of transcending the nation—and thus incorporate the ingrained and inalienable specificities of local cultural tastes and interests (Held *et al.*, 1999)—thereby embracing the nation as a source of consumer identification. As such, the next stage in our investigation, within numerous different national contexts, will focus on the practices of those cultural producers involved in the commercial inflection or erosion of locality within promotional initiatives, thereby allowing for a more comprehensive account of the ways in which these transnational advertising campaigns constitute the understanding and experiences of national identity.

References

Albrow, M. (1996). *The global age.* Stanford, CA: Stanford University.

Allen, J. (1992). Post-industrialism and post-fordism. In S. Hall, D. Held, & A. McGrew (Eds.), *Modernity and its futures* (pp. 168–204). Cambridge, UK: Polity.

Anderson, B. (1983). *Imagined communities: Reflections on the origin and spread of nationalism.* London: Verso.

Appadurai, A. (1990). Disjuncture and difference in the global cultural economy. *Theory, Culture & Society, 7*, 295–310.

Auge, M. (1995). *Non-places: Introduction to an anthropology of supermodernity.* London: Verso.

Bale, J (1998). Virtual fandoms: Futurescapes of football. In A. Brown (Ed.), *Fanatics: Power, identity and fandom in football* (pp. 265–278). London: Routledge.

Baudrillard, J. (1983). *Simulations.* New York: Semiotext(e).

Bell, E., & Campbell, D. (1999, May 23). For the love of money. *The Observer,* p. 22.

Bourdieu, P. (1984). *Distinction: A social critique of the judgement of taste* (R. Nice, Trans.). London: Routledge & Kegan Paul.

Castells, M. (1983). Crisis planning and the quality of life: Managing the new historical relationships between space and society. *Environment and Planning D: Society and Space, 1*(1), pp. 3–21.

Castells, M. (1996). *The rise of the network society.* Cambridge, MA: Blackwell.

Chadbourn, M. (1999, November 1). Why Lara Croft is too hot for the world too handle. *The Independent,* p. 14.

Cole, C. L. (1996). American Jordan: P.L.A.Y., consensus, and punishment. *Sociology of Sport Journal, 13*(4), 366–397.

Cole, C. L., & Andrews, D. L. (2000). America's new son: Tiger Woods and America's multiculturalism. In N. K. Denzin (Ed.), *Cultural studies: A research volume* (Vol. 5, pp. 109–124). Stamford, CT: JAI Press.

Dirlik, A. (1996). The global in the local. In R. Wilson & W. Dissanayake (Eds.), *Global local: Cultural production and the transnational imaginary* (pp. 21–45). Durham, NC; Duke University Press.

Du Gay, P., Hall, S., Janes, L., Mackay, H., & Negus, K. (1997). *Doing cultural studies: The story of the Sony Walkman.* London: Sage.

Fetto, J. (2000, July). Patriot games: National pride swells in the heartland, but the rest of America isn't too far behind. *American Demographics,* pp. 48–49.

Giulianotti, R. (1999). *Football: A sociology of the global game.* Cambridge, UK: Polity.

Hall, S. (1991). The local and the global: Globalization and ethnicity. In A. D. King (Ed.), *Culture, globalization and the world-system* (pp. 19–39). London: Macmillan.

Hannerz, U. (1996). *Transnational connections: Culture, people, places.* London: Comedia.

Harvey, D. (1985). The geopolitics of capitalism. In D. Gregory & J. Urry (Eds.), *Social relations and social structures* (pp. 128–163). London: Macmillan.

Harvey, D. (1993). From space to place and back again: Reflections on the condition of postmodernity. In J. Bird (Ed.), *Mapping the futures: Local cultures, global change* (pp. 3–29). London: Routledge.

Held, D., McGrew, A., Goldblatt, D., & Perraton, J. (1999). *Global transformations: Politics, economics and culture.* Stanford, CA: Stanford University Press.

Hirst, P., & Thompson, G. (1996). *Globalization in question: The international economy and the possibilities of governance.* Cambridge, UK: Polity.

Hobsbawm, E. J. (1990). *Nations and nationalism since 1870: Programme, myth, reality.* Cambridge, UK: Cambridge University Press.

Hobsbawm, E., & Ranger, T. (Eds.). (1983). *The invention of tradition.* Cambridge, UK: Cambridge University Press.

Hunter, S. (2000, March). Border-bending creative. *Boards Magazine* [Online]. Available: www.boardsmag.com/articles/magazine/200003/ideas.html

Jameson, F. (1991). *Postmodernism, or, the cultural logic of late capitalism.* Durham, NC: Duke University Press.

Leslie, D. A. (1995). Global scan: The globalization of advertising agencies, concepts, and campaigns. *Economic Geography, 71*(4), 402–425.

Levitt, T. (1983). *The marketing imagination.* London: Collier-Macmillan.

Luke, T. W. (1996). Identity, meaning and globalization: Detraditionalization in postmodern space-time compression. In P. Heelas, S. Lash, & P. Morris (Eds.), *Detraditionalization: Critical reflections of authority and identity* (pp. 109–133). Cambridge, UK: Blackwell.

Luke, T. (1999). Simulated sovereignty, telematic territoriality: The political economy of cyberspace. In M. Featherstone & S. Lash (Eds.), *Spaces of culture: City-nation-world* (pp. 27–48). London: Sage.

Morley, D. (1992). *Television, audiences and cultural studies.* London: Routledge.

Morley, D., & Robins, K. (1995). *Spaces of identity: Global media, electronic landscapes and cultural boundaries.* London: Routledge.

Ohmae, K. (1990). *The borderless world.* New York: HarperBusiness.

Perry, N. (1994). *The dominion of signs; Television, advertising, and other New Zealand fictions.* Auckland, New Zealand: Auckland University Press.

Pietersee, J. N. (1995). Globalization as hybridization. In M. Featherstone, S. Lash, & R. Robertson (Eds.), *Global modernities* (pp. 45–68). London: Sage.

Prendergrast, M. (1998). *For God, country and Coca-Cola: The unauthorized history of the great American soft drink and the company that makes it.* New York: Touchstone.

Reich, R. (1991). *The work of nations: Preparing ourselves for twenty-first-century capitalism.* New York: Knopf.

Robins, K. (1990). Global local times. In J. Anderson & M. Ricci (Eds.), *Society and social science: A reader* (pp. 196–205). Milton Keynes, UK: Open University.

Robins, K. (1991). Tradition and translation: National culture in its global context. In J. Corner & S. Harvey (Eds.), *Enterprise and heritage: rosscurrents of national culture* (pp. 21–44). London: Routledge.

Robins, K. (1997). What in the world's going on? In P. D. Gay (Ed.), *Production of culture/cultures of production* (pp. 11–66). London: The Open University.

Sassen, S. (2000). Whose city is it? Globalization and the formation of new claims. In F. J. Lechner (Ed.), *The globalization reader* (pp. 70–76). Maiden, MA: Blackwell.

Sloane, A. (1999, December 11). Echo of Europe. *The New Zealand Herald,* p. C6.

Smith, A. D. (1991). *National identity.* London: Penguin.

Tomlinson, J. (1999). *Globalization and culture.* Cambridge, UK: Polity.

Williams, R. (1983). *The year 2000.* New York: Pantheon.

7.8   Journalistic view

Surge in racist mood raises concerns on eve of World Cup

Jere Longman

Hamburg, Germany, June 3 [2006]—As he left the soccer field after a club match in the eastern German city of Halle on March 25, the Nigerian forward Adebowale Ogungbure was spit upon, jeered with racial remarks and mocked with monkey noises. In rebuke, he placed two fingers under his nose to simulate a Hitler mustache and thrust his arm in a Nazi salute.

In April, the American defender Oguchi Onyewu, playing for his professional club team in Belgium, dismissively gestured toward fans who were making simian chants at him. Then, as he went to throw the ball inbounds, Onyewu said a fan of the opposing team reached over a barrier and punched him in the face.

International soccer has been plagued for years by violence among fans, including racial incidents. But FIFA, soccer's Zurich-based world governing body, said there has been a recent surge in discriminatory behavior toward blacks by fans and other players, an escalation that has dovetailed with the signing of more players from Africa and Latin America by elite European clubs.

This "deplorable trend," as FIFA has called it, now threatens to embarrass the sport on its grandest stage, the World Cup, which opens June 9 for a month long run in 12 cities around Germany. More than 30 billion cumulative television viewers are expected to watch part of the competition and Joseph S. Blatter, FIFA's president, has vowed to crack down on racist behavior during the tournament.

Underlining FIFA's concerns, the issue has been included on the agenda at its biannual Congress, scheduled to be held this week in Munich. A campaign against bigotry includes "Say No to Racism" stadium banners, television commercials, and team captains making pre-game speeches during the quarterfinals of the 32-team tournament.

Players, coaches and officials have been threatened with sanctions. But FIFA has said it would not be practical to use the harshest penalties available to punish misbehaving fans—halting matches, holding games in empty stadiums and deducting points that teams receive for victories and ties.

Players and antiracism experts said they expected offensive behavior during the tournament, including monkey-like chanting; derisive singing; the hanging of banners that reflect neofascist and racist beliefs; and perhaps the tossing of bananas or banana peels, all familiar occurrences during matches in Spain, Italy, eastern Germany and eastern Europe.

"For us it's quite clear this is a reflection of underlying tensions that exist in European societies," said Piara Powar, director of the London-based antiracist soccer organization Kick It Out. He said of Eastern Europe: "Poverty, unemployment, is a problem. Indigenous people are looking for easy answers to blame. Often newcomers bear the brunt of the blame."

Yet experts and players also said they believed the racist behavior would be more constrained at the World Cup than it was during play in various domestic leagues around Europe, because of increased security, the international makeup of the crowds, higher ticket prices and a sense that spectators would be generally well behaved on soccer's grandest stage.

"We have to differentiate inside and outside the stadium," said Kurt Wachter, project coordinator for the Vienna-based Football Against Racism in Europe, a network of organizations that seeks to fight bigotry and xenophobia in 35 countries.

"Racism is a feature of many football leagues inside and outside Europe," said Wachter, who expects most problems to occur outside stadiums where crowds are less controlled. "We're sure we will see some things we're used to seeing. It won't stop because of the World Cup."

Particularly worrisome are the possibilities of attacks by extremist groups on spectators and visitors in train stations, bars, restaurants and open areas near the stadiums, Wachter and other experts said. To promote tolerance, he said his organization would organize street soccer matches outside World Cup stadiums.

Recent attacks in the eastern Germany city of Potsdam on an Ethiopian-born engineer and in eastern Berlin on a state lawmaker of Turkish descent, along with a government report showing an increase in right-wing violence, have ignited fears that even sporadic hate crimes and other intolerant behavior could mar the World Cup, whose embracing motto is A Time to Make Friends.

Far-right extremism is isolated on the fringe of German society, and the German government has intended to confront its Nazi past while preaching openness and tolerance. Germany has one of the world's lowest rates of violent crime. Still, an immigrant group called the Africa Council said it would publish a "No Go" guide for nonwhites during the World Cup, particularly for some areas of eastern Berlin and for surrounding towns of the state of Brandenburg.

In mid-May, a former government spokesman, Uwe-Karsten Heye, caused a furor when he tried to assist visitors by advising that anyone "with a different skin color" avoid visiting small and midsize towns in Brandenburg and elsewhere in eastern Germany, or they "may not leave with their lives."

These remarks received blunt criticism from high-ranking German officials. Wolfgang Schäuble, the minister of the interior, said there were no areas in which World Cup visitors should feel threatened, calling Germany "one of the safest places in the world."

Angela Merkel, Germany's chancellor, has warned that "anybody who threatens, attacks or, worse, kills anybody because of the color of his skin or because he comes from another country will face the full force of the law."

The Bundesliga in Germany is one of the world's top professional soccer leagues, and has not experienced widespread racism. Incidents involving racial abuse of black players are more prevalent in semiprofessional and amateur leagues in eastern Germany. One of the cities playing host to the World Cup, Leipzig, is in the former East Germany. Another, Berlin, was partly in East Germany.

After making a Nazi salute, which is illegal in Germany, Ogungbure of Nigeria was investigated by the authorities. But a charge of unconstitutional behavior against him was soon dropped because his gesture had been meant to renounce extremist activity.

"I regret what I did," Ogungbure said in a telephone interview from Leipzig. "I should have walked away. I'm a professional, but I'm a human, too. They don't spit on dogs. Why should they spit on me? I felt like a nobody."

Gerald Asamoah, a forward on Germany's World Cup team and a native of Ghana, has been recounting an incident in the 1990s when he was pelted with bananas before a club match in Cottbus. "I'll never forget that," he said in a television interview. "It's like we're not people." He has expressed anger and sadness over a banner distributed by a right-wing group that admonished, "No Gerald, You Are Not Germany."

Cory Gibbs, an American defender who formerly played professionally in Germany, said there were restaurants and nightclubs in eastern Germany—and even around Hamburg in the west—where he was told "You're not welcome" because he was black.

"I think racism is everywhere," said Gibbs, who will miss the World Cup because of a knee injury. "But I feel in Germany racism is a lot more direct."

Racist behavior at soccer matches is primarily displayed by men and is fueled by several factors, according to experts: alcohol; the perceived "us versus them" threat of multiculturalism in societies that were once more ethnically homogenous; the difficult economic transition of eastern European nations since the fall of the Berlin Wall; and crude attempts to unnerve opposing players during bitter, consuming rivalries.

Other observers say that the soccer stadium in Europe has become a communal soapbox, one of the few remaining public spaces where spectators can be outrageous and where political correctness does not exist and is even discouraged.

"Nowhere else other than football do people meet someplace and have a stage for shouting things as an anonymous mass," said Gerd Dembowski, director of a Berlin-based antiracist organization called Floodlight. "You can shout things you would never say in your normal life, let out your frustrations."

Not all the misbehavior can be traced to fans or to Europe. Players and coaches have also been transgressors.

Luis Aragonés, Spain's World Cup coach, was fined in 2004 after making racial remarks about the French star Thierry Henry. In March, in the Brazilian league, the defender Antonio Carlos was suspended for 120 days, and 4 additional matches, after an incident in which he shouted "monkey" at an opposing player who was black. But it was an incident in Spain on Feb. 25 that galvanized antiracist sentiment and prodded FIFA into taking a tougher stand against bigoted behavior. That match, in Zaragoza, was temporarily halted in the 77th minute by the referee, who threatened to cancel the remaining 13 minutes after Samuel Eto'o, the star forward for Barcelona, was subjected to a chorus of racial taunts. Eto'o threatened to leave the field. His coach and teammates eventually persuaded him to continue, and last month Barcelona won the European Champions Cup.

Eto'o has become one of the sport's most outspoken players on the subject of racism. "I'll continue to play," Eto'o, whose national team, Cameroon, did not qualify for the World Cup, said this week through his agent. "I'm not going to give up and hide and put my head down. I'll score goals against the teams whose fans are making rude noises."

Under pressure to curb what it acknowledged was an increase in racist incidents, FIFA in late March announced a stricter set of penalties that would apply for club and national team matches. The sanctions would include suspensions of five matches for players and officials who make discriminatory gestures, fines of $16,600 to $25,000 for each offense and two-year stadium bans for offending spectators. It also said teams, which receive 3 points in the standings for a victory, would have 3 points deducted on a first offense by misbehaving players, officials or fans.

Blatter, the FIFA president, told reporters that the 3-point deduction for abhorrent fan behavior would apply during the World Cup, then backed away from his comments in April. Blatter declined to comment for this article. And it remains unclear exactly what penalties will be levied against World Cup teams for offensive behavior by fans, coaches and players.

Nicolas Maingot, a FIFA spokesman, said World Cup sanctions would be made public later. But in an e-mail response to questions, he said: "Only racist abuses in the field of play will be punished. For fans, it will be impossible, due to the multinationality of the audience. In other words, it would be impossible to identify from which side would potential racist abusers come."

Critics counter that spectators are supposed to have their names on their tickets, so identifying offending fans should be relatively easy.

Onyewu, the American defender who was punched by an opposing fan in Belgium, said the man was identified through an anonymous tip and was barred from attending matches for two years. He said he did not retaliate because he believed that racist behavior reflected acts of a minority of fans.

"I'm anticipating a more professional environment in Germany because it's the World Cup," Onyewu said. Even so, he said, although antiracist efforts could restrict public behavior, "that's only helping the exterior."

He added, "The interior mind thinking, you can't really change that."

Index

Aaron, H. 93
achievement-striving 13–19
Acker, J. 165, 185, 191
Acosta, V. and Carpenter, L.J. 136, 139
Adams, N. and Bettis, P. 164, 167, 172, 178
Adelman, M.L. 336
Adidas 372, 376, 377
Adler, P.A. and Adler, P. 182, 206, 208, 212, 262
Adorno, T. 318
advertising, corporate 371–9; acting globally, thinking locally 373–5; America 372, 373, 374, 376; global anthems/local sensibilities 375–7
Afghanistan 301
Africa 88, 89, 101, 109–10, 290, 294, 310, 315, 322, 339, 380 see also South Africa
Africa Council 381
African Americans 53, 64, 65, 66, 67, 70, 85–7, 91–131, 154, 178, 204, 211, 244, 245, 247, 248, 249, 266, 268, 271–2, 285–6, 365
age 57, 58, 59, 62
Ajax 376
Alberto, C. 77–8
Albrow, M. 372
alcohol 247
Ali, Muhammad 70, 95, 117, 118, 119, 121
All-American Girls Baseball League 273, 276
Allen, D.R. 332, 338
Allen, P. 250
Allouch, H. 71
Amateur Athletic Union (AAU) 268, 273
amateur sports 1, 14–17, 200, 215, 216, 223, 224
Amaechi, John 255
América Futebol Clube 77, 78
Americanization 291, 293, 301, 309, 311, 315, 317, 318, 319

American Society for Cell Biology 226
American Tennis Association 85, 86
American Youth Soccer Organization (AYSO) 182, 183, 185, 186, 187, 191, 192
Andaraí, Rio de Janeiro 75, 76
Andrews, D. 125, 318, 319
Anquetil, J. 358
Appadurai, A. 307, 311, 332, 336, 347
Appiah, A. 94
Arab Americans 178
Aragonés, Luis 382
Arbena, J. 315, 316
Argentina 76, 79, 80, 82, 83, 121, 290, 325, 328, 329, 358, 365
Arguello, A. 121
Aristotle 99
Arledge, Roone 38–9
Arsenal 361, 376
Artfield, J. 188
Asamoah, Gerald 326, 381
Ashe, A. 86, 101
Asia 89, 303, 339; Asian Americans 178, 179; South Asia 332; South East Asia 294
Asinoff, E. 218
Astra 248, 249
Athens 88
Atlanta 124, 229
Australia 19, 46, 87, 93, 99, 145; 214–25, 301, 303, 318, 333, 334, 335, 336, 337, 344–5, 346, 349, 350, 373, 374; Aborigines 338 see also Donoghue, S.
Austria 358

Ba, Ibrahim 377
Bahrain 327
Baker, W. 308

383